SAN DIEGO PUBLIC LIBRARY

3 1336 00124 5852

D0770941

5852

628.5   Forster, C. F.
FOR   (Christopher F.)

         Environmental
         biotechnology

$105.00

DATE			

32 Y   c.1987   4/96
  9/88
  11/96

op 7/02   San Diego Public Library
37X 7/02
    4/02
32/8-97   SEP 3 0 1988

© THE BAKER & TAYLOR CO.

ENVIRONMENTAL BIOTECHNOLOGY

Ellis Horwood Series in
CHEMICAL ENGINEERING
Series Editor: Dr. DAVID SHARP, OBE, former General Secretary,
Society of Chemical Industry

*THERMODYNAMICS FOR CHEMISTS AND CHEMICAL ENGINEERS
M.H. CARDEW, University of Birmingham
ENVIRONMENTAL BIOTECHNOLOGY
C. F. FORSTER and D.A.J. WASE, University of Birmingham
MAJOR CHEMICAL HAZARDS
V. MARSHALL, University of Bradford
BIOLOGICAL TREATMENT OF WASTE-WATER
M. WINKLER, University of Surrey

Ellis Horwood Limited also publishes related titles in
APPLIED SCIENCE AND INDUSTRIAL TECHNOLOGY
INDUSTRIAL CHEMISTRY
BIOLOGICAL SCIENCES

* *In preparation*

ENVIRONMENTAL BIOTECHNOLOGY

CHRISTOPHER F. FORSTER
B.Sc., Ph.D., Dip.Biochem.Eng., C.Eng., F.I.Chem.E., M.I.W.P.C.
Lecturer in Civil Engineering
Department of Civil Engineering, University of Birmingham

and

D. A. JOHN WASE, B.Sc., Ph.D.
Senior Lecturer in Chemical Engineering
Department of Chemical Engineering, Biochemical Engineering Section
University of Birmingham

5852

ELLIS HORWOOD LIMITED
Publishers · Chichester

Halsted Press: a division of
JOHN WILEY & SONS
New York · Chichester · Brisbane · Toronto

First published in 1987 by
ELLIS HORWOOD LIMITED
Market Cross House, Cooper Street,
Chichester, West Sussex, PO19 1EB, England
The publisher's colophon is reproduced from James Gillison's drawing of the ancient Market Cross, Chichester.

Distributors:

Australia and New Zealand:
JACARANDA WILEY LIMITED
GPO Box 859, Brisbane, Queensland 4001, Australia

Canada:
JOHN WILEY & SONS CANADA LIMITED
22 Worcester Road, Rexdale, Ontario, Canada

Europe and Africa:
JOHN WILEY & SONS LIMITED
Baffins Lane, Chichester, West Sussex, England

North and South America and the rest of the world:
Halsted Press: a division of
JOHN WILEY & SONS
605 Third Avenue, New York, NY 10158, USA

© **1987 C. F. Forster and D. A. J. Wase/Ellis Horwood Limited**

British Library Cataloguing in Publication Data
Forster, C. F.
Environmental biotechnology. —
(Ellis Horwood series in chemical engineering).
1. Environmental protection   2. Biotechnology
I. Title   II. Wase, D. A. John
628.5   TD170.2

Library of Congress Card No. 87–3673

ISBN 0–85312–838–3 (Ellis Horwood Limited)
ISBN 0–470–20872–4 (Halsted Press)

Phototypeset in Times by Ellis Horwood Limited
Printed in Great Britain by Unwin Bros., Woking

COPYRIGHT NOTICE
All Rights Reserved. No part of this publication may be reproduced, stored in a retrieval system, or transmitted, in any form or by any means, electronic, mechanical, photo-copying, recording or otherwise, without the permission of Ellis Horwood Limited, Market Cross House, Cooper Street, Chichester, West Sussex, England.

Table of contents

1 **Aerobic processes**
C. F. Forster, Department of Civil Engineering, University of Birmingham, UK, and **D. W. M. Johnstone**, Sir William Halcrow and Partners, Swindon, Wiltshire, UK

2 **Anaerobic wastewater treatment process**
D. Barnes and **P. A. Fitzgerald**, School of Civil Engineering, University of New South Wales, Australia

3 **Mineral leaching with bacteria**
F. D. Pooley, Institute of Materials, University College Cardiff, UK

4 **Composting and straw decomposition**
A. J. Biddlestone and **K. R. Gray**, Department of Chemical Engineering, University of Birmingham, UK, and **Carol A. Day**, Microbial Developments Ltd.,

5 Solid waste
C. F. Forster, Department of Civil Engineering, University of Birmingham, UK, and **E. Senior,** Department of Bioscience and Biotechnology, University of Strathclyde, UK

6 **Agricultural alternatives**
Carol A. Day, Microbial Developments Ltd, Malvern Link, Malvern,
Worcs., UK, and **Stephen G. Lisansky**, Biotechnology Affiliates, Reading,
Berks, UK

7 Microbial control of environmental pollution
The use of genetic techniques to engineer organisms with novel catalytic capabilities
David J. Hardman, Biological Laboratory, University of Kent, Canterbury, UK

8 Continuous culture of bacteria with special reference to activated sludge wastewater treatment processes
G. Hamer, Institutes of Aquatic Sciences and Biotechnology, Swiss Federal Institute of Technology Zürich, Ueberlandstrasse 133, CH–8600 Dübendorf, Switzerland

11 Process engineering principles

M. S. Everett, Department of Chemical Engineering, University of Birmingham, UK

12 Biopossibilities: the next few years

C. F. Forster, Department of Civil Engineering, University of Birmingham, UK, and **D. A. J. Wase**, Biochemical Engineering Section, Department of Chemical Engineering, University of Birmingham, UK

Preface

The European Federation of Biotechnology has defined biotechnology as the integrated use of biochemistry, microbiology and chemical engineering in order to achieve the technological (industrial) application of the capacities of microbes and cultured tissue cells; environmental biotechnology is the specific application of biotechnology to the management of environmental problems, including waste treatment and pollution control, and their integration with non-biological technologies. On this basis, it would be foolish to claim that this book covers the field comprehensively; it does not; nor is it intended as a narrow book, to be used as a text for a specific course. What has been produced is a balanced selection of most of the main activities that can be considered as falling within the scope of environmental biotechnology together with an appraisal of the principles which are basic to the operation of these processes. The control of pollution is a significant part of the environment industry and, as such, is discussed in some detail. For example, there is considerable current concern over environmental pollution of agricultural land through a variety of sources, more often than not arising from man's activities. Solutions and potential solutions to the problem of land pollution are, therefore, provided, together with information on the treatment of effluents by a range of techniques. The disposal of refuse on landfill sites is also a potential source of environmental pollution. The problems and pitfalls of operating this type of solid waste disposal are discussed. However, environmental biotechnology must, by its very nature, examine all aspects of a process and, therefore, the potential for biogas generation at landfill sites is also examined.

Future technologies may well involve the use of genetically engineered microbes. Biotechnological advances in the manipulation of aromatic-degrading micro-organisms are also discussed together with an account of the problems of recalcitrant xenobiotics. Similarly, the potential of biological pest control and the management of biological nitrogen fixation are examined. The future is also addressed in a speculative, final chapter which evaluates the possibilities for biotechnology and its role within the environment industry.

The book should thus be of value to a wide range of readers. Thus, the undergraduate and graduate civil, chemical or biochemical engineer or biologist, the research worker, the industrialist or consultant who requires detailed information should all benefit from reading this text.

Christopher Forster
John Wase

1

Aerobic processes

C. F. Forster
Department of Civil Engineering, Birmingham University, UK
and
D. W. M. Johnston
Sir William Halcrow and Partners, Swindon, Wiltshire, UK.

1.1 INTRODUCTION

In terms of environmental biotechnology, the most significant aerobic processes are those used in the treatment and stabilisation of wastewaters. Many different designs of reactor are available for this purpose but, as a generalisation, they fall into one of two categories: homogeneous reactors and those with a fixed biofilm which is attached to an inert substratum. Some of these reactors can be thought of as being mutually interchangeable (e.g. activated sludge processes and trickling filters) whilst others are really only suitable for specific applications. However, all the various reactors must be capable of dealing with substrate and hydraulic loads which vary both diurnally and from day to day. The substrate loadings cannot be quantified on any general basis since they will tend to be site-specific but the hydraulic fluctuations could well vary from 0.5 DWF (dry weather flow) to 3, 6 or even 8 DWF. In other words the reactors under discussion must be thought of as being very resilient and, at best, as operating under only quasi-steady-state conditions.

1.2 DESIGN CRITERIA

1.2.1 Homogeneous reactors

The activated sludge process is the most common version of this type of reactor. In the case of domestic wastewater, the feedstock is usually sewage which has been screened to remove coarse solids, degritted and subjected to a settlement stage which removes some 60% of the suspended matter (together with, perhaps, 30% of the organic matter). Typically, therefore, settled sewage would contain, in the UK, 150–200 mg l^{-1} suspended solids, 150–200 mg l^{-1} of organic matter measured as biochemical oxygen demand (BOD) and 20–40 mg l^{-1} ammoniacal-nitrogen. The process itself consists of two stages: an aeration tank in which the settled sewage is contacted with air and the activated sludge solids for a predetermined period which could range from 4 to more than 24 h depending on the nature of the feedstock, the degree of treatment required and the mode of operation; and a settlement tank which separates the treated liquors from the activated sludge solids. This enables an essentially solids-free supernatant to be discharged and the solids to be recycled to the aeration tank. The process therefore can be thought as a continuous fermentation operating under washout conditions with solids feedback (Fig. 1.1). The activated sludge solids, often referred to

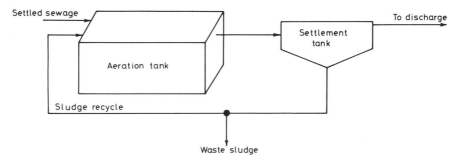

Fig. 1.1 — Schematic diagram of the activated sludge process.

as the mixed liquor suspended solids (MLSS), are a well flocculated mixture of bacteria and protozoa (Fig. 1.2).

A very wide range of bacterial species have been identified in activated sludge [1.1] and as a general rule, their classification to a species level is of little significance. Three main groups need to be considered:

— the floc-forming carbon oxidisers
— the filamentous carbon oxidisers
— the nitrifiers

The floc-formers are essential not only for the degradation of BOD but also to establish a stable floc which will settle rapidly to give a compact sludge in the settlement tank. The nitrifiers (*Nitrosomonas* and *Nitrobacter*) convert ammoniacial nitrogen to nitrate:

$$NH_3 + O_2 \xrightarrow{\textit{Nitrosomonas}} NO_2$$

$$NO_2 + O_2 \xrightarrow{\textit{Nitrobacter}} NO_3$$

Fig. 1.2 — Photomicrograph of activated sludge.

These species are essential if the process is required to produce an effluent which has a low ammoniacal-nitrogen concentration. The filamentous species are something of an anomaly. On the one hand it is claimed that they act as the skeleton around which the floc forms [1.2] whilst on the other they are linked to two specific operational problems; poor settlement (or 'bulking') and the formation of stable foams [1.3–1.5]. It has become essential, therefore, to be able to classify not only which filamentous species are present but also their abundance. It is possible to do this using the procedure developed at the TNO Institute [1.6]. This is based on the filament morphology and size and on their Gram and Neisser straining characteristics.

The protozoan species act as bacterial scavengers and ensure a low turbidity in the final effluent. Some 200 different species have been identified [1.7] but, arguably, it is the ciliated protozoa and in particular the stalked ciliates, such as *Vorticella* and *Opercularia* (Fig. 1.3), which are of greatest significance. A detailed assessment of the role of protozoans and the significance of the different species has been given by Curds and Cockburn [1.8] and by Curds [1.7–1.9].

In the context of sludge, the term 'activated' can therefore, be taken to mean that the biomass has:

— a flora with all the enzyme systems necessary for the degradation of the waste being treated
— a surface with good adsorbent properties
— the ability to form stable flocs and to settle readily under quiescent conditions

Fig. 1.3 —Electron micrograph of stalked ciliates in activated sludge.

In designing activated sludge systems, several parameters need to be considered (Table 1.1). The organic loading rate (OLR), sludge loading rate (SLR) or food to mass ratio (kg BOD kg^{-1} MLSS d^{-1}) is perhaps the most important as this defines the mode of operation and the hydraulic retention time:

$$\text{OLR (kg BOD kg}^{-1}\text{ MLSS d}^{-1}) =$$

$$\frac{\text{BOD (g l}^{-1}) \times \text{flow-rate (m}^3\text{ d}^{-1})}{\text{MLSS (g l}^{-1}) \times \text{aeration tank volume (m}^3)} \qquad (1.1)$$

$$= \frac{\text{BOD}}{\text{MLSS}} \times \frac{1}{t_r}$$

where t_r = hydraulic retention time.

There are essentially three operational modes; high-rate (OLR=0.5–5.0); conventional (OLR=0.25–0.45) and extended aeration (OLR=0.05–0.20).

High-rate processes are somewhat specialised and tend to be used for the partial treatment of wastes. The design choice therefore tends to be between conventional and extended aeration processes.

Extended aeration systems are often taken as being synonymous with

Table 1.1 — Parameters used in the design and operation of activated sludge plants

Parameter	Units
Organic loading rate	kg BOD (kg MLSS)$^{-1}$ d^{-1}
Sludge age	d
Hydraulic retention time	d
SVI or SSVI	—
Mass flux	kg SS m^{-2} h^{-1}

oxidation ditches [1.10]. As originally conceived, these were simply constructed, continuous ditches in which the aeration and the circulation of the ditch contents were both achieved by horizontally mounted surface aerators. However, the oxygen transfer capacity of the original rotor meant that the depth of the ditches was limited to about 1.8 m. This, in turn, meant that, for the treatment of large flows, large areas were required. This problem was overcome by the development of new rotors (the Mammoth system) and new configurations (the Carrousel process) [1.10] (Fig. 1.4). The main advantages of oxidation ditches, apart from their simplicity for small rural locations, are that (a) primary settlement frequently is not used, (b) there is a large 'buffering' capacity within the ditch, (c) the sludge is subjected to a significant amount of aerobic digestion (and, therefore, the amount of sludge for disposal is less), and (d) if double or triple ditches are used with alternating sequences of aeration and settlement [1.10] there is no need to provide a final settlement tank.

Having established the organic loading rate, some estimate of the operating MLSS concentration must be made. This is usually within the range 1.5–5.0 g l^{-1}. However, the value selected will depend on the type of waste being treated and its yield coefficient (i.e. kg MLSS produced kg^{-1} BOD removed) and the sludge age required for process. The sludge age (S) is calculated from:

$$S = \frac{\text{MLSS (g l}^{-1}) \times \text{aeration tank volume (m}^3)}{\text{Sludge wasted (kg d}^{-1}) + [\text{flow-rate (m}^3\text{ d}^{-1}) \times \text{effluent solids (g l}^{-1})]}$$

(1.2)

This is an important parameter when the system is being designed to achieve nitrification. Because the nitrifying species have long mean generation times, it is essential that a long sludge age is used if an adequate population of nitrifiers is to be maintained within the MLSS. The relationship between the minimum sludge age compatible with nitrification (S^*) and the pH (P) and temperature (T) of the liquors [1.11] is:

$$1/S^* = [0.18 - 0.15 (7.2 - P)] \exp [0.12 (T - 15)]$$

(1.3)

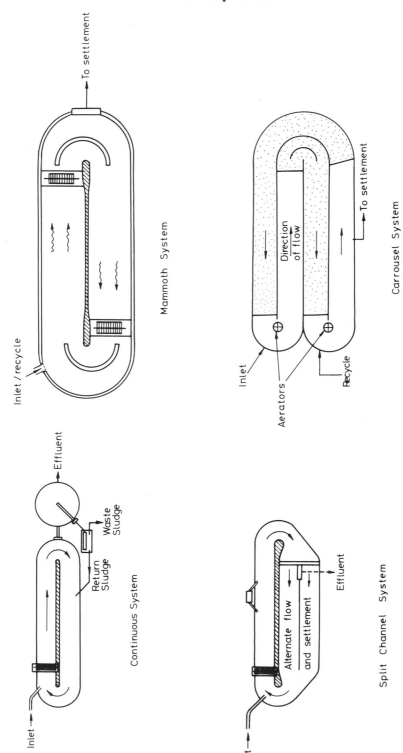

Fig. 1.4 — Various configurations for the operation of oxidation ditches.

This means that, at a neutral pH, a sludge age of 12 days is needed at a temperature of 10°C. Although it is possible to estimate the operational MLSS concentration (and therefore the daily sludge wastage), it must be recognised that, once the plant is in full operation, it may be necessary to adjust this figure as the settlement characteristics of the sludge fluctuate [1.12].

The operating dissolved oxygen (DO) concentration is chosen on the basis of the design requirements of the plant. Thus, if full nitrification is specified, a DO concentration of at least 2 mg l^{-1} would be selected whilst for other objectives (carbonaceous oxidation; denitrification) a lower value would suffice. These levels would be subject to control by dissolved oxygen electrodes. In the case of surface aerators (see Chapter 10; Fig. 1.5) the control is executed by altering the depth of immersion of the aerator sysem either by raising/lowering the liquid level in the aeration tank with an adjustable outlet weir or, less commonly, by a rise-and-fall gearbox fitted to the aerator.

Whatever level or method of control is used, it is essential that the aerators which are used are capable of transferring sufficient oxygen for the degree of treatment required. The daily carbonaceous oxygen requirements (R; kg day^{-1}) for conventionally loaded plants [1.13] can be calculated from

$$R = 0.75\ B + 0.048\ MV \tag{1.4}$$

For extended aeration systems treating unsettled sewage [1.14] the daily demand is:

$$R = B + 4.34\ N_H - 2.85\ N_T + 0.024\ MVr\theta^{(T-20)} \tag{1.5}$$

where B $=$ BOD removed (kg day^{-1})
N_H $=$ Ammoniacal-nitrogen removed (kg d^{-1})
N_T $=$ Total nitrogen removed (kg d^{-1})
M $=$ Mixed liquor suspended solids (kg m^{-1})
V $=$ Aeration tank volume (m^3)
r $=$ Endogeneous respiration rate. Taken as 3.9 mg 0$_2$ g^{-1} MLSS h^{-1}
θ $= 1.07$

Equation 1.5 takes account of all the processes taking place: carbonaceous oxidation, biomass respiration, the oxidation of ammonia to nitrate and any subsequent denitrification. In applying the equation, therefore, only those elements which are appropriate to the process being evaluated are used. Thus, for a temperature of 10°C and considering only carbonaceous oxidation, Equation 1.5 condenses to:

$$R = B + 0.048\ MV \tag{1.5a}$$

This expression is very comparable with that used for conventionally loaded aeration tanks (Equation 1.4).

(a)

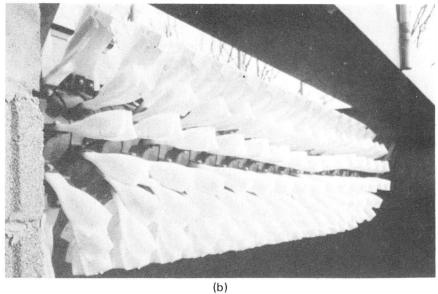

(b)

Fig. 1.5 — Surface aerators: (a) the Simcar aerator (by courtesy of Simon Hartley
Ltd); (b) a horizontally mounted cage rotor.

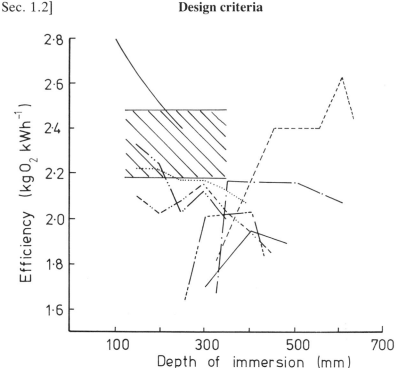

Fig. 1.6 — The variation in clean water oxygenation efficiency with depth of immersion for vertical shaft aerators.

These oxygen requirements are translated to an aerator size (i.e. hp) by use of an efficiency term expressed as kg O_2 $(kWh)^{-1}$. This step can be problematical as the data provided by the manufacturers of aeration equipment cover a wide range (Fig. 1.6). It is therefore desirable that the oxygen transfer efficiency of any new aerator be tested during the commissioning stage and that an appropriate penalty clause be included in the contract. The techniques for doing this are well documented and are relatively easy (see [10.38]), although the interpretation of results needs great care.

The final design decision that must be made is to determine the mixing regime within the aeration tank. The two extremes are (a) completely mixed, or (b) plug flow. A completely mixed system provides instantaneous dilution of the feedstock entering the aeration tank and, as such, can be used to protect the microbial flora of the activated sludge from toxic, inhibitory or highly oxygen-demanding components in that feedstock. However, it has been shown that completely mixed systems produce sludges which have a greater tendency for poor settlement than those in plug flow reactors [1.15]. Most aeration tanks have hybrid mixing regimes and the degree of longitudinal mixing can be described in terms of the Dispersion Number (DN) [1.16; 1.17]. Thus for a plug glow system, DN=0 and for a completely mixed tank

DN=1.0. A value for the Dispersion Number can only be obtained retrospectively using tracer studies. However, during the design stage it is worth examining all the possible flow patterns and adopting the configuration which gives the greatest operational flexibility (e.g. Fig. 1.7). An alternative

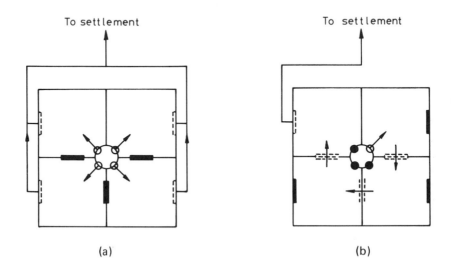

Fig. 1.7 — A potentially flexible layout for a four-pocket aeration tank: (a) completely mixed regime; (b) plug-flow configuration.

approach is to use the 'contact-tank' concept described by Rensink *et al.* [1.18]. This uses a small plug-flow tank to mix the return sludge and the incoming sewage prior to their entering the main aeration tank. In this way the occurrence of poor settlement can be minimised if not totally avoided.

Two special cases of the activated sludge process need to be considered. These are the Deep Shaft process and reactors in which pure oxygen is used. Pure oxygen (or oxygen-enriched air) can be used, in conjunction with the activated sludge process, in either of two ways: to provide supplementary capacity or as the sole source of aeration. Supplementary aeration capacity may be needed for several reasons. The works may, with time, have become overloaded to such an extent that the installed aerators cannot supply sufficient oxygen to enable nitrification or even the carbonaceous oxidation to be achieved adequately. Alternatively, the works may be subjected to a predictable seasonal overload (e.g. from the discharge of fruit or vegetable processing or at a large seaside resort), in which case it would be unreasonable to install conventional aeration capacity to meet these periodic peak loads. The Vitox process is probably the most successful way of providing supplementary oxygen. The process requirements are a supply of oxygen, a pump, pipework, a venturi and dispersal jets (Fig. 1.8). The pump is used to deliver liquid (settled sewage, final effluent or even mixed liquor) to the venturi. The oxygen is injected at this point where the pressure regime and turbulence are such that some 25 per cent of the gas dissolves immediately. A further 25 per cent dissolves in the subsequent pipework. When the liquid is injected into the aeration tank, the energy imparted by the jet provides a very thorough mixing of the oxygen (both dissolved and in the gaseous form) within the mixed liquors. The overall result is that the Vitox system can have an efficiency as high as 3 kg O_2 kWh^{-1} [1.19].

When oxygen is used as the sole aeration source, one of the prime process considerations is to minimise, if not to eliminate, the loss of oxygen at the liquid surface. There are essentially three ways of doing this [1.20]:

(i)   Covering the aeration tanks and allowing the surface aerators to operate in an atmosphere of pure oxygen.

(ii)   Circulating the biomass or the influent through a downflow bubble contactor which is separate from the main aeration tank.

(iii) Using specially designed diffusers which produce very fine bubbles with a low upflow velocity. In this way there is a high percentage of gas dissolution before the bubbles reach the surface.

In the UK, the covered tank system, as typified by the UNOX process (Fig. 1.9), is probably the most common process. However, whichever process is used, a supply of oxygen is required. This can be produced on-site cryogenically, or may be delivered to the works as a liquid and stored in insulated tanks, or oxygen-enriched air can be produced at the site by the process of pressure swing adsorption (PSA) (Fig. 1.10). This uses columns packed with molecular sieve having the ability to adsorb nitrogen and carbon dioxide from the air at pressures of 200–300 kPa. The gas resulting from this process, therefore, contains 75–90 per cent oxygen. Since the adsorption process is reversible, the packing can be reactivated by reducing the pressure to 100 kPa. In a typical system, three columns would be used; one producing gas, one on standby and one desorbing. The frequency of the pressurisation/decompression cycles can be adjusted to control the rate of production and the purity of the gas. However, it must be stressed that there is a need to incorporate adequate facilities for reducing the energy consumption when less oxygen is required by the mixed liquor ('turndown'). A lack of this ability has resulted in very wide variations in the oxygenation efficiency (kWh kg^{-1} BOD and ammonical-nitrogen oxidised) being reported [1.21]. During the design of a covered oxygenic reactor, special consideration must be given to plant safety. In particular, the gas space above the mixed liquor must be monitored for the pressure of volatile organics/hydrocarbons and this monitoring system must be linked to a shutdown and purge sequence.

The Deep Shaft process, which could be considered as a high-rate oxidation ditch operated in a vertical plane, was developed from fermentation technology. It consists of a single shaft (50–150 m deep × 0.5–10 m

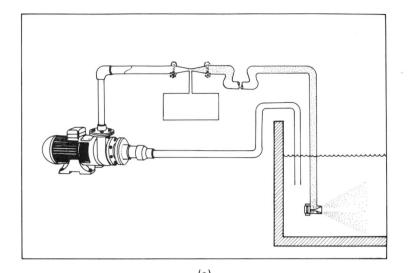

(a)

(b)

Fig. 1.8 — The Vitox side-stream injection system: (a) schematic diagram (by
courtesy of BOC Ltd); (b) an operational unit.

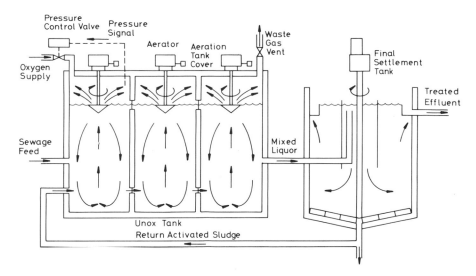

Fig. 1.9 — Schematic diagram of the Unox oxygen activated sludge process (by courtesy of Wimpey-Unox Ltd).

diameter; [1.22]) which is subdivided by a central core or a cruciform device (Fig. 1.11) so that there are upflow and downflow regions which give a circulation of the shaft contents. The flow-pattern is started by injecting air into the riser section at a relatively shallow depth. Airlift principles start the liquid movement and once the liquid velocity has reached 1–2 m s^{-1}, air is injected into the downcomer section. The velocity of the liquid is sufficient at this stage to carry the air bubbles downwards. The flow velocities are also sufficient to give high Reynolds numbers, minimal bubble coalescence and a high rate of surface renewal. Thus, there is a high rate of oxygen transfer. This is enhanced by the hydrostatic head resulting from this depth of the shaft. Typical figures for the transfer efficiencies are 3–4.5 kg kWh^{-1} [1.22]. Oxygen transfer efficiencies as large as this can support high sludge loading rates, 0.9 kg BOD kg^{-1} MLSS d^{-1} being typical.

The Deep Shaft process is, therefore, compact and can be operated at a high rate. It also has the advantage of being constructed largely below ground level. However, there is a major problem with the separation of solids from the mixed liquor. Microbubbles become attached to the solids and so disrupt settlement that the final effluent produced is of poor quality. To overcome this problem, a variety of techniques have been examined. These include vacuum degassing [1.23], flotation [1.24] and air-stripping [1.25]. Since none of these has proved to be totally satisfactory, current designs are being based on a hybrid reactor in which a reduced size shaft is used to treat a proportion of the load. The mixed liquors from this stage are then passed directly to an aeration tank in which the microbubbles are removed (by the action of the aerators) and any residual load is oxidised [1.26]. The solids from the aeration tank are then settled in the normal way,

Fig. 1.10 — A pressure swing absorption unit.

with the effluent being discharged and the concentrated sludge being recycled to the shaft stage (see Fig. 1.12).

1.2.2 Fixed biomass reactors

The trickling filter is the most widely used fixed biomass process. Essentially it is a packed bed reactor with a counter-current flow of air (upwards) and liquid. The biomass is grown on the packing as a film. The two significant features of the packing are, therefore, a high specific surface ($m^2 \, m^{-3}$) to maximise the area available for microbial colonisation and a high void space to permit the passage of air and liquid (see Table 1.2). The process can be designed in one of two modes: low-rate, in which case the packing is almost invariably stone as specified in BS1438/1971, or high-rate with a plastic packing.

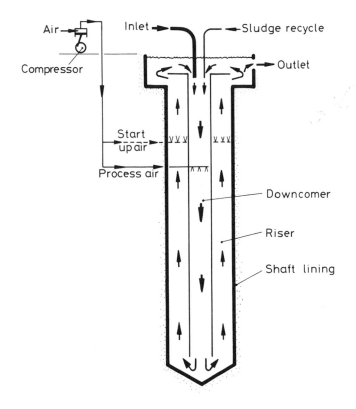

Fig. 1.11 — The Deep Shaft process.

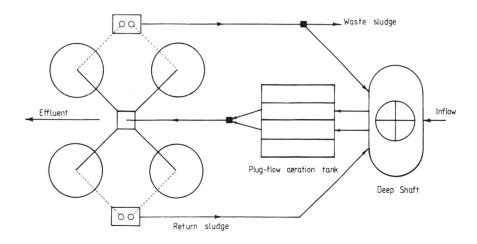

Fig. 1.12 — The second generation Deep Shaft process.

Table 1.2 — Properties of mineral media used in trickling filters

Media type	Specific surface ($m^2 m^{-3}$)	Voidage (%)
25 mm Slag	200–246	—
50 mm Slag	101–118	50
100–150 mm Slag	50	50
50 mm Granite	24–111	—
50 mm Crushed gravel	86–101	—
100–150 mm Slag	50	50

Stone filters have a depth of 1.5–2.5 m and may be circular or rectangular (Fig. 1.13). Circular filters should not have diameters in excess of 40 m and the dimensions of rectangular filters should not exceed 75 m (length) × 45 m (width). Whichever configuration is selected, provision should be made for good under-drainage so that there is a free removal of liquors and introduction of air. The feedstock for the process, nearly always sewage that has received primary settlement, is applied by distributors. In the case of circular filters, the distributors have a cruciform configuration (see Fig. 1.13) and are driven by water reaction, by water wheels or, at times, by electricity. Rectangular filters have full-width distributors which are driven either by water wheels or by cables.

The basic mode for the operation of stone filters is 'single-pass' or 'straight-through'. In other words, the sewage percolates gradually through the filter, passes into a settlement tank (often referred to as a humus tank) and is then discharged. Under these circumstances, the organic loading rate on the filter is in the range 0.06–0.12 kg BOD $m^{-3} d^{-1}$. If higher loading rates are required, either to uprate an overloaded system or to prevent an excessive area of filters being used, then the filters can be operated with recirculation or as alternating double filtration (ADF). These modes of operation can also be used to achieve a more complete treatment if the sewage contains a significant proportion of strong trade waste (e.g. from dairies or meat processing). Recirculation involves the dilution of the feed with settled final effluent using feed:recirculation ratios of 1:1–1:2. Three methods can be used for applying the recirculated liquors: a constant ratio, a constant recirculation flow-rate or a constant total flow to the filters. The organic loading rates that can result from using recirculation range from 0.09 to 0.15 kg BOD $m^{-3} d^{-1}$. Although recirculation increases the hydraulic loading rate, which results in a greater scouring within the bed, it also reduces the actual concentration of organics being applied to the filter. Since the removal kinetics are first-order, this reduction would be expected to result in a reduction in the removal efficiencies. At low recirculation rates, this does not occur. The reason is thought to be that the greater wetting results in more efficient use of the film. The interrelationship between

(a)

(b)

Fig. 1.13 — The trickling filter process: (a) circular filters; (b) rectangular filters.

surface wetting and performance can be seen from Fig. 1.14. This shows the hydraulic loading rates (L_v) which corresponds to the organic loading rates (L_s) for a range of influent BOD concentrations. The figure also shows the minimum values of L_v, which are compatible with the limiting irrigation ('wetting') rate of 1.5 $m^3 \ m^{-2} \ d^{-1}$, for two filter depths; 1.5 m and 2.0 m.

From this, it is easy to ascertain the actual hydraulic loading rate and then to determine the additional flow (obtained by recirculation) that is necessary to achieve the limiting value.

ADF uses two sets of filters and two humus tanks (Fig. 1.15). The flow sequence is changed, at 1–2 week intervals, so that conditions within the filters alternate between nutrient-rich (the first filter) and nutrient-limiting.

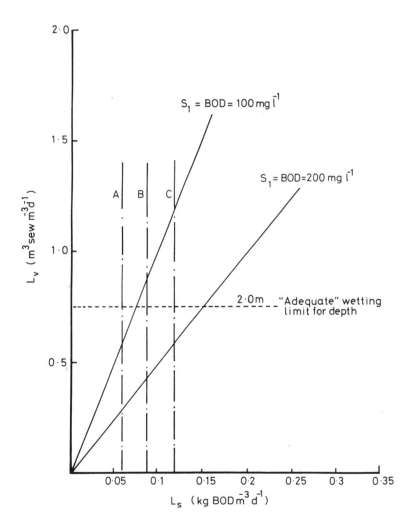

Fig. 1.14 — Nomogram to determine the minimum irrigation rate for conventional single-pass filtration.

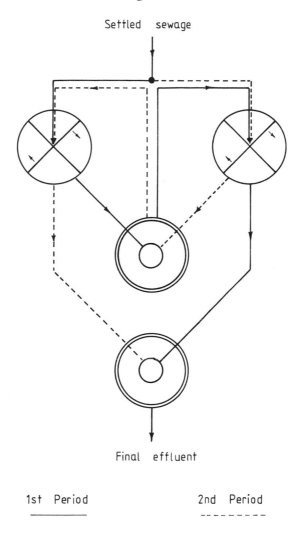

Fig. 1.15 — Sequence of operation for alternating double filtration: —— 1st period;
– – – 2nd period.

This, in turn, promotes heavy film growth and film reduction respectively.
The proper selection of the alternation frequency, therefore, means that
high loading rates (0.15–0.26 kg m^{-3} d^{-1}) can be applied without encounter-
ing the problem of heavy film growth blocking the void spaces in the upper
part of the filter ('ponding').

The biofilm produced in trickling filters has a more complex ecology than
activated sludge (Fig. 1.16). Bacteria (and occasionally fungi) form the
lowest trophic levels and it is these species which degrade the polluting
material, with carbon-oxidisers colonising the upper part of the reactor and
the nitrifiers occupying the lower portion where there is less competition for
oxygen and trace elements. Protozoans, rotifers and nematodes graze on the

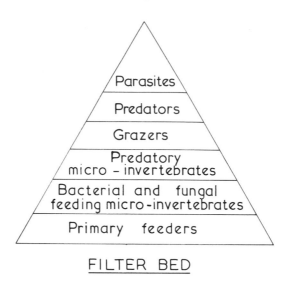

Fig. 1.16 — Trophic pyramid for the biofilm in trickling filters.

bacteria and, in turn, become prey for the higher species (e.g. fly larvae). The actual species involved in the ecological pyramid are not significant for design purposes. However, imbalances can cause operational problems (e.g. ponding; spring sloughing).

Although the most common design method in the UK is that based on the organic loading rate, various formulae do exist for calculating filter characteristics (Table 1.3). These are either empirical or are based on first-order kinetics. Their main parameters are:

$$
\begin{aligned}
L_i &= \text{influent BOD, mg l}^{-1} \\
L_e &= \text{effluent BOD, mg l}^{-1} \\
W &= \text{BOD load, kg d}^{-1} \\
V &= \text{volume of filter media, m}^3 \\
f &= \text{recirculation factor} = \frac{1 + \propto}{(1 + 0.1 \propto)^2} \\
\propto &= \text{recirculation flow: influent flow} \\
S &= \text{media specific surface, m}^2 \text{ m}^{-3} \\
Q &= \text{hydraulic loading rate, m}^3 \text{ m}^{-3} \text{ d}^{-1} \\
T &= \text{operational temperature, }^\circ\text{C} \\
k, m, n \text{ and } \theta &= \text{constants}
\end{aligned}
$$

However, as with many relationships of this type, the results that can be achieved by their use are only as good as the values used for the constants and the applicability of those values. In other words, care should be taken over their use and the results checked against accepted yardsticks.

Table 1.3 — Mathematical expressions relating to the operations of trickling filters

Source	Expression
National Research Council [1.27]	$\dfrac{L_i - L_e}{L_i} = \dfrac{1}{1 + 0.44\,[W/(fV)]^{0.5}}$
Bruce and Merkens [1.28]	$L_e = L_i \exp\left(-k\theta^{T-15}\,S/Q\right)$
Pike [1.29]	$L_e = L_i \exp\left(-k\theta^{T-15}\,S^m/Q^n\right)$

The plastic media that are used for high-rate filtration (Fig. 1.17) have a very high voidage and, in some cases, a specific surface which is significantly higher than that of stone packings (Table 1.4). They also have a low bulk density which means that they can be built as tower reactors up to 8–10 m high. In terms of design, there are six aspects that need to be considered, some of which are interrelated. These are the removal efficiency, the organic loading rate, the volume of media required, the aspect ratio (height:diameter), the irrigation rate, and whether to operate the process as a single filter or as a sequence of consecutive filters in 'cascade'. The efficiency is a predetermined factor, depending on the quality required of the final effluent. From this it is possible to derive the organic loading rate (Fig. 1.18) and hence the volume of media required. The choice of aspect ratio is more arbitrary. However, for a given volume of media better performances are

Fig. 1.17 — Various types of random pack plastic media.

Table 1.4 — Properties of plastic media used in high-rate biological filtration

Media type	Plastic	Bulk density (kg m^{-3})	Specific surface (m^2 m^{-3})	Voidage (%)
Flocor R.	u-PVC	40	240	95
Flocor ES	PVC	38	83	98
Actifil 50 E	Polypropylene	55	124	—
Filter YTH 1130	Polypropylene	64	190	—

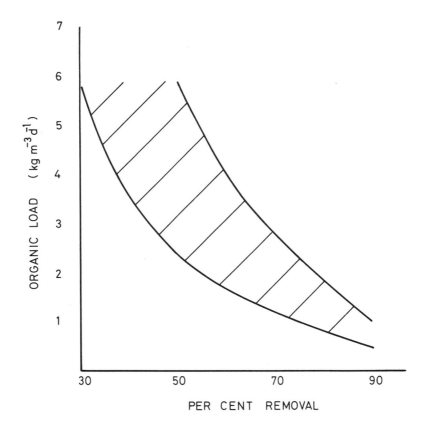

Fig. 1.18 — Performance envelope for plastic media filtration.

achieved from deep, small diameter filters than from reactors with smaller aspect ratios. This is due to an increased liquid residence time in the bed coupled with an improved wetting of the biofilm surface. As with stone filters, it is important to achieve an adequate minimum irrigation rate. This varies with the type of media being used as the packing but it is significantly higher (10–30 m^3 m^{-2} d^{-1}) than that required for stone packing.

An alternative method of calculating design criteria for high-rate filters is to use formulae based on first-order kinetics in a plug-flow reactor, as in, for example, Reference [1.30].

High-rate filtration using plastic media is most effect when being used to achieve a 50–60 per cent removal of BOD. However, if a high-strength industrial waste is being treated, a greater degree of treatment is often required. Under these circumstances, a 'cascade' process would be used, each stage being designed as a separate unit but with different influent BOD concentrations, removal efficiencies and loading rates. An alternative use for high-rate filters is to remove the initial load from an overloaded works (activated sludge or stone filters). Under these circumstances, a single filter would be adequate.

Another popular fixed biomass process is the rotary biological contactor (RBC). There are several different designs available commercially [1.29] but its basic form comprises a series of discs (2–3 m diameter) mounted on a shaft which is driven so that the discs rotate at right angles to the flow of settled sewage (Fig. 1.19). The discs, which are usually made of plastic, are located so that about 40 per cent of their area is submerged. The process is, therefore, one of alternating absorption — of pollutants and then of oxygen — by the biofilm which develops on the discs. This biofilm is protected from the weather by covering the reactors or by having them within buildings, and from rotational shear by limiting the speed of rotation to 0.5–10 revolutions per minute. The discs are arranged in groups which are separated by baffles. These minimise surging or short-circuiting. Excess biofilm that is sloughed off the discs tends to remain in the reactor trough. However, a final settlement tank should be used to protect the receiving watercourse.

Several techniques are available for the design of RBC's. These have been reviewed by Lumbers [1.31] who questions the suitability of all of them. However, for small reactors (less than a population equivalent of 250) it is reasonable to suggest that the design basis for a 30:20 effluent should be a loading rate of not more than 6 g BOD $m^{-2} d^{-1}$ and that, in the UK, the reactor tank should be compatible with CP 6297 [1.32]. For larger reactors readers are referred to the method based on the hydraulic loading rate per unit area [1.33; 1.34] or that using first-order kinetics [1.29].

The most recent type of fixed film process to be evaluated is the expanded or fluidised bed reactor. Indeed, its stage of development is such that there are no generally accepted design criteria. The basic features of these reactors are a solid support medium which is colonised by an appropriate microbial film, an upward flow of liquid sufficient to give either bed expansion or fluidisation, an oxygen transfer system and a means for obtaining an even horizontal distribution of the liquid flow across the bed. In addition, facilities must be provided for removing excess biofilm. The various differences in these basic aspects can best be illustrated by examining two processes which have to be developed to full-scale application: the Oxitron system (Dorr-Oliver Co. Ltd) and the Captor process (Simon-Hartley Ltd). The Oxitron reactors use sand (250–500 μm) as the support

Fig. 1.19 — Rotary biological contactor (by courtesy of Clearwater Systems Ltd).

medium and oxygen transfer is achieved by passing the feedstock (settled sewage) through an external downflow bubble oxygenator into which pure oxygen is injected. In the reactor described by Hoyland and Robinson [1.35], the average concentration of biomass within the reactor was 10–14 kg m^{-3}. The distribution of liquid is achieved by a downwards injection into a conical base [1.36]. Three methods have been developed for removing excess biomass from sand-based reactors [1.36–1.38]. All of them use shear to separate the sand from the biomass. The differences lie in the way in which the sludge is then thickened, whether the shear is done within the main reactor or externally and whether a final settlement tank is necessitated. The Captor process uses a unique support medium of reticulated foam pads which, it is claimed, can support a very high film density because of the large specific surface (see Chapter 9). The method of oxygen transfer is also different. A diffused air system is used within the reactor itself so that fluidisation is achieved by an air–liquid mixture. Biomass removal is effected by the simple process of taking pads from the reactor and passing them through rollers. This produces a concentrated sludge and leaves 'clean' pads to be returned to the reactor.

The final type of fixed biomass reactor that needs to be mentioned is the upflow filter. This can be thought of as a precursor to expanded bed reactors. It is also a process for which there are no clearly defined design criteria. The basic concept [1.39] is that of a packed bed reactor (using stone or plastic media) in which there is an upward flow of liquid so that the packing is totally submerged. Aeration is achieved either externally or by diffused air at the base of the reactor. The process is claimed to have the benefits of both the activated sludge system (hydraulic control) and trickling filters (fixed biomass). However, its application is not widespread.

1.3 OPERATIONAL ASPECTS AND PERFORMANCE

Although the design of aerobic wastewater treatment processes is based on sound scientific principles, their operation is often more of an art than a science. This mostly arises from the extreme variations that are found in the composition and nature of sewages; they vary diurnally, from day to day and from season to season. Not only are variations due to climatic conditions (mostly rainfall and temperature) but also due to changes in the effluents from industrial processes which may be discharged to public sewers.

The operation of sewage treatment processes can be said to be concerned with achieving a set of standard objectives under conditions of extreme variation and uncertainty. As a consequence, processes which are simple and robust are usually the easiest to operate. Very often processes are provided with sophisticated control and operational systems which are completely unwarranted. Like most industries the wastewater treatment industry is subject to fashion and an often misplaced desire to introduce the lastest technology whether it is justified or not. More often than not simple and robust processes do not need sophisticated control systems nor do they need over-sophisticated monitoring systems.

For routine operational purposes most sewage works can be operated from a knowledge of the flow rate, BOD, suspended solids and nitrogen determinations carried out on the influent, intermediate liquors and final effluents. While improvements in analytical techniques have produced methods for analysing an ever-increasing number of determinands in sewage, most (e.g. TOC) have little practical value in routine operations. Also, despite many recent developments, few instruments are available which can provide reliable information which is of immediate operational value, the exceptions being those for monitoring dissolved oxygen and suspended solids.

With regard to sampling frequency, it is impractical and unnecessary to sample all types of works on a daily basis. It is usual to consider the size of works, the effect that the effluent has on receiving watercourses, and the consequence of works failure when designing a sampling programme. However, no matter how frequently samples are taken, operations will always be carried out in an atmosphere of uncertainty and will be based on information which is, at best, recent history.

Before proceeding to discuss operation and control of sewage treatment systems in further detail, it is perhaps worth recalling two axioms which traditional sewage works managers used to expound — words of operational wisdom which are as relevant today as they were in the past. The first is that 'good sewage treatment starts with good trade effluent control'. The second is that 'if you take good care of the sludge the rest of the system takes care of itself'.

Regarding the first of these axioms it is beyond the scope of this text to discuss trade effluent control but it should be borne in mind that there is a vital need to prevent industrial discharges from poisoning or inhibiting the biological processes. Regarding the second axiom it is again beyond the scope of this chapter to discuss sludge treatment and disposal systems. However, it is worth stating that the largest proportion of the operational effort, problems, and costs of sewage treatment are usually associated with the treatment and disposal of sludge (see Chapter 5).

1.3.1 Preliminary treatment

Most aerobic treatment processes, whether they are homogeneous reactors or fixed biomass reactors, require some form of preliminary treatment. For domestic sewage systems this usually comprises removal of gross solids (screenings) and removal of grit. This vitally important aspect of wastewater treatment has been the subject of an intensive study [1.40; 1.41] in the UK and the reader is directed to this work for detailed discussion of the many problems associated with this often objectionable operation.

In general, screenings are dealt with either by systems which remove them from the flow (Fig. 1.20), or systems which chop them into small pieces and return the chopped material to the wastewater (Fig. 1.21). By and large, there are two schools of thought regarding the choice of system but sometimes it is governed by the size of the works. At large manned works it is a relatively easy matter to remove screenings using automatic or semi-automatic systems. This is not so easy at small rural works, especially if they have infrequent visits from mobile operators. In this case it is often easier to use a chopping and return to flow technique.

As a matter of principle it is better to remove screenings if possible, especially in works which have no primary settlement tanks. In cases where a removal technique is not used, care should be taken with the choice of device. Some types do not properly chop the screenings into small pieces but rather shred them into long thin strips which tend to reconstitute into rag balls in the downstream plant, causing considerable operational problems. In addition, unsatisfactorily chopped screenings can give rise to problems when ultimately disposed of if sludge is spread on agricultural land.

Fig. 1.20 — Automaticaly raked screen (by courtesy of Biwater Sewage Treatment).

1.3.2 Homogeneous reactors

General discussions on the overall performance of homogeneous reactors are difficult. The inherent uncertainties which accompany wastewater treatment, the variety of different processes and the dearth of good comparable operational data make it impossible to be precise about performance levels However, while the overall picture can be confusing, careful consideration shows that homogeneous reactors vary in only three principal respects:

(a) Method of oxygen supply
(b) Configuration
(c) Loading rate

All homogeneous reactors comprise different permutations of these

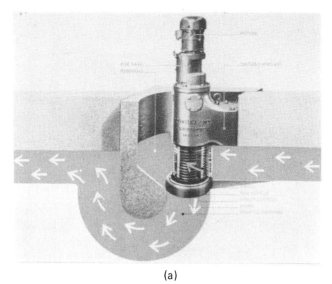

(a)

(b)

Fig. 1.21 — Comminutor systems: (a) Schematic diagram; (b) As installed.

elements and, differences in wastewater apart, it is these permutations which determine basic performance. Having set up a process with a specific tank configuration and method of aeration at a given loading rate, the ecology of the system is established and the performance in terms of effluent quality and sludge production is determined. This is of course an oversimplification, as other factors, such as the nature of sewage and changes in the rate of oxygen demand, also affect performance. Provided that each unit operation within a given process is not overloaded, the principal feature which governs effluent quality is the organic loading rate, which is operationally controlled in broad terms by controlling sludge wastage rate.

It is often claimed that effluent quality can be predicted from kinetic expressions but in practice this is of little real value; it is more useful to consider broad performance levels. For the treatment of domestic sewage the following approximate effluent quality can be expected:

	Range of organic loading $(kg\ kg^{-1}\ d^{-1})$	Effluent quality $(mg\ l^{-1})$
Extended aeration	0.05–0.2	High quality — fully nitrified BOD<10; SS<10; NH_3<5
Conventional aeration	0.2–0.45	About Royal Commission for 95% of the time. Fully nitrified at low end of range to non-nitrified at upper end
High rate	0.5–5.0	Such plants have high rate of removal of BOD per unit mass of sludge. Effluent quality would be about 30:20 on average provided supply of oxygen is adequate

It should be noted that the limits of these ranges are nebulous and that effluent varies throughout the diurnal cycle. Diurnal variations in flow rate may cause short-term changes in organic loading rate which can affect effluent quality, particularly if the aeration intensity is not sufficient to satisfy oxygen demand. For design purposes the maximum loading anticipated during the retention time should be used to calculate the required aeration intensity, otherwise sufficient dissolved oxygen may not be available to meet peak demand.

This leads to another feature which affects overall performance — the effective control of dissolved oxygen. Since installed aeration intensity should be based on peak loading, it is obvious that at other times the dissolved oxygen will increase unless there is some controlling mechanism. As previously stated, if full nitrification is required a DO concentration of at least $2\ mg\ l^{-1}$ is necessary somewhere in the aeration tank; concentrations above $2\ mg\ l^{-1}$ would simply be a waste of energy and money and would reduce the rate of oxygen supply, since the rate is directly proportional to the oxygen deficit.

Dissolved oxygen control can also affect quality in other ways, one of the most important being the introduction of anoxic zones into the aeration tanks of nitrifying systems to provide a means of denitrification. Although the production of a denitrified effluent in itself may have economic advantages and may be required for low nitrogen effluents, the main advantage is the operational one of preventing the phenomenon happening in the final settlement tank. Very often effluent quality is adversely affected by denitrification conditions in the final tank in which the gaseous nitrogen produced adheres onto the sludge particles, causing them to rise and be lost in the final effluent. Controlling denitrification within the aeration tank by reducing dissolved oxygen to less than 0.5 mg l^{-1} will minimise the problem.

Probably the most important feature in operating an activated sludge system is the control and operation of the final settlement tank (Fig. 1.22). If

Fig. 1.22 — A radial-flow final settlement tank.

this tank is overloaded with solids, biomass will be lost from the system at a rate faster than it can grow and the system will fail.

Final settlement tanks have two functions, clarification and thickening. Efficient performance demands that clarification is sufficient to meet the standard required by the effluent, and that the separated solids can be consolidated (or thickened) into a concentrated suspension to be recycled for maintenance of the process. Traditionally, clarification was the main concern in designing settlement tanks and the most commonly used design parameters were retention time and surface loading rate. More modern design philosophies are concerned with solids loading as this considers the thickening function. Probably the most successful addition to the theory has been the introduction of classical solids flux analysis [1.42, 1.43]. This theory predicts the maximum solids handling capacity of a tank from measurements of settling velocity at different solids concentrations, and it considers the effect of the underflow on solids withdrawal. A particular problem is the variability of the sludge settlement properties. Although much research has been carried out into sludge settlement no theory exists to account for all the variations. Therefore practical operation requires some measurement of sludge settleability. In fact, measurement of sludge settleability and control of sludge wastage rate are the most important aspects of activated sludge plant operation.

Traditionally, in the UK, settlement characteristics were assessed by allowing sludge to settle in a standard one-litre cylinder for 30 minutes. This produces a measure called the sludge volume index (SVI), the main disadvantage of which is that it is influenced by the presence of the walls of the small cylinder and by the concentration of solids, especially at high values.

In an attempt to overcome difficulties in the use of the SVI, the Water Research Centre developed and evaluated an alternative now known as the Stirred Specific Volume Index (SSVI) [1.44]. In this, settlement is carried out in a 10 cm diameter tube which incorporates a low-speed stirrer, thus reducing particle-bridging and wall effects. Evaluation of SSVI at 3.5 g l^{-1} shows that it correlates particularly well with sludge settling characteristics and that it can predict ($\pm 20\%$) the maximum solid handling capacity of a final settlement tank, except where sludge settlement is very bad [1.12].

As a guide to settlement characteristics it is convenient to consider four ranges of SSVI as follows:

Settlement	Range of SSVI (1 g^{-1}) at 3.5 g l^{-1}
Excellent	60–79
Good	80–99
Poor	100–119
Bad (bulked)	120–139

The operation of a settlement tank using a mass flux approach means keeping the applied solids loading, F_{app}, below the maximum flux rate, F_{max}, predicted from theory, i.e.

$$F_{app} = (Q_o/A + Q_u/A)C_f < F_{max} \tag{1.6}$$

where Q_o is the flow rate of sewage, Q_u is the rate of underflow, A is the surface area and C_f is the concentration of feed solids (i.e. MLSS).

It is possible to use the information derived from SSVI measurements in an operational environment. White [1.44] has shown that F_{max} can be obtained from the following empirical relationship:

$$F_{max} = 310 \, (SSVI)^{-0.77} \, (Q_u/A)^{0.68} \, \text{kg m}^{-2} \, \text{h}^{-1} \tag{1.7}$$

Thus for a given value of (Q_u/A), the operator can use Equations 1.6 and 1.7 to obtain a maximum MLSS concentration for a given rate of flow, or a given MLSS. The operator can then (if possible) alter the rate of return to accommodate the plant conditions. Alternatives to calculation are the nomograph given by White or the tabular system used by Johnstone et al. [1.45].

Although the use of mass flux and SSVI have proved useful tools in the design and operation of final tanks, they have little or no value in predicting final effluent quality. A comprehensive investigation by Chapman [1.46] studied the effect on effluent quality (C_e) of seven variables; MLSS, sidewater depth (SWD), influent flow-rate ($Q_f=Q_o+Q_c$), depth of stilling chamber, rake speed, underflow rate, and airflow rate. He found only the first three variables were significant and derived a best fit equation:

$$C_e = -180.6 + 4.03C_f + 133.24\,Q_f/A + SWD(90.16 - 62.54\,Q_f/A) \qquad (1.8)$$

Even this analysis does not take account of the filtering effect on the blanket, the settleability of the sludge particles, or the effects of weir shape, and therefore there are still no hard and fast rules for design or operation of final settlement tanks.

Although settlement problems can be coped with to a significant extent by use of the mass flux equations, activated sludge plants can suffer from a second biologically based operational problem: the formation of stable foams on the aeration tank (Fig. 1.23). These foams are very viscous and can

Fig. 1.23 — Stable foam on an activated sludge aeration tank.

have a depth of 0.5–30 cm. Their formation does not appear to have any detrimental effect on the oxidation of soluble BOD but they are unsightly, they can accumulate in the final settlement tanks giving rise to high suspended solids in the final effluent and, as they dry out or decompose, they can cause odour problems. In addition, the removal of foam can add to the operating cost of the plant. The main characteristic of these foams, apart from their stability, is that they contain high concentrations of biological solids (5–10% w/v), the dominant species of which are filamentous microbes (*Nocardia; Microthrix parvicella* or *Rhodococcus*) [1.4, 1.5, 1.47, 1.48]. The stimulus for foam formation is not known and, currently, the technique for getting rid of foams can have side-effects. For example, chlorination can produce an unknown range of chlorinated organic compounds and the use of anti-foams can have deleterious effects on oxygen transfer.

Despite variations in the settlement characteristics and the problems associated with foams, a correctly designed and well-maintained activated sludge plant can produce an effluent which is adequate for discharge into inland watercourses. The data presented in Table 1.5 are in broad agree-

Table 1.5 — Activated sludge performance data assessed in terms of the final effluent quality

Type of plant[a]	Daily flow $(m^3 d^{-1})$	BOD $(mg\,l^{-1})$	SS $(mg\,l^{-1})$	Amm.N $(mg\,l^{-1})$
CDA	240000	6	17	2
CDA	52000	22	20	5
EAC	25000	5	9	3
CSA	22500	11	11	13
EAM	6000	7	8	3
CSA	5750	29	40	6
CSA	4400	5	9	2

[a]CSA: Conventional plant; surface aeration
CDA: Conventional plant; diffused air
EAM: Extended aeration; Mammoth system
EAC: Extended aeration; Carrousel system

ment with most surveys into the performance of activated sludge systems. For example, the survey made by Booth [1.49] reported that 83 per cent reduced the BOD to less than 10 mg l^{-1} and 75 per cent produced effluents whose ammoniacal nitrogen concentrations were less than 10 mg l^{-1}.

Oxygen-activated sludge plants are sufficiently different to merit a brief but separate discussion. Thus, Table 1.6, which provides performance data from three studies, highlights the higher mixed liquor solids concentrations and sludge loading rates that can be used with this process. Other performance data from both full-scale and pilot-plant studies have been summa-

Table 1.6 — Unox–oxygen activated sludge plants: typical full scale operating data (by courtesy of Wimpey-Unox Ltd)

	Nature of feed[a]		
	A	B	C
Duration of study period (weeks)	31	25	4
Retention time in reactor (h)	1.54	4.1	13
(based on feed flow only)			
Mixed liquor suspended solids (mg l^{-1})	4 000	5 500	4 000
Sludge loading (kg BOD kg MLSS^{-1} day^{-1})	0.46	0.48	0.72
Sewage average characteristics:			
BOD (mg l^{-1})	109	453	1 560
COD (mg l^{-1})	268	730	2 500
Suspended Solids (mg l^{-1})	116	161	408
Effluent average characteristics:			
BOD (mg l^{-1})	5	21	25
COD (mg l^{-1})	56	68	159
Suspended Solids (mg l^{-1})	9	28	54
Sludge yield (kg sludge kg BOD removed^{-1})	0.53	—	—
Oxygen used (kg oxygen kg BOD removed^{-1})	0.95	—	—

[a]A: Settled domestic sewage
 B: Mixed industrial/domestic wastewater
 C: Industrial wastewater

rised by Forster [1.50]. This review covered not only the effluent quality produced but also the effect of sludge loading rate on the oxidation of BOD and ammoniacal nitrogen, the significance of sludge age on nitrification, the sludge production figures and the energy usage. The conclusions of this summary were that, although the process was more complex and required strict safety precautions, it did offer the facility of a compact, high-rate treatment for both domestic and industrial wastes. The only real problem with its performance was associated with the oxidation of ammonia.

1.3.3   Fixed film reactors

Like activated sludge systems, the quality of effluent obtained from fixed film reactors depends on many factors, not least of which is the performance of the humus tank. It is not uncommon for poor performance of biological filters to be attributed solely to the inadequate design of humus tank. Any inadequacies in humus tank capacity are exacerbated by the problem of 'spring sloughing'. In the winter months the lower temperatures cause a reduction in the activity of predators in the biofilm which in turn results in an accumulation of biomass within the filter. When ambient temperatures begin to increase again in the spring and normal predator activity levels are achieved, the excess biofilm is unloaded from the filters. Thus, the humus tanks are subjected to significantly higher loading rates than at other times of the year and, very frequently, this means that there is a noticeable increase in the concentration of solids discharged in the final effluent (see Fig. 1.24).

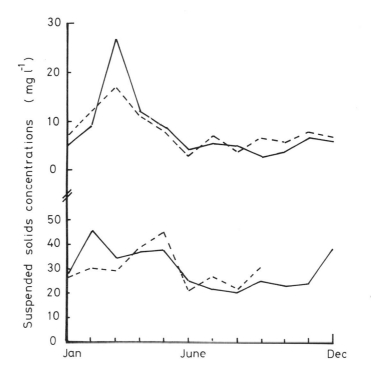

Fig. 1.24 — The suspended solids concentrations in the final effluent from two trickling filter works on consecutive years showing the impact of 'spring sloughing'.

Climatic conditions can also influence the performance of filters required to produce a nitrified effluent. In cold weather the first indication of effluent deterioration is loss of nitrification and this is often influenced by the location and position of the filter. Above-ground filters in isolated positions usually lose nitrification sooner than filters which are well sheltered from chilling winds. In theoretical terms, a sinusoidal variation would be expected and, indeed, such a pattern is used by the Sewage Treatment Optimisation Model (STOM) [1.51]. However, the seasonal variations noted in practice are not always so precise. For example, Booth [1.49] has shown that for a set of 45 filters, which produced annual mean ammoniacal nitrogen concentrations of less than 5 mg l^{-1}, only 16 produced their poorest quarterly mean in the coldest quarter (December to February). These data do not disprove the concept of a temperature effect; they simply emphasise how much other factors, such as the nature of the sewage and the type and size of the filter media, can affect performance. It is, therefore, difficult to be precise about performance levels of biological filters. However, for conventional filtration of domestic sewage the following can be used as a guide to the effluent quality which can be expected (see also Fig. 1.14):

Organic loading rate (kg BOD $m^{-3} d^{-1}$)	Expected effluent quality
0.06	Full nitrification
0.09	20 mg l^{-1} BOD: 30 mg l^{-1} SS; 3.5 mg l^{-1} NH_3 for 95% of time
0.12	20 mg l^{-1} BOD: 30 mg l^{-1} SS for 50% of time

The operation of biological filter plants is in some respects not a difficult process. In general, filters are not as flexible as activated sludge systems so that the operational options are limited. Vital to the successful operation is the need to keep dosing syphons and distributors clear of rags and screenings which have escaped preliminary treatment. The 1983 industrial dispute of the UK water workers illustrated very well the effect of removing basic cleaning operations from routine maintenance schedules: clogged distributors caused end-caps to be blown off and seals to break. The result was short-circuiting of the filters and, in some cases, sewage completely bypassing filters with only partially treated liquors reaching the humus tanks which themselves sometimes failed due to lack of desludging operations. A major development has been the introduction of the JETCLEAR™ system (Fig. 1.25). This is a simple mechanical device which prods the distributor holes and maintains effective distribution, thus reducing the need for manual cleaning. Developed by the Water Research Centre, trials have shown that the cleaning frequency can be cut from 6 hours per week to one per month with a similar reduction in flushing and rodding.

Under normal conditions, the operation of filter plants is a matter of controlling ponding, odours and flies. Ponding of filters is caused by an overgrowth of biomass on surfaces in the top layers of the bed and arises readily in low-rate filters. Filters with recirculation of effluent tend to be less susceptible to ponding, due not only to good wetting or irrigation rate but also to increased flushing of biomass. Ponding is indicated by a sudden increase in BOD of the filter effluent and by the formation of puddles or ponds on the surface of the bed. Ponding can be overcome in various ways, including recirculation of final effluent or increasing the rate of recirculation if already practised. Sometimes it is necessary to rake or fork the upper layers of the bed to loosen and turn the surface. This may also be needed in the early stages of increased recirculation until improved sloughing is

Fig. 1.25 — The JETCLEAR™ system (by courtesy of WRc Processes' JET-CLEAR is a trademark of the Water Research Centre).

achieved. If possible, resting of a filter for several days can alleviate ponding as can the introduction of a slug of chlorine (to about 30 mg l^{-1}.)

Flies often cause annoyance, especially if the filters are near to houses or industrial sites [1.52]. The main nuisance species are the 'filter fly' (Psychodids) and midges (Chironomids), and in elaborating control strategies it is an advantage to determine which species is responsible for the nuisance [see 1.53]. The techniques that are available for the control of fly nuisances are:

(a) To adjust the biofilm thickness so as to maximise the competition between the larvae of the two species (thick biofilms inhibit Chironomids but enhance Psychodids);

(b) To improve the wetting of the filter surface (*Psychoda* spp. emerge through dry media [1.54]);

(c) To use chemicals either against the adult fly, if 'resting places' around the works can be identified, or against the larvae [see 1.55]. However, in using chemical agents it must be remembered that tolerance against biocides can be developed and that the concentration of any toxic agent in the final effluent must be kept as low as possible so as to minimise the effect on the receiving watercourse.

Odours are frequently a problem with filters, particularly when operated as high-rate filters where there can be a large quantity of biomass respiring at a high rate. Ventilation rates may be inadequate to meet the oxygen demand

and the filter can contain a high proportion of anaerobic biomass. Under such circumstances it may be necessary to introduce forced ventilation. Odours can arise in high-rate filters not only from the filter itself but also from the humus sludge produced. In high-rate filters, humus sludges have high respiration rates so can readily turn septic on standing or when being subjected to further treatment (see Chapter 5). Odours sometimes arise from the distribution of sewage which has become septic either in rising mains or in preliminary treatment. Pre-aeration, recirculation of final effluent and chlorination can all be effective in freshening septic sewage.

1.4   CONCLUSIONS

The reactors described in this chapter are, of necessity, robust processes which are designed and operated on the basis of well-established empirical rules. In general, they perform well. However, one of the roles of the biotechnologist is to develop a sufficiently sound understanding of any process that is can be subjected to total control. This has not yet been achieved for aerobic reactors treating sewage or industrial wastewaters. Indeed, it is a point of contention whether it can or even should be done. The type of understanding needed almost invariably leads workers to develop theoretical mathematical models. At the present state of the art, these tend to have shortcomings (see Chapter 8). Indeed, Porter [1.56] has concluded that 'there are considerable difficulties in developing the theory to the point where high rate filters may be designed from knowledge of the waste alone'. There can be no doubt that this debate will continue: to model or not to model; to use theory or empiricism. Whatever the outcome, it is essential that the environmental biotechnologist takes a leading role in determining the answer so that, ultimately, processes are provided with the capacity of improved control. If this could be achieved, a much greater flexibility in discharge consent standards (in line with the prevailing conditions in the receiving watercourse) could be considered. This could, in turn, lead to savings in both capital and operational costs.

REFERENCES

[1.1] Pike, E. B. (1975) Aerobic bacteria. In *Ecological Aspects of Used-water Treatment,* Curds, C. R. and Hawkes, H. A. (eds), Academic Press, London, pp 1–64.

[1.2] Sezgin, M., Jenkins, D. and Parker, D. S. (1978) A unified theory of activated sludge filamentous bulking. *J. Wat. Pollut. Control Fed.,* **50,** 362–381.

[1.3] Blackbeard, J. R., Ekama, G. A. and Marais, G. V. R. (1986) A survey of filamentous bulking and foaming in activated-sludge plants in South Africa. *Wat. Pollut. Control,* **85,** 95–100.

[1.4] Segerer, M. (1984) Studies of scum formation in sewage works due to actinoymcetes. *Korr. Abwasser,* **31,** 1073–1076.

[1.5] Pipes, W. O. (1978) Actinomycete scum production in activated sludge processes. *J. Wat. Pollut. Control Fed.*, **50**, 628–634.

[1.6] Eikelboom, D. H. and van Buijsen, T. (1981) *Microscopic Sludge Investigation Manual.* TNO Research Institute, Delft, The Netherlands.

[1.7] Curds, C. R. (1975) Protozoa. In *Ecological Aspects of Used-water Treatment,* Vol. 1, Curds, C. R. and Hawkes, H. A. (eds), Academic Press, London, pp. 203–268.

[1.8] Curds, C. R. and Cockburn, A. (1970) Protozoa in biological sewage treatment processes: 2. Protozoa as indicators in the activated sludge process. *Wat. Res.*, **4**, 237–249.

[1.9] Curds, C. R. (1971) Computer simulations of microbial population dynamics in the activated sludge process. *Wat. Res.*, **5**, 1049–1066.

[1.10] Forster, C. F. (1983) Continuously-operated ditches. In *Oxidation Ditches in Wastewater Treatment,* Barnes, D. *et al.* (eds), Pitman Books, London, pp. 75–131.

[1.11] Downing, A. L. (1968) Factors to be considered in the design of activated sludge plant. In *Advances in Water Quality Improvement,* Gloyna, E. F. and Eckenfelder, W. W. (eds), Water Resources Symposium No. 1, University of Texas Press, pp. 190–202.

[1.12] Johnstone, D. W. M., Rachwal, A. J., Hanbury, M. J. and Critchard, D. J. (1980) Design and operation of final settlement tanks: use of stirred specific volume index and mass flux theory. *Trib. du CEBEDEAU*, **443**, 411–425.

[1.13] Boon, A. G. (1983) Aeration methods. In *Oxidation Ditches in Wastewater Treatment,* Barnes, D. *et al.* (eds), Pitman Books, London, pp. 173–187.

[1.14] Johnstone, D. W. M. and Carmichael, W. F. (1982) Cirencester Carrousel plant: some process considerations. *Wat. Pollut. Control*, **81**, 587–600.

[1.15] Tomlinson, E. J. (1976) *Bulking — a survey of activated sludge plants.* Technical Report TR 35, Water Research Centre.

[1.16] Tomlinson, E. J. and Chambers, B. (1979) *The effect of longitudinal mixing on the settleability of activated sludge.* Technical Report TR 122, Water Research Centre.

[1.17] Chambers, B. (1982) Effect of longitudinal mixing and anoxic zones on settleability of activated sludge. In *Bulking of Activated Sludge: Prevention and Remedial Methods,* Chambers, B. and Tomlinson, E. J. (eds), Ellis Horwood, Chichester, pp. 166–186.

[1.18] Rensink, J. H., Donker, H. J. G. W. and Ijwema, T. S. J. (1982) The influence of feed pattern on sludge bulking. In *Bulking of Activated Sludge: Prevention and Remedial Methods,* Chambers, B. and Tomlinson, E. J. (eds) Ellis Horwood, Chichester, pp. 147–165.

[1.19] Kite, O. A. and Garrett, M. E. (1983) Oxygen transfer and its measurement. *Wat. Pollut. Control*, **82**, 21–28.

[1.20] Boon, A. G. (1976) Technical review of the use of oxygen in the treatment of wastewater. *Wat. Pollut. Control*, **75**, 206–213.

[1.21] Blachford, A. J., Tramontini, E. M. and Griffiths, A. J. (1982) Oxygenated activated sludge process: evaluation at Palmersford. *Wat. Pollut. Control,* **81,** 601–618.

[1.22] Hemmings, M. L., Ousby, J. C., Plowright, D. R. and Walker, J. (1977) Deep Shaft — latest position. *Wat. Pollut. Control,* **76,** 441–451.

[1.23] Collins, O. C. and Elder, M. D. (1982) Experience in operating a Deep Shaft activated sludge process. *Public Health Engineer,* **10,** 153–158.

[1.24] Bolton, D. H. and Ousby, J. C. (1977) The ICI deep shaft effluent treatment process and its potential for large sewage works. *Prog. Wat. Technol.,* **8,** 265–273.

[1.25] Cox, G. C., Lewin, V. H., West, J. T., Bignal, W. J., Redhead, D. L., Roberts, J. G., Shah, N. K. and Waller, C. B. (1980) The use of the Deep Shaft process in uprating and extending existing sewage treatment works. *Wat. Pollut. Control,* **79,** 70–86.

[1.26] Robinson, A. B. and Cowen, R. (1985) Design and construction features of the second generation Tilbury Deep-Shaft plant. *Wat. Pollut. Control,* **84,** 515–522.

[1.27] National Research Council (1946) Sewage treatment at military installations. *Sewage Works J.,* **18,** 787–1028.

[1.28] Bruce, A. M. and Merkens, J. C. (1973) Further studies of partial treatment of sewage by high-rate biological filtration. *Wat. Pollut. Control,* **72,** 499–527.

[1.29] Pike, E. B. (1978) *The design of percolating filters and rotary biological contractors including details of international practice.* Technical Report TR 93, Water Research Centre.

[1.30] Hutchinson, E. G. (1975) A comparative study of biological filter media. Paper presented at the Biotechnology Conference, Massey University, May 1975.

[1.31] Lumbers, J. P. (1983) Rotating biological contactors: current problems and potential developments in design and control. *Public Health Engineer,* **11,** 41–45.

[1.32] British Standards Institution (1983) *Design and installation of small sewage treatment works and cesspools.* CP 6297, BSI, London.

[1.33] Steels, I. H. (1974) Design basis for the rotating disc process. *Eff. Wat. Trt. J.,* **14,** 431–445.

[1.34] Wilson, F. (1981) *Design Calculations in Wastewater Treatment.* E. and F. N. Spon, London.

[1.35] Hoyland, G. and Robinson, P. J. (1983) Aerobic treatment in 'Oxitron' BFB plant at Coleshill. *Wat. Pollut. Control,* **82,** 479–493.

[1.36] Cooper, P. F. and Wheeldon, D. H. V. (1982) Complete treatment of sewage in a two-stage fluidised-bed system. *Wat. Pollut. Control,* **81,** 447–464.

[1.37] Cooper, P. F., Wheeldon, D. H. V., Ingram-Todd, P. E. and Harrington, D. W. (1981) Sand-biomass separation with production of concentrated sludge. In *Biological Fluidised Bed Treatment of Water and Wastewater*, Cooper, P. F. and Atkinson, B. (eds), Ellis Horwood, Chichester, pp. 361–367.

[1.38] Hickey, R. and Owens, R. W. (1978) *Excess Growth Control System for Fluidised Bed Reactors*. US Patent No. 4177144.

[1.39] McHarness, D. D. and McCarty, P. L. (1973) *Field study of nitrification with the submerged filter*. US Environmental Protection Agency Report, EPA-R2-73-158.

[1.40] Sidwick, J. M. (1984) *Screening and grit in sewage: removal treatment and disposal: preliminary report*. Ciria Technical Note No. 119.

[1.41] Sidwick, J. M. (1985) *Screenings and grit in sewage: removal, treatment and disposal: Phase 2: further cost aspects of screening practice*. Ciria Technical Note No. 122.

[1.42] Dick, R. I. (1972) Gravity thickening of waste sludges. *Filtration and Separation*, **9**, 177–183.

[1.43] White, M. J. D. (1975) The settling of activated sludge — theory and practice. Symposium on the Application of Chemical Engineering to the Treatment of Sewage and Industrial Liquid Effluents, Instn Chem. Engrs Symp. Series No. 41, April 1975, pp. 1–19.

[1.44] White, M. J. D. (1976) *The settling of activated sludge*. Technical Report TR11, Water Research Centre.

[1.45] Johnstone, D. W. M., Rachwal, A. J., Hanbury, M. J. and Critchard, D. J. (1981) Design and operation of final settlement tanks. Paper presented at seminar on 'Future Trends in Sewage Treatment', Inst. Mun. Engrs, London, December 1981.

[1.46] Chapman, D. T. (1982) The influence of process variables on secondary clarification. Paper presented at 55th Water Pollution Control Federation Conference, St Louis, Missouri, September 1982.

[1.47] Greenfield, P. F., Pettigrew, A. E., Blackall, L. L. and Hayward, A. C. (1984) *Report No. 10: Actinomycete scum problems in activated sludge plants*. Department of Chemical Engineering, University of Queensland.

[1.48] Goddard, A. J. and Forster, C. F. (1987) The problem of stable foams in activated sludge plants. *Enz. Microbial Technol.*, **9**, 164–168.

[1.49] Booth, M. (1984) The alternative to aeration. Paper presented at symposium on 'Reducing Aeration Costs', *Inst. Water Pollut. Control*, Bristol, October 1984.

[1.50] Forster, C. F. (1985) *Biotechnology and Wastewater Treatment*. Cambridge University Press.

[1.51] Anon. (1981) *Sewage treatment optimisation model: User manual and description*. Technical Report TR 144, Water Research Centre.

[1.52] Painter, H. A. (1980) *A survey of filter fly nuisances and their remedies*. Technical Report TR 155, Water Research Centre.

[1.53] Woods, D. R., Williams, J. M. and Croydon, J. (1978) Fly nuisance control in treatment systems. *Wat. Pollut. Control*, **77**, 259–270.

[1.54] Otter, C. S. (1966) A physical method for the permanent control of *Psychoda* pests at wastewater treatment plants. *J. Wat. Pollut. Control Fed.*, **38,** 156–164.

[1.55] Harbott, B. J. and Penney, C. J. (1983) The efficiency of insecticide treatment of flies on biological filters. *Wat. Pollut. Control*, **82,** 571–581.

[1.56] Porter, K. E. (1985) High rate filters. In *Comprehensive Biotechnology,* Vol. 4, Robinson, C. W. and Howell, J. A. (eds), Pergamon Press, Oxford, pp. 963–981.

2

Anaerobic wastewater treatment processes

D. Barnes and P. A. Fitzgerald
School of Civil Engineering, University of New South Wales, Australia

2.1 INTRODUCTION

Two types of biological process are widely used for wastewater treatment:

— Aerobic processes in which the microbes use oxygen dissolved in the waste liquors (see Chapter 1).
— Anaerobic processes in which the microorganisms do not have access to freely dissolved oxygen, nor to other energetically favourable electron acceptors such as nitrate ions. In such circumstances microorganisms can use the carbon in organic molecules as the electron acceptor. The most widely used engineered anaerobic process in waste water treatment is that of sludge digestion; however, more sophisticated plants have been used for treating soluble, agricultural and industrial wastes and anaerobic systems have been investigated for treating settled municipal wastewaters.

The choice between aerobic and anaerobic processes for wastewater treatment has tended to favour the former because the systems were considered to be more reliable, more stable and better understood. However, anaerobic processes have several clear advantages [2.1]:

— Anaerobic processes generate less sludge than aerobic processes. The cost of sludge management can be significant due to the high moisture content (90–99.7%) of waste biological sludges. Aerobic processes are likely to yield between 0.5 and 1.5 kg of biomass (sludge) solids for each kg of BOD removed, while anaerobic processes are likely to yield only 0.1–0.2 kg for each kg of BOD removed.

— Anaerobic processes generate methane which can be used as a fuel source.
— Even without the use of methane as an energy source, the aeration energy requirements of aerobic processes exceed the mixing energy requirements of anaerobic processes.

The major disadvantages of anaerobic systems have been the slower rates of reaction when compared to aerobic processes [2.1]. Anaerobic processes therefore require larger plants. There is a lack of basic scientific knowledge of the processes and a lack of full scale operating experience and data. Hence the developments in anaerobic wastewater have been directed towards producing systems which have greater biological activity and are engineered as more compact plants and towards a greater understanding of the kinetics, microbiology and biochemistry of the processes.

2.1.1   Historical development

Systems harnessing anaerobic processes were reported in Europe approximately 100 years ago [2.2]. Septic tanks are sedimentation tanks in which the settled sludge undergoes anaerobic degradation. The solids separation and sludge digestion within a single tank were improved by provision of internal baffling in the Travis and Imhoff tanks; subsequently the two unit processes were separated and occurred in different tanks. Anaerobic sludge digestion is used to condition waste sludges, to reduce the mass of sludge solids and to reduce the number of pathogens in the sludge. The digesters are operated (usually) at approximately 35°C and use long hydraulic retention times (>20 d) without attempting to provide a mechanism to retain biomass for periods greater than the hydraulic residence time. A similar approach can be used to treat soluble and colloidal substrates based upon a stirred tank reactor; however, in order to reduce the size of the reactors the environmental and process conditions (pH, temperature, nutrients) are further optimised.

The development of high rate anaerobic processes requires not only that conditions are optimised for anaerobic degradation but that a high concentration of active biomass can be retained in the reactor. Two basic approaches have been used to increase biomass retention:

— Provide conditions which recycle sludge or engineer the reactors such that the sludge does not wash out at the same rate as the liquid. The anaerobic contact process provides a separate clarifier and recycles settled sludge, which is the same principle as used in the activated sludge (aerobic) process. The clarigester and upflow sludge blanket generate a dense granular sludge through which the wastewater passes at a rate which will not wash out the sludge solids.
— Provide a solid support on which the anaerobic biomass can grow and hence will be retained in the reactor. A range of solid support media has been reported in both upflow and downflow operation. For upflow systems the hydraulic flow rate through the reactor often specifies the

types of process; for example, using sand as a medium at low flows, the process is the anaerobic filter, while higher flows give the expanded and fluidised bed processes.

2.2 OVERALL PROCESS AND KINETICS

The majority of anaerobic wastewater treatment systems, operating in the mesophilic temperature range, will form the basis of work reported in this review. Cryophilic (<20°C) and thermophilic (>55°C) reactors have been studied; the majority of unheated systems (including septic tanks) are cryophilic. The microbial mixture within any reactor must reflect the organic molecules being degraded and the conditions within the reactor such as nutrients, mixing, and inlet arrangements.

The predominant species in the reactors are bacteria; however, there is a considerable degree of specialisation, in that the products from one bacterium are often the substrate for others and hence a balance between the bacterial numbers and the substrate concentrations must be maintained. For many years a simplified model was used to describe the anaerobic process in which large molecules were degraded to short-chain organic molecules (mainly volatile fatty acids) by 'acid forming' bacteria and these intermediate compounds were degraded to methane and carbon dioxide by 'methane forming' bacteria. The biochemistry is now perceived to be more complex, with the intermediate concentrations of volatile fatty acids the most important control parameters.

A detailed understanding of the thermodynamics and kinetics of anaerobic processes is not yet available; however, a simple overall analysis is possible based upon conventional reactor theory. Although the simplified kinetic model illustrates the basis for both municipal sludge digesters and high rate reactors, it should be stressed that such an approach provides few insights into the control of the reactions which occur.

2.2.1 Conventional kinetics

For a single substrate (S) being degraded by a microbial process, the rate of change of the substrate with time can be given by [2.3; 2.4):

$$\frac{dS}{dt} = -\bar{\mu}X\left(\frac{S}{K_s + S}\right) \tag{2.1}$$

where $\bar{\mu}$ is the maximum specific substrate utilisation rate,
X is the biomass concentration in the reactor, and
K_s is the substrate concentration at which the rate of reaction is half
the maximum rate — sometimes referred to as Monod's constant.

The equation can be written in terms of the maximum specific rate of uptake of substrate (k):

$$\frac{dS}{dt} = -kX\left(\frac{S}{K_s + S}\right) \tag{2.2}$$

The specific growth of the microorganism (μ) is given by

$$\mu = -\frac{dS}{dt}\frac{Y}{X} \tag{2.3}$$

where Y is the yield coefficient (kg biomass produced per kg of substrate removed).
  Hence

$$\mu = \bar{\mu}\left(\frac{S}{K_s + S}\right) \tag{2.4}$$

This simplified approach is clearly limited in its validity when applied to mixed microbial cultures (almost all wastewater treatment systems). For an interactive system such as mixed anaerobic cultures, the problems are compounded by difficulties in defining the active biomass and a lack of knowledge about the processes producing and consuming various substrtates. The rate-limiting step in the degradation scheme is probably the conversion of acetate into methane. Calculations based upon this assumption may be subject to error, especially where analytical data are not specific for acetate. To calculate the residence time for effective anaerobic degradation, data are required for the terms in Equation 2.4. The sludge age or mean cell residence time (θ_c) can then be calculated, where

$$\frac{1}{\theta_c} = \mu - K_d \tag{2.5}$$

in which K_d is the biomass decay constant and represents the death of the biomass.
  Approximate values of the factors in Equations 2.4 and 2.5 can be taken from the literature [2.5; 2.6] as:

$Y = 0.045$
$K_d = 0.02\ d^{-1}$
$\mu = 8.7\ d^{-1}$
$K_s = 165\ mg\ l^{-1}$ as COD for acetic acid.

Hence

$$\theta_c = \left(\frac{8.7 \times 0.045 \times S}{165 + S} - 0.02\right)^{-1} d \tag{2.6}$$

For low concentrations of acetic acid as may occur in conventional municipal sludge digesters, the values of K_s and S are likely to be similar and hence the value of θ_c will be approximately 5 days, as reported [2.7]. For systems which contain high concentrations of acetic acid (>200 mg l^{-1}) the value of θ_c reduces towards 2.5 d. However, in the presence of organic compounds which are more difficult to degrade, for example long chain fatty acids with K_s values of 2000 mg l^{-1} [2.7], the value of θ_c can be as high as 50 days. Most volatile acids in unstressed reactors are of low molecular weight, giving a mean cell residence time of at least 5 days.

Hence, for conventional stirred tank type reactors without any biomass retention or recycle, the minimum hydraulic retention time has to be 5 days. Other systems attempt to shorten the hydraulic residence time while retaining biomass for times in excess of 5 days.

2.3 BIOCHEMISTRY AND MICROBIOLOGY

2.3.1 Introduction

Recent advances in the understanding of microbiological and biochemical mechanisms of anaerobic digestion provide an opportunity for improved process control and optimisation, especially during start-up and for preventing digester instability. Despite the development of modern techniques for isolation and cultivation of strict anaerobes, and the availability of some data on microbial populations in municipal and animal waste digesters, little is known of the taxonomy of the microbial population. While the biochemistry of mixed culture fermentation systems is not yet fully elucidated, better understanding of the complex interrelated mechanisms involved has engendered a greater confidence in the large-scale industrial application of anaerobic digestion of wastes. These processes in the bacterially dominated biomass involve the conversion of complex organic material such as polysaccharides, lipids and proteins into methane and carbon dioxide. This symbiotic community, by having the ability to alter the fermentation pathways utilised, functions as a unified self-regulating system to maintain conditions of pH, oxidation/reduction potential (redox) and thermodynamic equilibria to optimise growth and hence maintain digester stability. According to their trophic requirements the bacteria may conveniently be divided into three broad categories. The first comprises hydrolytic bacteria, commonly referred to as acidogens, because they initially hydrolyse the substrate into short-chain organic acids and other small molecules. The second group are the heteroacetogens which produce acetic acid and hydrogen, and the third are the methanogens, which produce methane. This group may be further subdivided into hydrogen utilisers (lithotrophs) and acetic acid users (acetotrophs), Fig. 2.1.

Synergistic effects occur between these groups, such that different growth and yield rates may be recorded in co-culture or tri-culture from those observed in mono-culture, arising as a result of interactions such as interspecies hydrogen transfer [2.8]. Feedstocks containing oxidised sulphur

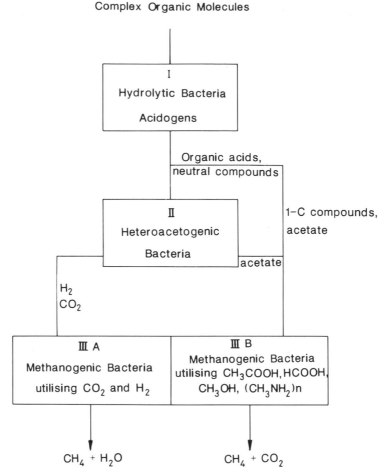

Fig. 2.1 — Schematic diagram showing the bacterial types and the degradation reactions which occur in anaerobic digestion.

and nitrogen may give rise to two additional groups of bacteria, the sulphate-reducers and the denitrifiers.

Cultural conditions other than substrate will affect the population distribution in mixed fermentation processes. One such parameter is temperature. Digesters may be operated at psychrophilic (<20°C), mesophilic (20–45°C) or thermophilic (50–65°C) temperatures. Thermophilic digestion has higher reaction rates, but this is frequently insufficiently advantageous to offset the cost of the additional heat energy required to maintain the higher temperature. In addition there is less species diversity [2.9], which can affect the ability of the system to adapt to different substrates [2.10] or inhibitory compounds.

Most engineered units, therefore, operate in the temperature range 34–38°C as a cost-effective compromise, which also allows more species diversity. Further discussion will refer mainly to mesophilic digestion.

2.3.2 Hydrolytic bacteria (Group I)
This functional group of bacteria hydrolyses macromolecules into soluble products, which can be taken up and converted into soluble short-chain organic molecules, some of which are listed by Zeikus (Table 2.1). Other

Table 2.1 — Products of anaerobic digestion (from [2.9])

Chemical species	Components with yields >0.2 mol mol^{-1} of substrate in an unstressed anaerobic digestion
Organic acids	Acetic acid, propionic acid, butyric acid, caproic acid, formic acid, lactic acid, succinic acid
Alcohols–ketones	Methanol, ethanol, iso-propanol, butanol, glycerol, acetone
Gases	Hydrogen, methane, carbon dioxide
Enzymes	Cellulase, alcohol dehydrogenase
Vitamins	Riboflavin, Vitamin B_{12}

products which may be present in small amounts include malonic acid, some longer chain fatty acids and fatty acid isomers, the concentrations of which depend upon feedstock characteristics and cultural conditions.

Members of this group (I) may be either strict anaerobes or facultative, and populations between 10^5–10^6 and 10^8–10^9 hydrolytic bacteria per ml of mesophilic sewage sludge, or 10^{10}–10^{11} per gram of volatile solids in sludge, have been found [2.8]. Isolates encompass a variety of genera including sporing and non-sporing gram-positive rods such as the proteolytic *Eubacterium*, cellulolytic Clostridia, *Acetobacterium*, strict anaerobes such as *Bacteroides* and *Bifidobacteria* and facultative Streptococci and Enterobacteriaceae. Gram-positive cocci are significant in piggery waste digestion. A recent investigation of 130 isolates from such a digester identified *Peptostreptococcus*, *Eubacterium*, *Bacteroides*, *Lactobacillus*, *Peptococcus*, *Clostridium* and *Streptococcus* [2.11].

The hydrolytic bacteria utilise a range of exo-enzymes such as proteases, lipases, amylases, cellulases and pectinases. These enzymes are frequently species-specific, and may be different from those of aerobic bacteria. The fermentation process hence solubilises natural substrates such as proteins, lipids and homo- and hetro-polysaccharides such as cellulose, starch, pectin and hemi-cellulose. Anaerobic degradation of lignin has not been thought feasible, due to the highly oxidative conditions normally required, although degradation of coniferyl alcohol, a basic lignin subunit, has recently been reported [2.12], and the presence of the intermediate phenyl propionic acid appears to support the concept of lignin fermentation via the anaerobic ferulate pathway. In addition to these natural substrates, anaerobic populations degrade phenols and sulphur compounds derived from such wastes as sulphur pulping processes, coal gasifier effluents and petrochemical wastewaters.

Fermentation products may vary with species and strain of bacteria, constitution and amount of feedstock and other cultural conditions such as pH, temperature and redox potential. Homo acid-forming species such as *Acetobacterium woodii* are generally product specific, but many hetero acid-forming bacteria such a *Lactobacillus brevis* have been described. Even conventional homo acid producers may have product variation. For example, *Lactobacillus casei* produces lactic acid as the sole end-product in non-energy limited batch culture, but produces nearly equivalent amounts of lactate, acetate and formate in energy-limited continuous culture. *Clostridium formoaceticum* forms only acetic acid during the logarithmic growth phase, but produces formic acid in addition during stationary phase at low pH, while butyrogens produce butyric acid in the presence of high acetate and proton concentration.

An important factor in hetero acid production is the concentration of hydrogen in the reactor. This affects both pH and the reduction–oxidation potential, E_h. Because of the broad speciation spectrum and versatility of the hydrolytic acidogenic group of bacteria, they are relatively tolerant of variation in cultural conditions, and a portion of this population is acidophilic. Mean generation times of 2–3 h have been recorded [2.13] — relatively low for anaerobic processes. The group, however, is adversely affected by low pH values and redox potentials E_h. In the event of hydrogen stress the organisms adopt alternative fermentation pathways in order to utilise more reduced compounds as hydrogen sinks, and hence control hydrogen concentration. For example, the normal production of acetic acid from glucose

$$C_6H_{12}O_6 + 2H_2O \rightarrow 2CH_3COOH + 4H_2 \qquad (2.7)$$
$$\text{glucose} \qquad\qquad\qquad \text{acetic acid}$$

produces four moles of hydrogen gas and two moles of acetic acid per mole of substrate. In the event of a hydraulic or concentration surge in feedstock to the digester, this population responds rapidly, producing excessive amounts of hydrogen and acetic acid, depressing the E_h and pH. If this process were to continue unchecked, the digester would 'sour' and fail. The acidogens, however, utilise feedback control loops, and adopt alternative biochemical pathways such as the production of propionic and butyric acids, thus aiding recovery of digester stability.

$$C_6H_{12}O_6 + 2H_2 \rightarrow 2CH_3CH_2COOH + 2CO_2 + 2H_2O \quad (2.8)$$
$$\text{glucose} \qquad\qquad \text{propionic acid}$$

$$C_6H_{12}O_6 \rightarrow CH_3CH_2CH_2COOH + 2CO_2 + 2H_2 \qquad (2.9)$$
$$\text{glucose} \qquad\qquad \text{butyric acid}$$

This role of hydrogen in controlling the production and consumption of intermediates accounts for production of some long chain (>4C) fatty acids which act as hydrogen sinks or storage. These processes are further discussed in the context of the trophic groups II and III (see Fig. 2.1).

2.3.3 Heteroacetogenic bacteria (Group II)

It was traditionally believed that the process of anaerobic digestion involved two main trophic groups, the acidogens and the methanogens. However, with the isolation of the S-organism [2.14] the significance of symbiotic acetogenic dehydrogenation of longer-chain fatty acids as a critical step in methanogenisis was recognised, and a separate group, the heteroacetogens, was acknowledged. Some workers classify the homoacetogenic bacteria such as *Acetobacterium woodii* as a separate fourth group, but here they have been included in the acidogenic category, Group I.

Two new species of heteroacetogens, *Syntrobacter wolinii* (a gram-negative rod) and *Synthrophomonas wolfii* (a non-phototrophic bacterium), have recently been described [2.15]. Populations of 4.2×10^6 of this group per ml of sewage sludge have been reported [2.8], and further identifications are anticipated. These bacteria are known to catabolise fatty acids such as propionate and butyrate, some alcohols and even aromatic organics such as benzoate, in this case with a mean generation time of 166 h [2.16], in association with methanogens.

The propionate and butyrate conversions may be written as:

$$CH_3CH_2COOH + 2H_2O \rightarrow CH_3COOH + CO_2 + 3H_2 \quad (2.10)$$
$$\text{propionic acid} \qquad\qquad\qquad \text{acetic acid}$$

$$CH_3CH_2CH_2COOH + 2H_2O \rightarrow 2CH_3COOH + 2H_2 \quad (2.11)$$
$$\text{butyric acid} \qquad\qquad\qquad \text{acetic acid}$$

The Gibbs free energy $\Delta G_0'$ of these reactions is not thermodynamically very favourable. The organisms can only derive energy from a reaction if the $\Delta G_0'$ under the cultural conditions is negative. Values of $\Delta G_0' = 48.1$ kJ and $\Delta G_r^0 = 71.67$ kJ have been derived for the propionate conversion [2.17; 2.18]. However, at low hydrogen partial pressures, the energetics of this reaction become more favourable, and biomass yield is increased, with a concomitant numerical reduction in Gibbs free energy (Fig. 2.2). From this it can be seen that heteroacetogenic dehydrogenation of propionate can only occur at $\log P_{H_2}$ (atmospheres) between -3.9 and -5.5, equivalent to approximately 3 to 126 ppm of hydrogen., Below 3 ppm of hydrogen, energy is not available from the reverse reaction of hydrogen conversion, and above 126 ppm of hydrogen propionate, conversion is thermodynamically unfavourable. This is confirmed by Heyes and Hall [2.19], who obtained concentrations of hydrogen between approximately 490 and 63 ppm in a continuously stirred tank reactor (CSTR) with hydraulic retention times of 8.2 and 14.5 days. These figures apply to conditions under which there are no mass transfer effects, and hence hydrogen is at similar concentration in all sectors of the reactors.

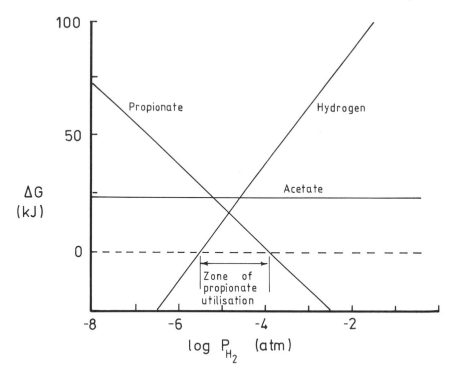

Fig. 2.2 — The effect of hydrogen partial pressure on the Gibbs free energy in
relation to fatty acids.

Mosey [2.20] has used E_h and the $NAD^+/NADH$ couple

$$NAD^+ + H^+ + 2e \rightleftharpoons NADH \qquad (2.12)$$

for steady-state kinetic modelling of hydrogen concentration in sewage
sludge digester gases, and predicted a concentration of 6–8 ppm of hydrogen
at $Eh = +260$ mV, representing a ratio of $[NADH]/[NAD^+] = 0.01$. The
predicted value rises by an order of magnitude for every -30 mV change in
E_h. For example, at $E_h = -290$ mV, hydrogen concentration would be
68 ppm of hydrogen, at $E_h = -320$ mV, 680 ppm of hydrogen is predicted,
and similarly 6800 ppm at $E_h = -350$ mV, equivalent to 6.8×10^{-3}
atmospheres.

More recently he used the following estimates of the kinetic constants for
hydrogen assimilation by methane bacteria at 35°C:

$Y = 1.04$ kg kg^{-1}
$b = 0.02$ d^{-1}
$k = 3.86$ kg kg^{-1} d^{-1}
$K = 2000$–4000 ppm in the gas

He compared calculated with actual measurements, and obtained good correlation at values of θ greater than 10 days, with most values falling in the range 50–100 ppm of hydrogen. The low hydrogen tension required for fatty acid conversion by the heteroacetogens explains why they have only been successfully grown in co-culture with hydrogen-utilising methanogens, and why the interlocking symbiosis and such phenomena as inter-species hydrogen transfer enhances the growth of both trophic groups (as referred to previously).

The utilisation of long-chain acids as electron sinks in the presence of excess hydrogen is caused by either hydraulic or organic digester overload. The group which primarily converts these back to usable stubstrates for methanogens are the heteroacetogens, producing acetic acid and hydrogen, both of which can be metabolised by Group III. However, the thermodynamics of this sensitive group indicate that increased hydrogen will stop or even reverse these reactions. A digester will therefore accumulate concentrations up to several thousand mg l^{-1} of propionate, butyrate and higher-chain organic acids when under stress. Provided the shock-load ceases or is minimised and suitable cultural conditions are maintained, the process will gradually recover as the methanogens utilise the hydrogen, and the heteroacetic bacteria recommence metabolising the longer-chain acids. It is therefore expected that there will be correlation between the presence of these acids and the hydrogen tension in the digester gas. In terms of this concept an early indicator of a stress induced impending digester failure would be the hydrogen concentration in the biogas. The advent of innovative instrumentation now enables cost-effective and accurate monitoring of this parameter [2.21].

The thermodymamic constraints discussed above dictate a close symbiotic relationship between Group II, the heteroacetogens and Group III, the methanogens. Mass transfer effects may alter local hydrogen concentrations and influence process kinetics. The precise nature of the observed synergism is not fully elucidated, because these bacteria, as a group, are not taxonomically or physiologically well characterised. Bio-energetics and yields may be species-affected; many questions remain unanswered, and much investigation still remains to be carried out.

2.3.4 Methanogenic bacteria (Group III)

This trophic group of bacteria is defined on the basis of utilisation of particular substrates to form methane. Group IIIA are chemolithotrophic and convert hydrogen and carbon dioxide to methane using gaseous hydrogen as an electron donor and incorporating hydrogen derived from water [2.22]:

$$CO_2 + 4H_2 \xrightarrow{2H_2O} CH_4 + 2H_2O \qquad (2.13)$$

This reaction also converts one ADP to ATP, hence is thermodynamically favourable.

The second group, IIIB, are presently known to metabolise acetate, formate, methanol and polymethylamines in methanogenesis [2.23]. The acetate conversion may be written as

$$CH_3COOH \rightarrow CH_4 + CO_2 \qquad (2.14)$$
$$\text{acetate} \qquad \text{methane}$$

This reaction generates only 0.25 mole of ATP, and is therefore thermodynamically relatively unfavourable [2.20].

The above reactions require specialist biochemical pathways, and enzymic co-factors unique to the group have been identified, in particular factor F_{430}, a nickel tetrapyrrole, and coenzyme F_{420}, a blue-green fluorescent compound which can be used as a diagnostic tool. The group as a whole displays a unique species diversity, including ecological, physiological and morphological variation. It includes gram-negative and gram-positive organisms, filaments, motile and non-motile rods, cocci, and lancet-shaped bacteria.

Cell walls contain pseudomurein instead of muramic acid, characteristic of conventional *Eubacteria*. Pseudomurein contains L-talosaminuronic acid instead of muramic acid. Some envelopes are polypeptide- or glycoprotein-based. Differences also occur in lipid composition and ribosomal sequencing. It is therefore considered that the methanogens belong to the *Archaebacteria*, a phylogenetically ancient group which also includes the extreme halophiles and the thermoacidophiles. Modern techniques for isolation and cultivation of anaerobic bacteria in general, and methanogens in particular, are enabling increased taxonomic and physiological characterisation. Populations of 10^6–10^8 organisms per ml of mesophilic sewage sludge have been isolated from digesters. These include the genera *Methanobacterium*, *Methanospirillum*, *Methanococcus*, *Methanosarcina* and *Methanothrix* [2.8]. Of these *Methanosarcina barkeri*, *Methanococcus mazei* and *Methanothrix soehngenii* have demonstrated ability to grow on acetate in pure culture with doubling times of 1–8 and 2–10 days or more [2.24]. All known methanogens except *Methanothrix soehngenii* can catabolise H_2 and CO_2 autotrophically.

Smith and Mah [2.25] and others [2.5] have reported that approximately 70–75% mole per mole of methane produced in anaerobic fermentation derives from the acetate pathway, hence approximately 25–30% mole per mole derives from autotrophism and catabolism of 1-C compounds. This is so despite the more favourable thermodynamics of the chemolithotrophic pathway, and indicates that hydrogen must be limiting.

The evolved biogas deriving from the methanogenic pathways in a healthy digester should therefore constitute:

$$70\%[CH_3COOH] \rightarrow CH_4 + CO_2 \qquad (2.15)$$

$$30\%[CO_2 + 4H] \xrightarrow{2H_2O} CH_4 + 2H_2O \qquad (2.16)$$

If all the carbon dioxide used in Equation 1.16 derives from 2.15, then the mole ratio of methane to carbon dioxide will be 50:20 or 2.5:1. This compares with conventional values of between 1:1 and 3:1. This biogas also includes water vapour, the concentration of which is related to the partial pressure of water under digester conditions of pressure and temperature. Where carbon dioxide exists in a ratio greater than predicted, this may be attributed to a lack of chemolithic methanogens in the biomass, or more probably to contributions from other groups. Fermentation of such substrates as starches, hexoses, pentoses and cellobiose by acidogens such as *Lactobacillus brevis* or *Thermoanaerobium brockii* produces carbon dioxide of the order of 80–131 mole per 100 mole from these substrates [2.9]. Heteroacetic conversions previously discussed (Section 2.3.3) similarly may produce carbon dioxide.

These carbonate conversions are further influenced by the physico-chemical balance of hydroxide, carbonate and bicarbonate in the digester. If a hydroxide such as sodium hydroxide is used for pH correction, it will absorb more carbon dioxide than if carbonates or bicarbonates were used. The concentration of methane in the biogas will therefore depend not only on microbial population, feedstock and cultural conditions such as buffering, pH and E_h, but also on influent composition.

Equations for biogas production from given substrates can be based on the elemental composition of the feedstock and its potential biodegradability or recalcitrance. However, it is difficult to account for the additional variations discussed above. Modern process design criteria are preferably based on bench or pilot scale digesters, and methane production commonly varies between 0.3–0.5 m^3 of CH_4 kg^{-1} of COD degraded.

The methanogens are the most culturally fastidious group in the symbiosis of anaerobic digestion. They require a broad spectrum of nutrients in order to grow, including carbon, phosphorus, nitrogen, sulphur, calcium, magnesium, potassium, sodium, organic nutrients such as amino-acids and vitamins and trace metals. Recent understanding of the trace metal requirements of methanogens has led to improved growth conditions in both pure culture and mixed fermentations. In addition to iron, zinc and manganese, it was established that methanogens require trace amounts of cobalt, molybdenum and nickel [2.26]. These elements are involved in prosthetic enzyme groups, for example the nickel tetrapyrrole prosthetic group of methyl CoM reductase, an essential enzyme of methanogenesis. Hydrogen and carbon dioxide are clearly essential nutrients for chemolithotrophic growth.

Speece and McCarty reported [2.27] the empirical equation for anaerobic biomass as $C_5H_9O_3N$, i.e. a molar ratio of C:N of 5:1, which is also approximately equal to the weight ratio. A ratio of N:P of 5:1 is widely applied to both aerobic and anaerobic biomass. A ratio of C:N:P for feedstock can therefore be calculated and a mean yield coefficient for the digester can be estimated, in order to differentiate between carbon incorporated into biomass and that evolved as CO_2 and CH_4. Mosey [2.21] has calculated theoretical yield coefficients based on ATP production: see Table 2.2. This shows, for example, that for a mixed culture growing on carbohyd-

Table 2.2 — Theoretical biomass yield coefficients (from [2.21])

| Substrate | Yield (kg kg^{-1}) | | |
	Acidogens	Methanogens	Mixed culture
Hydrogen		1.04	1.04
Acetic acid		0.04	0.04
Propionic acid	0.12	0.06	0.18
Butyric acid	0.20	0.09	0.29
Long-chain fatty acids	0.23	0.17	0.40
Carbohydrates	0.16	0.06	0.23
Fats	0.24	0.18	0.42
Proteins	0.06	0.07	0.13

rates, $Y=0.23$. From the empirical biomass formula, and inserting the traditional nitrogen/phosphorus ratio of $5:1$, a weight ratio of $C:N:P = 21.4:5:1$ is obtained. Adjustment of this carbon by the yield coefficient alters the ratio to $93C:5N:1P$. Most engineering data are expresed not in elemental carbon but in mg l^{-1} of BOD or COD. An estimate of the ratio of BOD:COD is $1:1.6$ for readily degradable wastes. From the conversion of carbon to carbon dioxide, the stoichiometric relationship between elemental carbon and COD is $32/12=2.6$. The relationship of $C:N:P$ for the previous model calculation may therefore be expressed as:

$$COD:N:P = 242:5:1 \qquad (2.17)$$

or

$$BOD:N:P = 151:5:1 \qquad (2.18)$$

Clearly these calculations depend on an analysed or assumed $N:P$ ratio and the derived yield coefficient. For example, using the yield coefficient of 0.04 for a mixed culture growing on acetic acid, the ratio would be

$$C:N:P = 535:5:1 \qquad (2.19)$$

The majority of mesophilic methanogens will not grow at pH values below 5.5. They employ oxidoreductase enzymes for hydrogen oxidation, and depend on the establishment of proton gradients for metabolism of acetate and 1-C compounds. Low pH values favour proton reduction to hydrogen, rather than hydrogen reduction to methane, and therefore methane production normally ceases. Empirical results have additionally shown that an upper pH limit of pH 8 is desirable. Although this has not been fully investigated, as pH 8.2 is a critical pH in bicarbonate/carbonate conversion there are many implications apart from enzymic pathways in terms of biogas stability and metal ion precipitation. In view of the pH range required, a good buffering system is obviously desirable in order to maintain digester stability. In situations of high nitrogen feeds, this buffering may be supplied naturally by the ammonia/ammonium couple ($NH_4^+ \rightarrow NH_3 + H^+$) which has an ionisation constant $pKa = 9.27$ at 35°C. This buffering system is useful, provided that the concentration of free ammonia does not become toxic (see Section 2.4.5).

In the absence of ammonium buffering, alkalinity may be added in the form of hydroxides, carbonates or bicarbonates, in which case the carbonate/bicarbonate couple becomes the controlling buffer system. In order to maintain stability in anaerobic processes, alkalinities as high as 6000 mg l^{-1} may be necessary. In general, a ratio of volatile fatty acids : alkalinity as $CaCO_3$ of at least 1:6 is considered advisable.

2.3.5 Reaction kinetics

Mathematical models developed for anaerobic systems can be used to predict the rate of substrate uptake, biomass yield and product formation [2.21; 2.28] and for the design and optimisation of treatment systems. While the overall kinetics (see Section 2) indicate the total solids retention time required for anaerobic methanogenesis, to predict the detail of the interlocking reactions requires a more complex model. There is a lack of data on specific effects within an anaerobic system, for example the concentration at which some intermediates become inhibitory; and currently the models can only serve as an indicator of effects rather than exact predictive tools.

Conventional steady state systems have been described by Monod kinetics, in terms of biomass concentration (X):

$$\frac{ds}{dt} = -kX \frac{S}{K_s + S} \tag{2.20}$$

Introducing the yield coefficient (Y) permits the equation to be written in terms of biomass:

$$\frac{dX}{dt} = kXY \frac{S}{K_s + S} \tag{2.21}$$

This equation can be further refined by the introduction of a coefficient to compensate for energy used by the bacteria themselves: a decay coefficient [2.29], to compensate for bacterial death (probably more appropriate to batch studies), or a maintenance coefficient [2.30]. In either case the term (bX) compensates for 'endogenous respiration':

$$\frac{dX}{dt} = kXY \frac{S}{K_s + S} - bX \tag{2.2.2}$$

where b = maintenance coefficient, hence

$$\mu = kY\frac{S}{K_s + S} - b \qquad (2.23)$$

At steady state $\mu = 1/\theta$ where θ is the nominal retention time of liquid within the reactor, or mean cell residence time in a continuously stirred tank reactor (CSTR). Table 2.3 summarises some of the constants determined from steady state experiments.

Table 2.3 — Values of kinetic constants (from [2.21])

Substrate	Temp. (°C)	Y (kg kg^{-1})	k (kg kg^{-1} d^{-1})	K_s (mg l^{-1})	b (d^{-1})
Acetic acid	35	0.04	8.1	154	0.019
	30	0.054	4.8	333	0.037
	25	0.05	4.7	869	0.011
Propionic acid	35	0.042	9.6	32	0.010
	25	0.051	9.8	613	0.040
Butyric acid	35	0.047	15.6	5	0.027
Long chain fatty acids	35	0.12	6.67	680	0.015
	25	0.12	4.65	1270	0.015
	20	0.12	3.85	1580	0.015
Glucose	37	0.173	30.0	23	0.8

The application of these principles to overall process design is illustrated in Section 2.2.1 in which the limiting retention time was calculated. This calculation is of restricted validity due to the usual constraints of Monod kinetics. For anaerobic systems it also assumes that the bacteria maintain a constant internal pH value of 7, that concentrations are constant throughout and that there are not mass transfer effects, for example that substrates including hydrogen are distributed equally throughout the liquid and biomass. In addition the kinetic parameters, particularly the maintenance coefficient b, require further determination (Table 2.3).

Despite the limitations in the accuracy of the kinetic parameters, some useful process information can be derived. For example, using the data in Table 2.3 and assuming θ is 10 days and the feedstock acetic acid concentration is 6000 mg l^{-1}, at a temperature of 35°C, the yield of biomass can be calculated:

$$\frac{1}{\theta_c} = kY\frac{S}{K_s + S} - b \qquad (2.23)$$

$$\frac{1}{10} = 8.1Y\frac{6000}{154 + 6000} - 0.019$$

$$Y = 0.015 \text{ kg kg}^{-1}$$

This type of calculation confirms the relatively low yield of biomass from mixed culture anaerobic processes referred to in Section 2.1. Similarly, the value of θ can be calculated and confirms that retention times of several days (3–10 d) are necessary for process stability.

The simple Monod type equations (2.1–2.8) are unsatisfactory for full scale digesters due to feedback inhibition and the non-steady state conditions which usually occur. Dynamic modelling is needed to predict and understand day to day process performance and hence informed operation. The equations are modified but require more complex computations.

Curves can be computed which quantify inhibition (or synergism) for factors such as pH, osmotic pressure, ion concentrations, toxins and gas concentrations. The kinetic constants can then be determined for specific conditions. For example, Fig. 2.2 illustrates the dynamic effect of hydrogen on the yield of propionate.

The mathematical description of the inhibitory effects by the Haldane function accounts for the competitive inhibition of an enzyme by the substrate. The previous equations are modified from the simple

$$\frac{ds}{dt} = kX\frac{S}{K_s + S} = \frac{kX}{1 + \frac{K_s}{S}} \qquad (2.1)$$

to

$$\frac{ds}{dt} = \frac{kX}{1 + \frac{K_s}{S} + \frac{S}{K_i}} \qquad (2.24)$$

where K_i is the inhibition constant.

The biomass concentration (X) strictly should be the concentration of the enzyme which is inhibited; this is assumed to be proportional to the biomass concentration. Mosey [2.21] has used this approach by applying a regulator function for the catabolism of propionic and butyric acids. The function is based on the redox potential at pH 7 of the hydrogen carrier NAD, known to be inhibited by hydrogen. He derived the regulatory function to modify the 'Monod' term $S/(K_s + S)$:

$$\frac{ds}{dt} = kX\frac{S}{(K_s + S)(1 + K'H)} \qquad (2.25)$$

where H is the concentration in ppm of hydrogen in the digester gas and K' is the calculated redox constant $= 0.0015$. Therefore

$$\frac{ds}{dt} = kX\frac{S}{(K_s + S)(1 + 0.0015H)} \qquad (2.26)$$

Clearly at low hydrogen concentrations the regulatory function approaches unity and there is no inhibition of the propionic and butyric acid catabolism. The rate of reaction is halved when the hydrogen concentration equals 670 ppm and at higher hydrogen concentrations will be further reduced.

2.4 TOXICITY AND INHIBITION

2.4.1 Introduction

Many substrates are essential to a microbiological process at low concentrations and hence stimulate growth. This effect was observed in anaerobic digesters at concentrations of 100 nM of nickel, 50 nM of cobalt and 50 nM of molybdenum [2.31], but at concentrations of over 100 mg l^{-1} for sodium or calcium salts (Table 2.4) [2.32].

Table 2.4 — Stimulatory and inhibitory concentrations of alkali and alka-
line-earth cations

Cation	Concentrations (mg l^{-1})		
	Stimulatory	Moderately inhibitory	Strongly inhibitory
Sodium	100–200	3 500–5 500	8 000
Potassium	200–400	2 500–4 500	12 000
Calcium	100–200	2 500–4 500	8 000
Magnesium	75–150	1 000–1 500	3 000

As concentrations increase above optimal, the rate of microbial activity decreases until the process is inhibited, as evidenced by lower activity than that achieved in the absence of the material; finally, at higher concentrations, activity ceases altogether. It is unfortunate that the majority of toxicity studies are reported in volume concentrations, and are not correlated with viable biomass. Clearly this is important, as it delineates the amount of toxin affecting a given weight of biomass, and represents how much an individual cell will have to detoxify.

Adaptation, also referred to as accommodation of acclimatisation, has been widely observed in microbial communities. The ability of an organism to adapt to a toxic or inhibitory substance may be constitutive or induced, and depends on the development of tolerance to the offending material, either by exposure over time to a given concentration or by exposure to a gradually increasing dose.

Many bacterial techniques of adaptation have been described, some of which will be examined in the following section.

2.4.2   Adaptation to toxins
Microbial adaptation is generally accompanied by extended lag times, after which growth recommences. Batch cultures may attain full yield, provided energy is not utilised in the adaptation process. Methods of adaptation range from macro-entrapment of toxins by biomass, to elegant cell envelope, cytoplasmic, enzymic and genetic alterations. Such accommodation frequently involves reproducible changes in protein patterns, and these may be detected at both cellular and subcellular levels by polyacrylamide gel electrophoresis (PAGE) [2.33].

Protein alterations may occur in enzyme pathways [2.34] to block metabolism of the harmful component or in transport systems [2.35] or cell walls to block uptake. Loss of specific outer membrane transport proteins has been recorded [2.36]. Similarly, organisms may produce endocellular binding proteins such as metallothioneins [2.37], or passivate toxins in cytoplasmic vacuoles or granules [2.38]. Non-specific exo-cellular binding by cell envelope material such as teichoic acids, polysaccharides and lipopolysaccharides also aids detoxification [2.39]. Many of these adaptations are known to be plasmid-mediated, such as the dual resistance of some *Staphylococcus aureus* strains to mercury and antibiotics.

In many cases toxicity involves inhibition of the essential genetic elements, as in the selective inhibition by zinc of RNA synthesis initiation in the RNA-polymerase I reaction [2.40], and interaction of hexavalent chromium with DNA, causing frameshift mutations and basepair substitutions, amplified by error-prone recombinational repair [2.41]. Zinc and silver affect the electron transport chain (ETC) [2.42], while zinc also inhibits the energy-dependent transhydrogenase reactions and NADH oxidation [2.43].

2.4.3   Antagonism and synergism
Antagonism and synergism in anaerobic digestion are not confined to particular salts, but have been widely observed in relation to the alkali and alkaline earth metals sodium, potassium, calcium and magnesium. The toxic effects of a particular cation present in a waste may be reduced or eliminated by the addition of another ion, an 'antagonist'. Conversely, toxicity may be increased by addition of a 'synergist'.

Some inhibitory effects can be explained in terms of transport systems. In passive transport the organism does not utilise cellular energy to absorb the substrate which simply crosses the cell wall according to the internal and external osmotic gradient. However, should the osmotic pressure of a particular component in the medium greatly exceed the internal concentration required by the bacteria, they will have to use cellular energy in order to export the excess. If more than one salt is present, competition for transport across the membrane may occur, and an endocellular balance is more likely. Active transport systems, in which cellular energy is expended, may similarly be affected by competition. For example, the low-affinity COR magnesium transport system which exists in *Escherichia coli* and other bacteria is multisubstrate, and also transports cobalt, nickel, manganese and iron at affinities four to ten times lower than for magnesium [2.35]. Hence magnesium transport is competitively inhibited by other cations, and this could lead to antagonism. Synergism results when a combination of cations is more toxic to the microbe than one on its own. Some cations which have been shown to cause antagonistic and synergistic effects are lised in Table 2.5 [2.44].

Table 2.5 — Antagonists and synergists in methanogenesis

Cation	Antagonist	Synergist
Na^+	Mg^{2+},K^+,K^+ and Mg^{2+},K^+ and Ca^{2+}	NH_4^+,Ca^{2+},Mg^{2+}
K^+	Na^+,Ca^{2+},NH_4^+	
Ca^{2+}	Na^+,K^+	NH_4^+,Mg^{2+}
Mg^{2+}	Na^+,K^+,Na^+ and Ca^{2+} and NH_4^+ or Mg^{2+}	NH_4^+,Ca^{2+}
NH_4^+	Na^+,Na^+ and K^+,Na^+ and Mg^{2+}	K^+,Ca^{2+},Mg^{2+}

Both antagonism and synergism are concentration dependent, although strictly this term should include a factor for biomass concentration. Interactions of sodium and potassium have been studied [2.45] in terms of their interactive effects on the kinetic constants, and the data are summarised in Table 2.6.

Table 2.6 — Antagonistic effect of sodium on a digester retarded by high concentrations of potassium (from [2.21])

Concentration (mg l^{-1})		Values of kinetic constants (Equation 2.23)				Retention time
Sodium	Potassium	Y (kg kg^{-1})	k (kg kg^{-1} d^{-1})	K_s (kg l^{-1})	b (d^{-1})	θ_c (d)
10	7 800	0.041 3	4.5	168	0.032 7	6.5
230	7 800	0.041 3	8.0	168	0.032 7	3.4
460	7 800	0.041 3	9.6	168	0.032 7	2.7
690	7 800	0.041 3	10.0	168	0.032 7	2.6
920	7 800	0.041 3	10.0	168	0.032 7	2.6

2.4.4 Kinetics of inhibition

The incorporation of the Haldane function into the rate equation for bacterial growth to provide a basis for dynamic modelling of hydrogen inhibition of fatty acid metabolism by heteroacetogens has been discussed in Section 2.3.5. Also, models are being developed for non-steady-state conditions [2.46]. The Recovery Pattern Model describes recovery of acetate-fed methanogenic systems from slug doses of a range of 30 toxicants of different type and concentration. Recovery patterns for the different toxicants were similar, while the shape of the curves resembled the classical dissolved oxygen sag curve. Therefore, the dissolved oxygen sag equation was used empirically as an initial recovery model, expressed as

$$G_1 = Ae^{-k_1 t} + Be^{k_2 t} \tag{2.27}$$

where G_1 = methane production,

t = time in days after toxicant addition,

A and B are empirically derived constants such that $A+B$ equal the control gas production,

k_1 and k_2 are the rate constants.

The model attempts to describe unsteady-state behaviour, and predictive recovery curves for cyanide, chloroform, formaldehyde and copper were constructed. From the curves the time of zero gas production and threshold and lethal toxicant doses can be estimated.

Two further models relied on traditional Monod-type kinetics: the first examined changes in the specific utilisation rate, k, and the half velocity constant K_s, according to the derived curves. The second was an inhibition coefficient (K_i) model, incorporating the classical inhibition equations derived by Lehninger [2.47].

All three models illustrated the importance of an adequate θ_c (SRT) for a given digester system. In this case it was necessary to overcome toxicity by the mechanisms previously discussed (Section 2.4.2). It was also found that extended periods of zero methane production do not necessarily indicate bacterial death.

2.4.5 Responses to toxicity

Successful acclimatisation has been observed in batch, semi-continuous and continuous cultures, including CSTR's and fixed film reactors. Systems examined include substrates such as H-coal wastewater, synthetic pulp mill sulphate evaporator condensate (SEC) waste and other toxicants [2.48–2.50]. In all of these studies adaptation was demonstrated, whereas shock loads of toxin to a non-acclimatised CSTR at 35°C with a θ_c of 50 d showed great sensitivity (Table 2.7). In contrast, the accommodated organisms in an anaerobic filter (AF) had much higher tolerances (Table 2.8). These authors also demonstrated reversible toxicity in which rapid recovery occurred on replacing the toxicant liquor with control medium [2.50].

An acclimatisation potential was calculated by dividing the highest

Table 2.7 — Influence of toxins on methane production [2.50]

Toxin	Concentration (mg l^{-1})	Time during which there was reduced methane production
Nickel	70	0
	80	3
	90	6
	100	11
Sulphide	100	2
	200	4
	300	6
	500	14
Formaldehyde	100	15
	150	23
	250	35
	500	35

Table 2.8 — Maximum concentration to cause no effects on acclimatised anaerobic filter [2.50]

Toxin	Maximum tolerable concentration (mg l^{-1})
Nickel	250
Sulphide	600
Formaldehyde	400

toxicant concentration that could be tolerated without significant decrease in methane production, by the threshold dose. The latter is defined as a concentration that will result in the onset of decreased gas production [2.51] and is generally reported as a 'less than' value. Results are presented in Table 2.9, obviously as 'greater than' values.

In addition to the observed affects of adaptation, θ_c and recovery time on toxicity and inhibition, other factors affecting the real toxicity of a given material in an anaerobic system include:

— The mass of microorganisms clearly will be significant, especially in cases such as polysaccharide detoxification. This would favour the high biomass/fixed film reactors over suspended biomass systems, as demon-

Table 2.9 — Acclimatisation potential for selected toxicants [2.50]

Toxicant	Acclimatisation potential
Ammonium	> 2.4
Chloroform	>25
Cyanide	>25
Formaldehyde	> 4
Nickel	> 5
Sulphide	>12

strated for volatile fatty acid buildup in a CSTR and an AFB (anaerobic fluidised bed) [2.52].

— Substrate interactions are significant in toxin passivation. For example, heavy metals react with anions to form salts. The toxic thresholds of such compounds can only be evaluated in terms of the capacity of the system as a whole to passivate them as insoluble precipitates such as metal chelates, carbonates, hydroxides, sulphides, and, in the case of such metals as silver and lead, the chlorides. Initial methodology for application of quantitative assessment of such interactions has been developed [2.53–2.55].

— pH must be maintained near pH 7, as it affects many reactions, for example the ammonia/ammonium couple previously discussed (Section 2.3.4). As the pH value increases the reaction equilibrium shifts to the right, so that the concentration of free ammonia will exceed that of ammoniun ion by progresively more as pH rises. At pH 7.2, 1% of the ammonia will be in the NH_3 form, while at pH 8.2, 10% is NH_3. In neutral anaerobic upflow filters (AUF's) containing heteroacetogens and methanogens, free ammonia concentrations above 80–100 mg l^{-1} could not be tolerated regardless of attempts to attain adaptation [2.56]. This figure is reported to be independent of pH, but clearly pH will affect the total ammonia-N tolerance. pH also affects the solubilities of many other compounds, including carbonates, hydroxides and sulphides of heavy metals.

— Microbial speciation is important, if there is insufficient diversity of speciation within the biomass, there is decreased ability to withstand, or adapt to, toxic shock.

Although most toxicity data will relate only to the specific reactor, feedstock and cultural process from which it was obtained, certain useful facts emerge, such as the importance of sludge retention time, indicating the potential value of fixed-film systems or retained sludge systems. Even these may be susceptible to certain toxins, for example surface-active agents which could lead to disruption or detachment of biomass and hence to washout.

There is a need for toxicities expressed as weight/volume concentrations in reactors to be correlated with the mass of microorganisms. Further, theoretical modelling of the many variable parameters has not yet been achieved. The process design, therefore, of a reactor to operate under a given set of variable constraints will probably still depend upon bench and pilot-plant studies to establish operational conditions.

2.4.6   Coping with toxicity

Of the many possible toxins which may inhibit full-scale digesters, a summary can be made of those most likely to occur under normal operational conditions. This would relate to the type of waste or wastes being treated, the frequency of factory operations such as tank washouts, hosing-down, and other processes. Toxins commonly encountered in industrial process wastewater include salinity, ammonia, sulphur, heavy metals and organics such as phenolics and detergents. These may all be toxic or inhibitory at certain concentrations giving rise to 'stuck' digesters. Many of the effects are reversible, and several methods may be used to attempt to overcome the inhibition. These include:

— Removal of the toxic liquid phase. Clearly this is most feasible for fixed film reactors.
— Dilution of the wastewater in order to reduce the concentration of toxicant.
— Addition of antagonists to an identified toxin; for example a slug of sodium chloride may be countered by potassium salts, provided the dose is not too high.
— Precipitation of the toxin, for example heavy metals could be precipitated as the chloride (mercury, silver, lead) or the sulphide or carbonate.
— Chelation of the offending material, for example by ethylene-diamine-tetra-acetic acid (EDTA).
— Absorption of the toxicant, for example onto activated carbon. This has been successfully demonstrated in anaerobic batch cultures of H-coal effluent containing up to 1500 mg l^{-1} of phenols at 20% v/v concentration [2.48]. The addition of 2500 mg l^{-1} of activated carbon enabled production of methane from a 12% v/v dilution, as opposed to 4% v/v as the maximum without carbon, a three-fold improvement. Adaptation times to the toxins were shortened in the presence of the carbon. This has also been demonstrated in anaerobic fluidised beds treating wood ethanol stillage [2.57]. Excess toxins are adsorbed into the carbon pore system, thus reducing the immediate toxic shock load. These are then subsequently available for slow biodegradation by tolerant or adapted organisms.

Clearly the cost-effectiveness of these techniques requires evaluation in terms of the severity and consequences of the toxicity, and the likelihood of success in reviving the digester.

2.4.7   Feedback inhibition
In the complex interlocking biochemical processes of acidogenesis and methanogenesis, various intermediates are formed, in addition to the final products. Significant among these are hydrogen (H_2), short chain organic acids, including the volatile fatty acids (VFA's), their isomers, and longer-chain VFA's. Feedback inhibition is exerted if the process becomes sufficiently unbalanced to allow significant accumulation of these intermediates. Hydrogen inhibition is so powerful that at concentrations of about 2000–5000 ppm H_2 degradation of substrate may cease altogether (see Section 2.3.3).

VFA inhibition depends on concentration and pH. The undissociated free acids such as CH_3COOH, CH_3CH_2COOH and not the radicals CH_3COO^-, $CH_3CH_2COO^-$ are mainly responsible for toxicity, as they can freely permeate the bacterial cell wall. This causes a change in internal cell pH, osmotic pressure, and possibly other effects, if the concentration is too high. Table 2.10 lists the pK_a of some common VFA's and shows that in order to maintain low concentrations of undissociated acids, pH must be maintained above pH 7. Even at this pH VFA's may become inhibitory at concentrations of approximately 2×10^3 mg l^{-1} as acetic acid, according to the particular configuration.

Table 2.10 — pK_a of volatile fatty acids commonly found in stressed digesters

Volatile fatty acid	pK_a
Acetic acid	4.76
Propionic acid	4.87
Iso-butyric acid	4.84
Butyric acid	4.81
Iso-valeric acid	4.77
Valeric acid	4.82

2.5   CONVENTIONAL DIGESTION PROCESSES

2.5.1   Septic tanks
In septic tanks wastewater passes through a long hydraulic residence time tank (>20 h). The solids which settle remain on the bottom of the tank

where the organic materials are subjected to anaerobic degradation. The UK design criteria for septic tanks [2.58] give the capacity (C) in litres, in terms of the design population (P) as

$$C = 180P + 2000 \qquad (2.28)$$

The per capita volume of 180 l accounts for 90 l of liquid plus 90 l of sludge storage. The liquid is made up from the per capita water use of 120 l to be stored for 12 h, that is 60 l plus an allowance of 30 l for infiltration or higher water consumption. The capacity is shared between two tanks, the first of $\frac{2}{3}C$ capacity, provided with a sloped floor to hold the sludge (Fig. 2.3). The sludge is removed periodically, often annually. Some sludge should be left in the tank to reseed the reactor for anaerobic activity.

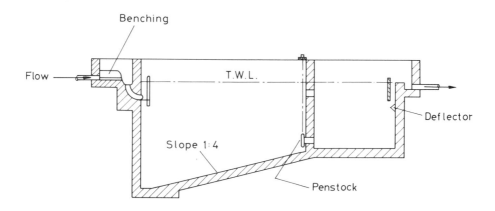

Fig. 2.3 — A typical design for a two-compartment septic tank.

Septic tanks are unstirred reactors which usually operate at temperatures below 25°C with no attempt to provide any mixing to facilitate the microbial activity. The mean cell residence time is controlled by the frequency of desludging. However, assuming that the tank is desludged annually and approximately one-sixth of the sludge is left to reseed the tank, the biomass remains in the system for approximately 50 days. While this residence time is sufficient to retain methanogenic activity at high temperatures (35°C), at ambient temperatures and with no mixing there is little methanogenesis. Similar effects occur within Travis and Imhoff tanks except that separate tanks or compartments are used to hold the sludge. This should provide more efficient solids separation by settlement.

2.5.2   Municipal sludge digestion
Sludge digesters are widely used in municipal plants and are fed with wasted primary sludges, scums and secondary biological sludges. The digested sludge is subsequently disposed of, often to land. It is important to stress that the sludges are digested to stabilise the solids so that handling is easier and

there are fewer odours. Digestion also reduces the number of pathogens in the sludge, further facilitating its handling and disposal. Anaerobic digestion is, therefore, a management process rather than merely a method for disposal or dewatering (see also Chapter 5).

As in any type of digestion carried out at a temperature above ambient, the heat budget is a critical design and operational factor [2.4]. In practice, many sludge digestion systems use two tanks (Fig. 2.4). The primary digester is heated (30–40°C) and mixed and contains actively digesting sludge. The secondary tank is neither heated nor mixed and is mainly for consolidation and storage (see Section 5.2.4). As such it is not amenable to even a basic technical evaluation.

The nature of municipal sludges makes it difficult to determine values for the constants in the kinetic equations (2.1–2.8). Digesters are therefore designed and operated on the basis of the highly pragmatic criteria outlined in Chapter 5 (Section 5.2.4) — the volumetric organic loading rate and solids retention time. However, the current philosophy in the UK is that there should be a greater process engineering input.

Thus, attention has been focused on improving the prime processing inputs; feeding, heating and mixing and using an overall sludge handling 'flow-sheet' concept [2.59]. Pre-thickening has also been advocated, with solids concentrations of 8–10% being discussed [2.59]. The same approach, applied to construction, has led to the development and use of prefabrication techniques for building digesters quickly (Fig. 2.5).

As sludge digesters do not usually retain biomass, the hydraulic and cell residence times are identical and are considerably greater than the values quoted in Section 2.2.1. This discrepancy is related to the following facts:

— The theory of stirred tank reactors assumed complete mixing of the substrate and biomass. In full scale digesters this does not occur, due to the large particle size of solids in the sludge and inadequate mixing which leads to pockets within the digester which are unfavourable for anaerobic processes, for example of low pH.
— The materials which have to be degraded are not simple organic molecules. Secondary sludges already have been subjected to aerobic biological oxidation, while primary sludges include the surface scums from primary sedimentation tanks and hence contain a high proportion of lipids which may be difficult to degrade. Table 2.11 illustrates that these lipids are a major substrate in sludge digesters and hence the overall reaction could be suboptimal. The 'ether extract' is a measure of lipid content and is reduced during the digestion; the loss of carbon is shown by the increased 'ash' (inorganic) content of the digested sludge.
— Toxicity can reduce biological activity; this can be critical when there is a high industrial component in municipal wastewaters (see Section 5.2.4).
— Process fluctuations such as variations in temperatures, retention time and pH can disrupt the process. A constant consistent feed of sludge is required to maintain efficient operation. While this is possible in pilot plant systems it is not always feasible in full scale practice.

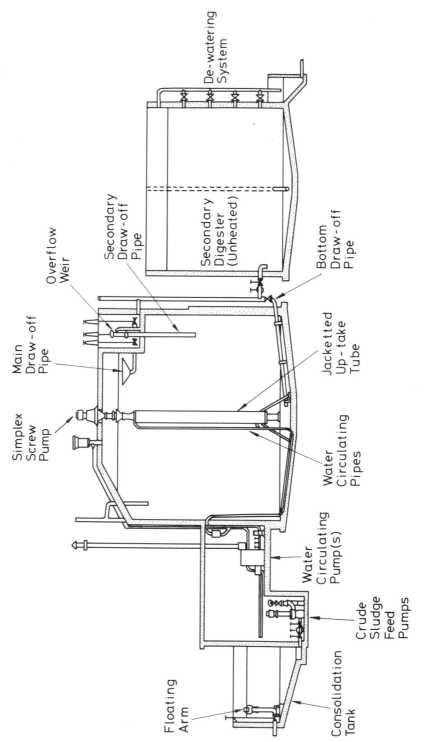

Fig. 2.4 — A two-tank digester for municipal sludges.

Fig. 2.5 — Prefabrication of anaerobic digesters.

Table 2.11 — Composition of municipal wastewater sludge

Constituent	Primary, dry solids basis		
	Primary sludge	Activated sludge	Digested sludge
Total nitrogen	4.6	8.0	3.4
Crude protein	28.8	50.0	21.2
Amino acids + ammonia	14.1	42.3	12.9
Total phosphorus	1.2	2.5	2.4
Ether extract	25.3	5.6	7.4
Crude fibre	13.0	0.2	3.8
Reducing sugars	1.8	—	0.1
Starch	1.5	—	0.1
Ash	17.8	17.8	31.5

There is no doubt that digestion of municipal sludge has a very positive future. However, the ideas currently being advanced in the UK, together with the possible requirements for an end-product containing very low pathogen counts, suggest that digestion could become part of an integrated sludge processing stream.

2.5.3 Stirred tank reactors

Flow-through anaerobic digesters of similar concept and design to those for sludge digesters have been used for domestic, industrial and agricultural wastewaters. The use of anaerobic reactors to treat domestic wastewaters has centered upon small low-cost systems, often harvesting the gas to use as a fuel source, an aspect which will not be discussed here. The treatment of strong industrial wastewaters from the food and beverage industries and slurries from intensive animal husbandry are the most widely quoted examples of simple flow-through anaerobic reactors. The majority of studies and plants have been single reactors in which a mixed microbial culture carries out the degradation. There is increasing interest in the use of two-stage systems, for which a simple stirred tank reactor has considerable merit as the first acid forming stage [2.60; 2.61).

The food and beverage industries tend to produce wastewaters containing high proportions of soluble or colloidal material of 'natural' origin, often with high concentrations of carbohydrates [2.62]. Specialised reactors treating these wastewaters are usually of relatively recent design, featuring reliable high volumetric performance but requiring continuous feeding and good mixing.

The loadings have been quoted as volatile solids m^{-3} d^{-1} as in sludge digestion, and as BOD and COD m^{-3} d^{-1} as a more conventional wastewater treatment process. In full scale operation the reactors can rarely exceed 4 kg COD or volatile solids m^{-3} d^{-1}; in laboratory or pilot plant studies two or three times these loadings can be achieved. As with sludge digesters there is no special retention of the biomass and hence high process loadings cannot be expected. The systems can be illustrated by the following examples.

Sugar beet pulps are difficult to degrade, since the pulps contain a high proportion of cellulose. Pretreatment with *Trichoderma harzianum* to hydrolyse the cellulose enzymatically improves degradability [2.63]. The pretreated pulps could be degraded at space loadings of 1 kg volatile solids m^{-3} d^{-1}; at higher loadings methane yields decreased and volatile acids accumulated. The feed contained 20 g volatile solids l^{-1} and yielded 0.74 m^3 of biogas per kg volatile solids applied.

Palm oil mill effluent [2.64; 2.65] is generated in the processing of oil palm fruit. Each tonne of crude palm oil which is produced [2.64] generates 2–3 tonnes of wastewater with a BOD of approximately 25 000 mg l^{-1}. The wastewater is at 45–70°C and hence thermophilic digestion may be appropriate. Laboratory scale reactors at 55°C were able to produce effluents with a BOD of less than 2000 mg l^{-1} at COD loadings of up to 4.5 kg COD

m^{-3} d^{-1}; biogas yields of 0.7–0.8 m^3 kg^{-1} volatile solids for 80–90% volatile solids reduction were achieved.

Wastes from soft drink bottling contain high concentrations of readily degradable soluble organic materials, often with significant amounts of sucrose. The wastewaters have COD concentrations between 50 and 150 000 mg l^{-1}. Conventional laboratory scale digestion [2.61] achieved satisfactory treatment at a loading of 1.28 kg volatile solids m^{-3} d^{-1} for 10 days hydraulic retention time and maintained the volatile acid concentrations at less than 200 mg l^{-1}. At a load of 2 kg volatile solids m^{-3} d^{-1} the methane yield decreased to almost undetectable amounts and the volatile acid concentration exceeded 2000 mg l^{-1}. Further increases in the load to the reactor converted it into an acid phase system which was loaded at between 4 and 16 kg volatile solids m^{-3} d^{-1} for retention times of between 7 and 2 days. Under these high loading conditions methane yields remained low and the biogas contained high concentrations of hydrogen (about 40%). The effluent from this reactor was treated in a packed bed methane phase digester loaded at 6.4 kg volatile solids m^{-3} d^{-1}. This separation of the acid and methane phases offers considerable savings in terms of volumetric loadings, gas production and usage [2.61]. Simple stirred tank digesters are probably the preferred technology for the first stage in the treatment of a high strength wastewater. The low engineering costs can be combined with a high organic loading rate (>10 kg volatile solids m^{-3} d^{-1}). The second (methane-forming) stage requires a lower loading rate in terms of the biomass in the reactor, because of the slower growth rate of methane-forming bacteria. For the second stage a more intensive treatment process which retains biomass, such as the fixed film or floc based reactors, would be favoured.

Animal slurries from intensive animal husbandry are of similar characteristics to municipal sludges with a high proportion of insoluble solids and non-biodegradable material. Completely mixed digesters of similar designs to municipal sludge digesters have been used to treat these wastes. The processes have been studied in some detail [2.66; 2.67] and several full scale plants are in operation for treating wastes from pigs [2.67; 2.69], cattle [2.66; 2.70] and poultry. In the majority of cases only 50% of the influent COD is removed from piggery and poultry [2.71] wastes and only 30% from cattle wastes. The high concentration of ammonium ions, particularly in pig and poultry slurries, provides good buffering against acidic conditions, but can begin to inhibit the degradation at concentrations greater than 4000 mgN l^{-1}. At 5000 mgN l^{-1} the rate may be reduced to 50% of the uninhibited values [2.72]. In practice the digesters can rarely be operated at greater than 4 kg volatile solids m^{-3} d^{-1}.

Wastewaters from piggeries are typical examples of the type of waste suited to this method of treatment. The digester can be engineered as for a municipal sludge digester or as a simpler low-cost tank system such as an excavated area lined with a synthetic membrane. Figure 2.6 illustrates a system treating slurry from a piggery which houses 1200 sows. The reactor has a capacity of 680 m^3 and was designed to treat 65 m^3 d^{-1} of slurry with

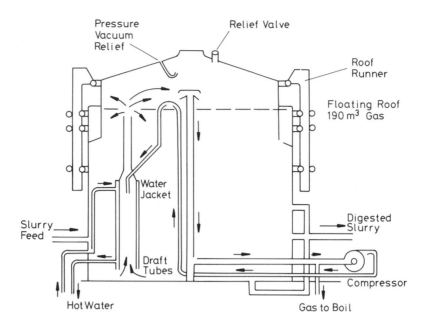

Fig. 2.6 — Digester design for treating animal slurry [2.68].

5–6% solids content — a loading of approximately 3.5 kg volatile solids m^{-3} d^{-1}. In practice it was difficult to maintain the design feed rate to the digester. The slurry solids were found to be approximately 2% and hence the daily feed volume was reduced to 20–30 m^3 d^{-1}, a hydraulic retention time of 20 days rather than the design figure of 10 days. At this loading the reactor system maintains conventional gas yields and composition (69% methane). The biogas is used as a fuel source to provide hot water for the piggery and digester and to generate electricity. With the reduced loading and biogas production there has been little nett energy generation. The example illustrates the problems which occur with many large-scale wastewater treatment systems, in that the inherent variability of the substrate means that full-scale operation is rarely as effective as laboratory studies carried out under controlled conditions.

2.6 FLOC BASED DIGESTERS

In anaerobic digestion, sludge retention time, θ_c or SRT, is a significant factor; in engineering practice this is frequently referred to as 'sludge age'. This is particularly significant in view of the relatively long mean generation times of the methanogens and acetogens. Attempts were therefore made to design reactors in which biomass could be retained and washout of the slower-growing organisms avoided. Sludge recirculation to maintain biomass density has long been practised in aerobic activated sludge plants, and this concept was initially introduced into anaerobic digestion as the anaerobic contact process, whereby sludge was recirculated from a settling tank back into a fully mixed digester. From this design evolved the Dorr–Oliver Clarigester, which was not mixed but incorporated a microbial sludge blanket, which process formed a natural precursor to the anaerobic upward flow sludge blanket (UASB). In addition several other commercial designs emerged, based on the anaerobic contact process with the similar objective of maximising SRT and hence optimising wastewater treatment; these include the Anamet Process and the Bioenergy Process.

2.6.1 Anaerobic contact process

This process was originally developed for treating biological wastes, for example from the food industry. Full-scale designs incorporated a primary reaction tank, which was fully mixed by either gas recirculation, sludge recirculation, or mechanical mixing (Fig. 2.7). Reaction rates were

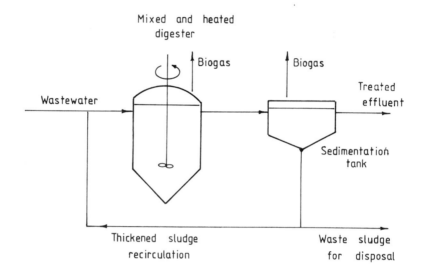

Fig. 2.7 — Typical layout for a stirred tank digester.

improved by increasing the temperature in the digester, either by using a warm influent, such as frequently occurs in the food industry, or by separate digester heating. The overflow from this unit passes to a clarifier, or settling tank, to concentrate the sludge by settlement. Thickening sludge was then recirculated to the primary digester to maintain high biomass densities, while clarified effluent was discharged. Biomass densities of 5–10 g l^{-1} VSS have been obtained from medium-strength wastewaters, with chemical oxygen demands (COD) of 2000–20 000 mg l^{-1}, and densities as high as 20–30 g l^{-1} VSS have been obtained for high strength wastewaters (20 000–80 000 mg l^{-1}, COD). These densities correlate with volumetric loadings of 2–6 kg COD m^{-3} d^{-1} for medium strength wastes and 5–10 kg

COD m^{-3} d^{-1} for high strength wastewaters [2.2]. This system was successfully applied at the Wilson and Company meat-packing plant in Minnesota, USA [2.73]. The waste stream contained about 70% protein, most of the remainder being lipids. The plant (Fig. 2.8) incorporates a vacuum degasser

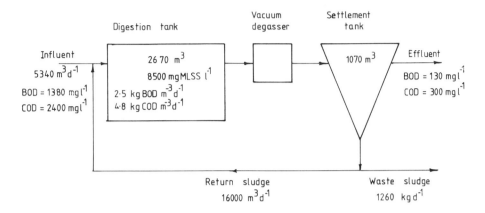

Fig. 2.8 — Digestion of meat-packing wastewater [2.73].

to remove gas from the sludge. However, the settlement properties remain poor and a high sludge return rate (3:1) is required to maintain the MLSS in the digester.

Problems with the anaerobic contact process were mainly related to sludge disruption in the digester, and failure of sludge separation in the settlement tank. Sludge disruption was generally caused by over-intensive mixing, and hence biomass dispersal. Failure of sludge to settle was caused by rising biomass, due to adherent gas bubbles. Attempts were made to overcome this by vacuum degasification (as in the Minesota plant), simple gravity settlement in a thickener, addition of polymers, addition of packing materials, centrifugation, flotation, air stripping, lamellar sedimentation, and thermal shock. The last three techniques resulted in patented processes.

The Anamet Process (AB Sorigona, Sweden and PEC Process Engineering Co., Switzerland) combines the anaerobic contact process with an aerobic phase, and incorporates lamellar sedimentation. The Bioenergy Process (Biomechanics Ltd, Smarden, Kent) uses cold thermal shock treatment temporarily to halt gasification of sludge in the settlement tank, thus enhancing sedimentation.

A further refinement of the anaerobic contact-process resulted in commercial development of the Dorr–Oliver Clarigester (Fig. 2.9). Wastewater enters the base of the unit via a multiport system, and flows upward through a bed of biomass in the lower compartment, which acts as the primary digestion tank. The effluent then passes further upwards in partial plug-flow to the upper compartment. The lower digestion compartment is not mixed, and relies on a dense sludge blanket for adequate waste/biomass interaction.

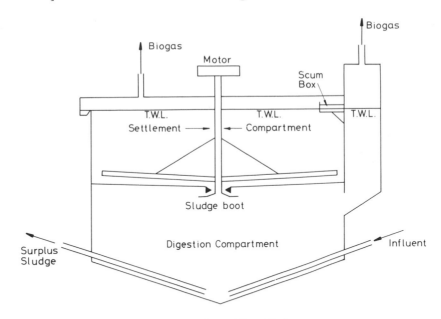

Fig. 2.9 — The Dorr–Oliver Clarigester.

The upper clarifier compartment is raked, to return settled sludge to the primary digester. The unit is also equipped with external sludge recirculation via a pump to return clarifier sludge to the digester. These units have been successfully applied to biological wastes, achieving BOD and COD removal rates above 80%. In treating a wine distilling waste (COD of 20 000 mg l^{-1}) a COD reduction of 97–98% was achieved, with a maximum space loading of 3.2 kg COD m^{-3} d^{-1} at a 6–9 day retention time and a tempera ture of 33°C [2.74]. As with previous process designs, the main limitation of the Clarigester is biomass retention, θ_c, and in this case average biomass densities of only 19 g l^{-1} were achieved. Further design modifications resulted in the development of the anaerobic upflow sludge blanket digester (UASB) in the Netherlands in the 1970s.

2.6.2   Anaerobic upflow sludge blanket process (UASB)
As with the Clarigester the biomass in the anaerobic upflow sludge blanket reactor is retained within the unit by development of highly settleable bacterial flocs, in the form of granules of 1–5 mm diameter (Fig. 2.10). This type of floc was achieved at a factory at Breda, Holland. Lettinga and Vinken [2.75] and coworkers found that high loadings could be applied once the granular sludge was formed. However, the granulation process did not occur with all wastes, for example slaughterhouse wastes and raw sewage did not cause granulation and rendering wastes only caused granulation at a slow rate. In many cases reactors could be seeded from an existing granulated sludge and, subsequently, could achieve high loading rates.

Development of granulated sludge is related to microbiological and

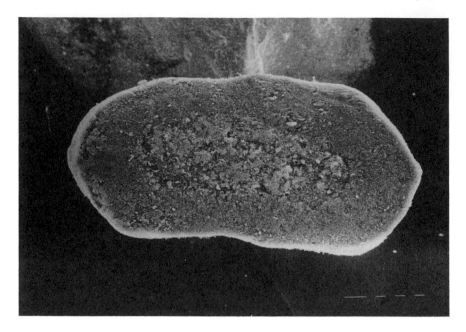

Fig. 2.10 — Granule (sectioned) from an upflow sludge blanket reactor (bar = 100 μm).

biochemical factors, feedstock characteristics, and reactor conditions. The hydraulic retention time has to be such that filamentous and other non-settling bacteria are washed out of the reactor, particularly during startup. Granulation is favoured [2.76] by a high proportion of short-chain organic acids (acetic and propionic) in the feedstock. Hence a two-stage process has been suggested, in which an acidification stage of short hydraulic retention time precedes the UASB. In many full-scale plants this occurs in the flow equalisation tanks or balance tanks required to ensure reliable hydraulic loadings. The feedstock is generally required to have a pH greater than 5.5 and sufficient alkalinity to ensure a stable operating pH; calcium also appears to be important.

It is important to separate biogas from the biomass to prevent carry-over of granules into the treated effluent. A submerged gas/liqid/solids separator creates a zone in which gas is disengaged and biomass can re-settle into the sludge blanket (Fig. 2.11). The baffles are arranged at an angle of approximately 50° and the separator is dimensioned such that gas bubbles provide sufficient agitation to prevent the formation of a scum layer and to minimise foaming. Wastes with a high lipid content require a skimmer device to remove foams.

For soluble wastes, mixing from the biogas generation is sufficient to ensure adequate treatment (70–85%). For wastes which contain undissolved solids, additional agitation may be needed. The UASB usually contains a dense intractable waste layer at the base of the reactor over which is the bed of granulated sludge and above which is a lighter floc blanket and the liquid

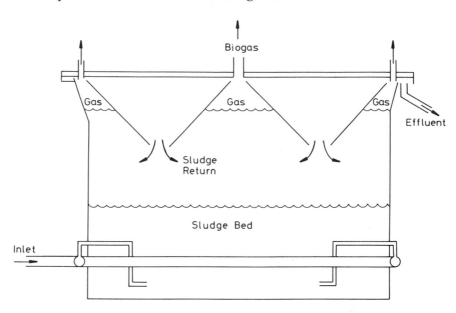

Fig. 2.11 — An upflow sludge blanket reactor.

phase. Tracer studies have shown that plug flow occurs through the granu-lated sludge bed with a minimum of channelling. The flocculated sludge zone acts as a well-mixed reaction in which the liquid or settlement zone is mainly plug flow [2.77].

The general conditions which favour the successful operation of a UASB have been summarised as [2.2; 2.75; 2.78]:

— Loadings of 12–15 kg COD $m^{-3} d^{-1}$ for wastes of COD $\geq$ 1000 mg l^{-1}.
— Feed strength not to exceed 10 000 mg l^{-1} COD; for high strength wastes effluent recycle has to be employed.
— Hydraulic loadings to retain biomass of $\leq$ 17 $m^3 m^{-2} d^{-1}$ in the reactor and of $\leq$ 50 $m^3 m^{-2} d^{-1}$ in the settling launder gap.
— Gas loadings of 70–200 $m^3 m^{-2} d^{-1}$ to prevent biomass washout.
— Feed inlets at the base of the reactor at one per 10 m^2 cross-section [2.78].

Several full-scale plants based upon these principles have been constructed [2.75; 2.78–2.80]. A plant of 4800 m^3 is used to treat effluent from a wheat starch factory in Victoria, Australia, following acidification and nutrient adjustment. The UASB is loaded at approximate 9.6 kg COD $m^{-3} d^{-1}$, treating a daily load of 46 tonnes COD to achieve an 85% COD reduction and producing 14 000 $m^{-3} d^{-1}$ of biogas with 70% methane content. The major applications of UASB's have been to food and agriculturally based wastewaters. However, the process has been demonstrated as being capable of treating a petrochemical effluent [2.80]. The wastewater from coal to oil conversion contained a high concentration of volatile fatty acids (8–13 g l^{-1})

and was treated at a loading rate of 7.2 kg COD m^{-3} d^{-1} reducing the COD by 83% with high methane yields. At higher loading rate (>8.5 kg COD m^{-3} d^{-1}) reduced treatment efficiency (<60%) was observed.

2.7 FIXED FILM REACTORS

While floc based reactors are comparable to aerobic suspended growth systems such as activated sludge, fixed film reactors can be compared to trickling filters. In anaerobic systems, the biomass is retained by attachment to an inert support medium and hence remains in the reactors for times longer than the hydraulic residence time. A range of support media has been used, depending on the type of rector and the process geometry.

2.7.1 Anaerobic filter

An anaerobic filter is similar in concept to the upflow filter used in water or tertiary wastewater treatment, but the media tend to be larger to prevent clogging. The first examples used rock media of 25–65 mm diameter [2.81; 2.82], giving approximately 50% void volume. The filters were tested on pretreated domestic wastewater and degradable soluble wastewaters. Subsequently, other types of support media have been used with void volumes [2.83] up to 96%. A high proportion of the biomass (50%) is not strictly attached to the support media, but is rather held in the interstitial spaces of the filters [2.2]. The hydraulic flow through the filters is low, so this interstitial biomass is retained. Wastewaters which contain a high concentration of suspended solids or a high degradable organic concentration tend to cause blockage or channelling within the filter.

Anaerobic filters have been used mainly for wastewaters which contain moderate organic concentrations (BOD 5000 mg l^{-1}) and low concentrations of suspended solids and preferably are warm [2.84]. The overall loadings possible rarely exceed 10 kg COD m^{-3} d^{-1} and for conventional 'stone' type media rarely exceed 5 kg COD m^{-3} d^{-1}. However, loadings as high as 20 kg COD m^{-3} d^{-1} have been reported for sludge heat treatment liquors for high void volume media, achieving a 67% COD treatment efficiency [2.85]. Analysis of the results by various workers on the treatment of carbohydrate based wastes indicates that at low loadings (2 kg COD m^{-3} d^{-1}) approximately 90% COD removal is possible, while at higher loading rates (8–16 kg COD m^{-3} d^{-1}), the removal efficiency is reduced to approximately 40%. Provided that the filters are not overloaded, they produce biogas at the standard rate of 0.5 m^3 kg^{-1} COD [2.84].

While the anaerobic filter process has been studied in some detail it has only found limited practical application. This may be attributable to [2.84]:

— the high cost of high void volume media,
— the restrictions imposed by suspended solids and high BOD wastewaters,
— the possible need for periodic backwashing

2.7.2 Stationary downflow reactors

Clogging in upflow filters can be overcome by using synthetic media of high void volume to create a high specific surface area and irrigating the wastewater over the media. The support media can be random packed units, tubes or sheeting arranged to achieve maximum contact between the liquid and the solid support/biomass. Downflow geometry has the advantage that the biogas rising against the flow can aid effective distribution without an expensive or complex distribution arrangement. The high void volume permits high loading rates and some suspended solids in the wastewater. Table 2.12 reports the overall performance of this type of wastewater treatment system.

Table 2.12 — Performance of downflow fixed film reactors

Wastewater	Loading rate ($kg\ COD\ m^{-3}\ d^{-1}$)	COD treatment efficiency
Bean processing [2.86]	9–18	87
Volatile fatty acids [2.86]	5–18	80
Sludge heat treatment liquor [2.85]	19	60
Piggery [2.87]	6	70
	40	27
Pear processing [2.87]	6–19	56
Rum distillation [2.87]	9	67
	13	57
Synthetic sewage [2.87]	7–14	75

2.7.3 Expanded and fluidised bed reactors (AEB's and AFB's)

In the early 1970s various workers [2.88–2.91] applied the principle of expanded and fluidised beds to anaerobic wastewater treatment systems. These processes have been applied to reduction of COD and BOD in both strong and weak wastewaters and to denitrification, but especially to pretreatment of industrial wastewater to sewer acceptance standards. The upflow reactor, containing approximately uniformly sized support medium on which biofilm can grow, is expanded, or fluidised, by the velocity of the influent plus a recycle loop (Fig. 2.12). Additional features may include a contact reactor [2.92] which also acts to concentrate any sludge carryover, or a biofilm reduction device to remove excess biofilm from the sand [2.93]. Biogas is collected from the top of both reactors.

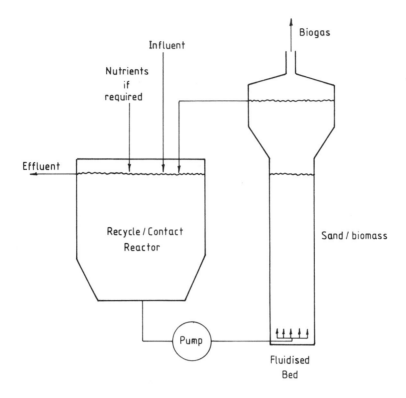

Fig. 2.12 — Schematic diagram of a fluidised bed digester.

The difference between expanded and fluidised beds is not clear cut. A popular definition is that expanded beds have an expansion of 10–20% of static height, while fluidised beds expand from 30–100% of static height [2.2]. Both systems are similar and will be discussed together. Their advantages over other high-rate reactors are:

— biomass washout is minimised due to adhesion to dense carrier particles;
— the fluidised particles are free to move, thus preventing clogging;
— the use of small, dense particles enables very high specific surface area, and hence large biomass volume for relatively small plant. This ensures high SRT, and aids stability in the event of transient high organic loads, or toxic slugs;
— shear forces create a thin, dense biofilm comprising mainly non-diffusion-limited, active biomass;
— removal of almost all readily degradable soluble BOD/COD can be achieved with average removal rates from 70% to 95% of total BOD/COD;
— high space loadings of 10–40 kg m^{-3} d^{-1} of COD have been reported

[2.93], with design figures of around 16 kg m^{-3} d^{-1} of COD more commonly employed;
— hydraulic retention times may be low, resulting in cost-effective installation and operation.

The major disadvantages of expanded/fluidised beds are:

— they must be highly engineered systems;
— power is required for the fluidisation process.

Full-scale plants have been developed in Britain, Australia and the United States of America, and at least three companies (Dorr–Oliver, Ecolotrol and Austgen Biojet) are offering fluidised bed treatment of wastewater worldwide. Clearly, the widespread adoption of anaerobic fluidised bed technology in the future will depend on satisfactory performance of existing installations.

Although primary reactor configuration is not critical, there is clearly a saving in space and distribution equipment if the utilisation of height is optimised, and further benefit from a reduction of turbulence and more effective biomass attachment. Primary design criteria include:

— an inlet system to create uniform flow distribution and hence even fluidisation across the reactor
— configuration and rating of the recycle loop;
— hydraulic retention time;
— reactor temperature;
— choice of medium.

An efficient inlet system is crucial to successful medium fluidisation. A fluidised bed has hydraulic properties which render it intrinsically unstable [2.94], resulting in channelling, with consequent uneven fluidisation and decreased efficiency due to reduction in the effective bed volume. Whereas fluidisation of small laboratory and pilot reactors is relatively simple, problems may be encountered on scale-up. Not only must the upflow be distributed evenly across the bed, but turbulence must be minimised above the inlet system to encourage biomass growth and adhesion to the medium particles. If turbulence is too great, biofilm formation is retarded, and inefficiencies occur. In order to accomplish fluidisation, the head loss of the inlet system must be much greater than that in the underdrain distribution system, as great as that across the bed itself [2.95]. This has been achieved by various techniques, including incorporation of a gravel layer, jets pointing downwards into a cone or trough, sometimes combined with a distributor plate, gravel layer, or vertical baffle systems. The type of distribution design will depend on:

— the nature of the wastewater, especially in terms of suspended solids;
— type of medium used;
— reactor size and configuration;
— cost-effectiveness.

In order to create sufficient head loss for successful fluidisation, narrow jets or porous ceramics have been used. These are applicable to soluble wastes, but caution must be exercised where, as would occur in most industrial or municipal wastewaters, particulate matter is present, and a practical balance must be achieved between orifice size and the head loss. Entry of support medium into the underdrain system must also be avoided, while sufficient inlet ports are required to achieve uniform fluidisation without 'dead spots'. Mixing has been studied in terms of the bioparticle distribution and the nature of the liquid flow through the reactor. The tendency of the liquid to spread out and mix during its passage through the reactor is termed 'dispersion', for which boundary conditions are:

— a completely mixed reactor, where dispersion is very high, due to a long hydraulic retention time or a high recycle rate;
— plug flow, in which little dispersion occurs, and flow is linear.

The situation in expanded and fluidised beds is controversial, some authors claiming that units are fully mixed [2.2] while others postulate plug flow [2.96]. It would appear that the difference lies in such factors as mixing caused by rising gas bubbles, bed height, recycle rate, Reynolds number and hydraulic retention time (HRT). Understanding of the distribution of bioparticles in expanded and fluidised beds has been equally confused. Studies with tracer particles in a fluidised bed with a depth of 1 m, particle diameter of 1 mm, upflow velocity of $21.6 \, \text{m}^3 \, \text{m}^{-2} \, \text{h}^{-1}$ and HRT of 2.8 min showed 80% dispersion in 30 s and 100% dispersion in less than 10 min [2.97]. Bioparticle mixing will be further discussed later in terms of medium selection.

While a high head loss across the inlet system enables efficient fluidisation and mixing, it also adds to the power consumption of the recycle pump and should therefore be optimised in terms of stability versus economy. Fluidisation should be minimised, without producing an unstable head loss curve, unfluidised zones, or blockage of the bed by suspended solids in the waste. As a liquid upflow is initiated in a bed or column of sand, head loss (or resistance to flow) increases proportionally to the flow according to D'Arcy's Law, where the hydraulic gradient is represented by head loss h over bed height L:

$$\frac{h}{L} = \frac{v}{K} \tag{2.29}$$

where K = the coefficient of permeability of the bed, and v = rise rate. As the flow increases, the head loss increases to a point of incipient fluidisation, when the particles start to lift. When flow is increased past this point the bed first expands, and then fluidises, with no further head loss increment. Head loss across the fluidised bed, h, is given by:

$$h = \frac{L(1 - \varepsilon)(\rho_s - \rho_e)}{\rho_e} \tag{2.30}$$

where ρ_s = density of particles
ρ_e = density of fluid
L = bed height
ε = bed porosity, or voidage

A porosity $\varepsilon = 0.4$ and density $\rho_s = 2650$ kg m^{-3} are commonly assumed for sand grains between 300 and 1000 μm diameter. It can be seen from Equation 2.30 that head loss across fluidised beds is approximately equal to the height L and is independent of particle size. The expanded bed height, L_e, can be calculated from the Richardson–Zaki equation:

$$Le = L\frac{1 - \varepsilon}{1 - (V_p/V_f)^n} \tag{2.31}$$

where V_f = superficial upflow velocity
V_p = single particle settling velocity
n = constant, approximately 4.5 for sand
and other terms are as previously defined.

These effects of increasing upflow on a bed of sand are illustrated diagrammatically in Fig. 2.13. Once a medium has been chosen for a given reactor design, provided the hydraulic loading rate remains constant, the recycle rate will only be varied within a narrow range and will be progressively stepped downwards to take account of decreasing bioparticle density as medium colonisation proceeds, otherwise carry-through of particles into the recycle loop will occur, and this is undesirable in terms of recycle pump wear, clogging of distribution systems, and effluent quality. Carry-over can be minimised by use of such devices as contact reactor tanks to allow settlement, and syphon-breakers; by correct choice of upflow rate for a given bioparticle system; and by avoiding wide fluctuations in hydraulic retention time (HRT). Optimum conditions established at pilot scale should not deviate greatly on scale-up.

Hydraulic retention time (HRT) is closely related to the recycle rate. For dilute wastes (<1000 mg l^{-1} COD) only short HRT's are required and liquid recycle may be minimised, with much of the fluidisation occurring as a result of the raw waste throughput, thus resulting in considerable energy saving.

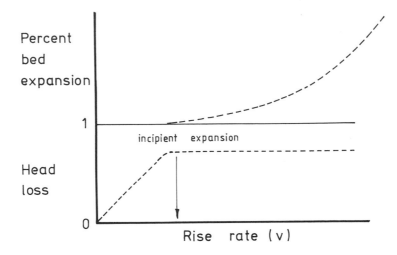

Fig. 2.13 — Head losses and bed expansion in a fluidised bed.

On the other hand, high strength wastes (BOD values as high as 30 000 mg l^{-1}) require extended HRT's for effective treatment. In these cases a high recycle rate is required to maintain fluidisation. Large variations in hydraulic loading rate are unfavourable to stable digester operation, and in such cases adequately sized balance tanks should be provided. Any anaerobic expanded or fluidised bed installation design must address the questions of operating temperature and the cost-benefits of more rapid treatment rates versus power costs of heating. This requirement for energy heat reactors is also related to HRT, inasmuch as a digester receiving a warm influent with a short HRT may not require further heating, while those with long HRT's are more affected by ambient temperature. In warm climates, external heating may not be necessary, and high rate anaerobic digesters are frequently operated at ambient temperatures even in Europe and the United States of America.

A most important design criterion for fluidised bed reactors is the support medium used, as fluidisation energy, the most significant process cost, may be minimised by smaller medium of lower density. Choice is usually based on cost-effectiveness and suitability for the given application. Biomass will adhere to and grow on a range of media. Some support materials which have been used are aluminium oxide particles, glass beads, anthracite, granular activated carbon (GAC), sand and polymeric particles. Of these sand is popular due to its cheapness and availability. It is graded within tight specifications, and approximately uniform sizes, in the range 0.2–1 mm, have been used. Whereas head loss across a fluidised bed is independent of particle size, the power required to fluidise particles is proportional to their size and density. The generalised expression for discrete particle settlement, V_p, is:

$$V_{\mathrm{p}} = \frac{4g(\rho_{\mathrm{s}} - \rho_{\mathrm{e}})D}{3C_{\mathrm{D}}\rho_{\mathrm{e}}} \tag{2.32}$$

where ρ_{s} = density of particle
ρ_{e} = density of fluid
D = diameter of particle
C_{D} = drag coefficient

Therefore, larger particles will result in increased power costs. A further advantage of smaller particles is their greater specific surface areas for biofilm attachment. The specific surface area, A, for spherical particles can be calculated from:

$$A = \frac{6(1 - \varepsilon)}{D} \tag{2.33}$$

Assuming $\varepsilon = 0.4$ for sand, we can calculate specific surface areas for spherical sand grains of mean diameters of 300 μm and 1 mm as follows:

$$A_{300\ \mu\mathrm{m}} = \frac{6(1 - 0.4)}{0.3 \times 10^{-3}} = 12\,000\ \mathrm{m^2\ m^{-3}}$$

$$A_{1\ \mathrm{mm}} = \frac{6(1 - 0.4)}{1 \times 10^{-3}} = 3600\ \mathrm{m^2\ m^{-3}}$$

These large specific surface areas compare with values of about 80 m^2 m^{-3} for stone used in trickling filters, and can generate 10–40 kg attached biomass m^{-3}. While these two factors favour a smaller sand size, the possibility of washout of the colonised bioparticle must be considered. The overall density, ρ_{pw}, of a spherical bioparticle is given by:

$$\rho_{\mathrm{pw}} = \frac{\rho_{\mathrm{s}} + \left[\left(1 + \dfrac{L}{r_{\mathrm{s}}}\right)^3 - 1\right]\rho_{\mathrm{bw}}}{\left(1 + \dfrac{L}{r_{\mathrm{s}}}\right)^3} \tag{2.34}$$

where ρ_{s} = density of support media
ρ_{bw} = density of wet biomass
r_{s} = radius of support particle
L = thickness of wet microbial layer = $r_{\mathrm{bp}} - r_{\mathrm{s}}$
r_{bp} = radius of bioparticle

The denser the medium, the less sensitive is the overall particle density to the biofilm thickness. The resultant decrease in overall particle density will clearly reduce settling velocity; however, the increased particle diameter will, conversely, increase settling velocity (Equation 2.32). The influence of carrier density can be determined by the ratio B [2.98]:

$$B = \frac{\rho_{bw} - \rho_e}{\rho_s - \rho_e} \qquad (2.35)$$

The two conflicting effects on settling velocity can be combined by using the equation for settling velocity (2.32) and incorporating the equations for the drag coefficient and Reynolds number:

$$C_D = \frac{F}{R^e} \qquad (2.36)$$

where R = Reynolds number
for $R < 2$, $F = 24$, $e = 1$ (Stokes' Law)
for $2 < R < 500$, $F = 18.5$, $e = 0.6$ (Transition Region)
for $R < 500$, $F = 0.44$, $e = 0$ (Newton's Law) and

$$R = \frac{V_p D \rho_e}{\mu} \qquad (2.37)$$

where μ = absolute viscosity and the other terms are as previously defined.
The resultant equation is as follows:

$$\frac{V_{bp}}{V_p} = \frac{(1 + B\bar{m})^{1/(2-e)}}{(1 + \bar{m})^{1/3}} \qquad (2.38)$$

where V_{bp} = settling velocity of bioparticle
m = ratio of biomass volume to support particle volume
and the other terms are as previously defined.
For spherical sand, graded between 250 and 300 μm, with a biofilm thickness of 100 μm, $\bar{m}$ = 4.15 and, since Transition Region conditions apply to most of the relevant particles, e = 0.6. Therefore for thin films, as found in fluidised beds, when $B < 0.3$ biofilm growth reduces settling velocity while if $B > 0.5$ the converse occurs (Equation 2.38; Fig. 2.14). Clearly if $B = 1$, as in the case of a biofloc, growth always increases settling velocity. For a fluidised bed at 20°C containing sand, with a density of 2650 kg m^{-3}, supporting a biofilm having a density of 1002 kg m^{-3}, from Equation 2.35:

$$B = \frac{1002 - 1000}{2650 - 1000} = 0.001$$

On this basis, therefore, support particles will rise within the fluidised bed as biofilm thickness increases, so that stratification occurs based on particle size. This has been confirmed by data showing that biofilm thickness at the

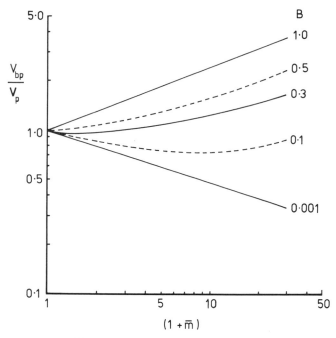

Fig. 2.14 — The effect of biomass growth on the settling velocities of particles in a fluidised bed.

top of a laboratory scale fluidised bed was 45 μm after 80 days, but was only 12 μm on sand taken from the middle of the bed [2.99]. If reactor fluid passes up the reactor by plug flow, the condition occurs in which the particles carrying the most biomass are located in the region of lowest substrate concentration, while small particles near the inlet are subject to high substrate concentrations which causes vigorous biofilm growth so that they ascend to the top of the bed, resulting in a dynamic equilibrium due to hydraulic sorting. Periodic sloughing of biomass from an inner core of the bioparticle occurs [2.100], probably attributable to decay due to low substrate concentration or mass transfer limitations though the thicker biofilm. The outer layers then succumb to shear forces generated by the difference between the buoyancy of a particle and its mass.

Several mathematical models have been developed to describe biofilm kinetics in anaerobic fluidised beds [2.96; 2.101–2.106]. Whereas a multidisciplinary approach, combined with the ready availability of microprocessors, has allowed better and more complex models to be developed, major limitations exist in measurement of the relevant kinetic parameters and constants, in addition to general dependence on assumptions such as sphericity, homogeneity of support particles, uniform biofilm thickness and the nature of mass transfer effects. Until these models are sufficiently developed and availability of reliable kinetic data enables confident prediction of such parameters as substrate utilisation and biofilm thickness and density, the approach of the engineer or biotechnologist to design of full-scale units must still be through bench, and subsequently pilot plant, studies for each particular application.

Experience with municipal sludge digesters has led to a general belief that anaerobic processes are less stable than aerobic processes. However, high rate reactors such as the expanded and fluidised beds have incorporated a higher level of engineering which, combined with improved knowledge of the microbiology and biochemistry of the digestion process, makes it feasible to monitor and control the units with greater reliability than was previously possible. Routine monitoring, which provides information about the progress of the digester during start-up or stress, should include:

— Total biogas flow; changes in this could represent a change in organic loading or some biochemical change. The measurement of gas flow is relatively simple but the reading does not indicate potential changes; more often it reflects events which have already significantly altered the process.
— Biogas composition; as the anaerobic systems are stressed there is usually an increasing proportion of carbon dioxide in the biogas, due to the greater sensitivity of the methane-forming bacteria. Although this does not represent a subtle change in cases of increased organic load, it is more senstive than biogas flow. The presence of oxygen and nitrogen in the biogas usually indicates air intrusion; oxygen is reported to be toxic to some strict anaerobes.
— Hydrogen concentration in the biogas; the critical role of hydrogen in controlling anaerobic processes means that monitoring the hydrogen concentrations can provide a rapid insight into changes in reactors. What is not clear is the concentration of hydrogen at which anaerobic systems are at risk and whether or not it is a universal indicator of shock organic or toxin load.
— Digester pH values decrease if the concentration of intermediate organic acids increases, but these have to be very high before pH values are significantly affected. Data are therefore often historical.
— Total volatile fatty acids — usually acetic and propionic acids increase if systems are stressed and reduce if the systems are underloaded.
— Separate analysis of the intermediate acids; when the systems are stressed, the concentration of longer carbon chain acids, for example propionic and heptanoic acid, increase more rapidly than the concentration of acetic acid.

Mechanical/electrical difficulties are usually the first encountered in start-up of any new unit operation and will not be discussed in detail. Such problems, frequently linked with design defects, may involve an unforeseen or altered process parameter, or may be due to imperfect communication between the design engineer and equipment suppliers. For example, pumps may be installed without the continuous flow variability envisaged by the plant designer, or they may generate more heat than anticipated. A further difficulty is that most fluidised bed reactors are designed for steady-state operation at design load. During start-up, the plant must operate at a small fraction of design rates. Process parameters may vary considerably during this period. For example, biomass has not yet colonised the fluidised sand grains and hence the particle density is much greater than at design steady-state, thus requiring a considerably higher upflow rate within the reactor than would be needed at steady-state.

It is likely that the factory employee(s) delegated to operate the new expanded or fluidised bed reactor will not have had any previous experience of this type of process. Even expertise with municipal digesters is not of much assistance as high-rate processes are much more engineered, and intrinsically require much more scrupulous monitoring. Frequently, there is nobody with the relevant expertise available to train and supervise the operator, which means that the initial processes may be operated under sub-optimal to adverse conditions, thus allowing little chance of successful start-up within a realistic time.

For the successful start-up of fluidised bed reactors:

— Ensure adequate communiction between design engineers and equipment suppliers so that the units will cope adequately from start-up to steady-state without excessive on-job modifications.
— Designers should either have a thorough understanding of all the ramifications of the process in terms of biomass characteristics and overall treatment performance, or should work closely with an expert.
— Feed quality and quantity and hence HRT and space loadings can be maintained constant by provision of adequately-sized balance tanks which may also serve as pre-digestors for acid production.
— Operators should be properly trained and closely supervised in the initial stages to prevent unnecessary setbacks.
— pH must be maintained at near neutral values, pH 7.0 ± 0.2. It may be necessary to install pH trimmer systems in addition to the major alkali dosing point in order to achieve this. Self-defouling electrodes are advisable.
— Temperature should not vary excessively. Best results in mesophilic digestors are obtained at temperatures of $36\pm1°C$.
— Feed loads should be applied in small increments, e.g. 0.5 kg m^{-3} d^{-1} of BOD. A few hours after stepping the load, volatile fatty acids and hydrogen should be monitored. This can be achieved by use of gas chromatography for volatile fatty acids which can give a full analysis to heptanoic acid in 25 min from time of sampling, and a hydrogen monitor for hydrogen, as previously described [2.21]. Loads should not be further increased until the VFA's are reduced to steady-state levels.
— The methane/carbon dioxide ratio should be monitored by gas chromatography to determine process efficiency. This analysis will also indicate presence of air leaks as evidenced by high nitrogen and oxygen concentrations.

Once a system has developed an appropriate biomass and has reached design load, the most likely upset will be either the discharge of a toxin or very variable loading. The former has to be prevented by appropriate management or pretreatment; however, it is not always possible to ensure a consistent feed to the reactor. This is often linked to operator education, but more frequently waste flow is interrupted by process scheduling or break-downs, in the factory supplying the waste.

If feed flow is turned off for the weekend due to a lack of conceptual understanding by the operator, or is interrupted by a cessation of production by the factory, both AFB's and AEB's are adversely affected. They will retain fluidisation at low HRT's due to recycle, but not where fluidisation is dependent on feedstock. They may also suffer temperature drop if depending on a warm feed for heating, and will also suffer biomasss loss (and consequent processing ability) due to endogenous respiration. The effects of organic load transients on a pilot plant anaerobic fluidised bed system have been described [2.92]. The fluidised bed was loaded at a base load of approximately 8 kg BOD m^{-3} d^{-1}, for a 1 h period; the influent strength was increased from 3000 mg l^{-1} to 38 500 mg l^{-1}, a 13-fold increase. The effluent quality initially deteriorated but within 400 min had recovered, much of the soluble BOD being due to volatile fatty acids. The greater the organic load transient the higher the effluent BOD. However, even for very high influent concentrations the system recovered relatively rapidly and was not permanently disrupted. Similarly, high biomass concentrations cushion AEB's and AFB's against toxic shock, thus rendering them more stable than suspended sludge systems.

In several laboratory and pilot scale studies on anaerobic fluidised beds high space loadings were achieved. A 0.646 m^3 fluidised bed has been used to treat brewery wastewaters [2.100]. The plant was loaded at up to 10 kg BOD m^{-3} d^{-1} with wastewaters of 30 000–40 000 mg l^{-1} of BOD. The plant always achieved in excess of 90% BOD removal and generated biogas which contained approximately 65% methane. Information on full-scale plants is less readily available. In Sydney, Australia, two large-scale plants have been constructed. An 80 m^3 fluidised bed loaded at 7.5 kg BOD m^{-3} d^{-1} is treating wastewater from a cereal processing plant which has a BOD of 1000–5000 mg l^{-1}. At a similar overall loading a 37 m^3 plant is treating wastewaters from a corn chip manufacturing process with influent BOD's in excess of 2000 mg l^{-1}. In both cases the plants are designed to reduce the BOD and suspended solids to less than 600 mg l^{-1} each, to meet sewer discharge standards [2.100].

2.8 CONCLUSIONS

Anaerobic processes for the treatment of wastewaters have not been widely used despite having several clear advantages over aerobic biological and chemical processes. The major advantage centres on the conversion of a high proportion of the influent organic carbon into methane and carbon dioxide. This loss of carbon represents an energy loss, making less energy available for the bacterial population to generate biomass and hence a lower generation of waste sludge than for aerobic biological processes. The biogas has considerable value as a fuel, but must be generated consistently.

Although anaerobic reactors such as septic tanks and municipal sludge digesters have been widely used for many years, the direct treatment of wastewaters is more recent. The interest in anaerobic treatment has been accelerated by the more stringent requirements to pretreat industrial wastewaters prior to sewer discharge, the need to reduce the energy costs of treatment, particularly for high strength wastewaters, and the unsuitability of alternative treatment methods for some types of wastewaters.

Recent work in gaining a better understanding of the biochemistry and microbiology is providing a basis for the operation and control of the reactors, while engineering improvements in terms of distribution systems, monitoring and control devices are increasing reliability. To date there are considerable numbers of laboratory and pilot plant studies but a relative scarcity of full-scale operating studies, particularly for the more recently developed processes.

It is interesting to note that the following quote was referring to waste-water treatment [2.107]:

'... no one system having so far established its claim to universal acceptance, and special cases will always demand special treatment, although the progress that has been made during the last few years in the system of biological treatment tends to show that in this direction the ultimate solution of this troublesome problem will be found'.

This quotation is relevant to anaerobic systems, and although it was written in the last century the basic concept that a combination of scientific and engineering expertise is needed to optimise processes is still relevant.

REFERENCES

[2.1] Forday, W. and Greenfield, P. (1983) Anaerobic digestion. *Effl. Water Tr. J.*, **23**, 405–413.

[2.2] Callander, I. J. and Barford, J. P. (1983) Recent advances in anaerobic digestion technology. *Process Biochem.*, **18**(4), 24–30.

[2.3] Eckenfelder, W. W. Jr (1980) *Principles of Water Quality Management*, CBI Publ. Co., Boston, Mass.

[2.4] Barnes, D. and Wilson, F. (1978) *Chemistry and Unit Operations in Sewage Treatment*, Applied Science Publishers, London.

[2.5] Lawrence, A. W. and McCarty, P. L. (1969) Kinetics of methane fermentation in anaerobic treatment. *J. Water Pollut. Cont. Fed.*, **41**, 1–17.

[2.6] Lawrence, A. W. (1971) Application of process kinetics to design of anaerobic processses. In *Anaerobic Biological Treatment Pro-*

cesses, Am. Chem. Soc., Advances in Chemistry 105, Chap. 9, Washington, DC.

[2.7] O'Rourke, J. T. (1968) *Kinetics of Anaerobic Treatment at Reduced Temperatures*, Ph.D. Thesis, Stanford University.

[2.8] Zeikus, J. G. (1980) Microbial populations in digestors. In *Anaerobic Digestion*, Stafford, D. A., Wheatley, B. I. and Hughes, D. E. (eds), Applied Science Publishers, London, pp. 61–90.

[2.9] Zeikus, J. G. (1980) Chemical and fuel production by anaerobic bacteria, *Ann. Rev. Microbiol.,* **34**, 423–464.

[2.10] Rudd, T., Hicks, S. J. and Lester, J. N. (1985) Comparison of the treatment of a synthetic meat waste by mesophilic and thermophilic anaerobic fluidised bed reactors. *Environ. Tech. Lett.,* **6**, 209–224.

[2.11] Ianotti, E. L., Fischer, J. R. and Sievers, D. M. (1982) Characterization of bacteria from a swine manure digester. *Appl. Environ. Microbiol.,* **43**, 136–143.

[2.12] Grbić-Galić, D. (1983) Anaerobic degradation of coniferyl alcohol by methanogenic consortia. *Appl. Environ. Microbiol.,* **46**, 1442–1446.

[2.13] Mosey, F. E. (1983) New developments in the anaerobic treatment of industrial wastes. *Effl. Water Tr. J.,* **23**, 85–93.

[2.14] Bryant, M. P., Wolin, E. A., Wolin, M. J. and Wolfe, R. S. (1967) *Methanobacillus omelianskii,* a symbiotic association of two species of bacteria. *Arch. Microbiol.,* **59**, 20–31.

[2.15] McIernay, M. J., Bryant, M. P., Hespell, R. B. and Costerton, J. W. (1981) *Syntrophomonas wolfei*, gen. nov. sp. nov., an anaerobic, syntrophic fatty acid oxidizing bacterium. *Appl. Environ. Microbiol.,* **41**, 1029–1039.

[2.16] Mountfort, D. O. and Bryant, M. P. (1983) Isolation and characterization of an anaerobic syntrophic benzoate-degrading bacterium from sewage sludge. *Arch. Microbiol.,* **133**, 249–256.

[2.17] Sahm, H. (1984) Anaerobic wastewater treatment. In *Advances in Biochemical Engineering/Biotechnology*, Fiechter, A. (ed.), Springer-Verlag, Berlin, pp. 83–115.

[2.18] McCarty, P. L. (1982) In *Anaerobic Digestion 1981*, Hughes, D. *et al.* (ed), Elsevier Biomedical Press, Amsterdam, **3**.

[2.19] Heyes, R. H. and Hall, R. J. (1981) Anaerobic digestion modelling — the role of H_2. *Biotechnol. Lett.,* **3**, 431–436.

[2.20] Mosey, F. E. (1983) Mathematical modelling of the anaerobic digestion process: Regulatory mechanisms for the formation of short-chain volatile acids from glucose. *Water Sci. Technol.,* **15**, 209–232.

[2.21] Mosey, F. E. (1983) Kinetic descriptions of anaerobic digestion. *Proc. 3rd Int. Symp. on Anaerobic Digestion,* Boston, 14–26 August 1983.

[2.22] Daniels, L., Fulton, G., Spencer, R. W. and Orme-Johnson, W. H. (1980) Origin of hydrogen in methane produced by *Methanobacterium thermoautotrophicum. J. Bacteriol.,* 141, 694–698.

[2.23] Zeikus, J. G. (1983) Metabolism of one-carbon compounds by chemotrophic anaerobes. *Adv. Microbiol. Physiol.*, **24**, 215–299.

[2.24] Huser, B. A., Wuhrmann, K. and Zehnder, A. J. B. (1982) *Methanothrix soehngenii* gen. nov. sp. nov., a new acetotrophic non-hydrogen-oxidizing methane bacterium. *Arch. Microbiol.*, **132**, 1–9.

[2.25] Smith, P. H. and Mah, R. A. (1966) Kinetics of acetate metabolism during sludge digestion. *Appl. Microbiol.*, **14**, 368–371.

[2.26] Schönheit, P., Moll, J. and Thauer, R. K. (1979) Nickel cobalt and molybdenum requirement for growth of *Methanobacterium thermoautotrophicum*. *Arch. Microbiol.*, **123**, 105–107.

[2.27] Speece, R. E. and McCarty, P. L. (1964) Nutrient requirements and biological solids accumulation in anaerobic digestion. *Adv. Water Pollut. Res.*, **2**, 305–322.

[2.28] Lawrence, A. W. (1967) *Kinetics of Methane Fermentation in Anaerobic Waste Treatment*, Ph.D. Thesis, Stanford University.

[2.29] McCarty, P. L. (1966) Developments in industrial microbiology. *Am. Inst. Biol. Sci.*, **7**, 144–155.

[2.30] Pirt, S. J. (1975) *Principles of Microbe and Cell Cultivation*, Blackwell, Oxford.

[2.31] Murray, W. D. and van den Berg, L. (1981) Effects of nickel, cobalt and molybdenum on performance of methanogenic fixed-film reactors. *Appl. Envrion. Microbiol.*, **42**, 502–505.

[2.32] McCarty, P. L. (1964) Anaerobic waste treatment fundamentals, part three, toxic materials and their control. *Public Works*, November, 91–94.

[2.33] FitzGerald, P. A. (1982) *Bacterial Responses to Heavy Metals*,. Honours Thesis, University of Sydney.

[2.34] Summers, A. O. and Silver, S. (1978) Microbial transformations of metals. *Ann. Rev. Microbiol.*, **32**, 637–672.

[2.35] Silver, S. (1978) Transport of cations and anions. In *Bacterial Transport*, Rosen, B. P. (ed.), Marcel Dekker, New York.

[2.36] Pan-Hou, H. S. K., Nichimoto, N. and Imura, N. (1981) Possible role of membrane proteins in mercury resistance of *Enterobacter aerogenes*. *Arch. Microbiol.*, **130**, 93–95.

[2.37] Olafson, R. W., Abel, K. and Sim, R. G. (1979) Prokaryotic metallothionein: preliminary characterization of a blue-green alga heavy metal-binding protein. *Biochem. Biophys. Res. Comm.*, **89**, 36–43.

[2.38] Holden, P. (1979) *Uptake of Heavy Metal by Soil Bacteria*, Honours Thesis, University of Sydney.

[2.39] Forster, C. F.. (1984) Activated sludge surfaces and their interactions with metals. *Proc. Int. Conf. on 'Heavy Metals in the Environment'*, Vol. 1, Heidelberg, September 1984, pp. 487–489.

[2.40] Nagamine, Y., Mizuno, D. and Natori, S. (1979) Selective inhibition by zinc of RNA synthesis initiation in the RNA polymerase I reaction. *Fed. Europ. Biochem. Soc. Lett.*, **99**, 29–32.

[2.41] Petrelli, F. L. and de Flora, S. (1977) Toxicity and mutagenicity of hexavalent chromium on *Salmonella typhimurium*. *Appl. Environ. Microbiol.*, **33**, 805–809.

[2.42] Bragg, P. D. and Rainier, D. J. (1974) The effects of silver ions on the respiratory chain of *Escherichia coli. Can. J. Microbiol.*, **20**, 883–339.

[2.43] Singh, A. P. and Bragg, P. D. (1974) Inhibition of energization of *Salmonella typhimurium* membrane by zinc ions. *Fed. Europ. Biochem. Soc. Lett.*, **40**, 200–202.

[2.44] Sheehan, G. J. (1981) *Kinetics of Heterogeneous Acidogenic Fermentations*, Ph.D. Thesis, University of Queensland.

[2.45] Kugelman, I. J. and Chin, K. K. (1971) Anaerobic biological treatment processes. In *Advances in Chemistry* Series 105, Am. Chem. Soc., Gould, R. F. (ed.), Washington, DC.

[2.46] Parkin, G. F. and Speece, R. E. (1982) Modeling toxicity in methane fermentation system. *J. Environ. Eng, Div., Proc. Am. Soc. Civ. Eng.*, **108**, 515–531.

[2.47] Lehninger, A. L. (1976) *Biochemistry*, Worth, New York.

[2.48] Fedorak, P. M., Knettig, E. and Hrudey, S. E. (1985) The effects of activated carbon on the methanogenic degradation of phenolics in H-coal wastewater. *Environ. Tech. Lett.*, **6**, 181–188.

[2.49] Benjamin, M. J., Woods, S. L. and Ferguson, J. F. (1984) Anaerobic toxicity and bio-degradability of pulp mill waste constituents. *Water Res.*, **18**, 601–607.

[2.50] Parkin, G. F., Speece, R. E., Yang, C. H. J. and Kocher, W. M. (1983) Response of methane fermentation systems to industrial toxicants. *J. Water Pollut. Cont. Fed.*, **55**, 44–53.

[2.51] Stuckey, D. C., Owen, W. F., McCarty, P. L. and Parkin, G. F. (1980) Anaerobic toxicity evaluation by batch and semi-continuous assays, *J. Water Pollut. Cont. Fed.*, **52**, 720–729.

[2.52] Asinari di San Marzano, C. M., Binot, R., Bol, T., Fripiat, J. L., Melchior, J. L., Perez, I., Naveau, H. and Nyns, E. J. (1981) Volatile fatty acids, an important state parameter for the control of the reliability and the productivities of methane anaerobic digestions. *Biomass*, **1**, 47–59.

[2.53] Callender, I. J. and Barford, J. P. (1983) Precipitation, chelation and the availability of metals as nutrients in anaerobic digestion. I Methodology. *Biotech. Bioeng.*, **25**, 1947–1957.

[2.54] Callender, I. J. and Barford, J. P. (1983) Precipitation, chelation and the availability of metals as nutrients in anaerobic digestion. II Applications. *Biotech. Bioeng.*, **25**, 1959–1972.

[2.55] Hayes, T. D. and Theis, T. L. (1978) The distribution of heavy metals in anaerobic digestion. *J. Water Pollut. Cont. Fed.*, **50**, 61–72.

[2.56] De Baere, L. A., Devocht, M., van Asshe, P. and Verstraete, W. (1984) Influence of high NaCl and NH_4Cl salt levels on methanogenic associations. *Water Res.*, **18**, 543–548.

[2.57] Tan, S. H. and McFarlane, P. N. (1984) Decolourization of wood-ethanol stillage using a granular activated carbon packed anaerobic expanded-bed reactor. *Proc. 16th Biotoechnol. Conf. on 'Forest Industries and Biotechnology'*, Massey University, Palmerston North, New Zealand, May 1984.

[2.58] British Standards Institution (1983) *British Standard Code of Practice for Design and Installation of Small Sewage Treatment Works and Cesspools*, BS6297:1983, British Standards Institution, London.

[2.59] Noone, G. P. and Brade, C. E. (1984) Anaerobic sludge digestion — Need it be expensive? III. Integrated and low-cost digestion. *Wat. Pollut. Control*, **84**, 309–328.

[2.60] Ghosh, S. and Klass, D. L. (1978) Two phase anaerobic digestion. *Process Biochem.*, **13**(4), 15–24.

[2.61] Ghosh, S. (1984) Feasibility of two phase anaerobic stabilization of industrial waste with simultaneous production of energy. *Environ. Tech. Lett.*, **5**, 373–382.

[2.62] Barnes, D., Forster, C. F. and Hrudey, S. E. (eds) (1984) *Surveys in Industrial Wastewater Treatment*, Volume 1, *Food and Allied Industries*, Pitmans, Boston, London, Melbourne.

[2.63] Labat, M., Garcia, J. L., Mayer, F. and Descamps, F. (1984) Anacrobic digestion of sugar beet pulps. *Biotech. Lett.*, **6**, 379–384.

[2.64] Ang, H. and Leong, L. (1984) Malaysian palm oil effluent treatment. *Effl. Water Tr. J.*, **24**, 73–79.

[2.65] Chin, K. K. and Wong, K. K. (1983) Thermophilic anaerobic digestion of palm oil mill effluent. *Water Res.*, **17**, 993–995.

[2.66] Mosey, F. E. and Faulkes, M. (1978) *Performance in laboratory-scale digestion of cow slurry at 35°C*. WRC Laboratory Report 737, Stevenage.

[2.67] Mosey, F. E. and Faulkes, M. (1978) *Laboratory-scale performance trials of the anaerobic digestion of pig slurry at 35°C*. WRC Laboratory Report 778, Stevenage.

[2.68] Summers, R., Hobson, P. N., Harries, C. R. and Fielden, N. E. H. (1984) Anaerobic digestion on a large pig unit. *Process Biochem.*, **19**, 77–78.

[2.69] Ianotti, E. L., Porter, J. H., Fischer, J. R. and Suvers, D. M. (1979) Changes in swine manure during anaerobic digestion, *Dev. Ind. Microbiol.*, **20**, 519–529.

[2.70] Hobson, P. N., Bousfield, S. and Summers, R. (1974) Anaerobic digestion of organic matter, *Crit. Rev. Env. Cont.*, **4**, 131–191.

[2.71] Aubart, Ch. and Fauchille, S. (1983) Anaerobic digestion of poultry wastes, Part 1 Biogas production and pollution decrease in terms of retention time and total solids content. *Process. Biochem.*, **18**(2), 31–37.

[2.72] Mosey, F. E. (1981) Anaerobic biological treatment of food industry waste waters. *Water Pollut. Cont.*, **80**, 273–291.

[2.73] Steffen, A. J. and Bedker, M. (1961) Operation of full-scale anaerobic contact treatment plant for meat-packing wastes. *Proc. Purdue Ind. Waste Conf.*, **16**, 423–437.

[2.74] Stander, G. J. (1967) Treatment of wine distillery wastes by anaerobic digestion. *Proc. Purdue Ind. Waste Conf.*, **22**, 892–907.

[2.75] Lettinga, G. and Vinken, J. N. (1980) Feasibility of the up-flow anaerobic sludge blanket (UASB) process for the treatment of low strength wastes. *Proc. Purdue Ind. Waste Conf.*, **35**, 625–634.

[2.76] Zoetemeyer, R. J. (1982) *Acidogenesis of Soluble Carbohydrate Containing Wastewaters*, Ph.D. Thesis, Amsterdam.

[2.77] Heertjes, P. M. and van der Meer, R. R. (1978) Dynamics of liquid flow in an upflow reactor used for anaerobic treatment of wastewater. *Biotech. Bioeng.*, **20**, 1577–1594.

[2.78] Lettinga, G. (1978) Feasibility of anaerobic digestion for the purification of industrial waste waters. *Europ. Abwassem. Symp.*, München, Germany, pp. 229–256.

[2.79] Mosey, F. E. (1981) *Anaerobic biological treatment plants (UASB-reactors) in Holland. Visit report.* Water Research Centre, 101-S, Stevenage.

[2.80] Nel, L. M., de Haast, J. and Britz, T. J. (1984) Anaerobic digestion of a petrochemical effluent using an upflow anaerobic sludge blanket reactor. *Biotech. Lett.*, **6**, 741–746.

[2.81] Coulter, J. B., Soneda, S. and Ettinger, M. B. (1957) Anaerobic contact process for sewage disposal. *Sew. Ind. Wastes*, **29**, 468–477.

[2.82] Young, J. C. and McCarty, P. L. (1967) The anaerobic filter for waste treatment. *Proc. Purdue Ind. Waste Conf.*, **22**, 559–574.

[2.83] Frostell, B. (1981) Anaerobic treatment in a sludge bed system compared with a filter system. *J. Water Pollut. Cont. Fed.*, **53**, 216–222.

[2.84] Mosey, F. E. (1977) *Anaerobic filtration: a biological process for warm trade waste waters.* Water Research Centre, TR48, Stevenage.

[2.85] Hall, E. R. and Jovanovic, M. (1982) Anaerobic treatment of thermal sludge conditioning liquor with fixed-film and suspended growth processes. *Proc. Purdue Ind. Waste Conf.*, **37**, 719–728.

[2.86] Kennedy, K. J. and van den Berg, L. (1982) Anaerobic digestion of piggery waste using a stationary fixed film reactor. *Agric. Wastes*, **4**, 151–158.

[2.87] van den Berg, L. (1984) Developments in methanogenesis from industrial waste water. *Can. J. Microbiol.*, **30**, 975–990.

[2.88] Beer, C. (1970) discussion of Seidel, D. F., Evaluation of anaerobic denitrification processes. *J. San. Eng. Div.*, ASCE, **96**, 1452–1454.

[2.89] Atkinson, B. and Davies, I. J. (1972) The completely mixed microbial film fermenter — a method of overcoming washout in continuous fermentation. *Trans, Inst. Chem. Eng.*, **50**, 208–216.

[2.90] Jeris, J. S. and Muëller, J. A. (1974) High rate biological denitrification using a granular fluidised bed. *J. Water Pollut. Cont. Fed.*, **46**, 2118–2128.

[2.91] Jeris, J. S. and Owens, R. W. (1975) Pilot-scale high rate biological denitrification. *J. Water Pollut. Cont. Fed.,* **47**, 2043–2057.

[2.92] Barnes, D., Bliss, P. J., Grauer, R. B. and Robins, K. (1984) Pretreatment of high strength wastewater by an anaerobic fluidised bed process. Part II. Response to organic load transients. *Environ. Tech. Lett.,* **6**, 73–78.

[2.93] Switzenbaum, M. S. (1983) Anaerobic fixed film wastewater treatment. *Enzyme Microb. Technol.,* **5**, 242–250.

[2.94] Norman, P. A. and Gould, B. W. (1984) Backwashing rapid sand filters. *Effl. Water Tr. J.,* **24**, 174–181.

[2.95] Coulson, J. M. (1983) *Chemical Engineering,* Pergamon Press, Oxford and New York.

[2.96] Mulcahy, L. T., Shieh, W. K. and la Motta, E. J. (1981) *A.I.Ch.E. Symp. Series,* **209**(77), 273–285.

[2.97] Ngian, K. F. and Martin, W. R. B. (1980) Biologically active fluidised beds: mechanistic considerations. *Biotech. Bioeng.,* **22**, 1007–1014.

[2.98] Andrews, G. F. and Tien, C. (1982) An analysis of bacterial growth in a fluidised bed adsorption column, *A.I.Ch.E.J.,* **28**, 182–190.

[2.99] Rockey, J. S. and Forster, C. F. (1982) Microbial attachment in anaerobic expanded bed reactors. *Environ. Tech. Lett.,* **6**, 115–122.

[2.100] Nicholas, P. (1985) pers. comm.

[2.101] Shieh, W. K., Sutton, P. M. and Kos, P. (1981) Predicting reactor biomass concentration. *J. Water Pollut. Cont. Fed.,* **53**, 1574–1584.

[2.102] Atkinson, B. and Davies, I. J. (1974) The overall rate of uptake (reaction) by microbial films. Part I — A biological rate equation. *Trans. Inst. Chem. Engrs,* **52**, 248–259.

[2.103] Williamson, K. and McCarty, P. L. (1976) A model of substrate utilisation by bacterial films. *J. Water Pollut. Cont. Fed.,* **48**, 9–24.

[2.104] Harremoes, P. (1978) Biofilm kinetics. In *Water Pollution Microbiology,* Mitchell, R. (ed.), Vol. 2, John Wiley, New York, pp. 82–109.

[2.105] Andrews, G. F.. (1982) Fluidised bed fermenters: a steady state analysis. *Biotech. Bioeng.,* **24**, 2013–2030.??

[2.106] Rittman, B. E. and McCarty, P. L. (1980) Model of steady state biofilm kinetics, *Biotech. Bioeng.,* **22**, 2343–2357.

[2.107] Moore, E. C. S. (1898) *Sanitary Engineering,* Batsford, London.

3

Mineral leaching with bacteria

F. D. Pooley
Institute of Materials, University College, Cardiff, UK

3.1 INTRODUCTION

The knowledge that microorganisms play a significant role in the concentration and distribution of elements in the lithosphere has been appreciated by both microbiologists and geologists for many years. This is especially true of many metals which are essential components of the complex biological reactions necessary to maintain the metabolism of most microorganisms. These elements can be directly involved in intracellular biochemical reactions and as a result may accumulate or be excreted in concentrated forms by organisms. Conversely, extracellular chemical activity, initiated or catalysed by microorganisms or the organic compounds they excrete, may result in by-products which serve as sources of nutrients or energy necessary for their subsequent growth. Iron and sulphur are both important examples of elements which may be both oxidised or reduced by a variety of microorganisms in a corresponding diversity of natural environments providing an important source of energy for growth.

The term bacterial leaching is used to describe, in general, the extraction or solubilisation of metals from minerals contained either in a rock matrix or in the form of concentrated mineral products from conventional ore processing plants. In the majority of cases, the major sources of the commercial metals are in ore bodies in which the metals occur mainly as sulphide minerals. Table 3.1 briefly lists the more important mineral forms which are the natural source of those metals which have been the subject of bacterial leaching investigations. Extraction of the metal from these sulphide minerals is conveniently accomplished by their aqueous oxidation from sulphide to the soluble sulphate, thus producing solutions from which the metals may more readily be recovered.

The chemical conditions under which natural bacterially aided sulphide

Table 3.1 — Major sulphide mineral forms and economic occurrence

Iron (Fe)	FeS_2 as pyrite and marcasite, FeS_{1+x} as pyrrhotite. Produced as a source of sulphur and iron but present in most sulphide ore bodies.
Copper (Cu)	$CuFeS_2$ (chalcopyrite), Cu_2S (chalcocite), $CuFeS$ (bornite), CuS (covellite) main sources of copper (worldwide distribution), often in association with other base metal sulphide minerals.
Zinc (Zn)	ZnS (sphalerite) main source of zinc metal, often associated with PbS lead sulphide. Zinc sulphide ores are also an important source of cadmium. Worldwide occurrence.
Nickel (Ni)	NiS (millerite), $FeNiS$ (pentlandite) primary sources of nickel, often in association with copper sulphide minerals.
Cobalt (Co)	$CuCo_2S_4$ (carrolite) produced in association with copper sulphide minerals.
Molybdenum (Mo)	MoS_2 (molybdenite) main source of molybdenum in association with copper sulphide minerals.
Lead (Pb)	PbS (galena) main source of lead often found in association with zinc sulphide, also a major source of silver. Worldwide occurrence.
Silver (Ag)	Ag_2S (argentite) major silver mineral, always found in association with other metal sulphide minerals.
Arsenic (As)	$AsFeS$ (arsenopyrite) sources of arsenic, often occurring as a contaminant mineral in many sulphide ore bodies.

mineral leaching takes place are normally acidic, sulphuric acid being the major solvent. This is always fortified by the presence of varying amounts of the powerful oxidising agent ferric iron. Also present in all bacterially influenced reactions will be the biochemical products of microbial synthesis. These compounds may either directly influence the kinetics of the sulphide mineral oxidation or provide a nutrient source for heterotrophic organisms which maintain a suitable chemical environment for the growth of the autotrophic organisms involved in mineral leaching. Bacterial leaching depends essentially, therefore, upon the production of sulphuric acid and ferric iron, both of which are produced by bacterial oxidation of reduced sulphur compounds and ferrous iron respectively.

There are an increasing number of mesophilic, moderate and extreme thermophilic organisms which have been characterised by their ability to oxidise sulphur and/or ferrous iron. Many of these organisms have been shown to enhance the oxidation rate of sulphide minerals manyfold when compared with simple chemical oxidation systems. This has stimulated much research into the ways in which such organisms can be harnessed practically to develop new simple and economical hydrometallurgical processes for the treatment of metalliferous ores and sulphide mineral concentrates.

3.2   MICROORGANISMS INVOLVED IN SULPHIDE MINERAL LEACHING

By far the most important group of bacteria which are involved in sulphide mineral leaching are the acidophilic thiobacilli which form part of the family Thiobacteriaceae. They are characterised by a chemosynthetic metabolism and the ability to use the oxidation of inorganic sulphur and its compounds to produce energy for growth. They are therefore referred to as chemolithotrophs. They have been shown [3.1] to consist of three categories of bacteria. These include the autotrophs which derive their carbon for growth solely from carbon dioxide, the mixotrophs which can utilise carbon derived from organic compounds as well as carbon dioxide, and the heterotrophs whose sole source of carbon is obtained from organic substrates. The majority of the thiobacilli species are mesophilic bacteria which have an optimum temperature for growth between 30 and 35°C. However, moderately thermophilic species have been isolated which grow best at temperatures of 45–50°C.

Not all thiobacilli are useful for the purposes of sulphide mineral leaching, some because they are unable to grow at the low pH levels necessary to enhance mineral oxidation, others because of their inability to utilise sulphur when it is initially in a solid sulphide mineral form. Although not able to involve themselves directly in sulphide oxidation, some thiobacilli species can cooperate in mineral leaching by utilising the by-products of such reactions which will be both organic and inorganic in character. They are able to use organic compounds as a source of carbon and reaction products, such as elemental sulphur or soluble sulphur compounds, as an energy source.

In order of importance, the thiobacilli which are involved in mineral leaching are *Thiobacillus ferrooxidans, T. thiooxidans, T. acidophilus* and *T. organoporus. T. ferrooxidans* is by far the most important of the above species and has been the most extensively studied [3.2–3.7]. This species is able to utilise not only inorganic sulphur compounds but also ferrous iron simultaneously as oxidisable inorganic substrates. Many strains of this organism have been isolated, their differentiation being based upon their capacity to oxidise either elemental sulphur or various sulphide minerals. Of most importance from a leaching point of view are strains with capacity for rapid sulphide mineral oxidation.

T. ferrooxidans is an aerobic, acidophilic, autrophic, rod-shaped bacterium which is active over a pH range 1.5–5.0 with an optimum pH for growth of 2.0, although it can be adapted to grow at lower pH values [3.8]. Mesophilic strains have an optimum temperature for growth of 35°C but this does vary with strains. It requires a source of nitrogen, phosphate and trace amounts of calcium, magnesium and potassium. Its energy for growth is obtained from the oxidation of ferrous iron, soluble and insoluble sulphides, sulphur and soluble sulphur compounds. *T. ferrooxidans* can be found in a wide range of natural environments but its presence can readily be detected where there are concentrations of sulphide minerals.

T. thiooxidans is also an acidophilic, autotrophic, rod-shaped mesophilic baterium which grows on elemental sulphur and soluble sulphur compounds but is unable to oxidise ferrous iron or insoluble sulphides. Its conditions for optimum growth are similar to those of *T. ferrooxidans*, i.e. temperature 30–35°C and pH 2.0, but it can grow within the pH range 1.5–6.0.

T. acidophilus and *T. organoparus* are mesophilic, mixotrophic, acidophilic, rod-shaped bacteria which oxidise only elemental sulphur for growth. They grow at pH 1.5–5.0 with an optimum pH of 2.5–3.0. Being unable to oxidise insoluble sulphides, their role in mineral leaching may be one of only consuming organic compounds excreted by *T. ferrooxidans* which are detrimental to the latter organism's growth.

Although the thiobacilli are the most important group of microorganisms involved in mineral leaching, especially the various strains of *T. ferrooxidans*, other mesophilic, acidophilic, iron-oxidising bacteria with a role to play in mineral leaching have been isolated. One of these which may be of importance is *Leptospirillum ferrooxidans* [3.9]. This is an autotrophic vibroid cell, capable of forming spirals of joined cells, which oxidises only ferrous iron. It is able to leach sulphide minerals under acid conditions indirectly by its ability to produce ferric iron, thus promoting chemical leaching. Its optimum temperature and pH range for growth are 30° and 1.5–5.0 respectively.

In recent years, moderately and extremely thermophilic and acidophilic bacteria which are able to oxidise iron, sulphur and mineral sulphides have been isolated [3.10–3.12] and this has extended the temperature range over which mineral leaching might be performed. Moderately thermophilic thiobacilli have been demonstrated to be heterotrophic with optimum temperatures for growth between 45 and 60°C. Strains of thermophilic organisms of a sulfolobus type, both mixotrophic and heterotrophic, have been isolated which grow within a temperature range of 55–85°C.

It is only under laboratory conditions that the leaching of sulphide minerals is performed with pure bacterial cultures. These have been shown [3.13] to produce poorer results when compared with enriched cultures from local sites where sulphide mineral oxidation is occurring. Under natural leaching conditions, many organisms other than the active leaching bacteria will be present and microbial interaction will be an important part of the process; examples of such microbial interaction have been noted [3.14].

It is unlikely that any engineered microbial leaching process will employ a pure bacterial culture. Enriched cultures obtained from the same site as the mineral to be treated or from a locality containing minerals of a similar chemistry are most likely to serve as the source of the culture. Emphasis is placed upon the tolerance of the culture to the metals released from the minerals being leached and its ability to oxidise both sulphur and iron. *T.*

ferrooxidans can tolerate 40 g l^{-1} iron, 70 g l^{-1} copper, 119 g l^{-1} zinc, and 70 g l^{-1} nickel [3.15–3.19], and strains can be made adaptable by successive sub-culturing to a variety of metals such as cobalt, uranium, chromium, and arsenic. A much lower tolerance has been displayed to mercury and selenium. The presence of these and other inhibitory metals may therefore influence leaching results.

3.3 THE CHEMISTRY OF SULPHIDE MINERAL OXIDATION BY BACTERIA

Some doubt still surrounds the actual role of bacteria in the oxidation of sulphide minerals because of the inability to separate those reactions which are solely promoted by bacteria from those which are simply chemical. Reference is often made to direct and indirect attack in bacterial leaching systems; these terms relate to dissolution of the sulphide mineral matrix directly by bacteria and dissolution of the matrix with ferric iron produced by the bacterial oxidation of ferrous iron. As it is practically impossible to isolate each form of reaction experimentally, it is the sum of both that is normally observed in leaching systems, a sum which is usually much greater in magnitude than the individual components of the reaction. The oxidation reactions taking place during the bacterial leaching of the sulphide minerals can best be considered by examining the oxidation of pyrite (FeS_2), a mineral form of ferrous sulphide. Pyrite can be considered to be the most important sulphide mineral substrate as far as the active leaching bacteria are concerned. It contains almost equal quantities of ferrous iron and sulphur which are the principal sources of energy of such bacteria. Pyrite is also the most common of the naturally occurring sulphide minerals and is present as an accessory mineral in practically all commercial sulphide ore deposits. Two equations can be written to represent the autooxidation of this mineral in the presence of oxygen, water and sulphuric acid, as follows:

$$2FeS_2 + 7O_2 + 2H_2O \rightarrow 2FeSO_4 + 2H_2SO_4 \qquad (3.1)$$

$$2FeS_2 + 2H_2SO_4 + O_2 \rightarrow 2FeSO_4 + 2H_2O + 4S \qquad (3.2)$$

In Equations 3.1 and 3.2, ferrous sulphate is formed while elemental sulphur is an additional product in the second equation. These reactions take place (under ambient conditions) at a very slow rate due to the formation of reaction product layers such as sulphur on the surfaces of pyrite particles, resulting in diffusion-controlled reactions.

When the oxidation of pyrite is considered in the presence of iron and sulphur oxidising bacteria, the reactions shown in Equations 3.1 and 3.2 are modified by bacterial oxidation of the ferrous sulphate and elemental sulphur which would be formed during its chemical oxidation, as follows:

$$4FeSO_4 + 2H_2SO_4 + O_2 \xrightarrow{\text{bacteria}} 2Fe_2(SO_4)_3 + H_2O \qquad (3.3)$$

$$2S + 3O_2 + 2H_2O \xrightarrow{\text{bacteria}} 2H_2SO_4 \tag{3.4}$$

With ferrous sulphate and elemental sulphur now oxidised to produce ferric sulphate and sulphuric acid respectively, the oxidation of pyrite proceeds under different chemical conditions, ferric sulphate reacting with pyrite as follows:

$$FeS_2 + Fe_2(SO_4)_3 \xrightarrow{\text{bacteria}} 3FeSO_4 + 2S \tag{3.5}$$

The ferrous sulphate and sulphur which are formed in Equation 3.5 are again oxidised by bacteria to ferric sulphate and sulphuric acid as shown in Equations 3.3 and 3.4. An overall equation representing the oxidation of pyrite in the presence of bacteria can now be written in the form:

$$4FeS_2 + 15O_2 + 2H_2O \xrightarrow{\text{bacteria}} 2Fe_2(SO_4)_3 + 2H_2SO_4 \tag{3.6}$$

This reaction proceeds rapidly and is chemically controlled. Reaction products such as sulphur do not form on the pyrite mineral surface as they are oxidised by bacteria.

Fig. 3.1 illustrates graphically the rate at which pyrite can be leached bacterially. The iron released into solution from the mineral is accompanied by a corresponding increase in sulphate and also sulphuric acid as indicated by the drop in the pH. Not all the sulphide in the pyrite is oxidised immediately to sulphate during the leach; a portion is converted initially to elemental sulphur before it also is oxidised to sulphuric acid.

Similar equations can be written for the bacterially assisted oxidation of other sulphide minerals such as those of copper and zinc. Chalcopyrite ($CuFeS_2$), the most important copper mineral, is leached in the presence of bacteria in the following manner:

$$CuFeS_2 + 2Fe_2(SO_4)_3 \longrightarrow CuSO_4 + 5FeSO_4 + 2S \tag{3.7}$$

Again the reaction by-products ferrous iron and sulphur are oxidised by bacteria to ferric iron and sulphuric acid. In a similar manner the dissolution of sphalerite (ZnS) will also produce some ferric iron, as ferrous iron is an integral part of most natural zinc sulphide samples. The leaching of sphalerite can therefore be represented as follows:

$$ZnS + Fe_2(SO_4)_3 \longrightarrow ZnSO_4 + 2FeSO_4 + S \tag{3.8}$$

The reaction products again represent suitable substrates for bacterial oxidation. In general the leaching by bacteria of all metal sulphides can be represented by the following equation:

$$MS + Fe_2(SO_4)_3 \longrightarrow MSO_4 + 2FeSO_4 + S \tag{3.9}$$

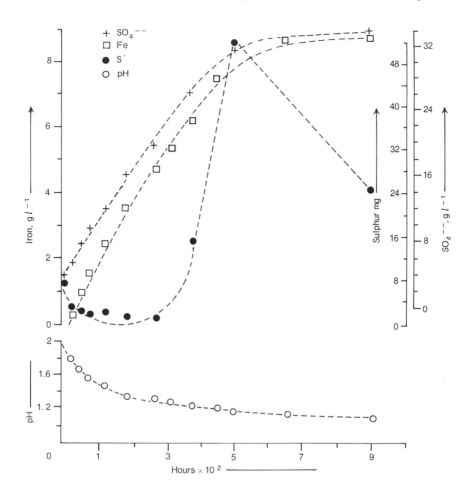

Fig. 3.1 — Results obtained from the bacterial leaching of a 53 μm pyrite sample at a solids concentration of 2% by weight in the presence of 1×10^9 cells ml^{-1} of *T. ferrooxidans*.

This equation demonstrates why the iron and sulphur oxidising bacteria are so important in maintaining such reactions. Their oxidation of the ferrous iron and sulphur maintain the chemical conditions necessary for the dissolution of the sulphide mineral by maintaining levels both of ferric iron and of sulphuric acid.

3.4 THE EXPLOITATION OF BACTERIAL SULPHIDE MINERAL OXIDATION

The ways in which the oxidation of sulphide minerals by bacteria can be utilised in the minerals industry are many and varied. They all rely, however, upon the promotion of the growth of bacteria capable of oxidising ferrous iron and reduced sulphur compounds, in either a soluble or an initially solid form. The purpose of developing processes which depend upon the growth of microorganisms arises from the continual search for methods of extracting metals which are less energy-intensive, more economically viable and environmentally more attractive. Bacterial oxidation of sulphide minerals is an attractive method for the production of metals from ores or concentrates for a number of reasons, which include the following:

(a) It is flexible and can be employed to treat a variety of individual sulphide minerals or mineral mixtures.
(b) The manner in which it can be applied varies from simple fixed bed percolation to stirred tank leaching systems.
(c) It does not require high operating temperatures or pressures.
(d) It is self generating in terms of solvent in the form of ferric sulphate solution.
(e) Any liquid effluents it produces are in an aqueous form which can be conveniently neutralised, while no noxious gaseous by-products are formed.
(f) It is not scale dependent.
(g) It can be employed in close proximity to the production source of the minerals to be treated.
(h) It involves reactions which cannot be reproduced by simple chemical means alone.

There are also some inherent disadvantages in the use of a bacterial leaching system for the recovery of metals, the most important of which is the need to maintain the presence of an active culture of the desired microorganisms. This requires the control of reaction temperature and the input of compounds and elements essential to maintain their growth. It is also essential to ensure that anything detrimental to their growth, in either soluble or solid form, does not contaminate the leaching process. Bacterial leaching is also a much slower process than competitive chemical leaching processes. Mineral oxidation rates in the presence of bacteria are closely related to the growth rate of the microorganisms involved and these are relatively inflexible.

Sulphide mineral oxidation of bacteria can be employed to establish a number of routes for the processing of minerals which can be categorised as follows:

(a) The extraction of metals from low grade ores by dump, heap and *in situ* leaching methods.
(b) The total leaching of single or mixed mineral concentrates by fixed bed percolation or agitated reactors.
(c) The partial leaching of mixed mineral concentrates to remove impurities or render the mineral suitable for processing by other techniques.
(d) Employment of a bacterial leaching system to generate lixiviant in the

form of acid ferric sulphate solutions to treat independently other ore types not suitable in character to support bacterial growth.

So far the only applications of bacterial leaching to have been pursued on a commercial scale are dump, heap and *in situ* leaching operations. However, extensive investigations and feasibility trials have been and are still being conducted to investigate possible in-plant operations of bacterial oxidation.

3.5   DUMP AND HEAP LEACHING

Dump and heap leaching mainly involves the extraction of metal values from mining wastes or marginal ores which are either too low in grade to be treated profitably by conventional methods or too complex to be concentrated for smelter treatment. Heap leaching differs from dump leaching because of its application to ore types which are more rapidly leached and are higher in contained values. They are first mined then crushed to a suitable size for leaching and transported to the prepared leaching area and formed into a heap specifically to be leached. Heap leaching is therefore concerned with the recovery of the contained metals from an ore in a period of months, whereas it may take years to recover the same percentage of metal from the leaching of low grade waste dump which can be considered as a metal scavenging operation. Bacterially aided heap leaching operations are employed in many parts of the world for the recovery of copper, especially where the ores treated are already partially oxidised from their original sulphide form. The knowledge gained from the experience of heap formation for leaching purposes is now being exploited extensively in other chemical leaching operations, such as the recovery of gold with dilute cyanide solutions.

Dump leaching operations are also practised in many countries and this is perhaps the most widely used bacterial leaching technique. It is applied to the treatment of material normally considered as waste from large open pit mining operations of disseminated porphyry copper deposits which have accumulated over a number of years. It is interesting to note that approximately 15 per cent of copper is recovered by dump leaching operations in the United States of America [3.20]. This leaching method produces a 'pregnant' solution of a generally lower metal concentration than does heap leaching. Both heap and dump operations simulate natural bacterial leaching processes, the main difference being that they are controlled and constructed to optimise metal extraction.

Both dumps and heaps are formed of broken ore in layers on an impermeable sloping base which is prepared to ensure that the solutions percolating through the ore are collected and not lost by seepage to ground water. Leach liquor, in the form of acid ferric sulphate solution containing bacteria, is pumped to the top of the ore piles and allowed to percolate through them. The solutions may be applied by ponding, spraying or injection. The spraying method usually employs perforated plastic pipes laid in a pattern across the top of the ore and has the advantage that better oxygenation and a more uniform wetting of the dump or heap surface is achieved. Improved contact of mineral and solution is claimed [3.21], however, by use of a solution injection system, especially where excessive evaporation may occur due to arid weather conditions. Metal-rich solutions emerging from the dump are channelled to collection ponds to be pumped to a treatment plant where the desired metal may be recovered. Metal recovery may consist of a simple precipitation step or more sophisticated routes involving either ion exchange or solvent extraction to remove and concentrate the metal from the leach solution. This is then followed by either an electrowinning or a selective precipitation stage. Barren leach liquors, containing mainly dissolved iron, are either pumped to oxidation ponds to regenerate them or returned directly to the heap or dump. In the oxidation ponds, bacteria convert ferrous iron in the leach liquor to the ferric form prior to recycling it. The outline of a typical heap or dump leaching operation for a copper ore is illustrated by Fig. 3.2 in which solvent extraction is employed to remove and concentrate the copper from the leach solution prior to electrowinning of the metal.

Dump leaching, for example, is used at the Kennecott Chino mine in New Mexico, USA, where the daily production of minewaste is some 7×10^4 tonnes. The dumps are 25–30 m in height. Copper is removed from the resultant pregnant liquors (typically having a concentration of about 1.4 g Cu l^{-1}) by the addition of scrap iron. This induces a surface deposition of 'cement' copper which is then removed by high-pressure jets for further purification. The daily yield of the cement copper at this mine is 45–50 tonnes.

The rate of extraction of metal from a large scale percolation leaching operation involving a heap or a dump of ore is dependent upon many factors. Some are related to the characteristics of the ore treated, others to the maintenance of an active culture of the desired microorganisms in contact with the material. Of most importance is the rate of percolation of solutions and the penetration of air into the packed layers of ore. These are markedly influenced by its particle size characteristics, and the proportion of voids present. Rapid and continuous percolation rates will result in a quick transfer of oxygen and leach solutions into packed beds of material and a transfer of dissolved metals out, but may produce leach solutions low in metal content and also result in a washout of the bacteria contained in the ore. Too rapid a percolation rate can also produce a transport of finer material to the base of the dump or heap which can result in its compaction and subsequent blockage. The particle size of material treated also controls the amount of exposed surface area available for bacterial leaching. However, reducing particle size to increase available surface area for reaction produces a reduction in percolation and aeration rates. A balance, therefore, has to be produced which will optimise metal production and this is normally established by pilot leaching operations employing ore samples of varying degrees of fineness. Metal production rates are also very dependent

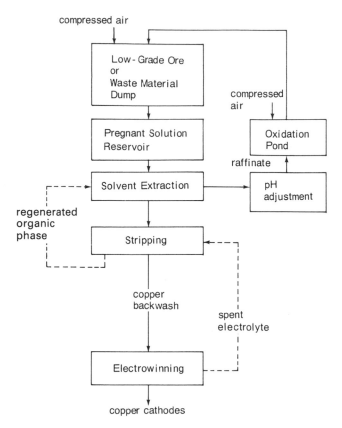

Fig. 3.2 — Outline flowsheet of a typical bacterial heap or dump operation for the recovery of copper metal.

on the mineralogical characteristics of the ore treated, its mineral grain size and porosity being important factors. If the particle size of material leached is not controlled, the application rate of leach solutions will depend upon the percolation depth, the surface area of material leached and the required metal loading of the final leach solutions. Most dump and heap leaching operations are conducted in a cyclic manner with rest periods between solution applications. This has been found to be important for air incorporation into the mass of ore [3.22]. Experiments have also shown that the introduction of compressed air into a copper leach dump can increase metal extraction rates by as much as 25 per cent [3.23].

Bacterial activity will vary dramatically within a mound of ore, being more prominent in areas where conditions favour their growth, such as those portions which are adequately aerated. As sulphide mineral oxidation reactions are exothermic, those areas towards the middle of a dump, which are insulated, may heat up and restrict the growth of mesophilic bacterial strains, yet allow the growth of thermophiles. Once initiated, the bacterial leaching and subsequent metal production from a heap or dump of ore are difficult to control, maintenance of permeability and hence flow of solution and air incorporation being the prominent practical parameters necessary to maintain bacterial activity and metal leaching rates [3.24].

3.6   *IN SITU* BACTERIAL LEACHING OF ORE

In situ leaching refers to those situations where minerals can be leached without removing them from the ground by mining methods. It has found a use in old underground mine workings and low grade deposits where ore cannot be economically mined but where sufficient metal remains to finance its extraction by a bacterially aided leaching method. Existing mine road-ways or new access tunnels driven into the ore provide the channels and collection areas for the leach solutions which are introduced into the ore. The ore may be initially fractured by explosives to increase its permeability and surface area for leaching, and solutions may be injected or sprayed onto the broken material underground. Solutions percolating to the lowest levels in the deposit are pumped to the surface for metal recovery and then regenerated and recycled.

This method of leaching ore has the advantage that it does not disturb the surface of the deposit or leave large piles of leached waste as unsightly remnants of an operation. It is also unaffected by surface weather conditions. *In situ* leaching is a much more difficult process to control. Leach solutions may migrate in unpredicted directions with the possibility of contaminating natural groundwaters. The method has been employed in both copper and uranium deposits [3.25–3.27] as a scavenging method for metal recovery. There are many mines in the world where *in situ* leaching is occurring but is not encouraged. Once mines containing sulphide ores are developed, they soon become contaminated with iron and sulphur oxidising organisms. If conditions are favourable, i.e. mine workings are wet, then bacterial leaching can be a considerable nuisance and cost as acid-bearing mine waters are often produced on a large scale. These acidic solutions are expensive to remove from the mine, because of the corrosion they produce in pumps and the piping. They require to be neutralised once they have been returned to the surface before disposal.

3.7   MINERAL CONCENTRATE LEACHING

The conventional route for the production of most metals initially involves the extraction or concentration of the metal-bearing mineral from its ore at the mine site. These mineral concentrates, which are usually an order of magnitude higher in metal content than the original ore, are then sold and transported large distances to be processed by pyrometallurgical or hydro-metallurgical techniques and turned into the refined metal. It is rare to find situations where concentrates are refined to metal on the mine site because of the capital and operating costs involved. However, it would be a great financial advantage to mining companies if this were possible.

Bacterial leaching of concentrates of a single metal or mixed metal sulphide has been investigated as a possible process for such purposes, but the technique has to compete on economic grounds with the existing custom and practice. Its main drawbacks as a process are its relatively slow leaching rates and often incomplete dissolution of certain minerals. Bacterial leaching of concentrates has certain advantages which include its feasibility for the small scale treatment of concentrates in remote locations where their transportation costs are high and production of acid by conventional means for leaching is financially prohibitive.

Laboratory investigation using small scale pilot plant has shown that copper can be economically produced from a chalcopyrite concentrate [3.28], and Fig. 3.3 illustrates the proposed process which is capable of producing leach solutions containing 30–50 g l^{-1} of copper at rates of 560–725 mg l^{-1} h^{-1}. Subsequent development has shown that these rates of extraction can be increased by using silver as a catalyst [3.29].

Other studies have indicated that zinc, copper and cadmium can also be bacterially leached from mixed sulphide concentrates containing lead sulphide [3.30; 3.31]. Pilot plant studies, employing a circuit which is illustrated by Fig. 3.4, produced results in which overall extractions of the dissolved metals exceeded 94% with the leach residue containing the upgraded lead mineral. The processes outlined have also extended to the treatment of nickel-bearing samples [3.32–3.24].

Another area of potential application of concentrate leaching is in the selective removal of undesirable contaminants from mineral products prior to their sale for treatment by conventional smelters. The value of mineral concentrates is closely linked to the level of impurities they contain, and removal or reduction in the level of penalty elements such as arsenic can markedly influence the financial viability of a mining operation.

Many mines also produce small quantities of sulphide mineral concentrate as a by-product in the recovery of non-sulphide minerals of such metals as tin and tungsten. These are usually disposed of or stored for future treatment but do not generally contribute to the revenue of the mining operation. Treatment of these sulphide by-products by bacterial leaching could contribute to the income of a small mine and also alleviate the disposal problems associated with such materials.

It appears that, in the future, bacterial leaching processes will become of increasing interest not only to producers of mineral concentrates but also to their purchasers. Applications are most likely to be expected in the treatment of mixed sulphide concentrates produced from complex ore bodies where at present recovery of metals is sacrificed to obtain concentrates of sufficient grade for present-day marketing requirements. Purchasers of concentrates have yet to consider incorporation of bacterial leaching techniques into metal refining plants either as a process for cleaning and improving the grade of their incoming concentrate feeds or as a possible technique for recovery of metal from matte and slag and other smelter waste products.

In the past few years the interest of mining companies in the bacterial leaching field has centred around the use of the process to enhance gold and

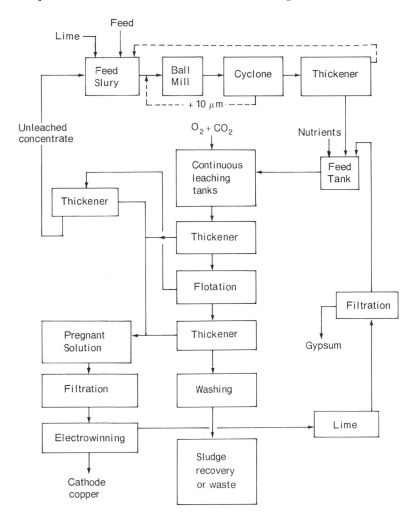

Fig. 3.3 — Outline flowsheet of a bacterial leaching process suggested for the production of copper from copper concentrates (after [3.28]).

silver recovery from refractory ores where these metals are locked in sulphide minerals such as pyrite (FeS_2) and arsenopyrite (FeAsS). The objective in the oxidation of these precious-metal-bearing sulphides is to release the gold and silver they contain so that it can be recovered by conventional cyanide leaching methods. Research and development in this particular area has been stimulated by the buoyant price of both metals and also by the fact that other methods of extraction are not able to produce a sufficiently high recovery of the contained value. Fig. 3.5 illustrates a typical flowsheet that has been proposed for the treatment of such a concentrate. It has been demonstrated by both laboratory and pilot testwork that such a process is feasible [3.34] and several small plants treating high grade gold-bearing sulphide concentrates are planned.

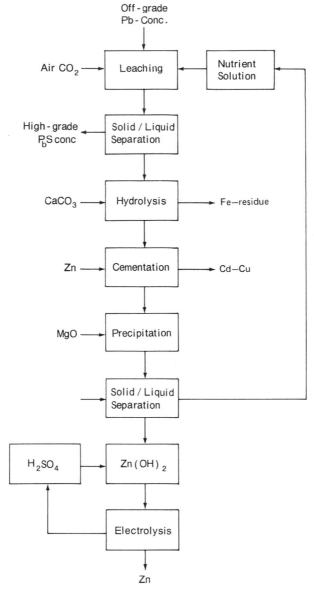

Fig. 3.4 — Proposed flowsheet for the bacterial treatment of a mixed sulphide concentrate containing lead, zinc, copper and cadmium (after [3.30]).

A similar application relating to the removal of sulphur occurring in coal in the form of pyrite is also receiving consideration internationally. Various investigations have evaluated the desulphurisation of coal using bacteria; this has been shown to be a practical [3.35–3.37] and economically viable route to the precombustion removal of pyrite from coals [3.38].

The amount of sulphur in coals varies from < 1 to > 10 percent. One

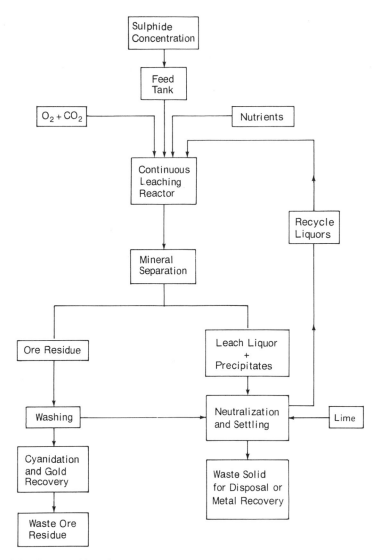

Fig. 3.5 — Proposed flowsheet designed for the bacterial treatment of a gold-bearing sulphide concentrate.

study, using coal with a fairly typical pyritic sulphur content of 3.1 per cent, showed that within 5 days about 97 per cent of the sulphur could be removed [3.39].

3.8   UTILISATION OF BACTERIALLY GENERATED SOLVENTS

Many metalliferous ores can be treated by leaching methods to extract metal but do not contain mineral ingredients capable of sustaining an active population of iron and sulphur oxidising bacteria. Similarly, other ore types do contain such components but release soluble metal products which are detrimental to the growth of microorganisms. Typical of these ore types are those containing uranium as the commercial metal. In such cases it has been found possible to leach the uranium by using bacterially generated acid ferric sulphate solutions produced independently of the ore leaching process itself. This leaching method has been shown to be a viable method by the uranium industry, the two stages it entails being optimised separately for hotter temperature and pH. Acid ferric sulphate solutions are generated in a separate reactor to leach uranium-bearing ore and the uranium is then recovered from the leach solution. Barren solutions containing predominantly ferrous iron can then be recycled to the bacterial reactor for regeneration [3.40;3.41]. A similar system can also be envisaged for the treatment of oxide ores of zinc and copper.

Indirect use of bacteria and bacterially generated solvents has also been demonstrated on a laboratory basis, to show that this procedure is suitable for the rapid treatment of sulphide ores where leaching is not the desired outcome. A surface treatment of sulphide minerals with bacterial solutions has been shown to influence their superficial chemical properties, thus altering their response in such processes as froth flotation. This technique is being evaluated as a method of enhancing the physical separation of pyrite from coal in fine coal flotation circuits and is suggested as an alternative method to the total leaching of pyrite from coal [3.42].

Bacterially generated acid ferric sulphate solutions and the ability to regenerate such solutions have also attracted interest from a number of industries other than mining. It has been demonstrated that these solutions can be employed to de-rust and clean corroded steel surfaces such as those encountered in the tanks of large ships employed to transport oil. Any industry where acid ferric sulphate solutions are used can be considered to be a potential user of a bacterial process to produce such solutions.

3.9 CONCLUSIONS

The ability of certain microorganisms to oxidise iron and reduced sulphur compounds has attracted an increasing interest in the minerals engineering field over the past two decades. Their use as a means of dissolving or leaching sulphide minerals offers attractive alternative routes to the production of certain metals. Bacterial leaching technology so far developed has almost duplicated natural leaching situations (and processes have been successfully applied to the recovery of copper and uranium from low grade ores and mine wastes).

Although uranium does not occur naturally as a sulphide, its principal form, UO_2, is frequently associated with pyritic minerals. Leaching occurs either indirectly, with acidic ferric sulphate producing UO_2SO_4 which is soluble, or directly, with *T. ferrooxidans* effecting the oxidations:

$$2UO_2 + O_2 + H_2SO_4 \longrightarrow 2UO_2SO_4 + 2H_2O \qquad (3.10)$$

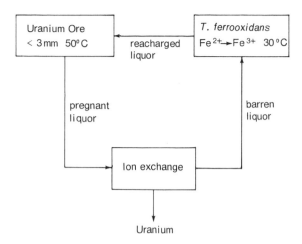

Fig. 3.6 — A leaching scheme for uranium ore [3.43].

The outline for a uranium leaching scheme, giving a recovery of up to 90 per cent, is shown in Fig. 3.6.

More sophisticated in-house mineral leaching systems have not yet been commissioned although several possible applications have been demonstrated. A greater understanding of the basic mechanisms of bacterial mineral leaching is still required as published results relating to the oxidation of various minerals differ greatly with respect to the rate and amount of oxidation obtained. This would indicate that considerable information is still necessary to determine the most efficient types of bacteria, the manner in which they should be cultivated and also the way in which they should be utilised and contacted with the minerals to be leached. It has become obvious that bacterial leaching is not a standard process which will treat any variety of minerals or ores fed to it. Leaching processes employing bacteria will have to be tailored to suit the mineral ore being treated and this will require the development of a variety of reactor designs and leaching conditions, thus creating some challenging research prospects.

REFERENCES

[3.1] Rittenburg, S. C. (1969) The roles of exogenous organic matter in the physiology of chemolithotrophic bacteria. *Adv. Microbial Phys.*, **3,** 159.

[3.2] Temple, K. L. and Colmer, A. R. (1951) The autotrophic oxidation of iron by a new bacterium *T. ferrooxidans*. *J. Bacteriol.*, **62,** 605.

[3.3] Unz, R. F. and Lundgren, D. G. (1961) A comparative nutritional study of three chemo-autotrophic bacteria *T. ferrooxidans, T. thiooxidans, F. ferrooxidans. Soil Science*, **92,** 302.

[3.4] Tuovinen, O. H., Niemela, S. I. and Gyllenberg, H. G. (1971) Effect of mineral nutrients and organic substances on the development of *T. ferrooxidans. Biotech. Bioeng.,* **13,** 517.

[3.5] Mackintosh, M. E. (1971) Nitrogen fixation by *T. ferrooxidans. J. Gen. Microbiol.,* **66,** i.

[3.6] Tuovinen, O. H. and Kelly, D. P. (1972) Biology of *T. ferrooxidans* in relation to the microbiological leaching of sulphide ores. *Zeitschrift für Allgemeine, Mikorbiologie,* **12,** 311.

[3.7] Torma, A. E. (1977) The role of *T. ferrooxidans* in hydrometallurgical processes. In *Advances in Biochemical Engineering,* Ghose, T. K., Fiechter, A. and Blakebrough, N. (eds), Vol. 6, Springer-Verlag, Berlin, p. 1.

[3.8] Silverman, M. P. (1967) Mechanism of bacterial pyrite oxidation. *J. Bacteriol.,* **94,** 1046.

[3.9] Balashova, V. V., Vedenina, I. Ya. and Markasyan, G. E. (1974) The autotrophic growth of *Leptospirillium ferrooxidans. Mikrobiologiya,* **43,** 581 (English translation, p. 491).

[3.10] Brierly, C. C., Brierly, J. A., Norris, P. R. and Kelly, D. P. (1980) Metal tolerance microorganisms of hot, acid environments. In *Microbial Growth and Survival in Extremes of Environment,* Gould, G. W. and Corry, J. E. (eds), Academic Press, London, p. 38.

[3.11] Brierly, J. A. and Lockwood, S. J. (1977) The occurrence of thermophilic iron-oxidising bacteria in a copper leaching system. *FEMS Microbiol. Lett.,* **2,** 163.

[3.12] Norris, P. R., Brierly, J. A. and Kelly, D. P. (1980) Physiological characteristics of two facultatively thermophilic mineral-oxidising bacteria. *FEMS Microbiol. Lett.,* **7,** 119.

[3.13] Norris, P. R. and Kelly, D. P. (1978) Dissolution of pyrite (FeS_2) by pure and mixed cultures of some acidophilic bacteria. *FEMS Microbiol. Lett.,* **4,** 143.

[3.14] Tsuchiya, H. M. and Trivedi, N. C. (1974) Microbial mutualism in ore leaching. *Biotech. Bioeng.,* **16,** 991.

[3.15] Lawrence, R. W. (1974) *Bacterial Extraction of Metals from Sulphide Concentrates,* Ph.D. Thesis, University of Wales.

[3.16] Atkins, A. S. (1976) *Studies of the Oxidation of Ferrous Sulphide in the Presence of Bacteria,* Ph.D. Thesis, University of Wales.

[3.17] Pinches, A., Al-Jaid, F. O. and Williams, D. J. A. (1976) Leaching of chalcopyrite concentrates with *T. ferrooxidans* in batch culture. *Hydrometallurgy,* **2,** 87.

[3.18] Torma, A. E., Walden, C. C., Duncan, D. W. and Branion, R. M. R. (1972) The effect of carbon dioxide and particle surface area on the microbiological leaching of a zinc sulphide concentrate. *Biotech. Bioeng.,* **14,** 777.

[3.19] Torma, A. E. (1976) *Microbiological Extraction of Cobalt, Nickel and Copper from Sulphide Ores and Concentrates,* Australian Patent No. 474,361.

[3.20] Madsin, B. W., Groves, R. D., Evans, L. G. and Pooter, G. M.

(1975) *Prompt copper recovery from mine strip waste,* US Bur. Mine, R.I. 8012.

[3.21] Bruynesteyn, A. and Cooper, J. R. (1974) Leaching of Canadian ore in test deposits. In *Solution Mining Symp. AIE,* Aplon, F. F. and McKinney, W. A. (eds), Chapter 20, p. 268.

[3.22] Harris, J. A. (1969) Development of a theoretical approach to the heap leaching of copper sulphide ores. *Proc. Aust. Inst. Min. Metall.,* **230,** 81.

[3.23] Moodry, R. P. (1976) Compressed air injection into sulphide leach dump. *Proc. 105th AIME Meeting,* Las Vegas, Nevada.

[3.24] Murr, L. E. (1980) Theory and practice of copper sulphide leaching in dumps and *in situ. Min. Sci. Engng,* **12**(3), 121.

[3.25] Pings, W. B. (1968) Bacterial leaching. *Min. Ind. Bull. Col. Sch. Mines,* **2,** 1.

[3.26] Duncan, D. W. and Bruynesteyn, A. (1971) Enhancing bacterial activity in a uranium mine. *CIM Bull.,* **64,** 32.

[3.27] Fisher, J. R. (1966) Bacterial leaching of Elliot Lake uranium ore. *CIM Bull.,* **59,** 588.

[3.28] Bruynesteyn, A. and Duncan, D. W. (1971) Recent advances in the microbiological leaching of sulphide concentrates. *Can. Metall. Quart.,* **10,** 57.

[3.29] Bruynesteyn, A., Lawrence, R. W., Wizsolyi, A. and Hackl, R. (1983) An element sulphur producing biohydrometallurgical process for treating sulphide concentrates. In *Recent Progress in Biohydrometallurgy,* Rossi, G. and Torma, A. E. (eds), Associazione Mineraria Sarda, Cagliari, p. 151.

[3.30] Torma, A. E. and Subramanian, K. N. (1974) Selective bacterial leaching of a lead sulphide concentrate. *Int. J. Min. Proc.,* **1,** 125.

[3.31] Torma, A. E. (1978) Complex lead-sulphide concentrate leaching by microorganisms. In *Metall. Appl. Bacterial Leaching, Related Microbial Phenomena,* Murr, L., Brierly, J. and Torma, A. (eds), Academic Press, New York, p. 375.

[3.32] Dutrizac, J. E. and MacDonald, R. J. C. (1974) Percolation leaching of pentlandite ore. *CIM Bull.,* **169,** 169.

[3.33] Duncan, D. W. and Trussell, P. C. (1964) Advances in the microbiological leaching of sulphide ore. *Can. Metall. Quart.,* **3,** 43.

[3.34] Livesey-Goldblatt, E., Norman, P. and Livesey-Goldblatt, D. R. (1983) Gold recovery from arsenopyrite-pyrite ore by bacterial leaching and cyanidation. In *Recent Progress in Biohydrometallurgy,* Rossi, G. and Torma, A. E. (eds), Associazione Mineraria Sarda, Cagliari, p. 642.

[3.35] Razzell, W. E. and Trussell, P. C. (1963) Microbial leaching of metallic sulphides. *Appl. Microbiol.,* **11,** 105.

[3.36] Dugan, P. R. and Apel, W. A. (1978) Microbial desulphurisation of coal. *Metall. Appl. Bacterial Leaching, Related Microbial Phenomena,* Murr, L., Torma, A. and Brierly, J. (eds), Academic Press, New York.

[3.37] Ponsford, A. P. (1966) Microbial activity in relation to coal utilization. II Coal and Hydrocarbons, *British Coal Utility Res. Assoc. Bull.*, **30,** 41.

[3.38] Silverman, M. P., Rogoff, M. H. and Wender, I. (1963) Removal of pyrite sulphide from coal by bacterial action. *Fuel*, **42,** 113.

[3.39] Detz, C. M. and Baruinchok, G. (1979) Microbial desulphuration of coal. *Mining Congress J.*, **75,** July.

[3.40] Livesey-Goldblatt, E., Tunley, T. H. and Nagy, I. F. (1977) Pilot plant bacterial film oxidation of recycled acidified uranium plant ferrous sulphate leach solution. *Conf. Bacterial Leaching*, Schwartz, W. (ed.), Verlag Chemie, New York, p. 175.

[3.41] Derry, R., Garrett, K. H., Le Roux, N. W. and Smith, S. E. (1977) A bacterially assisted process for leaching uranium ores. In *Geol. Mining Extract. Process Uranium*, Jones, M. J. (ed.), Institute of Mining and Metallurgy, London, p. 56.

[3.42] Pooley, F. D. and Atkins, A. S. (1983) Desulphurisation of coal using bacteria by both dump and process plant techniques. In *Recent Progress in Biohydrometallurgy*, Rossi, G. and Torma, A. E. (eds, Associazione Mineraria Sarda, Cagliari, p. 511.

[3.43] Johnson, D. B. (1985) The leaching of mineral ores using bacteria. *Ind. Biotech.*, **5**(3), 60–62.

4

Composting and straw decomposition

A. J. Biddlestone, K. R. Gray
Department of Chemical Engineering, Birmingham University, UK
and
Carol A. Day
Microbial Developments Ltd, Malvern Link, Malvern, Worcs, UK

4.1 INTRODUCTION

Traditionally, man has used the inedible parts of plants in a variety of ways: for bedding for animals, or for thatch, for instance. His waste was, in any case, returned to the soil along with dung and urine, thus to some extent conserving nitrogen and maintaining fertility. In the more highly developed countries with large urban populations, this is no longer possible. Grain is grown intensively, leaving huge quantities of waste for disposal. Animals, too, are intensively herded, giving rise to large quantities of slurries which are potentially highly polluting. Recent research into composting as a means of disposal, both of slurries and of vegetable remains, is therefore described, along with possible biotechnological solutions of the problems arising from straw disposal direct to soil.

4.2 COMPOSTING OF ORGANIC WASTES

Many of the environmental problems of current concern are due to local accumulations of organic wastes which are too great for the basic degradation process inherent to nature. Where possible these wastes are reused; sugar beet tops, brewers' grains and some chopped straw are used for animal feed. Some material is used to prepare compost substrates for mushroom production and a relatively small amount for high grade compost for horticulture. A small but increasing amount of separated refuse is being used for refuse-derived fuels. After this the remainder is largely regarded as low grade waste to be disposed of by the cheapest route possible, which is usually a compromise between financial and environment considerations. Landfill, incineration and incorporation into the soil are all used in the UK. Current major environmental issues include field burning of excess straw, odour complaints from the spreading of anaerobic sludges, disposal of sewage sludge to land, and agricultural codes of practice limiting the quantity of manure which can be spread per hectare. In all these problem areas composting offers both a production process for an end product of value and a waste treatment process to render low grade organic waste less obnoxious to the environment. It provides a means of obtaining a stable product by biological oxidative transformation. The humified product comes quickly into equilibrium with the ecosystem in which it is placed without causing the major disruption associated with raw wastes.

Composting is an exothermic process of biological oxidation in which organic material is decomposed by a mixed microbial population in a warm, moist, aerobic environment. During the process degradable organic substrate undergoes chemical and physical transformation to give a stable humified end-product. The product is of value in agriculture both as an organic fertiliser and as a soil improver.

Wastes amenable to composting vary from the heterogeneous organic/inorganic mixture in urban refuse to the more homogeneous farm manures, crop residues, sewage sludges and night soil. During the composting process most of the oxygen demand of the wastes is met, the organic materials are converted to more stable products, carbon dioxide and water are released and heat is evolved. Under natural conditions the degradation process takes place slowly, on the surface of the ground at ambient temperature and mainly under aerobic conditions. The natural process of breakdown can be accelerated by gathering the material into heaps to conserve part of the heat of fermentation so that the temperature of the mass rises and faster reaction rates are obtained. This accelerated process is composting. Important process factors include an appropriate carbon to nitrogen ratio and the necessary blending of diverse materials to provide a suitable matrix for aeration purposes. Manures, sewage sludges and many vegetable wastes have a low carbon to nitrogen ratio and a high moisture content, and are difficult to aerate. They need to be blended with an absorbent solid matrix which provides extra carbon and an appropriate mixture structure. Cereal straw is an obvious choice as it has a fairly rigid structure, even when wet, but other bulking agents such as wood chips, refuse, leaves and shredded tyres have been used.

4.3 PROCESS PRINCIPLES

The process of composting is a complex interaction between the organic waste, micro-organisms, moisture and oxygen. The waste material will normally have an indigenous mixed population of micro-organisms. When the moisture content and oxygen concentration are brought to a suitable level microbial action increases. In addition to oxygen and moisture, the micro-organisms require for their growth and reproduction a source of carbon, micronutrients such as nitrogen, phosphorus and potassium and certain trace elements. These additional requirements are usually provided by the waste materials. In using the organic waste as a food source the micro-organisms reproduce themselves and release carbon dioxide, water, other organic products, and energy. Some of the energy released by the biological oxidation of carbon is used in metabolism, the remainder is given off as heat (Fig. 4.1).

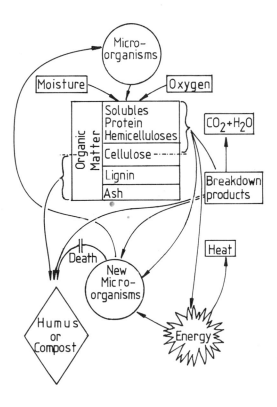

Fig. 4.1 — The composting process.

The final product, compost, comprises the more resistant residues of the organic matter, breakdown products, the biomass of dead micro-organisms and some living micro-organisms, together with products from further chemical reaction between these materials.

4.3.1 Microbiology
Composting is a dynamic microbial process brought about by the activities of a succession of various microbial groups each of which is appropriate to an environment of relatively limited duration. A list of the main classes of organisms involved in the composting process is given in Table 4.1.

Table 4.1 — Organisms in composting

Microflora (very small plants)	Bacteria	Very tiny, enormous numbers. Many varieties—spheres, rods, filaments. Some form spores. Size range 1–8 μm
	Actinomycetes	These have slender branched filaments. Flourish under hot, fairly dry conditions. Filaments 0.5–2 μm diameter
	Fungi, moulds, yeasts	Larger organisms. Usually form filaments and spores (pseudohyphal yeasts). Several varieties. The thermophilic ones very important. Size range 3–50 μm
	Algae	Prefer wet conditions. Size range 10–100 μm
	Viruses	Extremely small. Need a host organism, bacterium or actinomycete, to live on. Size: head 0–1 μm diameter, tail 0.2 μm long
Microfauna (very small animals)	Protozoa	Move around with whips or hairs. Some prey on the bacteria. Size range 5–80 μm
Macroflora (larger plants)	Macro-fungi	or Higher Fungi. Grow up through the compost heap with fruiting body in the air above. Size of head about 25 mm diameter
Macrofauna (small soil animals)	Millipedes, centipedes	Millipedes mainly vegetarian. Centipedes carnivorous. Sizes: millipedes 20–40 mm long, centipedes 30 mm long
	Mites, springtails	Wide range of sizes. Some are vegetarian, others carnivorous. Size range 0.1–2 mm
	Worms	*Eisenia foetida*, or manure worm, very important in the manure heap. Size range 30–100 mm.
	Also ants, termites, spiders and beetles	

There are many different species, up to 2000 of bacteria and at least 50 of fungi, within each genus. The species can be subdivided according to the temperature ranges of their activity. Psychrophiles prefer temperatures below 20°C, mesophiles 20–40°C and thermophiles above 40°C. The organisms which flourish during the final stage of composting are essentially mesophiles.

Although the bacteria are present in large numbers, 10^8–10^9 per gram of moist compost, they are of very small size (1–8 μm) and form less than half of the total microbial mass. Some species form endospores which can withstand considerable heat and dessication. The actinomycetes develop far more slowly than most bacteria and fungi and are ineffective competitors in the early stages of composting. They are more prominent in the later stages of the process when they can become abundant and the white or grey colour typical of these organisms is clearly visible some 10 cm below the surface of the composting mass. They are numerically less prominent than bacteria, being of the order of 10^5–10^8 per gram of moist compost.

Fungi are important in the decomposition of cellulose and the environment of composting masses should be adjusted to optimise the activities of these organisms. Temperature is an important consideration as the fungi will die out as the temperature rises above about 55°C, reinvading from cooler zones as the temperature falls.

Studies on the populations of bacteria, actinomycetes and fungi during composting have been made by a number of workers. Chang Yung and Hudson [4.1] give data on the changes in numbers of all of these organisms during the composting of wheat straw. Hayes and Lim [4.2] also give experimental data on changes in the populations of these organisms during the composting of wheat and rice straw for mushroom production. At the commencement of composting they found that the aerobic thermophilic bacteria dominate, while in the later stages bacterial numbers decline and the actinomycetes population increases. Fermor and Wood [4.3] and Atkey and Wood [4.4] also provide information on the microbial succession of a wide range of species of mesophilic and thermophilic bacteria, actinomycetes and fungi during the composting of wheat straw to provide a mushroom substrate. de Bertoldi et al. [4.5] have reported the microbial changes during the composting of urban solid waste (60%) with sewage sludge (40%) in a static heap system with forced aeration. Over 50 days of composting they found an increase in cellulolytic fungi and actinomycetes with a corresponding decrease in the numbers of bacteria. Fungi isolated from the static heap system included both thermophilic strains (at 50°C) and mesophilic strains (at 28°C). An increase in ligninolytic fungi was also reported and it is suggested that lignin decomposition is enhanced in static systems. Agitation of the material for other purposes disturbs the growth of hyphae within the mass.

Viruses are organisms of considerable importance because of the diseases of plants, animals and humans for which they are responsible. They are non-cellular organisms which are far smaller than the cells or filaments of bacteria and protozoa. The virus particle requires for its reproduction a viable host organism and various strains are specific to certain hosts. When diseased material is passed through a composting process the numbers of pathogenic viruses are greatly reduced, a predominantly temperature–time effect.

The protozoa are simple unicellular organisms. Most soil protozoa feed upon preformed organic matter such as bacteria, algae and other strains of protozoa. Only certain strains of bacteria are susceptible to attack: others are entirely unsuitable, as are actinomycetes and yeasts. It is suspected that the protozoa maintain a control on the expansion of the bacterial population. When environmental conditions such as moisture and temperature become unsuitable for growth the protozoa can enter a cyst form and withstand adverse conditions for a considerable time.

As the compost mass cools from its peak temperature it is accessible to a wide range of the soil animals. These feed upon other animals, animal excreta and the organic material remains. They normally require well aerated conditions and adequate moisture and prefer temperatures in the range of 7–13°C. Many of the soil animals make a major contribution to breakdown in the composting mass due to physical maceration; breaking the material into smaller particles exposes greater surface area for subsequent attack by microflora. They also make a contribution to the mixing of the various constituents. In temperate climates the earthworm plays a major role in the final stages of composting and in the subsequent incorporation of organic matter into the soil; in arid and semiarid climates this function is usually undertaken by the termite [4.6]. The macrofauna build up tissues which are rich in nitrogen and are easily decomposed. With fairly short lives, their mass is a reservoir of nitrogenous matter which is continuously replenished and broken down.

4.3.2 Biochemistry

Organic waste materials, whether of industrial, urban or agricultural origin, are mixtures of sugars, proteins, fats, hemicelluloses, cellulose, lignin and minerals in a wide range of concentrations as shown in Table 4.2. The fractions contained in plant material will depend upon the age of the plant, its type and environment. Fresh green material contains much water-soluble matter, proteins and minerals. As the plant ages, minerals tend to return to the soil and low molecular weight compounds are converted to higher molecular weight compounds, expecially the hemicelluloses, cellulose and lignin. In the case of animal detritus composition will depend upon the type of animal and its feed.

Composting is both a building up and a breaking down process. The cell wall of the micro-organism attacking the organic matter is the significant factor. Simple low molecular weight carbon compounds, such as soluble sugars and organic acids, can pass through the cell wall easily and be metabolised and mineralised, providing energy and being built up into larger polymers. The longer chain components of the organic wastes cannot pass through the cell wall and cannot be used without being broken down into simpler compounds. This is accomplished by some of the micro-

Table 4.2 — Composition of organic wastes

Fraction	% (dry weight)
Hot/cold water solubles (sugars, starches, amino acids, urea, ammonium salts)	2–30
Ether/alcohol solubles (fats, oils, waxes)	1–15
Protein	5–40
Hemicelluloses	10–30
Cellulose	15–60
Lignin	5–30
Ash	5–25

organisms exuding extracellular enzymes which hydrolyse the long chain polymers into simpler compounds, Fig. 4.2. Virtually all micro-organisms present in composting masses can assimilate the resulting fragments but only certain organisms can carry out the hydrolysis.

The extent of the biochemical changes taking place during composting is indicated by the results of Chang Yung [4.7] who composted wheat straw with added ammonium nitrate, Fig. 4.3. The straw had lost 50% of its dry weight in 60 days with the majority of the loss in the first 34 days. The loss of total dry weight could be accounted for almost entirely by the loss in hemicelluloses and cellulose. The greater rate of loss occurred over the first 5 days, averaging 2.7% per day, as compared with an average of about 1.3% per day over the following 30 days. The hemicellulose content declined steadily over the 34-day period from 37% to 18% of the initial dry weight. Cellulose degradation slowed down during the middle of the cycle, presumably because the fungal population declined as the temperature rose above 55°C. The cellulose content was 46% at commencement, falling to 12% of the initial dry weight after 34 days of composting. The ethanol-soluble fraction, which contains the simpler carbon compounds, decreased very little, being continually replaced by the breakdown of longer chain plymers. The most resistant fraction, lignin, is extremely resistant to enzyme attack, the degradation being restricted to a small microbial group of higher fungi. de Bertoldi *et al.* [4.8] suggest that lignin decomposition is enhanced in static composting systems because fungal hyphae may grow undisturbed by the movement of material found in agitated systems.

4.3.3. Temperature–time profile
When organic wastes are gathered together for composting, the insulating effect of the materials conserves the heat released by biological activity and causes a rise in temperature. The subsequent composting process may

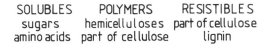

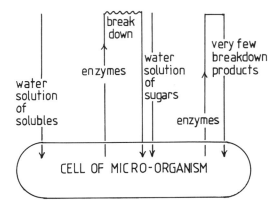

Fig. 4.2 — Food supply.

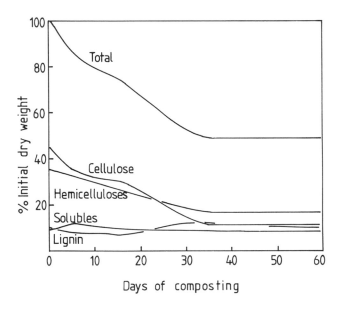

Fig. 4.3 — Decomposition of straw in a compost box.

conveniently be divided into four stages: mesophilic, thermophilic, cooling down and maturing, Fig. 4.4.

At the commencement of composting the wastes are at ambient temperature and are slightly acidic. In the first or mesophilic stage, the indigenous micro-organisms multiply rapidly, the temperature rises to about 40°C and the mass becomes increasingly acidic as organic acids are produced. Above about 40°C the indigenous mesophiles start to be killed off and the thermophiles take over. These raise the temperature towards 60°C when the fungi start to be deactivated. Above 60°C the reaction is continued by the actinomycetes and spore-forming bacteria. The pH of the material starts to turn alkaline as ammonia is liberated during the breakdown of protein molecules. During the thermophilic phase the more readily degradable substances such as simple sugars, starch, fats and proteins, are rapidly consumed, and the reaction rate decreases as the more resistant materials are encountered. The rate of heat generation then becomes equal to the rate of heat loss from the mass; the temperature peak is reached. The heap then enters the cooling down phase. In some instances, usually when composting old wastes, a number of temperature peaks occur.

At this point in an adequately agitated heap the material can be said to have reached stability. The easily convertible materials have been decomposed, the major oxygen demand has been met, the material is no longer attractive to flies and vermin and it will not give off bad odours, because the readily accessible nitrogen and sulphur have been bound up in new micro-organisms.

During the cooling down stage which follows the temperature peak the pH drops slightly but remains alkaline. Thermophilic fungi reinvade the mass from the cooler regions and together with the actinomycetes attack the long chain polysaccharides, hemicelluloses and cellulose, breaking them down into simpler sugars, which may then be utilised by a wider range of micro-organisms. The rate of energy release now becomes very small and the temperature of the mass falls to ambient.

The three stages of mesophilic, thermophilic and cooling down, occur fairly rapidly, being completed in days or weeks, depending on the type of composting system used. The final stage, maturing, occurs over several months during which mass loss and heat evolution arc small. Complex chemical reactions occur between the lignin residues of the original waste and the proteins from dead micro-organisms to form humic acids. The material will not heat up on turning nor go anaerobic in storage nor rob nitrogen from the soil when incorporated. The final pH of the compost is slightly alkaline.

High temperatures have frequently been considered a necessary requirement for good composting. In fact decomposition is suppressed at excessively high temperatures because the growth of the micro-organisms is inhibited; only a few species show activity above 70°C. The threshold of suppression is about 60°C and thus for rapid composting high temperatures for long periods should be avoided. A temperature of the order of 60°C is useful, however, in controlling thermosensitive pathogenic organisms. It is

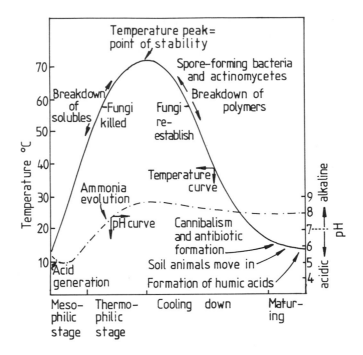

Fig. 4.4 — Temperature and pH variations in a compost heap.

therefore necessary to balance the requirements of pathogen destruction against the encouragement of those organisms which are the main decomposers of long chain polymers. An optimum of 55°C is recommended. Finstein *et al.* [4.9] suggest that temperature control can be achieved by using forced pressure ventilation throughout the process. Such a system removes heat by evaporative cooling and a temperature feedback control system is used to link a temperature sensor placed in the composting mass with the air blower. Such a system facilitates water removal in high moisture content situations.

4.4 PROCESS PARAMETERS

The breakdown of organic wastes during the composting process is a dynamic and complex ecological process in which temperature and food availability are constantly changing. The numbers and species of organisms present change markedly during the process. The rate of progress towards the mature end-product is dependent on several interrelated process parameters. These include nutrient supply, particle size, moisture level, structural strength, aeration, agitation, pH and size of heap. It is desirable to adopt the most suitable operating conditions within the prevailing economic constraints. The complexity of the processing plant, and the quality of the final product, will depend upon the nature of the organic waste to be processed and the level of investment available.

4.4.1 Separation

It is preferable that a compost product should contain as high an organic matter content as possible and a minimum of non-organic debris. This is of particular importance when processing some wastes, particularly from urban sources, the composts from which can contain significant levels of trace metals such as copper, lead, nickel and zinc. Thus, with such wastes, it is desirable to remove as much glass, metal, plastic and debris as is economically possible. On a very small scale such separation may be manually undertaken. On a large scale a variety of devices are available for such separations. Where sewage sludge is used it should be mainly from domestic and not industrial sources to avoid heavy metal contamination.

4.4.2 Particle size

The smaller the size of the particles of the organic waste, the greater is the surface area exposed to microbial attack, thus theoretically allowing a higher rate of reaction. Very small particles, however, pack tightly together, giving material with a high bulk density having narrow pores and channels within it. This restricts the diffusion of air into the mass and carbon dioxide out of the mass, thereby reducing the rate of reaction. The high bulk density may cause excessive loads on mechanised turning equipment, particularly when the materials have a high moisture content.

A compromise on particle size is therefore necessary. For mechanised plants with agitation and forced aeration the particle size may be as low as 12.5 mm after shredding. For naturally aerated static heaps and windrows a particle size of approximately 50 mm is appropriate. In large scale plants particle size reduction may be achieved using hammer mills or raspers or by self-abrasion in rotary drums.

4.4.3 Nutrients

The composting process depends upon the activity of micro-organisms which require a source of carbon to provide energy and material for new cells together with a supply of nitrogen for cell proteins. To a lesser extent there is a requirement for phosphorus, potassium, calcium, sodium, magnesium, sulphur, iron and traces of other elements such as cobalt and zinc. In most composting situations the requirement for these nutrients is adequately met from the original organic waste; only the carbon/nitrogen (C/N) ratio and occasionally the phosphorus level may need adjustment.

Chemical analysis of micro-organisms established that on average they contained 50% carbon C, 5% nitrogen N and 0.25–1.0% phosphorus P on a dry weight basis [4.10]. Since approximately 50% of the organic carbon in the composting materials is converted to carbon dioxide, an initial C/N ratio of about 25/1 should be optimum if no nitrogen is lost. A higher ratio involves the oxidation of excess carbon, the organisms passing through many life cycles to achieve a final C/N ratio of 10/1. With C/N ratios lower than 25/1, as in the case of sewage sludge and manures, nitrogen will be lost as ammonia, often in considerable amounts. The loss of nitrogen by volatilisation of ammonia can be partially offset by the activity of nitrogen-fixing bacteria, mainly in association with mesophilic temperatures in the later stages of decomposition. It is suggested that biological nitrogen fixation is inhibited by the presence of ammonia and by high temperatures [4.8] and is thus associated with the later stages of the process. The uncertainty of nitrogen losses makes accurate prediction of initial C/N requirements difficult but in practice a ratio in the range 25/1 to 30/1 is recommended. For low initial C/N ratios the loss of nitrogen as ammonia may be partially suppressed by the addition of extra phosphate, such as superphosphate or basic slag, but this may not be practicable on cost considerations.

4.4.4 Additives
Various claims have been made regarding the use of chemical, herbal or bacterial supplements to increase the rate of composting. Apart from the possible need for extra nitrogen, most wastes amenable to composting contain a wide range of micro-organisms and all the nutrients required. There is some evidence that the onset of the thermophilic phase could be speeded up by recycling some product compost to the feed. This was the case with a large scale rotary drum system where no separation of material, except for removal of ferrous scrap and some textiles, was carried out. In a composting plant where pulverisation was carried out prior to composting, the recycling of actively composting materials did not have any significant effect.

Bulking agents are normally necessary to ensure an open matrix for air diffusion when composting finely divided organic solids such as sewage sludge and animal manure slurries. Wood chips have been favoured as the bulking agent in aerated pile systems for sewage sludge [4.11; 4.12]; Higgins [4.13] proposed pulverised tyres as an alternative; Biddlestone *et al.* [4.14] used straw when composting manure slurries, sewage sludge and vegetable wastes.

4.4.5 Moisture content
Water is essential to the composting process as the nutrients for the micro-organisms must dissolve in water before they can be assimilated. At moisture contents below 30% on a fresh weight basis the biological reactions slow down markedly and may cease below 20%. At too high a water content the voids within the matrix become waterlogged, limiting access of oxygen to the micro-organisms. Some materials, such as paper, readily lose structural strength when very wet, collapsing into an impervious mass. Straw-type materials, however, can tolerate a high moisture content. Thus optimal moisture content varies and depends upon the physical state and size of the particles. An optimum moisture content in the range 50–60% is recommended but higher values are possible when using bulking agents.

Water is produced during the composting process by microbial action and is lost by evaporation into the air stream. Where forced aeration is applied moisture loss can be excessive and it may be necessary to supply additional water to the composting mass. This can be supplied by the addition of sewage sludge or other liquid wastes. Problems of water loss are naturally more severe in hot climates. It is important to recognise the interrelation between moisture content, particle size and aeration in terms of the movement of air within the interstices of the composting matrix.

4.4.6   Free air space

A composting mass can simplistically be considered as a three-phase matrix of solids, water and gas. The matrix is a network of solid particles that contains voids and interstices of varying size. The voids between particles are filled with gas (oxygen, nitrogen, carbon dioxide), water or a mixture of gas and water. If the voids are completely filled with water then oxygen transfer is greatly restricted. It is an oversimplification to assume that there is a discrete water volume and gas volume within the void space, but this is the traditional approach of soil mechanics and can be used to define a porosity and free air space for a composting matrix [4.15]. The porosity of the composting mass is defined as the ratio of the void volume to the total volume and the free air space within the matrix is defined as the ratio of the gas volume to total volume.

The optimum moisture content for a particular composting mass varies and depends upon the physical state and particle size; thus different materials can hold different moisture levels whilst still maintaining an adequate free air space. However, experimental work by Jeris and Regan [4.16] on the effect of moisture content in various feed materials on free air space and on the oxygen consumption rate of mixed refuse samples suggests that a minimum free air space of 30% should be maintained for a wide variety of composting situations.

4.4.7   Aeration requirements

Oxygen is essential for the metabolism of the aerobic species of micro-organisms responsible for composting. Aeration is possible by natural gaseous diffusion into the composting mass, by turning the material regularly by hand or with a machine, or by forced aeration from a fan. Natural diffusion frequently fails to supply adequate oxygen in the early stages of the process, leading to anaerobic conditions in the lower central regions of the mass of material.

Aeration has other functions in the composting process. A flow of air removes the carbon dioxide and moisture produced in the microbial reaction and also removes heat by evaporative heat transfer. The latter is particularly significant in high rate, mechanised, composting systems. Oxygen requirements vary throughout the process, being low in the mesophilic stage, increasing to a maximum in the thermophilic stage and decreasing towards zero through the cooling down and maturing stages.

The stoichiometric oxygen requirements can be determined if the chemical composition of the organic matter and the extent of degradation during the process are known. For example, the oxidation of proteinaceous material may be represented by the following equation:

$$C_{16} H_{24} O_5 N_4 + 16.5 O_2 \rightarrow 16 CO_2 + 6 H_2O + 4NH_3 \qquad (4.1)$$

$$352 \qquad 528 \qquad + HEAT \text{ released}$$

Thus, based on this equation, 1.5 g oxygen will be required per gram of the material oxidised. This theoretical requirement will vary from about 1.0 g oxygen g^{-1} organic material for highly oxygenated wastes such as cellulose, to 4.0 g oxygen g^{-1} material for saturated hydrocarbons. In practice the composting mass will comprise a mixture of materials with differing theoretical oxygen demands and varying degradability such that typically only 40% of the organic matter may be oxidised. Also in practice more air than the stoichiometric level should be supplied to ensure aerobic conditions throughout the mass. There may also be a controlling requirement in relation to heat and water removal in some composting situations.

Wiley and Pearce [4.17] recommend aeration rates to supply 6–19 mg oxygen $h^{-1} g^{-1}$ volatile solids in the composting mass. An alternative recommendation is that the oxygen level in the air within the mass should be maintained at an oxygen concentration between 10 and 18%. Measurement of oxygen concentration within the mass presents difficulties and in practice it is more realistic to use an indirect parameter to indicate that aerobic conditions are being maintained. In forced aeration systems temperature feedback control of the air supply is a possibility [4.9].

4.4.8 Agitation

In natural aeration composting systems the lower central regions of the composting mass may become anaerobic because the rate of diffusion of oxygen into the mass is too low for metabolic requirements. In such cases turning the material by hand or by machine allows air to reach these deficient regions. Agitation also helps to break up larger pieces of material; exposing fresh surfaces to microbial attack. Control of the agitation process ensures that most of the material is subjected to the high temperature of the thermophilic base. However, too much agitation can lead to excessive cooling and drying of the composting mass and shearing of actinomycete and fungal mycelium. Turning heaps of material can be expensive in machine or labour costs and the frequency of turning is a compromise between economics and the requirements of the process. Flintoff [4.18] considers that turning a windrow heap 3 or 4 times should be sufficient.

Agitation in mechanised plants is usually achieved by means of slowly rotating drums, augers, or especially designed arms. These move through the materials, turning and mixing. Excess agitation may also destroy the physical structure of the materials, creating a wet impervious mass. Drums are generally rotated at 0.5–1.0 rev min^{-1} continuously. Gray *et al.* [4.19] suggest that in mechanised plants short periods of vigorous agitation should be alternated with periods of no agitation.

4.4.9   Heat production and heap size

The various organic compounds present in composting masses each have a different value for the heat of combustion. Three materials commonly found, proteins, carbohydrates and lipids, have heats of combustion within the range 9–40 kJ g^{-1}. Lipids generally contain about twice as much energy per gram as do proteins or carbohydrates. This energy is released during the biological oxidation of the composting process. The stoichiometric chemical oxygen demand (COD) for this oxidation, if the composition of the waste is known, can be determined from the chemical equations. For example, if the composting mass was proteinaceous, as represented by Equation 4.1, the chemical oxygen demand would be 1.5 g COD g^{-1} organic material. The heat release per gram of material can then be estimated because most organic compounds have a heat of combustion of about 14.2 kJ g^{-1} COD of the organic material. The total heat release would then depend upon the amount of material oxidised.

It is difficult to estimate heats of reaction when composting wastes because of the heterogeneous mixture comprising the mass. However, if there is some knowledge of the major constituents a chemical oxygen demand calculation could estimate possible levels of heat release.

Heat production may also be determined directly by experimentation. Wiley [4.20] studied the heat release when pulverised refuse was composted and concluded that, over 8–10 day cycles, it amounted to approximately 7 × 10^3 kJ kg^{-1} of initial volatile solids. Mote and Griffis [4.21] determined heat production rates from composting two organic materials, obtaining values in the range 20–28 W kg^{-1} of initial dry mass.

The amount of heat produced is sufficient such that in large composting masses high temperatures in the range 80–90°C can be reached [4.22]. This is well beyond the optimum temperature of 55°C and forced aeration evaporative cooling may well be necessary in such cases. Small masses of material have high surface/volume ratios and hence much of the material has to act as insulation. It is preferable to have at least 1 tonne of material to ensure that a reasonable proportion of the mass reaches a satisfactory temperature. For heaps composting under natural aeration conditions the material should not be piled over 1.5 m high or 2.5 m wide, otherwise diffusion of oxygen to the centre will be impeded. The heap can be elongated into a windrow of any convenient length.

4.5   PRACTICAL PROCESSES

A summary of the recommended values of the important process parameters is given in Table 4.3. The requirement is to translate these parameters into low-cost but reliable composting systems. The complexity of the composting equipment and the degree of approach to the recommended values of the parameters vary considerably from the simple heap situation to the highly sophisticated mechanical urban plant.

Recent interest in composting has been in response to the need to deal

Table 4.3 — Optimum composting parameters

Parameter	Value
C/N ratio of feed	25/1 to 30/1
Particle size	12.5 mm for agitated systems and forced aeration
	50 mm for windrows and natural aeration
Moisture content	50–60% (higher values possible when using bulking agents)
Free air space	about 30%
Air flow	0.6–1.8 m^3 air day^{-1} kg^{-1} volatile solids during thermophilic stage, or maintain oxygen level at 10–18%
Temperature	55°C
Agitation	No agitation to periodic turning in simple systems.
	Short bursts of vigorous agitation in mechanised systems
Heap size	Any length, 1.5 m high and 2.5 m wide for heaps and windrows using natural aeration. With forced aeration heap size depends on need to avoid overheating

hygienically with large quantities of urban refuse and sewage sludge and the increasing need to recycle crop residues and animal manures in agriculture.

For the composting of agricultural, horticultural and garden wastes relatively simple processing schemes are still employed. Agitation is rare but forced aeration is sometimes used. Widely varying inputs of capital investment, running costs and labour are to be found in a variety of processing arrangements. Because of the fairly low monetary value of composts, sophisticated processes cannot be afforded in most agricultural situations and process conditions frequently fall short of the recommended levels listed in Table 4.3.

The composting of garden wastes is a long-practised simple manual technique [4.23]. In complete contrast, during the past 50 years some 30 different processing schemes for up to 500 t of refuse per day have been introduced for composting urban waste, with varying success. Equipment for feed preparation and compost product finishing are similar to many of these processes. The decomposition stage, however, has varied widely, being attempted in pits, cells, silos, digesters and drums.

A wide variety of organic materials suitable for compost production are produced by human communities and agriculture. Table 4.4 lists some of these materials, with very approximate values for their carbon/nitrogen (C/N) ratios. The C/N ratio of some materials, such as manures and sewage, is below the recommended value; this can lead to excessive ammonia loss during composting. These are best mixed with materials having a high C/N ratio such as straws and woody-type wastes. Materials which have high moisture contents should be mixed with materials of low moisture content to give a material which will compost readily. This occurs with animal manures and straw, sewage sludge and straw or woodchips, and sewage sludge and refuse.

The pretreatment available in preparing the materials for the composting reaction will vary and will depend on whether the composting system is essentially small scale and manual or large scale and mechanical. In manually intensive systems various types of material can be differently prepared. Fresh green materials such as weeds and vegetable trimmings can be used without pretreatment. Coarse materials such as crop stalks are best broken before use. This can be done by chopping in equipment such as a chaff cutter. Leaves, rice bran and straws can be used without pretreatment. Woody materials such as sugar cane trash, treebark and sawdust should be steeped in water for several days or placed in a pit with moist soil for several weeks. Urban refuse is suitable for composting after some degree of pretreatment. This usually takes the form of salvage recovery, a pulverisation stage, magnetic recovery of ferrous metals, removal of plastics and textiles, and adjustments to moisture content and C/N ratio. The order and degree of pretreatment varies according to the type of composting system used and the nature of the refuse.

4.5.1 Simple heap and windrow systems

In simple heap systems the prepared material is formed into long heaps known as windrows, either manually or using equipment such as tipper lorries or front end loaders. The height and width of the approximately triangular sectioned heaps can vary but it is recommended as a general guide that simple heaps using natural aeration should be approximately 1.5 m high and 2.5 m wide. The windrows may be any length and are usually arranged according to the shape of the site. The windrow area should preferably be concreted in order to withstand the movement of vehicles; however, such concreting may be expensive for low cost installations. The windrows may be left standing for several months, until the temperature begins to fall, or they may be occasionally turned. The aims of turning the heaps are to provide aeration, reduce particle size, and ensure that all material is subjected to the high temperature of the thermophilic stage. The last requirement is achieved by turning the outer parts of the heap into the centre of the reconstructed heap. Turning of windrows may be achieved in several ways of different effectiveness. For very small installations manual labour may be used, but more frequently tractor-mounted bucket loaders are used. Larger installations may use specially designed mobile processors which straddle the heap and turn, aerate and, if necessary, add moisture. Turning

Table 4.4 — Approximate composition of organic wastes suitable for composting

Material	C/N ratio
Urine	0.8
Dried blood	3
Nightsoil, dung, sewage sludge	8
Bone meal	8
Coffee pulp	8
Farmyard manure	14
Brewers' wastes	15
Water hyacinths	16
Grass, weeds	20
Refuse	35
Leaves	60
Wheat straw	80
Rice straw	100
Fresh sawdust	500
Paper	Infinity

is a time-consuming operation and some simple systems have used stakes or bamboo poles to create channels within the heaps to improve natural convective aeration.

Several simple heap composting systems have been reported, using a variety of organic wastes. In Europe and the USA mixed farm systems involve the use of front-end loaders with forks and in some cases flat-bed manure spreaders. The organic wastes, usually from animal houses, are loaded into a flat-bed manure spreader which shreds the wastes, aerates them and throws them into a pile about 1.25 m high. The machine is gradually moved along to form a long heap. A series of vertical holes to ground level and 1 m apart are next made through the mass with a 75 mm diameter stake. Another section of heap is then made and aeration holes created. Where possible, some green vegetable material is added to the material in the manure spreader. Such heaps have reached 70°C within a week and then cool to 30°C after a month when they are turned with a front-end loader. After 2–3 months the compost is ready for use. Farmers in Europe are also using a 'moving windrow' technique. A flat-bed manure spreader with side belt elevator is used to lay out a windrow up to 2 m high alongside the moving machine. In practice a small triangular shaped windrow is laid out first; this is readily permeated by adequate air. After 3–4 days, when most of the high rate oxygen demand has been met, a layer of new material is added to the side. The heap is not subsequently turned.

In the tropics, the improved Indore process is still remarkably pertinent.

In this technique the organic wastes are composted in pits approximately 9 m by 4.5 m by 1.2 m deep, Fig. 4.5. Vegetable wastes are put on in 150 mm layers, followed by manure in 50 mm layers and a sprinkling of earth, wood ashes and water. Layering is continued to a height of 1.2 m and vertical aeration vents are made. The heap is turned by hand two or three times and further water is added as necessary. The method has been used in recent years with marked success by Dalzell at Medak Agricultural Centre, India [4.24].

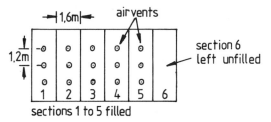

Plan view showing completed compost heap

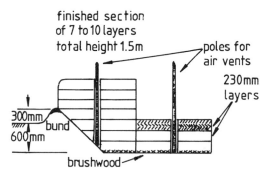

Each 230mm layer contains urine–earth/wood ashes, weeds/leaves, manure, coarse wastes.

Fig. 4.5 — Partly built pit compost heap showing layers of ingredients.

A study tour of organic waste recycling in China reported several techniques of composting [4.25]. Human and animal wastes are layered into a heap with chopped plant stalks, similar to the Indore process. A typical heap comprises 40% crop stalks, 30% agricultural wastes/refuse and 30% animal manures, excreta or night soil. The dimensions of the heap are 1 m high, 2–3 m wide at the top, 4 m wide at the bottom and 6–7 m long, Fig. 4.6. When building the heap sets of bamboo poles, 100 mm in diameter, are laid horizontally every 1.5–2 m along the heap at a height of about 300 mm above the base. Each set is connected with bamboo poles stood vertically to provide aeration channels. When completed the heap is covered with mud about 30 mm thick. The bamboos are removed after 24 h, leaving airways for ventilation. After 4–5 days a temperature of 60–70°C is reached. Turning of the heap is practised after 2 weeks and the compost is used after 2–4 months. A similar approach is reported for the composting of a mixture of night soil, water hyacinths and leaves in Central Thailand [4.26]. Bamboo poles are used for aeration channels and rice straw as a covering to control heat loss from the heap. The rate of composting is reported as being most rapid when sufficient leaves are added to the night soil and water hyacinth mix to give an initial C/N ratio of 30.

Other examples of simple heap systems have been reported in the literature. Shuval *et al.* [4.27] consider night soil composting. Paatero [4.28] and Shea *et al.* [4.29] report the composting of dewatered sewage sludge. Hyde and Consolazio [4.30] composted the wastes from various food manufacturing processes. Biddlestone *et al.* [4.14] describe experiments on the composting of animal manure slurries, dewatered sewage sludge and vegetable wastes when intimately mixed with straw, the straw being incorporated at a level of 5–10% of the total mass. Fig. 4.7 shows the ARMIX Processor developed for mixing these materials and forming the heaps.

4.5.2   Forced aeration windrow processes

In order to increase the rate of decomposition and to reduce or remove the need for turning, some windrow processes force-aerate the heaps from air channels or pipes beneath the windrows. The air may be sucked through the heap and into the channels, or blown from the channels, through the heap to atmosphere. There are advantages and disadvantages to both these methods of aeration.

Several forced aeration windrow processes have been installed in the USA for the composting of dewatered sewage sludge with wood chips as bulking agent. The Beltsville process [4.11] uses sludge of 78% moisture content with wood chips in the volume ratio of 1:2. The combined materials are laid out in windrows on top of perforated pipes, covered with a layer of finished compost, and air is drawn through the perforated pipe. The heap is composted for 4 weeks, then removed and stored for a further 4 weeks. The wood chips are then recovered by screening. In order to achieve effective screening the moisture content of the compost needs to have been reduced to about 40%. Singley *et al.* [4.31] have produced a detailed design and operating manual for such a system. Finstein *et al.* [4.9] compare two 36 t heaps of sludge and woodchips, one with suction aeration, the other with blown aeration. Their recommendation is that a blown air system with interactive feedback temperature control of the blower should be used as the best means of preventing excessive temperatures being reached.

de Bertoldi *et al.* [4.8] composted a mixture of sewage sludge and the organic fraction of urban refuse in three 2 t heaps that were identical apart from their aeration systems. The urban waste and sludge were mixed in the proportion 60:40 (w/w) respectively. The initial moisture content was 67%. Heap 1 followed a turning system on a twice-a-week cycle. Heap 2 used a vacuum-induced aeration system, the blower being activated by a timer providing 40 s suction every 13 min. Heap 3 was a forced pressure blown system with temperature feedback; the blower operated for 40 s every 13

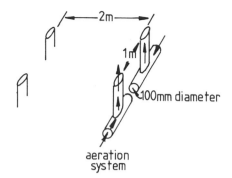

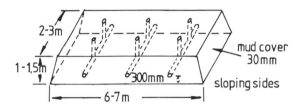

Fig. 4.6 — Chinese high-temperature heap.

Fig. 4.7 — Armix Processor for blending materials and forming heaps.

min below 55°C and operated continuously above 55°C. The conclusion reached from the experiment was that the forced pressure blown system was the most rapid of the three processes tested, and led to the production of the best product in terms of lower moisture content and a higher degree of humification and stabilisation.

In the absence of a forced aeration system, oxygen supply can become the limiting factor. The authors have carried out experiments on the composting of a variety of organic materials with straw. The temperature profiles of 5 t heaps comprising vegetable waste (leeks) with 5% by weight of straw with and without forced aeration were significantly different. The forced aeration heap was blown for 7 min every hour by a blower delivering $2.8 \, m^3 \, min^{-1}$ at 160 mm water head. The heat release in the heap relying on natural aeration was considerably less than the forced aeration heap.

4.5.3 Mechanised processes

The modern large scale urban composting process usually comprises refuse storage facilities, feed preparation equipment, a biological breakdown stage and final product upgrading, Fig. 4.8. Refuse collection vehicles discharge their contents into deep hoppers or onto flat concreted areas from where it is conveyed by moving floors, overhead grabs or front-end loaders. The material is then prepared by size reduction, separation of unwanted and salvageable materials, and then adjustment of moisture. Size reduction can be carried out in wet pulverisers which consist of a slightly inclined drum, typically 3 m in diameter and up to 10 m long, rotating at $3–10 \, rev \, min^{-1}$ with a throughput of about $10 \, t \, h^{-1}$. Alternatively, dry pulverisers can be used; these are either rasping or hammer mill types, although ball mills have been used in a few installations. The power requirements of pulverisers depend mainly upon the final size of the outlet material; for reduction to 50 mm about $8 \, kWh \, t^{-1}$ is required, whilst reduction to 12.5 mm requires about 20 $kWh \, t^{-1}$. After size reduction separators are used to remove ferrous metals, sheet plastics and rags. Prior to composting, the moisture content of the material is adjusted, if necessary, by the addition of water or sewage sludge.

The biological degradation stage is carried out in windrows/accelerated windrows or in more sophisticated mechanised units. Mechanised units vary from automated windrow systems with continuous automatic turning equipment, to totally enclosed silos which achieve extensive breakdown of the material within a few days.

In automated windrow systems the material is usually placed in troughs or between walls. The base of the composting area has provision for blowing or sucking air. Agitation is provided by a turning device which moves along the walls on rails or wheels. The residence time in the heaps varies from 4 to 12 days depending upon the particular design.

Rotating drum units basically consists of a cylinder up to 4 m in diameter and 40 m long, inclined slightly to the horizontal, Fig. 4.9. Refuse, usually without pulverisation, is fed to the higher end. The refuse is physically broken down by attrition and abrasion as the drum rotates continuously at about $1–2 \, rev \, min^{-1}$. Various sizes of screen may be incorporated into the

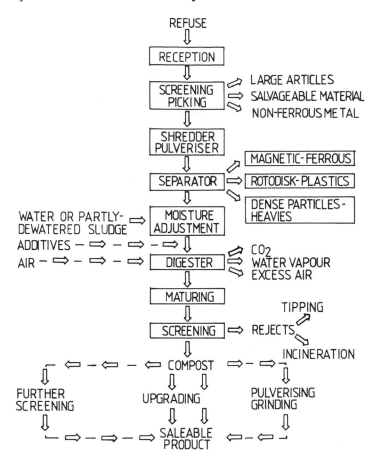

Fig. 4.8 — Flow diagram of a typical composting plant process.

sides or the end of the drum to separate the material. The rejects may be separately disposed of or returned to the inlet of the drum. Some designs of drum include fans to provide forced aeration. The residence time in the drum is typically 2–3 days, after which the material is usually put into windrow heaps for several weeks.

Vertical silo systems may be circular or rectangular in cross-section and may have more than one floor. The material passes through on a continuous batch principle. The simplest form of circular silo is a single floor unit which holds 1 day's batch of refuse. A number of such towers are provided to give the required residence time of 4–5 days. Air is usually supplied through a perforated floor. Agitation may be provided either by vertical screw or auger devices, or by horizontal rotating arms or ploughs.

In multi-floored silos, typically 8 m in diameter by 12 m high, the refuse is fed in at the top in approximately 50 t batches and gradually moves downwards. The floors may be in segments which are hinged to open and discharge the material to the floor below. Some designs have perforated

Fig. 4.9 — Rotating drum composting unit.

floors and rotating arms which force the composting material through the perforations to the floor below. A more sophisticated design has hinged trap doors in each floor which open at predetermined times to allow rotating arms to push the material through to the floor below. Aeration is provided either through the floor or through the rotating arms.

A single silo may contain up to 200 t of material which can release substantial amounts of heat; this may raise the temperature beyond the recommended level of 55°C. Excess air is often provided to effect cooling by evaporation of water into the air stream and, in order to prevent the materials from becoming too dry, provision for water addition on each floor is usually made. Aeration rate may be controlled from floor to floor. The extent of instrumentation and automation provided for silo systems varies according to the design. Residence times are in the range 4–20 days, 8 days being most common. Some systems make provision for subsequent windrowing while others have a simple storage area of 2–3 weeks capacity. Some recent schemes are offering a highly mechanised forced aerated composting unit with a short residence time of 1–2 days followed by a simple windrowing period of 2–3 weeks. This reduces the level of capital investment.

4.6   ADVANTAGES AND USE OF COMPOSTING

4.6.1   Yields of compost

The breakdown of organic material during composting results in the loss of approximately 30–40% of the organic matter to carbon dioxide and water. Thus the mass of compost product produced is significantly less than that of the raw materials supplied. There may be additional losses from any separation processes. Predicting yield is difficult. Only part of the organic matter will be degraded; any non-degradable fraction in the feed will pass through the process into the product unless separated. The water content is difficult to predict. Water is required by the micro-organisms and is also lost by evaporation into the air stream. In dry climates it is sometimes necessary to add water to maintain a sufficient level for microbial action.

A simple pit system in the tropics composting a mixture of crop/ vegetable wastes, manure, weeds, wood ashes and urine earth is likely to have a wet basis yield of about 40%. A single pit charged with approximately 18 t will provide about 7 t of product. It is quite likely that water will have been added during the turning operations. An urban refuse composting plant in Europe is likely to produce 40 t of product from 100 t refuse input on a wet weight basis, but some organic matter in the form of sewage sludge is likely to have been added at the degradation stage. Urban refuse plants in semiarid and tropical areas tend to have a higher proportion of degradable materials than European plants and can achieve 50% yields on a wet weight basis. Simple garden compost boxes containing garden and kitchen wastes typically have yields of 40–50%.

It can then be seen that in passing organic wastes through a composting process the final weight of compost is no more than half that of the original wastes; the volume reduction is even greater. This can significantly reduce the cost of transport.

4.6.2   Costs of production
The cost of production and the cost of process equipment vary considerably from the manually intensive simple heap process to the more sophisticated mechanical process. In simple pit or heap operations the main cost is for labour. Recent experience of pit composting in the tropics indicates that the production and spreading of 1 t of compost requires 2–3 man-days. A highly mechanised urban waste composting factory of typically 500 t day^{-1} input of refuse will have a capital cost of the order of £12 000 t^{-1} d^{-1} of refuse treated. In a very recent review of the cost of composting refuse/sewage sludge in the USA, Savage and Golueke [4.32] indicate that the capital costs for a 400 t d^{-1} plant arc approximately $8.6 million for a turned windrow system and $14.9 million for a silo or in-vessel unit. For such a size of unit the total cost per tonne of waste handled is $18 for the turned windrow and $27 for the silo system; this covers both capital and operating costs but not the revenue from sales of product compost and recovered metal. Economic surveys of composting operations worldwide show significant variations in costs. Economic analysis must take account of local factors for labour, interest charges, land charges and equipment costs.

4.6.3   Composition
The composition of compost products varies widely and reflects mainly the composition of the organic materials used. Table 4.5 indicates the range of compositions normally encountered. Composts prepared from urban wastes

Table 4.5 — Composition range of matured composts

Substance	Composition range % by weight, dry basis
Organic matter	25.0–80.0
Carbon	8.0–50.0
Nitrogen (as N)	0.4–3.5
Phosphorus (as P)	0.1–1.6
Potassium (as K)	0.4–1.6
Calcium (as CaO)	7.0–1.5

tend to be lower in organic matter and the major plant nutrients than those made from garden/farm wastes. Composts from urban wastes can also contain significant quantities of trace metals; several field trials have examined the take-up by crops of these metals from soils treated with such composts [4.33]. The level of heavy metal trace elements should be monitored to prevent a build-up of toxicity in the soil.

4.6.4 Advantages and application

The importance of recycling organic wastes is being increasingly recognised. The addition of fresh organic wastes to any ecosystem can create problems because of the high oxygen demand of the wastes, or from competition for nitrogen, or from the effects of intermediate compounds, or the release of ammonia. Composting provides a means of obtaining a stable product by biological oxidative transformation. The humified product comes quickly into equilibrium with the ecosystem in which it is placed without causing the major disruption associated with raw wastes. It provides a means of combining together low value straw-type wastes with human and animal wastes that pose a problem of hygienic disposal. At the temperatures achieved in composting there is a significant kill of pathogenic organisms, weeds and seeds.

Compost is primarily a soil conditioner and to some extent a fertiliser. When compost is added to the land it breaks down, releasing the major plant nutrients, N, P and K plus minor and trace elements. It is attractive to soil fauna. The gummy constituents and fungal/actinomycete mycelia help to bind the soil particles into crumbs while its organic components increase the water-holding capacity of the soil. These factors greatly increase the stability of the soil to wind and water erosion. One of the major uses for urban compost in Europe is in the stabilisation of steep vineyard slopes in France and Germany.

It is improbable that a harmful level of mature compost could be applied unless high levels of toxic trace metals are present. In temperate climates organic matter added to the soil is broken down over a period of years and hence is usually applied once every 3–4 years. In tropical conditions it is broken down much more quickly and annual dressings of compost are appropriate. A recommended level of application in these conditions is from 15 t ha^{-1}. If heavier dressings are used, reductions should be made in the quantities of inorganic fertilisers applied. In dryland farming conditions in the semiarid tropics, there are many tracts of soil which would support much larger yields of crops given better soil and water management. There is evidence to show that on poorer soils, if the level of production is increased, deficiencies appear which are not seen under the traditional pattern of farming. Such deficiencies can be prevented by the use of organic manures and composts. Through its ability to supply the minor and trace elements to the soil, and to improve soil structure and water-holding capacity, the use of compost with inorganic fertilisers may well increase the response to that fertiliser. In considering the combined use of composts and inorganic fertilisers it should be noted that composts vary widely in composition, depending upon the raw materials used in their preparation. Additionally nutrients are released more slowly from composts than from very soluble inorganic fertilisers; consequently the effects of compost can last for more than one season. Dalzell *et al.* [4.24] suggest that the percentages of the major nutrients which become available in the year of application are N 25%, P 100%, K 80%.

A recent and interesting use of compost has involved the passing of malodorous air through active compost heaps (see Chapter 12). The obnoxious chemicals are absorbed onto the compost and then broken down by the micro-organisms. When handling large volumes of malodorous air the pressure drop through the compost bed needs to be kept small and the bed occasionally watered if necessary to prevent dehydration.

4.7 PUBLIC HEALTH CONSIDERATIONS

Pathogens are agents which cause infections in man and animals. They may belong to any of the main classes of micro-organisms, bacteria, actinomycetes, fungi, viruses and protozoa. They also belong to the macrofauna, helminths/nematodes or intestinal worms. Most of these pathogenic organisms are mesophilic, preferring temperatures below 40°C, being adapted to the body temperatures of man and animals. The majority normally succumb at higher temperatures if exposed for a long enough time, Table 4.6. There are, however, a few pathogens which are spore-forming bacteria; these form highly resistant endospores which can withstand great heat and dessication and then proliferate when environmental conditions improve.

Most organic wastes from human and animal communities—nightsoil, raw and even digested sewage sludge, abbattoir wastes, animal manures and bedding, and refuse—will be contaminated with pathogens. There is an increasing need for the organic matter and the plant nutrients which it contains to be returned to the land. However, it is essential from a public health viewpoint that the waste be brought into a biologically acceptable

Table 4.6 — Lethal conditions for common pathogens and parasites

Disease	Organism	Lethal conditions (moist heat)
Non-spore-forming bacteria		
Brucellosis	*Brucella abortus*	10 min—60°C
Cholera	*Vibrio cholerae*	15 min—55°C
Contagious abortion	*Vibrio fetus*	5 min—56°C
Diptheria	*Corynebacterium diptheriae*	10 min—58°C
Dysentery	*Shigella* species	60 min—55°C
Food poisoning	*Salmonella* species	20 min—60°C
Leptospirosis (Weil's disease)	*Leptospira* species	10 min—50°C
Plague	*Yersinia pestis*	5 min—55°C
Staphylococcal infections	Staphylococci	30 min—60°C
Streptococcal infections	Streptococci	30 min—55°C
Tuberculosis	*Mycobacterium tuberculosis*	20 min—60°C
Typhoid fever	*Salmonella typhi*	20 min—60°C
Spore-forming bacteria		
Anthrax	*Bacillus anthracis*	10 min—100°C
Botulism	*Clostridium botulinum*	5 h—100°C 5 min—120°C
Gas gangrene	*Clostridium* species	6 min—105°C
Tetanus	*Clostridium tetani*	3–25 min—105°C
Viruses		
Foot and mouth disease		30 min—56°C
Scrapie		withstands 2 h—100°C
Serum hepatitis		10 h—60°C
Swine fever		1 h—78°C
Intestinal worms		
Round worm	*Ascaris lumbridoides*	1 h—55°C
Tape worm	*Taenia saginata*	few min—55°C

state with few pathogens present. Little hazard will then be presented either to those handling the waste or to those consuming the crops.

In a composting process there are several barriers to the survival of pathogenic organisms; the temperature–time relationship is a barrier and pathogens are also destroyed or controlled by competition for food with other organisms, antagonistic relationships and antibiotic or inhibiting substances such as ammonia. It is important to note that above a certain temperature level thermal death is time-dependent. A higher temperature for a short period of time or a lower temperature for a longer duration can be equally effective. Based on known time–temperature relationships, heat inactivation of most pathogens is normally effective under the conditions common to composting. Temperatures of 55–60°C for periods of a few minutes to a few days are typically effective. However, although most disease and parasitic organisms are killed, a few spore-forming bacteria, if present, can survive temperatures in excess of 100°C. Examples are the aerobic spore-forming *Bacillus* species, notably that causing anthrax, and the anaerobic spore-forming *Clostridium* species, which cause tetanus, botulism and gas gangrene. These organisms are likely to survive the composting process.

It is quite clear that it is impossible to guarantee that a particular composting process will produce a product which is entirely free of pathogens. However, if composting is correctly effected a sufficiently hygienised product should be obtained. Totally enclosed mechanically agitated systems may be more desirable in this respect than the occasionally turned windrow heap. In a mechanically agitated totally enclosed digester the heat is spread fairly evenly throughout the mass, and there should be no major cool static pockets. In a windrow heap, however, there is a large variation in temperature and aeration. There is a cool outer layer, cool pockets at the lower edges, possibly an anaerobic region at the centre bottom and a high temperature region just above the middle. By periodic turning of the heap cooler areas may be brought into the hot centre, but a number of turnings may be necessary to obtain the required degree of sterilisation.

A composting mass is a hot-bed of microbial activity. Air passing through the wastes will pick up organisms and their spores and eject them into the atmosphere surrounding the compost plant. This is true both of pathogenic organisms and of the normally innocuous ones. Under certain conditions, usually very high microbial concentrations, some of the latter can cause allergic lung disease. Probably the most important are Farmer's Lung and related syndromes arising from the inhalation of the spores of thermophilic fungi and thermophilic actinomycetes. Consequently, in composting plants it is advisable not to release dusty spore-laden air into enclosed working areas nor to carry out windrow turning operations in roofed buildings.

A number of tests of pathogen survival in composting systems have been reported. It is evident that, in a composting mass which is well agitated or is turned fairly often or is well insulated so that all material is exposed to the higher temperatures for a period of several hours, all the common pathogenic organisms investigated were significantly destroyed. Composting material is not the natural environment for pathogens and they will tend to be eliminated in such an ecosystem. In those situations, in which highly resistant spore-forming pathogens may be found, the organisms are very likely to be present in the soil and the composting process will not offer a degree of sterilisation of those organisms better than the soil to which the product is to be applied.

Some recent publications have extensively reviewed the literature on the presence and survival of pathogens in composting systems [4.34–4.36].

4.8   COMPOSTING—CONCLUSIONS

The importance of recycling organic wastes is being increasingly recognised. The composting process provides a means of hygienic disposal of organic waste material and provides a product which when added to the soil will add nutrients, reduce leaching from the soil, increase the water-holding capacity and improve soil stability. In arid and semiarid regions return of compost to the land is essential for maintaining soil stability and humus content. In temperate climates the compost process is more important in waste disposal processes as a means of reducing both odour and pathogen levels.

4.9   STRAW DECOMPOSITION

Whilst the review on composting has shown that this process can utilise considerable amounts of straw, particularly when used in combination with slurry from intensive animal rearing, there is still an excess of cereal waste produced in the UK and, for that matter, in much of the world.

At the moment burning of cereal straw and stubble in the fields seems to be the only economic answer the UK farmer has in disposing of this excess. Even though the National Farmers' Union have stressed the importance of careful straw burning in their 'Code of Practice', environmentalists are increasingly concerned at the pollution risk, the damage caused to the hedgerows with their fauna and flora, and the loss of nutrients to the soil. Farmers themselves are becoming aware of public opinion related to these problems, and an increasing number now incorporate straw by ploughing in, or direct-drilling through straw residues in the autumn, and resign themselves to the fact that these alternative methods may ultimately lead to reduced crop yields in following years.

4.10   THE PHYTOTOXIC NATURE OF DECOMPOSING STRAW

Living and dead plant tissues constitute a major part of the soil environment and are the primary source of organic matter available for decomposition. The major constituents of plants that enter the soil are cellulose (40%), hemicellulose (30%) and lignin (25%) with the remainder made up of oils, proteins, nucleic acids, etc. These materials are ultimately decomposed through the action of biological and chemical processes with many simple and complex chemicals being produced, some of which can affect plant growth adversely. Early investigations were mainly concerned with the possible effects of crop residues and their decomposition products on soil productivity. Pickering (in Pickering and Bedford [4.37]) was one of the earliest investigators who found that decomposition products were toxic to plants. Since then many researchers have agreed with and expanded on these findings and an excellent review by Patrick *et al.* [4.38] covers the work of these early scientific investigations into the detection and assay of phytotoxins, their specific effects on plants and the specificity of certain phytotoxins to different plant species. In this connection, it was found that leaving wheat straw on the surface of soil occasionally caused yield reduction of the succeeding wheat crop and it was suggested that adverse effects were due, in part, to phytotoxic substances produced by rotting crop residue [4.39; 4.40]. Moreover, aqueous acidic extracts of cereal straw caused measurable root and shoot stunting in wheat, corn and sorghum [4.41]. In Australia, Kimber [4.42] investigated the influence of rotted wheat straw on wheat and oat seedling growth for short periods of time. Under aseptic conditions to eliminate the effects of pathogens and nitrogen immobilis-ation, he found that the degree of inhibition varied with the time of rotting. Root and shoot growth were measured at various time intervals during the course of the experiment. Early root growth was inhibited by as much as 30–42% for both oat and wheat seedlings in extracts from straw rotted for 2–6 days. On the other hand, whereas oat shoot growth was little affected, wheat shoot growth was similarly inhibited. However, it was also found that some varieties of straw actually stimulated wheat root growth by as much as 40% after 2 days of rotting. For longer periods of rotting, the extracts became slightly toxic, and overall the differences from control growth were not significant.

As well as demonstrating root and shoot inhibition by wheat straw in water, Tang and Waiss [4.43] attempted to isolate those compounds which were very toxic to seedlings. By a combination of column and gas–liquid chromatography they isolated salts of acetic, propionic and butyric acids from the toxic fraction and found that the amounts of these acids increased gradually, particularly acetic acid, during up to 12 days of rotting as did the toxicity of the straw extracts analysed. They grew wheat seeds in test tubes with agar, medium and purified straw extracts. The seeds were allowed to germinate and grow for 7 days before the longest primary root was measured. The results showed that the short-chain fatty acids were impor-tant phytotoxic compounds of decomposing straw extracts, producing maximum wheat root inhibition at 12 days of rotting, and were derived from the cellulose component of straw [4.44].

4.10.1   Phytotoxins as growth inhibitors

It was observed that in wet seasons, direct drilling of cereals often led to poor establishment of seedlings [4.45], because toxic substances were produced by anaerobic microbial activity on the unburnt straw of the preceding crop and incorporated with the seed during the drilling process. Lynch [4.46] subjected wheat straw to aerobic and anaerobic decomposition in suspen-sions of soil. He found that the products of the aerobic process stimulated the root extension of barley seedlings, whereas the anaerobic fermentation yields products which inhibited growth. Under aerobic conditions the straw was degraded rapidly with less accumulation of soluble carbon products, but the straw subjected to anaerobic conditions produced more soluble carbon, the majority of which was composed of organic acids. On analysis of the organic fraction, the major component was found to be acetic acid. He also demonstrated that products from this anaerobic fermentation of straw inhibited the root growth of barley seeds, whereas the aerobic decomposition gave rise to products which in fact caused a stimulation of root growth. In a later study [4.47] it was found that the initial concentration of acetic acid in freshly harvested straw was 180 mM but that within 6 h of incorporation of the straw into soil this level fell to 10 mM. The majority of this drop was due to water uptake, but this residual level remained relatively stable for about 12 days. Although the initial concentration of acetic acid detected in dry straw did not result from microbial processes, the relatively steady concentration of 10 mM acetic acid detected over a much longer period presumably did result from microbial fermentation and could be harmful to root growth. Acetic acid concentration was also found to decline exponentially with distance from the incorporated straw. Though natural diffusion of acetic acid through the soil would account for some of this decline, it had been earlier found [4.48] that the acid can be immobilised readily by micro-organisms. This is consistent with the field observation that phytotoxic damage occurred only when seedling roots came into close contact with straw [4.49].

Although it was already known in general terms that microbial decomposition of crop residues can impede plant establishment [4.50; 4.51], Harper and Lynch [4.52] suggested that the requirements for seed germination and seedling growth should be determined so that their precise interactions with micro-organisms could be explained. In their study, Harper and Lynch provided a more detailed analysis of the conditions used in the study of interactions between non-pathogenic micro-organisms and both seed and emerging seedlings of barley. Barley seeds were treated with micro-organisms or their metabolites and were germinated and grown under conditions that in the absence of treatment were known to be favourable for plant development. As part of their study, products of straw fermentations in dilute mineral solution were used which contained acetic acid (15 mM), propionic acid (4 mM) and butyric acid (1 mM) [4.46]. Also used were soil solutions containing similar concentrations of the acids [4.48]. Germination, root and shoot growth of barley seeds were found to be inhbited when in contact with both of these solutions.

To demonstrate the effects of acetic acid on germination and seedling growth, Fig. 4.10 gives the results of two small laboratory experiments where different concentrations of acetic acid were incorporated into an agar medium. Fig. 4.10a shows that when surface-sterilised wheat and barley seeds are in close contact with acetic acid (buried in agar in Petri dishes), low concentrations of acetic acid have a profound inhibitory effect on germination, demonstrable at a concentration of only 0.07% acetic acid, whilst 50% of both wheat and barley seeds are inhibited by a concentration of 0.15% acetic acid. Fig. 10b shows that when germinated surface-sterilised wheat and barley seeds are grown for 7 days in tubes of agar under similar

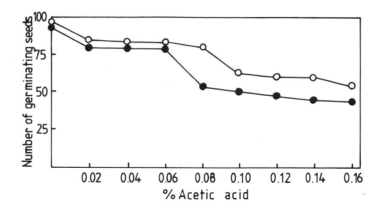

Fig. 4.10a — Effects of acetic acid on wheat and barley seed germination and seedling root growth: (a) Inhibition of seed germination by acetic acid (averaged results from 100 seeds for each concentration): wheat, ●; barley, ○.

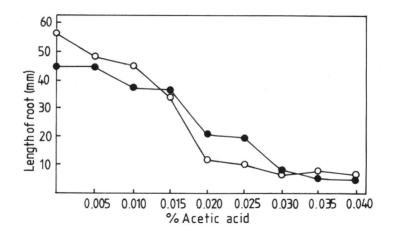

Fig. 4.10b — Effects of acetic acid on wheat and barley seed germination and seedling root growth: (b) Inhibition of seedling root growth by acetic acid (averaged results from 20 seedlings for each concentration): wheat, ●; barley, ○.

experimental conditions, a concentration of only 0.02% acetic acid leads to a 60% reduction in root length against control seedlings, which seems to demonstrate that even minimal levels of acetic acid can adversely affect root extension.

4.10.2 Field trials

It was found that crop yields were reduced when straw residues from preceding crops had not been removed [4.50;4.53]; under temperate conditions when cereals are direct-drilled in autumn in the presence of straw these reductions have been attributed primarily to the production of phytotoxins by micro-organisms under anaerobic conditions [4.48;4.49]. The immobilisation of available soil nitrogen in the microbial population which decomposes straw also contributes to the decrease in yield [4.45]. Losses in the weight of straw contained within mesh bags have been followed under field conditions [4.55; 4.56], but these studies were not combined with an examination of changes in the potential of the straw to act as a substrate for phytotoxin production by micro-organisms. Comparing the effects of burnt and unburnt straw on the yields of wheat in clay soils with differing cropping histories and irrigation levels, Lynch *et al.* [4.57] extracted samples from around the drill slits to recover the seeds and seedlings. Again, root and shoot measurements were taken, percentage seed germination recorded, and soil water extracts taken for examination by GLC analysis [4.46]. The presence of straw in wet autumn conditions did not affect seed germination, although it retarded the growth of young plants and decreased the extent of tillering so that there were fewer ears and a smaller grain yield. Although no organic acids were found in any of the soil solutions, they pointed out that this did not prove their absence close to the decomposing straw.

Harper and Lynch [4.58] later used a mesh bag technique to follow the decomposition of straw under field conditions. Following oat straw decomposition over the course of a year, they found that all samples lost weight most rapidly in autumn, but in winter there was a marked reduction in the rate of decomposition. In the spring the rate of weight loss increased slightly again but slowed down during the summer months. Buried and slit samples lost a total of 80% by weight but surface samples lost only 60%. This loss in weight resulted primarily from the degradation of hemicellulose and cellulose. The potential of recovered straw samples to produce acetic acid declined steadily during decomposition, coinciding with the losses of dry weight and hemicellulose and cellulose. They found that once 50% of these compounds had been decomposed in the buried straw samples (after approximately 50 days), further accumulation of phytotoxin did not occur. However, the other samples retained their phytotoxic potential until the spring, although much reduced.

4.11   INCORPORATION OF CELLULASE PRODUCERS

The problems of reduced cereal yield following direct-drilling through straw residues in the autumn, and build-up of phytotoxic acetic acid from anaerobic microbial activity, are now well known. More recent research is aimed at the possibility of using micro-organisms to speed up or alter the process in some way. It seems feasible that many cellulolytic fungi could be grown commercially, as they now are for cellulase production, and added to stubble as a liquid spray behind the tractor during straw incorporation to accelerate decomposition in the soil. In that event, phytotoxic levels of acetic acid would be produced earlier and subsequently utilised earlier by microbial activity in the soil, so that when cereal crops were sown in the autumn there would be a reduced incidence of phytotoxic effects on crop yield. There are many indigenous fungi, found both on rotting straw and in the soil, which are capable of cellulolytic activity and which could be utilised as a novel 'Stubble Digester' [4.59–4.63].

With this possibility in mind the author has studied the effects of added cellulolytic fungi on straw decomposition in soils. Soil classification for ease of straw incorporation in the UK can be divided into three simple main categories—easy, intermediate and difficult [4.64]—and using this simple classification three soil types [4.65] were chosen for the experiment: WICK 1, YELD and EVESHAM 2, respectively. Six mixed fungal cultures containing different *Trichoderma*, *Penicillium* and *Chaetomium* species were formulated and added to chopped barley straw to give a total concentration of 1×10^6 spores g^{-1} straw. Lynch and Harper [4.66] had earlier demonstrated that the use of a nitrogen-fixing organism along with cellulolytic fungi increased the decomposition rate of straw because of cooperative nitrogen fixation. This is due to the fact that there is an extra demand for nitrogen during straw decomposition by cellulolytic micro-organisms which can be supplemented by nitrogen-fixing micro-organisms. It was therefore decided to include such a micro-organism in five of the six mixed fungal cultures. Fifteen gram quantities of treated straw were mixed with the three non-sterile soil types (at 20% moisture content) to give a straw/soil ratio of 0.15:1, sealed inside loose plastic bags to provide a micro-environment and stored in individual plastic containers with a lid to exclude daylight. These containers were left undisturbed at ambient temperature from September through to April.

The results (Table 4.7) showed that with all mixed fungal cultures (1–6) and all three soil types (A–C) there was a definite, though variable, increase in straw decomposition in comparison with straws which were untreated. Although these results are preliminary, it is interesting to note that the mixed fungal cultures which did not contain the nitrogen-fixing micro-organism (A3, B3, C3) furnished the least increase in straw decomposition for each soil type. This agrees with the findings of Lynch and Harper [4.66] and Kimber [4.54]. Immobilisation of soil nitrogen on straw residues is likely to lead to certain soil micro-organisms receiving an inadequate nitrogen supply, making them less able to utilise the products of straw degradation. This, in turn, will lead to an increase in phytotoxic concentration. However, as would probably be expected after a time-interval of 8 months, there was no evidence of phytotoxic levels of acetic acid found from GLC analysis either of soil or of straw aqueous extracts [4.58].

4.11.1   Practical problems in the application of the new technology
Although the aim is, ideally, to obtain a single cellulolytic fungal species which gives the best overall straw decomposition rate, that is only part of the answer. From a manufacturing point of view, large-scale fermentation of a novel fungus species will depend on initial problem-solving exercises relating to economies of scale. To gain maximum biomass production from any one fungal fermentation run, the growth conditions need to be optimised by

Table 4.7 — Effect of the addition of cellulolytic microbial mixes (1×10^6 organisms g^{-1} straw) on the decomposition of barley straw after a period of 8 months (September to April)

Treatment[a]	Weight loss (%)	Increased weight loss vs control	Decomposition rate (kg d^{-1}) [4.58]
A1	56.67	28.63	0.002 36
A2	48.67	20.63	0.002 03
A3	41.75	13.71	0.001 74
A4	55.33	27.29	0.002 31
A5	62.00	33.96	0.002 58
A6	57.19	29.19	0.002 38
Control A	28.04	—	0.001 17
B1	83.16	40.49	0.003 47
B2	53.68	11.01	0.002 37
B3	50.88	8.21	0.002 12
B4	74.04	31.38	0.003 09
B5	62.81	20.14	0.002 62
B6	76.84	34.17	0.003 20
Control B	42.67	—	0.001 78
C1	78.95	32.51	0.003 29
C2	62.81	16.37	0.002 62
C3	52.28	5.84	0.002 18
C4	65.61	19.17	0.002 73
C5	67.72	21.28	0.002 82
C6	74.74	28.30	0.003 11
Control C	46.44	—	0.001 94

[a]Soil types: A=WICK 1; B=YELD; C=EVESHAM.
Phytotoxic levels of acetic acid were not detected in any soil or straw washings.

the monitoring of numerous small-scale fermentations using variable pH, temperature, oxygen and nutrient supply before a choice is ultimately made. Up till now most fungal fermentations, particularly submerged fermentations, have been optimised for maximum production of their metabolites, such as enzymes and antibiotics, rather than purely maximum biomass production. In the end, optimisation will probably be a compromise between biomass production and the cost of the fermentation.

From the retail point of view, the farmer will not buy a biological 'stubble digestion' product unless it is known to work and will give him a return for his money. At the moment it may be argued that the burning of cereal residues in the field costs the farmer nothing, but that is debatable. On the negative side, he loses nutrients and could otherwise increase his soil stability and fertility, and there is a fire control and pollution risk. However, burning straw in the fields does reduce the pest load in the soil, and can thus lead to a reduction in the incidence of plant diseases as well as 'rogue' wild grasses, etc. Convincing the farmer of the efficacy of the product leads to other research and development problems. The fungal product must obviously still retain its cellulolytic activity following drying and long-term storage. It will need to be added to the straw in sufficient quantities to improve straw decomposition rate over as short a time period as possible, so that there will be minimal levels of phytotoxins present at the time of sowing. Moreover, the fungal species will need to compete successfully with the indigenous soil microflora. These problems can only be really answered by full evaluation at the field trial stage.

Although the idea of a 'Stubble Digester' seems promising, many cellulolytic fungal species are capable of degrading only easily accessible cellulose contained in the leaves and nodes of straw residues. Harper and Lynch [4.67] reported that cellulose contained in the internodes is particularly hard for cellulolytic fungi to degrade. Even more resistant to cellulolytic activity is, of course, the lignin fraction of cereal residues which would probably be completely undegraded over the time period when a stubble digestion product would be used. Nevertheless, there is considerable current research into lignin biodegradation relevant to straw decomposition [4.68;4.69] and therefore even this very intractable problem might well be solved in the coming years.

REFERENCES

[4.1] Chang Yung and Hudson, H. J. (1967) The fungi of wheat straw compost: ecological studies. *Trans. Br. Mycol. Soc., 50*(4), 649–666.

[4.2] Hayes, W. A. and Lim, W. C. (1979) Wheat and rice straw composts and mushroom production. In *Straw Decay and its Effect on Disposal and Utilisation,* Grossbard, E. (ed.), John Wiley, New York, pp. 85–94.

[4.3] Fermor, T. R. and Wood, D. A. (1979) The microbiology and enzymology of wheat straw mushroom compost production. In *Straw Decay and its Effect on Disposal and Utilisation,* Grossbard, E. (ed.), John Wiley, New York, pp. 105–112.

[4.4] Atkey, P. T. and Wood, D. A. (1983) An electron microscope study of wheat straw composted as a substrate for the cultivation of the edible mushroom. *J. Appl. Bact., 55,* 293–304.

[4.5] de Bertoldi, M., Valleni, G. and Pera, A. (1983) The biology of composting. *Waste Management and Res., 1,* 157–176.

[4.6] Edwards, C. A. (1974) Macroarthropods. *Biology of Plant Litter Decomposition,* Dickson, C. H. and Pugh, G. J. F. (eds), Academic Press, London and New York, pp. 533–554.

[4.7] Chang Yung (1967) The fungi of wheat straw compost: biochemical and physiological studies. *Trans. Br. Mycol. Soc., 50*(4), 667–677.

[4.8] de Bertoldi, M., Valleni, G., Pera, A. and Zucconi, F. (1982) Comparison of three windrow compost systems. *Biocycle, 23*(2), 45–50.

[4.9] Finstein, M. S., Miller, F. C., Strom, P. F., MacGregor, S. T. and Psarianos, K. M. (1983) Composting ecosystem management for waste treatment. *Bio/Technology,* **1**(4), 347–353.

[4.10] Alexander, M. (1977) *Introduction to Soil Microbiology,* John Wiley, New York.

[4.11] Epstein, E., Willson, G. B., Burge, W. D., Mullen, D. C. and Enkiri, N. K. (1976) A forced aeration system for composting wastewater sludge. *J. Wat. Pollut. Control Fed.,* **48**(4), 688–694.

[4.12] MacGregor, S. T., Miller, F. C., Psarianos, K. M., and Finstein, M. S. (1981) Composting process control based on interaction between microbial heat output and temperature. *Appl. Environ. Microbiol.,* **41**(6), 1321–1330.

[4.13] Higgins, A. J. (1983) Reducing costs for bulking agents. *Biocycle,* **24**(5), 34–38.

[4.14] Biddlestone, A. J., Gray, K. R. and Cooper, D. J. (1985) Development of straw based techniques for composting organic wastes. *Environmental Health,* **93**(3), 67–71.

[4.15] Haug, R. T. (1980) *Compost Engineering: Principles and Practice,* Ann Arbor Science, Michigan.

[4.16] Jeris, J. S. and Regan, R. W. (1973) Controlling environmental parameters for optimum composting: moisture, free air space and recycle. *Compost Sci.,* **14**(2), 8–15.

[4.17] Wiley, J. S. and Pearce, G. W. (1955) A preliminary study of high rate composting. *Proc. ASCE, J. San. Eng. Div.,* **81**(846), 1–27.

[4.18] Flintoff, F. (1976) *Management of Solid Wastes in Developing Countries,* World Health Organisation Publications, South East Asia Office, New Delhi, India.

[4.19] Gray, K. R., Sherman, K. and Biddlestone, A. J. (1971) A review of composting: the practical process. *Process Biochemistry,* **6**(10), 22–28.

[4.20] Wiley, J. S. (1957) Liquid content of garbage and refuse. *Proc. ASCE, J. San. Eng. Div.,* **83**(1411), 1–11.

[4.21] Mote, C. R. and Griffis, C. L. (1982) Heat production by composting organic matter. *Agric. Wastes,* **4**, 65–73.

[4.22] Spohn, E. (1970) Composting by artificial aeration. *Compost Sci.,* **11**(3), 22–23.

[4.23] Gray, K. R. and Biddlestone, A. J. (1976) The garden compost heap. *J. Royal Hort. Soc.,* **101**, 540–544, 594–598.

[4.24] Dalzell, H. W., Gray, K. R. and Biddlestone, A. J. (1979) *Composting in Tropical Agriculture,* International Institute of Biological Husbandry, Ipswich, UK.

[4.25] FAO (1977) China: recycling of organic wastes in agriculture. *FAO Soils Bulletin,* **40**, FAO, Rome.

[4.26] Polprasert, C., Wangsuphachart, S. and Muttamara, S. (1980) Composting nightsoil and water hyacinth in the Tropics. *Compost Sci./Land Utilization,* **21**(2), 25–27.

[4.27] Shuval, H. I., Gunnerson, C. G. and Julius, D. (1978) *Nightsoil Composting,* P.U. Report RES 12, World Bank, Washington, DC.

[4.28] Paatero, J. (1979) Fertiliser from sewage sludge. *Environ. Pollution Management,* **9**(6), 169–172.

[4.29] Shea, T. G., Braswell, J. and Coker, C. S. (1979) Bulking agent selection in sludge composting facility design. *Compost Sci./Land Utilization,* **20**(6), 20–21.

[4.30] Hyde, M. A. and Consolazio, G. A. (1982) Composting of food processing waste sludges. *Biocycle,* **23**(1), 58–60.

[4.31] Singley, M. E., Higgins, A. J. and Rosengaus, M. F. (1982) *Sludge Composting and Utilisation: a Design and Operating Manual,* New Jersey Agricultural Experiment Station, Cook College, Rutgers University, New Brunswick, NJ 08903, USA.

[4.32] Savage, G. M. and Golueke, C. G. (1986) Major cost elements in co-composting. *Biocycle,* **27**(1), 33–35.

[4.33] Gray, K. R. and Biddlestone, A. J. (1980) Agricultural use of composted town refuse. In *Inorganic Pollution and Agriculture,* Ministry of Agriculture, Fisheries and Food, Reference Book 326, HMSO, London, pp. 279–305.

[4.34] Finstein, M. S., Lin, K. W. R. and Fishchler, G. E. (1982) *Sludge Composting and Utilization: Review of the Literature on Temperature Inactivation of Pathogens,* New Jersey Agricultural Experiment Station, Cook College, Rutgers University, New Brunswick, NJ 08903, USA.

[4.35] Higgins, A. J. (1983) Technical issues involving sludge and compost use. *Biocycle,* **24**(1), 40–44.

[4.36] Golueke, C. G. (1983) Epidemiological aspects of sludge handling and management. *Biocycle,* **24**(4), 50–58.

[4.37] Pickering, S. U. and Duke of Bedford (1914) The effect of one crop on another. *J. Agric. Sci.,* **6**, 136.

[4.38] Patrick, Z. A., Tousson, T. A. and Koch, L. W. (1964) Effect of crop residue decomposition products on plant roots. *Ann. Rev. Phytopath.,* **2**, 267.

[4.39] McCalla, T. M. and Army, T. J. (1961) Stubble mulch farming. *Adv. Agronomy,* **13**, 125–196.

[4.40] McCalla, T. M. and Haskins, F. A. (1964) Phytotoxic substances from soil micro-organisms and crop residues. *Bact. Rev.,* **28**, 181.

[4.41] Guenzi, W. D. and McCalla, J. M. (1962) Inhibition of germination of seedling development by crop residues. *Soil Sci. Soc. Am. Proc.,* **26**, 454.

[4.42] Kimber, R. W. L. (1967) Phytotoxicity from plant residues. I. The influence of rotted wheat straw on seedling growth. *Aust. J. Agric. Res.,* **18**, 361.

[4.43] Tang, C. S. and Waiss, A. C. (1978) Short-chain fatty acids as growth inhibitors in decomposing wheat straw. *J. Chem. Ecol.,* **4**, 225.

[4.44] Barbera, D. A., Gunn, K. B. and Haynes, J. C. (1976) Effects of straw residues on the growth of cereals. *Agric. Res. Council, Letcombe Lab. Ann. Report 1975*, pp. 29–31.

[4.45] Ellis, F. B., Barber, D. A. and Graham, J. P. (1975) Seedling development in the presence of decaying straw residues. *Agric. Res. Council, Letcombe Lab. Ann. Report 1975*, pp. 39–40.

[4.46] Lynch, J. M. (1977) Phytotoxicity of acetic acid produced in the anerobic decomposition of wheat straw. *J. Appl. Bact.*, **42**, 81.

[4.47] Lynch, J. M., Gunn, K. B. and Painting, L. M. (1980) On the concentration of acetic acid in straw and soil. *Plant and Soil*, **56**, 93.

[4.48] Lynch, J. M. (1978) Production and phytotoxicity of acetic acid in anaerobic soils containing plant residues. *Soil Biol. Biochem.*, **10**, 131.

[4.49] Cochran, V. L., Elliott, L. F. and Papendick, R. I. (1977) The production of phytotoxins from surface crop residues. *Soil Sci. Soc. Amer. J.*, **41**, 903.

[4.50] McCalla, T. M. and Norstadt, F. A. (1974) Toxicity problems in mulch tillage. *Agric. Environ.*, **1**, 153.

[4.51] Lynch, J. M. (1976) Products of soil micro-organisms in relation to plant growth. *CRC Crit. Rev. Microbiol.*, **5**, 67–102.

[4.52] Harper, S. H. T. and Lynch, J. M. (1980) Microbial effects in the germination and seedling growth of barley. *New Phytol.*, **84**, 473.

[4.53] Elliott, L. F., McCalla, T. M. and Waiss, A. (1978) Phytotoxicity associated with residue management. In *Crop Residue Management Systems*, Oschwald, W. R. (ed.), Am. Soc. Agronomy.

[4.54] Kimber, R. W. L. (1973) Phytotoxicity from plant residues. III. The effect of toxins and nitrogen immobilisation on the germination and growth of wheat. *Plant and Soil*, **38**, 534–535.

[4.55] Brown, P. L. and Dickey, D. D. (1970) Losses of wheat straw residue under simulated field conditions. *Soil Sci. Soc. Am. Proc.*, **34**, 118.

[4.56] Smith, J. H. and Douglas, C. L. (1971) Wheat straw decomposition in the field. *Soil Sci. Soc. Am. Proc.*, **35**, 269.

[4.57] Lynch, J. M., Ellis, F. B., Harper, S. H. T. and Christian, D. G. (1980) The effect of straw on the establishment and growth of winter cereals. *Agriculture and Environment*, **5**, 321.

[4.58] Harper, S. H. T. and Lynch, J. M. (1981) The kinetics of straw decomposition in relation to its potential to produce the phytotoxin acetic acid. *J. Soil Sci.*, **32**, 627.

[4.59] Lynch, J. M., Slater, J. H., Bennett, J. A. and Harper, S. H. T. (1981) Cellulase activities of some aerobic micro-organisms isolated from soil. *J. Gen. Microbiol.*, **127**, 231–236.

[4.60] Viesturs, V. E., Apsite, A. F., Laukevics, J. J., Ose, V. P. and Bekers, M. J. (1981) Solid-state fermentation wheat straw with *Chaetomium cellulolyticum* and *Trichoderma lignorum*. *Biotech. Bioeng. Symp.*, **11**, 359–369.

[4.61] Lynch, J. M. (1983) *Soil Biotechnology—Microbiological Factors in Crop Productivity*, Blackwell Scientific Publications, Oxford.

[4.62] Lynch, J. M. (1983) Microbial utilisation of straw in agriculture. In *Biotech 83 Conf. Proc.*, Online Publications, London.

[4.63] Lynch, J. M. and Elliott, L. F. (1983) Aggregate stability of volcanic ash and soil during microbial degradation of straw. *Appl. J. Environ. Microbiol.*, **45**, 1398–1401.

[4.64] Thomasson, B. and Davies, B. (1964) Straw incorporation. *Farmer's Weekly,* July 13.

[4.65] *Soil Survey of England and Wales* (1983) Rothamsted Experimental Station, Harpenden, Herts, UK.

[4.66] Lynch, J. M. and Harper, S. H. T. (1983) Straw as a substrate for cooperative nitrogen fixation. *J. Gen. Microbiol.*, **129**, 251–253.

[4.67] Harper, S. H. T. and Lynch, J. M. (1981) The chemical components and decomposition of wheat straw leaves, internodes and nodes. *J. Sci. Fd Agric.*, **32**, 1057–1062.

[4.68] Lynch, J. M., Harper, S. H. T., Chapman, S. J. and Veal, D. A. (1984) Biodegradation of lignocelluloses in agricultural wastes. In *Anaerobic Digestion and Carbohydrate Hydrolysis of Waste,* Ferrero, G. L., Ferranti, M. P. and Naveau, H. (eds), Elsevier, New York.

[4.69] Mishra, C., Rao, M., Seeta, R., Srinivasan, M. C. and Deshpande, V. (1984) Hydrolysis of lignocelluloses by *Penicillium funiculosum* cellulase. *Biotech. Bioeng.*, **26**, 370–373.

5

Solid waste

C. F. Forster
Department of Civil Engineering, Birmingham University, UK
and
E. Senior
Department of Bioscience and Biotechnology, Strathclyde University, UK

5.1 INTRODUCTION

Civilised societies, by their very nature, generate waste as both liquids and solids. The disposal of these wastes in ways which neither constitute a public health hazard nor create an unacceptable impact on the environment is, therefore, a major challenge. Within the field of environmental biotechnology, the solid wastes whose processing and disposal involves the most significant effort, in terms of both volume and cost, are the sludges generated by the treatment of sewage and the solids discarded as domestic refuse.

5.2 SEWAGE SLUDGE: AN INTRODUCTION

Conventional physico-chemical treatment of sewage or wastewater will produce significant quantities of residual solids. A proportion of these accumulates at the primary settlement stage; the rest is the excess biomass produced by the biological oxidation of the carbonaceous pollutants in the wastewaters. The quantities of solid waste resulting from the treatment of sewage are given in Table 5.1 It must be recognised that these figures are expressed in terms of dry matter and that, in fact, as handled initially, the solids exist as suspensions, the consistency of which can be very variable, ranging from 1–10% dry solids (DS). The handling, processing and disposal of sludge solids is therefore a major consideration in the design and operation of any wastewater treatment plant. A considerable financial input

Table 5.1 — Sludge production data [5.1; 5.2]

Country	Annual production (tons DS $\times$ 10^3)
Belgium	10
France	800
West Germany	1300
Italy	1200
UK	1240
USA	4500
Canada	500

is also involved. Indeed in the UK, some 40% of the revenue costs for sewage treatment are associated with sludge treatment and disposal. In general, the techniques that are used for the processing of sludge are those which achieve a degree of dewatering. The choice of process or processes in any sludge handling sequence tends, therefore, to be governed by the disposal mode which is appropriate to that particular sludge and treatment site. In this context, it must be recognised that in reality there is no such commodity as 'sewage sludge'; rather, there is a range of sludges depending for their characteristics on their origin and degree of treatment [5.3]. Each type of sludge (Table 5.2) has different properties in relation to, for

Table 5.2 — Types of sewage sludge

Sludge	General description
Primary	Produced from primary settlement. Contains raw sewage solids. Concentration = 3–4%.
Humus	The excess biofilm from trickling filters. Typical concentration = 2%.
Activated	Flocculated biomass (bacteria + protozoa) produced in the activated sludge process. Concentration (as wasted) = 8–12 g l^{-1}.
Secondary	Activated or humus.
Co-settled	Mixture of primary and secondary solids produced in primary settlement tanks.
Raw	Untreated in any way. Usually refers to primary or co-settled sludges.

example, pumping, chemical conditioning and filtration. Thus the type of sludge being processed will affect the choice of treatment mainly by its effect on the process economics.

In the UK (as in many other countries) the main disposal route for sludge is to land. However, there are constraints to this practice. These will be discussed in detail later but essentially they are aimed at limiting the dissemination of heavy metal ions and pathogenic/parasitic organisms into the environment. Each area for the reception of this type of disposal will have different characteristics and therefore different sets of constraints. It is for this reason that the disposal mode can influence the processing sequence.

5.3 PROCESSING

5.3.1 Thickening

As produced and wasted, the various types of sewage sludge do not have a high solids concentration. Modern philosophies on sludge handling dictate that, in most cases, a degree of dewatering should be achieved before the main processing sequence. One of the simplest ways of doing this is extended gravity settlement or thickening. In fact, one can differentiate between primary and secondary thickening [5.4]. Primary thickening is applied to sludges directly after wastage. The process itself can be operated in a batch or continuous mode and the rate of thickening can be assisted by incorporating a 'picket fence' in the thickening tank design. Thickening is caused by the compressive forces of the sludge in the upper part of the tank squeezing water out of the solids at the bottom. A 'picket fence' (see Fig. 5.1) therefore assists this basic mechanism by:

— releasing gas bubbles
— preventing bridging by the solids
— providing void channels for the upflow of water

Typically the spacing between the vertical rods is 100 mm and the rotational speed is such that the peripheral velocity is between 0.5 and 3.0 m min^{-1}. Performance data for this type of process are given in Tables 5.3 and 5.4. The design of thickening tanks is somewhat arbitrary and batch trials are often used to provide design data [5.8]. However, the development of the 'frozen image centrifuge' [5.9] has provided a rapid technique for predicting the thickenability of sludges and, thus, for designing thickening tanks.

Secondary thickening is applied to sludges that have been treated by anaerobic digestion (Section 5.2.4). The problems with this type of thickening are usually associated with the presence of microbubbles of the biogas formed during the digestion process. These tend to become attached to the solids and retard or even inhibit settlement. Secondary thickening, therefore, is usually preceded by some process which promotes gas disengagement. The processes that have been used include the use of very shallow thickeners, rapid cooling, vacuum degassing and aeration [5.10]. Of these, aeration appears to be the most promising. Not only are the microbubbles

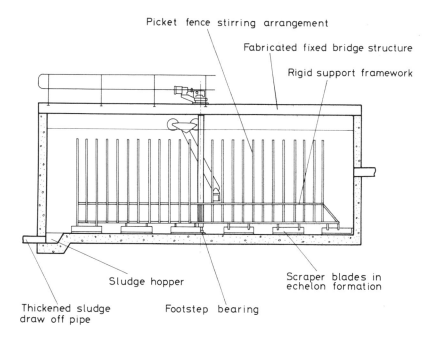

Fig. 5.1 — Typical picket fence thickener.

Table 5.3 — Performance of primary thickeners

| Solids concentration (% dry matter) | | |
Feed	Output	Reference
4.7	6.8[a]	[5.5]
3.9	7.6[b]	[5.5]
2.5	4.3	[5.6]
1.1–3.3	5.5–6.0	[5.7]

[a] Manual control.
[b] Automatic control.

Table 5.4 — Operational criteria for the thickening of surplus activated and thermally conditioned sludges (courtesy of Emschergenossenschaft)

	Tank diameter (m)	Surface load $(m^3\,m^{-2}\,d^{-1})$	Mass load $(kg\,DS\,m^{-2}\,d^{-1})$
Activated	32	4.56	100
Conditioned	20	3.36	120

stripped from the liquors but the resultant removal of carbon dioxide from solution can bring about a sufficiently large increase in pH to inhibit any further methanogenic activity, an activity which is also diminished by the presence of oxygen. Typical performance data are given in Table 5.5. The

Table 5.5 — Performance of pre-aerated consolidation tanks for thickening digested sludge (from Hurley *et al.* [5.10])

Treatment works	Method	Period (h)	Intensity (m^3 air m^{-3} h^{-1})	Initial solids (% DS)	Solids volume after 7 days (% initial)
Mogden	Venturi	1	5	2.0	50
		2	5	2.0	59
Basingstoke	Venturi	1	5	2.6	52
	Coarse bubble	2–10	1–5	2.6	45
	Coarse bubble	10–16	1	2.5	48

cost of using aeration in this way has been estimated as being £0.27 m^{-3} (for a 100 000 population-equivalent works) with a total energy requirement of less than 2 kWh m^{-3} [5.10].

Thickening can also be achieved by using centrifuges or flotation. Although many variants of these processes are available, none has found a wide application in the UK Water Industry. The performance and characteristics of the various types of centrifuge have been reviewed by the Institute of Water Pollution Control [5.11] and an appraisal of the use of flotation has been provided by Melbourne and Zabel [5.12] and by Maddock and Tomlinson [5.13]. It must be recognised, however, that whichever technique is used to achieve sludge thickening, thick sludges do have distinct and pronounced non-Newtonian properties. It is therefore essential that the degree of thickening is not such that the resultant sludge cannot be pumped. For primary sludges, a solids concentration of about 12% is the critical point. However, the precise value depends on the nature and source of the sludge solids and there is, currently, an inadequate understanding of the factors which influence sludge rheology for valid predictions to be made or precise control criteria established [5.14; 5.15].

Nevertheless, the rheological characteristics can be measured. Currently, this can be done using a simple tube viscometer (Fig. 5.2). Thus, by measuring the sludge level in the reservoir in relation to time and applying Equations 5.1 and 5.2, the values of the constants in the basic rheological equation (5.3) can be derived:

$$\tau_\omega = \frac{D\Delta P}{4\ L} \tag{5.1}$$

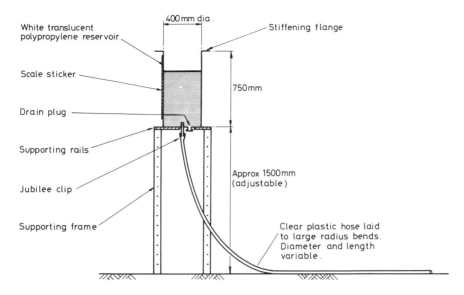

Fig. 5.2 — Tube viscometer for determining the rheological properties of sludge.

$$\Delta P = \rho_s gh \tag{5.2}$$

$$\tau_\omega = \tau_0 + K \left[\frac{8V}{D} \right] \tag{5.3}$$

where

τ_ω = wall shear stress
D = tube diameter
L = tube length
ρ_s = sludge density
h = head
V = velocity of flow
T, K and n = constants

For primary sludge, the values for τ_0 and K have been shown to vary with the solids concentration [5.16]. Thus:

$$\tau_0 = 4.353S - 14.08 \tag{5.4}$$

$$K = 0.0736S - 1.233 \tag{5.5}$$

where S=solids concentration (%).

Using all these equations it is possible to calculate the pressure drop in sludge pipelines of any diameter (e.g. Fig. 5.3).

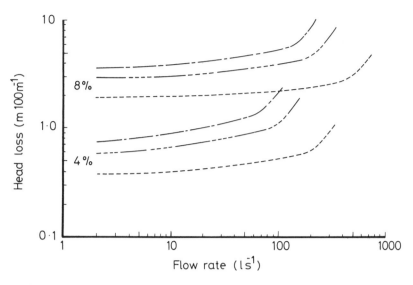

Fig. 5.3 — Head loss/flow curves at 5°C for sludges having solids concentrations of
8% and 4%: pipe diameter = 450 mm – – – – – –; pipe diameter = 300 mm
——— – – – ———; pipe diameter = 250 mm ——— – ———.

5.3.2 Filtration

Sludges may be dewatered to an even greater extent by filtration. In the UK,
probably the most common process is the filter press (Fig. 5.4). The unit
consists of a series of plates which are suspended from a side-bar or an
overhead beam. The plates are recessed so that chambers are formed
between them. Filter cloths are fitted over each plate and the entire

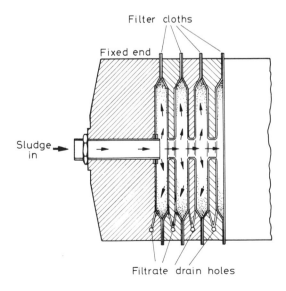

Fig. 5.4 — Schematic diagram of a filter press.

assemblage is held in position by either screws or hydraulic pressure. Pumps
are then used to fill the press with sludge and to provide the driving force for
the filtration, the maximum pressure being of the order of 690 kPa. At the
end of the cycle, when the flow of filtrate stops, the pressure is released, the
plates are separated and the cake removed. The disposal of the cake can be
facilitated if the press is located on the first floor of a building and the cake
can drop directly into containers for removal. Alternatively, a conveyor-belt
can be used for transferring the cake from underneath the press to a disposal
point. Filter pressing is, therefore, a batch process with a single cycle,
including washing the press components (when necessary) using high-
pressure jets, taking 3–14 h.

The operational costs of pressing can be optimised by using the approach
described by Hoyland *et al.* [5.17]. This recognises that, after the filling
stage, there are two distinct stages to filter pressing (Fig. 5.5): one in which

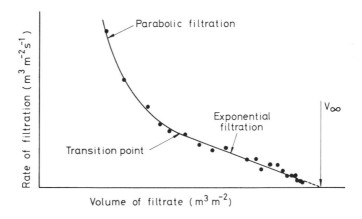

Fig. 5.5 — Typical rate of filtration during filter pressing (from [5.17]).

the filtration curve is parabolic and a second in which it is exponential. On
the basis of the mathematics of this second phase, the rate of filtration is
given by:

$$\frac{\mathrm{d}V}{\mathrm{d}t} \propto V_{\infty} - V \qquad\qquad (5.6)$$

where V = filtrate volume ($m^3 \, m^{-2}$).

Therefore, by following the filtration cycle and plotting $\mathrm{d}V/\mathrm{d}t$ against V,
it is possible to predict V_{∞} and the 'degree of completion' (V/V_{∞}). This
means that a final cake can be produced which is neither too hard nor too
soft. This approach can be linked to microprocessors so that the pressing
cycle can be controlled automatically.

The recent development of membrane filters may also offer a method of producing a high solids cake in a shorter time than in conventional presses [5.18]. In this system, every other plate can be inflated with air (using pressures up to 800 kPa) before a firm cake is formed. However, it must be recognised that the installation of membrane plates is expensive and their economic benefits need to be assessed with care [5.19].

The belt press is possibly the second most popular option for sludge filtration in the UK. This process utilises two continuous belts (a porous filter belt and an impervious press belt) in conjunction with a series of rollers (Fig. 5.6). The configuration of these rollers may vary between designs but

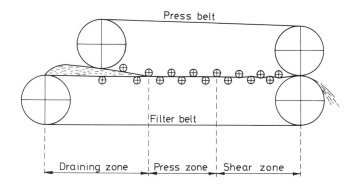

Fig. 5.6 — Schematic diagram of a belt press.

the basic principle of operation is the same. The sludge, which has been fed evenly across the width of the belt, drains under gravity for the initial phase. As the belts then pass between the rollers, pressure and, later, shear are applied. The extent of dewatering that is achieved, therefore, depends on the rentention time and the clearance between the belts. Both of these are adjustable. A typical cake produced by belt pressing would have a solids concentration of about 25% [5.20].

Although filter presses and belt presses are used for dewatering about 75% of sludges, vacuum filters are used in the UK. The most widely used design is the rotating drum filter (Fig. 5.7). The drum consists of a series of compartments, each of which can be subjected to either a vacuum (40–90 kPa) or a positive pressure. The filter medium may be a cloth, a wire screen, or close-packed wire coils fitted with their axis in the direction of rotation. Sludge would be fed into a reservoir through which the drum passed with a typical speed of 5 mm s^{-1}. A mat of wet solids would become attached to the filter medium as the result of the vacuum applied to the submerged cell. The vacuum would be continued as the drum rotated to provide the driving force for the filtration process. Immediately prior to completing one revolution, the vacuum would be released and a slight pressure applied. This aids the release of the cake. As a general rule, this cake contains more moisture than that produced by a filter press. However, the process does have the

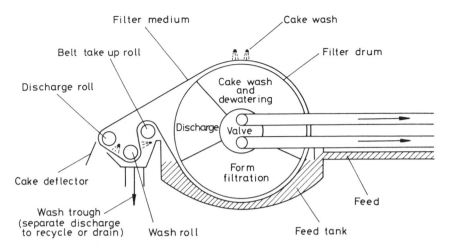

Fig. 5.7 — Schematic diagram of a rotary vacuum filter.

advantage of being continuous. The operational characteristics of vacuum filtration have been appraised by Nelson and Tavery [5.21]; this report also includes a 'trouble-shooting' guide and equipment inspection programme.

Whichever method of filtration is used, it must be remembered that the filtrate will have a BOD value which at times is appreciable (Table 5.6). The liquors from these processes, therefore, need to be returned to the works inlet and an allowance must be made for the load they represent at the design stage.

Table 5.6 — Typical values (mg l^{-1}) for the strength of the liquors produced by dewatering proceses (from Forster [5.22])

Treatment	BOD	Amm-N
Filter press	2550	274
Belt press	800	—
Vacuum filter	414	355

5.3.3 Conditioning

Most of the sludges that are generated by the various wastewater treatment processes cannot be dewatered by filtration very easily. Therefore, they must receive a pretreatment to improve their filterability. This is conditioning. As a general rule, the process entails the addition of chemicals which act as coagulants or flocculants. These chemicals may be inorganic salts (lime; ferric chloride; ferrous sulphate; aluminium chlorohydrate) or specially formulated organic polymers with a range of molecular weights and ionic affinities. The proper application of polymers can best be learnt from the

Polyelectrolyte Users' Manual produced by Lockyear *et al.* [5.23]. This provides not only a comprehensive listing of the polymers available in the UK but also details of testing equipment and producers. One of the most basic tests is the measurement of the specific resistance to filtration, *r*.

The rate of filtration, making no allowance for cake compressibility, is given by:

$$\frac{dV}{dt} = \frac{PA^2}{\mu(VC + RA)} \tag{5.7}$$

which, at constant pressure, can be written as:

$$\frac{t}{V} = \frac{\mu C}{2PA^2}V + \frac{\mu R}{PA} \tag{5.8}$$

where

$$
\begin{aligned}
V &= \text{volume of filtrate at time } t \\
P &= \text{applied pressure} \\
A &= \text{filter area} \\
\mu &= \text{filtrate viscosity} \\
C &= \text{solids concentration} \\
R &= \text{resistance of the filter cloth}
\end{aligned}
$$

Values for *r* can be measured, quite simply, in the laboratory using a Buchner funnel, a graduated receiver and a vacuum source that can be controlled at the standard value of 49 kPa (see Fig. 5.8). Thus, by measuring

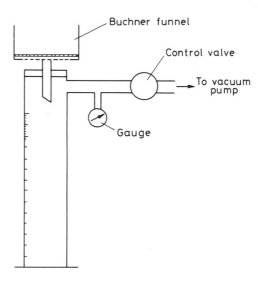

Fig. 5.8 — Buchner funnel apparatus for the measurement of specific resistance to filtration.

the filtrate volume at fixed times, it is possible, by plotting (t/V) against V, to calculate the value of r. A value which is greater than $10-50 \times 10^{11}$ m kg^{-1} is indicative of poor filterability. As can be seen from Table 5.7, most sludges

Table 5.7 — Typical values for the specific resistance to filtration of various sludges.

Type of sludge	Specific resistance ($\times 10^{11}$ m kg^{-1})
Primary	1000–1500
Humus	500–3000
Activated	1000–4000
Digested	1000–2500
Primary/activated + lime/copperas	14

do not filter well unless they have been conditioned.

Whatever type of conditioner is used (i.e. inorganic or polymer), it is essential that no more than the optimum dose be used. Excessive, uncalculated dosages are not only wasteful and over-expensive but also at times, result in a deterioration in filterability. The optimum dose can, of course, be determined from a series of specific resistance measurements, but this is time-consuming. A simpler way is to use capillary suction time (CST) measurements. In its simplest form, the CST apparatus is a rectangle of absorbent paper (Whatman No. 17; 90×70 mm) which is seated between two Perspex blocks (Fig. 5.9). The upper piece is fitted with a sludge reservoir and three electrodes located on two concentric circles. These electrodes are coupled to an amplifier and a stop-clock. When a sludge sample is placed in the reservoir, filtration occurs under the capillary suction pressure of the paper and filtrate diffuses outwards. On reaching the electrodes set on the inner circle, the timer is started. When the filtrate front reaches the third electrode, the clock is stopped. More advanced models use multiple radii and enable the CST concept to be related to the specific resistance [5.24].

These methods, therefore, enable the filterability of any particular combination of sludge and conditioner to be assessed so that the most effective conditioner and its optimum dose can be determined. Dosages are usually expressed as a percentage of the dry solids concentration and typical values are:

    Raw sludge   — lime (20%) + copperas (10%)
    Digested sludge — aluminium chlorohydrate (5–8%)
                    — polymers (1–8%)

When using conditioners, it must be remembered that the amount of sludge

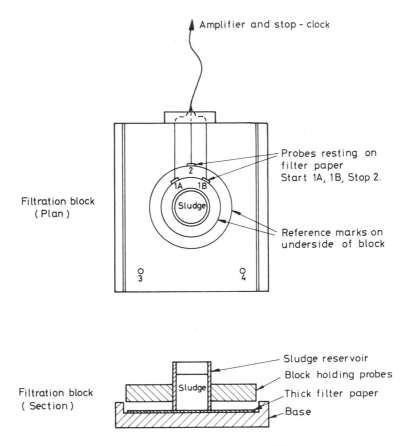

Fig. 5.9 — Apparatus for the measurement of capillary suction time.

will be increased and that the size of the increase will depend on the type and quantity of conditioner used. For example, lime and copperas can amount to 50 per cent of the final cake. Details of the type of cake produced by conditioning/filtration are shown in Table 5.8.

5.3.4   Anaerobic digestion
Anaerobic digestion (a fermentation process in which the end-products are, in the main, carbon dioxide and methane) can be, and is, carried out both in the cold and at elevated temperatures, although the most common process is mesophilic digestion. Its main features are that the sludge should be held for a period of time (traditionally about 30 days) at a temperature of 30–37°C and a more or less neutral pH, under anaerobic conditions. Under these circumstances, the putrescible fraction of the sludge (lipids, carbohydrates, proteins) is degraded, initially by hydrolytic and acidogenic bacteria and then by methogenic species. As can be seen from Chapter 2 and Fig. 5.10, acetate, hydrogen and carbon dioxide can all act as precursors to methane. However, in most systems, about 70 per cent of the methane is formed from

Table 5.8 — Filtration performance data

Type of sludge	Conditioner	Solids concentration (%)	
		Initial	Cake
Filter press			
Primary/humus	Lime/copperas	6.5	35–39
	Aluminium chlorohydrate	7.0	40
Digested	Lime/copperas	4.6	37
	Aluminium chlorohydrate	4.6	30
	Polymer	4.1	30
Vacuum filter			
Primary/humus	Lime/ferric chloride	—	20–30
	Polymer	—	25–38
Digested	Lime/ferric chloride	—	25–32
	Polymer	—	25–32
Belt press			
Primary/humus	Polymer	4.2–9.4	20.5–24.5

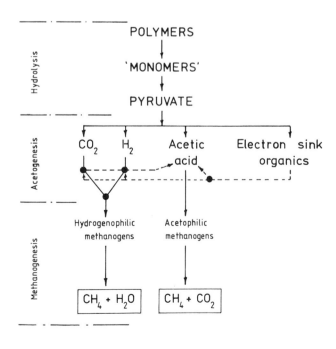

Fig. 5.10 — Simplified metabolic pathway for the degradation of biopolymers to methane.

the acetate methyl group by the acetophilic methanogens (e.g. *Methanothrix* spp.; *Methanosarcina* spp.) Hydrogenophilic methogens such as *Methanobacterium* spp. produce the rest of the methane from hydrogen and carbon dioxide. However, these steps frequently involve what are almost symbiotic relationships between fermentative bacteria, obligate proton reducers, acetogenic proton reducers and methanogens [5.25; 5.26]. Since hydrogen can be inhibitory to some of these species, the partial pressure of hydrogen can be thought of as a regulator of both intermediate fatty acid catabolism and methane production. As such, it is essential that the hydrogen concentration is maintained at a low level. If the sludge contains high concentrations of sulphate, these can be reduced to sulphides by the sulphate-reducing bacteria (e.g. *Desulphovibrio* spp.). These species compete with the methanogens for the methane precursors acetate and hydrogen, and, since their ultilisation of these compounds is more effective than that of the methanogens, methane production is reduced.

The features that can be considered as the secondary parameters for the sound operation of a mesophilic digester are good mixing and an efficient heat transfer system. The former is important to minimise stratification, grit settlement and scum formation. It also enhances gas removal and assists in maintaining an even temperature throughout the reactor. Essentially there are two types of mixing: mechanical devices and gas recirculation [5.27]. A typical gas recirculation rate for mixing would be 0.94 m^3 free gas m^{-2} tank area h^{-1} [5.28]. Tracers can be used to check the efficiency of mixing: tritium to label the aqueous phase and gold-198 to monitor the solids. The energy required for mixing varies from 2 to 14 W m^{-3} [5.28]. Heat transfer can be achieved either by direct steam injection or by using an exchange medium, usually water. In either case, the initial heat is acquired by burning some of the digester gas.

The main design parameters for sludge digesters are the solids retention time and the volumetric loading rate based on the volatile solids (i.e. kg volatile matter m^{-3} d^{-1}). Even allowing for the fact that there is a differentiation between high-rate and conventional-rate digestion, there is a wide variation in what is considered to be 'standard'. For example, retention times are quoted within the range 10–30 days and loading rates from 0.48 to 8.5 kg m^{-3} d^{-1}. However, it has been reported that methanogens can be washed out of the digester at retention times of less than 12 days [5.12] and that operational difficulties, both temporary and persistent, can occur when the loading rates are less than 1.71 kg m^{-3} d^{-1} [5.29]. It is not unreasonable, therefore, to suggest that a digester should be designed on the basis of a 20-day retention time and a loading rate of 2 kg m^{-3} d^{-1}. An alternative is to calculate the digester capacity on the basis of the population equivalent (N) being served. Thus:

$$\text{Capacity (m}^3) \; = \; 1.8 \times 25 \times 10^{-3} \times N \tag{5.9}$$

This formula [5.17] assumes a *per capita* sludge production of 1.8 litres d^{-1}

at a dry solids content of 4.5% (equivalent to a dry solids loading rate of 1.8 kg m^{-3} d^{-1}).

The sludge feedstock to most digesters would contain 3–6 per cent solids and about 75 per cent of these solids would be volatile. During the digestion process, about 50 per cent of the volatile matter would be converted to biogas, the average yield being of the order of 1 m^3 biogas kg^{-1} volatile dry solids destroyed. However, in making comparative judgements between different digesters (i.e. loading rates and performance), it is essential that the true volume of the digester is known accurately and allowances made for reductions in this volume as a result of accumulated rags and grit. These reductions can be significant, 30–50 per cent having been reported [5.30; 5.31].

In recent years considerable attention has been paid to uprating digesters. One of the main points of focus has been the thickening of sludge prior to digestion [5.31; 5.32]. This has several implications:

— New digesters can be built to more compact specifications
— Existing plant can be used to treat greater quantities of sludge
— Existing digesters can be operated at increased solids retention times.

The advantages accruing from the final implication are that there is (a) an increased gas production and (b) a smaller volume of sludge for final disposal [5.32] (see Fig. 5.11).

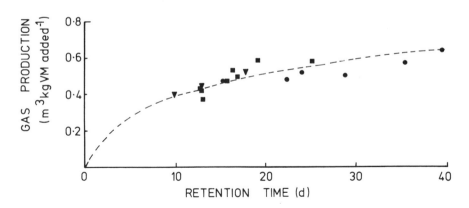

Fig. 5.11 — The effect of retention time on the production of gas in anaerobic sludge digesters: Works A ▼; Works B ■; Works C ●.

Whatever the design basis, it is essential that the chemistry of the digester contents be monitored regularly and key parameters maintained with recognised limits. The main control parameters are volatile fatty acids, alkalinity and pH. The former should be maintained below 200–500 mg l^{-1} (measured as acetic acid). At concentrations above this, methanogenic activity can be inhibited. The acceptable range for bicarbonate alkalinities is 3500–5000 mg l^{-1} whilst that for pH is 7.0–7.5. There is normally no need for pH adjustments to be made as there should be a natural buffering capacity within the reactor due to the interactions between ammonium and bicarbonate ions. If it is necessary to enhance this, carbonate/bicarbonate can be added. However, it must be remembered that alkali metal ions can be toxic at high concentrations, the limits being 3.5–5.0 g l^{-1} for sodium and 2.5–4.5 g l^{-1} for potassium.

Other toxic agents which can be present in sludge are heavy metal ions, detergents and chlorinated hydrocarbons (Table 5.9). The best control

Table 5.9 — Concentrations of toxic materials causing significant inhibition (20%) of the digestion process [5.12]

Toxin	Concentration (mg kg^{-1}DS)
Chloroform	15
Trichlorethane	20
Carbon tetrachloride	200
Nickel	2000
Cadmium	2200
Copper	2700
Zinc	3400
Anionic detergent	15 000–20 000

strategy is to limit the concentrations of these materials in the sewage which produces the sludge by controlling the trade effluent discharges to the sewers. However, in formulating any trade effluent control policy it must be noted that the effect of toxic agents appears to be additive [5.33]. Although the absolute gas production rates will vary from plant to plant and, as such, cannot be used as a measure of plant performance, any significant decrease in gas yield can be taken as indicative of a potential problem. The composition of the gas can also be used in the same way, a rise in the carbon dioxide level being a distinct warning signal [5.31].

The gas that is normally produced from sludge digestion will contain 65–70 percent methane and its gross calorific value (CV) can be estimated from $CV = (334 \times \text{methane percentage})$ kJ m^{-3}, in other words, 22–24 MJ m^{-3}. The way in which the potential of this energy is realised will depend on the plant and local circumstances. If it is not merely burnt in a flare, it can be used to maintain the digester temperature, to generate electricity or even as an automotive fuel. However, as the usage becomes more sophisticated, so the costs needed to realise the energy potential increase.

Whatever option is selected for using the gas, adequate safety precautions must be enforced. A suitable Code of Practice is that published by the British Anaerobic and Biomass Association [5.34].

As can be seen from the data in Table 5.10, the performance of anaerobic

Table 5.10 — Typical performance data for mesophilic anaerobic digesters

Loading rate (kg VDS m^{-3} d^{-1})	1.0–1.7	1.27–1.36	0.97–1.36	1,09–2.5
Retention time (d)	19–23	31–33	18.5–28.1	15–40
Reduction in VDS (%)	47–54	47–50	36–47	36–44
Gas yield (m^3 kg Δ VDS)	0.83–1.18	1.07–1.25	0.84–1.22	1.22–1.44
Reference	IWPC	Booker	Eves	Hemsley and
	[5.12]	[5.35]	[5.30]	Lattern [5.36]

digesters is remarkably consistent. Even so, current philosophies hold that improvements to the process can be achieved in terms of economics and cost-efficiency [5.31; 5.37]. The capital costs of digesters designed and constructed on a 'conventional' basis are given by [5.38]:

$$\text{Civil costs} \quad (\text{£'000}) \left\{ \begin{array}{l} = 0.57 \times (\text{digester capacity})^{0.69} \quad (5.10) \\ = 0.47 \times (\text{digester capacity})^{0.72} \quad (5.11) \end{array} \right.$$
$$\text{Mechanical costs}$$

These costs (third quarter, 1976) are based on a retention time of 30 days and a feedstock solids concentration of 4.5%. Significant savings in these capital costs can be achieved by using prefabricated or 'package' digesters [5.37; 5.39]. The construction details of this type of modular unit are provided by Noone *et al.* [5.37] and performance data (for an 18 000 population-equivalent plant) by Bradford *et al.* [5.40]. These data show that a package-digester can achieve performances that are quite comparable with those produced by conventional digesters. If the solids concentration of sludge after the digestion period is too low, then post-digestion consolidation will be necessary. In fact many of the digesters operated in the UK are two-tank systems [5.10]: a fully covered, fully anaerobic tank and a final consolidation tank (Fig. 5.12) which may or may not be covered. Digested sludge consolidates less readily than most primary sludges and therefore secondary digesters tend to function poorly as thickeners. The main reasons for this are continued gas evolution and micro-bubble hold-up.

Of the various techniques that have been suggested for improving solid/

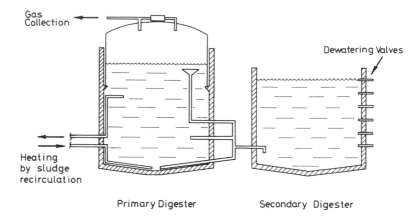

Fig. 5.12 — Typical arrangement for the two-stage digestion of sludge.

liquid separation, some form of aeration has been found to be the most promising [5.10]. Various types of aeration device have been used — coarse bubble, venturis, surface aerators — and using aeration intensities of 0.5–5 m^3 air m^{-3} sludge h^{-1} for periods of 2 h, a 50% volumetric reduction of a 2.5% (DS) sludge was achieved in 10 days or less. This must be compared with the period of 90–100 days to thicken an unaerated sludge to the same extent. The sludge pH appears to be an important feature. During aeration, this increases to a value of > 8.0 as carbon dioxide is stripped from solution. This elevation prevents any further production of methane gas during the thickening process. It is essential, therefore, that the thickening stage is completed before the pH drops to a level where methanogenesis can recommence. It would appear that this process can take 5–7 days. Similar results to those reported by Hurley *et al.* [5.10] have been described by Price and Alder [5.32]. However, it cannot be said that the process has been fully optimised in terms of aeration intensity, aeration time or the depth of aeration/settlement tank.

Anaerobic digestion can also be operated in the thermophilic range (50–55°C). This process can achieve digestion in a shorter time and with a higher gas production than a comparable mesophilic digester [5.41]. However, as a process, it has had little commercial success.

5.3.5   Aerobic digestion
Sludges may also be digested aerobically, the ultimate objective being to effect stabilisation of the sludge solids. The basic process requirements are good aeration, good mixing and an aeration time which is sufficient for the putrescible organic matter to be oxidised by bacterial respiration. Although aerobic digestion has been studied for over 25 years and although it is used considerably in North America, is is not a process which has had any real popularity in the UK. However, the development of auto-heating, thermophilic digestion appears to be changing these attitudes [5.42]. Auto-heating,

arguably the most interesting aspect of aerobic digestion, is the ability of aeration (or oxygenation) to induce a significant temperature rise in the sludge. This increase in temperature is caused by free energy being released as organic matter is converted to new cell material. The total energy released (F, kcal l^{-1}) can be calculated from $\Delta F = 3.5E(\Delta COD)$, where E is the efficiency of the retention of heat and COD has units of g l^{-1}. Since the heat released, expressed as kcal l^{-1}, is approximately equal to the temperature change and since the thermal efficiency (E) is about 70 per cent [5.43], the temperature rise that is achieved (T) can be expressed as $T = 2.4(COD)$.

The requirements for auto-heating have been summarised by Jewell and Kabrick [5.43]. They are:

(a) There should be sufficient biogradable organics in the incoming sludge to generate between 25 and 35 kcal l^{-1}.
(b) Oxygen transfer efficiencies should exceed 10 per cent (that is to say, more than 10 per cent of the oxygen supplied should be used in the biochemical reactions).
(c) The reactors should be well insulated.
(d) The product of temperature and sludge retention time should exceed 150 degree-days [5.44].

As can be seen from the data in Table 5.11, the process of digestion can be

Table 5.11 — Performance data for auto-thermal aerobic digestion.

Reference	Loading rates		ΔT (°C)	Δ VSS (%)
	(kg VS $m^{-3} d^{-1}$)	(kg COD $m^{-3} d^{-1}$)		
Cohen [5.44][a]	6.9–9.6	—	13–23	34–47
Jewell and Kabrick [5.45][a]	10	—	40	40
Matsch and Drnevich [5.43][b]	6.1–8.5	—	36	30–45
Morgan et al. [5.47][b]	—	6.8–15.7	37–39	36–52
Booth and Tramontini [5.46][a]	3.4–7.7	—	40–50	17–25

[a] Oxygenation.
[b] Aeration.

fuelled either by air or by oxygen. Both systems can achieve and maintain thermophilic conditions, using retention times ranging from 3 to 10 days, and can achieve a significant reduction in the concentration of volatile solids in the sludge. The Environmental Protection Agency have set the criterion for successful digestion as being a 40 per cent reduction in volatile solids (VS) and, in general, the systems used as the source of the data given in Table 5.11 can meet this standard. However, there are many yardsticks by which sludge stability can be judged [5.22]. These include the oxygen uptake rate of the ultimate sludge (<1.5 mg oxygen g^{-1} VS h^{-1}), the BOD of the sludge (< 0.2 kg BOD kg^{-1} VS) and the development of odours by sludge stored at 25°C. Certainly the results reported by Booth and Tramontini [5.46] indicate that their system is capable of producing an end-product which meets the BOD 'standard'. The data presented by Morgan and his co-workers [5.47] do not contain BOD measurements but their COD values (1.77 kg COD kg^{-1}VS) are not dissimilar to those of Booth and Tramontini (1.23 kg COD kg^{-1}VS). It is not unreasonable, therefore, to suppose that the BOD values are also similar. If this is the case, then the aerobic thermophilic process does produce stable sludges; in addition, it achieves a high removal of pathogens.

There are two possible disadvantages to the process. The first is that it does produce a sludge whose dewatering characteristics are not good, relative to the initial sludge. The second is that this type of digestion, as opposed to the anaerobic process, does consume energy. Typical values for the energy consumption are 0.7–4.4 kWh kg^{-1} VS oxidised [5.46; 5.47]. It can be seen, therefore, that thermophilic aerobic digestion can provide a degree of sludge stabilisation that is similar to that achieved by mesophilic anaerobic digestion. This means that there may be a need to choose between these processes. A comparison by Riegler [5.48] suggests that anaerobic digestion should be the choice at large treatment works ($> 50\ 000$ population) whilst aerobic digestion would be more appropriate for smaller units. Franzen and Hakanson [5.49] offer a similar suggestion. Although performance data are available for individual units, there is also a need for generalised scale-up and optimisation procedures.

5.4   SLUDGE DISPOSAL

5.4.1   Land disposal
In the EEC countries some 6×10^6 tonnes (DS) of sludge are produced each year and about 30 per cent of this is disposed of to agricultural land [5.4]. There can be significant benefits from doing this in terms of both crop productivity and land reclamation [5.50]. Digested sludge, considered as a slurry, will typically contain nitrogen, phosphorus and potassium in the following elemental concentrations (expressed on a dry solids basis) [5.51]:

N = 5.1%
P = 1.6%
K = 0.4%

The availability of this nitrogen to crops is 50–85 per cent whilst that of the phosphorus is 20–100 per cent (compared to superphosphate). Liquid digested sludge, therefore, has a definite manurial value in terms of these elements. Other types of sludge contain lower nutrient concentrations and are, thus, less attractive to farmers. No sludges contain much potassium and, therefore, sewage sludge cannot be considered as a complete fertiliser. Nevertheless, the application of sludge to agricultural land can enhance crop yields [5.50].

There are two problems associated with this practice: the dissemination of pathogens and the presence of toxic elements in the sludge. The spread of pathogens can certainly be controlled by applying some form of disinfectant process to the sludge before allowing it to go to land (see Section 5.4). However, such processes are not, at the moment, used very often in the UK. Rather the philosophy is to employ a combination of stabilisation and restriction. The stabilisation processes accepted by the UK 'guidelines' [5.51] are digestion, storage or the use of lime. The restrictions stipulate no grazing intervals and time limits for the growing and harvesting of certain crops. Alternatively, sludge can be buried or injected below the soil surface, thus ensuring that pathogens cannot come in contact with crops or grass. This also prevents odour problems. Officially, two pathogens are of concern: *Salmonella* spp. and the human beef tapeworm [5.52]. However, other pathogenic species, particularly parasites, may also be present in sludge, for example *Brucella abortus* [5.53] and *Ascaris suum* [5.54]. Although there is concern about salmonellosis, it would appear that the UK 'guidelines' are quite adequate for the control of this disease. In Britain, only one outbreak in food animals has been specifically associated with sludge disposal. Moreover, this all but negligible figure is not due to inadequate surveillance. The Zoonoses Order, 1975 makes salmonellosis in food animals a notifiable disease and, as such, subject to veterinary investigation. It is, perhaps, not an exaggeration to say that in Britain there is not a *Salmonella* problem. The prevalence of parasitic worms in the human population of the UK is not known precisely, since even when detected the disease is not one which is notifiable. However, it is not thought to be widespread. The occurrence in food animals is detectable on slaughtering and, on this basis, is not considered to be particularly widespread in the UK. In other countries this is not the case. The philosophy of disease control by stabilisation/restriction is also effective for deactivating worm eggs in sludge, provided that the restriction phase is properly applied [5.52]. Anaerobic digestion does destroy the infectivity of eggs and deactivation also occurs during the 'no-grazing' interval.

The problems associated with metal ions in sludge and the control procedures adopted for minimising the environment impact have been reviewed by Matthews [5.1]. Only a broad outline of the procedure will, therefore, be given in terms of limits. Thus, the application of toxic elements is controlled at a rate such that the concentration of any toxic element in the soil does not exceed the limit concentration above which its effect is pronounced or unacceptable. Alternatively, a limit may be placed on the concentration of specific metals in the sludge. In making this type of assessment, two toxicological effects must be considered: the phytotoxicity which reduces crop quality and yield, and the zootoxicity whereby metals accumulate in crops to levels which are toxic during the consumption of those crops. The metals which are thought to be significant and the limit concentrations selected vary from country to country. For example, the Federal Republic of Germany specifies a sludge concentration for cadmium of 20 mg kg^{-1} whilst in Denmark the limit is 8 mg kg^{-1}. The UK 'guidelines' place limits on a range of elements. These limits vary with the type of land receiving the sludge (Table 5.12) and are based on a 30-year application

Table 5.12 — Elemental application rates for various metal concentrations

	Limit rate[a] (kg ha^{-1})	Concentration in sludge (mg kg^{-1})	Concentration in soil (mg kg^{-1})	Elemental application rate (tonnes ha^{-1} y^{-1})
Zinc	560	1650	40	$\frac{560-(2.2\times40)}{1650}\times\frac{1000}{30}=9.5$
Cadmium	5	34	1	$\frac{5-(2.2\times1)}{34}\times\frac{1000}{30}=2.7$
Lead	1000	150	30	$\frac{1000-(2.2\times30)}{150}\times\frac{1000}{30}=207.6$
Copper	280	400	15	$\frac{280-(2.2\times15)}{400}\times\frac{1000}{30}=19.7$
Nickel	70	30	10	$\frac{70-(2.2\times10)}{30}\times\frac{1000}{30}=53.3$
Zinc Equivalent	560	2690	150	$\frac{560-(2.2\times150)}{2690}\times\frac{1000}{30}=2.9$

[a] From UK 'guidelines'.

period and an active soil depth (for arable land) of 0.2 m. The application rate for any element is calculated from:

$$\text{Rate (tonnes DS ha}^{-1}\text{y}^{-1}) = \frac{A-B}{C}\times\frac{1000}{D} \qquad (5.12)$$

where A = addition limit (from Table 5.12)
B = concentration of available element in soil, kg ha^{-1}
   = 2.2(concentration in mg $^{-1}$DS)
C = total concentration in the sludge, mg kg $^{-1}$DS
D = application period (i.e. 30 years)

The permissible sludge application rate is then fixed by the lowest elemental rate. This concept does assume an equal yearly rate over the 30-year period. However, this can be exceeded. Up to one-fifth of the total amount can be added in one application, but after such an addition no more can be added until the running average drops to the 30-year average.

The metal which is probably of greatest concern is cadmium. Indeed, the US Federal regulations give detailed criteria only for this element. The main concern with cadmium is its zootoxicity [5.55]. On the basis of the review presented by Matthews [5.1], the other metals which must be considered as significant are copper, zinc and nickel. These are phytotoxic elements and, since their effect can be additive, are frequently considered together. However, there is debate as to the precise values for their comparative toxicities, hence the concept of zinc equivalent (ZE),

$$ZE = Zn + 2Cu + 8Ni \tag{5.13}$$

which is based on the comparative toxicity values of 1:2:8, is now used only in the UK. However, if it is necessary to assess the phytotoxicity of these, or any other, elements, a method has been suggested by Davis *et al.* [5.56]. This is based on the length of root generated by specific varieties of maize and barley in pot-trials.

The proper use of the various national regulations/guidelines can, therefore, prevent sludge being a vector for the dissemination of either pathogens or toxic elements into the environment. What is perhaps of concern is whether metal contamination of sludges will result in their being applied at such low rates that the sludge is unacceptable to the farmer (i.e. the sludge applications are providing insufficient nitrogen). Under these circumstances, even more stringent trade effluent control would be required to prevent toxic metals entering the sewerage system. However, this merely moves the problem from one of sewage sludge disposal to one of a concentrated industrial sludge disposal, which has its own specific difficulties. What is needed is some means of reclaiming the metals from industrial sludges or of detoxifying biological sludges.

5.4.2 Sea disposal

The use of the sea for sludge disposal is an important aspect of UK strategy with some 10×10^6 wet tonnes year being dumped in this way. Other European countries are less enthusiastic about this approach [5.4; 5.57]. The disposal of sludge (and other solids) is controlled by means of annual licences issued by the Ministry of Agriculture, Fisheries and Food (in England and Wales). These licences, which specify the dumping location together with the quantity and quality of the material being dumped, are drafted so as to conform to the requirements of two international agreements: the London Convention and the Oslo Convention. In this way, the indiscriminate dumping of toxic material is prevented. Any potential impact on the marine environment is controlled, by regular monitoring. The results of these surveys suggest that sludge dumping has no significant effect on the marine biota [5.58; 5.59]. In the light of these conclusions there is a need to question whether any EEC ban on sea dumping, which, according to Calcutt and Moss [5.4], would cost the UK Water Industry an additional £30 × 10⁶ per year, can be tolerated.

5.4.3 Incineration

Although incineration is not widely used in the UK, it plays a significant part in the sludge disposal strategies of several European countries (e.g. France, 30%; Denmark, 10%). However, there are situations, in the UK, where there is a no real alternative, other routes being unavailable or the sludge being seriously contaminated. There are esssentially two designs for sludge incineration: the multiple hearth and the fluidised bed. Details of the design and operational criteria for these incinerators may be found elsewhere [5.60–5.62]. Whichever design is used, one of the major considerations will be the energy balance of the process and the requirement for supplementary fuel. Thus, there is a need to assess the energy content of the sludge. This can be done in terms of its calorific value or its heat release potential. According to Jank [5.63], the calorific value (C) of sludges may be calculated from:

$$C = 260.5V - 1537 \text{ kJ kg}^{-1}\text{DS} \qquad (5.14)$$

where V = volatile matter (%). The heat release potential (H) may be found [5.61] from:

$$H = \frac{C \times d}{100 - d} \qquad (5.15)$$

where d = dry solids concentration (%). This latter parameter is important as it determines whether or not the sludge is autothermal. The minimal conditions for autothermicity are a heat release potential of 5400 kJ kg^{-1} of water to be evaporated [5.61]. It is therefore essential that both the solids concentration and the organic/volatile fraction are as large as possible. In this context, it is better to incinerate raw sludge since digested sludge has lost some of its energy potential in the form of biogas (see Table 5.13). Also, consideration can be given to increasing the organic content by incorporating oily sludges from industry.

5.5 SLUDGE SANITISATION

5.5.1 Pasteurisation

This is a process which is used mainly in Switzerland and West Germany to control the dissemination of *Salmonella* during the application of sludge to agricultural land. The basic requirements are that the sludge should be heated to 70°C and held at this temperature for 30 min. The designs and operating conditions of the various processes currently available have been discussed in detail by Huber and Mihalyfy [5.66]. Only a summary (Table 5.14) will therefore be given here. The reactors can be operated as either

Table 5.13 — Typical calorific values of sewage sludge

Sludge type	Reference	Calorific value (kJ kg^{-1} DS)	
		a	b
Cake (vacuum filter)	Dickens et al. [5.62]	—	11350–19400
Cake (filter press)	Smith et al. [5.64]	15 792	15 228
Cake (filter press)	Tench et al. [5.65]	25 040	—

[a] As reported.
[b] Calculated from Equation 5.14.

Table 5.14 — Pasteurisation processes (summarised from Huber and Mihalyfy [5.66])

Process	Type	Througput (m^3 d^{-1})	Energy Requirements	
			Heat (MJ m^{-3})	Electrical (kWh m^{-3})
Sulzer	Batch	—	134–160	2.4–5.4
Alpha	Batch	30–40	105–147	6.5–9.0
CFP	Batch	3–20	120–160	2.4–4.0
MTS	Semi-continuous	4–9[a]	—	1.4–1.8
Alfa Laval	Continuous	4[a]	130	3.6

[a] m^3 h^{-1}.

batch or continuous processes, the heating usually being achieved by sequential heat exchangers. Heat exchange units are also used to recover energy after pasteurisation. This reduces costs and also brings the sludge temperature down to a level which is compatible with mesophilic anaerobic digestion (see Section 5.2.4). The inclusion of digestion as a post-pasteurisation process has been found to be necessary to prevent the regrowth of enterobacteria. On the basis of the Swiss experiences, pasteurisation is quite capable of achieving the legal limit of 100 enterobacteria g^{-1}. In addition, it was found that parasitic eggs were rendered non-viable.

An alternative concept is currently being evaluated in Germany and the UK. This process is based on burning biogas in the sludge using submerged combustion units [5.67]. The operational conditions which the UK reactor is aiming to achieve are a temperature of 55°C and a holding time of 3 h.

5.5.2 Heat treatment

This process uses much more severe conditions than those dictated by pasteurisation — typically a high pressure and a temperature of about 200°C. The main objectives of heat treatment are:

— to condition the sludge prior to dewatering
— to produce solids which are inert and stable

The process can certainly condition sludges well. Everett [5.68] has shown that heat treatment can reduce the specific resistance to filtration from 1000 × 10^{11} to 1 × 10^{11} m kg^{-1} for activated sludge and from 10 × 10^{11} to 0.5 × 10^{11} m kg^{-1} for digested sludge. However, the author is not aware of there having been any bacteriological studies on heat treated sludges, although the conditions are such that the resultant sludge ought to be sterile.

As a process, heat treatment no longer has any great popularity in the UK. It is, however, used in France and Germany. At the Bottrop Plant, sludge is preheated in steps to 195°C at a pressure of 15 bar before being passed to the main reactor, the operating conditions of which are:

temperature	220°C
pressure	25 bar
conditioning time	30 min
steam consumption	70 kg m^{-3} sludge
throughput	3 × 80 m^3 h^{-1}

A major problem with the heat treatment process is the strength of the liquors. These can have COD values as high as 25000 mg l^{-1} and allowance must be made for this load in designing the main bio-oxidation stage. However, it must be recognised that the biodegradability of heat treatment liquors is not great and that, therefore, a residue of organic carbon will remain after treatment.

5.5.3 Thermophilic digestion

Thermophilic digestion, be it aerobic or anaerobic (see Sections 5.2.5 and 5.2.4), will achieve a significant degree of sanitisation. Current philosophies indicate that aerobic digestion would be the preferred process. The effect of this type of digestion on the numbers of *Salmonella* spp. in sludge is, therefore, shown in Table 5.15.

5.5.4 Irradiation

The use of irradiation to produce sterile material is now not uncommon (e.g. foodstuffs, medical disposables). It was, therefore, quite logical to examine the potential of irradiation for producing sludges with significantly reduced pathogen and parasite concentrations. In commercial terms this meant the use of radionuclide sources (cobalt-60 and caesium-137) and electron beam (EB) accelerators. Both Co-60 and EB machines are currently available. Units based on Cs-137 should, however, be considered as processes of the

Table 5.15 — Effect of aerobic thermophilic digestion on the numbers of *Salmonella* spp. in sludge

Reference	Temperature (°C)	*Salmonella* count	
		Raw	Digested
Morgan *et al.*	54	2250[a]	0[a]
[5.47]	52	5150[a]	0[a]
	46	1400[a]	6[a]
Booth and Tramontini	68	1700[b]	0[b]
[5.46]	69	2500[b]	0[b]

[a] MPN.
[b] Number per 100 ml.

future, although there is a commercial Cs-137 plant for the disinfection of sludge at Albuquerque, New Mexico and test plants elsewhere in the USA. The development and design of all these processes, in relation to sludge treatment, have been reviewed by White [5.69] and the basic characteristics of their radiations are summarised in Table 5.16. Perhaps the main points to

Table 5.16 — Summary of irradiation methods

Method	Emission	Energy (MeV)	Half-life (years)
Co-60	γ-rays	1.17 and 1.33	5.27
Cs-137	γ-rays	0.66	30
EB	β-rays	1.5[a]	—

[a] Typical value.

note are that Cs-137 has a much longer decay half-life than Cs-60 and that the energy of the γ-rays emitted by Cs-137 are lower than those of Cs-60. This means that, although Cs-137 would need to be replaced less often, about four times as much would be required initially to give the same output as a Co-60 source.

Whilst it is accepted that it is the total absorbed dose which determines the extent of death or inactivation, there does appear to be some disagreement over the design dose for sludge disinfection plants. Plants have been designed to give dosages of both 0.3 and 0.4 Mrad (1 Gy = 100 rad) whilst official studies have recommended that at least 0.5 Mrad should be used for liquid sludges and 1.0 Mrad for dry solids [5.69]. To a certain extent, the dose will depend on the operational conditions and the species involved. The susceptibility of individual species is assessed as the absorbed dose (krad) needed to reduce the population by 90 per cent — the D_{10} value. Typical values are given in Table 5.17. However, it must be recognised that factors such as dissolved oxygen, temperature and the presence of other chemicals can produce synergistic effects. Thus, the inactivation of *Streptococcus faecalis* by a dose of 0.4 Mrad is tenfold greater in digested sludge than in raw sludge [5.70].

The process costs of the three types of irradiation have been examined by White [5.69]. Some of these results are summarised in Table 5.18 and show that, in cost terms, Cs-137 has a distinct advantage. However, the dosage, the type of sludge and the throughput (both existing and projected) will influence the unit costs. The selection of the irradiation process is, therefore, site-specific. In more general terms, the cost of irradiating sludge is comparable with that of pasteurisation. Irradiation processes, however, do produce some beneficial side-effects in the form of a better settlement of the final stage and lower BOD concentrations in the sludge liquors.

The irradiation of sludge must certainly, therefore, be thought of as a viable process for disinfection. What is not absolutely clear at the moment is whether disinfection is necessary. In the UK, this degree of pathogen removal is not thought to be needed. However, EEC philosophies do support disinfection and in the USA the need for sludge disinfection is also recognised, irradiation being specifically mentioned (although this is linked with the beneficial use of by-product Cs-137). Much of the development work has, therefore, been done in these countries, in Canada and in Japan [5.73–5.78].

5.6   SLUDGE UTILISATION

Although the application of sludge to agricultural land may be considered as using sludge, there are limitations to the quantities of sludge that can be used in this way. These limitations stem from the presence of toxic metal ions and trace organic compounds. Furthermore, there is a philosophy which argues that the complex chemicals in sludge (both matrix and biomass) should not be discarded so lightly. The potential uses of sludge were reviewed over a decade ago [5.79] and from time to time during the intervening period suggestions have been made to supplement or enhance ideas [e.g. 5.80; 5.81]. However, few, if any, of these have matured beyond the suggestion stage. It could therefore be argued that developments (to commercial processes) in the following areas:

— sludge detoxification
— direct product recovery
— conversion to secondary products

constitute the greatest biotechnological challenges in the field of sludge processing.

Table 5.17 — D_{10}-values for biological species relevant to sludge disposal

Species	D_{10} (krad)	Reference
Escherichia coli, K12	27	
Salmonella tryphimurium, LT2	16	Massachusetts
S. tryphimurium, R6008	105	Institute of
Streptococcus faecalis	125	Technology [5.70]
Poliovirus, type 2	185	
Ascaris ova	45–62	Yeager and O'Brien [5.71]
Spore-forming bacteria	192	Carrington and Harman [5.72]

Table 5.18 — Energy requirements and costs for a throughput of 130 m^3 d^{-1} and a dose of 0.3 Mrad (from White [5.69])

	Energy	Cost ($£m^{-3}$)[b]
Co-60	460 kCi	0.95
Electron beam	1.3×10^6 kWh[a]	1.06
Cs-137	1840 kCi	0.58

[a] Yearly basis.
[b] Amortised over 20 years.

5.7 LANDFILL TECHNOLOGY: AN INTRODUCTION

Regardless of the method of waste treatment, a solid residue almost always remains for ultimate disposal, traditionally by landfill. Currently, there are plenty of landfill sites available, and, in spite of the fact that the volume of waste produced per head tends to increase with time [5.82], this situation is likely to continue; the only problem will be the increasing isolation and distancing of the site from the waste source, leading to an increase in uncontrolled tipping. This, even in 1984, was reported to account for 10.3, 17.5 and 35% of the total wastes disposed of in France, Greece and Eire, respectively [5.83].

With increasing populations consuming finite resources, there has been emphasis on investigating the possibilities of recycling waste materials. However, it is now evident that even with current technology, mere disposal of solid waste to landfill represents a saving of at least 65% when compared with any reprocessing operation [5.84] and this disposal route is therefore favoured at present. Moreover, with the recognition that a valuable energy source, methane, can be generated in high volumes from emplaced wastes, emphasis is now swinging towards the recovery of this gas, and site practices have changed accordingly.

Whichever way landfill sites are viewed, whether for ultimate disposal, or as anaerobic filters (for liquid effluent treatment) of anaerobic digesters (for the generation of methane), full control and exploitation of the bioreactor will never be achieved without a much more complete understanding of the fundamental microbiology and biochemistry of the refuse catabolic processes. It is particularly unfortunate, therefore, that in spite of an increasing number of papers on landfill, there is still very little fundamental information of this type available. Thus, although this problem was clearly recognised by Filip and Küster in 1979 [5.85] and restated by Jones and Grainger in 1985 [5.86], even now few definitive studies have been reported.

5.8 REFUSE COMPOSITION, LANDFILL SITES AND REFUSE EMPLACEMENT STRATEGIES

The composition of refuse differs between countries and cultures, and also with time [e.g. 5.85; 5.86]. Thus, although in developed countries refuse composition is likely to become ever more uniform, significant differences are at present apparent even over relatively short distances. For instance, even within the UK, plastics, and vegetable and putrescible wastes account respectively for 7 and 25% of the refuse of England and Wales compared with 11 and 18% in Central Scotland [5.82].

Examination of the chemical composition of refuse [e.g. 5.86; 5.87] shows that the biodegradable fraction, which has been increasing with time, currently approximates to 70% of the total. Recent trends in foodstuff marketing methods suggest that plastics and paper will be increasingly responsible for future compositional changes. Elemental changes could therefore result, with a possibility of nitrogen and/or phosphorus limitation [5.88], leading to protracted periods of landfill stabilisation.

The primary objective of site selection or design is to protect surface and ground waters. One way to achieve this is by containment of the waste within an impermeable barrier. Materials considered for this possible use include clays, fine grain soils, soil/cement admixes, concrete, asphaltic compositions and polymeric membranes. One examination of leachate migration through three clays (kaolinite, montmorillonite and illite) found that the most important factors for predicting metal-ion permeability were solution pH, ionic composition and the clay's ion exchange capacity [5.89]. However, permeability tests must be made under realistic conditions. For instance, hydraulic conductivities of clay liners can be 10–1000 times higher than values obtained in laboratory tests on either undisturbed or recompacted samples of the material. Indeed, Lee and Jones [5.90] reported that there is no demonstrated evidence that a few feet of clay can provide long-term containment for wastes, and concluded that without pretreatment this method of disposal could pose a greater threat to public health than the burial of many radioactive wastes of equivalent toxicity. As an alternative to containment, aquifers may be protected by attentuation involving slow leachate migration through, for example, silt.

Although refuse emplacement strategies vary considerably from country to country, the trend in the UK is towards covering the material at the end of the working day, in other words, a cell emplacement strategy. Analogies between a honeycombed landfill site (which contains a multitude of solid-state closed cultures) and more conventional fermenters are therefore not valid. Landfill systems are extremely complex, since they can be irregularly stratified both horizontally and vertically at irregular time intervals [5.91]. Consequently they are subject to multidirectional temperature, gas, liquid, Eh, pH, enzyme activity, electron acceptor and vectorial solute flow gradients. Further complicating factors include molecular properties such as water solubility, lipid/water partition coefficients, volatility, molecular size, charge, shape and functional groups, microbial attachment, interspecies interactions, bi-directional diffusion across oxic–anoxic interfaces, overlapping habitats and activity-domains of microbial species and the various interfaces which occur. Mixed, interdependent microbial systems are a feature of landfill sites, occurring particularly as attached growth containing close associations of diverse species on nutrient-rich solid surfaces. These associations are strongly influenced by chemical gradients, particularly of electron donors and acceptors and hydrogen.

5.9   REFUSE DEGRADATION

Before transportation to the site, refuse can be subjected to processing, e.g. milling, shredding, and baling [5.92], which may ultimately exert considerable influence on landfill catabolic processes. In a typical landfill in which cell emplacement strategy has been employed, the site as a whole acts as a series of batch cultures at various stages of decomposition subjected to dramatic changes due to random perturbations by, for example, the ingression of oxygen-containing water or xenobiotic molecules. In this case, a simple model would be an individual batch culture with the results interpreted for the site as a whole but with due regard to the time sequence of filling. Alternatively, for the more traditional landfill (progressively filled without daily cover), a fed batch model with repeated seeding of invertebrate and microbial inocula could be used.

Initially refuse catabolism, accompanied by physical and chemical reactions, is dominated by aerobic processes during which labile molecules are rapidly degraded by a range of invertebrates (mites, millipedes, isopods, nematodes and eutrachids) and microbial species (fungi, bacteria and actinomycetes); see Chapter 4. Mixotrophic substrate utilisation is then replaced by sequential catabolism as macromolecules such as lignocelluloses, lignin, tannins and melanins are slowly dissimilated, provided that oxygen does not become limiting. The actual length of this period varies considerably and in part depends on the preliminary processing which can alter the availability of oxygen. The most successful method of assessing the extent of decomposition depends on the differing rates of catabolism of cellulose and lignin [5.86]. Thus, cellulose:lignin ratio estimates of 4.0, 0.9–1.2 and 0.2 have been reported for unfermented refuse, active or partially stabilised landfill and well stabilised landfill respectively, as the lignin component becomes progressively more recalcitrant. Clearly the semi-recalcitrant polymer content increases with time. Xenobiotics behave similarly; their effective degradation is more likely under aerobic conditions and may involve constitutive or inducible enzymes, co-metabolism, plasmid transfer, mutations, and other mechanisms of genetic transfer. Ultimately, C:N organic fraction ratios of $\geqslant$ 55:1 can be achieved, possibly limiting to aerobic breakdown mechanisms.

During this stage, the raised temperature (up to 80°C) and the presence of abiotic antimicrobial molecules result in the death or inactivation of pathogens such as *Salmonella* spp. and Polio Virus type 1 [5.93], insect larvae and plant seeds. Thus, temperature has been used as an indicator of landfill behaviour [5.94]. Although temperature increases have the positive effect of accelerating microbial activity and growth, there is also the negative effect of reduced solubility of the limiting oxygen. Carbon dioxide, in turn, can also influence metabolic rate by effecting a pH reduction, although this can in fact promote polymer hydrolysis. Finally, the significant production of water by microbial metabolism [e.g. 5.95] can add considerably to the site water balance.

The *in situ* depletion of molecular oxygen results in a slowing of heat production, and oxygen entry by convection is correspondingly diminished. Simultaneously, the accumulation of carbon dioxide during the composting stage establishes microaerophilic conditions which select for enrichment firstly of facultative anaerobic bacteria and then of obligate anaerobes as the redox conditions become suitably reduced. It is perhaps fortunate that these species do not suffer from the same nitrogen and phosphorus element limitations as the aerobes. Unlike aerobic metabolism (where complete mineralisation is often achieved by a single bacterial species), anoxic dissimilation characteristically requires the cooperative metabolism of a mixed population. These interacting microbial associations are able to use a variety of inorganic acceptors, often in sequence according to the energy liberated from a common electron donor. Since most of the bacteria require a specific electron acceptor, the sequence leads to distinct changes in bacterial populations. Species able to use the more oxidised acceptors gain a thermodynamic, and thus a kinetic, advantage.

During hydrolysis and fermentation, fermentative bacteria (which require no external electron acceptor, and therefore do not depend on gradients of acceptors) hydrolyse polymers such as polysaccharides, lipids, protein and nucleic acids and ferment the resulting monomers to gaseous metabolites such as hydrogen and carbon dioxide, and to straight- and branched-chain fatty acids together with compounds such as ethanol, lactate and succinate. Product distribution of the individual compounds can vary considerably and depends on a number of interrelated factors such as redox potential, growth rate, molecular configuration and hydrogen concentration. Filip and Küster [5.85] found that associations between fermentative bacteria and those which catabolise their products are often very close, since fermentation reactions are usually only thermodynamically possible at very low concentrations of hydrogen. Even without inhibition, hydrogen concentration still often influences the reaction. For example, at low concentrations, the balance is shifted towards more oxidised products (particularly acetate) and more energy is conserved as ATP, an effect also seen when low concentrations of lactate are maintained [5.96]. Both sulphate-reducing and methanogenic bacteria thus play key roles by removing toxic metabolites, directing electron flow to reduced end-products and enhancing growth rates, whilst, at the same time, supplying essential growth factors [5.97].

In acetogenesis, there are two types of acetogenic bacteria (see Chapter 2), the hydrogen-producing acetogens, which gain energy for growth by completely dissimilating alcohols and organic acids into acetic acid and hydrogen (and occasionally carbon dioxide), and the homoacetogens, which catabolise carbohydrates, hydrogen and carbon dioxide or one-carbon compounds into acetic acid [5.97]. The major difference between the two types of acetogen is that the hydrogen-producers must grow in co-culture with an obligate hydrogen sink bacterium (such as a nitrate reducer, sulphate reducer or methanogen) to maintain a low partial pressure of hydrogen [e.g. 5.98], otherwise inhibitory fatty acids accumulate.

In methanogenesis, the carbon dioxide utilising methanogens are limited in two ways. Firstly, anoxic landfill sites generally lack high concentrations of inorganic electron acceptors, such as nitrate and sulphate. Secondly, homoacetogens can also consume carbon dioxide by reduction to acetic acid, thus competing with the methanogens for hydrogen. To date, eight substrates have been reported for methogenic bacteria, of which four, carbon dioxide/hydrogen, acetic acid, methanol and trimethylamine, have been confirmed for landfill (G. B. Kasali, unpublished observations).

The electron donor and electron acceptor components of emplaced material direct the way in which the various metabolic groups of organisms will interact. The situation is made even more complex (Fig. 5.13) because, except for carbon dioxide, these materials are used sequentially and thus can limit sequentially the various reactions and interactions. For example, sulphate is, in high concentrations, reduced by sulphate-reducing bacteria to hydrogen sulphide (energetically more favourable than methane production from hydrogen, carbon dioxide and acetate [5.99]), thus excluding methanogens. Conversely, in the absence of sulphate, sulphate-reducing bacteria may act as syntrophic acetogens on intermediates such as lactic acid or ethanol, switching from sulphate reduction to hydrogen formation by proton reduction [5.100].

5.10   LANDFILL PRODUCTS AND SITE EXPLOITATION

Characteristically, landfill sites generate two types of products from decaying refuse; leachate and gas. The former is water which has percolated through emplaced waste carrying with it soluble and suspended substances;

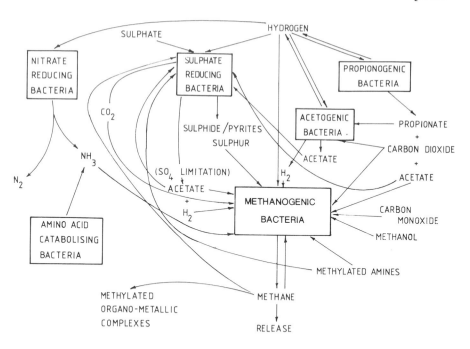

Fig. 5.13 — Microbial interactions in terminal anoxic catabolism.

its composition is influenced by several complex interacting first- and second-tier factors. First-tier factors include the site geology, hydrogeology, hydrometeorology, the waste composition (including electron donors and acceptors, microbial inoculum and moisture content), refuse emplacement strategy, cover permeability, topography, vegetation cover and site after-use. The season and age of the site are also important. These, in turn, direct the second-tier variables, such as redox state, pH and temperature, together with physico-chemical reactions including acidification, volatilisation, precipitation, solution, sorption and ion exchange. When the refuse absorptive capacity [5.101] is exceeded through infiltration by precipitation, ground or surface water or microbially produced water, leachate is produced. However, some leachate is often formed before the field capacity (55% w/w of the absorbent proportion) is reached [5.102] due either to the heterogeneity and channelling of the waste or to high intensity short duration rainfall. The absorptive capacity of refuse varies, depending on pretreatment, degree of compaction, and composition. Pulverising or shredding, for example, results in a threefold increase (estimated by Marriott [5.103] to be 125 l m^{-3}). The proportion of paper in refuse (increasing progressively with time, see Fig. 5.14) is also important, since paper can absorb more than 250% its own weight of water [5.105].

Leachate contains soluble compounds (including dispersed organic phases) and inorganic materials, together with microorganisms such as bacteria and viruses. Many materials detected in leachate from domestic

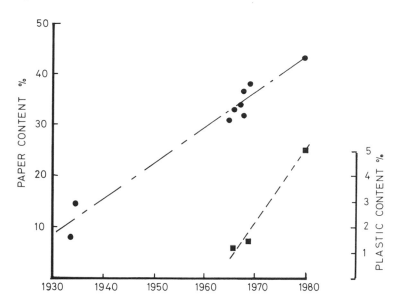

Fig. 5.14 — The variation in the paper and plastics content of domestic refuse [5.104].

refuse and co-disposal landfills are listed in Tables 5.19 and 5.20, which would be much more extensive if sites which had received major inputs of industrial waste were also included [5.107]. There is, as yet, no reliable method of predicting leachate composition and concentration. Brice *et al.* [5.108] examined the chemical composition of leachate derived from six ground refuse fractions (putrescibles, fines <20 mm, commercial paper, plastics, clean paper and dirty paper) in short- and long-term studies, and concluded that greater concentrations of species would go into the solution during repetitive tests rather than in protracted equilibrium tests. Results such as these, however, are of only limited value without consideration of the impacts of each leachate, singly and in combination, in individual refuse fractions (and the percentage contribution of each component). Moreover, although shredded refuse produces higher peak concentrations of matter in leachate than unprocessed refuse under similar conditions of landfill [5.109], it has also been reported that concentrations of components are relatively independent of the flow rate through the waste [5.110]. The heavy metal fraction, however, has received considerable attention, due to potential contamination of water supplies. In general, there is a linear relationship between the logarithm of the weight of the metal released per gram of refuse and the gross pH of the leachate, although copper and chromium are exceptions [5.111].

During the early stages of a typical landfill, aerobic catabolism leads to high fatty acid concentrations (see Table 5.21), a lowering of pH and solubilisation of metals which then complex with the free acids [5.112]. With the change to microaerophilic conditions, the redox potential falls, the pH

Table 5.19 — Composition of leachates from UK sites (concentrations in mg l^{-1}) (from [5.106])

	Recently tipped		Old waste	
pH	7.1	6.9	7.1	7.2
BOD	7250	8000	55	63
COD	11 600	11 050	96	124
NH$_3$-N	340	576	34	47
Total VFA	2805	3672	<4	<2
o-PO$_4$	0.22	0.03	0.03	<0.02
Chloride	2103	—	520	747
Iron	160	240	0.1	0.55
Sodium	2500	900	380	440

rises and the metals start to precipitate as sulphides and carbonates [5.113], resulting in reduced leachate concentrations. The picture can be further complicated if heavy metal complexes are formed with ammonium ions at low Eh, or with humic acids.

The composition of landfill leachate changes through either short-term factors (seasonal climatic conditions) or long-term factors (waste catabolism), with the latter the major determinants [5.114]. As mentioned previously, the initial stages of landfill degradation are acidogenic. Leachate from these phases is characterised by high BOD, COD and TOC values (see Table 5.21) and low concentrations of high molecular weight materials (such as humic and fulvic acids), heavy metals and sulphate. The change to the methanogenic stage has a dramatic effect on leachate, with BOD, COD and TOC falling and humic and fulvic materials increasing.

Detection of groundwater contamination [5.115] can involve the use of chemical and/or biological markers. Typical chemical markers include elevated concentrations of ammonia, chloride, iron, manganese, magnesium, potassium, sodium and TOC; the presence of filamentous bacteria has also been taken to be indicative of leachate contamination.

The best method of leachate control is prevention by the use of low permeability cover [5.116] to minimise water ingression [5.117]. The overall effect of this, however, would be to decrease the rate of refuse decomposition [5.118]. Alternatively, one can either provide a barrier which is less permeable than the surroundings (discussed previously), or rely on attenuation through natural microbiological and physico-chemical processes in the zones surrounding the site. Heavy metals have been found to be strongly attentuated with only limited remobilisation (except for nickel [5.119] and lead [5.120]), the process being controlled by buffering with carboxylic acids and enhanced by formation of soluble bicarbonate and sulphates. Acid–base reactions of this type increase pore fluid pH, favour precipitation of heavy metals and increase base-exchange capacity.

Table 5.20 — Identified constituents or leachate from refuse and co-disposal landfill sites

ELEMENTS

ALUMINIUM	COBALT	NICKEL
ARSENIC	COPPER	POTASSIUM
BARIUM	IRON	SELENIUM
BERILIUM	LEAD	SILICON
BORON	MAGNESIUM	SILVER
CADMIUM	MANGANESE	SODIUM
CALCIUM	MERCURY	STRONTIUM
CHROMIUM	MOLYBDENUM	ZINC

INORGANIC RADICALS

AMMONIUM	FLUORIDE	PHOSPHATE
BICARBONATE	NITRATE	SULPHATE
CHLORIDE	NITRITE	SULPHIDE
CYANIDE		

ALIPHATICS

ACETIC ACID		METHYL HEXYL KETONE
ACETIC ACID, ESTER	HEPTANOL	2 METHYL PANTANOIC ACID
BUTANOL	HEXANE	4 METHYL PANTANOIC ACID
2 BUTYL ALCOHOL	HEXANOIC ACID	2 METHYL PROPANOIC ACID
iso-BUTYLAMINE	HEXANOIC ACID, BUTYL ESTER	MYRISTIC ACID
sec-BUTYLAMINE	HEXANOIC ACID, ETHYL ESTER	δ- NONALACTON
t-BUTYLAMINE	HEXANOIC ACID, HEPTYL ESTER	OCTANE
BUTYRIC ACID	HEXANOIC ACID, HEXYL ESTER	OCTANOIC ACID
iso-BUTYRIC ACID	HEXANOIC ACID, METHYL ESTER	1-OCTANOL
BUTYRIC ACID, ESTER	HEXANOIC ACID, OCTYL ESTER	OLEIC ACID
BUTYRIC ACID, PROPYL ESTER	HEXANOIC ACID, PENTYL ESTER	PALMITIC ACID
CARBON TETRACHLORIDE	HEXANOIC ACID, PROPYL ESTER	PENTANOIC ACID
CAPROIC ACID	1-HEXANOL	iso-PENTANOIC ACID
iso-CAPROIC ACID	HEXANONE	PENTANOIC ACID, ETHYL ESTER
CHLOROFORM	HEXENE	PROPIONIC ACID
DIALKOXYDIMETHOXY PROPANE	KETONES	iso-PROPYL ALCOHOL
DICHLOROETHANE	LAURIC ACID	SQUALENE
DICHLOROMETHANE	METHANOL	STEARIC ACID
DIETHYL ETHER	METHYL ACETATE	TETRACHLOROETHYLENE
DISULPHIDES	METHYLAMINE	TRIALKYL PHOSPHATE
ETHANOL	METHYLENE CHLORIDE	TRICHLOROETHYLENE
ETHYL ACETATE	2 METHYL BUTANOIC ACID	TRIMETHYLAMINE
ETHYL BUTYL ETHER	3 METHYL BUTANOIC ACID	3,5,5 TRIMETHYL HEXANOIC ACID
ETHYL ESTER	2 METHYL BUTYRIC ACID	VALERIC ACID
ETHYL HEXANOL	DIMETHYL KETONE	iso-VALERIC ACID
HEPTANE	METHYL ETHYL KETONE	VINYL CHLORIDE
HEPTANOIC ACID	METHYL iso-BUTYL KETONE	

AROMATICS

2-(4-ACETYL PHENYL) PROPAN-2-OL	2,6-DI-t-BUTYL-4-METHYL PHENOL	LIGNIN
ALKYL BENZENES	DIETHYL PHTHALATE	3 METHYL INDOLE
C6 ALYL PHENOL	DIMETHYL BENZOIC ACID	METHYL NAPHTHALENE
BENZALDEHYDE	DIMETHYL t-BUTYL PHENOL	NAPHTHALENE
BENZENE	DIOCTYL PHTHALATE	PHENOL
BENZOIC ACID	DIPROPYL PHTHALATE	PHENYL ACETIC ACID
BENZYL ALCOHOL	DISULPHIDES	2 PHENYL ETHANOL
BUTYL BENZENE SULPHONAMIDE	ETHYL BENZENE	PHENYL PROPANOL
t-BUTYL CRESOL	ETHYL METHYL BENZENE	PHENYL PROPIONIC ACID
t-BUTYL METHOXY PHENOL	ETHYL METHYL THIOINDONE	PHTHALATES
t-BUTYL PHENOL	m-ETHYL PHENOL	STYRENE
CHLOROTRIISOPROPYL BENZENE	p-ETHYL PHENOL	TANNIN
CRESOLS	FULVIC ACID	TOLUENE
m-CRESOL	HUMIC ACID	o-XYLENE
p-CRESOL	KETONES	p-XYLENE
DI-t-BUTYL CRESOL		

ACYCLICS

t-BUTYL CYCLOHEXANE
CYCLOHEXANE
CYCLOHEXANE HEXANOIC ACID
CYCLOHEXANOL
CYCLOHEXANONE

TERPENES

α-BICYCLIC SESQUITERPENE
CAMPHANE
CAMPHOR
FENCHONE
TERPINEOL
α-TERPINEOL
THUJONE

Table 5.21 — Identified minor constituents of landfill gas

ACETONE	DISULPHIDES	n-NONANES
ARGON	DIMETHYL SULPHIDE	NONENES
BENZENE	ETHANE	n-OCTANE
C_3-SUBSTITUTED BENZENES	ETHANOL	OCTANES
C_4-SUBSTITUTED BENZENES	ETHYL ACETATE	OCTENES
BUTYL BENZENE	ETHYL BUTANOATE	n-PENTANE
BUTYL BENZENES	2 ETHYL-1-HEXANOL	iso-PENTANE
DICHLOROBENZENE	ETHYL MERCAPTAN	PENTANES
DICHLOROBENZENES	ETHYL PENTANOATE	PENTAN-2-ONE
ETHYL BENZENE	ETHYLENE	PROPANE
PENTYL BENZENES	HEPTANE	PROPAN-1-OL
PROPYL BENZENES	HEPTANES	PROPAN-2-OL
n-BUTANE	n-HEXANE	PROPYL CYCLOHEXANES
iso-BUTANE	HEXANES	SULPHIDES
BUTANE THIOL	HEXENES	TERPENE
1-BUTENE	C_4-C_{14} HYDROCARBONS	TERPENES
BUTYL ALCOHOL	HYDROGEN SULPHIDE	α-TERPINENE
BUTAN-1-OL	LIMONENE	TETRACHLOROETHYLENE
iso-BUTAN-1-OL	MERCAPTAN SULPHUR	TOLUENE
BUTAN-2-OL	METHANE THIOL	1,1,1 TRICHLOROETHANE
BUTAN-2-ONE	METHANOL	TRICHLOROETHYLENE
DECANES	METHYL ETHYL KETONE	n-UNDECANE
n-DECANE	2 METHYL FLURAN	UNDECANES
DECENES	METHYL PENTANOATE	UNDECENES
DICHLORODIFLUOROMETHANE	METHYL STYRENE	XYLENE
DIETHYL ETHER	NONANES	XYLENES

It has been shown that migrations of materials such as *n*-butyric acid, phenol, *p*-chlorophenol and dimethyl phthalate through the saturated zone surrounding the landfill site were all approximately similar, although final concentrations differed because the rates of degradation differed, *n*-butyric acid and phenol being dissimilated most rapidly. This sort of reaction can be examined by radiorespirometry [5.121] to establish optimum conditions for *in situ* underground treatment. However, even after degradation, there is still the possibility that refractile metabolic end-products will remain to threaten groundwater supplies.

If natural attenuation mechanisms are unable to cope with pollution from landfill leachate then collection and treatment are necessary. Treatment, either by using the refuse tip itself (site exploitation) or by external means, must be both environmentally acceptable and also low-cost.

Perhaps the most satisfactory method of site exploitation is through controlled anaerobic decomposition, which accelerates landfill stabilisation (discussed later). Alternatively, the leachate may be recycled through the refuse mass by either surface irrigation or subsurface distributor inoculation, thus using the landfill as a plug-flow anaerobic filter with feedback. By use of either method, the rate of addition can be controlled to optimise the

biological treatment in respect of residence time, depth of fill and maintenance of refuse mass temperature [5.113]. Recycling by spray irrigation also
promotes evapotranspiration [5.118], the volatilisation of low molecular
weight organic compounds and the oxidation and subsequent precipitation
of metals such as iron, although the total volume available for recirculation,
of course, increases with time [5.122].

The overall effect of leachate recycle is to increase moisture content and
movement [5.123] through the refuse mass, promoting microbial degradation, particularly if provision is made for pH control and/or nutrient
supplementation by sludge seeding and surface settlement [5.124; 5.125]. In
addition, precipitation of metallic sulphides may result, although concentrations of ammonia, chloride and COD can remain high, thus necessitating
further treatment before ultimate discharge [5.118; 5.123]. Other problems
include difficulties in achieving high rates of liquid flow through the refuse
mass, possible 'hard pan' formation, and difficulties in lateral movement of
liquid into surrounding surface or groundwater.

Soil application has been extensively used, although care must be taken
to choose a soil type of appropriate permeability, particle size and stability,
and to maintain these infiltration characteristics by appropriate dosing
regimes: any anoxic conditions within the soil will decrease the degradation
rate. Initial addition establishes gradients of electron donors and acceptors,
oxygen and temperature, leading to microbial stratification with sorption at
first controlling TOC removal. Once sorption is exceeded, microbial catabolism takes over, aided by dilution with water retained in the soil (below field
capacity). Although land treatment is low-cost [5.126], problems can result,
particularly in winter, due to high leachate volumes, low evapotranspiration
rates and low microbial activity. Even under better environmental conditions, heavy metal accumulation [5.127] and the formation of a relatively
impermeable surface 'hard pan' as the insoluble salts of iron, manganese and
calcium precipitate, may still occur [5.128]. In addition, high concentrations
of organic chemicals and heavy metals may result in differential plant death
[5.129], only avoided by pretreatment [5.128; 5.130]. Thus, whilst spray
irrigation of landfill leachate on a sandy soil which supported permanent
pasture grass had no adverse effect, calcium oxide, magnesium oxide and
phosphorus pentoxide were shown to accumulate. Although it has a direct
phytotoxic effect on foliage, leachate contains all essential plant nutrients,
but studies by Menser on subirrigated sand cultures of soybean showed that
these were unbalanced, and the process needed careful regulation [5.131].

Aerobic treatment can be either direct or on recycled leachate. Whilst
oxidation ditches, clay inclined planes and more complex methods have
been tried, the principal treatment is the aeration lagoon, which in one
report gave a 70% BOD reduction over several months' retention time.
Problems arose over toxic metals and high molecular weight materials,
particularly humic and fulvic acids which have also been implicated in
reports of a seven-fold selective reduction of natural phenols [5.132]; a
further report indicated TOC removals of 97–99%, accompanied by high

heavy metal reductions, provided that care was taken to avoid phosphorus limitation by maintaining an adequate COD:P ratio [5.133]. Aeration lagoons effectively reduce the high ammonium concentrations in landfill leachate. Smith [5.134] described a treatment involving cyclic aeration and settlement, resulting in significant improvements in ammonium removal relative to the volume of air utilised. Reduced running costs are also possible with aquatic plants which can saturate the leachate with oxygen and promote aerobic bacterial oxidation [5.135].

Trickling filters, activated sludge and rotating biological contractors (see Chapter 1) have all been used for treatment of landfill leachate, either alone or mixed with wastewater. Often nutrient supplementation [5.118] is required, although treatment with, for example, phosphate also can precipitate heavy metals as organophosphates. These treatments have resulted in BOD and COD reductions as high as 99% [5.123] and 95% [5.136] respectively, together with significant removal of ammonia (by a combination of bacterial nitrification and cell assimilation [5.118; 5.132]), iron (>98%), manganese (>92%) and zinc (>94%) [5.118]; however, recalcitrant organic molecules need further treatment. Temperature can be a major limiting factor, since in temperate climates the lowest temperatures occur with the highest leachate volumes. Sludge bulking may be exacerbated by the low phosphate levels often encountered [5.137]. Finally, metal accumulation within flocs has also been shown to be a problem.

Anaerobic treatment by lagooning removed 80–90% of the COD within 40–50 days at 25°C (but only 50% at 10°C) [5.138]. However, digesters are perhaps more promising, with performances reported only marginally below aerated lagoons and a claimed 50% decrease in installation and operating costs [5.133; 5.139]. Unfortunately, there are potential problems from accumulation of ammonia and heavy metal toxicity, although this can be treated [5.133]. Model systems removed >96% of the BOD, but methane yields were disappointing [5.130]. Optimisation of methane production in a reactor rather than the landfill is superficially attractive, but it would be necessary to inhibit methanogenesis within the refuse mass, by either rapid water elution or leachate recycle. Whilst this could provide high concentrations of fatty acids, it would also promote heavy metal solubilisation, giving further problems, and is unlikely to be financially worth while.

Since physico-chemical treatments do not remove as much organic material as biological processes, they are preferably used in conjunction with biologically stabilised leachates. Although many physico-chemical treatments, including chemical coagulation and precipitation, carbon adsorption, reverse osmosis, resin adsorption, chemical oxidation (including ozonolysis), stripping and irradiation have been examined, no one treatment has been found to be totally effective. For example, ozone, activated carbon, weak base anion exchange resin, strong base anion exchange resin, and membrane reverse osmosis resulted in TOC reductions of 48, 86, 53, 82–85 and 91–96% respectively [5.133]. Conversely, chemical coagulation and precipitation in the presence of lime, alum, ferric chloride, ferrous sulphate and polymers removed little organic matter, although high removals of both heavy metals and suspended matter were observed [5.140].

5.11   TOXIC AND HAZARDOUS WASTES AND CO-DISPOSAL

Toxic and hazardous waste disposal, either alone or with refuse, to landfill needs careful site selection and choice of liner material [5.141]. Geological strata with an inherent permeability to distilled or tap water of 10^{-7} cm s^{-1} or less are thought to be suitable for the disposal of many types of hazardous wastes. Often toxic and hazardous liquid wastes and sludges (defined in terms of toxicity, carcinogenicity, mutagenicity, corrosivity, inflammability, radioactivity or reactivity [5.142]) are either stabilised or solidified before landfill disposal [5.143]. With inorganic stabilising reagents, such as cements, fixation depends on hydration, whereas organic polymers such as polyester resins rely on physical encapsulation by the formation of an inpermeable boundary, and careful testing is necessary.

Of batch and column methods, batch extraction offers advantages through greater reproducibility and simplicity whilst the column approach is more realistic in simulating leaching processes occurring *in situ*. Comparisons of groundwater quality at selected landfills with leaching test results show that, except for barium, metal concentrations were less than those released in the tests, whilst concentrations of inorganic non-metallic molecules were higher. Thus, leaching tests alone could not be used to predict the environment impact of waste disposal, and site-specific hazard assessment testing methods have therefore been developed [5.144].

Successful co-disposal of toxic and hazardous wastes with emplaced refuse needs consideration of waste type (solid, sludge or liquid), compatibility of reactive species, loading rate, evapotranspiration, leachability rate, refuse (type, quantity, density and age), temperature and site water balance [5.101; 5.103; 5.145]. Although fresh refuse has greater absorptive and buffering capacities than old, sulphate, chloride and iron are only poorly attenuated when rapid liquid additions are made to low density material. Liquid disposal should therefore be, in general, to old, completed areas of sites, with the added advantage of simpler leachate control [5.101], although arsenic and selenium (which are quite mobile in relatively pure clay minerals, particularly under alkaline conditions) should not be included.

Attenuation mechanisms can be physico-chemical or microbiological. Thus, for co-disposal of barium-containing salts the major attenuation mechanisms were shown, in tests, to be physico-chemical processes, particularly adsorption. Microbial activity was also indirectly implicated, however, since microbially produced carbon dioxide and bicarbonate precipitated barium carbonate, although the presence of fatty acids effected significant mobilisation as organic complexes.

Radioactive wastes are also subject to some microbiological transformation. Whilst co-disposal of radionucleotides such as ^{3}H, ^{58}Co, ^{85}Sr and ^{134}Cs required only indirect microbial intervention (since strontium and cobalt removals were attributed to sulphide and basic carbonate precipitation, while caesium concentration reductions were attributed to ion exchange with the solid refuse), co-disposal of soluble arsenicals [5.146] required direct microbial involvement with reduction and methylation to di- and tri-methylarsine.

Although co-disposal of toxic and hazardous molecules could affect *in situ* microbial degradative processes, no evidence of any catabolic process inhibition was found by Knox [5.147], and no significant changes were found when cyanides, phenols, heavy metals and pesticides were co-disposed with domestic refuse and mixtures of refuse and sewage sludge in test lysimeters. Nevertheless, leachates from toxic and hazardous waste co-disposal sites have the added complication of the toxic materials. Lime flocculation will remove dispersed organic phases, preventing inhibition, whilst inoculum enrichment is reported to have furnished a microbial population capable of TOC reductions in excess of 90% provided that nitrogen, phosphorus and potassium were supplied in non-limiting concentrations [5.148].

However, although leachates from toxic and hazardous waste- and co-disposal sites can often be treated successfully by combinations of physico-chemical and microbiological methods, the costs involved may make these methods of disposal of liquids and sludges increasingly less attractive.

5.12   CONTROL, OPTIMISATION AND EXPLOITATION OF LANDFILL GAS

Landfill gas (see Table 5.21) can be a liability as well as an energy recovery opportunity. Releases, which can be monitored by aerial thermography, can give rise to odours, groundwater acidification, and reduced crop yields (including complete die-back); consequently discharge limits have been imposed [5.149]. To comply with these limits, gas migration controls have been installed, such as cut-off barriers or trenches filled with gravel in shallow sites, and gas extraction systems or air injection systems in deeper sites (>20 ft deep) [5.150]. Alternatively, gas seals of natural materials or fabricated membranes may be employed [5.151]. Once gas migration has been controlled, the problem is dealt with by flaring or by soil sieving. Low pore size soils trap reduced malodorants which are subsequently oxidised by aerobic microbial species [5.152; 5.153].

Over the years, the most significant change in landfill gas composition has been the increase in methane content as refuse and site practices have changed. Interest in recovery has increased correspondingly over the last decade, with the USA having 81 facilities on line or planned in 1984. Similarly, the European Community has increased operational sites from two in 1982 to 36 in 1983 [5.83]. In addition, gas recovery is now practised or planned in Brazil, Canada, Switzerland and Japan as well as in the UK [5.154].

As a largely untapped resource, landfill gas has vast potential, since 200 × 10^9 ft^3 in the USA and 200 million therms in the UK could be realised annually [5.155]. However, until sold, it is a waste product and represents a liability to the site owner.

Landfill gas recovery in the USA has been practised on sites varying from 6 to 600 ha and averaging 67.6 ha [5.156]. Characteristically, refuse depths have been between 6 and 90 m with an average of 30 m [5.149]. The feasibility of commercial gas extraction can be assessed on the basis of 1 to 2 million tonnes of in-place refuse, an average refuse depth of 13 m, an active fill area of 16 ha, a refuse intake of 400 tonnes d^{-1}, the landfill either recently closed or preferably still active, and a market for the gas in close proximity.

A theoretical maximum methane yield of 0.266 m^3 kg^{-1} dry refuse has been calculated. However, this calculation is based on a number of assumptions which, according to Ham, are not valid in landfill and consequently he suggested that a more realistic figure for recoverable methane was 0.047 m^3 kg^{-1} [5.157]. Comparisons of actual and theoretical gas production rates are difficult to make, since little information on real systems is available, and such figures as exist are, typically, determined by indirect methods [5.158] rather than the much more valid radiotracer technique [5.91].

Ham [5.157] reviewed 38 reports of gas production rates from municipal refuse in which laboratory studies, lysimeters, pilot-scale landfills and test landfills were used to examine gas generation from untreated refuse and digested refuse, with and without sludge supplementation. Ranges of estimated, measured and theoretical rates were reported as 3.7–190, 0.21–400 and 16–450 l kg^{-1} y^{-1}. It was concluded that during the more active period of methane production a reasonable rate of generation would be between 3.1 and 37 l kg^{-1} y^{-1}.

Methanogenic species are particularly susceptible to the effects, both direct and indirect, of interacting environmental variables (Fig. 5.15), which, in turn, are controlled by gross site factors. Refuse composition is the major determinant of both gas quality [5.157] and rate of production [5.159]. There is little reported work on potential inhibitors, although it has been shown [5.114] that heavy metals, whose toxicity depends on a variety of factors, have little influence on the sensitive methogenic species. Pretreatment can result in dramatic changes. Particle size reduction from 250 to 10 mm resulted in quadruple rates of gas production, possibly as a result of increased surface area, or due to increased oxygen, since there was a shift in the fermentation balance to carbon dioxide.

Incremental increases of 10% up to 65% in the refuse moisture content resulted in more pronounced changes with low density refuse (0.25 t m^{-3}) than with compacted refuse (0.80 t m^{-3}) due to increased bacterial mobility which, in turn, promoted hydrolysis and subsequent methanogenesis. Conversely, at constant moisture content (21%), a density increase from 0.32 to 0.47 t m^{-3} resulted in a gas production rate increase from 410 to 845 ml d^{-1} kg^{-1} dry refuse [5.158]. However, the percentage water content for optimum gas production rates is still not known. Thus, two studies have suggested water-saturated refuse as optimal [5.158], whereas the work of Farquhar and Rovers [5.160] suggested an optimum between 60 and 80% wet weight and that of Marriott [5.103] between 55 and 60% (w/v).

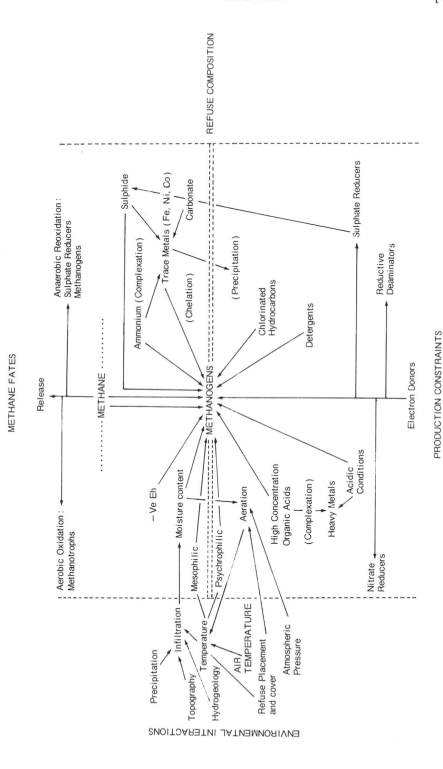

Fig. 5.15 — Methane production constraints and fates in landfill [5.91].

However, laboratory studies have indicated that the overall reaction rate is chemically controlled and as such is not subject to diffusional mass transfer limitations in the presence of high moisture contents [5.161].

Changes in gas production rate are also apparent when moisture moves through the refuse mass. Klink and Ham [5.162], for example, demonstrated methanogenic rate increases of between 25 and 50% in the presence of moisture movement, even when the total moisture content was constant, and concluded that moisture content and movement were separate variables affecting landfill methanogenesis. Further increases when the water was replaced by landfill leachate were attributed to distribution of basic nutrients, methanogenic precursors and pH.

Although fermentation of unsaturated refuse often produces hydrogen, it is absent at elevated moisture regimes, when the methane:carbon ratio progressively increases because more carbon dioxide dissolves.

Finally, increased moisture content can be inhibitory by cooling the refuse, increasing the redox potential and thus changing the fermentation balance [5.160].

Laboratory studies show that increases in temperature generally increase gas production; thus in one laboratory study, a temperature increase from 22 to 33°C was accompanied by a gas production increase of 70%. Further work [5.163] showed that the optimum temperature for methanogenesis was 41°C and no evolution was detected between 48 and 55°C. Landfill temperature is changed by microbial metabolism (in turn directed by emplaced refuse dry density, specific surface area, water content, refuse temperature, refuse composition and availability of electron acceptors, particularly oxygen), heats of neutralisation and solar energy, all of which are balanced by heat loss to the atmosphere and to the surrounding soil and leachate. However, the rapid temperature increases which have been reported can often be equated with aerobic metabolism, since subsequent anaerobiosis is usually accompanied by temperature reductions [5.163].

Nyns and Pauss [5.159] demonstrated highest gas yields from refuse with an alkalinity of $16 \, g \, CaCO_3 \, kg^{-1}$ total solids, concluding that in the presence of low alkalinity fatty acids would accumulate at the expense of methane. This was confirmed at an operating landfill by Ehrig [5.114] who reported that an acetic acid:alkalinity ratio of <0.8 was required before methogenesis was initiated. Such a buffering capacity in the refuse mass can be achieved by adding calcareous material, although this could represent a significant cost. A full scale landfill site presents complications not encountered in the laboratory, and optimisation of gas production provides a particular challenge to the operator, for the strategy chosen must not interfere with day-to-day site operation. Rees [1.158] has suggested a first lift of low density (0.35 t m^{-3}) refuse, diluted with material such as wood, paper or pulverised or aerobically stabilised refuse, placed at the base and allowed to decompose aerobically to raise the temperature and to produce water. After filling, water should be added through a central well, rising at a rate of 1–2 m y^{-1} and thus maintaining the acetogenic and methanogenic phases in balance.

To reduce heat loss, an insulating layer of refuse approximately 4 m in depth should be placed above the reactive zone. Stegmann [5.164] also advocates an initial uncompacted aerobic layer for a period of between six and nine months, after which he suggested that second lifts of refuse should be supplemented with recycled leachate. For each of these strategies, water (leachate) plays a key role. Control of the site water balance is therefore vital to prevent abstraction difficulties such as partial flooding of extraction wells due to high water tables.

Landfill gas is recovered by means of vertical or horizontal perforated pipes or domes of polythene sheeting. Pumps or blowers can increase the recovery efficiency, although care must be taken to prevent suction of air into the refuse mass. After condensate and particulate removal, landfill gas can be used as a low grade fuel (17–20 MJ m^{-3}) to fire bricks, raise steam or heat greenhouses. Alternatively, after purification to give 34–37 MJ m^{-3} it can be used for pipeline injection or liquefaction at 200 bar for fuel. Other possibilities include conversion to electricity or products such as methanol and chemical feedstock, hydrocarbon fuel replacement and coal replacement.

5.13   METHODS OF STUDY

Landfill systems are essentially complex. *In situ* investigations are exacerbated by the problems normally associated with field work on a working site; consequently there is a need to complement such work with ecologically relevant laboratory studies under defined and controlled conditions, but mirroring those of the natural habitat.

Homogeneous models, such as chemostats at steady-state, are very limited; Wimpenny *et al.* [e.g. 5.165], who recognised this problem, advocated heterogeneous models. Harder *et al.*, however, argued that both homogeneous and heterogeneous models should be used, hand-in-hand [5.166].

These models cannot cope with mutually exclusive niches, such as nitrate reduction; however, linked homogeneous chemostats do not suffer from these limitations. Multi-stage laboratory models can be used for sequential reactions, overlapping niches, nutrient gradients, microbial competition, synergism and antagonism, species diversity and interfaces. Although these systems provide more realistic models than single-stage systems, constraints still remain, such as step changes rather than true gradients. Moreover, surface phenomena, extremely difficult to model, are essentially absent. Unfortunately in environments such as landfill, large varieties of organic and inorganic surfaces are present for microbial attachment.

In spite of this, it is clear that collection and utilisation of landfill gas is likely to continue and expand, for on the one hand the composition of refuse increasingly favours gas production (Fig. 5.15), whilst on the other the potential of such sites is also increasingly being recognised by a public which is simultaneously becoming less tolerant of pollution by leachate, by methane *per se*, or by malodours. Thus, although the problem is in part economic (and the recent fall in oil prices will to some extent affect thinking), ultilisation, however low the price, is often going to be preferable to mere flaring, which otherwise would have to be adopted to prevent pollution, hazards and malodours. Thus, a recent exploitation of landfill has been that at the Rossman landfill, with a peak summer production of 40 000 $m^3 d^{-1}$. It would appear that other landfill sites possess similar potential and are therefore likely to be similarly exploitable [5.167].

Although similar criteria apply to many European sites, there is likely to be an even more powerful anti-pollution lobby, because of high population densities and proximity to sites. It is therefore clear that developments of the type mentioned in this chapter are likely to increase. Clearly there is a swing towards the utilisation of landfill gas as a positive resource. Moreover, there seems little doubt that the sorts of anti-pollution pressures mentioned above will continue. Landfill gas utilisation would appear to be here to stay.

REFERENCES

[5.1] Matthews, P. J. (1983) Agricultural utilisation of sewage sludge in the United Kingdom. *Wat. Sci. Technol.*, **15**, 135–150.

[5.2] Vincent, A. J. and Critchley, R. F. (1984) A review of sewage sludge treatment and disposal in Europe. In *Sewage Sludge Stabilisation and Disinfection*, Bruce, A. (ed.), Ellis Horwood, Chichester, pp. 550–570.

[5.3] Wood, R. (1975) The utilisation of sewage sludge. *Effl. Wat. Trt. J.*, **15**, 455–457.

[5.4] Calcutt, T. and Moss, J. (1984) Sewage sludge treatment and disposal — the way ahead. *Wat. Pollut. Control*, **83**, 163–171.

[5.5] Brade, C. E., Noone, G. P. and Whyley, J. (1984) Progress in anaerobic digestion — heating, cooling and thickening. In *Sewage Sludge Stabilisation and Disinfection*, Bruce, A. (ed.), Ellis Horwood, Chichester, pp. 158–173.

[5.6] Taylor, K., Clark, E. I. and Sourbutts, K. (1984) Sludge dewatering at Bolton sewage-treatment works. *Wat. Pollut. Control*, **83**, 71–81.

[5.7] Gough, A. J. and Pearce, M. J. (1983) Cannock sludge thickeners — process design. *Wat. Pollut. Control*, **82**, 255–366.

[5.8] Lockyear, C. F. (1978) *Pilot-scale experiments on continuous gravity thickening of activated sludge*. Technical Report TR 97, Water Research Centre.

[5.9] Lockyear, C. F. and White, M. J. D. (1979) *The WRC thickenability test using a low-speed centrifuge*. Technical Report TR 118, Water Research Centre.

[5.10] Hurley, B. J. E., Rachwal, A. A. J. and Hatton, C. J. (1984) Consolidation of digested sludge. In *Sewage Sludge Stabilisation and Disinfection*, Bruce, A. (ed.), Ellis Horwood, Chichester, pp. 239–260.

[5.11] Institute of Water Pollution Control (1978–1981) *Manuals of British Practice in Water Pollution Control. Sewage Sludge I, II and III.* Maidstone, Kent, IWPC.

[5.12] Melbourne, J. D. and Zabel, T. F. (eds) (1977) *Flotation for Water and Waste Treatment.* Water Research Centre.

[5.13] Maddock, J. E. L. and Tomlinson, E. J. (1980) The clarification of effluent from an activated sludge plant using dissolved air flotation. *Wat. Pollut. Control*, **79**, 117–125.

[5.14] Frost, R. C. (1982) *Prediction of friction losses for the flow of sewage sludge in straight pipes.* Technical Report TR 175, Water Research Centre.

[5.15] Rose-Innes, I. H. and Nossel, S. (1983) The rheology and pumping of thickened activated sludge. *Wat. Sci. Technol.* **15**, 59–76.

[5.16] Papacrivopoulos, D. (1985) *Pumped desludging of primary sedimentation tanks at Minworth.* MSc. Thesis, Birmingham University.

[5.17] Hoyland, G., Day, M. and Baskerville, R. C. (1981) *Getting more out of the filter press.* Technical Report TR 173, Water Research Centre.

[5.18] Pietila, K. A. and Jourbert, P. J. (1981) Examination of process parameters affecting sludge dewatering with a diaphragm filter press. *J. Wat. Pollut. Control Fed.*, **53**, 1708–1716.

[5.19] Bruce, A. M. and Lockyear, C. F. (1982) Uprating sludge treatment processes. *Wat. Pollut. Control*, **81**, 425–443.

[5.20] Moore, J. G. (1983) The design and construction of Springfield sewage-treatment works. *Wat. Pollut. Control*, **82**, 37–41.

[5.21] Nelson, J. K. and Tavery, M. A. H. (1978) Chemical conditioning alternatives and operational control for vacuum filtration. *J. Wat. Pollut. Control Fed.*, **50**, 507–517.

[5.22] Forster, C. F. (1985) *Biotechnology and Wastewater Treatment.* Cambridge University Press.

[5.23] Lockyear, C. F., Jackson, P. J. and Warden, J. H. (1983) *Polyelectrolyte users' manual.* Technical Report TR 184, Water Research Centre.

[5.24] Bruce, A. M. and Baskerville, R. C. (1981) A note on a new development of sludge filtrability. *Proc. 1st Eur. Symp. on Treatment and Use of Sewage Sludge*, CEC, Brussels, pp. 25–28.

[5.25] Zehnder, A. J. B., Ingvorsen, K. and Marti, T. (1982) Microbiology of methane bacteria. In *Anaerobic Digestion 1981*, Hughes, D. E. *et al.* (eds), Elsevier Biomedical Press, Amsterdam, pp. 45–70.

[5.26] Mah, R. A. (1983) Interactions of methanogens and non-methanogens in microbial ecosystems. *Proc. 3rd Int. Symp. on Anaerobic Digestion*, Massachusetts, p. 13–22.

[5.27] Rundle, H. and Whyley, J. (1981) A comparison of gas recirculation systems for mixing of contents of anaerobic digesters. *Wat. Pollut. Control*, **80**, 463–480.

[5.28] Thompson, J. L. and Michaelson, A. P. (1984) Design aspects of the new anaerobic digesters at Bury. In *Sewage Sludge Stabilisation and Disinfection*, Bruce, A. (ed.), Ellis Horwood, Chichester, pp. 92–106.

[5.29] Swanwick, J. D., Shurben, D. G. and Johnson, S. (1069) A survey of the performance of sewage sludge digestion in Great Britain. *Wat. Pollut. Control*, **68**, 639–661.

[5.30] Eves, E. G. (1981) Hogsmill Valley Works: twenty years on. *Wat. Pollut. Control*, **80**, 543–462.

[5.31] Noone, G. P. and Brade, C. E. (1982) Low-cost provision of anaerobic digestion. *Wat. Pollut. Control*, **81**, 479–510.

[5.32] Price, G. J. and Adler, M. (1985) The economic advantages of sludge thickening at Avonmouth sewage treatment works. *Wat. Pollut. Control*, **84**, 394–406.

[5.33] Mosey, F. E. (1976) Assessment of the maximum concentration of the heavy metals in crude sewage which will not inhibit the anaerobic digestion of sludge. *Wat. Pollut. Control*, **75**, 10–20.

[5.34] Anon. (1982) *Anaerobic Digestion: A Code of Practice of Safety in and around Anaerobic Digesters*. British Anaerobic and Biomass Association Ltd, Reading.

[5.35] Booker, D. I. J. (1981) Beddington sewage-treatment works, Croydon — Some operating experiences, 1969–1979. *Wat. Pollut. Control*, **80**, 356–377.

[5.36] Hemsley, J. and Lattern, A. (1984) Automation and uprating of anaerobic digesters. In *Sewage Sludge Stabilisation and Disinfection*, Bruce, A. (ed.), Ellis Horwood, Chichester, pp. 125–145.

[5.37] Noone, G. P., Brade, C. E. and Whyley, J. (1984) Progress in anaerobic digestion — prefabrication of digesters. In *Sewage Sludge Stabilisation and Disinfection*, Bruce, A. (ed.), Ellis Horwood, Chichester, pp. 107–124.

[5.38] Anon. (1981) *Sewage treatment optimisation model: user manual and description*. Technical Report TR 144, Water Research Centre.

[5.39] Wolinsky, W. K. (1984) A cost comparison of prefabricated and conventional digesters. In *Sewage Sludge Stabilisation and Disinfection*, Bruce, A. (ed.), Ellis Horwood, Chichester, pp. 488–498.

[5.40] Bradford, A., Hatfield, D. and Wright, P. (1985) Sludge digestion: a package of conventional approach. *Wat. Pollut. Control*, **84**, 356–365.

[5.41] Farrell, J. B. (1984) Recent developments in sludge digestion in the United States and a view of the future. In *Sewage Sludge Stabilisation and Disinfection*, Bruce, A. (ed.), Ellis Horwood, Chichester, pp. 317–329.

[5.42] Gunson, H. G. and Morgan, S. F. (1982) Aerobic thermophilic digestion of sewage sludge. *Effl. Wat. Trt. J.*, **23**, 319–320.

[5.43] Jewell, W. J. and Kabrick, R. M. (1980) Autoheated aerobic thermophilic digestion with aeration. *J. Wat. Pollut. Control Fed.* , **52**, 512–523.

[5.44] Cohen, D. B. (1977) A comparison of pure oxygen and diffused air digestion of waste activated sludge. *Prog. Wat. Tech.*, **9**, 691–702.

[5.45] Matsch, L. C. and Drnevich, R. F. (1977) Autothermal aerobic digestion. *J. Wat. Pollut. Control. Fed.*, **49**, 296–310.

[5.46] Booth, M. G. and Tramontini, E. (1984) Thermophilic sludge digestion using oxygen and air. In *Sewage Sludge Stabilisation and Disinfection*, Bruce, A. (ed.), Ellis Horwood, Chichester, pp. 292–316.

[5.47] Morgan, S. F., Littlewood, M. H., Winstanley, R. and Gunson, H. G. (1984) Aerobic thermophilic digestion of sludge using air. In *Sewage Sludge Stabilisation and Disinfection*, Bruce, A. (ed.), Ellis Horwood, Chichester, pp. 278–292.

[5.48] Reigler, G. (1982) Aerobic or anerobic sludge stabilisation. *Korr. Abwasser*, **29**, 790–794.

[5.49] Franzen, G. and Hakanson, L. (1983) Thermophilic aerobic digestion of sewage sludge. *Vatten*, **39**, 213–216.

[5.50] Coker, E. G., Davis, R. D., Hall, J. E. and Carlton-Smith, C. H. (1982) *Field experiments on the use of consolidation sewage sludge for sludge for land reclamation: Effects of crop yield and composition and soil conditions, 1976–1981.* Technical Report TR 183, Water Research Centre.

[5.51] Healey, M. G. (1984) Guidelines for the utilisation of sewage sludge on land in the United Kingdom. *Wat. Sci. Tech.*, **16**, 461–471.

[5.52] Pike, E. B. and Davis, R. D. (1984) Stabilisation and disinfection — their relevance to agricultural utilisation of sludge. In *Sewage Sludge Stabilisation and Disinfection*, Bruce, A. (ed.), Ellis Horwood, Chichester, pp. 61–91.

[5.53] Bell, J. C., Argent, V. A. and Edgar, D. (1979) The survival of *Brucella abortus* in sewage sludge. *Proc. Conf. Utilisation of Sewage Sludge on Land*, Water Research Centre, pp. 475–483.

[5.54] Lewis-Jones, R. (1985) The effects of process factors on the removal of slude pathogens, PhD Thesis, UMIST.

[5.55] Davis, R. D. and Coker, E. G. (1980) *Cadmium in agriculture with special reference to the utilisation of sewage sludge on land.* Technical Report TR 139, Water Research Center.

[5.56] Davis, R. D., Carlton-Smith, C. H., Johnson, D. and Stark, J. H. (1985) Evaluation of the effects of metals in sewage sludge disposal. *Wat. Pollut. Control*, **84**, 380–393.

[5.57] Fish, H. (1983) Sea disposal of sludge: the UK experience. *Wat. Sci. Tech.*, **15**, 77–88.

[5.58] McIntyre, A. D. (1977) *A review of the effects of the disposal of sewage sludge to sea.* Technical Note No. 6, Research and Development Division, Department of the Environment.

[5.59] Norton, M. G. (1978) The control of monitoring of sewage sludge dumping at sea. *Wat. Pollut. Control*, **77**, 402–407.

[5.60] Burton, D. and Conway, E. (1983) Early operating experiences of sludge incineration at Douglas Valley. *Wat. Pollut. Control*, **82**, 521–534.

[5.61] Grieve, A. (1978) Sludge incineration with particular reference to the Coleshill plant. *Wat. Pollut. Control*, **77**, 314–323.

[5.62] Dickens, R., Wallis, B. and Hrundel, J. (1980) Fluidised bed incineration of sewage sludge at Esher, 1976–1978. *Wat. Pollut. Control*, **79**, 431–441.

[5.63] Jank, B. E. (1975) Discussion on Thomas, J., Sludge incineration; New aspects of multiple hearth furnace and fluidised bed incineration. *Prog. Wat. Tech.*, **7**, 935–946.

[5.64] Smith, J. T., Griffin, B. G. and Grahame, A. W. (1978) Commissioning and initial operation of the Coleshill incineration plant. *Wat. Pollut. Control*, **77**, 324–345.

[5.65] Tench, H. B., Phillips, L. F. and Swanwick, K. H. (1972) The Sheffield sludge incineration plant. *Wat. Pollut. Control*, **71**, 176–185.

[5.66] Huber, J. and Mihalyfy, E. (1984) Experiences with the pre-pasteurisation of sewage sludge with heat recovery. In *Sewage Sludge Stabilisation and Disinfection*, Bruce, A. (ed.), Ellis Horwood, Chichester, pp. 381–398.

[5.67] Kidson, R. J. and Ray, D. L. (1984) Pasteurisation by submerged combustion together with anaerobic digestion. In *Sewage Sludge Stabilisation and Disinfection*, Bruce, A. (ed.), Ellis Horwood, Chichester, pp. 399–411.

[5.68] Everett, J. G. (1972) Dewatering of wastewater sludge by heat treatment. *J. Wat. Pollut. Control. Fed.*, **44**, 92–100.

[5.69] White, K. H. (1984) Ionising radiation to treat sludge: energy sources and future prospects. In *Sewage Sludge Stabilisation and Disinfection*, Bruce, A. (ed.), Ellis Horwood, Chichester, pp. 462–487.

[5.70] Massachusetts Institute of Technology (1980) *High energy electron treatment of wastewater liquid residuals.* Final Report to the National Science Foundation.

[5.71] Yeager, J. G. and O'Brien, R. T. (1983) An evaluation of irradiation as a means to minimise public health risks from sludge-borne pathogens. *J. Wat. Pollut. Control. Fed.*, **55**, 977–983.

[5.72] Carrington, E. G. and Harman, S. A. (1984) The effect of gamma irradiation and subsequent storage upon *Salmonella* and other bacteria in sewage sludge. In *Sewage Sludge Stabilisation and Disinfection*, Bruce, A. (ed.), Ellis Horwood, Chichester, pp.546–550.

[5.73] Remini, W. C. (1981) *Executive strategy plan for beneficial uses program cesium-137 sewage sludge irradiation.* US Department of Energy, NE-0014 NTIS, Springfield, Va.

[5.74] Homan, P. S., Hartwigsen, C. C. and Zak, B. D. (1982) *Bibliography of the beneficial uses sewage sludge irradiation project,*

1974–1982. Sandia Report SAND 82–1550, Sandia Research Laboratories, Albuquerque, New Mexico.

[5.75] Lessel, T. and Suess, A. (1981) Europe's experience with sludge irradiation. *54th Annual Conf.. Wat. Pollut. Control. Fed.*

[5.76] Luscher, D. (1980) Operating experiences with a sewage sludge hygienization plant. *Sulzer Technical Review,* **2**, 70–76.

[5.77] Suess, A., Lessel, T. and Haisch, A. (1983) Technical and economic aspects of irradiation. *Proc. EEC Workshop on Disinfection of Sewage Sludge,* Bruce, A., Havelaar, A. H. and L'Hermite, P. (eds), D. Reidel Pub. Co., pp. 179–190.

[5.78] Takenisha, M. and Sakamoto, A. (1982) Radiation treatment of wastewater. *Proc. Conf. Ind. Applications of Radioisotopes and Radiation Technology,* IAEA, Vienna, pp. 217–233.

[5.79] Forster, C. F. (1973) Sludge: Waste or raw material? *Effl. Wat. Trt. J.,* **13**, 697–699.

[5.80] Carberry, J. B., McCaffery, T. F. and Clurie, R. M. (1978) Protein recovery from waste activated sludge. In *New Processes in Wastewater Treatment and Recovery,* Mattock, G. (ed.), Ellis Horwood, Chichester, pp. 374–404.

[5.81] Hand, P. (1985) Earthworm biotechnology. *Ind. Biotech.,* **5**(1), 41–43.

[5.82] Anon. (1984) *Review of Refuse Disposal in Central Scotland,* Report prepared for Scottish Development Agency by Coopers and Lydbrand Associates.

[5.83] E.E.C. (1984) General statistics. *Biomass News Int.,* **1**, 17.

[5.84] Chynhoweth, D. (1978) Waste disposal statistics. *County Council Gazette,* **70**, 268.

[5.85] Filip, Z. and Küster, E. (1979) Microbial activity and the turnover of organic matter in a municipal refuse disposed of in landfill. *Eur. J. Appl. Microbiol. Biotechnol.,* **7**, 371.

[5.86] Jones, K. L. and Grainger, J. M. (1983) The application of enzyme activity measurements to a study of factors affecting protein, starch and cellulose fermentation in domestic refuse. *Eur. J. Appl. Microbiol. Biotechnol.,* **18**, 181.

[5.87] Marchant, A. J. (1981) Practical aspects of landfill: management of landfill gas — a local authority view. In *Landfill Gas Symposium Papers,* Harwell, Paper 7.

[5.88] Kaiser, E. R. (1975) Physical–chemical characters of municipal refuse. In *Proc. Int. Symp. Energy Recovery from Refuse,* University of Louisville, Ky.

[5.89] Griffin, R. A. and Shimp, N. F. (1976) Leachate migration through selected clays. In *Gas and Leachate from Landfill: Formation, Collection and Treatment,* Genetelli, E. J. and Cirello, J. (eds), EPA-600/9-76-004.

[5.90] Lee, G. F. and Jones, R. A. (1984) Is hazardous waste disposal in clay vaults safe? *J. Am. Water Works Assoc.,* **76**, 9, 66.

[5.91] Senior, E. and Balba, M. T. M. (1987) Landfill biotechnology. In

Biotechnology Applied to Environmental Problems, Wise, D. L. (ed.), CRC Press, BOCA Raton, Fl, in press.

[5.92] Diaz, L. F., Savage, G. M. and Golueke, C. G. (1982) *Resource Recovery from Municipal Solid Wastes, Vol. I, Primary Processing*, CRC Press, Boca Raton, Fl.

[5.93] Wigh, R. J. (1984) *Landfill research at Boone County field site*, US National Technical Information Service, Springfield, Va., Report No. PB 84–161546.

[5.94] Crutcher, A. J., Rovers, F. A. and McBean, E. A. (1982) Temperature as an indicator of landfill behaviour. *Water, Air and Soil Pollut.*, **17**, 213.

[5.95] Venkataramania, E. S., Ahlert, R. C. and Corbo, P. (1984) Biological treatment of landfill leachates. *CRC Crit. Rev. Environ. Control*, **14**, 333.

[5.96] Thauer, R. K. and Morris, J. G. (1984) Metabolism of chemotrophic anaerobes: old views and new aspects. In *The Microbe 1984. II: Prokaryotes and Eukaryotes*, Kelly, D. P. and Carr, N. G. (eds), SGM Symp. 36 (II), Cambridge University Press, p. 123.

[5.97] Zeikus, J. G. (1983) Metabolic communication between biodegradative populations in nature. In *Microbes in their Natural Environments*, Slater, J. H., Whittenbury, R. and Wimpenny, J. W. T. (eds), SGM Symp. 34, Cambridge University Press, p. 423.

[5.98] Mountfort, D. O. and Bryant, M. P. (1982) Isolation and characterisation of anaerobic syntrophic benzoate-degrading bacterium from sewage sludge. *Arch. Microbiol.*, **133**, 249.

[5.99] Laanbroek, H. J. and Veldkamp, H. (1982) Microbial interactions in sediment communities. *Phil. Trans. Royal Soc. London, Ser. B.*, **297**, 533.

[5.100] Cappenberg, Th.E. (1975) A study of mixed continuous cultures of sulfate-reducing and methane producing bacteria. *Microb. Ecol.*, **2**, 60.

[5.101] Campbell, D. J. V. (1983) Understanding water balance in landfill sites. *Wastes Management*, **73**, 594.

[5.102] Pohland, F. G. (1972) *Landfill stabilisation with leachate recycle*, Ann. Prog. Report EPA, EP-00658, Washington, DC.

[5.103] Marriott, J. (1981) Some aspects of control of leachate from landfill sites. *Solid Wastes*, **71**, 513.

[5.104] Forster, C. F. (1973) Food from the waste cycle. *Reclamation Industries International*, July/August, 26–29.

[5.105] Dilaj, M. and Lenard, J. F. (1975) Stop leachate problems. *Water Waste Eng.*, **12**, 10, 27.

[5.106] Robinson, H. D. and Maris, P. J. (1979) *Leachate from domestic waste: generation, composition and treatment. A review*. Technical Report TR 108, Water Research Centre.

[5.107] Reinard, M., Goodman, N. L. and Barker, J. F. (1984) Occurrence and distribution of organic chemicals in two landfill leachate plumes. *Environ. Sci. Technol.*, **18**, 953.

[5.108] Brice, J. B., McGahan, D. J. and Rees, J. F. (1984) *The chemical composition of leachate derived from various fractions of domestic refuse*, UKAEA, Harwell, Report AERE-R 10938.

[5.109] Ham, R. K. and Bookter, T. J. (1982) Decomposition of solid waste in test lysimeters. *J. Environ. Eng. Div., ASCE*, **108**, (EE6), 1147.

[5.110] Raveh, A. and Avnimelch, Y. (1979) Leaching of pollutants from sanitary landfill models. *J. Wat. Pollut. Control Fed.*, **51**, 2705.

[5.111] Josephson, J. (1982) Immobilization and leachability of hazardous wastes. *Environ. Sci. Technol.*, **16**, 219A.

[5.112] Harmsen, J. (1983) Identification of organic compounds in leachate from a waste tip. *Water Res.*, **17**, 699.

[5.113] Rees, J. F. (1982) Landfill management and leachate quality. *Effl. Wat. Trt. J.*, **22**, 457.

[5.114] Ehrig, H. J. (1983) Quality and quantity of sanitary landfill leachate. *Waste Management Res.*, **1**, 53.

[5.115] Tester, D. J. and Harker, R. J. (1982) Groundwater pollution investigations in the Great Ouse basin. II Solid waste disposal. *Wat. Pollut. Control*, **81**, 308.

[5.116] Chian, E. S. K. and deWalle, F. B. (1976) Sanitary landfill leachates and their treatment. *J. Environ. Eng. Div., ASCE*, **102**, EE2, 411.

[5.117] Khan, A. Q. (1982) Control of water inflow to landfill sites. In *Landfill Leachate Symposium*, Harwell, Paper 2.

[5.118] Robinson, H. D. and Maris, P. J. (1985) The treatment of leachates from domestic waste in landfill sites. *J. Wat. Pollut. Control Fed.*, **57**, 30.

[5.119] Campbell, D. J. V., Parker, A., Rees, J. F. and Ross, C. A. M. (1983) Attenuation of potential pollutants in landfill leachate by Lower Greensand. *Waste Management Res.*, **1**, 31.

[5.120] Loch, J. P. G., Lagas, P. and Haring,. B. J. A. M. (1981) Behaviour of heavy metals in soil beneath a landfill; results of model experiments. *Sci. Total Environ.*, **21**, 203.

[5.121] Deeley, G. M., Skierkowski, P. and Robertson, J. M. (1985) Biodegradation of [^{14}C] phenol in secondary sewage and landfill leachate measured by double-vial radiorespirometry. *Appl. Environ. Microbiol.*, **49**, 867.

[5.122] Robinson, H. D., Barber, C. and Morris, P. J. (1982) Generation and treatment of leachate from domestic wastes in landfills. *Wat Pollut. Control*, **81**, 465.

[5.123] Barber, C. (1983) Treatability and treatment of leachate from domestic wastes in landfills. *Reclamation 83 Papers*, Industrial Seminars Ltd, p. 362.

[5.124] Mather, J. D. (1977) Attenuation and control of landfill leachate. *J. Inst. Solid Wastes Management*, **67**, 362.

[5.125] Tittlebaum, M. E. (1982) Organic carbon content stabilisation through landfill leachate recirculation. *J. Wat. Pollut. Control. Fed.*, **54**, 428.

[5.126] Tomson, M. B., Dauchy, J., Hutchins, S., Curran, C., Cook, R. C. J. and Ward, C. H. (1981) Groundwater contamination by trace level organics from a rapid infiltration site. *Water Res.*, **15**, 1109.

[5.127] Scott, M. P. (1982) Options for the treatment of municipal and chemical waste leachate. *Public Hlth. Eng.*, **10**, 119.

[5.128] Chan, K. Y. (1982) Changes to a soil on irrigation with a sanitary landfill leachate. *Water, Air and Soil Pollut.*, **17**, 295.

[5.129] Pavacic, J. W. (1983) A leachate recirculation project. *Public Works*, **114**, 68.

[5.130] Bull, P. S., Evans, J. V., Wechsler, R. M. and Cleland, K. J. (1983) Biological technology of the treatment of leachate from sanitary landfills. *Water Res.*, **17**, 1473.

[5.131] Menser, H. A. (1981) Irrigating with landfill leachate. *Biocycle* **22**, 39.

[5.132] Stegmann, R. (1982) Design and construction of leachate treatment plants in West Germany; current status. In *Landfill Leachate Symposium Papers*, Harwell, Paper 11.

[5.133] Chian, E. S. K. and deWalle, F. B. (1977) *Evaluation of leachate treatment, Volume II. Biological and Physical–Chemical Treatment Processes*, EPA-600/2-77/186b.

[5.134] Smith, P. G. (1984) Removal of ammonia from landfill leachates and other wastewaters. *Public Hlth Eng.*, **12**, 159.

[5.135] Lavigne, R. A. (1979) The treatment of landfill leachate using a 'living filter'. *Compost Sci./ Land Util.*, **20**, 3, 24.

[5.136] Zapfe-Gilje, R. and Mavinic, D. S. (1981) Temperature effects of biostabilisation of leachate. *J. Environ. Eng. Div.*, *ASCE*, **107**, EE4, Proc. Paper 16430, 653.

[5.137] Palit, T. and Qasim, S. R. (1977) Biological treatment kinetics of landfill leachate. *J. Environ. Eng. Div.*, *ASCE*, **103**, EE2, 353.

[5.138] Cossu, R. (1984) Laboratory investigation of leachate treatment by anaerobic lagooning. *Ing. Amb.*, **13**, 226.

[5.139] Boyle, W. C. and Ham, R. K. (1974) Biological treatability of landfill leachate. *J. Wat. Pollut. Control Fed.*, **46**, 860.

[5.140] Thornton, R. J. and Blanc, F. C. (1973) Leachate treatment by coagulation and precipitation. *J. Environ. Eng. Div.*, *ASCE*, **99**, E4, Proc. Paper 9946, 535.

[5.141] Green, W. J., Lee, G. F., Jones, R. A. and Pallt, T. (1983) Interaction of clay soils with water and organic solvents: implications for the disposal of hazardous wastes. *Environ. Sci. Technol.*, **17**, 278.

[5.142] Gunn, A. (1983) Hazardous wastes disposal or dispersal. *Soil and Water*, **19**, 4.

[5.143] Tittlebaum, M. E., Seals, R. K., Cartledge, F. K. and Engels, S. (1985) State of the art on stabilisation of hazardous organic liquid wastes and sludges. *CRC Crit. Rev. Environ. Control*, **15**, 179.

[5.144] Lee, G. F. and Jones, R. A. (1981) Application of site-specific hazard assessment testing to solid wastes. In *Hazardous Solid Waste Testing: First Conference*, ASTM STP 760, Conway, R. A. and Malloy, B. C. (eds), p. 331.

[5.145] Pearce, P. (1983) Landfilling: a long-term option for hazardous waste disposal? *UNEP Indutry and Environment Special Issue*, 57.

[5.146] Hounslow, A. W. (1980) Groundwater geochemistry: arsenic in landfills. *Groundwater*, **18**, 331.

[5.147] Knox, K. (1983) Treatability studies on leachate from a co-disposal landfill. *Environ. Pollut. Ser. B.*, **157**.

[5.148] Kosson, D. D. and Ahlert, R. C. (1984) *In situ* and on-site biodegradation of industrial landfill leachate. *Environ. Progress*, **3**, 176.

[5.149] Strearns, R. P. (1980) Landfill methane: 23 sites are developing recovery systems. *Solid Wastes Management/RRJ*, June, 56.

[5.150] Bogardus, E. R. (1984) Should you recover landfill gas? *Biocycle*, **25**, 48.

[5.151] Cheyney, A. C. and Moss, H. D. T. (1981) Landfill gas as an energy source. In *Landfill Gas Symposium*, Harwell, Paper 9.

[5.152] Baker, J. M., Peters, C. J., Perry, R. and Knight, C. P. V. (1984) Odour problems associated with solid waste disposal. *Public Hlth Eng.*, **12**, 115.

[5.153] Bohn, H. L. (1975) Soil and compost filters of malodorant gases. *J. Air Pollut. Control Assoc.*, **25**, 953.

[5.154] Gill, T. (1985) Landfill gas — A fuel from waste for industry. *Ind. Biotech.*, **5**(3), Conference Article 3:1:85.

[5.155] Marchant, A. J. (1982) The sweet smell of success? Landfill gas its problems and uses. *Wastes Management*, **72**, 236.

[5.156] Parry, G. D. R. (1981) Afteruse of landfill sites. In *Landfill Gas Symposium*, Harwell, Paper 8.

[5.157] Ham, R. K. (1979) Predicting gas generation from landfills. *Waste Age*, November, 50.

[5.158] Rees, J. F. (1981) Major factors affecting methane production in landfills. In *Landfill Gas Symposium*, Harwell, Paper 2.

[5.159] Nyns, E. J. and Pauss, A. (1984) Production of methane by anaerobic digestion of domestic refuse. In *Proc. Int. Symp. Anaerobic Digestion and Carbohydrate Hydrolysis of Waste*, Luxembourg, p. 30.

[5.160] Farquhar, G. J. and Rovers, F. A. (1973) Gas production during refuse decomposition. *Water, Air and Soil Pollut.*, **2**, 483.

[5.161] deWalle, F. B., Chian, E. S. K. and Hammerberg, E. (1978) Gas production from solid waste in landfills. *J. Environ. Eng. Div., ASCE*, **104**, EE3, 415.

[5.162] Klink, R. E. and Ham, R. K. (1982) Effects of moisture movement on methane production in solid waste landfill samples. *Resour. Recov. Conserv.*, **8**, 29.

[5.163] Hartz, K. E., Klink, R. E. and Ham, R. K. (1982) Temperature effects: methane generation from landfill samples. *J. Environ. Eng. Div., ASCE*, **108**, EE4, 629.

[5.164] Stegmann, R. (1981) Landfill gas problems — summary of West German experience. In *Landfill Gas Symposium*, Harwell, Paper 6.

[5.165] Wimpenny, J. W. T., Coombs, J. P. and Lovitt, R. W. (1984) Growth and interactions of microorganisms in spatially hetero-geneous ecosystems. In *Current Perspectives in Microbial Ecology*, Klug, M. J. and Reddy, C. A. (eds), ASM, Washington, DC, p. 291.

[5.166] Harder, W., Dijkhuizen, L. and Veldkamp, H. (1984) Environ-mental regulation of microbial metabolism. In *The Microbe 1984. II: Prokaryotes and Eukaryotes*, Kelly, D. P. and Carr, N. G. (eds), SGM Symp. 36(II), 51.

[5.167] Raab, J. (1985) Biogas resources developed in Oregon. *Public Works*, **116**, 64–65.

6

Agricultural alternatives

Carol A. Day
Microbial Developments Ltd, Malvern Link, Malvern, Worcs., UK
and
Stephen G. Lisansky
Biotechnology Affiliates, Reading, Berks., UK

6.1 INTRODUCTION

Particularly in the more developed countries, high agricultural yields are obtained through intensive farming. High stocking levels are generally maintained by use of antibiotics and intensive crop cultivation, together with high levels of nitrogenous fertiliser and the use of chemical pesticides to maintain yields. Forage has to be available over winter months, necessitating careful preservation.

Man cannot live without food, and there is therefore little doubt that intensive agricultural practices will continue in the future, although many of the means currently in use to attain such an intensity are open to criticism. New biotechnological alternatives to current practices not open to such criticism are now being developed, offering a means of avoiding many of our current problems; some of these developments form the subject of this chapter.

6.2 INTRODUCTION TO PROBIOTICS

The indiscriminate and increasing use of antibiotics given in low dosage, both as a growth stimulant and as a preventative measure against stress-related gastrointestinal disturbances in farm animals, is causing mounting ferred from one bacterial cell to another at conjugation through a transmissible plasmid which is usually a circular piece of extrachromosomal DNA capable of replication. An antibiotic given at low dosage over a period of time leads to a marked increase in numbers of drug-resistant micro-organisms, particularly the Enterobacteriaceae residing in the mammalian gut, because of the transfer of these R factors. R factors are now frequently found in both commensal and pathogenic gut-colonising Enterobacteriaceae. Having evolved in some farm animals, transferable drug resistance has now been found in the gut microflora of man. A *Salmonella* infection amongst cattle successfully treated with therapeutic doses of antibiotics may not, at first sight, give cause for alarm. However, these bacteria too can acquire transferable resistance. Spread to man by contaminated meat, *Salmonella* organisms containing R factors can pass them on to the normal commensal micro-organisms found in the human gastrointestinal tract, which in turn transfer resistance to human pathogenic Enterobacteriaceae. This seemingly endless vicious circle can repeat itself with many different antibiotics, and more complex multiple-resistance R factors have now evolved. By this mechanism, many pathogenic micro-organisms now show increasing antibiotic resistance, and concern at this development has prompted much research over the last few decades into the use of lactic acid bacterial preparations as a safer alternative to low-dose antibiotics for the prevention and possible treatment of stress-related gut disturbances in farm animals.

6.3   HISTORY OF PROBIOTICS

Several commercial 'anti-stress' products are now available, incorporating single or mixed cultures of lactic acid bacteria, such as *Lactobacillus acidophilus* and *Streptococcus faecium*, along with electrolytes and vitamins. Marketed as oral pastes and gels or dissolvable powders, they have had a mixed reception in the UK over the last few years. Although many animal trials of probiotics have been performed in the United States, as yet there is little evidence of proven efficacy under UK farming conditions. However, several research institutes are now conducting such trials.

One of the earliest references to the possible value of lactic acid bacteria to health was made by Metchnikoff [6.1] who attributed the longevity of the Balkan people to their regular ingestion of fermented milk. Since then there has been fluctuating interest in the use of lactic acid bacteria as dietary aids until the evolution and recognition of transferable drug resistance. The modern production of livestock now places a tremendous amount of stress on young farm animals. Farm management practices dictate that the young animal, separated from its mother soon after birth, is reared on an artificial diet to achieve a rapid gain in weight in as short a time period as possible. Scouring, enteritis and diarrhoea are a common occurrence at this time and it is believed that these conditions arise as a result of an imbalance in the intestinal microflora. This imbalance occurs because of the lack of implantation in the gut by normal non-pathogenic micro-organisms which are diet to achieve a rapid gain in weight in as short a time period as possible. Scouring, enteritis and diarrhoea are a common occurrence at this time and it is believed that these conditions arise as a result of an imbalance in the intestinal microflora. This imbalance occurs because of the lack of implantation in the gut by normal non-pathogenic micro-organisms which are usually obtained from the mother when reared under natural conditions. Research has been conducted using lactic acid bacterial cultures to try to combat the onset of enteritis as a preventative measure and also to alleviate or stop the diarrhoea once it has arisen.

Comparison of gnotobiotic animals with normally reared animals has shown that the physiological characteristics of the gastrointestinal tract change when deprived of a normal intestinal microflora, leading to reduced intestinal weight due to poor development and excess liquids in the caecum and colon, Clarke and Bauchop [6.2] showed that these changes could be reversed once normal microflora were re-established. It was also found that the normal microflora of the gut had an inhibitory effect on pathogenic micro-organisms. Oral introduction of *Shigella* spp. into gnotobiotic animals soon brought about enteritis and diarrhoea, but the same dosage of *Shigella* spp. introduced into animals with a normal gut microflora had little effect and was soon eliminated from the gastrointestinal tract. Other researchers have obtained similar results when animals were exposed to other pathogenic. micro-organisms, such as *Clostridium* spp., *Staphylococcus* spp. and enteropathogenic *Escherichia coli*.

6.4   THE LACTOBACILLI AS PROBIOTIC ORGANISMS

There is a wealth of information on the role of *Lactobacillus* spp. in the maintenance of health in the gastrointestinal tract of both animals and man. Most researchers agree that the antibacterial role of these lactic acid bacteria lies in their ability to produce sufficient acid to inhibit other micro-organisms, and to attach to sites on the intestinal villi at the expense of other bacterial species. Moreover, certain strains of *Lactobacillus* spp. not only possess anti *E. coli* activity but also produce metabolites which are capable of neutralising the effects of enterotoxins produced by many gut-colonising micro-organisms. *Lactobacillus* organisms have been isolated from many regions of the gastrointestinal tract, and similarities in the composition and proportion of gut microflora of many warm-blooded animals have been recorded. Establishing themselves within a few hours of birth [6.3], *Lactobacillus* spp. soon alter the overall pH of the immature gut so that protection against enteropathogenic micro-organisms is afforded at a very early age. In the early studies of animal intestinal microflora much work was undertaken to identify the *Lactobacillus* spp. involved. The three most dominant species isolated were *Lactobacillus acidophilus*, *L. bulgaricus* and *L. bifidus*. *L. bulgaricus* was found to be a high acid producer but was not credited with the ability to survive through the digestive tract to a degree sufficient for intestinal implantation to take place [6.4]. However, later studies have shown that *L. bulgaricus* does possess both anti-*E. coli* and anti- *E. coli*-enterotoxin activity [6.5] and that the addition of this micro-organism to pig milk replacer at the time of weaning has a beneficial effect. *L. bifidus* and *L. acidophilus* also survive the digestive tract and both could be thought potential candidates for oral implantation. *L. bifidus* and *Actinomyces bifidus*), an organism found in the intestines of infants on a diet of human milk [6.6], was found to be difficult to grow *in vitro*, for many strains require complex growth factors found only in human milk. *L. acidophilus*, however, is found not only in the gastrointestinal tract of infants and young animals fed on a diet of cows' milk but also in many healthy adult animals. The fact that *L. acidophilus* survives throughout the digestive tract and can be cultivated *in vitro* relatively easily, makes it one of the *Lactobacillus* spp. of choice for oral implantation.

6.5   MECHANISMS OF THE PROBIOTIC ACTION OF THE LACTOBACILLI

The inhibitory action of *Lactobacillus* spp. to other micro-organisms owes much to their ability to produce acid. *L. acidophilus*, being a homofermentative organism, produces over 85% lactic acid from the fermentation of glucose, and it is this production of lactic acid which establishes an acid condition in the intestines of most animals. Many enteropathogenic micro-organisms prefer a neutral or slightly alkaline environment and so acidity alone can be quite inhibitory to many of them. Also, *L. acidophilus* is a facultative anaerobe and consequently thrives in the intestinal environment. Under such circumstances the lactobacilli have a distinct advantage over other micro-organisms in the struggle for nutrients.

6.5.1   Specificity of strains

Many lactic acid bacteria are known to adhere to the epithelial surfaces lining the gastrointestinal tract of many animals, but as researchers have shown, this adherence not only seems to be tissue-selective within the various regions of the alimentary tract itself but, in some cases, is also species–specific [6.7; 6.8]. Fuller [6.9; 6.10] found that lactobacilli attached to the epithelial lining of the chicken crop within hours of hatching. Their constant presence, unaffected by diet constituents or abrasion, means that a low pH is maintained in the crop which keeps the upper intestine free from harmful bacterial invasion. If lactobacilli from a non-avian source are introduced, they do not adhere or establish themselves in the crop and are washed through the gastrointestinal tract with ingested material. Only avian lactobacilli were capable of adherence to crop epithelium; a symbiotic relationship had probably evolved between them and the epithelial cells of the crop [6.9]. In pigs and calves, too, it was found that a number of lactic acid bacteria were capable of attachment, particularly to the gastric epithelium [6.11]. Barrow *et al.* [6.12], using *in vitro* techniques, demonstrated that lactic acid bacteria of porcine origin adhered in the greatest numbers, particularly strains of *Lactobacilus fermentum* and *Streptococcus salivarius*. However, they did not attach to columnar epithelial cells from excised procine small and large intestine, and other lactic acid bacteria of non-porcine origin did not adhere to either tissue. The specificity of these micro-organisms was further demonstrated by Mayra-Makinen *et al.* [6.13] who found porcine strains of *L. fermentum* capable of *in vitro* adherence to columnar epithelial tissue of pigs, in contrast to the findings of Barrow *et al.* [6.12]. This gives further credence to the increasing observation that adhering strains of lactic acid bacteria can be highly species- and tissue-specific.

6.5.2 Antimicrobial metabolites of the lactobacilli

One of the predominant intestinal micro-organisms in mammals is *E. coli*. *E. coli* and *L. acidophilus* co-exist in the same intestinal environment, but the acid produced by the lactobacilli usually suppresses *E. coli* and a balance between the organisms is established. A vigorous strain of *L. acidophilus* tends to become dominant in this situation and exerts a strong influence by competing with other microflora for nutrients and attachment sites in the gut [6.14] and so keeps the coliform micro-organisms at a low level. Many researchers have found that some strains of lactic acid bacteria also produce various antimicrobial metabolites. Wheater *et al.* [6.15] referred to these anti-bacterials under the broad term 'lactobacillin', but Vincent *et al.* [6.16], when investigating the antibacterial activity of *L. acidophilus*, decribed the active substance produced as 'lactocidin'. They found that lactocidin demonstrated broad-spectrum activity against many enteric bacteria but that pathogenic gram-negative organisms were most susceptible to a crude extract of lactocidin. *L. acidophilus* was later shown to produce other antibiotic-like substances, such as acidolin, acidophilin and bacteriocins; similarly *L. bulgaricus* was also found to produce inhibitory proteins. De Mitchell and Kenworthy [6.5] suggested not only that *L. bulgaricus* showed antagonism towards the *E. coli* organisms themselves but that some of its metabolites also demonstrate cell-free anti-enterotoxin activity. The effi-cacy of a selected strain was tested by the addition of *L. bulgaricus* to diets in a feeding trial using young pigs exposed to haemolytic *E. coli* at the time of weaning. Beneficial responses to the dietary inclusion of *L. bulgaricus* and its metabolites was demonstrated. Although there was only a 10% reduction in the recovery of haemolytic *E. coli* from the experimental group of piglets versus those recovered from the control group, there was a significant improvement of up to 30% in both weight gain and reduction in scouring and mortality in those piglets receiving *L. bulgaricus*. This suggested that most benefit seemed to have been derived from the anti-enterotoxin activity of the organism, a fairly specific mode of action. Other lactic acid bacteria have also been found to produce anti-microbial cell-free metabolites, for example *Streptococcus faecium* [6.17] and *S. diacetylactis* [6.18], active against many enteric pathoghenic micro-organisms, such as *E. coli* and *Salmonella* spp. The subsequent isolation, characterisation and purification of some of these inhibitory proteins [6.19] has further demonstrated the specificity of these metabolites.

6.6 MANUFACTURE OF *LACTOBACILLUS* BASED PROBIOTICS

It is the net effect of the properties possessed by many lactic acid bacteria (e.g. lactic acid production, adherence capability, anti-microbial and anti-enterotoxin activity, as well as high tolerance to low pH and bile [6.13]) which promotes and maintains a normal intestinal environment. It is also these very properties which must be retained when manufacturers produce lactic acid bacteria commercially for incorporation into probiotic preparations. An excellent review by Klaenhammer [6.20] highlights the importance of strain selection and fermentation conditions in the full-scale production of *L. acidophilus*. Although the biological activity of such preparations for probiotic use is of prime importance, viability and stability of lactic acid bacterial concentrates is of equal importance. It was found that environmental and cultural conditions could affect the phenotypic response of *Lactobacillus* cultures during growth. Under conditions of nutritional deficiency, *Lactobacillus* spp. can adopt a filamentous morphology resulting in a 'rough' colonial appearance when subcultured onto agar. 'Smooth' colonies from bacillary forms of *L. acidophilus* grown under more favourable conditions were found to be far more resistant to the environmental stresses of concentration processes, freezing and freeze-drying. It would seem logical, therefore, in the development of fermentation procedures, for manufacturers to choose those conditions which would encourage the growth of bacillary forms and so enhance the long-term stability of their products. Because of all these factors which must be considered, there is no easy route to the production of lactic acid bacterial cultures for probiotic use. Once a probiotic has been developed, animal feed trials need to be performed to judge the efficacy of the product. Many such trials have been performed in the United States, but there is a paucity of such data from Europe.

6.7 CURRENT APPLICATIONS OF *LACTOBACILLUS* PROBIOTICS

6.7.1 Lactobacilli in the treatment of pigs

Various lactic acid bacterial cultures, especially *L. acidophilus*, have been evaluated as possible probiotics for the alleviation of stress-related scouring and diarrhoea in young pigs. The times when piglets are most vulnerable to stress-related gastrointestinal infections are during the first week of life, during weaning, and when they are first moved to growing and fattening pens. Scouring and diarrhoea in pigs at these times is caused by a number of organisms (predominantly haemolytic *E. coli*) which can result in impaired herd performance, colibacillosis and ultimately death from dehydration. Whereas the microflora of the gastrointestinal tract of normal pigs is dominated by lactic acid bacteria, during stressful times, their presence diminishes and is replaced by haemolytic *E. coli* [6.21; 6.22]. Earlier, Kenworthy and Crabb [6.23] had observed that, at the onset of gastroenteritis, haemolytic *E. coli* appeared in the jejunum and ileum of young pigs. Chopra *et al.* [6.24] also found an increase in *E. coli* numbers at this time. They observed that in normal pigs there is a natural balance between lactic acid bacteria and coliforms in the gastrointestinal tract which becomes greatly disturbed when diarrhoea is present. In scouring pigs, haemolytic strains of *E. coli* increase dramatically. With colibacillosis and other stress-related gastrointestinal disturbances a major cause of economic loss in the pig industry, and transferable drug resistance causing many strains of haemolytic *E. coli* to be resistant to an increasing number of antibiotics, the use of lactic acid bacterial preparations is seen as a possible safe alternative.

Kohler and Bohl [6.25] reported that the feeding of *L. acidophilus* to piglets prior to their transport resulted in a dramatic reduction in stress-related piglet death, and Redmond and Moore [6.26] similarly found that *L. acidophilus* cultures fed to a pig herd suffering from enteritis brought about a significant reduction in scouring. In a review by Sandine *et al* [6.22] which cites many references to this early work, it is noted that not only does *L. acidophilus* supplementation reduce the onset and persistence of scouring in pigs, it also indirectly brings about beneficial gains in weight. Other lactic acid bacteria have also been shown to demonstrate antimicrobial and growth stimulatory activity. A concentrate of *Streptococcus faecium* developed in Sweden was evaluated and found to be useful as a growth stimulant for weaned and growing pigs [6.27]. Muralidhara's group supplemented the diet of bottle-fed newborn pigs with frozen concentrates of *L. lactis*. They found not only that *L. lactis* reduced the number of faecal coliforms and the incidence of scouring in the pigs, but that this suppression persisted for at least 30 days after treatment was discontinued due to the continuing colonisation of epithelium by *L. lactis* [6.28]. They also found that piglets receiving both colostrum and lactobacilli did not produce any scouring when challenged with haemolytic *E. coli*. De Mitchell and Kenworthy [6.5] supplemented the diet of early weaned pigs with broth cultures of different species of lactobacilli organisms and found many species were capable of inhibiting the growth of *E. coli*. In particular, they found *L. bulgaricus* produced high levels of an anti-enterotoxin metabolite. When studying the attachment of lactic acid bacteria to the gastric epithelium in pigs, Barrow *et al.* [6.21] found that a specific strain of *L. fermentum* which was capable of good adhesion reduced the numbers of *E. coli* found in the stomach and duodenum. However, they found only moderate success in the prevention of scouring, due partly to the low numbers of lactobacilli administered ($>10^6$ organisms). It has been suggested that an effective dosage rate is 10^8–10^9 organisms, administered on a daily basis.

6.7.2   Lactobacilli for transported cattle

L. acidophilus has also been found to suppress enteric bacteria in other animal species. Cattle are transported at some stage in their lives and during transit can be subjected to the stresses of overcrowding, fear, lack of food and undue movement. Trovatelli and Matteuzzi [6.29] found that, after transit, those cattle normally on high-roughage diets had very low concentrations of *Lactobacillus* organisms in the rumen compared to those cattle on high-grain rations. Consequently, the former cattle had little inoculum to start fermentation again once the cattle were in their new environment and so were prone to stress-related gastrointestinal bacterial infections. During the initial period of settling in, *Lactobacillus* supplements have been used to avert these problems and are believed to have greatest value in 're-conditioning' the rumen at this time. In similar trials, Crawford [6.30] found that cattle given *Lactobacillus* supplementation during this settling-in period showed statistically significant benefits in terms of weight gain and feed efficiency conversion when compared with control animals. Gilliland *et al.* [6.31] fed *L. acidophilus* cultures obtained from two different sources to young calves. They found that those calves fed *L. acidophilus* from a bovine source showed a higher incidence of lactobacilli in the faeces, whereas those fed *L. acidophilus* from a human source produced a greater decrease in coliform numbers. This is further evidence that it is important to be selective in the choice of *Lactobacillus* strain used for any possible probiotic use, and in the end only full-scale animal trials will confirm that choice.

6.7.3   *Lactobacillus* supplementation in poultry

Compared with other animal species, there are a lot more data available on *Lactobacillus* supplementation in poultry. The immune system in the young poults is immature, and they are quite susceptible to bacterial and viral enteritis. When affected, they are reluctant to move and have a depressed appetite with accompanying diarrhoea; if the infection is severe, death will eventually occur. The degree of mortality depends on the pathogenicity of the primary invading agent which may be bacterial (e.g. *Campylobacter* spp., *E. coli* and *Salmonella* spp.), fungal (e.g. *Candida* spp.), viral (e.g. adenovirus, rotavirus, etc.) or parasitic. In normal healthy poultry the crop is dominated by lactobacilli with many species attaching to the crop epithelium as well as being found in the ileum and caecum [6.32; 6.33].

Under natural rearing conditions, young poultry are more resistant to *E. coli* enteric infections than the neonatal pig or calf, presumably because of close contact with litter as soon as they are hatched. However, when reared under modern, artificial intensive conditions susceptibility to enteric disease is increased due to a decrease in lactic acid bacterial load and a subsequent delaying of colonisation by lactobacilli on the one hand, and an increase in bacteriological stress due to overcrowding and *E. coli* invasion on the other. Fuller [6.33] showed that *Lactobacillus* fed to healthy chicks soon after hatching resulted in an improved growth rate during the first 3 weeks of life. He also found [6.34] that *Streptococcus faecium* played a significant protective role in the duodenum of the chicken. Earlier, Tortuero [6.35] had found that *L. acidophilus* supplementation to growing chicks under commercial conditions led to a marked increase in lactobacilli throughout the gut with an almost total disappearance of coliform bacteria. A statistically significant improvement in broiler growth rate and feed efficiency was also observed when Dilworth and Day [6.36] evaluated the addition of differing levels of *Lactobacillus* cultures to broiler diets. When summarising the results of trials performed by various American universities, Crawford [6.30] found similar results. He also found that there was a consistent improvement in the production of large eggs by *Lactobacillus*-supplemented layer birds along with a simultaneous reduction in feed uptake, so confirming other researchers' findings that feed efficiency was significantly improved.

6.8   CONCLUDING COMMENTS

With lactic acid bacteria widely distributed in nature and becoming an important part of the intestinal micoflora of young, warm-blooded animals shortly after birth, it would seem pertinent in the light of all these findings to suggest that probiotic administration could be of immense benefit to animals during stressful times, as an alternative to low-dose antibiotic prophylaxis. However, as has been demonstrated, the application of biotechnology in this instance is not that simple. Any prospective manufacturer of probiotics has a lot to take into account. The selection of the right species and strain of lactic acid bacteria that will colonise the gut of many animals, that will produce enough lactic acid to achieve an inhibitory low pH and that may also produce antimicrobial and anti-enterotoxin metabolites may, at first sight, be a large enough hurdle to climb to start with. Sarra *et al.* [6.37] demonstrated recently that many *L. acidophilus* strains possess genetic heterogeneity and in their studies divided these strains into four genetic groups. This research suggests that *L. acidophilus* demonstrates a certain amount of 'host specificity' and obviously this has an important bearing when selecting suitable strains for probiotic use. Selection and corroboration by animal trials is only the beginning. Another important aspect to be taken into account is that the selected probiotic strain should be resistant to many of the growth-promoting antibiotics used in commercial livestock farming. Even as probiotics are being introduced the concept is a novel one for many farmers and it is likely that they will be used simultaneously with growth promoters as a cautionary measure until they have proven efficacy. Dutta and Devriese [6.38] have demonstrated that many lactobacilli are resistant to the more common growth promotants used today, but it is an important point that must be borne in mind. Other choices that must be made are production ones; whether the growth medium will encourage the correct phenotypic form to grow to maximum viable numbers in a commercial fermentation plant, and whether the micro-encapsulation technique or cryoprotectant chosen produces a viable and stable product.

However, as with the successful commercialisation of *E. coli* vaccines, probiotics will no doubt ultimately find their place as a safe alternative to low-dose antibiotics for the prevention and treatment of stress-related gut disturbances in farm animals.

6.9 INTRODUCTION TO LEGUME INOCULANTS

Nitrogenous fertilisers have become increasingly expensive due to fossil fuel shortages, and environmentalists and conservationists have increased public and political awareness of the possibilities of chemical pollution. Consequently, attention is now being focussed on the processes of biological nitrogen fixation as an alternative to fertiliser nitrogen.

The agricultural importance of nitrogen fixation has led to extensive research on the bacteria which are capable of forming a symbiotic relationship with leguminous plants. One such genus is the *Rhizobium* species which have been isolated from the root nodules of various legumes such as peas, lupins, clovers, soybeans and lucerne.

6.10 THE *RHIZOBIUM* BACTERIA

Some of the earliest research was undertaken by Hellriegel and Wilfarth [6.39] who examined the nodules found on the roots of *Pisum sativum*. They suggested that the nodules were formed by the action of bacteria and that nodulation enabled the plants to fix nitrogen. Beijerinck [6.40] later isolated pure cultures of such nodule-forming bacteria, now classified as *Rhizobium leguminosarum*.

6.10.1 Classification and specificity

Later researchers found that all the *Rhizobium* species isolated from nodules resemble each other very closely but show a considerable degree of host specificity. For example, those isolated from lupins cannot successfully induce nodule formation in peas and vice versa. However, *Rhizobium* species isolated from peas will form a symbiotic relationship with lentils, broad beans and other members of this particular legume group. So it has been possible to classify the bacteria into a series of 'cross-inoculation' groups according to their activity. The bacteria capable of nodulating the plants in one of these groups are considered a *Rhizobium* sp. (Table 6.1). This grouping of leguminous plants with their respective *Rhizobium* species has been particularly useful to the inoculant manufacturer. Since the initial classification of 'cross-inoculation' groups, taxonomists and inoculant manufacturers alike have focussed attention on other characteristics and techniques whereby *Rhizobium* spp. can be further characterised, such as

Table 6.1 — Host specificity of *Rhizobium* species

Rhizobium species	Host species group
R. japonicum	Glycine spp. (Soybean)
R. leguminosarum	Pisum spp. (Pea)
R. lupini	Lupinus spp. (Lupin)
R. meltiloti	Medicago spp. (Lucerne)
R. phaseoli	Phaseolus spp. (Bean)
R. trifolii	Trifolium spp. (Clover)

Note: The Rhizobiaceae were reclassified in 1982; the slow-growing non acid-producing root-nodule bacteria have been placed in the genus *Bradyrhizobium*. *Rhizobium japonicum*, therefore, is now *Bradyrhizobium japonicum*.

speed of growth [6.41], induced antibiotic resistance [6.42], immunofluorescence [6.43] and longevity [6.44]. Thus strains can now be selected which are capable of nodulating one particular plant species or variety, and from these, the best nitrogen-fixing bacteria can be chosen as a specific inoculant.

6.10.2 Invasion, penetration and nodule formation
Rhizobium species invade the roots of leguminous plants and initiate the formation of root nodules, within which they develop as intracellular symbionts and fix dinitrogen. Rhizobial cells penetrate the root hairs of the legume plant and travel into the root via a special tube, the 'infection thread'. This thread is thought to develop from an invagination of the plasmalemma from where it proceeds to the root cortex. Here the rhizobia infect the cells and stimulate them into division to form the young nodules. It was once thought that invasion only occurred in tetraploid cells but evidence suggests that this is not the case [6.45]. Division also occurs in cells before penetration by the infection thread. In young nodules, the bacteria occur mainly as rods, but in later growth form a variety of shapes, becoming spherical, branched or club-shaped, and are known as 'bacteroid' [6.46]. These bacteroids clump together in small groups and become surrounded by host membrane within the nodule. Once nodules are forming with large numbers of specific rhizobia present in the host, deformation of the root hairs occurs with subsequent 'branching' and 'curling' [6.47].

There has been much research into the basic mechanism of rhizobial attraction to the root hairs of legumes. Dazzo and Hubbell [6.48] and Brill [6.49] have suggested that there is a specific interaction between the root hair surfaces and specific *Rhizobium* species. They thought that lectins were possibly produced by the host plant and these were capable of binding the rhizobial cells to the root hair surfaces. However, this work has not been successfully repeated. Gaworzewska and Carlile [6.50] demonstrated positive chemotaxis of *Rhizobium leguminosarum* towards root exudates produced by the host, the edible pea. However, it is suggested that this process is not symbiont-specific, for they found that the rhizobial bacteria were also attracted to exudates from many other plants, non-legumes included. In addition, *Escherichia coli*, as well as other *Rhizobium* species, were attracted to the edible pea root exudate. Other researchers have suggested that inhibition, rather than attraction, may be the answer to host specificity [6.45; 6.51].

6.10.3   Nitrogen fixation in *Rhizobium* spp.

When grown separately, neither the leguminous plant nor the *Rhizobium* bacteria can fix nitrogen, but upon interaction between the two this new property is acquired. This is the essence of the symbiotic relationship in that they both benefit from the association. The legume provides energy from its carbon sources to the bacteria, and the rhizobia provide fixed nitrogen which is utilised by the legume. This sphere of influence also extends for a short distance away from the roots so that other plants, such as companion grasses, also benefit from the availability of fixed nitrogen.

A unique characteristic of active nodules is the presence of a red pigment, leghaemoglobin. Like mammalian haemoglobin, leghaemoglobin possesses an important property in that it can bind with and immobilise oxygen. Equally important is the fact that this process is reversible. Sited in the host cytoplasm, the importance of this protein which is produced by the legume [6.52] could be appreciated when it was realised that a dilemma exists in terms of oxygen need. Rhizobia are strict aerobes in that they can only grow and multiply in the presence of oxygen. However, the enzyme they produce, nitrogenase, is inactivated by high levels of oxygen and will only fix dinitrogen in a reduced atmosphere. It is likely, therefore, that the leghaemoglobin provides the necessary regulation of oxygen diffusion within the nodules. It combines with molecular oxygen so that the nitrogenase is not inhibited, but the combined oxygen can become available at respiratory sites for oxidative metabolism in the host cytoplasm close to the bacteroids [6.53]. The structural organisation of the nodule also promotes the rapid removal of the products of nitrogen fixation, the accumulation of which can inhibit fixation.

As well as demonstrating the action of nitrogenase in the reduction of dinitrogen to ammonia, several workers found that nitrogenase can also catalyse the reduction of a variety of other substrates. Particularly important was the demonstration that nitrogenase can reduce acetylene to ethylene and this has led to a quick and effective method of evaluating legume–*Rhizobium* associations, both in the laboratory and in the field [6.54; 6.55]. Such evaluation studies demonstrated that *Rhizobium* strains varied widely in their ability to fix dinitrogen and stimulate legume growth. Burton *et al* [6.56] showed that certain leguminous hosts were capable of working with a wide range of rhizobia, whilst others were highly specific, only forming an active symbiotic relationship with one particular *Rhizobium* strain. Within cross-inoculation groups, it was demonstrated that some legume species responded similarly to inoculation with certain strains of rhizobia. This subsequently led to the formation of 'effectiveness groupings' and inoculant manufacturers were able to produce and offer 'multiple host' inoculants alongside the specific inoculants.

6.11   IS *RHIZOBIUM* INOCULATION NECESSARY?

6.11.1   Natural distribution

Rhizobium species can persist for some time in soil but are probably unable to grow successfully in competition with members of the free-living microflora. Soils under wheat cultivation may have fewer than 10 *Rhizobium* cells per gram of soil. Following the growth of a flourishing legume crop the same soil can contain 10^5–10^7 organisms per gram of soil. In the absence of fertiliser nitrogen rhizobial bacteria are therefore a vitally important source of nitrogen and reduce the need for expensive fertilisers. Often, however, a leguminous crop will develop poorly in a given plot of soil because the nodule bacteria specific for it are either absent or present in such small numbers that effective nodulation does not occur. For this reason, lucerne is usually pre-inoculated for the UK market. However, it is a widely held assumption that indigenous strains of *Rhizobium* spp. are present in the soil in adequate numbers for legumes, such as clover, commonly used in the UK. This assumption is not necessarily valid. For instance, if a legume is infected with the wrong *Rhizobium* species, ineffective nodules can be formed. These do not contain leghaemoglobin and therefore do not fix dinitrogen but are a drain on the plant's carbon resources. Because the rhizobia give nothing in return, the host legume does not thrive and this is possibly one of the causes for the lack of persistence of clovers often seen in mixed swards. The density of effective nodule bacteria normally present in the soil is therefore extremely variable, depending upon factors which include the nature of the soil, the crop and any previous agricultural treatment. So, when a leguminous crop is introduced into either an area where it has not previously grown, or a soil where in previous years the legumes have grown poorly, inoculation of the seed with specific rhizobial symbionts would seem advisable to encourage satisfactory nodulation and nitrogen fixation.

6.11.2   Environmental factors

Much research is documented on the influence of environmental factors, particularly nitrogen presence, on the *Rhizobium*–legume association. Legume strains are often chosen for yield, especially for areas where fertiliser nitrogen has already been applied. Such strain selection is starting to produce legumes which have a lower nitrogen-fixing ability, but it would seem have a correspondingly better tolerance to the presence of fertilizer nitrogen. However, Gibson [6.57] found that both nodulated and nitrogen-fertilised legumes grew equally efficiently. Oghoghorie and Pate [6.58] also showed that in nodulated plants in soils containing fertiliser nitrogen, both nitrogen fixation and nitrate assimilation mechanisms were being utilised.

Using the field pea (*Pisum arvense*) they demonstrated that the roots were taking part of their nitrogen from nitrate reduction, whereas fixed dinitrogen was being supplied to the nodules and shoots, even though Silsbury [6.59] found that fixation of atmospheric nitrogen required far more energy than assimilation of mineral nitrogen.

6.12   RHIZOBIA IN THE FIELD

Most clovers in the UK are grown with one or more companion grasses as a mixed sward. Livestock grazing on such a mixed sward can improve their liveweight gain, in the case of sheep by as much as 25%, compared with grass alone, largely due to increased protein and dry matter content. Apart from this obvious advantage, the companion grass can benefit from the *Rhizobium*–legume association. As the sphere of influence can extend a little way into the soil, fixed dinitrogen can become available to the grass roots. However, an actively dinitrogen-fixing legume will utilise most of the nitrogen itself, leaving little in the soil for other plant species. The major soil source of fixed dinitrogen originates from dead nodules, roots and shed leaves. Simpson [6.60] found that *Trifolium repens* competes for nitrogen in late spring and early summer, but later the legumes succumb to temperature and water stress with subsequent death of parts of the plant, releasing up to 4% of its available nitrogen to the soil. So, trying to maximise the yield of both clover and companion grasses and also maintain the mixture over a number of years has been difficult to achieve. Many farmers find that they need to over-sow their pastures in subsequent years due to the lack of persistence of the clovers, particularly in areas where fertiliser nitrogen has been regularly added.

6.12.1   Effects of grazing and cutting

Grazing obviously adds another form of environmental stress on the growing legumes. Simpson [6.60] observed variations when evaluating the effects of the regrowth of different legume species after cutting during a 3-year field trial. This was dependent on the time of year when the cuts were performed as well as the particular species under investigation. Gibson [6.61] also found wide variations in effects of defoliation on growing legumes, ranging from little effect at all to severe retardation of growth and nodule activity with subsequent nodule shedding. This variation was dependent not only on the legume species studied but also on the conditions of the experiment, whether in the laboratory situation or in a full field trial where other environmental variables exerted an influence. However, the results of legume field trials under simulated grazing conditions must be taken with a certain amount of reservation. It has been shown that trials under true grazing conditions can give different results when compared to simulated grazing trials with regular cutting. In one set of field trials, different varieties of white clover were studied. Whereas under simulated grazing conditions the regrowth and persistence of all varieties were very similar, under true hard grazing conditions the larger-leaved varieties such as Sonja and Donna showed a marked lack of persistence when compared to the smaller-leaved varieties such as Kent [6.62]. So, not only is it important to choose the right set of conditions for the field trials themselves, it is also important to choose the right legume species and varieties for the investigation. Sonja and Donna, for example, are more suited to the lighter grazing of cattle.

6.12.2   Strain selection for the field

Once thought to be obligate symbiotes, *Rhizobium* spp. are now known to grow and fix nitrogen on a defined medium in the laboratory [6.63]. However, Date and Roughley [6.64] pointed out that for large-scale production of rhizobia, retention of the dinitrogen-fixing capabilities of the organisms was obviously paramount when formulating a medium. Therefore, inoculant manufacturers have not only spent a lot of time and research in selecting the right strains and species of *Rhizobium* for the various legumes currently grown, but also taken care to produce a viable product which has retained dinitrogen-fixing ability, contains enough bacteria to be competitive in the natural environment, and has an economic storage life. The product itself has been produced in a variety of forms, such as a liquid broth, a frozen concentrate and a freeze-dried or oil-dried preparation, and has also been incorporated into a peat-based carrier. In the past, various carrier media, such as coal dust, bagasse and lignite, have been tried and tested but so far the peat-based carrier has proved to give the best protection to the rhizobia, both in the packaged form and in the soil environment [6.41]. To be effective, the carrier medium must be non-toxic, have good absorption capacity, be easy to mix and sterilise and be cost-efficient. A low-salt, good quality peat-based carrier has been found to possess all these criteria. Once flash-dried and milled the peat is ready to accept the rhizobial inoculum. The pH of the peat is adjusted to 6.8 with lime, and the inoculum sprayed on as a broth culture to give a final moisture content of approximately 40%. After incubation for 72 h at 28°C the product is ready for packaging and distribution. It has been found that, prepared in this way, the rhizobia will carry on growing for about 5 weeks but after this time viable counts will start to fall unless the product is kept at 4°C or lower. Maintained in this way, the product will remain viable for up to one year.

6.12.3   Inoculation of legume species

Currently there are two main ways in which legume species can be inoculated with the rhizobial preparations, either as direct application of the product to the soil alongside large-seeded legumes at planting, or by pre-inoculation of the small-seeded legumes. There are advantages in using either method. By direct application in the furrow alongside the seed, more rhizobia per seed can be added and these will have less chance of being affected by any chemical protectants which may be coated on the seeds. Also this method of application can be used to stimulate already growing legumes which may not be effectively nodulated. On the other hand, pre-inoculation of the seeds with the rhizobial preparation is an effective method of implanting the bacteria close to the root zone of the developing seedlings. It is the current practice of many seed producers and merchants to pre-inoculate legume seeds with rhizobial inoculants before distribution, but Vincent and Scott Smith [6.44] have demonstrated that the viability of rhizobia falls off with subsequent storage of the prepared seeds. By the time the farmer comes to plant these pre-inoculated seed preparations, there is no guarantee that rhizobia are present in sufficient numbers to compete with the indigenous microflora in the soil. Therefore, inoculant manufacturers advise that rhizobial preparations be mixed with the seed just before planting to ensure a successful *Rhizobium*–legume association. To ensure thorough mixing of seed and inoculant preparations, research has been undertaken to find an effective adhesive. Based on either a sugar or a gum arabic preparation, there are several brands currently on the market specifically for use with peat-based rhizobial inoculants, and Waggoner *et al.* [6.65] have found that inoculation efficiency has been greatly increased by the use of such adhesives.

6.13   TESTING EFFECTIVENESS OF INOCULANTS

As Date [6.66] suggests, the only real way to test a *Rhizobium* inoculant is to run field trials to check that the bacteria are able to compete with other highly infective rhizobia present in the soil, that the rhizobial strain chosen will produce nodules on the host and that this symbiotic relationship is beneficial to both host and bacteria in terms of nitrogen fixation. However, until the present day, no really comprehensive trials have been organised, the only information of note being the work of Evers [6.67]. His principal aims were to investigate the inoculation potential itself, together with the use of adhesives, by inoculating a white clover with a host-specific *Rhizobium* sp. From his results, he suggested that clover inoculation was essential for areas with fine sandy soils. In addition, he recommended that inoculated clovers be used in clay soil areas, even though they may possess indigenous *Rhizobium* spp., for there would be no guarantee that those present in the soil would be specific for white clover, or in sufficient numbers to ensure good root nodulation. However, he did not investigate overall yields, or persistence of the clover.

   Currently, the author is involved in a much more comprehensive trial, aimed at providing answers to these problems, and involving eight varieties of white clover on two sites — an uncultivated upland region of Wales, and a well-cultivated and fertilised site in lowland Scotland. So far the results of this trial have shown (Fig. 6.1) that inoculated clover establishes better (this could be clearly seen even in 1983, the establishment year), with improved yields (Fig. 6.2) even under drought conditions (Tables 6.2 and 6.3). Uninoculated clover yields were adversely affected by fertiliser nitrogen

(a)

(b)

Fig. 6.1 — Beulah white clover/companion grass mixture, Welsh site, no nitrogen, just before second cut, first year, showing the increase in herbage, particularly clover, on the inoculated plot (b) compared with the uninoculated plot (a).

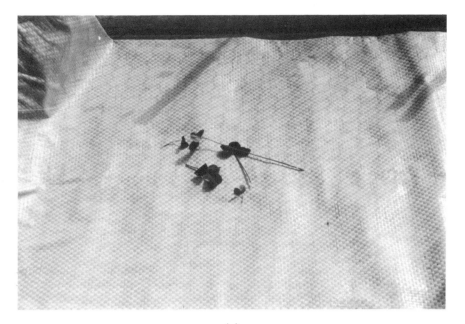

(a)

(b)

Fig. 6.2 — Comparison of yields of clover separated from (a) uninoculated and (b)
inoculated plots, just before second cut, first year.

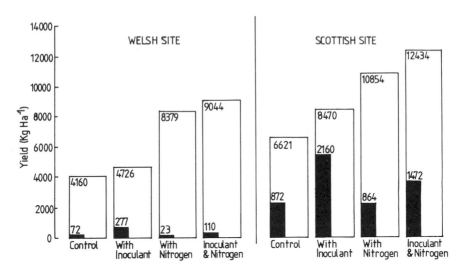

Fig. 6.3 — Total average dry matter yields (kg ha⁻¹) for the first harvest year: total
grass and clover yields — white columns; clover yields only — black columns.

addition, but inoculated clovers fared much better, though not as well as the
inoculated clovers without additional nitrogen. (The Scottish site showed
clearly the effects of residual fertiliser when compared with the Welsh;
Table 6.2.) The percentage clover cover was also found to be better for
inoculated clovers, indicating that clover persistence benefits from inoculation, as shown in Table 6.4 which compares dry matter figures for both grass
and clover. Finally, (Fig. 6.3), comparisons of the total dry matter yield
show that the best responses, overall, arose through sowing inoculated
clovers and subsequently fertilising with nitrate, even though the clover
yields themselves were repressed by the nitrogen. (These results will be
published in more detail when the trial is completed [6.69].)

6.14   CONCLUDING REMARKS

With the world's rapidly expanding population, and agriculture near its peak
of productivity, other sources of high protein crops are being investigated.
The rapid soya price rise over the last few years has led to much research into
other legume forage crops, such as peas and beans. Lupins, with an average
protein content of 35%, are also witnessing a small but significant revival in
Europe, particularly the white variety *Lupinus albus*. All these legumes
could benefit from inoculation with a host-specific *Rhizobium* sp. Another
area of research is in the reclamation and utilisation of man-made waste
areas, such as coal and mineral tips. Although usually hostile to plant life,
over the years a natural flora has evolved to take advantage of these barren
places. The possibility of using forage legumes to increase the nitrogen

Table 6.2 — Average total dry matter yield of clover (kg ha^{-1}) at first cut following establishment year

Clover variety[a]	Treatment at welsh site				Treatment at Scottish site			
	Control	With inoculant	With nitrogen	Inoculant plus nitrogen	Control	With inoculant	With nitrogen	Inoculant plus nitrogen
Kent[a]	7.58	77.74	5.76	37.09	376.65	2371.36	362.91	624.33
S184[b]	19.43	74.60	5.09	46.96	646.03	1503.43	462.36	967.20
Huia[c]	20.38	100.22	4.36	32.46	555.53	1283.03	538.55	1618.29
Donna[c]	11.23	182.00	5.11	74.77	657.15	1275.25	761.43	1372.25
Menna[c]	13.79	66.90	0.00	26.99	459.56	1574.58	401.62	1289.40
Olwen[c]	29.79	94.54	10.64	53.27	1139.52	1930.44	715.00	1065.27
Milkanova[d]	36.82	138.78	6.30	85.58	729.70	1298.71	619.74	645.45
Nesta[d]	17.28	95.87	3.41	48.86	736.11	1436.56	812.63	1177.63

[a] Immediately before sowing, the clover seed was coated with a specially selected *Rhizobium* sp., host-specific for white clover, on a peat-based carrier/adhesive system, at a final concentration of 10^5 organisms g^{-1} clover seed. The clover seed and companion-grass (perennial rye-grass S24) were sown and subsequently treated according to standard procedures.
[b] Small leaf.
[c] Medium-small leaf.
[d] Medium-large leaf.
Chosen from NIAB recommendations [6.68].

Table 6.3 — Average total yield DM clover (kg ha^{-1}) for the first harvest year

Clover variety	Treatment at Welsh site				Treatment at Scottish site			
	Control	With inoculant	With nitrogen	Inoculant plus nitrogen	Control	With inoculant	With nitrogen	Inoculant plus nitrogen
Kent	43.27	225.86	18.49	80.38	403.37	2637.45	456.17	751.34
S184	72.17	275.50	13.60	76.83	750.05	1902.29	676.63	1118.03
Huia	70.35	230.91	18.96	57.40	718.60	1804.22	803.20	2130.94
Donna	72.46	426.81	26.03	149.24	879.69	1987.14	1168.79	1971.93
Menna	62.27	186.38	18.42	86.20	593.48	2034.14	690.23	1689.30
Olwen	82.30	195.54	23.10	155.61	1547.51	3022.07	1165.26	1570.81
Milkanova	122.10	398.71	46.77	194.93	916.29	1688.22	814.59	971.25
Nesta	51.95	278.35	15.55	82.09	1169.47	2201.21	1136.54	1571.75

Table 6.4 — Percentage clover cover cover to ryegrass at the last cut (on DM yields kg ha^{-1}) for the first harvest year

Clover variety[a]	Treatment at welsh site				Treatment at Scottish site			
	Control	With inoculant	With nitrogen	Inoculant plus nitrogen	Control	With inoculant	With nitrogen	Inoculant plus nitrogen
Kent	2.99	11.39	0.415	1.757	17.61	37.60	11.64	14.74
S 184	4.54	14.64	0.289	1.190	26.95	39.65	18.33	15.89
Huia	4.00	13.42	0.536	1.051	31.14	39.99	18.88	26.22
Donna	4.80	18.19	0.677	2.980	33.87	42.87	23.29	28.97
Menna	4.25	9.93	0.582	2.510	30.70	41.31	23.71	22.63
Olwen	4.38	8.14	0.381	4.410	39.28	47.99	26.99	26.32
Milkanova	7.05	18.94	1.359	5.024	32.77	40.65	17.63	13.56
Nesta	3.09	12.54	0.397	1.233	35.60	41.58	21.98	24.86

build-up in the soils of these waste areas has been investigated [6.70]. Here, again, rhizobial inoculants could assist in the establishment and growth of legumes and companion grass species in areas which are low in soil nitrogen. Perhaps the most interesting and probably the most daunting area of research is in gene transference. Already it has been proved possible to transfer the nitrogen-fixing (nif) gene by conjugation in *Klebsiella pneumoniae* [6.71], and Helsinki [6.72] suggests that plasmids may be utilised to transfer such genes. To transfer such nitrogen-fixing genes from *Rhizobia* spp. to non-leguminous plants would seem to be the ultimate goal of present and future research, and although not yet attained, there is now little doubt that this goal will achieved in the future.

6.15 SILAGE MAKING: AN INTRODUCTION

The art of making silage as a method for the preservation of high moisture content animal fodder has been known for thousands of years, though the complex biochemical and microbiological changes which occur during the ensiling process are only recently being understood. Modern-day farmers harvest grass forage in the UK whilst it is still at a relatively young stage of growth demonstrating a high content of fermentable sugars (water-soluble carbohydrates, WSC's) and a low fibre content. Whether the crop is picked up immediately (direct-cut) or left in the fields to wilt for several hours (pre-wilt) depends upon the climatic conditions at the time of harvest, but the farmer ideally wants to ensile a crop with an average dry matter content of 25–30%. In many temperate countries, such as the UK, the rainfall pattern in late spring and early summer often means that a pre-wilt is not always possible and with a harvested crop of <25% dry matter, (DM), the farmer invariably uses a silage additive in order to achieve a good fermentation and so minimise in-silo losses.

Stored in silage clamps, silos or 'big bales' with sufficient consolidation and external sealing to ensure anaerobic conditions, the natural ensiling process passes through various stages. Initially, trapped atmospheric oxygen in the newly ensiled forage is utilised by plant enzymes in the still respiring crop, but this soon becomes exhausted and anaerobiosis results [6.73]. At this time, the natural lactic acid bacteria present in small numbers on the crop [6.74] begin to multiply rapidly to 10^9–10^{10} g^{-1} using the released sugars from the broken grass cells as a primary source of energy. Due to a combination of high lactic acid output and an inherent acid tolerance, lactic acid bacteria soon become the dominant bacterial species in silage [6.75]. Under ideal conditions, the pH stabilises at around 3.8–4.2, depending on dry matter content, and the silage is effectively preserved after a few weeks. However, when the DM content of cut forage is less than 25% conditions are no longer ideal, and poor preservation can often result, particularly if WSC levels are also low (as they often are in temperate grasses because of the climate). Inadequate consolidation and poor sealing of the clamp can also lead to poor preservation and high in-silo nutrient losses due to ingress of air (oxygen). Under such circumstances, lactic acid bacteria are inhibited and the silage will not reach an effective pH 4.0. Therefore, other bacterial species, such as Enterobacteriaceae and *Clostridium* spp. which are normally inhibited by a low pH, will be able to grow and utilise the lactic acid, protein and residual WSC's with a consequent loss of nutritive value in the silage (Figs. 6.4 and 6.5).

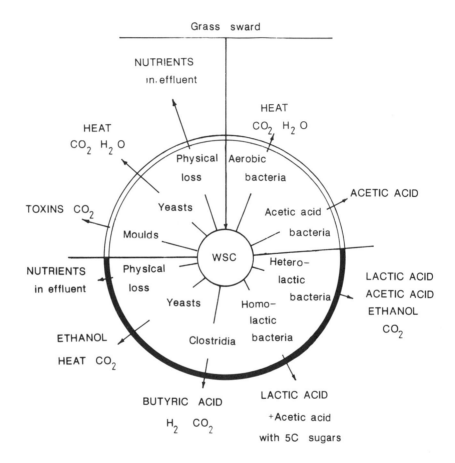

Fig. 6.4 — The fate of energy in silage fermentation.

Clostridium species with an optimum pH for growth of 7.2 are not inhibited until the pH falls to below 5.5. Therefore, in poorly preserved wet silages they can soon dominate the silage microflora. *Clostridium* spp. also prefer a higher water activity for growth and therefore prefer low DM silages [6.76; 6.77]. Saccharolytic species, such as *Clostridium tyrobutyricum*, utilise water-soluble carbohydrates and lactic acid during growth, and in a silage which may already have a low lactic acid concentration there will inevitably be a rise in pH due to the production of butyric acid which is

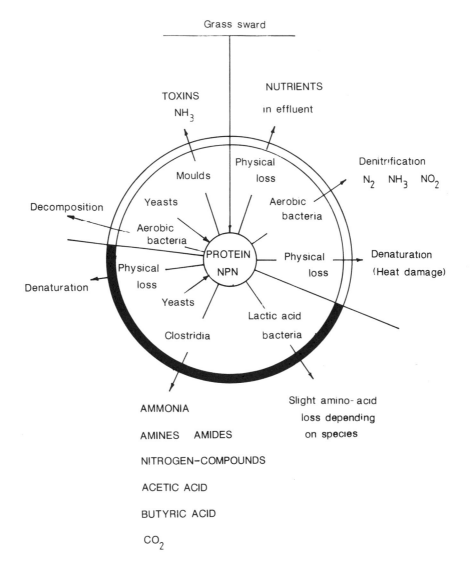

Fig. 6.5 — The fate of protein in silage fermentation.

weaker than lactic acid [6.78]. Proteolytic species, such as *C. sporogenes*, also utilise many of the amino-acids in silage, producing predominantly butyric acid and ammonia [6.79]. These reactions help to further enhance the development of *Clostridium* spp. with the silage environment during this secondary fermentation. Typical reactions of *Clostridium* spp. are shown in Fig. 6.6.

In practice the achievement of rapid anaerobic conditions at the clamp or silo is not always guaranteed. Neither is it easy to attain the ideal DM in cut forage because of climatic variations. Therefore, over the years, there has

TYPICAL REACTIONS OF SACCHAROLYTIC CLOSTRIDIUM SPP.

$$Glucose \longrightarrow Butyric\ acid\ +\ 2CO_2\ +\ 2H_2$$

$$2\ Lactate \longrightarrow Butyric\ acid\ +\ 2CO_2\ +\ 2H_2$$

TYPICAL REACTIONS OF PROTEOLYTIC CLOSTRIDIUM SPP.

1   Deamination

$$Lysine \longrightarrow Acetic\ acid\ +\ Butyric\ acid\ +\ 2NH_3$$

2   Decarboxylation

$$Glutamic\ acid \longrightarrow \gamma\text{-Amino-butyric\ acid}\ +\ CO_2$$

3   Stickland reaction

$$Alanine\ (ox.)\ +\ 2\ Glycine\ (red.) \longrightarrow 3\ Acetic\ acid\ +\ 3NH_3\ +\ CO_2$$

Fig. 6.6 — Typical reactions of *Clostridium* species.

been much research into the use of chemical treatments which could influence silage preservation.

6.16 SILAGE ADDITIVES

There are basically two major groups of silage additives, grouped according to their effects on the fermentation process: fermentation inhibitors and fermentation stimulants [6.80; 6.81]. Fermentation inhibitors include the acid additives such as sulphuric and formic acid, and preservatives such as formaldehyde and paraformaldehyde. Stimulants include carbohydrate sources such as molasses and grain, and a growing number of additives which incorporate lactic acid bacteria and enzymes.

6.16.1   Fermentation inhibitors

Although practised as early as 1885, direct acidification of forage crops did not become popular until Virtanen [6.82] recommended the use of mineral acids to lower the pH to a level which was thought to be inhibitory to plant and microbial enzymes. Experience has shown that silages with a pH at or below 3.0 (easily achieved with strong mineral acids) were unpalatable to the animals, and even when eaten were liable to cause acidosis in the rumen. He calculated the amount of acid needed to lower the pH of forages to 3.6–4.0, a level which was more palatable to the animals, yet still inhibitory to some detrimental fermentation processes. Although sulphuric acid and mixtures of sulphuric and hydrochloric acid were popular additives in many Northern European countries, they gradually fell into disuse because of their corrosive nature and handling problems associated with the use of these acids. Dirks and Von Kapff (see Watson and Nash [6.83]) first suggested the additional use of organic acids in the 1920's. Using a mixture of formic and hydrochloric acid sprinkled over the ensiled crop, they achieved moderate success. Failures at this time were mainly attributed to the difficulties of achieving even distribution throughout the crop, but with the advent of flail-type forage harvesters and collection wagons, formic acid could be sprayed directly onto forage immediately after cutting. With more successful and consistent results, formic acid additives became commercially available in the 1950's. Although weaker than mineral acids, formic acid reduces the pH to below 4.0 if applied at a concentration proportional to the dry matter content of the forage. Ryegrass crops of 17% dry matter or less need higher levels of formic acid to achieve pH 4.0 [6.84]. Formic acid achieves its antibacterial activity by a combination of its hydrogen ion concentration and bactericidal action of undissociated acid [6.85; 6.86]. Though inhibitory to *Clostridium* spp., Enterobacteriaceae and some strains of *Strepotococcus* spp. and *Pediococcus* spp., formic acid at this pH does not totally suppress *Lactobacillus* spp. [6.87] and thus some microbial activity remains. Barry *et al.* [6.88] also found that as the concentration of formic acid addition to forage was increased there was a decrease in the levels of lactic and acetic acids produced, as would be expected, and an increase in protein nitrogen and water-soluble carbohydrates (WSC's) due to the increasing inhibition of proteolytic and respiratory micro-organisms. Formic acid treatment, however, has led to some poor-quality unstable silages being made.

Whereas Crawshaw *et al.* [6.89] found the aerobic stability of formic acid-treated silage to be good, other researchers have not always found this to be the case. Henderson *et al.* [6.90] demonstrated that some yeasts were tolerant to formic acid and contributed to aerobic deterioration in some cases once the clamps were opened for feeding. The fact that up to 50% formic acid content can be lost from the forage during the process of ensilage has also led to cases of poor silage preservation. However, commercial preparations of formic acid are still widely used in the UK and North European countries.

Other organic acids have been evaluated as potential silage additives. Acetic acid, propionic acid and acrylic acid [6.87; 6.91] were found to be less effective than formic acid in restricting fermentation activity. Being weak acids and so needing higher application rates to achieve fermentation inhibition also meant that they were not cost-effective.

Amongst the preservatives, formaldehyde (a 40% aqueous solution of formalin) was used commercially in the 1930's because of its known bacteriostatic properties [6.92]. Renewed interest in its use was shown when Browen and Valentine [6.93] studied formaldehyde-treated lucerne. At moderate levels of application they observed that formaldehyde protected the plant protein from microbial attack in the rumen. However, it was found that formaldehyde used alone had disadvantages. Losses during field application could be high due to its volatility, and even the silo the proportion of formaldehyde applied at the time of ensilage gradually declined with time due to decomposition, so that by 100 days only 20% of the original concentration remained. This led to more silage failures due to a combination of butyric acid fermentation as the concentration of formaldehyde declined, and consequent aerobic instability at feed-out [6.94]. More concentrated levels of application gave further problems. The plant protein protection afforded by moderate application of formaldehyde could lead to the rumen micro-organisms being actually starved of degradable nitrogen when higher levels of formaldehyde were used, so that there was reduced protein digestion in the small intestine [6.95]. Rauramaa and Kreula [6.96] has also noted that 'free' formaldehyde could be transferred to milk. Most of these disadvantages disappeared when mixtures of formaldehyde and formic acid were used. The mixture was effective in reducing proteolysis and butyric acid fermentation [6.94], yet did not depress protein digestibility and led to an increase in voluntary dry matter intake of silage. Mixtures of formaldehyde with formic or sulphuric acid became commercially available in the 1970's. Less volatile than formaldehyde, paraformaldehyde (a solid polymer containing up to 90% formaldehyde) was found to restrict fermentation and prevent extensive protein breakdown [6.97]. However, even though it controls clostridial fermentation at low rates of application, paraformaldehyde does not inhibit all silage microflora.

6.16.2   Fermentation stimulators

Additives which actively stimulate the fermentation processes in silage have also been used for many years. The addition of molasses has been found to increase both dry matter and lactic acid contents, with a consequent reduction of pH which is inhibitory to spoilage micro-organisms yet still allows lactic acid bacteria to grow, although addition of molasses to crops low in WSC's such as legumes was only beneficial if relatively high application rates (around 40–50 g kg^{-1} or more) were used. At such rates of application, not all of the available carbohydrates would be converted to lactic acid by the *Lactobacillus* spp. naturally present in the silage and so there would be quite high residual levels of WSC's still present at the end of fermentation. Once the silo was open to the atmosphere for feed-out, Weise [6.98] found that these residual WSC's were open to attack by yeasts, so leading to loss of dry matter because of aerobic deterioration. Whittenbury [6.99] also suggested that, owing to the high levels of fructose present in molasses, heterofermentative bacteria would be encouraged to grow. This would reduce the lactic acid content of the silage and so lead to instability of allowing clostridial fermentation to take place.

The latest group of fermentation stimulation products to become commercially available are those which incorporate lactic acid bacteria and/or enzymes, known collectively as microbial or biological silage additives. The advent of such additives owes much to the wealth of research over the last few years into the microbiological and biochemical processes occurring during the silage fermentation.

6.17   ROLE OF THE LACTIC ACID BACTERIA IN SILAGE ADDITIVES

The quality of a natural silage fermentation relies heavily on the numbers and types of lactic acid bacteria present on the forage at the time of ensiling. Of the four lactic acid bacterial genera associated with silage, *Lactobacillus*, *Pediococcus*, *Streptococcus* and *Leuconostoc*, the Lactobacillaceae tend to dominate the silage microflora with time. In the early stages, once anaerobiosis has been established, the cocci multiply rapidly due to their pH range (6.5–5.0 with an optimum of 5.5), though certain pediococci can survive at pH 4.0 due to their higher acid tolerance [6.100]. As the pH falls belows 5.5, the lactobacilli become dominant and remain so throughout the preservation period. Initiated by homofermentative lactobacilli such as *Lactobacillus plantarum* and *L. curvatus*, it has been found that by the end of the ensiling period 75–95% of the lactobacilli present were heterofermentative species predominated by *L. buchneri* and *L. brevis*. This was attributed to the fact that heterofermentative lactobacilli are more tolerant to the acetic acid which they also produce [6.75]. It has also been shown that there can be a shift from a homolactic to a mixed fermentation by some homofermentative lactic acid bacteria induced by substrate limitation including re-fermentation of lactic acid [6.101]. In temperate regions where the sugar content of forages can be low, the demand for water-soluble carbohydrates by the lactic acid bacteria in silage can outstrip supply and this shift in fermentation pattern could occur, so reinforcing the domination by heterofermentative lactic acid bacteria. The importance of these natural fermentation patterns is illustrated by the reactions of *Lactobacillus* spp. in Fig. 6.7. As can be seen, in terms of energy and DM conservation, the homolactic fermentation of WSC's is the preferred pathway in order to preserve the maximum nutritive value of the silage with no loss in DM and an insignificant loss in energy. The growth of heterofermentative *Lactobacillus* spp. in silage leads to the production of ethanol and carbon dioxide with subsequent loss in DM and

REACTIONS OF HOMOFERMENTATIVE LACTOBACILLUS SPP.

Glucose $\longrightarrow$ 2 Lactic acid

Fructose $\longrightarrow$ 2 Lactic acid

No loss in DM and insignificant loss in energy

Arabinose $\longrightarrow$ Lactic acid + Acetic acid

Xylose $\longrightarrow$ Lactic acid + Acetic acid

No loss in DM and insignificant loss in energy

REACTIONS OF HETEROFERMENTATIVE LACTOBACILLUS SPP.

Glucose $\longrightarrow$ Lactic acid + Ethanol + CO_2

20% loss in DM and 1.7% loss in energy

3-Fructose $\longrightarrow$ Lactic acid + Acetic acid + 2 Mannitol + CO_2

5% loss in DM and 1.0% loss in energy

Arabinose $\longrightarrow$ Lactic acid + Acetic acid

Xyiose $\longrightarrow$ Lactic acid + Acetic acid

No loss in DM and insignificant loss in energy

Fig. 6.7 — Typical reactions of *Lactobacillus* species.

energy [6.100]. Because of these factors, most biological silage additives contain species of lactic acid bacteria which will encourage a homolactic fermentation in silage.

6.17.1   Strain selection in additive formulation
The criteria for inclusion of lactic acid bacteria in a silage additive product were laid down by Whittenbury [6.102]. He suggested that the chosen species should (1) grow rapidly and be capable of rapid domination over indigenous silage microflora, (2) be homofermentative and so produce lactic acid from the available WSC's, (3) be acid tolerant to at least pH 4.0, (4) be able to ferment hexoses, pentoses and fructans, (5) not produce dextran nor

have any action on organic acids, and (6) possess a growth temperature capability up to 50°C. Certain strains of *Lactobacillus plantarum* possess all these properties and therefore this has been the species of choice for inclusion in biological silage additives. However, because *Lactobacillus* spp. are slow to grow until the pH of silage falls below 5.0, they are rarely incorporated into a product alone. *Pediococcus* or *Streptococcus* spp. are also usually added because these species are active within the pH range of 5.0–6.5. Therefore, by mirroring what happens in the natural fermentation, the cocci will dominate fermentation in the early stages of ensilage very rapidly and be superseded below pH 5.0 by the homofermentative *Lactobacillus plantarum* [6.103]. It has been shown in laboratory experiments that biological silage additives incorporating such mixed species of lactic acid bacteria are capable of producing a rapid drop in pH in 24 h [6.104]. Such a rapid fermentation will help to conserve the energy and protein value of the silage by inhibiting the growth of *Clostridium* spp. and restricting the growth of heterofermentative lactic acid bacteria by homofermentative domination.

6.17.2   Additional requirements for microbilogical additives

Apart from the selection of lactic acid bacterial strains, any bacterial silage additive should contain enough viable bacteria to outnumber and dominate the indigenous population when added to the cut crop, a minimum of 10^5–10^6 organisms g^{-1} forage [6.105]. When biological silage additives and inoculants were first used commercially to ensile grass in the UK, there was much controversy over their use. Early inoculants were based upon lactic acid bacterial strains at viable numbers which were known to ensile corn silage successfully. However, ensiled corn contains an adequate supply of fermentable sugars and so ensiles without difficulty [6.106]. On the other hand, green forage crops, particularly those grown in temperatate regions, can be low in WSC's (less than 8–20% of DM) and biological additives containing these lactic acid bacteria alone did not always give satisfactory fermentation due to the exhaustion of available sugars before a satisfactory pH could be reached. Also, additives tend to be used when DM content is <25% and, coupled with low WSC's, these early inoculants were unable to prevent clostridial secondary fermentation. Even more failures were observed when mixed forages of ryegrass and clover or other legumes such as lucerne were ensiled. Legumes are more highly buffered than grasses due to higher organic acid and protein levels and therefore more lactic acid needed to be produced by the bacteria to achieve a similar low pH than if grasses were ensiled alone, an almost impossible task if these forages were both wet and low in fermentable sugars.

It soon became obvious, therefore, that a way of increasing the level of fermentable sugars within the forage itself was necessary, for although plant enzymes are capable of slowly producing some extra WSC by hydrolysis of hemicelluloses to pentose sugars, there is still a large untapped source of potentially fermentable sugars within the unbroken plant cells. The quantity and type of carbohydrate present in forage is dependent upon the species, the growing climate and the methods of cultivation. Most carbohydrates in forages can be divided into structural carbohydrates composed of lignin and cellulose (the fibre content) and storage carbohydrates which include fermentable sugars (Fig. 6.8). In grasses of temperate zones fibre levels

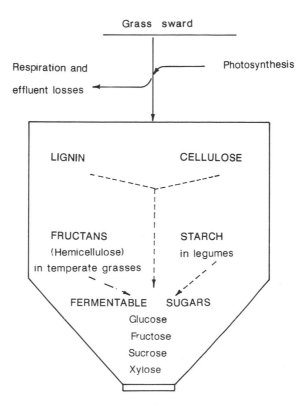

Fig. 6.8 — The enzymatic conversion of grass carbohydrates to fermentable sugars.

generally account for 30–40% of DM; the main storage carbohydrates, fructans or hemicelloses, 5–7% of DM; and actual fermentable sugars in grasses up to 10% DM, consisting mainly of fructose, glucose and sucrose [6.107]. In legumes, starch is the main storage carbohydrate. Over the last few years, second-generation biological silage additives have evolved with the addition of various blends of enzymes which will hydrolyse many of these normally inaccessible storage polysaccharides to hexoses and pentoses which can then be utilised by the homofermentative lactic acid bacteria. The structural carbohydrates, however, remain inaccessible, for lignin and cellulose are difficult to hydrolyse effectively under the normal conditions found in silage. The enzyme kinetics of cellulases are slow, and as these enzymes require elevated temperatures and prolonged time periods to bring about really effective hydrolysis, they are really of little benefit. However, there are many hemicellulases and amyloglucosidases readily and economically available from fungal sources which together can bring about a rapid hydrolysis of the hemicellulolytic components of non-structural carbohydrates in low DM grass silages over the temperature and pH ranges of the normal silage environment.

An important point to note with the inclusion of such enzymes in biological silage additives is that the hexoses and pentoses produced by them should be matched with the fermentation capability of the lactic acid bacteria in the product. Whereas 6-carbon sugars are utilised by homofermentative and heterofermentative lactobacilli, the pentoses can only be utilised by a relatively small number of lactobacilli [6.108]. *Lactobacillus plantarum* strains have been isolated from grass silage which can also utilise pentoses, and these particular strains should be used with an enzyme blend which produces them (Fig. 6.7). The production of pentoses is particularly useful because both the pentose-utilising homo-and heterofermentative lactobacilli strains yield lactic and acetic acid with no loss in DM or energy.

The most recent biological additives to appear on the market are those which contain enzymes only. The cellulolytic and hemicellulolytic enzymes contained in these products convert storage polysaccharides in grass to hexoses and pentoses which are then utilised by the lactic bacteria naturally present on the forage. However, as previously stated, most natural silages tend towards a population of heterofermentative lactic acid bacteria with subsequent DM losses due to the production of ethanol and carbon dioxide (Fig. 6.7). With enzyme-only additives, therefore, the conversion of WSC's to lactic acid is more likely to be less energy conservative then if homolactic bacteria had been included. If the enzymes present in these additives also produce pentoses as well as hexoses, the 5-carbon sugars may not be utilised because of the relatively sparse distribution of pentose-utilising lactic acid bacteria in natural silages [6.108].

It would seem to be advantageous, therefore, to incorporate both hemicellulolytic enzymes and homofermentative lactic acid bacteria in a biological silage additive to cover all possible ensiling conditions. Additives which contain homofermentative lactic acid bacteria only will work well if there is sufficient WSC content to support their nutritional requirements and so achieve a low pH and stable fermentation. However, in forages with low WSC content the bacteria could be starved of nutrients long before a stable pH is reached, and thus would not be able to inhibit the growth of clostridial bacteria. On the other hand, additives containing only enzymes rely on the natural, predominantly heterofermentative lactic acid bacteria to produce enough lactic acid to lower the pH.

Although there may be sufficient WSC's due to the enzymes' hydrolytic activity, heterofermentative lactic acid bacteria are less energy efficient than homofermentative bacteria, leading to nutritional loss. Should the forage at ensiling also have a low indigenous lactic acid bacterial population, the period taken for the pH to fall sufficiently to inhibit other micro-organisms may be extended for several days, time enough for spoilage micro-organisms to start affecting the course of fermentation. By incorporating hemicellulo-lytic enzymes *and* homofermentative lactic acid bacteria, both these problems can be overcome.

6.17.3 Silage clamp management

Good clamp management is particularly necessary when using biological silage additives. Because the lactic acid bacteria will not start rapid multipli-cation until anaerobic conditions are established, rapid filling, consolidation and sealing of a clamp is a vital first step towards a good fermentation and maximum preservation of nutrients. Should aerobic conditions persist due to poor management, other micro-organsims which are normally inhibited by anaerobiosis can rapidly. Yeasts, in particular, are undesirable in silage. After initial rapid multiplication, aerobic species such as *Candida* spp. and *Pichia* spp. lie dormant under anaerobic conditions until the silage clamp is exposed to the atmosphere for feeding. Aerobic deterioration of silage at the clamp face can be rapid and lead to total loss of nutrients (Fig. 6.9) with

ANAEROBIC

$$Glucose \longrightarrow 2\ Ethanol\ +\ 2CO_2\ +\ 15400\ calories$$

(100% loss in DM, 9% loss in energy)

AEROBIC

$$Glucose\ +\ 6O_2 \longrightarrow 6CO_2\ +\ 6H_2O\ +\ 169400\ calories$$

(100% loss in DM, 100% loss in energy)

Fig. 6.9 — Typical reactions of yeasts.

the production of carbon dioxide, water and heat [6.109; 6.110]. Apart from *Clostridium* spp., yeasts can also be a problem if anaerobic conditions develop rapidly, yet achievement of a low pH is delayed. Tolerant to fairly acid conditions, anaerobic yeasts such as *Torulopsis* spp. compete for sugars alongside the lactic acid bacteria which are then fermented to ethanol and carbon dioxide [6.85] with subsequent DM loss and excessive in-silo temper-atures (Fig. 6.9). Therefore, biological silage additives must be able to initiate a rapid fermentation and retain a low pH throughout the ensilage and preservation period. As already stated, delay can result in nutrient loss.

6.17.4   Effects of types of bacterial species in aditives

Although the total number of lactic acid bacteria should be 10^5–10^6 organisms g^{-1} forage in order to achieve bacterial domination in silage, equally important are the relative numbers of bacterial species within the product and their fermentation capability and stability. Most biological silage additives contain at least two species of lactic acid bacteria: a *Streptococcus* sp. or preferably, a *Pediococcus* sp. acting as a pre-starter to bring the pH down rapidly to at least 5.0, and a *Lactobacillus* sp. which can take over and increase the acidity to a stable pH 3.8–4.2 according to DM. Experience has shown that a *Lactobacillus:Pediococcus* ratio of 3:1 achieves the most rapid and stable fermentation in grass silage. Products which contain predominantly *Pedicoccus* spp. or *Streptococcus* spp. bring the pH down to 5.0 satisfactorily, but there is then usually a delay in further pH fall until the indigenous *Lactobacillus* spp. can reach sufficient numbers to complete fermentation. This is a danger period, particularly in low DM silages, for *Clostridium* spp. can still survive and multiply in silage at pH 5.0 [6.76], and silages kept at this pH for any length of time will soon go 'butyric' from the action of proteolytic clostridia utilising the amino acids (Fig. 6.6). Until such time as standards are legally applied to biological silage additives, there is no stipulation in the UK, as yet, for commercial producers of biological additives to prove the efficacy of their products and so lactic acid bacterial ratios are rarely quoted.

6.17.5   Manufacturing considerations

As far as prime production of lactic acid bacteria in fermenters is concerned, pediococci and streptococci are much cheaper to produce. They are not so fastidious in their nutritional requirements as lactobacilli, grow to higher viable numbers in fermenters, survive freeze-drying better, and remain more stable under normal farm storage conditions. Even so, the choice of which coccal species to incorporate into a product must be dictated by their capability to reproduce rapidly in restricted aerobic and anaerobic conditions and achieve a pH below 5.0 quickly so that clostridia and other spoilage micro-organisms do not have a chance to become active. Even more important is the choice of *Lactobacillus plantarum* strain. Ideally, the chosen strain should have originated from its natural environment, i.e. a well-preserved grass silage; be capable of rapid multiplication in order to dominate the silage microflora; be also capable of a high output of lactic acid and be acid-tolerant to at least pH 4.0. Apart from these basic conditions, the *Lactobacillus* strain should also be able to utilise pentoses as well as hexoses, particularly if hemicellulolytic enzymes producing pentoses are incorporated into the final product. In other words, the enzymes and lactic acid bacteria in a product should be complementary. Basic fermentation production of *Lactobacillus* spp. needs to be more rigorously controlled. By choosing a high lactic acid output strain, final harvest yields are invariably lower than from a low acid-producing strain, probably because of subtle changes in bacterial cell wall permeability and stability. Neutralisation with alkali to keep the fermentation at the strain's optimum growth pH is obviously important but so is the continuous monitoring of, say, lactate concentration in the growth medium to ward off a further drop in yield due to toxic metabolite build-up. Therefore, optimisation of growth conditions is imperative when producing strains of *Lactobacillus* spp. which have been chosen for particular beneficial characteristics such as lactic acid output. As a drop in yield is further reflected at the recovery and freeze-drying stage, careful choice of cryoprotectants is also necessary, with long-term storage trials performed to establish long-term bacterial viability in commercial products. The technological and economic choices to be made for the inclusion of lactic acid bacteria and enzymes into biological silage additives are therefore not easy ones, but successful biotechnology companies must bear responsibility for the long-term efficacy of their products.

6.18 EFFECTIVENESS OF BIOLOGICAL SILAGE ADDITIVES

Long-term monitoring of the efficacy of some biological silage additives 'in the field' by the author's Company is summarised in Table 6.5 which gives the mean results of approximately 400 silage analyses (predominantly of grass forages) over a 3-year period in the UK. These results demonstrate that biological silage additives can be a positive aid to fermentation, particularly in low DM conditions. Both pH and ammonia nitrogen means are in the 'very good' fermentation category, but it must be stated that these analyses possess a 'negative' bias, for farmers will usually only use an additive when difficult ensiling conditions are expected (such as low DM content). So in that respect these results are particularly encouraging.

6.18.1 Some effects of nitrate fertilisers

In 1985, the ensiling conditions were mostly poor with a cold and wet climate over most of the UK. This is reflected by slightly higher means for both pH and ammonia nitrogen content, and a doubling of the coefficient of variation for ammonia nitrogens over previous years. In Figs 6.10, 6.11 and 6.12, silage analyses and gas–liquid chromatographs of volatile fatty acids are given for three different silage 'types'. Fig. 6.10 is a typical example of an excellent fermentation at low DM with good nutritional preservation, whereas conversely Fig. 6.11 shows an example of a typical 'butyric' silage profile with a high pH, ammonia nitrogen and butyric acid content. As well as being left in the field for 6 days because of continuous rain, and picked up directly in desperation, the poor ensilage of this particular grass crop was compounded by bad clamp management, too, for sealing and consolidation of the clamp was poor, so the results are not surprising. However, the results shown in Fig. 6.12 are distinctly untypical. Farmers, on request, usually receive a copy of their silage analyses, but gas–liquid chromatographs of silages are a basic research tool and are recently sent as a normal analytical procedure. Therefore, a farmer receiving such an analysis would be con-

Table 6.5 — Grass silage analyses of 400 clamps sampled during 1983–85 representing approximately 300 000 t silage treated with biological additives.

	Silage analyses 1983				Silage analyses 1984				Silage analyses 1985			
	Mean	SD[a]	Variance	$C_v(\%)$[b]	Mean	SD[a]	Variance	$C_v(\%)$[b]	Mean	SD[a]	Variance	$C_v(\%)$[b]
Dry matter (%)	22.85	4.580	20.970	20.00	21.70	4.430	19.640	20.40	20.74	3.830	14.690	18.48
pH	4.01	0.296	0.088	7.40	3.98	0.329	0.108	8.26	4.16	0.527	0.277	12.37
Ammonia–N (% of total N)	7.17	3.023	9.140	42.20	7.68	3.920	15.380	51.00	9.84	8.259	68.219	83.94
Crude protein (%)	14.14	2.880	8.300	20.40	16.00	2.560	6.550	16.00	15.32	2.505	6.277	16.35
MAD fibre (%)	36.98	4.270	18.260	11.50	33.30	4.153	17.230	12.50	36.44	3.763	14.160	10.33
'D' value %	61.46	3.450	11.930	5.60	64.40	3.360	11.280	5.20	61.88	3.020	9.131	4.88
Metabolisable energy (MJ kg^{-1})	9.73	0.479	0.299	4.90	10.30	0.542	0.2940	5.30	9.86	0.492	0.242	4.99
Digestible crude protein (g kg^{-1})	81.70	19.99	399.69	24.50	107.00	20.950	438.900	19.60	101.77	21.690	470.650	21.32

[a] SD = Standard deviation.
[b] C_v = Coefficient of variation.

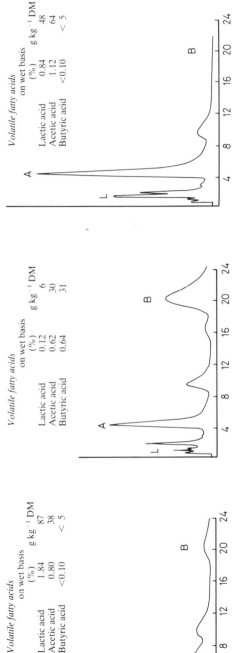

Volatile fatty acids

on wet basis

	(%)	g kg⁻¹ DM
Lactic acid	1.84	87
Acetic acid	0.80	38
Butyric acid	<0.10	< 5

Silage analysis

Dry matter	21.2
pH	3.7
Ammonia–N (% of total N)	6
Crude protein %	16.3
MAD fibre %	37.3
'D' value %	61.2
Metabolisable energy (MJ kg⁻¹)	9.8
Digestible crude protein (g kg⁻¹)	109

First cut ryegrass (Scotland) picked up following 1 day's pre-wilt after a previous week of rain.

Fig. 6.10 — Analysis and gas–liquid chromatograph of average 1985 well-preserved silage.

Volatile fatty acids

on wet basis

	(%)	g kg⁻¹ DM
Lactic acid	0.12	6
Acetic acid	0.62	30
Butyric acid	0.64	31

Silage analysis

Dry matter	21.0
pH	5.6
Ammonia–N (% of total N)	27
Crude protein %	15.5
MAD fibre %	42.3
'D' value %	57.1
Metabolisable energy (MJ kg⁻¹)	9.1
Digestible crude protein (g kg⁻¹)	103

First cut ryegrass (Yorkshire, UK) picked up after lying in field for 6 days because of continuous rain.

Fig. 6.11 — Analysis and gas–liquid chromatograph of a 1985 silage suffering from secondary fermentation.

Volatile fatty acids

on wet basis

	(%)	g kg⁻¹ DM
Lactic acid	0.84	48
Acetic acid	1.12	64
Butyric acid	<0.10	< 5

Silage analysis

Dry matter	17.5
pH	4.7
Ammonia–N (% of total N)	19
Crude protein %	12.4
MAD fibre %	41.9
'D' value %	57.5
Metabolisable energy (MJ kg⁻¹)	9.2
Digestible crude protein (g kg⁻¹)	78

First cut ryegrass (Cornwall. UK) direct cut in rain and picked up 3 weeks after nitrate application.

Fig. 6.12 — Analysis and gas–liquid chromatograph of a 1985 silage, showing nitrate interference.

vinced that his silage had undergone secondary fermentation. Given the evidence of the silage analysis results alone, this would seem to be the case with a pH of 4.7 and an ammonia nitrogen of 19%. However, the GLC trace discounts this assumption for there is no detectable level of butyric acid evident. This is not an isolated case, for, in 1985, particularly in very wet silages, a number of similar analyses have been reported. There seems to be no connection with silage additive use, for this phenomenon has been observed in untreated silages as well as silage treated with molasses, acids and biologicals. The one consistent feature with all of these results has been the fact that the forage has been cut and ensiled too soon after fertilizer nitrogen application to the crop, sometimes as early as only 2–3 weeks following application. With the cold and wet conditions of 1985, the grass had not had sufficient time to convert these nitrates into plant protein and thus, at ensiling, there was an excess of nitrates both on and within the forage.

It is well known that high nitrate levels on forage at ensilage can affect the subsequent fermentation. Smith [6.107] found that the WSC content of grass was negatively correlated with the level of nitrates applied to the crop because of the rapid growth of the herbage. With levels commonly found exceeding 100 g kg^{-1} total nitrogen (TN) in commercial field samples [6.111], it is likely that under these conditions, the lactic acid bacteria in silage are not able to reduce the pH sufficiently to stop clostridial activity due to substrate limitation. However, the results given in Fig. 6.12 show that secondary fermentation has not occurred in this particular silage.

It has been further shown that, under moderately acid conditions in silage, nitrates will be reduced eventually to ammonia via its reduction product nitrite [6.112]. The released ammonia then gradually raises the pH to a level when clostridial activity can start (pH 5.0) and a badly fermented silage will result. A few *Clostridium* spp. and certain strains of lactic acid bacteria can even utilise the nitrates themselves [6.113] so that secondary fermentation can be rapid at this time. However, it is known that nitrites (NO_2^-) will inhibit the growth of *Clostridium* spp. [6.114] and therefore, even at a higher pH, butyric acid production may not take place. This condition may arise because, although Spoelstra [6.112] found that nitrate reduction in laboratory silos stopped after about 10 days, Oshima and McDonald [6.115] found that nitrates could remain at high levels throughout the ensilage and preservation period. Therefore, if nitrates are being continually but slowly reduced to nitrites over a long period of time, clostridial growth could be totally suppressed even though the pH may be in the region of 5.0. This could be the case for the silage in Fig. 6.11, which was sampled 3 months after ensilage. As Spoelstra [6.116] stated in his review on nitrates in silage, nitrate degradation can inhibit clostridial growth by the temporary accumulation of nitrites and nitrogen gases even though the ammonia produced counteracts the acidification and raises the pH to a level where clostridial activity can take place. Therefore, even though the ammonia level of 19% TN (Fig. 6.12) has been sufficient to raise the pH to 4.7, there has been no secondary fermentation, so it would be reasonable to suggest that most of this ammonia nitrogen has been derived from nitrate reduction and not from the proteolytic activity of clostridial bacteria. If more ammonia is eventually produced, however, the pH may rise even further to a point when even the nitrite content is unable to inhibit clostridial activity. Once secondary fermentation has occurred and butyric acid is produced, it would be difficult to determine whether excess nitrates had been the initial cause of the problem unless the silage had been analysed on a regular basis. The effects of excess nitrates on the silage fermentation need to be further researched.

6.19   FUTURE PROMISE OF BIOLOGICAL SILAGE ADDITIVES

During the last few years biological silage additives have been gaining more acceptance as biotechnology companies have researched into and adapted their products to suit green forage and silaging conditions. An increasing number of farmers and silage contractors are realising that biological additives can be a safer alternative to the use of acids in terms of their ease of handling and non-corrosive properties for both man and machine. Prime producers of silage acids are beginning to come to terms with these trends and are turning to the production of biological alternatives themselves, as are companies who sell molasses who are now including lactic acid bacterial concentrates with their silage aid products. In this respect, it looks as though biological silage additives are here to stay. However, no-one must be complacent. As more and more of these products come into the market (in fact, there has been quite an explosion over the last couple of years) there will inevitably come a time when only the best will survive, either by natural selection or by statutory regulations (EEC Directive 70/524: Silage Aids). The complexity of the microbiology and biochemistry of the silage fermentation is not, as yet, completely understood and in that respect, further research and development into the benefits of biological silage additive use is essential.

6.20   BIOPESTICIDES — AN INTRODUCTION

The remainder of this chapter reviews the need for alternatives to chemical pesticides and describes some of the biological alternatives available. It concentrates primarily on the microorganisms which can replace chemical pesticides and concludes with a few of the changes which may make biopesticides more attractive to users and the chemical industry.

6.20.1   Do we need alternatives to chemical pesticides?
Pesticides are used to suppress insects, weeds, and diseases which reduce the yield obtained from a particular crop. An investment has been made in the land, seed, fertiliser, equipment and time; weeds reduce the return on this investment, insects and disease can occasionally eliminate it completely. A

significant number of these problems can be avoided or solved with synthetic chemicals. There is little doubt that modern developed agriculture benefits enormously from the range and potency of the chemical armoury arrayed in its favour. However, chemical pesticides have not proved a complete solution to crop protection. There are numerous insects which, by virtue of their habitat and behaviour, remain uncontrolled and continue to damage valauble crops; similarly, various diseases and weeds remain unchecked. In addition, pests are beginning to escape from chemical control by developing resistance, mainly to certain insecticides and fungicides; there are cases reported where the acquisition of resistance to a particular chemical leads to enhanced resistance to other chemicals, compounding the problem further (Table 6.6).

Table 6.6 — Number of species of Arthropoda with reported cases of resistance through 1980

	Pesticide group					
Order	Dieldrin/ BHC	DDT	OP[a]	Carb.[b]	Pyr.[c]	Other
Diptera	107	106	60	11	6	1
Lepidoptera	40	40	31	14	8	2
Coleoptera	55	24	26	9	3	19
Homoptera	13	13	28	9	3	4
Heteroptera	16	8	6	—	—	—
Other insects	23	21	7	2	1	2
Acarina	15	17	42	6	1	30
Total	269	229	200	51	22	58

[a] Organo-phosphates.
[b] Carbamates.
[c] Pyrethroids.

A rapidly breeding insect can become resistant very quickly. In the year that pyrethroid insecticides were introduced into the United Kingdom, growers reported a need to apply higher rates by the end of a single, four-month season. Recent reports indicate that 2000 times more pyrethroid may now be required to control the glasshouse whitefly than when the chemical was introduced.

In addition to resistance, the increasing use of chemicals has prompted concern over their residual effects on users and other non-target organisms, and on the environment in general. Some controversies have been well publicised, like those over DDT and 2,4,5-T, although, despite its being banned in many countries, DDT is used in Africa at over 30 000 tonnes per year at present. Other chemicals are being subjected to closer scrutiny or outright bans. Allowable levels of ethylene dibromide (EDB) have been reduced in stored grain, citrus and other fruits. The chemical now replacing EDB is methyl bromides, which has shown oncogenic effects and mutagenic potential [6.117].

6.20.2   The biological alternative

The use of biological agents to control pests has been known and practised for a long time. The Chinese used Pharoah's ants to control pests in their grain stores; mynah birds were brought to Mauritius in 1762 to control red locusts; dogs and many other animals have been used to control insects and rodent pests.

Domestic cats, which are thought to be the first biological control agents, played such a significant role in rat control that their persecution in the Middle Ages may well have contributed to the spread of bubonic plague in Europe. However, their effects on non-target organisms were unpredictable and in those days, no tests were required for registration. In 1815 the cats introduced to Ascension Island for rat control virtually exterminated the sea birds.

Many insects are controlled by other insects which prey on or parasitise their hosts. The 'classical' form of biological control is defined as the introduction of a host-specific, self-reproducing, host-seeking parasite or predator from an exotic source which will complement the naturally occurring flora and fauna, and thus maintain the pest species at sub-economic levels. Cottony cushion scale was successfully controlled by Australian ladybirds in California as early as 1888, and in Israel, most of the 20+ insect pests of citrus have been controlled by classical methods.

Organisations such as the Commonwealth Institute of Biological Control in Britain or the Australian CSIRO specialise in finding and utilising natural enemies of pest species. Successes include the use of myxomatosis viral disease of rabbits and the introduction of the fish *Gambusia affinis* to eat mosquito larvae in ponds and water courses. In crop protection, self-sustaining introductions include the fungus *Aschersonia aleyrodidis*, which successfully controls the citrus whitefly in Florida, and the use of ten parasites and a predator species in the Northeastern United States to control the alfalfa weevil, *Hypera postica*.

'Augmented' biological control is the selective use, establishment or encouragement of biotic agents to suppress particular pests. At present there are several noteworthy examples of predatory and parasitic insects used in protecting the European cucumber and tomato crops. The spider mite predator, *Phytoseuilus persimilis*, is very effective against the red spider (two-spotted) mite *Tetranychus urticae*; similarly the whitefly parasite *Encarsia formosa* controls the glasshouse whitefly *Trialeurodes vaporariorum*. Both of these pests are resistant to chemical control. The development of these insects as biological control agents during the 1960's and

1970's led to their commercialisation throughout Europe and in a number of other parts of the world.

In the United Kingdom, it is estimated that approximately 80% of cucumber nurseries and 50% of the tomato industry now obtain reliable and cost-effective control by using *Phytoseuilus* as a replacement for acaricidal sprays that are applied 20–25 times during the life of the crop. Beneficial insects are produced and supplied commercially in Australia, Canada, Finland, France, Israel, The Netherlands, Norway, Sweden, the United Kingdom and the United States.

Other biological alternatives include 'sterile release', whereby a population is inundated with non-fertile insects. Advances are being made in the use of pheromones and other chemicals extracted from insects or based on naturally occurring behaviour-orienting compounds. These are used to attract insects to traps to determine the optimal spraying time, reducing pesticide use, cost and the likelihood of resistance. They also are used to disrupt mating, leading either the males or the females to the wrong places to find mates, thereby reducing the population [6.118].

6.21   MICROBIAL PESTICIDES

The use of microorganisms as pesticides is more recent and has had some notable successes [6.119]. At present, there are a number of bacteria, fungi and viruses which have been introduced as commercial pesticides, frequently after skilful production and formulation efforts.

6.21.1   Bacteria

Bacteria are ubiquitous in nature and have a versatile metabolism which allows them to live in every part of the biosphere. Altogether, over 90 species of bacteria which infect insects have been described. Most belong to the families Pseudomonadaceae, Enterobacteriaceae, Lactobacillaceae, Micrococcaceae and Bacillaceae (Table 6.7). The majority of the commercial strains belong to the genus *Bacillus*; the most widely used products are made from *Bacillus thuringiensis* (Bt) [6.120], of which there are over 22 serotypes (determined by flagellar antigens). Members of the group are toxic to lepidopteran, dipteran, and coleopteran insects.

Bt species are used for the control of caterpillar pests, mosquitoes and blackflies. A second commercial type is *Bacillus popilliae* for the control of Japanese beetles. A third, *Bacillus sphaericus*, is considered to a be a highly promising pathogen for mosquito control but is not yet in commerical production.

6.21.1.1   *Bacillus thuringiensis*

Bt was discovered in silkworms in Japan in the early part of the 20th century. The first commerical product was produced in France in 1938 and was based on a strain which also made a toxin dangerous to man, called the beta-

Table 6.7 — Bacteria pathogenic to insects [6.121]

Bacteria	Susceptible insects
Pseudomonadaceae	
Pseudomonas aeruginosa	Grasshoppers
Pseudomonas septica	Scarab beetle, striped ambrosia beetle
Vibrio leonardia	Greater wax moth, European corn borer
Enterobacteriaceae	
Serratia marcescens	Butterfly, moth and skipper
Escherichia coli and *Enterobacter aerogenes*	
Proteus vulgaris, *P. mirabilis* and *P. retigeri*	Grasshoppers
Salmonella schottmuelleri var. *alvei*	Honey bee, greater wax moth
Salmonella enteritidis and *Shigella dysenteriae*	Greater wax moth
Lactobacillaceae	
Diplococcus and *Streptococcus* spp.	Cockchafer, silk worm, gypsy moth, processionary moth, greater wax moth
Micrococcaceae	
Micrococcus spp.	Green June beetle, sawflies, houseflies, various Lepidoptera, European corn borer and cutworms
Bacillaceae	
Bacillus thuringiensis and *B. cereus*	Various butterflies and moths
B. popillieae and *B. lentimorbus*	Scarab beetles
B. sphaericus	Mosquitos
B. larvae	Honey bees
B. moritai	Flies
Clostridium novyi and *C. perfringens*	Greater wax moth

exotoxin. Various methods were developed to remove this toxin from the commercial product by processing the fermentatin broth. Dulmage [6.122] isolated Bt HD-1, an exotoxin-free strain of Bt Kurstaki which is now the active ingredient in most commercial strains of Bt used against Lepidoptera. HD-1 is effective against a broad range of caterpillar pests but is often not the most active strain against any particular pest. The science of Bt has been reviewed most recently by Aronson *et al.* [6.120].

The market for Bt is not large, representing slightly over 0.1% of the world pesticide market, yet it is over 90% of all microbial pesticide sales. The two commercial strains are serotype 3A3B (HD-1) used against caterpillars, and H-14, effective against mosquitoes and blackfly.

During the production of modern strains of Bt, the cells produce a resistant endospore and a protein crystal. The crystal, or parasporal body, contains a toxin [6.123; 6.124] which becomes insecticidal after digestion due to the alkaline environmemnt and proteases found in the mid-guts of susceptible species. The intact crystal is non-toxic. The crystal varies amongst the many serotypes and isolates of Bt, producing a varied spectrum of activity against different insects.

6.21.1.2 Bt 3A3B

The toxic moiety is thought to be a peptide of 68 000 daltons molecular weight [6.125, 6.126]. The released toxin attacks the epithelial lining of the insect gut, disrupting the cell membranes; the lining breaks down, the contents mix with the insect haemocoel and death quickly follows.

In commercial use, Bt 3A3B is specific to caterpillars because the conditions found within the caterpillar's stomach are specifically appropriate to activate the Bt toxin, having the correct degree of alkalinity (man, for example, has an acid stomach), the correct array of digestive enzymes and a specific chemistry of the stomach wall cell which allows the Bt toxins to bind. The action of Bt is seen almost immediately after the insect has eaten a small amount; feeding ceases and the insect becomes moribund, caterpillars dying between 2 and 5 days later.

Various products such as Dipel, Thuricide, Biobit and Bactospeine are available based on 3A3B, both as wettable powders or as flowable liquid formulation. These are applied by conventional spray equipment, although new developments in application technology and in the assessment of efficacy may allow the use of novel equipment requiring lower doses of Bt to be effective.

However, not all caterpillars are controlled by Bt, e.g. the *Heliothis* caterpillar complex which damages cotton. Other lepidopterous cotton pests bore into the cotton flower bud and do not ingest a lethal dose of Bt. There may also be substances on the cotton leaf which inactivate the toxin.

6.21.1.3 Bt H14

Bt H14, or Bt *israelensis*, is a mosquito larvicide first identified in 1977 [6.127]; the organism has some similarities in its biology and safety to 3A3B but is effective against a range of disease-carrying and nuisance mosquitoes and blackflies. Amongst others, the World Health Organisation has carried out extensive tests to demonstrate the bacterium's efficacy and safety, and its use is growing. Commercial products based on BtH14 include Teknar, Skeetal, Vectobac and Bactimos.

Its toxin is produced differently from that of 3A3B, seemingly having three associated proteins rather than only one. When solubilised, the toxin has been reported to cause death in mice following injection and to have haemolytic properties, neither characteristic being present in 3A3B. It is described as radically different in its 'entomocidal behaviour' biochemical and serological properties, DNA homology and physical appearance of the crystal in electron micrographs' [6.128].

6.21.1.4   Bt Beta-exotoxin

Some strains, such as the early commercial strains, produce the beta-exotoxin, an ATP anologue. Despite its mammalian toxicity, it is especially toxic to house-fly larvae, not needing to be ingested to be effective. Few products based on the exotoxin are registered for use in the west, Finland, and probably Italy, being the only countries involved.

6.21.1.5   The future of Bacillus thuringiensis

Although formulations scientists and innovative application technology have improved current Bt products, the most significant further advances will come from biochemists and geneticists. DNA probes and plasmid curing have been used to show that the genes which control the synthesis of the crystal production are located on a small number of high molecular weight plasmids [6.129]; 6.130]. The evidence of this was reviewed by Dean [6.128; 6.131], including results from various workers on transducing phages and the transformation of protoplasts.

The toxic protein has been cloned into *E. coli* and *B. subtilis* and has been expressed, even during the vegetative growth phase [6.132]. One company has successfully cloned the lepidopteran toxin into tobacco cells which have been regrown into whole plants in which every cell expresses the toxin. These plants are 'resistant' to insects; after eating leaf tissue the caterpillars die before doing any significant damage [6.133].

Proteins from different strains have been combined, thereby expanding the activity spectrum of the recombinant strain [6.134]. Wholly new strains have been reported with activity against additional groups of insects such as Coleoptera (beetles). Kreig *et al.* [6.135; 6.136] were the first to report such a new strain, *B. thuringiensis* variety *tenebrionis*, but were followed by Herrnstadt *et al.* [6.137] with *B. thuringiensis* variety *sandiego*. The initial report of this strain included the cloning and expression of its toxin gene in *E. coli* and the comment that 'The entire assemblages of molecular genetic technology can be brought to bear on the fragment of DNA that contains the nucleotide sequence coding for *B.t.s.d.* toxin protein with the aim of producing novel genes that have improved transcription/translation properties, encode protein with enhanced toxicity or with altered host specificity'.

Whiteley *et al.* [6.129] isolated genes for toxic protein, deduced the amino acid sequence for the active site of protein from the DNA sequence of the gene, and elucidated the composition of the crystal.

The mode of action at the molecular level is not yet proved but receptors such as phosphatidyl choline and *N*-acetyl galactosamine may be the target sites for the toxin [6.138]. Himeno *et al.* [6.139] proposed that nucleotide derivatives participate in the action of the toxin.

Hardy [6.121] speculated on the possibility of using computer graphics to model the interaction between the toxin and insect receptors which could lead to prediction of insecticidal protein structures. After the secondary and tertiary structure of the protein is known, the active site can be described; this could lead eventually to custom-built biological insecticides.

New biotechnological techniques may make a contribution through increases in potency by modification of the plasmid complement of the bacterium, which controls the synthesis of the protein [6.140]. This would both reduce the cost of production and provide the starting place for new, more easily used formulations. Alternatively, production of asporogenic strains may reduce production costs by avoiding the 'waste' of metabolic energy on spore production and may make the product more acceptable in certain countries which baulk at releasing live microorganisms into the environment [6.141].

In the shorter term, a variety of more specifically targeted products may be developed. In 1985, Sandoz successfully field-tested a new product, Javelin, which was based on NRD-12, a 3A3B strain discovered by Norman Dubois of the United States Forest Service. Although the strain was discovered and characterised for its enhanced effect against Gypsy Moths, Javelin's improved effects are against *Spodoptera*, a pest of vegetables and in some countries of cotton. New products for control of Coleoptera based on the two strains cited above find a variety of markets, especially for control of Colorado Potato Beetle.

6.21.2 Fungi

Over 400 species of fungi are known to attack insects and mites. Examples are found in most groups of fungi, although the Deuteromycetes and Phycomycetes contain most of the useful species [6.142].

Fungi usually infect their hosts by direct invasion and are therefore able, unlike most bacteria and viruses, to attack pests without first being ingested. In addition, a major feature of fungi is their ability to sporulate on the dead bodies of their hosts. By this means they can spread throughout a population, creating an epizootic. They control not only the insects they land on, but the entire host population for extended periods. In some cases, the timely application of a sufficient number of fungal propagules at an early stage can control pests effectively for the duration of the crop.

Unfortunately, to be effective, fungi are fairly fastidious in their requirements for humidity and temperature. If the humidity or the temperature varies too far from the optimum for the fungus, the control of the insect pests will be slow at best and it is unlikely that the desired epizootic will develop.

It is for this reason that several of the presently commercial pesticides based on fungi are targeted to glasshouse pests. Glasshouses are expensive to build and to run; therefore they are generally used to produce higher-value crops like flowers or out-of-season vegetables. Since the potential cash loss to pests or diseases is so great, and the proportion of total operating costs represented by pesticide purchase and application is small, glasshouse operators tend to use more chemicals per unit area than other growers. This high use leads to resistance earlier than it might otherwise occur and creates a demand for biopesticides sooner than in other market sectors [6.143].

In order to make effective use of a fungus, applying it at the right time and in the optimum amount, it is necessary to understand the aetiology of the pest problem. When do the pests arrive, from where, what makes attacks worse, why do they sometimes not come at all? One must understand how the pest interacts both with the crop and with other members of the pest complex.

Despite the limitations cited above, fungi do have promise as cost-effective biopesticides. A number of fungi are either in commercial use or in development [6.144].

6.21.2.1   *Metarhizium anisopliae*

M. anisopliae is the best known of all entomopathogenic fungi, having been first described approximately 100 years ago as the green muscardine fungus. It was also the first fungus to be produced on a large scale. Using a peg which penetrates the epicuticle, the fungus forms a subepicuticular plate from which hyphae are generated. The insect is killed by invasion and the fungus resporulates on the cadaver.

M. anisopliae infects a number of different types of insects including spittle bugs in pasture and sugar cane, for which is it used commercially in Brazil. It has been combined with a virus for control of the rhinoceros beetle, a major destroyer of palms in the the South Pacific. Recent reports suggest that it can also be used to control Brown Planthopper, a pest in rice in parts of the Far East. A number of UK universities and research institutes as well as a variety of companies have active interests in the further development of this fungus.

6.21.2.2   *Beauveria bassiana*

Colorado Potato Beetle is the potentially commerical target of *B. bassiana*; it has been used for this purpose for some years in the USSR in a commercial preparation known as Boverin. It has been the object of extensive experimentation in the USA and has achieved control almost as effectively as the best available pesticides. After invasion of the insect, *B. bassiana* produces beauvericin, a cyclodepsipeptide toxin.

6.21.2.3   Nomurea rilevi
N. rileyi was investigated for many years by Ignoffo's group in collaboration with Abbott Laboratories for the control of lepidopterous pests in soybeans. Grown on solid media, it was apparently difficult to obtain enough spores cheaply enough to consider its commercial use.

6.21.2.4   Entomophthorales
Various species of the Enterophthorales, including especially *Erynia neo-aphidis*, have been studied as potential biopesticides. However, members of this group present a somewhat contrary problem in that the ones which have proved easy to grow were not very effective, whereas other more virulent species have been more difficult to grow *in vitro*. These problems are now being overcome by scientists at King's College, London, and Rothamsted Experimental Station.

6.21.2.5   Verticilium lecanii
V. lecanii is the only entomopathogenic fungus on which successful commercial products are based, a development which followed almost 10 years of research at the Glasshouse Crops Research Institute. Strains of this fungus control aphids and whitefly, sometimes for months, in the protected environment of the glasshouse. Successful trials have been conducted in many countries. Simultaneously research is being conducted by scientists at King's College, London, to understand the genetic basis for vigorous epizootics, thereby leading to the development of improved strains.

6.21.2.6   Hirsutella thompsonii
H. thompsonii was produced briefly as Mycar in the USA for control of citrus mites. It did not perform as expected, possibly due to the dry weather or to it being mixed with incompatible fungicides. Despite excellent research by McCoy [6.145], Mycar is no longer available.

6.21.2.7   The future of fungal pesticides
The principal reason for the failure of entomopathogenic fungi to achieve commercial success has been their lack of absolutely predictable effectiveness. This does not have to be 100% control all the time; but it has to be a cost-effective minimum, enough to allow the user to apply it with confidence. Substantial effort is required in the future to understand the aetiology of the pest, to predict the consequences of crop/pest/biopesticide interactions, in order to refine the 'use recommendations' and provide consistently successful control.

Genetic engineering of fungi has not progressed as rapidly as that for bacteria and viruses. Nevertheless, recent developments should enable scientists to use genetic engineering to achieve a better understanding of the relationship between fungal genetics, biochemistry and physiology. This should, in turn, lead to better products and more interest in this versatile group of organisms.

6.21.3   Viruses

Over 1200 insect host–virus associations have been described of which almost three-quarters are in Lepidoptera [6.146]. Most of these associations have merely been noted observationally, without the intention of seeking means of insect control.

Most attention has been paid to one group of viruses, the baculoviruses, following a WHO recommendation in 1973. This recommendation was based on the non-occurrence of vertebrate pathogens in this viral group; they were considered at the time to be the most likely to be safe. However, other groups, the cytoplasmic polyhedrosis viruses, entomopoxviruses and iridoviruses, contain potential insect biopesticides that may now be considered candidates for development.

Two reasons can be adduced for a broadening of the research spectrum. The first is that new techniques, developed in the present biotechnological innovation wave, can be applied to safety testing of viruses to give greater assurance than was hitherto possible about their behaviour in mammals. Nucleic acid probes and genetic 'tagging' can be used to obtain an understanding that was not possible a few years ago. The second reason is that, to date, no cross-infection between an insect virus and a vertebrate has been observed and it is considered unlikely to occur [6.147]. (*Bacillus thuringiensis* is closely related to *B. anthracis* but this has not proved a major handicap to its development.)

6.21.3.1   Baculoviruses

Baculoviruses are double-stranded DNA viruses which have biopesticides in three groups: the Nuclear Polyhedrosis Viruses (NPVs), the Grandulosis Viruses (GVs), and non-occluded viruses.

They infect insects after ingestion; the susceptibility of many species of insects varies over several orders of magnitude depending on the age of the insect. Clearly, application timing becomes a critical matter in attempting to control the maximum number of insects with the minimum amount of virus. Entwhistle and Evans [6.146] suggest that frequency of application is more important than dosage per application; they believe it is important to ensure newly hatched larvae are consistently exposed to an appropriate viral dose before they grow old and insensitive.

The effectiveness of the control obtained in the field will also depend substantially on the method of application as well as on the rate of application of the viruses. Small viral particles (inclusion bodies) must be made to land on the target foliage or the control effort will be pointless.

Although the NPVs and GVs formulate themselves, by wrapping up in a proteinaceous matrix thought to provide some protection from ultraviolet light, formulation of viral pesticides is a new technology, only just being tackled by the commercial concerns involved in this field.

Many of the viruses studied are very specific in their action. *Neodiprion sertifer* NPV has only mild cross-infectivity to closely related species. While specificity enhances environmental and operator safety, it does little to enlarge the potential market. However, several viruses, notably *Autographa californica* NPV, have a broader spectrum of activity and may find bigger potential markets.

6.21.3.2   *The future of viral pesticides*

One key area in which new research in likely to prove beneficial is ecological and epizootological studies. The spread, residual detection, and survival characteristics of viruses should be understood in order to optimise their use. Although many studies have been carried out over the years, the data have been transferred into practice relatively slowly [6.147]; increasing commercial interest should accelerate this process. New techniques, in particular the use of innocuous oligonucleotide sequences to tag the viral genome, will have a major impact on the speed, breadth and accuracy of the ecological studies which can be carried out. This technique is being pioneered by the NERC Institute of Virology in Oxford.

Recombinant DNA technology has been used to insert new sequences into the gene for the polyhedral proteins which can then be used for synthesis of novel proteins. These new proteins could include the protein toxins of *Bacillus thuringiensis*, thereby potentially enhancing the toxic effects of the virus.

Yet another area where new biotechnological methods may have an impact is on production cost. Most viruses are made in the living insect; a few can be grown in insect cell culture, a technique which provides more uniformity but is no less expensive. Improving the technology of insect cell culture, selecting or engineering higher-yielding viruses, or even producing eukaryote viruses in prokaryotes, could have a significant effect on the competitiveness of viral biopesticides against chemical competition.

6.22   THE FUTURE OF BIOPESTICIDES

Until relatively recently, biopesticides did not attract much interest from commercial firms. Many companies attempted to make and sell products based on *Bacillus thuringiensis* but most gave up fairly quickly. Bt could not be made or marketed in the same pattern as chemicals, it was unlikely to find a market a large as most companies required of their chemical products, and new and better chemicals were being invented at a high rate. In addition, the uncertainties of registration and the non-patentability of most microorganisms discouraged entrants to the commercial field.

Twin revolutions have completely changed the present situation.

The first revolution is the change in future perspectives for the chemicals business. The public are uneasy about the use of chemicals, about chemical residues in their food, about hazardous effects on the environment. They would prefer alternatives; this preference has manifested itself in regulatory guidelines which provide a tiered testing system which utilises what is already known about many microorganisms. Less expensive registration procedures encourage more companies to develop products. At the same time, procedures for the registration of chemicals get no easier and many chemicals already registered are having their safety questioned.

New market opportunities are opening up for biopesticides as chemicals are banned or their use restricted. The discovery of new chemicals becomes an ever more costly exercise. The substantial consolidation in the pesticide industry suggests that fewer companies can afford to sustain the cost of bringing wholly novel chemicals to market.

Simultaneously, a second revolution has occurred in what biotechnology can do and, more importantly, in the perception of what it might be able to do: engineering of genes and of proteins; the production of bacterial toxins in plants, in other bacteria, in viruses; a rapid increase in understanding of the mechanism of action of fungi and in the ecology of viruses. These changes contribute to a belief that the traditional limitations of biopesticides — slow action, limited and unpredictable efficacy, non-patentability, small markets, etc. — may now be overcome.

Inevitably many expectations will be disappointed. It is likely, however, that patience and excellence will be rewarded and biopesticides will provide a profitable future for some.

REFERENCES

[6.1] Metchnikoff, E. (1980) *Prolongation of Life*, Putnam & Sons, New York.

[6.2] Clarke, R. T. Y. and Bauchop, T. (1977) *Microbial Ecology of the Gut*, Academic Press, New York.

[6.3] Sandine, W. E. (1978) Role of *Lactobacillus* in the intestinal tract. *J. Fd Prot.*, **42**, 259.

[6.4] Kulp, W. L. and Rettger, L. F. (1924) A comparative study of *Lactobacillus acidophilus* and *Lactobacillus bulgaricus*. *J. Bact.*, **9**, 357.

[6.5] De Mitchell, I. G. and Kenworthy, R. (1976) Investigation on a metabolite from *Lactobacillus bulgaricus* which neutralises the effect of enterotoxin from *Escherichia coli* pathogenic for pigs. *J. Appl. Bact.*, **41**, 163–174.

[6.6] Hawley, H. B., Shepard, P. A. and Wheater, D. M. (1959) Factors affecting the implantation of lactobacilli in the intestine. *J. Appl. Bact.*, **22**, 360.

[6.7] Savage, D. C. (1977) Microbial ecology of the gastrointestinal tract. *Ann. Rev. Microbiol.*, **31**, 107.

[6.8] Savage, D. C. (1979) Introduction to mechanisms of association of indigenous microorganisms. *Am. J. Clin. Nutr.*, **32**, 113.

[6.9] Fuller, R. (1973) Ecological studies on the *Lactobacillus* flora associated with the crop epithelium of the fowl. *J. Appl. Bact.*, **36**, 131–139.

[6.10] Fuller, R. (1979) Bacterial attachment in the epithelium of the alimentary tract. *ARC Res. Rev.*, **5**, 31.

[6.11] Fuller, R., Barrow, R. and Brooker, B. E. (1978) Bacteria associated with the gastric epithelium of neonatal pigs. *Apl. Environ. Microbiol.*, **35**, 582–591.

[6.12] Barrow, P. A., Brooker, B. E., Fuller, R. and Newport, M. J. (1980) The attachment of bacteria to the gastric epithelium of the pig and its importance in the microecology of the intestine. *J. Appl. Bact.*, **48**, 147–154.

[6.13] Mayra-Makinen, A., Manninen, M. and Gyllenburg, H. (1983) The adherence of lactic acid bacteria to the columnar epithelial cells of pigs and calves. *J. Appl. Bact.*, **55**, 241–245.

[6.14] Fuller, R. (1972) Bacteria that stick in the gut. *New Scientist*, **30**, 506.

[6.15] Wheater, D. M., Hersch, A. and Mattick, A. T. R. (1951) Lactobacillin: an antibiotic from lactobacilli. *Nature*, **168**, 659.

[6.16] Vincent, J. G., Veomett, R. C. and Riley, R. F. (1959) Antibacterial activity associated with *Lactobacillus acidophilus*. *J. Gen. Microbiol.*, **12**, 123.

[6.17] Kvanta, E. (1980) *Fermentation of fodder*, US Patent No. 4,210,673.

[6.18] Delaney, J. M., Daly, C. and Herlihy, M. (1979) Bacteriocin type inhibitors produced by *Streptococcus lactis* subspecies *diacetylactis*. *Soc. Gen. Microbiol Quart.*, **6**, 159.

[6.19] Mehta, A. M., Patel, K. A. and Dave, P. J. (1983) Purification and properties of the inhibitory protein isolated from *Lactobaccillus acidophilus* AC1. *Microbios*, **38**, 73–81.

[6.20] Klaenhammer, T. R. (1982) Microbiological considerations in selection and preparation of *Lactobacillus* strains for use as dietary adjuncts. *J. Dairy Sci.*, **65**, 1339–1349.

[6.21] Barrow, P. A., Fuller, R. and Newport, M. J. (1977) Changes in the microflora and physiology of the anterior intestinal tract of pigs weaned at 2 days, with special reference to the pathogenesis of diarrhoea. *Infect. Immun.*, **18**, 586–595.

[6.22] Sandine, W. E., Muralidhara, K. S., Elliker, P. R. and England, D. C. (1972) Lactic acid bacteria in food and in health: a review with special reference to enteropathogenic *Escherichia coli* as well as certain enteric diseases and their treatment with antibiotics and lactobacilli, *J. Milk Fd Technol.*, **35**, 691–702.

[6.23] Kenworthy, R. and Crabb, W. E. (1963) The intestinal flora of young pigs with reference to early weaning and *Escherichia coli* scours. *J. Comp. Path.*, **73**, 215.

[6.24] Chopra, S. L., Blackwood, A. C. and Dale, D. G. (1983) Intestinal microflora associated with enteritis of early weaned pigs. *Can. J. Comp. Med. Vet. Sci.*, **21**, 29.

[6.25] Kohler, E. M. and Bohl, E. M. (1964) Prophylaxis of diarrhoea in newborn pigs. *J. Am. Vet. Med. Assn.*, **144**, 1294.

[6.26] Redmond, H. E. and Moore, R. W. (1965) Biologic effect of introducing *Lactobacillus acidophilus* into a large swine herd experiencing enteritis. *Southern Vet.*, summer edition, 287.

[6.27] Kornegay, E. T. and Thomas, H. R. (1973) *Bacterial and yeast preparations for starter and grower rations.* Research Report No. 151, Virginia Polytechnic Inst., Blacksburg, VA, USA.

[6.28] Muralidhara, K. S., Sheggeby, G. G., Elliker, P. R., England, D. C. and Sandine, W. E. (1977) Effect of feeding *Lactobacillus* on the coliform and *Lactobacillus* flora of the intestinal tissue and faeces from piglets. *J. Fd Prot.*, **40**, 288.

[6.29] Trouvatelli, L. D. and Matteuzzi, D. (1976) Presence of bifidobacteria in the rumen of calves fed different rations. *Appl. Environ. Microbiol.*, **32**, 470.

[6.30] Crawford, J. S. (1979) Probiotics in animal nutrition. *1979 Arkansas Nutrition Conference*, pp. 45–55.

[6.31] Gilliland, S. E., Bruce, B. V., Bush, L. J. and Staley, T. E. (1979) Effect of feeding *Lactobacillus acidophilus* on the intestinal and fecal flora of young dairy calves. *J. Dairy Sci.*, **62**, 45.

[6.32] Fuller, R. and Turvey, A. (1971) Bacteria associated with the intestinal wall of the fowl (*Gallus domesticus*). *J. Appl. Bact.*, **34**, 617–622.

[6.33] Fuller, R. (1977) The importance of lactobacilli in maintaining normal microbial balance in the crop. *Br. Poultry Sci.*, **18**, 85.

[6.34] Fuller, R., Houghton, S. B. and Brooker, B. E. (1981) Attachment of *Streptococcus faecium* to the duodenal epithelium of the chicken and its importance in colonisation of the small intestine. *Appl. Environ. Microbiol.*, **41**, 1433–1441.

[6.35] Tortuero, F. (1973) Influence of the implantation of *Lactobacillus acidophilus* in chicks on growth, feed conversion, malabsorption of fat syndrome and intestinal flora. *Poultry Sci.*, **52**, 197.

[6.36] Dilworth, C. and Day, E. J. (1978) *Lactobacillus* cultures in broiler diets. *75th Ann. Meeting, Soc. Assoc. Agric. Sci.*, p. 18.

[6.37] Sarra, P. G., Magri, M., Bottazzi, V. and Dellaglio, F. (1980) Genetic heterogeneity among *Lactobacillus acidophilus* strains. *Antonie van. Leeuwenhoek*, **46**, 169–176.

[6.38] Dutta, G. N. and Devriese, L. A. (1981) Sensitivity and resistance to growth promoting agents in animal lactobacilli. *J. Appl. Bact.*, **51**, 282–288.

[6.39] Hellriegel, H. and Wilfarth, H. (1888) Supplement to *Z. Ver. Rubenzucker-Ind. Dtsch. Reichs.*

[6.40] Beijerinck, M. W. (1888) *Botan. Ztg.*, **46**, 725.

[6.41] Vincent, J. M. (1974) In *Biology of Nitrogen Fixation*, Quispel, (ed.), American Elsevier, New York.

[6.42] Beyon, J. L. and Josey, D. P. (1980) Demonstration of heterogeneity in a natural population of *Rhizobium phaseoli* using variation in intrinsic antibiotic resistance. *J. Gen. Microbiol.*, **118**, 437.

[6.43] Bohlool, B. B. and Schmidt, E. L. (1980) The immunofluorescence approach in microbial ecology. *Adv. Microbial Ecol.*, **4**, 203.

[6.44] Vincent, J. M. and Scott Smith, M. (1982) Evaluation of inoculant viability on commercially inoculated legume seed. *Agron. J.*,, **74**, 921–923.

[6.45] Sprent, J. I. (1979) *The Biology of Nitrogen-Fixing Organisms*. McGraw-Hill, Maidenhead.

[6.46] Bassett, B., Goodman, R. N. and Novacky, A. (1977) Ultrastructure of soybean nodules. I. Release of rhizobia from infection thread. *Can. J. Microbiol.*, **23**, 572–582.

[6.47] Yao, P. Y. and Vincent, J. M. (1969) Host specificity in the root hair 'curling factor' of *Rhizobium* species. *Aust. J. Biol. Sci.*, **22**, 413–423.

[6.48] Dazzo, F. and Hubbell, D. H. (1975) Cross-reactive antigens and lectin as determinants of symbiont specificity in the *Rhizobium*–clover association. *Appl. Microbiol.*, **30**, 1017–1033.

[6.49] Brill, W. J. (1977) Biological nitrogen fixation. *Scient. Am.*, **236**, 68–81.

[6.50] Gaworzewska, E. T. and Carlile, M. J. (1982) Positive chemotaxis of *Rhizobium leguminosarum* and other bacteria toward root exudates of legumes and other plants. *J. Gen. Microbiol.*, **128**, 1179–1188.

[6.51] van Egeraat, A. W. S. M. (1975) The growth of *Rhizobium leguminosarum* on the root surface and in the rhizosphere of pea seedlings in relation to root exudates. *Plant & Soil*, **42**, 381–386.

[6.52] Verma, D. P. S. and Bal, A. K. (1976) Intracellular site of synthesis and localisation of leghaemoglobin in root nodules. *Proc. Nat. Acad. Sci.*, **73**, 3843–3847.

[6.53] Oppenheim, J. and Marcus, L. (1970) Correlation of ultrastructure in *Azotobacter vinelandii* with nitrogen source for growth. *J. Bact.*, **101**, 286–291.

[6.54] Masterson, C. L. and Murphy, P. M. (1976) Application of the acetylene reduction technique to the study of nitrogen fixation by white clover in the field. In *Symbiotic Nitrogen Fixation in Plants*, Nutman, P. S. (ed.), Cambridge University Press.

[6.55] Hardy, R. W. F. and Holsten, R. D. (1977) In *A Treatise on Dinitrogen Fixation*, Hardy, R. W. F., and Gibson, A. H. (eds), John Wiley, New York.

[6.56] Burton, J. C., Martinex, C. J. and Curley, R. L. (1977) *Rhizobia inoculants to various leguminous species*, Information Bulletin 101, Nitragin Co., Milwaukee, Wisconsin, USA.

[6.57] Gibson, A. H. (1965) The carbohydrate requirements for symbiotic nitrogen fixation: a 'whole-plant' growth analysis approach. *Aust. J. Biol. Sci.*, **19**, 499–515.

[6.58] Oghoghorie, C. G. O. and Pate, J. S. (1971) The nitrate stress syndrome of the nodulated field pea (*Pisum arvense* L.). *Plant & Soil.*, special volume, 185–202.

[6.59] Silsbury, J. H. (1977) Energy requirements for symbiotic nitrogen fixation. *Nature*, **267**, 149–150.

[6.60] Simpson, J. R. (1976) Transfer of nitrogen from 3 pasture legumes under periodic defoliation in a field environment. *Aust J. Exp. Anim. Husb.*, **16**, 863.

[6.61] Gibson, A. H. (1977) The influence of the environment and managerial practices on the legume–*Rhizobium* symbiosis. In *A Treatise on Dinitrogen Fixation*, Section IV, Agronomy and Ecology, Hardy, R. W. F. and Gibson, A. H. (eds), John Wiley, New York.

[6.62] Anon. (1984) *Recommended Varieties of Herbage Legumes, 1984*, National Institute of Agricultural Botany, Cambridge.

[6.63] Barber, L. E. (1979) Use of selective agents for recovery of *Rhizobium meliloti* from soil. *Soil Sci. Soc. Am. J.*, **43**, 1145–1148.

[6.64] Date, R. A. and Roughly, R. J. (1977) In *A Treatise on Dinitrogen Fixation*, Section IV, Agronomy and Ecology, Hardy, R. W. F. and Gibson, A. H. (cds), John Wilcy, New York.

[6.65] Waggoner, J. A., Evers, G. W. and Weaver, R. W. (1979) Adhesive increases inoculation efficiency in white clover. *Argon. J.*, **71**, 375–378.

[6.66] Date, R. A. (1976) In *Symbiotic Nitrogen Fixation in Plants*, Nutman, P. S. (ed.), Cambridge University Press.

[6.67] Evers, G. W. (1980) *Clover inoculation on S. E. Texas soils*, Texas Agricultural Experiments Station, March 1980.

[6.68] Anon. (1984) *UK National List Trials*, National Institute of Agricultural Botany, Cambridge.

[6.69] Day, C. A. Evaluation of a host-specific *Rhizobium* peat-based inoculant on the establishment and persistence of white clover in a grass/clover sward (to be published).

[6.70] Dancer, W. S., Handley, J. F. and Bradshaw, A. D. (1977) Nitrogen accumulation in kaolin mining wastes in Cornwall. II. Forage legumes. *Plant & Soil*, **48**, 303–314.

[6.71] Dixon, R. A. and Postgate, J. R. (1971) Transfer of nitrogen-fixation genes by conjugation in *Klebsiella pneumoniae*. *Nature*, **234**, 47–48.

[6.72] Helsinki, D. (1977) Plasmids as vectors for gene cloning. In *Genetic Engineering for Nitrogen Fixation*, Hollander, A. (ed.), Plenum Press, New York.

[6.73] Sprague, M. A. (1974) Oxygen disappearance in alfalfa silage (*Medicago sativa* L.). *Proc. 12th Grassl. Conf., Moscow*, **3**, 651.

[6.74] Stirling, A. C. and Whittenbury, R. (1963) Sources of lactic acid bacteria occurring in silage. *J. Appl. Bact.*, **26**, 86.

[6.75] Beck, T. (1972) The quantitative and qualitative composition of the lactic acid bacterial population of silage. *Landwirtschaftliche Forschung*, **27**, 55.

[6.76] Gibson, T. (1965) Clostridia in silage. *J. Appl. Bact.*, **28**, 56.

[6.77] Weissbach, F., Schmidt, L. and Hein, E. (1974) Method of anticipation of the run of fermentation in silage making based on chemical composition of green fodder. *Proc. 12th Grassl. Conf., Moscow*, **3**, 663.

[6.78] Edwards, R. A. and McDonald, P. (1978) The chemistry of silage. In *Fermentation of Silage — a Review*, McCullough, M. E. (ed.), National Feed Ingredients Association, Iowa, p. 29.

[6.79] Mead, G. C. (1971) The amino acid-fermenting clostridia, *J. Gen. Microbiol.*, **67**, 47.

[6.80] McCullough, M. (1977) Silage and silage fermentation. *Feedstuffs*, March 28, p. 49.

[6.81] McDonald, P. (1981) *The Biochemistry of Silage*, John Wiley, New York.

[6.82] Virtanen, A. I. (1933) The AIV method of processing fresh fodder. *Eur. J. Exp. Agric.*, **1**, 143.

[6.83] Watson, S. J. and Nash, M. J. (1960) *The Conservation of Grass and Forage Crops*, Oliver & Boyd, Edinburgh.

[6.84] Henderson, A. R. and McDonald, P. (1976) The effect of formic acid on the fermentation of ryegrass ensiled at different stages of growth and dry matter levels. *J. Br. Grassl. Soc.*, **31**, 47.

[6.85] Beck, Th. (1978) In *Fermentation of Silage — a Review*, McCullough, M. E. (ed.), National Feed Ingredients Association, Iowa, p. 61.

[6.86] McDonald, P. and Henderson, A. R. (1974) The use of fatty acids as grass silage additives. *J. Sci. Fd Agric.*, **25**, 791.

[6.87] Woolford, M. K. (1975) Antimicrobial effects of mineral acids, organic acids, salts and sterilising agents in relation to their potential as silage additives. *J. Br. Grassl. Soc.*, **33**, 131.

[6.88] Barry, T. N., Mundell, D. C., Wilkins, R. J. and Beever, D. E. (1978) The influence of formic acid and formaldehyde additives and type of harvesting machine on the utilisation of nitrogen in lucerne silages: 2; changes in amino-acid composition during ensilage and their influence on nutritive value. *J. Agric. Sci., Camb.*, **91**, 717–725.

[6.89] Crawshaw, R., Thorne, D. M. and Llewelyn, R. H. (1980) The effect of formic and propionic acids on the aerobic deterioration of grass silage. *J. Sci. Fd Agric.*, **31**, 685.

[6.90] Henderson, A. R., McDonald, P. and Woolford, M. K. (1972) Chemical changes and losses during the ensilage of wilted grass treated with formic acid. *J. Sci. Fd Agric.*, **23**, 1079.

[6.91] Wilson, R. F., Woolford, M. K., Cook, J. E. and Wilkinson, J. M. (1979) Acrylic acid and sodium acrylate as additives for silage. *J. Agric. Sci., Camb.*, **92**, 409.

[6.92] Watson, S. J. (1939) The science and practice of conservation: grass and forage crops, *Fertiliser & Feeding Stuffs J.*, London.

[6.93] Brown, D. C. and Valentine, S. C. (1972) Formaldehyde as a silage additive. I. The chemical composition and nutritive value of frozen lucerne, lucerne silage, and formaldehyde-treated lucerne silage. *Aust. J. Agric. Res.*, **23**, 1093.

[6.94] Barry, T. N. (1975) Effect of treatment with formaldehyde, formic acid and formaldehyde-acid mixtures on the chemical composition and nutritive value of silage, *N.Z. Journ. Agric. Res.*, **18**, 285.

[6.95] Siddons, R. C., Evans, R. T. and Beevers, D. E. (1979) The effects of formaldehyde treatment before ensiling on the digestion of wilted grass silage by sheep. *Br. J. Nutr.*, **42**, 535.

[6.96] Rauramaa, A. and Kreula, M. (1977) On the formaldehyde content of the silages prepared with formaldehyde-containing preservatives. *J. Sci. Agric. Soc. Finl.*, **49**, 199.

[6.97] Wilson, R. F. and Wilkins, R. J. (1978) Paraformaldehyde as a silage additive. *J. Agric. Sci., Camb.*, **91**, 23.

[6.98] Weise, F. (1967) The action of food quality sugar as a safety additive for grass silage. *Landwirtschaftliche Forschung*, **20**, 171.

[6.99] Whittenbury, R. (1968) Microbiology of grass silage. *Process Biochem.*, Feb., p. 27.

[6.100] McDonald, P. and Whittenbury, R. (1973) In *Chemistry and Biochemistry of Herbage*, Butler, G. W. and Bailey, R. W. (eds), Academic Press, New York, Vol. **3**, p. 33.

[6.101] London, J. (1976) The ecology and taxonomic status of the lactobacilli. *Ann. Rev. Microbiol.*, **30**, 279.

[6.102] Whittenbury, R. (1961) *An investigation of the lactic acid bacteria*, Ph.D. Thesis, University of Edinburgh.

[6.103] Carpintero, C. M., Henderson, A. R. and McDonald, P. (1979) The effects of some pre-treatments on proteolysis during the ensiling of herbage. *Grass & Forage Sci.*, **34**, 311.

[6.104] Henderson, A. R. and McDonald, P. (1984) The effect of a range of commerical inoculants on the biochemical changes during the ensilage of grass in laboratory studies. *Res. Dev. Agric.*, **1**, 171.

[6.105] Gross, F. (1969) Directing the silage process with additives. *Proc. 3rd Gen. Meet. Eur. Grassl. Fed., Braunschweig*, pp. 139–145.

[6.106] Wilkinson, J. M. (1978) The ensiling of forage maize: effects on composition and nutritive value. In *Forage Maize*, Bunting, E. S. (ed.), Agricultural Research Council, London, p. 201.

[6.107] Smith, D. (1973) The non-structural carbohydrates. In *Chemistry and Biochemistry of Herbage 1*, Butler, G. W. and Bailey, R. W. (eds), Academic Press, New York.

[6.108] Kandler, O. (1983) Carbohydrate metabolism in lactic acid bacteria. *Antonie van Leeuwenhoek*, **49**, 209.

[6.109] Henderson, A. R., Ewart, J. M. and Robertson, G. M. (1979) Studies on the aerobic stability of commercial silages. *J. Sci. Fd Agric.*, **30**, 223.

[6.110] Woolford, M. K. (1984) *The Silage Fermentation*. Microbilogy Series, Vol. 14, Marcel Dekker, New York.

[6.111] Henderson, A. R. and McDonald, P. (1975) The effect of delayed sealing on fermentation and losses during ensilage. *J. Sci. Fd Agric*, **26**, 653.

[6.112] Spoelstra, S. F. (1983) Inhibition of clostridial growth by nitrate during the early phase of silage fermentation. *J. Sci. Fd Agric.*, **34**, 145.

[6.113] Bousset-Fatianoff, N., Gouet, P., Bousset, J. and Contrepois, M. (1971) Research on nitrate in forages and silages. 2. Origin of nitrate catabolism in silages and the degree of degradation as a function of conservation treatment. *Annales de Biologie Animale, Biochemie et Biophysique*, **11**, 715.

[6.114] Woolford, M. K.)1975) Microbiological screening of the straight chain fatty acids (C1–C12) as potential silage additives. *J. Sci. Fd Agric.*, **26**, 219.

[6.115] Oshima, M. and McDonald, P. (1978) A review of the changes in nitrogenous compounds of herbage during ensilage. *J. Sci. Fd Agric.*, **29**, 497.

[6.116] Spoelstra, S. F. (1985) Nitrates in silage. *Grass & Forage Sci.*, **40**, 1.

[6.117] Anon. (1984) *Pesticides and Toxic Chemical News*, Food Chemical News Inc., Washington, DC, 7 March, p. 20.

[6.118] Jones, O. T. O and Kelly, D. (1986) Biotechnological innovation in the use of behaviour modifying chemicals in crop protection. In *Biotechnology and Crop Improvement and Protection*, Day, P. (ed.), BCPC Monograph No. 34, BCPC Publications, Thornton Heath, pp. 173–184.

[6.119] Quinlan, R. J. and Lisansky, S. G. (1983) Microbial insecticides. In *Biotechnology, a Comprehensive Treatise*, Dellweg, H. (ed.), Verlag Chemie, New York.

[6.120] Aronson, A. I., Beckman, W. and Dunn, P. (1986) *Bacillus thuringiensis* and related insect pathogens. In *Microbiological Reviews*, March 1986, American Society for Microbiology, pp. 1–24.

[6.121] Hardy, G. A. (1986) Bacteria are a plant's best friend. In *Biotechnology and Crop Improvement and Protection*, Day, P. (ed.), BCPC Monograph No. 34, BCPC Publications, Thornton Heath, pp. 151–160.

[6.122] Dulmage, H. T. (1970) Insecticidal activity of HD-1 — a new isolate of *Bacillus thuringiensis* var. *alesh*. *J. Invertebr. Pathol.*, **15**, 232–239.

[6.123] Dulmage, H. T. (1981) Insecticidal activity of isolates of *Bacillus thuringiensis* and their potential for pest control. In *Microbial Control of Pests and Plant Diseases 1970–1980*, Burges, H. D. (ed.), Academic Press, London, pp. 193–222.

[6.124] Luthy, P., Cordier, J.-L. and Fischer, H.-M. (1982) *Bacillus thur-*

ingiensis as a bacterial insecticide: basic considerations and application. In *Microbial and Viral Pesticides*, Kurstak, E. (ed.), Marcel Dekker, New York, pp. 35–74.

[6.125] Faust, R. M. and Bulla, L. A., Jr (1982) Bacteria and their toxins as insecticides. In *Microbial and Viral Pesticides*, Kurstak, E. (ed.), Marcel Dekker, New York, pp. 75–208.

[6.126] Fast, P. G.)1981) The crystal toxin of *Bacillus thuringiensis*. In *Microbial Control of Pests and Plant Diseases 1970–1980*, Burges, H. D. (ed.), Academic Press, London, pp. 223–248.

[6.127] Goldberg, L. J. and Margalit, (1977) A bacterial spore demonstrating rapid larvicidal activity against *Anopheles sergentii*, *Uranotaenia unquiculata*, *Culex univitattus*, *Aedes aegypti*, and *Culex pipens*. *Mosquito News*, **38**, 355–358.

[6.128] Dean, D. H. (1984) Biochemical genetics of the bacterial insect-control agent *Bacillus thuringiensis:* basic principles and prospects for genetic engineering. In *Biotechnology and Genetic Engineering reviews*, Vol. 2. Russell, G. E. (ed.), Intercept, Newcastle, pp. 341–364.

[6.129] Whiteley, H. R., Schnepf, H. E., Kronstad, J. W. and Wong, H. C. (1984) Structural and regulatory analysis of a cloned *Bacillus thuringiensis* crystal protein gene. In *Genetics and Biotechnology of Bacilli*, Ganesan, A. T. and Hoch, J. A., (eds), Academic Press, London, pp. 375–386.

[6.130] Carlton, B. C. and Gonzalez, J. M., Jr (1984) Plasmid-associated delta endotoxin production in *Bacillus thuringiensis*. In *Genetics and Biotechnology of Bacilli*, Ganesan, and Hoch, J. A. (eds), Academic Press, London, pp. 387–400.

[6.131] Dean, D. H. *et al.* (1982) In *Proc. 3rd Int. Coll. on Invertebrate Pathology*, 6–10 September 1982, Brighton, UK, pp. 11–12.

[6.132] Shivakumar, A. G., Gundling, G. J., Benson, T. A., Casuto, D., Miller, M. F. and Spear, B. B. (1986) Vegatative expression of the delta-endotoxin genes of *Bacillus thuringiensis* subsp. *kurstaki* in *Bacillus subtilis*. *J. Bact.*, **166**(1), 194–204.

[6.133] Anon. (1986) Tobacco plant's health warning to insects, *New Scientist*, 17 April, **110** (1504), 18.

[6.134] Klier, A. and Rapoport, G. (1984) Cloning and heterospecific expression of the crystal protein genes from *B. thuringiensis*. In *Bacterial Protein Toxins*, Alouf, J. E., Fehrenbach, F. J., Freer, J. H. and Jeljaszewicz, J. (eds), FEMS Symposium No. 24, Academic Press, London, pp. 65–72.

[6.135] Krieg, A., Huger, A. M., Langenbrook, G. A. and Schnetter, W. (1983) *Bacillus thuringiensis* var. *tenebrionis*: ein neuer gegenuber Larven von Coleopteren wirksamer Pathotyp. *Z. Ang. Ent.*, **96**, 500–508.

[6.136] Krieg, A., Huger, A. M., Langenbrook, G. A. and Schnetter, W. (1984) Neue Ergebniss über *Bacillus thuringiensis* var. *tenebrionis* unter besonderer Berücksichtigung seiner Wirkung auf den Kartof-felkafer (*Leptinotarsa decemlineata*). *Ang. Schadlingskede., Pflanzenshutz, Umweltschutz*, **57**, 145–150.

[6.137] Herrnstadt, C., Soares, G. C., Wilcox, E. R. and Edwards, D. L. (1986) A new strain of *Bacillus thuringiensis* with activity against Coleopteran insects. *Biotechnology*, **4**, 305–308.

[6.138] Ellar, D. J., Thomas, W. E. Knowles, B. H., Ward, S., Todd, J., Drobniewski, F., Lewis, J., Sawyer, T., Last, D. and Nichols, C. (1985) Biochemistry, genetics, and mode of action of *Bacillus thuringiensis* delta-endotoxins. In *Molecular Biology and Microbial Differentiation*, Hoch, J. A. and Setlow, P. (eds), *Proc. Int. Spore Conf*. No. 9, pp. 230–240.

[6.139] Himeno, M., Koyama, N., Funato, T. and Komano, T. (1985) Mechanism of action of *Bacillus thuringiensis* delta-endotoxin in insect cells *in-vitro*. *Agric. Biol. Chem.*, **49**(5), 141–146.

[6.140] Lindow, S. E. (1986) *In vitro* construction of biological control agents. In *Biotechnology and Crop Improvement and Protection*, Day, P., (ed.), BCPC Monograph No. 34, BCPC Publications, Thornton Heath, pp. 185–200.

[6.141] Lisansky, S. G. (1985) Microbial insecticides. In *Biotechnology and Its Application to Agriculture*, Copping, L. G. and Rodgers, P. (eds), BCPC Monograph No. 32, BCBP Publications, Thornton Heath, pp. 145–152.

[6.142] Lisansky, S. G. and Hall, R. A. (1983) Fungal insectides. In *Fungal Technology*, Vol. 4, *Filamentous Fungi*, Edward Arnold, London.

[6.143] Lisansky, S. G. (1985) Production and commercialisation of pathogens. In *Biological Pest Control for Profit (The Glasshouse Experience)*, Hussey, N. W. and Scope, N. (eds), Blandford Press, Poole, Dorset.

[6.144] Faull, J. L. (1986) Fungi and their role in crop protection. In *Biotechnology and Crop Improvement and Protection*, Day, P. (ed.), BCPC Monograph No. 34, BCPC Publications, Thornton Heath, pp. 161–172. pp. 141–150.

[6.145] McCoy, C. W. (1981) Pest control by the fungus *Hirsutella thompsonii*. In *Microbial Control of Pests and Plant Diseases 1970–1980*, Burges, H. D. (ed.), Academic Press, London, pp. 499–512.

[6.146] Entwhistle, P. F. and Evans, H. F. (1985) Viral control. In *Comprehensive Insect Physiology, Biochemistry and Pharmacology*, Vol. 12, *Insect Control*, Kerkut, G. A. and Gilbert, L. I. (eds), Pergamon Press, Oxford, pp. 347–412.

[6.147] Evans, H. (1986) Viruses. A realistic alternative in crop protection? In *Biotechnology and Crop Improvement and Protection*, Day, P. (ed.), BCPC Monograph No. 34, BCPC Pubblications, Thornton Heath, pp. 161–172.

7

Microbial control of environmental pollution: the use of genetic techniques to engineer organisms with novel catalytic capabilities

David J. Hardman
Biological Laboratory, University of Kent, Canterbury, Kent, UK

7.1 INTRODUCTION

The release of xenobiotic compounds into the natural environment, whether indirectly as a result of dumping waste materials or more directly by application of herbicides or pesticides, has resulted in widespread environmental contamination. The toxic nature of a number of these compounds originally passed unnoticed, chiefly because of the belief in the ability of the natural microbial community to metabolise all organic compounds. This belief was encapsulated in Gale's proposition of 'microbial infallibility' [7.1] which suggested that, because of the ubiquitous presence of microorganisms in the natural environment and the extensive catabolic potential of such organisms, any compound released into the biosphere would eventually be mineralised.

This sense of security began to falter with the appearance of undegraded pesticides, such as dichlorodiphenyltrichloroethane (DDT), in food-chains and the resultant biomagnification, or concentration, of the compounds in higher animals as predator capatured prey (Fig. 7.1). These observations led to investigations into the ability of natural microbial populations to detoxify xenobiotic compounds in the natural environment. Such studies, often using soil columns or microcosms [7.2–7.4], led to a realisation that a number of the compounds thought to be nonbiodegradable were susceptible to degradation as long as they were sufficiently similar in structure to the natural substrates of catabolic pathways already present in the microbial populations [7.5]. Findings such as these led to a reappraisal of selection and adaptation mechanisms existing in microorganisms.

The fate of a compound in the environment is determined by a number of

aquatic
environment 10^0

↓

phytoplankton

↓

zooplankton

↓

small fish 10^6

↓

large fish

↓

osprey 10^8

Fig. 7.1 — Biomagnification of dichlorodiphenyetrichloroethane (DDT) (numbers represent approximate concentration factors).

physical, chemical and biological factors. The type of soil, its mineral and organic content, moisture, oxygen content and temperature will all affect the rate of degradation as a result of nonbiological processes such as adsorption, oxidation, photolysis, hydrolysis and catalytic decomposition and by affecting the microbial communities present in the soil. For example, Kaufmann [7.6] found that the degradation of the herbicide Dalapon (the disodium salt of 2,2'-dichloropropionic acid) was mediated by bacteria in silty or sandy loams, but in loam and silty clays numerous fungi were involved. The chemical structure of the compound also determines the rate of degradation. Whilst one structure is biodegradable, further or different substitutions of the molecule can lead to greater recalcitrance (Fig. 7.2).

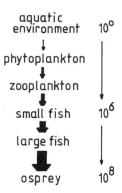

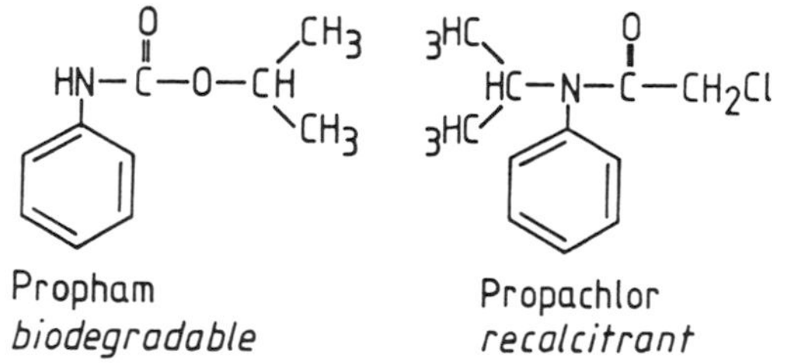

Propham
biodegradable

Propachlor
recalcitrant

Fig. 7.2 — The effect of substitution on biodegradability.

This occurs because the new structure can no longer be recognised by the natural catabolic systems present in the environment.

The biological fate of a novel compound entering the environment may be complete mineralisation, partial degradation, accumulation or polymerisation (Fig. 7.3). Compounds which are completely degraded — mineralised

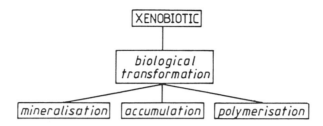

Fig. 7.3 — The biological fate of xenobiotic compounds in the environment.

to carbon dioxide, water, ammonia, sulphates and phosphates — are usually metabolised by complete metabolic pathways and, as such, can be utilised as sources of carbon and energy by the microbial community. Those degraded to a greater or lesser extent are usually transformed as a result of co-metabolism [7.7; 7.8]. That is, the compound cannot act as a growth substrate but, whilst utilising other substrates, the organism(s) may catalyse the transformation, a consequence of which is that such compounds are only transformed slowly. An example of this is seen in Fig. 7.4 where *Pseudomonas*

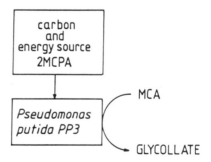

Fig. 7.4 — Cometabolism of monochloroacetate (MCA) by *Pseudomonas putida* PP3, whilst utilising 2-monochloropropionate (2MCPA) as a carbon and energy source.

putida cannot utilise monochloroacetate (MCA) as a carbon source but, whilst utilising 2-monochloropropionate (2MCPA), the organism can catalyse the dehalogenation of MCA [7.9]. The inability to use MCA as a carbon source arises because the dehalogenase system of *P. putida* PP3 is not induced by MCA. A third group of compounds is those which are totally recalcitrant with no known organisms being capable of any transformations. These compounds include synthetic plastics and some aromatic hydrocarbons.

Almost all environments possess a very diverse population of microorganisms. Even in very extreme environments, of high temperature or low pH, a few monocultures exist. It is the heterogenous nature of these natural populations which result in the degradation of so many xenobiotic compounds.

A single organism may possess the catabolic ability to catalyse the transformation of one compound to a second compound but then not possess the enzymic systems for further degradation. These may be supplied by a second organism and so on, such that communities of organisms possessing complementary catalytic capabilities become established and the compound is degraded (Fig. 7.5).

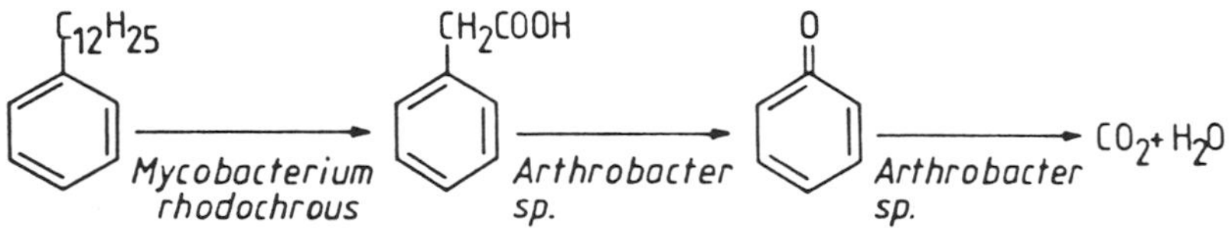

Fig. 7.5 — Synergistic degradation of dodecylcyclohexane (after Bull and Slater [7.10]).

The synergistic degradation of a xenobiotic compound can also prevent the build-up of toxic intermediates, as in a number of instances partial degradation leads to the production of a compound more toxic to the natural community than the original substrate. It is not within the scope of this chapter to discuss in detail the role of microbial consortia in the biodegradation of xenobiotic compounds, but it is important to realise the involvement of such heterogenous biocatalysts in the degradation of these compounds when considering the engineering of strains to perform degradative tasks. Further information on the role of microbial communities is provided in a review by Bull and Slater [7.10].

By the utilisation of the natural detoxification pathways present in microbial communities, the pollution control industry has harnessed, or is planning to harness, microbes for waste management, particularly for the control of organic pollutants and especially haloorganic compounds. The rest of this chapter will examine the various ways by which microorganisms, or communities of organisms, can be manipulated to catalyse the required reactions and the potential of recombinant DNA techniques for expanding the use of these biocatalysts.

7.2   THE EVOLUTION OF NATURAL DETOXIFICATON SYSTEMS

The vast potential of natural communities to degrade novel compounds was recognised from the beginning of the studies on biodegradation. Even from these studies, it was observed that a challenge with a new substrate resulted in a time lapse before the onset of degradation, whilst on subsequent additions, the substrate was degraded with a much reduced induction period

[7.11; 7.12]. During the initial time lapse before degradation is observed a population of microorganisms adapts, or is selected, so as to be able to degrade the compound. The degradation leads to a proliferation of the population which may then be seen to persist for at least 2–3 months, after the substrate has been exhausted [7.13]. Thus, on subsequent additions of the compound the microorganisms capable of degrading it are already present, hence the onset of degradation is much faster.

The utilisation of haloalkanoic acids as sources of carbon and energy necessitates the cleavage of the carbon–halogen bond. Microorganisms capable of utilising chloro-, bromo- and fluorosubstituted alkanoic acids are readily isolated from the soil environment [7.14–7.18].

If, however, a sample of soil is suspended in a buffered solution, serially diluted and placed directly onto solid media containing one of the halosubstrates, the resulting microbial growth is very poor. On the other hand, if the soil sample is first placed in a salts-medium containing the substrate and incubated for 4–7 days, then samples are taken and plated, the ensuing microbial growth is substantially enhanced. These isolates are able to utilise the substrate as the sole source of carbon and energy [7.14]. From such observations it would appear that, in order to isolate organisms capable of effective growth on these substrates, a period of enrichment, or selection, is required. Once the carbon–halogen bond is cleaved, the products are readily metabolised by the central metabolic pathways of the microorganisms. The period of enrichment may thus be required to select for organisms capable of the carbon–halogen bond cleavage. The catalytic ability is conferred by the possession of one or more of a family of inducible enzymes collectively known as dehalogenases [7.15]. These enzymes catalyse the hydrolytic cleavage of the carbon–halogen bond, yielding hydroxyalkanoic acids from monosubstituted compounds and oxoalkanoic acids from disubstituted ones.

The dehalogenation system represents the rate-limiting step in the utilisation of the substrate [7.19]. Therefore, the selection process presumably involves increasing the rate of dehalogenation by increasing the levels of the dehalogenase proteins. This could be achieved in one of three ways: (i) selection of constitutive mutants; (ii) selection for gene duplication; or (iii) selection of strains with more than one dehalogenase, obtained through the activity of a gene-transfer mechanism. Few of the strains isolated have demonstrated constitutive dehalogenase production. Weightman and Slater [7.20] isolated a mutant strain of *Pseudomonas putida* PP3 which possessed elevated levels of dehalogenase activity, and they suggested that this was due to a gene duplication event. However, in a number of enrichment studies, the resultant isolates possess more than one active dehalogenase form ([7.14]; Tsang, Bull and Hardman, unpublished data). During the enrichment phase, organisms with elevated substrate-capturing enzymes would be at a selective advantage. The aggregation of dehalogenase structural genes into a single organism would ensure enhanced specific activities for dehalogenase and so provide selective advantage.

The addition of a novel substrate to the natural environment, by whatever route, may well trigger the same sort of selective response. As such, this represents *in vivo* genetic engineering. In response to the presence of a new substrate, organisms not originally capable of efficient use of the compound are 'engineered' by the transfer of genetic information, so leading to the aggregation of the necessary catabolic functions and enabling utilisation of the novel compound. This genetic flux would involve random exchange of genetic material. However, once the advantageous permutation had been obtained, the 'new' organism would be at a selective advantage. These mechanisms presuppose that the laboratory observations of exchange of genetic material between organisms, even across species and genus barriers, also occurs in the natural environment. Some studies have shown that this does occur, even if at a much reduced frequency [7.21].

7.3   CATABOLIC PLASMIDS

7.3.1   Physical and genetical overview
Since the publication of evidence for the transmissibility of drug resistance among the Enterobacteria the important of extrachromosomal genetic elements, or plasmids [7.22], in the transfer of genetic information from one organism to another has become apparent.

The term catabolic plasmid (degradative or metabolic plasmid) refers to those replicons which encode one reaction, or a multistep reaction sequence, leading to the transformation or mineralisation of a substrate. The presence of catabolic plasmids in a bacterial community enables the organisms to share a pool of degradative genes. In this way, the plasmids increase the biochemical versatility of the population. The deposition of catabolic genes on self-transferring replicons facilitates the spread of esoteric phenotypes from an initial minority of the population to the majority when such phenotypes confer a selective advantage. In this way, the population can maintain the potential to utilise substrates only encountered intermittently whilst not causing a metabolic drain on the whole population in the absence of the novel substrate. Recently, such mechanisms have been observed with a catabolic plasmid encoding the dehalogenase genes of a *Pseudomonas* species [7.23]. When this organism was cultured in a chemostat, utilising 2MCPA as a sole source of carbon and energy, the whole population was capable of growth on succinate and 2MCPA and 100% of those cells tested contained the catabolic plasmid (Fig. 7.6). However, when the carbon source was changed to succinate, the component of the population capable of utilising 2MCPA fell to below detectable levels and, although it fluctuated with time, the plasmid could not be detected. Once 2MCPA was restored as the carbon source, the 2MCPA utilisers again represented 100% of the population and a catabolic plasmid could be detected. In the absence of the halosubstrate the members of the population possessing the plasmid rapidly declined, but whilst the decline was to below detectable levels, the catabolic potential was not lost completely as, on addition of the halosubstrate, the catabolic ability was still available to the population as a whole.

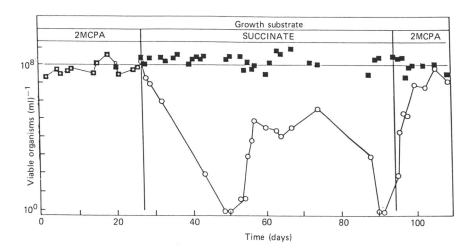

Fig. 7.6 — The role of plasmids in the maintenance of catabolic potential under non-selective conditions: ■=growth on succinate; ○=growth on 2-monochloropropionate (2MCPA) (after Hardman *et al.* [7.23]); see text for details.

The information carried on catabolic plasmids may extend the substrate range of a host by encoding a complete pathway, so providing a novel route by which the host may utilise the substrate or may complement chromosomally encoded pathways leading to extension of existing pathways or the linkage of two metabolic routes. Complementation in this fashion is of particular importance if existing mechanisms lead only to the partial degradation of the compound, resulting in accumulation of potentially toxic metabolites. These plasmids may also provide enzymes which catalyse reactions already present in the chromosomally encoded systems but which possess different substrate specificities. Plasmids with molecular weights ranging from 1.5 to greater than 900 kilobases (kb) have been isolated from natural bacteria. Those used to construct cloning vectors are usually small (2–10 kb) whilst catabolic plasmids form part of the larger end of the spectrum. As such, these molecules are hard to handle, and, although techniques have been developed for their study [7.24], with the exception of a few, little is known about their structural organisation.

Although catabolic plasmids have been isolated from a wide variety of bacteria, they have been most frequently identified in the Pseudomonads (Table 7.1). The wide variety of catabolic plasmids found in this genus provides one explanation for the extensive catabolic capabilities these organisms possess. The physical size of these plasmids enables them to encode a large number of genes. A plasmid with a molecular weight of 150 kb contains sufficient DNA to encode approximately 150 genes. This means that, even in the instances where a number of phenotypic markers have been associated with a given plasmid, such as multiple drug resistances [7.25] or the 12 catabolic enzymes which catalyse the cleavage of toluene and meta-

Table 7.1 — Natural catabolic plasmids

Name	Substrate	Host
pJP1 and others	2,4-D and halopesticides	*Alcaligenes paradoxus*
pUU220	Haloalkanoates	*Alicaligenes* sp.
—	Nicotine	*Arthrobacter oxidans*
—	Lactose	*Escherichia coli*
RAF	Raffinose	*Escherichia coli*
SCR	Sucrose	*Escherichia coli*
—	Lactose	*Klebsiella pneumoniae*
CAM	D-Camphor	*Pseudomonas putida*
SAL and others	Salicylate	*Pseudomonas* sp.
NAH and others	Naphthalene	*P. putida*
OCT	Octane	*P. oleovorans*
XYL	Xylene	*P. arvilla*
TOL and others	Toluene, *m*-xylene, *p*-xylene	*P. putida*
NIC	Nicotine,	*P. convexa*
	3,5,Xylenol	*P. putida*
pAC25	3-Chlorobenzoate	*P. putida*
	p-Cresol	*P. putida*
pWW17	Phenylacetate	*Pseudomonas* sp.
pUU204 and others	Haloalkanoates	*Pseudomonas* sp.
—	Urea	*Providencia stuartii*
—	Lactose	*Salmonella typhimurium*
LAC	Lactose	*Yersinia enterocolitica*

and para-xylenes, encoded by the TOL plasmid [7.4], large regions of the plasmid encode no recognisable phenotypes. Our knowledge, therefore, even about the relatively well studied archetypal TOL plasmid (pWWO; [7.26; 7.27]), is limited to the regions of catabolic function, plasmid replication and transfer.

Macroevolutionary events [7.28] lead to insertion, deletion or rearrangement of DNA sequences in replicons. Such recombinational events alter the structural integrity of the plasmid and as such may affect the expression of genes carried on the plasmid by repositioning structural genes downstream of promoter sequences [7.29] or removing insertionally inactivating sequences. Recombination between two phenotypically defined plasmids can lead to the coexistence of the two as an aggregate or cointegrate [7.30] in a single organism. This may overcome the natural exclusion mechanisms, or incompatibility mechanisms, which usually prevent replicons belonging to the same incompability group coexisting in a single host. In this way recombinational events enhance the metabolic potential of the host.

The TOL plasmids provide further insight into the nature of the effects of recombinational events on natural vectors. Closely related replicons may undergo homologous recombination, the frequency of which is directly related to the degree of structural homology between the plasmids. The importance of homologous recombination in the evolution of catabolic plasmids is demonstrated by the alkane degradation plasmids, in that the TOL, XYL, SAL and NAH plasmids show high degrees of homology [7.31; 7.32].

Inter- and intra-plasmidic recombination may lead to the shuffling of genes on catabolic plasmids, resulting in new combinations of genes, so extending the catabolic pathways encoded on the plasmids. However, this does not provide a mechanism by which entirely new catabolic genes can be acquired. One way this is achieved is through recombination between the plasmid and the host chromosome. The movement of plasmid DNA into and out of the chromosome has been demonstrated, indeed the TOL plasmid has been found in an integrated form [7.33].

A strain of *Pseudomonas syringae* pv. *phaseolicola* possesses a 150 kb plasmid which can replicate autonomously or can integrate into the bacterial chromosome. Subsequent excision events are, however, imprecise, leading to the production of a family of plasmids ranging in size from 35 kb to 270 kb, some of which contain large segments of chromosomal DNA [7.34].

Imprecise excision of integrated forms may explain the acquisition of novel sequences. The mobilisation of chromosomal segments by the plasmid R68–45 [7.35] can result in sequences as large as 150 kb becoming part of 'new' plasmids [7.36]. Recombinational events may explain the structural and genetic diversity of plasmids; the process enables the translocation and fusion of separately evolved sequences of DNA (Fig. 7.7). Evolution of

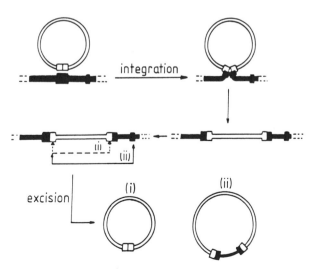

Fig. 7.7 — Recombination: modular evolution of catabolic plasmids: (i) precise excision; (ii) imprecise excision leading to exchange of genetic material from one replicon to the other.

plasmids by the exchange of discrete sequences has been termed 'modular evolution' [7.31]. These modular mechanisms enable the fusion of sequences of DNA encoding whole sections of catabolic pathways from discrete replicons, creating new catabolic potential and new catabolic plasmids.

There is, however, one other mechanism by which new catabolic potential can be gained, that is by the incorporation of transposable elements. Transposons range in size from 750 to 50 000 base pairs and are structurally defined by repeated DNA sequences at the termini. Any piece of DNA flanked by identical insertion sequences could act as a transposon, thus virtually any gene on the chromosome could exist as a transposon [7.38]. Transposon insertion may represent a mechanism for genetic acquisition but may also lead to changes in phenotypic expression by influencing the regulation of existing structural genes. This may result from insertional mutation of structural or regulatory function of an associated DNA sequence, or as a consequence of a promoter or termination sequence encoded by the transposon.

The structural diversity of the TOL plasmids, ranging in size from 115 kb to 270 kb, all of which encode the same catabolic potential, is explained by the observation that the sequence encoding the degradative pathway can be transposed from one replicon to another. However, there is not a single transposition unit. Several studies on independently isolated Resistance plasmids — *tol* hybrids — revealed a wide variation in the amount of TOL DNA present in the hybrid plasmids. There are two molecular components to the *tol* region [7.39]: a 56 kb segment, encoding the *tol* genes, which behaves in a manner similar to a transposable element [7.40; 7.41]; and a 39 kb segment within that sequence, defined by 1.4 kb direct repeat sequences at the termini which is capable of precise excision [7.42].

The transposable region on the TOL plasmids encodes a complete catabolic pathway. Clustering of chromosomal genes specifying consecutive steps in a catabolic pathway has been described for regions of the *Pseudomonas putida* chromosome [7.43]. Such clustering, into pseudo-operons, whilst enabling coordinated gene expression, also increases the chance of the cotransfer of functionally related genes. If the gene cluster were situated between two insertion sequences then transpositional events could enable exchange of a complete functional unit from the original replicon to another. Cotransfer of such genes is important as many catabolic pathways will only function in their entirety.

7.3.2 Catabolic plasmids as natural vectors

The flux of genetic material to and from plasmid genomes is well documented. The modular nature of plasmid evolution can explain the diverse nature of the catabolic phenotypes associated with this group of plasmids. It does, however, indicate that these plasmids may only be transient structures and that only when the environmental conditions suppress the genetic flux do 'stable' forms exist. When a catabolic function is associated with a particular plasmid, further structural change in the plasmid is suppressed by providing a selective pressure to inhibit further modificaton, in this instance by the continual supply of a novel substrate.

The plasticity of catabolic plasmids provides the mechanism by which exchange of genetic material can lead to the 'creation' of an organism capable of efficient utilisation of a novel substrate during an enrichment phase such as that described for the haloalkanoic acid-utilising organisms. In that study, six isolates, capable of growth on chloro-acetic and propionic acids, were seen to possess one of a series of plasmids ranging in size from 150 kb to 290 kb. Loss of the plasmid from three of these strains was associated with loss of dehalogenation capability and so ability to grow on the substrate [7.23]. On this bassis there are two possibilities which might arise from the flux of genetic material between two organisms in the original enrichment culture. On the one hand, it could lead to the accumulation of the dehalogenase structural genes onto a common ancestral plasmid, which then underwent further structural reorganisation during movement between strains. Alternatively, it could also lead to the genes becoming associated with five different plasmids. In other studies of the dehalogenase systems it has been proposed that the dehalogenase structural genes are encoded on transposons [7.44; 7.45].

Isolation and enrichment studies, using inocula from the natural environment, result in the isolation of organisms capable of degrading a large number of xenobiotic compounds. Genetic mechanisms have been described which enable the reassortment of coordinately functioning genes and so provide a means for the production of new combinations of catabolic functions enabling degradation of complex xenobiotic molecules.

Conventional recombinant DNA techniques permit the transfer of genetic information from one organism to another. However, the cloned foreign DNA only encodes a small number of genes, often only a single structural gene encoding one protein catalysing a specific reaction. When considering genetic techniques for the production of microbial strains, capable of environmental detoxificaton, the conventional recombinant techniques are of limited value. To date the genetic manipulation of microorganisms for this purpose has largely involved the harnessing of the natural genetic exchange mechanisms to engineer the required organisms. It will be seen, however, that recombinant DNA technology can be used to refine these degradative capabilities. Most of the work in this field has been directed towards the production of microbial strains capable of degrading halogenated compounds.

7.4 HALOXENOBIOTICS AND GENETIC ENGINEERING

Haloorganic compounds are one of the largest groups of environmental pollutants. They are highly toxic, often bioconcentrated and recalcitrant. Large amounts of these compounds are used as fire retardants, paints and varnishes, refrigerants, solvents, herbicides and pesticides. In true pollutant fashion these compounds find their way into the environment, directly or indirectly, where their toxicity has led to the United States Environmental

Protection Agency listing 70 such compounds among a total of 129 'priority pollutants' [7.46]. The persistence and toxicity of these compounds is caused by the carbon–halogen bond which is not easily cleaved. The presence of a halosubstitutent or an additional substituent converts a biodegradable compound into a recalcitrant one (Fig. 7.8).

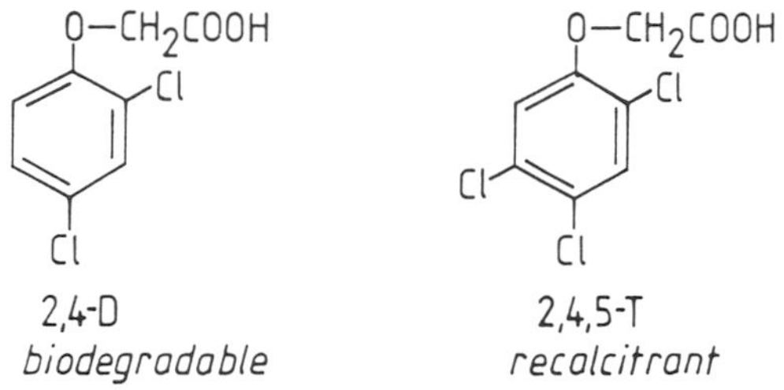

Fig. 7.8 — The effect of halogen substitution of biodegradability.

Studies have shown that naturally occurring microoganisms can metabolise haloaromatic and haloaliphatic compounds, and there is little doubt that this is an important factor determining the fate of halo-compounds in the environment. Naturally occurring halogenated compounds have been identified [7.47] produced as fungal metabolites, fungal and bacterial bactericidal compounds, marine algal and sponge metabolites and mammalian compounds (thyroxin and a bromo-substituted compound found in the cerebrospinal fluid of man). The presence of such compounds in the natural environment, as agents produced to inhibit growth of competing species, provides one reason for the ability that microorganisms have to transform them. A mechanism of natural detoxification is seen, for example, in bacterial resistance to chloramphenicol. In this specific instance the detoxification mechanism is one of acylation but in other instances dehalogenation would also provide the desired detoxificaton. Man's contribution to the pool of halogenated compounds is thus seen against a background of natural compounds and degradative mechanisms.

As already described, a prerequisite for the degradation of a xenobiotic compound in the natural environment is the presence of a structurally related natural compound already present in that environment. These natural mechanisms may initially be inefficient at catalysing the transformation of the xenobiotic because of kinetic limitations caused by the substrate specificity of the biocatalyst. This may eventually be overcome by hyperproduction of the catalyst(s), by inactivation or changes in regulatory control, gene duplication leading to a dosage effect, or by mutational divergence creating an enzyme with altered substrate specificities. Futher adaptation may result from the adaptive plasticity of the microorganisms through genetic rearrangement or gene recruitment.

One major problem for a geneticist wishing to construct a 'super-bug'

capable of degrading one or more xenobiotic compounds is the lack of
knowledge about the degradative pathways involved in the transformations.
After three decades of work in this area and a plethora of papers, few
catabolic pathways have been determined. The two most understood
pathways are those involved in the degradation of the chlorobenzoates and
chlorophenoxyacetates.

The catabolic machinery for the degradation of aromatic compounds
requires modification in order that haloaromatic compounds may be
degraded. The substrate specificities of the chromosomally encoded
β-ketoadipate (*ortho-*) pathway enzymes result in an inability to degrade
chlorocatechol, the metabolic intermediate resulting from the first two steps
in the degradation of chlorobenzoates or chlorophenoxyacetates (Fig. 7.9).

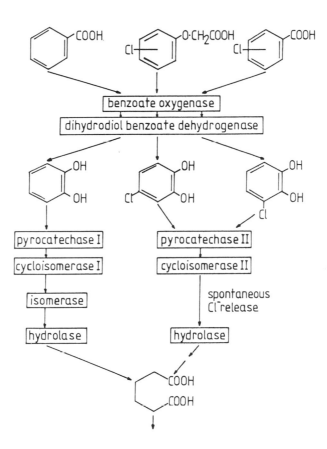

Fig. 7.9 — A comparison of the enzymes involved in the *ortho-* and modified *ortho-*
pathways for the degradation of benzoate, chlorobenzoate and chlorophenoxyacetate.

The first two transformations are catalysed by the same enzymes involved in
the degradation of the unsubstituted benzoate to catechol, namely benzoate
oxygenase and the dihydrodiol benzoate dehydrogenase. However, the

chromosomally encoded pyrocatechase I which promotes the ring cleavage of catechol cannot act on the chloro-derivative.

The ring cleavage of chlorocatechol is mediated by a modified *ortho*-pathway oxidizing chlorocatechol to chloro-*cis, cis*-muconic acid involving pyrocatechase II. This enzyme acts specifically on the chlorocatechol rather than the non-substituted parent molecule. The dehalogenation appears to be a spontaneous reaction during the activity of the second modified enzyme cycloisomerase II which is active towards both the halosubstituted and parental molecules. After the activity of hydrolase II, an enzyme very different from the β-ketoadipate enzyme, the normal and modified pathways converge and result in the enventual formation of succinate which is mineralised by the central metabolism of the organism. This modified pathway, identified in *Pseudomonas* sp. B13 [7.48; 7.49], illustrates the importance of broad-specificity enzymes when considering the degradation of halogenated hydrocarbons. *Pseudomonas* sp. B13 possesses isofunctional enzymes which complement the activity of the highly specific enzymes in the β-ketoadipate pathway. The critical steps in this catabolic pathway are the ring-cleavage pyrocatechases I and II, the cycloisomerases I and II and the hydrolases I and II. Whilst it is not clear whether all the genes involved in the modified *ortho*-pathway are plasmid encoded, it is known that the novel isofunctional enzymes are encoded on the plasmid pWR1 in *Pseudomonas* sp. B13 [7.50] or pAC25 in a 3-chlorobenzoate (3cba) utilising strain of *Pseudomonas putida* [7.51]. Thus, the novel catabolic potential resulted from the acquisition of degradative plasmids encoding isofunctional enzymes overcoming the substrate limitations imposed by the chromosomally encoded enzymes.

The idea of constructing catabolic pathways was introduced by Reineke and Knackmuss [7.50] when they 'constructed' a pseudomonad capable of degrading 4-chlorobenzoate (4cba). By the process of conjugation, which involves donor-recipient direct cell contact, it is possible to mediate transfer of a plasmid from the donor cell to the recipient. Cells resulting from such matings are known as transconjugants. Reineke and Knackmuss produced a transconjugant from a mating experiment between *Pseudomonas putida* PaW1 (possessing the TOL plasmid pWWO) and *Pseudomonas* sp. B13 (pWR1), the 3cba-utilising organism. The new strain was capable of utilising 4cba because of the transfer of the toluate 1,2-dioxygenase gene encoded by pWWO to *Pseudomonas* sp. B13. The native 1,2-dioxygenase encoded by the B13 chromosome could not catalyse the conversion of 4cba to 4-chlorodihydro-1,2-dihydroxygenzoate but the pWWO enzyme could (Fig. 7.10).

A similar result was seen when a culture of *Pseudomonas putida* or *P. aeruginosa* harbouring pAC25 was cocultured with a strain harbouring the TOL plasmid in a chemostat [7.51]. Under normal circumstances the TOL and pAC 25 plasmids cannot coexist in the same host because when supplied with the halosubstrate their combined pathways lead to the production of toxic chlorinated metabolites. The derivation of a 4cba-utilising strain resulted from deletion events occurring in both plasmids

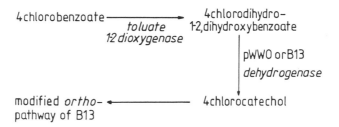

Fig. 7.10 — The role of pWW0 encoded enzymes in the degradation of 4-chlorobenzoate.

which prevented the lethal synthetic combination. The deletion events appear to have occurred as a result of homologous recombination between the two parental plasmids as both demonstrate a high degree of structural homology.

The first plasmid to be associated with the catabolism of a halogenated organic compound was reported by Pemberton and Fisher [7.52] and Fisher *et al.* [7.53] and presented evidence for the plasmid-mediated degradation of 2,4-dichlorophenoxyacetic acid (2,4-D) in *Acaligenes paradoxus*. Subsequent studies have resulted in the isolation of other plasmids encoding degradative mechanisms for 2,4-D which can be placed into two classes on the basis of incompatibility, associated resistance to mercury, molecular weight and host range [7.54].

Although the degradation of 2,4-D had been observed, reports on the biodegradation of the trichloro-derivative (2,4,5-T) were sparse. It was the construction of a bacterial strain capable of degrading this compound which represented the first organism to be engineered to degrade a specific compound.

Kellogg and his coworkers used a process which they termed 'plasmid-assisted molecular breeding' [7.55]. Samples from a number of waste-dumps were mixed with a variety of bacterial strains derived from other investigations which contained a number of catabolic plasmids. The culture was maintained in a chemostat and supplied with increasing concentrations of 2,4,5-T over a period of 8–10 months. At the end of this period, organisms were isolated which were capable of degrading 2,4,5-T. The authors suggested that the presence of the various catabolic plasmids promoted, by as yet unspecified interactions, the formation of the strain, hence 'plasmid-assisted molecular breeding'. It should, however, be noted that the procedures adopted do not rule out the possibility of a more direct selective enrichment — one or more waste-dump microorganisms. One of the organisms isolated by this procedure was *Pseudomonas cepacia* strain AC1100. This organism could utilise 2,4,5-T or 2,4,5-trichlorophenol as its sole source of carbon and energy [7.56]. This strain harboured two plasmids but, whilst there was circumstantial evidence for their involvement in the degradative capability of the host organism [7.57], the precise role of the plasmids in 2,4,5-T degradation has not been determined.

7.5   RECOMBINANT DNA TECHNIQUES

The *in vivo* genetic selection described so far can provide an organism capable of degrading a specific compound. However, such techniques require long periods of selection (8–10 months as described in the example above) and rely on random assortment of the genetic material to produce the desired catabolic system. The use of recombinant DNA techniques enables the experimenter to piece together a defined catabolic sequence and introduces the possibility of controlling the expression of specific genes. With the *in vivo* techniques, the levels of expression are determined by the regulatory mechanisms encoded by the plasmid sequences and little can be done to influence the levels of individual enzymes. However, by cloning specific genes downstream of promotor sequences, on expression vectors, elevated levels of the gene product can be obtained.

However, the application of cloning techniques to the manipulation of such genes should not be seen as a panacea, providing the wherewithal to produce microbial systems to solve all the problems of pollution control. There are a number of limitations to the use of cloning strategies to produce the 'super-bug':

(a)   the multistep nature of degradative pathways;
(b)   the novel nature of the degradative organisms;
(c)   the limited knowledge of individual catabolic pathways;
(d)   considerations about the release of engineered organisms into the environment.

The first of these has already to be alluded to: the complex structure of xenobiotic compounds necessitates multistep pathways to enable complete mineralisation. Cloning one or two genes into an organism will only enable it to degrade the compound if the new gene products complement existing catabolic systems. To this extent cloning will broaden the organism's metabolic capabilities. Application of these techniques will thus only allow a more defined engineering of the organism.

An example of this was provided by Lehrbach *et al.* [7.58]. These workers used an alternative approach to produce a 4cba-utilising strain of *Pseudomonas* sp. B13. In the previous experiment, the introduction of the TOL plasmid into this organism resulted in a mutation in the TOL plasmid which prevented the formation of toxic halometabolites normally produced as a result of the TOL-specified *meta*-pathway for the degradation of 3-chlorocatechol. Lehrbach and coworkers cloned a single gene (*xyl*D) from the TOL plasmid into *Pseudomonas* sp. B13 which alone enabled growth on 4cba. This work was extended [7.58] to include the cloning of a gene (*nah*G) from the napthalene degradation plasmid NAH7 [7.59], which enabled the host to convert salicylate and chlorosalicylate to catechol or chlorocatechol, so enabling the organism to utilise new substrates.

These manipulations are directed towards creating organisms capable of degrading only one or two specific compounds. The recent observation that ligninase systems are capable of catalysing the degradation of halogenated substrates may point the way to the use of very broad-specificity enzyme systems in cloning strategies and indeed extend the systems suggested by Weightman *et al.* [7.60]. These involved linkage of broad-specificity enzymes, which catalyse the first steps in the degradation of aromatic compounds and are also capable of catalysing the transformation of the halogenated analogues, with the modified *ortho*-ring cleavage pathway of, for example, *Pseudomonas* sp. B13. As such, this would produce an organism capable of degrading a whole range of mono- and dihalogenated aromatic compounds (Fig. 7.11). It should be noted that to date even this

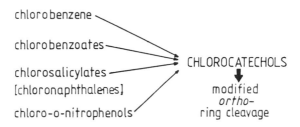

Fig. 7.11 — A generalised catabolic pathway for the degradation of haloaromatic compounds.

strategy has only been used to produce organisms capable of growth on one or two substrates. Often this ability has also depended on ill-defined mutational events subsequent to the *in vitro* manipulations, thus our understanding of the genetic mechanisms involved is not yet sufficient to enable direct production of the desirable genetic configurations. This may be a reflection of our lack of knowledge about the genetics of those organisms important in biological treatment. Whilst cloning strategies are well worked for *Escherichia coli* and a few *Bacillus* and *Streptomyces* species, the cloning procedures for the pseudomonads have to date largely consisted of manipulation of catabolic plasmids or parts thereof.

The lack of knowledge about the metabolic pathways also limits the extent to which recombinant DNA techniques may be used to enhance progress in this field. Without this understanding, it is not possible to identify the genes which would most beneficially be cloned, usually those which limit substrate range or the rate of substrate utilisation. The advantages of this are graphically seen in the case of the two systems described, where the critical steps limiting the substrate range of the pathway were seen to be encoded by three enzymes of the β-ketoadipate pathway.

When considering the use of recombinant DNA techniques it is a prerequisite that vector systems exist for the proposed host. For a number of the organisms involved in pollution control well-defined vectors do not exist. One possible way around this problem is by the use of broad-host range vectors, for example the vector R300B [7.61]. The host range of this plasmid

includes *Escherichia coli, Pseudomonas aeruginosa, Methylophilus methy-
lotrophus* and species of the *Acinetobacter, Alcaligenes, Klebsiella, Pro-
teus, Providencia, Rhizobium, Rhodopseudomonas, Salmonella* and *Serra-
tia* genera. The use of such vectors is, however, in its infancy and one major
problem of these systems is one of stability.

The stability of the host-vector is of importance if the organism is to be
released into the environment. The use of engineered organisms in dealing
with environmental pollution outside the laboratory has yet to be tested.
The proposals for manipulating natural isolates, then returning them to the
environment to deal with specific pollution problems, is appealing, but is it
feasible? The simple act of removing an organism from the environment and
culturing it in the laboratory, often under relatively nutrient-rich conditions,
will result in a selection of mutations which fit the organism to the new
environment. Replacing this organism into the original environment, having
supplied it with a novel catabolic function which enables it to utilise a
substrate not available to the rest of the microbial community, does in
theory give the organism a competitive advantage. However, the environment will contain other sources of assimilable carbon; toxic waste dumps
usually contain many chemicals, including ones more readily assimilable.
Under such conditions the construct would need to be very stable to ensure
better utilisation of the target compound. Little or nothing is known about
the stability of recombinant strains in the natural environment. In addition,
the original natural population, well adapted to the environment, is likely to
out-compete the genetically improved strain.

The use of recombinant DNA techniques to produce biological pollution
control agents may be at an early stage, but one technique which may prove
useful in the foreseeable future is that of the genetic probe. The selection of
organisms capable of transforming a novel compound often relies on the
utilisation of the compound as a growth substrate. If the growth is only poor
or the substrate is only co-metabolised then these isolation techniques will
not result in the identification of these degradative capabilities. It would thus
be of use to develop genetic probes to detect specific gene sequences in
plasmids and chromosomes which could be used to identify catabolic
potential even if the potential is not being expressed. Such probes have been
developed for the TOL plasmids. Sayler *et al.* [7.62] used DNA–DNA
hydridization techniques to detect catabolic genotypes in environment
samples. The method could detect one bacterial colony harbouring the TOL
plasmid among 10^6 colonies of *Escherichia coli*. Such a powerful tool would
be of great value in the isolation of cryptic catabolic functions [7.63].

7.6 CONCLUSIONS

The release into the environment of xenobiotic compounds which do not
readily enter the elemental cycles for carbon, nitrogen, sulphur or phosphorus, has resulted in pollution of the biosphere. These chemicals exhibit
transitory or permanent accumulation and lead to adverse effects on the
natural flora and fauna.

Pollution management can be considered at two levels: firstly prevention, where potentially toxic compounds are contained and degraded before they enter the environment, or secondly at the level of removal once the chemical has entered the environment. In view of the complex physicochemical and biological interactions in the biosphere, it is likely that in the short term the utilisation of engineered organisms will be most profitably put to use in the former situation.

Whilst there is still a large gap between the advances in the use of directly engineered organisms as laboratory detoxification sytems and that of an applied technology, the advances do indicate that such organisms could be utilised on site to remove potential pollutants from waste-streams, whilst the chemicals are contained under defined conditions.

Industrial wastes and waste waters are rarely simple solutions containing a single compound. In view of the restricted way in which we can manipulate single organisms, it seems likely that the most efficient biological detoxification systems will consist of microbial consortia derived from *in vivo* and *in vitro* manipulations of individuals or communities of organisms.

Our present understanding of the physiological, biochemical and genetical interactions between community components, makes the establishment of such consortia a qualitative procedure based solely on the ability of the consortia to effectively detoxify the growth environment. To unlock the full potential of the biotechnological control of pollution a greater understanding of the kinetics of individual systems is required.

REFERENCES

[7.1] Alexander, M. (1965) Persistence and biological reactions of pesticides in soils. *Soil Sci. Soc. Am. Proc.,* **29,** 1–7.

[7.2] Hale, M. G., Hulcher, F. H. and Chappel, W. E. (1957) The effects of several herbicides on nitrification in a field soil under laboratory conditions. *Weeds,* **5,** 331–341.

[7.3] Holstun, J. T. and Loomis, W. E. (1956) Leaching and decomposition of 2,2'-dichloropropionic acid in several Iowa soils. *Weeds,* **4,** 205–217.

[7.4] Broda, P., Downing, R., Lehrbach, P., McGregor, I. and Meulien, P. (1981) Degradative plasmids: TOL and beyond. In *Molecular Biology, Pathogenicity and Ecology of Bacterial Plasmids,* Levy, S. B., Clowes, R. C. and Koenig, E. L. (eds), Plenum Press, New York, p. 511.

[7.5] Hill, I. R. (1978) Microbial transformations of pesticides. In *Pesticide Microbiology. Microbiological Aspects of Pesticide Behaviour in the Environment,* Hill, I. R. and Wright, S. J. L. (eds), Academic Press, London, p. 137.

[7.6] Kaufman, D. D. (1964) Microbial degradation of 2,2'-dichloropropionate in 5 soils. *Can. J. Microbiol.,* **10,** 843–852.

[7.7] Horvath, R. S. (1972) Microbial co-metabolism and the degradation of organic compounds in nature. *Bact. Rev.,* **36,** 146–155.

[7.8] Jensen, H. L. (1963) Carbon nutrition of some microorganisms decomposing halogen-substituted aliphatic acids. *Acta. Agric. Scand.*, **13**, 404–412.

[7.9] Slater, J. H. (1981) Mixed cultures and microbial communities. In *Continuous Culture Fermentation*, Bushell, M. E. and Slater, J. H. (eds), Academic Press, London, p. 1.

[7.10] Bull, A. T. and Slater, J. H. (1982) Environmental microbiology: biodegradation. *Phil. Trans. R. Soc. Lond. B*, **297**, 575–597.

[7.11] Audus, L. J. (1960) Microbiological breakdown of herbicides in soils. In *Herbicides and the Soil*, Woodford, E. K. and Sagar, G. R. (eds), Blackwell, Oxford, pp. 1–9.

[7.12] Macgregor, A. N. (1963) The decomposition of dichloropropionate by soil microorganisms. *J. Gen. Microbiol.*, **30**, 497–501.

[7.13] Percich, J. A. and Lockwood, J. L. (1978) Interactions of atrazine with soil microorganisms: population changes and accumulation. *Can. J. Microbiol.*, **24**, 1145–1152.

[7.14] Hardman, D. J. and Slater, J. H. (1981) Dehalogenases in soil bacteria. *J. Gen. Microbiol.*, **123**, 117–128.

[7.15] Jensen, H. L. (1960) Decomposition of chloroacetates and chloro-propionates by bacteria. *Acta Agric. Scand.*, **10**, 83–103.

[7.16] Little, M. and Williams, P. A. (1971) A bacterial halidohydrolase. Its purification, some properties and its modification by specific amino acid reagents. *Eur. J. Biochem.*, **21**, 99–109.

[7.17] Senior, E., Bull, A. T. and Slater, J. H. (1976) Enzyme evolution in a microbial community growing on the herbicide Dalapon. *Nature*, **263**, 476–479.

[7.18] Tonomura, K., Futai, F., Tanake, O. and Yamaoka, T. (1965) Defluorination of monofluoroacetate by bacteria. Part I. Isolation of bacteria and their activity of defluorination. *Agric. Biol. Chem.*, **29**, 1324–1328.

[7.19] Slater, J. H., Lovatt, D., Weightman, A. J., Senior, E. and Bull, A. T. (1979) The growth of *Pseudomonas putida* on chlorinated aliphatic acids and its dehalogenase activity. *J. Gen. Microbiol.*, **114**, 125–136.

[7.20] Weightman, A. J. and Slater, J. H. (1980) Selection of *Pseudomonas putida* strains with elevated dehalogenase activities by continuous culture growth on chlorinated alkanoic acids. *J. Gen. Microbiol.*, **121**, 187–193.

[7.21] Gowland, P. C. and Slater, J. H. (1984) Transfer and stability of drug resistance plasmids in *Escherichia coli* K12. *Microbial Ecol.*, **10**, 1–13.

[7.22] Lederberg, J. (1952) Cell genetics and hereditary symbiosis. *Phys. Rev.*, **32**, 403–430.

[7.23] Hardman, D. J., Gowland, P. C. and Slater, J. H. (1986) Large plasmids from soil bacteria enriched on halogenated alkanoic acids. *Appl. Environ. Microbiol.*, **51**, 44–51.

[7.24] Gowland, P. C. and Hardman, D. J. (1986) Isolation of large plasmids. *Microbiological Sciences,* in press.

[7.25] Jacoby, G. A. and Matthews, M. (1979) The distribution of β lactamase genes on plasmids found in *Pseudomonas. Plasmid,* **2,** 41–47.

[7.26] Williams, P. A. and Murray, K. (1974) Metabolism of benzoate and methylbenzoate by *Pseudomonas putida (arvilla)* mt-2. Evidence for the existence of a TOL plasmid. *J. Bact.,* **120,** 416–423.

[7.27] Worsey, M. J., Franklin, F. C. H. and Williams, P. A. (1978) Regulation of the degradative pathway enzymes coded for by the TOL plasmid (pWWO) from *Pseudomonas putida* mt-2. *J. Bact.,* **134,** 757–764.

[7.28] Cohen, S. N., Brevet, J., Cabello, F., Change, A. C. Y., Chou, J., Kopecko, D. J., Kretschmer, P. J., Nisen, P. and Timmis, K. (1978) Macro and microevolution of bacterial plasmids. In *Microbiology-1978,* Schlesinger, D. (ed.), Am. Soc. Micro., p. 217.

[7.29] Schupp, T., Toupet, C., Stalhammar-Carlemaim, M. and Meyer, J. (1983) Expression of a Neomycin phosphotransferase gene from *Streptomyces fradiae* in *Escherichia coli* after intraplasmidic recombination. *Mol. Gen. Genet.,* **189,** 27–33.

[7.30] Clowes, R. C. (1972) Molecular structure of bacterial plasmids. *Bact. Rev.,* **36,** 361–405.

[7.31] Lehrbach, P. R., McGregor, I., Ward, J. M. and Broda, P. (1983) Molecular relationships between *Pseudomonas* INC P-9 degradative plasmids TOL, NAH and SAL. *Plasmid,* **10,** 164–174.

[7.32] Yen, K.-M., Sullivan, M. and Gunsalus, I. C. (1983) Electron microscope heteroduplex mapping of naphthalene oxidation genes on the NAH7 and SAL1 plasmids. *Plasmid,* **9,** 105–111.

[7.33] Meulien, P. and Broda, P. (1982) Identification of chromosomally integrated TOL DNA in cured derivatives of *Pseudomonas putida* PAW1. *J. Bact.,* **152,** 911–914.

[7.34] Curiale, M. S. and Mills, D. (1982) Integration and partial excision of a cryptic plasmid in *Pseudomonas syringae* pv. *phaseolicola. J. Bact.,* **152,** 797–802.

[7.35] Haas, M. J. and Holloway, B. W. (1976) R factor variants with enhanced sex factor activity in *Pseudomonas aeruginosa. Mol. Gen. Genet.,* **144,** 243–251.

[7.36] Morgan, A. F. (1982) Isolation and characterisation of *Pseudomonas aeruginosa* R plasmids constructed by interspecific mating. *J. Bact.,* **149,** 654–661.

[7.37] Kopecko, D. J. (1980) Specialised genetic recombination systems in bacteria: their involvement in gene expression and evolution. *Progr. Molec. Subcell. Biol.,* **7,** 135–234.

[7.38] Kopecko, D. J. (1980) Involvement of specialised recombination in the evolution and expression of bacterial genomes. In *Plasmids and Transponsons. Environmental Effects and Maintenance Mecha-*

nisms, Stuttard, C. and Rozee, K. R. (eds), Academic Press, London, p. 165.

[7.39] Pemberton, J. M. (1983) Degradative plasmids. *Int. Rev. Cytol.,* **84,** 155–183.

[7.40] Inouye, S., Nakazawa, A. and Nakazawa, T. (1981) Molecular cloning of gene *xyl*S of the TOL plasmid: evidence for the positive regulation of the *xyl*DEGF operon by *xyl*S. *J. Bact.,* **148,** 413–418.

[7.41] Nakazawa, T., Inouye, S. and Nakazawa, A. (1980) Physical and functional mapping of RP4-TOL plasmid recombinants: analysis of insertion and deletion mutants. *J. Bact.,* **144,** 222–231.

[7.42] Downing, R. G., Duggleby, C. J., Villems, R. and Borada, P. (1979) An endonuclease cleavage map of the plasmid pWWO-8, a derivative of the TOL plasmid of *Pseudomonas pevtida* mt-2. *Mol. Gen. Genet.,* **168,** 97–99.

[7.43] Leidigh, B. J. and Wheelis, M. (1973) The clustering on the *Pseudomonas putida,* chromosome of genes specifying dissimilatory functions. *J. Mol. Envoln.,* **2,** 235–242.

[7.44] Kawasaki, H., Yahara, H. and Tonomura, K. (1984) Cloning and expression in *Escherichia coli* of the haloacetate dehalogenase genes from *Moraxella* plasmid pUO1. *Agric. Biol. Chem.,* **48,** 2627–2632.

[7.45] Slater, J. H., Weightman, A. J. and Hall, B. (1985) Dehalogenase genes of *Pseudomonas putida,* PP3 on chromosomally located transposable elements. *Mol. Biol. Evoln.,* **2,** 557–567.

[7.46] Keith, L. H. and Tiellard, W. A. (1979) Priority pollutants I — a perspective view. *Env. Sci. Technol.,* **13,** 416–423.

[7.47] Suida, J. F. and De Bernardis, J. F. (1972) Naturally occurring halogenated organic compounds. *Lloydia,* **36,** 107–143.

[7.48] Dorn, E., Hellwig, M., Reineke, W. and Knackmuss, H.-J. (1974) Isolation and characterisation of a 3-chlorobenzoate-grown pseudomonad. *Arc. Microbiol.,* **99,** 61–70.

[7.49] Dorn, E. and Knackmuss, H.-J. (1978) Chemical structure and biodegradability of halogenated organic compounds. *Biochem. J.,* **174,** 85–94.

[7.50] Reineke, W. and Knackmuss, H.-J. (1980) Hybrid pathway for chlorobenzoate metabolism in *Pseudomonas* sp. B13 derivatives. *J. Bact.,* **142,** 467–473.

[7.51] Chatterjee, D. K., Kellogg, S. T., Hameda, S. and Chakrabarty, A. M. (1981) Plasmid specifying total degradation of 3-chlorobenzoate by a modified *ortho*-pathway. *J. Bact.,* **146,** 639–646.

[7.52] Pemberton, J. M. and Fisher, P. R. (1977) 2,4-D Plasmids and persistence. *Nature,* **268,** 732–733.

[7.53] Fisher, P. R., Appleton, J. and Pemberton, J. M. (1978) Isolation and characterisation of the pesticide-degrading plasmid pJP1 from *Alcaligenes paradoxus. J. Bact.,* **135,** 789–804.

[7.54] Don, R. H. and Pemberton, J. M. (1981) Properties of six pesticide degradation plasmids isolated from *Alcaligenes paradoxus* and *A. eutrophus. J. Bact.,* **145.,** 681–686.

[7.55] Kellogg, S. T., Chatterjee, D. K. and Chakrabarty, A. M. (1981) Plasmid-assisted molecular breeding: a new technique for enhanced biodegradation of persistent toxic chemicals. *Science,* **214,** 1133–1135.

[7.56] Kilbane, J. J., Chatterjee, D. K., Karns, J. S. and Kellogg, B. T. (1982) Biodegradation of 2,4,5-trichlorophenoxyacetic acid by a pure culture of *Pseudomonas cepacia. Appl. Environ. Microbiol.,* **44,** 72–78.

[7.57] Ghosal, D., You, I.-S., Chatterjee, D. K. and Chakrabarty, A. M. (1985) Plasmids in the degradation of chlorinated aromatic compounds. In *Plasmids in Bacteria,* Heliniski, S. N., Cohen, D., Clewell, D., Jackson, D. and Hollanender, A. (eds), Plenum Press, New York, p. 667.

[7.58] Lehrbach, P. R., Zeyer, J., Reineke, W., Knackmuss, H.-J. and Timmis, K. N. (1984) Enzyme recruitment *in vitro*: use of cloned genes to extend the range of haloaromatics degraded by *Pseudomonas* sp. strain B13. *J. Bact.,* **158,** 1025–1032.

[7.59] Yen, K.-M. and Gunsalus, I. C. (1982) Plasmid gene organization: naphthalene/salicylate oxidation. *Proc. Natl. Acad. Sci. USA,* **79,** 874–878.

[7.60] Weightman, A. J., Don, R. H., Lehrbach, P. R. and Timmis, K. N. (1983) The identification and cloning of genes encoding haloaromatic catabolic enzymes and the construction of hybrid pathways for substrate mineralisation. In *Genetic Control of Environmental Pollutants,* Omenn, G. S. and Hollaender, A. (eds), Plenum Press, New York, p. 47.

[7.61] Barth, P. T. and Grinter, N. J. (1974) Comparison of the doxyribonucleic acid molecular weights and homologies of plasmids conferring linked resistance to streptomycin and sulfonamides. *J. Bact.,* **120,** 618–630.

[7.62] Sayler, G. S., Shields, M. S., Tedford, E. T., Breen, A., Hooper, S. W., Sirotkin, K. M. and Davis, J. W. (1985) Application of DNA–DNA colony hybridisation to the detection of catabolic genotypes in environmental samples. *Appl. Env. Microbiol.,* **49,** 1295–1303.

[7.63] Trevors, J. T. (1985) DNA probes for the detection of specific genes in bacteria isolated from the environment. *Trends Biotechnol.,* **3,** 291–293.

8

Continuous culture of bacteria with special reference to activated sludge wastewater treatment processes

G. Hamer
Institutes of Aquatic Sciences and Biotechnology, Swiss Federal
Institute of Technology, Zürich, Dübendorf, Switzerland

8.1 INTRODUCTION

The theoretical basis for the growth of bacteria and other microbes in continuous flow chemostat culture resulted from the original work of Monod [8.1] and of Novick and Szilard [8.2] published in 1950. By 1961, it had become possible for Herbert [8.3] to present a comprehensive theoretical analysis of a wide selection of possible continuous culture systems as a result of the extensive experimental studies with continuous culture systems carried out during the previous decade. The theoretical basis of continuous culture systems has also been presented in detail by Málek and Fencl [8.4] and by Pirt [8.5]. Continuous culture has proved to be a most valuable research tool for investigating the physiology of microbes, but its potential in the microbial process industries remains relatively restricted, with one major exception. This exception is in aerobic sewage and wastewater biotreatment, where both activated sludge processes with their many variants [8.6], and trickling filters or biological beds [8.7], are operated in a continuous flow mode. In simple terms, activated sludge processes are processes in which biodegradable pollutants present in the water undergoing treatment are oxidised by dispersed bacterial flocs, whilst in trickling filters the pollutants are oxidised as the water undergoing treatment flows over films of bacteria attached to stationary solid support media. Recently, hybrid aerobic processes have been developed in which the oxidation of biodegradable pollutants results from the action of moving films of microbes growing either on solid supports such as sand which is fluidised by the flow of polluted water through the bioreactor [8.8], or on rotating discs that are partially submerged in the polluted wastewater undergoing treatment [8.9]. In addition to these aerobic biotreatment processes, analogous anaerobic wastewater treatment processes have also been developed [8.10] and considerable expansion in this area of wastewater treatment technology can be predicted for the future. In addition to wastewater treatment processes, both anaerobic and aerobic waste sewage sludge treatment processes are also frequently operated on a continuous flow basis (see Chapters 1 and 2). Many of the above-mentioned processes were developed prior to the establishment of the theoretical basis for continuous culture, hence application of continuous culture theory to such processes is essentially retrospective.

The activated sludge process (see Chapter 1) was originally developed by Ardern and Lockett between 1914 and 1921 [8.11] for the effective removal of bulk biodegradable carbonaceous pollutants from municipal sewage containing a significant fraction of trade and industrial wastewater. The numerous variants [8.6] of the process are the most widely distributed and, in terms of throughput, the largest engineered processes [8.12], being used for the biotreatment of both municipal sewage and industrial wastewater with process objectives that include nitrification/denitrification sequences in addition to carbonaceous pollutant removal. In spite of their importance, detailed understanding of the process biology of activated sludge processes is markedly lacking, and the impact of continuous culture theory on either process effectiveness or process improvement is negligible. However, in the future this *status quo* is likely to change provided it is allowed to do so by sanitary engineering practitioners.

In addition to continuous flow activated sludge processes, batch processes found limited application in the early days of sewage and wastewater biotreatment [8.13], and recently small numbers of sequencing batch systems [8.14] have been installed.

8.2 BACTERIAL GROWTH REQUIREMENTS

The essential requirements for the growth of any bacterial culture are:

(1) a viable inoculum;
(2) an energy source and a carbon source;
(3) all other essential nutrients for biomass synthesis;
(4) an absence of growth inhibitors;
(5) appropriate physico-chemical conditions in the culture environment

8.3 BATCH REACTORS

Provided all these requirements are satisfied simultaneously in a well-mixed batch culture containing discretely dispersed bacteria that multiply by binary fission, the rate of increase in bacterial biomass with respect to time will be proportional to the bacterial biomass concentration, so that:

$$dx/dt = \mu x \tag{8.1}$$

where dx/dt is the growth rate, μ is the specific growth rate constant, x is the bacterial biomass concentration measured on a dry weight basis, and t is time. Growth in accordance with Equation 8.1 is described as either logarithmic or exponential growth and only occurs when both environmental conditions and bacterial biomass composition remain constant.

For the qualitative assessment of growth it is essential to relate the formation of bacterial biomass to the utilisation of substrates, nutrients and energy by means of appropriate yield coefficients. The yield coefficient concept was originally introduced by Monod [8.15] to describe heterotrophic growth on single carbon energy substrates, but has since been extended to account for the utilisation of other nutrients and for energy requirements and to describe product formation [8.16]. The bacterial biomass yield coefficient for heterotrophic growth on carbon energy substrates, $Y_{x/s}$, is defined as:

$$Y_{x/s} = -dx/ds \tag{8.2}$$

where ds is the infinitely small decrease in the carbon energy substrate concentration that corresponds to the infinitely small increase in bacterial biomass concentration, dx. Under constant growth conditions the yield coefficient will remain constant, so that if at an initial time t_0 the bacterial biomass and carbon energy substrate concentrations are x_0 and s_0 respectively, and at a final time t they are x and s respectively, then:

$$x - x_0 = Y_{x/s}(s_0 - s) \tag{8.3}$$

Although yield coefficients are frequently thought to be essentially constant, changing culture conditions affect them markedly, so that in all real systems it is possible, by manipulation of culture conditions, to optimise yield coefficients. For either wastewater or waste sludge biotreatment processes minimisation of the bacterial biomass yield coefficient is a primary objective of process optimisation.

The only other basic relationship required for the quantitative description of bacterial growth is that between the specific growth rate constant and the limiting substrate concentration. Several such relationships have been proposed and their validity has been discussed by Powell [8.17]. By far the most widely used relationship is that attributed to Monod:

$$\mu = \mu_m s/(s + K_s) \tag{8.4}$$

where μ_m is the maximum value of μ when s greatly exceeds K_s, which is a saturation constant equal to the value of s when $\mu = \mu_m/2$.

The Monod relationship both provides a good approximation to what is observed in actual growth processes and is a mathematically tractable expression, Fig. 8.1.

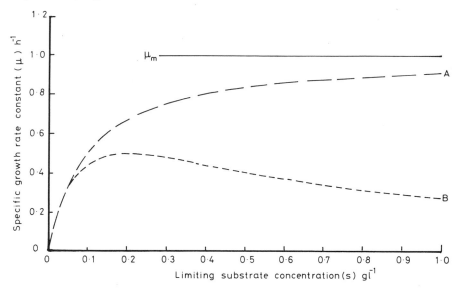

Fig. 8.1 — The Monod relationship, which describes the effect on the specific growth rate constant of (A) non-inhibiting limiting substrate concentration; and (B) inhibitory limiting substrate concentration ($\mu_m = 1.0\ \mathrm{h}^{-1}$, $K_s = 0.1\ \mathrm{g\ l}^{-1}$, $K_i = 0.4\ \mathrm{g\ l}^{-1}$).

Equations 8.1, 8.2 and 8.3 can be used to describe ideal bacterial growth in any bioreactor for which the flow characteristics can be described. However, many factors affect the growth process such that ideal growth is rarely, if ever, achieved, and prior to the extension of the discussion to bacterial growth in continuous flow bioreactors certain of the factors encountered in real systems will be considered.

In batch cultures, exponential growth continues as long as the limiting substrate concentration, s, greatly exceeds the saturation constant, K_s, i.e. $\mu = \mu_m$. However, when the limiting substrate approaches exhaustion, i.e. the condition mentioned above no longer applies, growth will deviate from the exponential pattern, and when the limiting substrate becomes completely exhausted no further growth occurs.

8.3.1 Oxygen-limited batch growth

In the case of aerobic bacterial batch cultures, oxygen, unlike other nutrients and most other substrates, is supplied continuously because of both its inordinately low solubility in water and a potentially high demand, and hence oxygen presents a special case when it becomes growth limiting. With obligate aerobic bacteria, oxygen limitation results in linear growth, but when oxygen limitation occurs in cultures of facultative anaerobic bacteria, alternative metabolic pathways are invoked to compensate for restrictions in the oxygen supply. In the especially relevant case of some of the facultative anaerobic denitrifying (nitrate reducing) bacteria, a progressive change from oxygen to nitrate as electron acceptor occurs with reducing dissolved oxygen concentrations [8.18].

From the two-film hypothesis for the physical absorption of gases in liquids [8.19], the oxygen supply R_{Ox}, can be written as:

$$R_{Ox} = K_L a(C_{Ox}^* - C_{Ox}) \qquad (8.5)$$

where K_L is the overall liquid side transfer coefficient, a is the specific gas–liquid interfacial area, C_{Ox}^* is the equilibrium dissolved oxygen concentration corresponding to the gas phase oxygen partial pressure, and C_{Ox} is the actual liquid phase dissolved oxygen concentration (see Chapter 10).

Just as with any other substrate and/or nutrient, the yield coefficient concept can be applied to oxygen, i.e.

$$Y_{x/Ox} = -dx/ds_{Ox} \qquad (8.6)$$

where $Y_{x/Ox}$ is the weight of bacterial biomass produced per unit weight of oxygen utilised, and dx is the increase in bacterial biomass corresponding to ds_{Ox}, the oxygen utilised during an infinitely small time interval dt. The rate of change of the dissolved oxygen concentration in an exponentially growing aerobic culture is:

$$dC_{Ox}/dt = R_{Ox} + ds_{Ox}/dt \qquad (8.7)$$

Substituting for ds_{Ox} from Equation 8.6 into Equation 8.7 gives:

$$dC_{Ox}/dt = R_{Ox} - dx/Y_{x/Ox}dt \qquad (8.8)$$

The maximum oxygen supply rate, $(R_{Ox})_m$, is reached when $C_{Ox}=0$, i.e.

$$(R_{Ox})_m = K_L a C_{Ox}^* Ox \qquad (8.9)$$

and remains constant, no longer able to increase with increasing demand. Under such conditions $dC_{Ox}/dt=0$. For oxygen limited growth, combining Equations 8.8 and 8.9 and rearranging gives:

$$dx/dt = K_L a C_{Ox}^* Y_{x/Ox} \qquad (8.10)$$

i.e. linear growth occurs, provided K_L, a, C_{Ox}^* and $Y_{x/Ox}$ remain constant, until another substrate or nutrient becomes growth limiting and the stationary phase of growth commences.

8.3.2 Maintenance energy concept

The stationary phase of the batch growth cycle is generally considered to be characterised by a constant number of bacterial cells and a slowly decreasing dry weight of cells present in the culture. It is hypothesised that the decrease in cell weight results from endogenous carbonaceous substrate utilisation to satisfy the maintenance requirements of the non-growing cells. Essentially this phenomenon is thought to involve the degradation of both storage products and those cellular constituents that have become redundant when no growth occurs, to produce energy and carbon dioxide.

The maintenance energy concept has been extended to growth conditions, as it seemed plausible that the energy consuming maintenance processes occurring in resting cells also occur during growth. Maintenance energy requirements are considered to be growth rate independent and the conventional way of accounting for them is incorporation of an endogenous metabolic rate constant, μ_e, in Equation 8.3 such that

$$\mu = [\mu_g s/(s+K_s)] - \mu_e \tag{8.11}$$

where μ is now the observed specific growth rate constant and μ_g the real maximum specific growth rate constant in the absence of endogenous metabolism. For exponential growth to occur, i.e. when $s \gg K_s$, μ_e must be negligible, suggesting that endogenous metabolism might not necessarily occur during growth. Under non-growth conditions, i.e. when $s=0$, $\mu=-\mu_e$, endogenous metabolism manifests itself in depression of $Y_{x/s}$ and is a convenient, frequently all-embracing, but not necessarily accurate means of explaining yield coefficient depression, particularly in continuous flow culture systems operating at extended hydraulic and biomass residence times.

8.3.3 Lysis and cryptic growth

In all bacterial cultures, death and lysis are the ultimate consequences of life, but in spite of this these processes are generally ignored, although when linked together with cryptic growth they provide an equally plausible explanation for $Y_{x/s}$ depression as does the maintenance energy concept under both growth and starvation conditions. The phenomena of bacterial death and lysis have been little studied at temperatures either within or close to the optimum range for growth, and at such temperatures it still remains unclear whether death and lysis occur either sequentially or simultaneously. However, if one defines a dead bacterium as a bacterium totally devoid of biochemical activity, it can be concluded that death and lysis occur simultaneously at normal growth temperatures. The killing of bacteria at elevated temperatures clearly occurs and allows dead cells, in an essentially 'fixed' state, to exist. The very limited data available concerning bacterial cell death/lysis within the temperature range for their growth [8.20] suggest that lysis occurs both in the absence of and during growth and in the latter case is growth rate dependent, such that the specific death/lysis rate constant, k_{dl}, can best be expressed as:

$$k_{dl} = b\mu + c \tag{8.12}$$

where b and c are system dependent constants. Irrespective of whether cryptic growth on lytic products occurs or not in a bacterial culture undergoing some degree of death/lysis, the death/lysis process manifests itself in $Y_{x/s}$ depression. Such depression will obviously be minimised when cryptic growth occurs, but because of the energy requirements for cryptic growth, carbon from lytic products will not only be converted into new bacterial biomass but also degraded to carbon dioxide to produce energy. The maximum possible bacteria biomass yield coefficient for cryptic growth, $Y_{x/s}$, is 0.67, but under real growth conditions will always be <0.67 because either the conditions for cryptic growth are non-optimal or some of the lytic products produced are either only slowly biodegradable or even non-biodegradable.

8.3.4 Growth inhibition

The widespread existence of bacteriostatic and bactericidal agents clearly indicate that bacteria are susceptible to the action of various chemicals, which depending on their nature either inhibit bacterial growth or kill bacteria. A well-known example of a bacterial growth inhibitor is phenol, whilst chlorine is the best known and most widely used chemical bactericidal agent. The presence of inhibitory chemicals in bacterial culture systems can be either intentional or unintentional and it is this latter context that is particularly pertinent in the case of polluted wastewater. The unintentional presence of inhibitors in biological sewage and wastewater treatment processes arises from the presence of inhibitory pollutants (substrates), the production of inhibitory partial degradation products or intermediates and inhibitory compound release resulting from cell lysis.

The theory concerning bacterial response to growth inhibitors is directly based on the kinetics of enzyme inhibition and makes the somewhat gross assumption that a bacterium behaves as if it were an enzyme. Such an analogy results in the concept of essentially two primary types of inhibition: competitive inhibition, where the inhibitor competes with the growth-limiting substrate for uptake, thereby affecting the affinity for this substrate; and non-competitive inhibition, where the inhibitor reacts at a site other than the site of uptake of the growth-limiting substrate and does not directly affect the affinity for this substrate. In both cases inhibition is accounted for by the introduction of a term α, defined as

$$\alpha = (i+K_i)/K_i \tag{8.13}$$

where i is the inhibitor concentration and K_i the inhibition constant, into the Monod relationship, i.e. for competitive inhibition

$$\mu = \mu_m s/(s+\alpha K_s) \tag{8.14}$$

and for non-competitive inhibition

$$\mu = \mu_m s/\alpha(s+K_s) \tag{8.15}$$

It should be noted that α is always >1.

Both substrate and product inhibition can be considered as cases of non-competitive inhibition. For inhibition by the growth-limiting substrate, s can be substituted for i in Equation 8.13 so that Equation 8.15 becomes:

$$\mu = \mu_m/[1+K_s/s+(s+K_s)/K_i] \tag{8.16}$$

When inhibition by the growth-limiting substrate occurs, $s \gg K_s$, so that Equation 8.16 is frequently simplified to:

$$\mu = \mu_m s K_i/(s K_i + K_s K_i + s^2) \tag{8.17}$$

which is generally referred to as the Haldane equation. The typical relationships between μ and s for both a non-inhibitory substrate and an inhibitory substrate are shown in Fig. 8.1, for the values of μ_m, K_s and K_i indicated in the figure caption. In the former case μ asymptotically approaches μ_m as s increases, whilst in the latter case μ reaches a distinct maximum and then declines markedly as inhibition becomes more pronounced with increasing substrate concentration.

In addition to the effect that they have on the specific growth rate constant, some inhibitors can also depress biomass yield coefficients by uncoupling growth from carbon energy substrate oxidation to varying degrees. Such mechanisms are clearly advantageous in wastewater treatment where minimisation of biomass (sludge) production is an established process objective.

8.3.5 Flocculent growth

The aggregation of bacteria to form flocs and the formation of thick bacterial films on solid surfaces are phenomena which arise from the adhesive properties of bacterial cells. Various terms are used interchangeably to describe bacterial aggregation, but a most important mechanistic distinction must be drawn between flocculation, i.e. the coming together of previously discretely dispersed cells, and flocculent growth, i.e. the non-dispersion of cells after binary fission. Flocculent growth is essential for the effective functioning of activated sludge treatment processes.

The physical interaction between two bacteria arises from the summation of a wide range of attractive and repulsive forces, each contributing in a more or less dominant manner. Two discretely dispersed bacterial cells will flocculate when they have sufficient kinetic energy to overcome the energy barrier from the direction of infinite separation, whereas flocculent growth of two bacterial cells occurs when they have insufficient energy to overcome the energy barrier from the direction of zero separation [8.21] as is evident from Fig. 8.2. Consequently, when a bacterial floc is disrupted by high shear conditions, the bacteria will not necessarily re-flocculate when quiescent conditions are re-established. Further, the growth of bacteria as either flocs or discretely dispersed cells does not indicate either the presence or absence

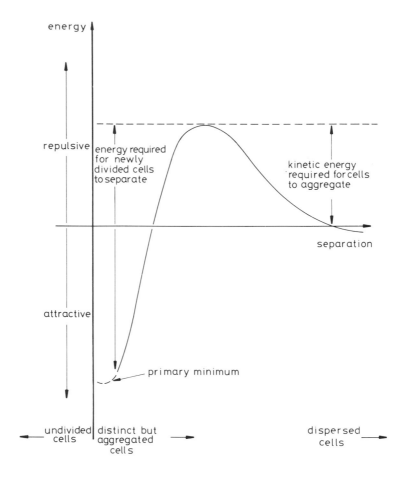

Fig. 8.2 — Energy-separation diagram for two micro-organisms showing distinction
between aggregation and flocculent growth.

of an energy barrier to flocculation but the depth of the primary minimum in
Fig. 8.2. For discretely dispersed bacteria to flocculate it is necessary for a
strengthening of the attractive forces in the primary minimum and, possibly,
a weakening of the energy barrier opposing flocculation to occur. However,
the force between bacterial cells is only one of the factors affecting
flocculation. The collision frequency between the bacterial cells, which
increases as the square of the concentration, also influences flocculation
kinetics.

The growth of bacterial flocs does not follow a similar pattern to the
growth of discretely dispersed bacteria, because once a floc exceeds a critical
size growth becomes limited by the diffusion of substrates and nutrients,
particularly oxygen, to each bacterium comprising the floc. By analogy with
the growth of mould pellets, bacterial flocs are considered to grow in
accordance with the cube root law, i.e. a situation where growth is restricted

to the outer layers of the floc. In the case of bacterial flocs such an approach is undoubtedly an over-simplification because bacterial flocs are rarely spherical in shape, comprise a relatively broad size distribution and are subject to mechanical shearing. Unfortunately, few data concerning either bacterial floc size distribution or floc structure are available, so that in order to account for diffusional resistances it is necessary to adopt an approach that disregards these aspects.

One such approach to the problem of flocculent growth, which is applicable to both batch and continuous cultures, has been proposed by Characklis [8.22] who, in the absence of equilibrium floc size distribution data, has approached the questions of overall growth and substrate utilisation in bacterial flocs by considering the flux of limiting substrate into the floc by diffusion on the basis of uni-dimensional transfer and subsequent uptake at the surface of the bacteria, in accordance with Monod-type saturation kinetics. A more common approach to this problem is to modify the kinetic expression used to account for diffusional resistance, but such an approach essentially mistakes the mass transfer rate for the reaction rate. Using the former approach, and designating the limiting substrate concentration at the bacterial surface as s', the rate of substrate uptake can be expressed as:

$$-ds'/dt = x[\mu_m s'/(s'+K_s)]/Y_{x/s} \tag{8.18}$$

If the substrate uptake (reaction) rate, r, is considered on a unit area of bacterial surface basis, then

$$r = (\mu_m x/Y_{x/s} A)[s'/(s'+K_s)] \tag{8.19}$$

where A is the bacterial surface area.

In systems where the bacterial biomass concentration remains essentially constant, r may be rewritten as:

$$r = k_1 s'/(s'+K_s) \tag{8.20}$$

where

$$k_1 = \mu_m x/Y_{x/s} A$$

The flux of limiting substrate to the bacterial surface, N_s, is:

$$N_s = \mathbb{D}(s-s')/w \tag{8.21}$$

where s is the bulk liquid limiting substrate concentrations, $\mathbb{D}$ the molecular diffusivity of the limiting substrate in the bacterial floc, and w the thickness of the diffusion zone. As limiting substrate accumulation does not occur at the bacterial surface, the reaction rate can be equated to the flux so that:

$$k_1 s'/(s'+K_s) = \mathbb{D}(s-s')/w \tag{8.22}$$

Eliminating s' from Equation 8.22 results in a quadratic equation in terms of r, i.e.

$$r^2 - r[k_1 \mathbb{D}(s+K_s)/w] + \mathbb{D}sk_1/w = 0 \tag{8.23}$$

The real root of Equation 8.23 is

$$r = k_1 s / [(K_s + k_1 w / \mathbb{D}) + s] \tag{8.24}$$

which can then be incorporated into the material balance expressions for growth and limiting substrate utilisation in various bioreactors.

8.3.6 Diauxic growth

When a monospecies bacterial culture is presented simultaneously with two utilisable carbon energy substrates under nutrient sufficient conditions, such as pertain in batch cultures, the bacteria usually first utilise the substrate that supports the highest growth rate, whilst the enzymes necessary for utilisation of the second substrate remain repressed until the first substrate is exhausted. The phenomenon of sequential substrate utilisation is described as either diauxie growth or diauxic [8.15]. In spite of the fact that bacteria are frequently presented with a multiple choice of substrates satisfying a single physiological requirement in natural environments and process situations, remarkably little attention has been devoted to diauxie. Yoon *et al.* [8.23] have sought to model diauxic growth with an equation in which each substrate exhibits competitive inhibition of the utilisation of the other substrates, which obviously has application when an inhibitory, biodegradable intermediate product builds up in the culture, but does not strictly describe diauxic growth when the second substrate exhibits no inhibitory effect on the utilisation of the first substrate. Hence, it would seem more appropriate to model diauxic growth on the basis of uninhibited utilisation of the first substrate and non-competitive inhibition of utilisation of the second substrate by the first, i.e.

$$\mu = [\mu_{m1}s_1/(s_1+K_{s1})] + [\mu_{m2}s_2K_{i1}/(s_1+K_{i1})(s_2+K_{s2})] \tag{8.25}$$

where the subscripts 1 and 2 refer to the first and second substrates according to preferential utilisation. However, Equation 8.25 fails to indicate a lag between the two growth phases which is commonly encountered.

Such a clear preference for one utilisable substrate to the total exclusion of another would place a bacterium at a serious disadvantage in either nutritionally poor or nutritionally variable environments. In the case of mixed bacterial cultures where all species utilise both substrates, diauxie would be expected, whilst in bacterial cultures comprising species that utilise either one or other of the substrates, one would expect simultaneous utilisation of the dual substrate mixture.

8.3.7 Temperature effects on growth

Temperature is a most important factor affecting both the physiological and biochemical potentials of microbes. The three main temperature ranges used in classification are (i) psychrophilic growth, where the optimum temperature is <10 °C; (ii) mesophilic growth, where the optimum temperature is between 15 and 40 °C; and (iii) thermophilic growth, where the optimum temperature is >50 °C. Those microorganisms that can only grow well at temperatures within one of the defined ranges are considered to be obligate with respect to the particular temperature range, whilst those that are able to grow well in an additional temperature range to that which includes their optimum growth temperature are described as facultative with respect to the additional range. Obligate thermophiles and obligate psychrophiles, as opposed to their facultative counterparts, are optimally adapted for growth in the thermophilic and psychrophilic temperature ranges, respectively, and are not struggling to survive and function under such conditions.

As far as microbial processes are concerned, the effect of temperature on overall reaction rates has received inadequate attention with respect to both process research and process operation. For chemical reactions, an increase in temperature usually enhances the reaction rate and, by analogy, it is generally assumed that a similar effect occurs in the case of microbially mediated reactions, but only within any one of the temperature ranges appropriate for psychrophilic, mesophilic or thermophilic growth. As far as microbes are concerned, they exhibit maximum critical temperatures above which growth ceases within two or three degrees.

Most biotreatment processes are operated at mesophilic temperatures, usually close to the minimum of the mesophilic range. However, in a recent review of developments and trends in biotreatment Zlokarnik [8.24] suggested that, because many industrial wastewaters are produced at high temperatures, realistic possibilities exist for considering biotreatment of such wastewaters at thermophilic temperatures, where enhanced reaction rates might offer distinct advantages. Obviously, because of discharge quality standards, hot effluents cannot be discharged directly into surface waters, but cooling post-treatment is equally appropriate as cooling pre-treatment.

Unlike many chemical reactions that occur under essentially homogeneous conditions, all microbially mediated processes occur under heterogeneous conditions. The heterogeneous nature of microbial systems will be of considerable significance in any analysis of the effects of temperature on such systems. Further, microbially mediated processes involve a complex sequence of biochemical reactions, none of which may be rate limiting as far as the overall process is concerned. The rate limiting step in most microbial systems is usually a resistance to mass transfer.

As far as bacterial systems are concerned, the simplest system that can be devised for analysis is one where a pure monoculture grows, in accordance with Monod-type kinetics, as discretely dispersed cells in a defined liquid growth medium, in a completely mixed bioreactor where no wall effects occur, on a single carbon energy substrate. For such a system, it is possible to hypothesise concerning the several potential effects of temperature. Clearly identifiable effects include (i) effects on the maximum specific growth rate constant of the culture; (ii) effect on the affinity of the bacteria for the growth-limiting substrate; (iii) effect on endogenous metabolism and maintenance requirements; and (iv) effect on the specific death and lysis rate constants of the culture. Experimental evidence suggests that, within a specific temperature range, a temperature increase will enhance the maximum specific growth rate constant, the rate of endogenous metabolism and the affinity of the microorganisms for the growth-limiting substrate, but that effects on the specific death and lysis rate constants occur primarily at temperatures above the optimum range for growth. The overall effect of increasing temperature is, within limits, to increase the maximum potential growth rate of the culture, but with a concomitant decrease in the yield coefficient for the conversion of the limiting carbon energy substrate into microbial biomass.

In heterogeneous process systems the effects of temperature frequently stem from changes in physical properties that result from the changes in temperature. Physical properties that are primarily affected in this way in bacterial process systems include gas solubilities, liquid phase viscosity and liquid phase diffusivities. The solubility of oxygen is of key importance in aerobic bacterial processes, as in such systems oxygen transfer frequently becomes the rate limiting step in the process. For example, in an ideal continuous flow aerobic bacterial process operating under carbon energy substrate limitation where the maximum possible rate of supply of oxygen just exceeds the actual rate of demand, an increase in temperature could result in the process becoming oxygen rather than carbon energy substrate limited because of a solublity dependent reduction in the oxygen transfer rate. In addition, an enhanced oxygen demand resulting from a reduction in the microbial biomass yield coefficient at enhanced temperature will also adversely affect the maintenance of carbon energy substrate limitation. If a similar change and effect were to occur in wastewater treatment processes, biodegradable carbonaceous pollutants would no longer be effectively removed by microbial oxidation from the water undergoing treatment. Liquid phase diffusivities will be enhanced by increases in temperature, and in multiphase microbiological process systems such enhancement can be expected to affect overall process rates favourably by the reduction of the rate limiting resistance for interphase transfer of the overall reaction rate limiting nutrient.

8.3.8 Co-oxidation and co-metabolism

The terms co-oxidation, co-metabolism and fortuitous oxidation have all been used to describe the oxidation and degradation of non-growth substrates by microbes and have become virtually synonymous. Co-oxidation was originally defined by Foster [8.25] as the phenomenon whereby actively growing microbes oxidise a compound but do not utilise either carbon or energy derived from the oxidation. Co-metabolism was originally defined by

Jensen [8.26] to extend the above definition of co-oxidation to include other reactions, e.g. dehalogenations (see Chapter 6), in addition to oxidations, but did not include the obligate requirement for the presence of a growth substrate. More recently, both definitions have been subject to criticism on the grounds that they describe metabolic phenomena which can readily be encompassed by the existing terms for metabolism, anabolism and catabolism. However, some microbial oxidations that satisfy Jensen's definition of co-metabolism are merely a reflection of the non-specific nature of particular mono-oxygenases, and it has been proposed that the transformation of non-growth substrates in the absence of a co-substrate should simply be referred to as a fortuitous activity [8.27]. The currently accepted definition of co-metabolism is the transformation of a compound, which is unable to support cell replication, in the requisite presence of another transformable co-substrate.

The capacity for co-metabolism and fortuitous activity seems to occur most frequently in hydrocarbon-utilising bacteria, where both anthropogenic and xenobiotic pollutants are transformed by such mechanisms.

In wastewater treatment processes, biotransformation of pollutants in the absence of bacterial growth also occurs as a result of the activities of endoenzymes present in non-viable bacteria, as discussed by Jones [8.28], and as a result of exoenzymes excreted by viable bacteria, but the magnitude of such effects has yet to be defined.

The most important feature with respect to the several mechanisms described above is that they result in a zero biomass yield coefficient, because they involve either partial oxidation to intermediates or complete oxidation to CO_2 with all the energy produced being dissipated as heat, thereby making such mechanisms ideal for biotreatment. However, it should be noted that in some cases of co-metabolism some energy derived from non-growth substrate degradation can be used to fix carbon from the growth substrate as biomass.

8.3.9 Predation

It is generally agreed that the numerous species of bacteria present are the most important microbes responsible for the removal of biodegradable pollutants in activated sludge treatment processes, and as a result the rôles of all other organisms are frequently ignored. However, in activated sludge processes, the actions of predatory protozoa present in the complex mixed biocenosis comprising the process culture are so important with respect to effluent discharge quality that predator–prey relationships involving protozoa and the discretely dispersed bacteria present in the process system must be considered if realistic process descriptions are to be developed.

Essentially, the biomass present in activated sludge processes can be divided into three distinct categories: dispersed bacteria that are not removed by sedimentation; flocculated bacteria that are easily removed by sedimentation and are recycled to maintain process intensity; and protozoa, predominantly ciliated, peritrichous species of the sessile type that attach themselves to the bacterial flocs [8.29] and hence are recycled together with the flocs and thereby maintained in the process system. The protozoa constitute some 5 per cent of the total biomass and their rôle is to feed on any discretely dispersed bacteria present in the system, thus reducing the suspended solids present in the treated water. Because of the size of the flocs, it is assumed that the ciliated protozoa do not ingest flocculated bacteria, and further it is also assumed that they do not utilise soluble carbon energy substrates.

In culture systems where predation occurs, the growth of the predator and the prey are generally considered separately. For the prey, i.e. the discretely dispersed bacteria, one has to consider both growth on soluble carbon energy substrates and utilisation by the protozoan predators, so that:

$$dx_b/dt = \mu_b x_b - \mu_p x_p / Y_{xp/xp} \tag{8.26}$$

where subscript b refers to the bactria, subscript p to the protozoa, and the yield coefficient $Y_{xp/xp}$ is the dry weight of protozoan biomass produced per unit dry weight of bacterial biomass consumed. The growth of the protozoan predators can be expressed as:

$$dx_p/dt = \mu_p x_p \tag{8.27}$$

In classical predator–prey models, it is usual to assume that the specific growth rate constants in Equations 8.26 and 8.27 are first-order with respect to the respective substrate concentrations, i.e. soluble carbon energy substrate concentration in the case of the bacteria and bacterial concentration in the case of protozoa. However, for the bacteria it would seem more plausible to apply Monod-type kinetics.

8.4 CONTINUOUS REACTORS

8.4.1 Mixing in continuous flow bioreactors

The analysis of growth in any bioreactor operating in a continuous flow mode involves definition of both the flow characteristics of the bioreactor and the kinetics of the pertinent biological processes that are occurring. The flow characteristics of all continuous flow reactors can be described by the residence time distribution of material passing through the reactor. The two extremes with respect to residence time distribution are the perfect plug flow reactor on the one hand, and the completely mixed reactor on the other hand. As far as single phase systems are concerned, both extremes and a complete range of intermediate situations can be imagined. However, in bioreactors in which bacterially mediated processes are occurring, the question of mixing becomes much more difficult to define. Whilst it is possible to have a discretely and uniformly dispersed suspension of bacteria in a liquid, thereby satisfying the condition of perfect macro-scale mixing, marked gradients will undoubtedly occur at interfaces on the micro-scale. Therefore, in the case of bacterial suspensions in bioreactors, a completely mixed system is one in which macro-scale inhomogeneities do not occur, i.e. no segregation of bacteria occurs. Whilst in plug flow systems, a distinct macro-scale concentration gradient exists throughout the system. In systems where flocculent growth of bacteria occurs, differentiation between homogeneous and non-homogeneous systems on the macro-scale becomes increasingly fraught with difficulty.

In a completely mixed continuous flow reactor, the residence time distribution curve for parcels of fluid passing through the reactor takes a negative exponential form, as does the washout curve for such reactors. However, the mean residence time, t, for parcels of fluid passing through the rector is:

$$t = V/F \tag{8.28}$$

where V is the liquid volume in the reactor and F the rate of flow of fluid into and out of the reactor, assuming no accumulation of liquid in the reactor. The residence time is rarely used for the description of continuous flow bacterial bioreactor systems, where dilution rate, D, defined as

$$D = F/V \tag{8.29}$$

is favoured. In terms of dilution rate, the bacterial biomass washout equation corresponding to the appropriate residence time distribution is:

$$dx/dt = -Dx \tag{8.30}$$

In the case of ideal plug flow bacterial bioreactors, the residence time of all parcels of fluid passing through the system is the same and is equal to V/F. Ideal plug flow bacterial bioreactors are only infrequently encountered, but non-ideal plug flow systems, with varying degrees of backmixing, are commonly encountered variants in activated sludge process technology. However, the closest approach to ideal plug flow operation is achieved in cascades (series) of more than six completely mixed tanks operating without intermediate feeds.

The previous paragraphs concern the liquid/bacteria phases in bioreactors, but in all aerobic systems one must, in addition, consider the gas phase, comprising either air or mixtures of air enriched with oxygen. As is clear to all operators of sparged bioreactors, the mean residence time of the gas phase is markedly less than that of the liquid/microbe phases. Hence, depending on the bioreactor configuration, mode of agitation and power input, a gas phase can be either in plug flow or completely mixed. The degree of mixing of the gas phase affects the driving force for gas–liquid mass transfer and has important implications with respect to gaseous substrate/nutrient conversion.

8.4.2 Growth in continuous flow bioreactors

From the viewpoint of describing bacterial growth in continuous flow bioreactors, it is stirred tank continuous flow systems which are completely mixed with respect to the macro-scale of mixing and operating under steady-state condition that are the most easily analysed. Essentially, the method of analysis that is adopted involves quantification of all processes that tend either to increase or to decrease the concentrations of bacteria, limiting substrate and products. As product production is not an objective of wastewater treatment, it will be ignored in the analysis presented here. A completely mixed continuous flow bioreactor in which bacteria are growing is shown diagrammatically in Fig. 8.3. It is assumed that the liquid volume in

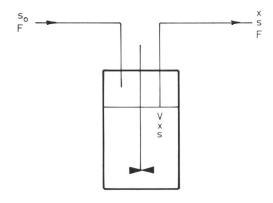

Fig. 8.3 — Continuous flow, completely mixed, stirred tank bioreactor showing flows and concentrations (symbols are defied in the text).

the bioreactor, V, and the liquid flow rates into and out of the bioreactor, F, are constant, i.e. no liquid utilisation, evaporation or accumulation occurs. The concentration of bacteria in the feed is assumed to be zero and in the bioreactor to be x. The corresponding concentrations of limiting substrate are assumed to be s_o and s, respectively.

Material balance equations for bacterial biomass and limiting substrate in such a system can be established by equating, during an infinitely short time interval, dt, the accumulation of either bacterial biomass or limiting substrate to the processes that tend to increase and decrease accumulation, i.e. production (growth), utilisation, inflow and outflow. Hence, for bacterial biomass, the material balance equation is:

$$Vdx = V\mu x dt - Fx dt \qquad (8.31)$$

where neither inflow nor utilisation is relevant, and for limiting substrate, the material balance equation is:

$$Vds = Fs_odt - Fsdt - V\mu xdt/Y_{x/s} \qquad (8.32)$$

where production is irrelevant. Dividing Equations 8.31 and 8.32 by Vdt gives

$$dx/dt = (\mu - D)x \qquad (8.33)$$

and

$$ds/dt = D(s_o - s) - \mu x/Y_{x/s} \qquad (8.34)$$

respectively, where $F/V = D$.

For steady-state operation, dx/dt and ds/dt will be zero, and expressing the steady state values of x and s as $\bar{x}$ and $\bar{s}$, respectively, Equation 8.33 can be written as

$$(\mu - D)\bar{x} = 0 \qquad (8.35)$$

or

$$\mu = D \qquad (8.36)$$

and Equation 8.34 can be written as

$$D(s_o - \bar{s}) - \mu\bar{x}/Y_{x/s} = 0 \qquad (8.37)$$

The Monod relationship, Equation 8.4, can be rewritten in terms of the steady-state limiting substrate concentration as:

$$\mu = \mu_m\bar{s}/(\bar{s} + K_s) \qquad (8.38)$$

Substituting D for μ from Equation 8.36 into Equation 8.38 and rearranging gives:

$$\bar{s} = K_sD/(\mu_m - D) \qquad (8.39)$$

Making the same substitution from Equation 8.36 into Equation 8.37 gives:

$$\bar{x} = Y_{x/s}(s_o - \bar{s}) \qquad (8.40)$$

Eliminating $\bar{s}$ from Equation 8.39 gives:

$$\bar{x} = Y_{x/s}[s_o - K_sD/(\mu_m - D)] \qquad (8.41)$$

A typical diagram of $\bar{x}$ and $\bar{s}$ with respect to D for a single-stage, completely mixed, continuous flow, bacterial bioreactor or chemostat is shown in Fig. 8.4, for the values of μ_m, $Y_{x/s}$ and s_o indicated in the figure caption. As can be seen, both $\bar{x}$ and $\bar{s}$ remain essentially constant for a wide

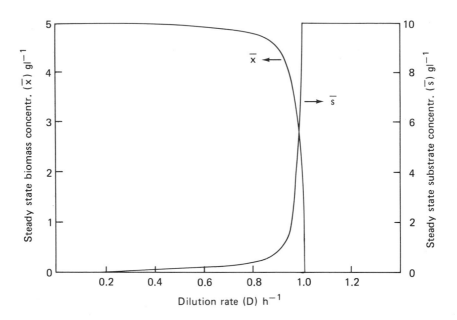

Fig. 8.4 — Theoretical relationships between the steady-state microbial biomass concentration, the steady-state limiting substrate concentration and the dilution rate for a simple chemostat ($\mu_m = 1.0 \text{ h}^{-1}$, $K_s = 0.1 \text{ g l}^{-1}$, $Y_{x/s} = 0.5$, and $s_o = 10 \text{ g l}^{-1}$).

range of dilution rates. However, when D approaches μ_m, a precipitous decrease in $\bar{x}$ and a simultaneous sharp increase, in $\bar{s}$, from close to zero concentration, occurs. The point at which $\bar{x}=0$ and $\bar{s}=s_o$ is the critical dilution rate, equal to the maximum value of the specific growth rate constant, above which complete washout occurs in perfectly mixed systems.

In practice, one rarely encounters perfect mixing, and hence it is important to account for segregation of parts of the growing microbial population, particularly the frequently observed phenomenon of wall growth. Many bacteria are able to adhere to and grow on solid surfaces. During long duration continuous cultures, bacterial build-up on the submerged surfaces of bioreactors almost inevitably occurs, and such wall growth modifies overall bioreactor performance characteristics. In many respects, retention of captive bacterial biomass in continuous flow bioreactors closely resembles continuous flow bioreactor operation with bacterial biomass recycle. It is particularly important, when undertaking biotreatability studies for specific wastewaters in non-biomass recycle type laboratory-scale bioreactors, to be aware of the potential effects of any wall growth. Failure to account for such effects can result in the undersizing of scaled-up units, particularly if geometrical similarity is maintained, because volume increases as the cube of the linear dimensions whereas surface area only increases as the square of the linear dimensions.

A simple model for wall growth can be established by assuming a situation where the process involves the growth of an active mono-layer of bacterial cells, on the surface of a nutrient-starved, constant thickness of non-growing biofilm from which, under equilibrium conditions, no net build-up of growing bacterial cells occurs and excess production after division is discharged into the bulk liquid. To illustrate the effects on performance of wall growth in a continuous flow bioreactor, it can be assumed that the growth rates of both the attached and the dispersed populations obey Monod-type saturation kinetics and that both growing populations exhibit the same specific growth rate constant. Hence, under steady-state conditions, the material balance equations for bacterial bio-mass and growth limiting substrate will be:

$$\mu \bar{x} + \mu \bar{x}_w - D\bar{x} = 0 \tag{8.42}$$

and

$$D(s_o - \bar{s}) - \mu(\bar{x} - \bar{x}_w)/Y_{x/s} = 0 \tag{8.43}$$

respectively, where $\bar{x}_w$ is the dry weight of growing attached bacterial cells per unit volume of liquid culture. Substituting Equation 8.42 into Equation 8.43 gives:

$$\bar{x} = Y_{x/s}(s_o - \bar{s}) \tag{8.44}$$

Substituting for x from Equation 8.44 and μ from the Monod relationship, Equation 8.38, into Equation 8.43 gives:

$$\bar{s}^2(DY_{x/s} - \mu_m Y_{x/s}) + \bar{s}(\mu_m \bar{x}_w + \mu_m Y_{x/s} s_o - DY_{x/s} s_o + DY_{x/s} K_s)$$
$$- DY_{x/s} s_o K_s = 0 \tag{8.45}$$

Equation 8.45 is a quadratic in terms of $\bar{s}$. However, when $D < \mu_m$, only one of the roots is positive and has a real meaning. The effect of wall growth on $\bar{x}$ and $\bar{s}$ is shown in Fig. 8.5 for the values of the constants listed in the figure caption.

Activated sludge biotreatment processes frequently comprise a series of stages (see Chapter 1), hence it is necessary to consider bacterial growth and limiting substrate utilisation in multi-stage systems both with and without intermediate feeds. Obviously, the simplest of such systems is one comprising two completely mixed bioreactors. In such systems, it should be noted that the liquid volume of the feed flow rate into and the limiting substrate concentrations in each stage are not necessarily identical. For the two-stage system, with each stage completely mixed, and intermediate feed, as shown in Fig. 8.6, the analysis to stage 1 is identical to that for a single-stage system as considered earlier. However, for the analysis of stage 2, it is necessary to consider inlet flows from two different sources, i.e. the outflow from stage 1,

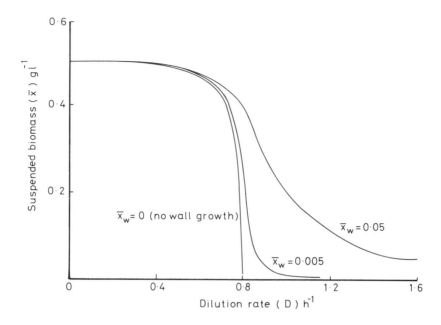

Fig. 8.5 — The effect of wall growth on the steady-state biomass concentration in a chemostat culture ($Y_{x/s} = 0.5$, $\mu_m = 0.8$ h^{-1}, $s_o = 1.0$ g l^{-1}, $K_s = 0.02$ g l^{-1}.

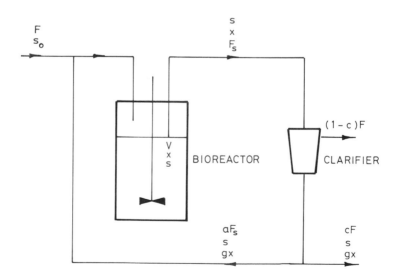

Fig. 8.6 — Continuous flow, completely mixed, stirred tank bioreactor with clarifier and recycle of a concentrated microbial biomass (symbols are defined in the text).

F_1, and the intermediate feed, F_{o2}, so that the dilution rate D_2 for stage 2 will be:

$$D_2 = (F_{o2}+F_1)/V_2 \qquad (8.46)$$

In an analogous manner to that used for the single-stage continuous flow bioreactor, material balance equations for bacterial biomass and limiting substrate can be established by equating accumulations against the increases and decreases occurring in an infinitely short time interval, dt. Hence, for bacterial biomass one has:

$$V_2dx_2 = V_2\mu_2x_2dt+F_1x_1dt-F_2x_2dt \qquad (8.47)$$

and for the growth limiting substrate one has:

$$V_2ds_2 = F_1s_1dt+F_{o2}s_{o2}dt-F_2s_2dt-V_2\mu_2x_2dt/Y_{x/s} \qquad (8.48)$$

where $F_2=F_{o2}+F_1$. Dividing Equations 8.47 and 8.48 by V_2dt gives:

$$dx_2/dt = \mu_2x_2 + F_1x_1/V_2 - D_2x_2 \qquad (8.49)$$

and

$$ds_2/dt = F_1s_1/V_2 + F_{o2}s_{o2}/V_2 - D_2s_2 - \mu_2x_2/Y_{x/s} \qquad (8.50)$$

For steady-state operation, Equations 8.49 and 8.50 can be rewritten as:

$$(\mu_2 - D_2)\bar{x}_2 + F_1\bar{x}_1/V_2 = 0 \qquad (8.51)$$

and

$$F_1s_1/V_2 + F_{o2}s_{o2}/V_2 - D_2\bar{s}_2 - \mu_2\bar{x}_2/Y_{x/s} = 0 \qquad (8.52)$$

respectively. From Equation 8.51,

$$\mu_2 = D_2 - F_1\bar{x}_1/V_2\bar{x}_2 \qquad (8.53)$$

and

$$\bar{x}_2 = F_1\bar{x}_1/V_2(D_2 - \mu_2) \qquad (8.54)$$

Equation 8.54 indicates that, in a two-stage system, provided $\bar{x}_1$ is finite, $\bar{x}_2$ will also be finite, irrespective of the value of D_2 employed, so that washout can only occur in stage 2 after washout has occurred in stage 1.

Substituting μ_2 from Equation 8.53 and $\bar{x}_1$ from Equation 8.40 into Equation 8.52 gives

$$\bar{x}_2 = Y_{x/s}F_1s_{o1}/V_2D_2 + F_{o2}s_{o2}/V_2D_2 - \bar{s}_2 = 0 \qquad (8.55)$$

By assuming Monod-type saturation kinetics in stage 2 and by substituting $\bar{x}_2$ from Equation 8.55, Equation 8.57 can be solved for $\bar{s}_2$.

For the special case where the two stages are of equal volume and where no intermediate feed is introduced, $F_{o2}/V_2 = 0$ and $F_1/V_2 = D_2$, so that Equation 8.55 becomes:

$$\bar{x}_2 = Y_{x/s}(s_{o1} - \bar{s}_2) \tag{8.56}$$

and Equation 8.53 becomes:

$$\mu_2 = D_2(\bar{x}_2 - \bar{x}_1)/\bar{x}_2 \tag{8.57}$$

In such a system, x_2 will not differ significantly from $\bar{x}_1$ and μ_2 will approach zero, for all conditions other than those existing either when D_1 approaches the critical value for washout or when inhibition is occurring.

For a series (cascade) of completely mixed stages which, in the absence of intermediate feeds, begins to approach the plug flow situation, the system will be operated close to the critical dilution rate for washout from each stage. Where the stages are each of equal volume, V, and the total number of stages is n, the overall dilution rate in such a system, D_T, will be:

$$D_T = F/nV \tag{8.58}$$

The most essential feature of continuous flow activated sludge processes is that the process comprises, in addition to an aerated bioreactor for biodegradation, an unaerated clarifier for biomass separation by gravity settling and a facility for recycling, from the clarifier to the bioreactor, settled (concentrated) microbial biomass. Hence, if continuous culture theory is to be applied to activated sludge processes, both the clarifier and the recycle loop must be incorporated in the analysis. Such a system, comprising a completely mixed bioreactor, a clarifier and a loop for partial biomass recycle, was first analysed by Herbert [8.3] and is shown in Fig. 8.6.

For such a system, the overall dilution rate, D, is F/V, where F is the liquid flow rate into and out of the whole system and V is the volume of the bioreactor. The liquid flow out of the bioreactor, F_s, is given by:

$$F_s = F/(1-a) \tag{8.59}$$

where a is the fraction of the bioreactor outflow that is recycled. If it is assumed that the bacteria biomass is concentrated by a factor g in the clarifier, the bacterial biomass recycled to the bioreactor is $aF_s gx$.

Material balance equations for bacterial biomass and limiting substrate can be established for the bioreactor in a similar manner as for non-biomass recycle bioreactors with the modification that any additions to the bioreactor by recycle must now be incorporated. For bacterial biomass, the accumulations during an infinitely short time interval dt can be expressed as:

$$Vdx = V\mu xdt - F_s xdt + aF_s gxdt \qquad (8.60)$$

and that for limiting substrate as:

$$Vds = Fs_o dt + aF_s sdt - F_s sdt - V\mu xdt/Y_{x/s} \qquad (8.61)$$

It should be noted that no concentration of soluble limiting substrate occurs during sedimentation and that the soluble limiting substrate concentration is identical in all process streams except the feeds to the overall system and to the bioreactor. Dividing Equations 8.60 and 8.61 by Vdt and substituting for F_s from Equation 8.59 gives:

$$dx/dt = \mu x - Dx/(1-a) + agDx/(1-a) \qquad (8.62)$$

and

$$ds/dt = D(s_o - s) - \mu x/Y_{x/s} \qquad (8.63)$$

Equation 8.63 is identical with Equation 8.34, i.e. the equation of a completely mixed bioreactor without bacterial biomass recycle. Under steady-state conditions $dx/dt=0$, so that Equation 8.62 can be rewritten as:

$$[\mu - D(1-ag)/(1-a)]\bar{x} = 0 \qquad (8.64)$$

Therefore

$$\mu = D(1-ag)/(1-a) \qquad (8.65)$$

Substituting for μ from the Monod relationship (Equation 8.38) gives:

$$\bar{s} = DK_s(1-ag)/[\mu_m(1-a) - D(1-ag)] \qquad (8.66)$$

Substituting μ from Equation 8.65 into the steady-state form of Equation 8.63 (i.e. Equation 8.37) gives:

$$\bar{x} = Y_{x/s}(s_o - \bar{s})(1-a)/(1-ag) \qquad (8.67)$$

A typical diagram of $\bar{x}$ and $\bar{s}$ with respect to D for a single-stage, completely mixed, continuous flow bioreactor with partial biomass recycle is shown in Fig. 8.7 for the values of μ_m, $Y_{x/s}$, s_o, a and g listed in the figure caption.

The steady-state concentration of biomass, hx, in the overflow stream from the clarifier can be obtained by establishing a bacterial biomass balance for the clarifier assuming neither liquid accumulation nor biological activity in the clarifier. Hence,

$$F_s\bar{x} = aF_s g\bar{x} + cFg\bar{x} + (1-c)Fh\bar{x} \qquad (8.68)$$

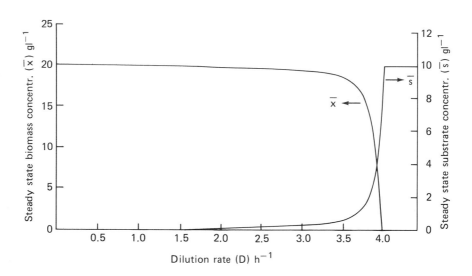

Fig. 8.7 — Theoretical relationships between the steady-state microbial biomass concentration, the steady-state limiting substrate concentration and the dilution rate for a chemostat with microbial biomass concentration and recycle ($\mu_m = 1.0 \text{ h}^{-1}$, $K_s = 0.1 \text{ g l}^{-1}$, $Y_{x/s} = 0.5$, $s_o = 10 \text{ g l}^{-1}$, $a = 0.2$ and $g = 4$).

where h is the factor by which the biomass concentration is reduced by settling and c is the fraction of the liquid flow through the system, F, that leaves the system with the waste bacterial biomass stream, Substituting for F_s from Equation 8.59 gives:

$$h = [(1-ag)-cg(1-a)]/(1-a)(1-c) \qquad (8.69)$$

8.5 PROCESS BIOLOGY OF ACTIVATED SLUDGE SYSTEMS

When one seeks to describe the process biology of activated sludge type biotreatment processes (see Chapter 1), numerous process features have to be taken account of in the analysis. These include:

(i)   bacterial growth with carbon dioxide and potential product production;

(ii)   co-oxidation and co-metabolism, involving no bacterial growth;

(iii)   yield coefficient variability, as a result of changing environmental conditions;

(iv)   substrate or nutrient microbe interactions, based on substrate or nutrient affinities;

(v)   multiple and variable growth limiting substrates and nutrients, serving identical physiological functions;

(vi)   solid and/or immiscible substrates;

(vii)   physico-chemical imbalances in process feeds;
(viii)   restricted availability of essential nutrients;
(ix)   growth inhibition by toxic pollutants;
(x)   maintenance energy requirements;
(xi)   death, lysis and 'cryptic' growth;
(xii)   flocculent growth and floc breakage;
(xiii)   flocculation of particulate and colloidal substrates and/or nutrients and non-biodegradable matter;
(xiv)   simultaneous and/or sequential heterotrophic and autotrophic growth and mixotrophy;
(xv)   variable nitrogen metabolism;
(xvi)   incomplete mixing and segregation;
(xvii)   oxygen gradients;
(xviii)   sequences of operating conditions;
(xix)   variations in volumetric flow rates;
(xx)   variations in feed compositions;
(xxi)   biological activity during biomass settling and recycle;
(xxii)   protozoan predation;
(xxiii)   exo-enzyme activity;
(xxiv)   non-biological, biomass associated, removal mechanisms;
(xxv)   non-biological, equipment or system associated, removal mechanisms;
(xxvi)   the use of lumped parameters instead of individual pollutant concentrations.

Such a list can only be incomplete, but it serves to emphasise the complexity of activated sludge processes and the numerous process features that must be considered when one seeks to establish realistic equations that effectively describe overall process operation and which can provide an effective basis for process design.

Clearly, applying appropriate parts of the growth theory discussed earlier, the effects of many of these features of activated sludge processes can be evaluated. Unfortunately, an overall general lack of real process data, particularly rate constants, exists and a completely comprehensive model embracing a broad spectrum of the listed features has yet to be developed. However, some individual features have been examined in isolation. For example, Hamer and co-workers have examined flocculent growth with recycle coupled with the question of viability [8.30; 8.31], of either interaction or neutralism [8.32], of death, lysis and 'cryptic' growth [8.33–8.35], of temperature effects and particulate substrate utilisation [8.36], of mixed substrates [8.37] and of biological activity in clarifiers [8.38], but these approaches only represent the 'tip of the iceberg'.

Some 15 years ago, Pirt [8.39] made a plea for increased expenditure on microbiological research oriented towards wastewater treatment processes. Regrettably, this plea has been very largely ignored in spite of the undoubted importance of the wastewater treatment as the single most efficient means for maintaining the quality of natural water resources. To develop effective solutions for some of the challenges of the present and the future, recently discussed by Stumm [8.40], will require much improved understanding of the process microbiology of biotreatment systems.

REFERENCES

[8.1] Monod, J. (1950) La technique de culture continue; théorie et applications. *Ann. Inst. Pasteur,* **79**, 390–410.

[8.2] Novick, A. and Szilard, L. (1950) Description of the chemostat. *Science,* **112**, 715–716.

[8.3] Herbert, D. (1961) A theoretical analysis of continuous culture systems. *Soc. Chem. Ind. Monograph No. 12*, 21–53.

[8.4] Málek, I. and Fencl, Z. (1966) *Theoretical and Methodological Basis of Continuous Culture of Microorganisms,* Czechoslovak Academy of Sciences.

[8.5] Pirt, S. J. (1975) *Principles of Microbe and Cell Cultivation*, Blackwell, Oxford, UK.

[8.6] Committee on Water Polution Management (1980) Engineering design variables for the activated sludge process. *J. Environ. Engng Div., Proc. ASCE,* **106**, 473–503.

[8.7] Winkler, M. (1981) *Biological Treatment of Wastewater*, Ellis Horwood, Chichester, UK.

[8.8] Cooper, P. F. and Atkinson, B. (eds) (1981) *Biological Fluidized Bed Treatment of Water and Wastewater*, Ellis Horwood, Chichester, UK.

[8.9] Antonie, R. L., Kluge, D. L. and Mielke, J. H. (1974) Evaluation of a rotating disk wastewater treatment plant. *J. Wat. Pollut. Contr. Fed.,* **46**, 498–511.

[8.10] Stuckey, D. C. (1982) Anaerobic treatment of industrial wastewater in developing nations. In *Management of Industrial Wastewater in Developing Nations*, Stuckey, D. C. and Hamza, A. (eds), Pergamon Press, Oxford, UK.

[8.11] Ardern, E. and Lockett, W. T. (1914) Experiments on the oxidation of sewage without the aid of filters. *J. Soc. Chem. Ind.,* **33**, 1–19.

[8.12] Marshall, V. C. (1974) Water borne waste: Report of the Institution of Chemical Engineers Working Party. *Chem. Eng.,* suppl., 1–67.

[8.13] Reeve, D. A. D. (1973) Secondary treatment. In *Advances in Sewage Treatment*, Institution of Civil Engineers, pp. 27–38.

[8.14] Irvine, R. L., Alleman, J. E., Miller, G. and Dennis, R. W. (1980) Stoichiometry and kinetics of biological waste treatment. *J. Wat. Pollut. Contr. Fed.,* **52**, 1997–2006.

[8.15] Monod, J. (1942) *Recherches sur la Croissance des Cultures Bactériennes*. Hermann, Paris.

[8.16] Herbert, D. (1976) Stoichiometric aspects of microbial growth. In *Continuous Culture 6*, SCI/Ellis Horwood, Chichester, UK, pp. 1–30.

[8.17] Powell, E. O. (1967) The growth rate of micro-organisms as a function of substrate concentration. In *Microbial Physiology and Continuous Culture,* Powell, E. O., Evans, C. G. T., Strange, R. E. and Tempest, D. W. (eds), HMSO, London, pp. 34–55.

[8.18] Mechsner, K. and Hamer, G. (1985) Denitrification by methanotrophic/methylotrophic bacterial associations in aquatic environments. In *Denitrification in the Nitrogen Cycle,* Golterman, H. L. (ed.), Plenum Publ. Corp., pp. 257–271.

[8.19] Lewis, W. K. and Whitman, W. G. (1924) Principles of gas absorption, *Ind. Engng. Chem.,* **16**, 1215–1221.

[8.20] Drozd, J. W., Linton, J. D., Downs, J. and Stephenson, R. J. (1978) An *in situ* assessment of the specific lysis rate in continuous cultures of *Methylococcus* sp. (NCIB 11083) grown on methane. *FEMS Microbiol. Lett., 4,* 311–314.

[8.21] Ash, S. G. (1979) Adhesion of microorganisms in fermentation processes. In *Adhesion of Microorganisms to Surfaces,* Ellwood, D. C., Melling, J. and Rutter, P. R. (eds), Academic Press, London, pp. 57–86.

[8.22] Characklis, W. G. (1978) Microbial reaction rate expressions. *J. Environ. Engng Div., Proc. ASCE,* **104**, 531–534.

[8.23] Yoon, H., Klinzing, G. and Blanch, H. W. (1977) Competition for mixed substrates by microbial populations. *Biotechnol. Bioengng,* **19**, 1193–1210.

[8.24] Zlokarnik, M. (1983) Bioengineering aspects of aerobic waste water purifications: developments and trends. *Ger. Chem. Engng,* **6**, 183–197.

[8.25] Foster, J. W. (1963) Hydrocarbons as substrates for microorganisms. *Antonie van Leeuwenhoek,* **28**, 241–274.

[8.26] Jensen, R. A. (1963) Carbon nutrition of some microorganisms decomposing halogen-substituted aliphatic acids. *Acta Agric. Scand.,* **13**, 404–412.

[8.27] Stirling, D. I. and Dalton, H. (1979) The fortuitous oxidation and cometabolism of various carbon compounds by whole cell suspension of *Methylococcus capsulatus* (Barth). *FEMS Microbiol. Lett.,* **5**, 315–318.

[8.28] Jones, G. L. (1973) Bacterial growth kinetics: measurement and significance in the activated sludge process. *Water Res.,* **7**, 1475–1492.

[8.29] Pike, E. B. and Curds, C. R. (1971) The microbial ecology of activated sludge processes. *Soc. Appl. Bacteriol. Symp. Ser.,* **1**, 123–147.

[8.30] Hamer, G. (1983) The application of continuous culture theory to activated sludge processes. *Chem. Ing. Tech.,* **55**, 478–479.

[8.31] Hamer, G. (1983) A biotechnological approach to the treatment of wastewater from petrochemicals manufacture. *Instn Chem. Engrs Symp. Ser.,* **77**, 87–101.

[8.32] Hamer, G. (1984) Continuous culture kinetics and activated sludge processes. In *Continuous Culture 8*, SCI/Ellis Horwood, Chichester, UK, pp. 169–184.

[8.33] Hamer, G. (1985) Lysis and 'cryptic' growth in wastewater and sludge treatment processes. *Acta Biotechnol.*, **5**, 117–127.

[8.34] Mason, C. A., Bryers, J. D. and Hamer, G. (1986) Activity, death and lysis during microbial growth in a chemostat. *Chem. Engng Commun.*, **45**, 163–176.

[8.35] Mason, C. A., Hamer, G. and Bryers, J. D. (1982) The death and lysis of microorganisms in environmental processes. *FEMS Microbiol. Rev.*, **39**, 373–410.

[8.36] Hamer, G. and Bryers, J. D. (1985) Aerobic thermophilic sludge treatment: some biotechnological concepts. *Conservation & Recycling*, **8**, 267–284.

[8.37] Hamer, G., Egli, T. and Mechsner, K. (1985) Biological treatment of industrial wastewater: a microbiological basis for process performance. *J. Appl. Bacteriol. Symp. Suppl.*, **59**, 1275–1405.

[8.38] Hamer, G. (1986) Incompatibilities between process biology and performance in activated sludge processes. *Instn Chem. Engrs Symp. Ser.*, **96**, 19–32.

[8.39] Pirt, S. J. (1972) The microbiological means for the improvement of effluent purification. In *Association of River Authorities Year Book*, pp. 119–123.

[8.40] Stumm, W. (1986) Water, an endangered ecosystem. *Ambio*, **15**, 201–207.

9

Cell immobilisation

Colin Webb
Department of Chemical Engineering UMIST, Manchester, UK

NOMENCLATURE

Symbol	Definition	Dimensions
A_f	surface area of microbial film	L^2
D	dilution rate	T^{-1}
f_p	fraction of the reactor occupied by particles	—
$k_L a$	volumetric oxygen transfer coefficient	T^{-1}
K_m	Monod coefficient	$M L^{-3}$
L	film thickness	L
m_p	amount of biomass associated with a particle	M
n	Richardson–Zaki exponent	—
n_p	number of particles per unit reactor volume	L^{-3}
ΔP	pressure drop	$M L^{-1} T^{-2}$
r_s	radius of solid support particle	L
R	specific rate of reaction	T^{-1}
R_f	specific rate of reaction for microbial film	T^{-1}
R_p	specific rate of reaction for a particle	T^{-1}
R_s	specific rate of reaction for freely suspended cells	T^{-1}
R_v	volumetric rate of reaction	$M L^{-3} T^{-1}$
S_{in}	inlet concentration of limiting substrate	$M L^{-3}$
U	superficial liquid velocity	$L T^{-1}$
U_i	superficial liquid velocity at infinite dilution	$L T^{-1}$
U_{mf}	minimum fluidising velocity	$L T^{-1}$
V_i	total volume of immobilised aggregates within a reactor	L^3
V_l	liquid volume within a reactor	L^3
V_R	volume of the reaction zone within a reactor	L^3
V_T	total volume of reactor	L^3

V_v	void volume	L^3
x	concentration of freely suspended cells	$M\,L^{-3}$
Y_c	yield of cells from glucose	—
ε	bed voidage	—
λ	effectiveness factor	—
μ	specific growth rate	T^{-1}
μ_{max}	maximum specific growth rate	T^{-1}
ρ	liquid density	$M\,L^{-3}$
ρ_{bw}	wet biomass density	$M\,L^{-3}$
ρ_f	density of biofilm	$M\,L^{-3}$
ρ_{pw}	net particle density	$M\,L^{-3}$
ρ_s	solids density	$M\,L^{-3}$

9.1 INTRODUCTION

When a microbial population exists in the form of single cells dispersed throughout a liquid medium, its physical behaviour is governed by the properties of the bulk liquid. In other words the individual cells behave as elements of the fluid within which they are suspended. Hence, when process liquors are removed from a vessel containing such a dispersed microbial population, a proportion of the total cell population will also be removed. This represents a severe limitation to the operation of such systems, since it is often desirable that the cells be retained for further (continuous or repeated batch) use. In order that cells can be retained they must be separated from the bulk liquor. This can most readily be achieved if the cells can be arranged so as to exhibit physical (hydrodynamic) characteristics which differ from those of the bulk liquor, in which case they can be thought of as being immobilised.

Cell immobilisation, then, is the process by which cells are confined to a certain defined region of space in such a way as to exhibit hydrodynamic characteristics which differ from those of the surrounding environment. This is most usually achieved by significantly increasing the effective size or density of the cells by aggregation or by attachment of the cells to some support surface. Thus flocculated cells in the form of large aggregates where cells are attached to others can be considered to be immobilised if the flocs can be readily separated from the bulk liquid by relatively coarse screens or by rapid sedimentation. Cells which are attached to solid particles of sufficiently high relative density to enable their ready separation from the bulk liquid are another example of immobilised cells.

The immobilisation of cells can be a natural process (both of the above examples commonly occur in nature) or can be induced by chemical or physical means but, in general, if advantage is to be taken of the properties of immobilised cells then some provision has to be made to promote or encourage the immobilisation. It is the development of techniques to effect this artificial or induced immobilisation that has caused the recent massive increase in awareness of the advantages that immobilised cells can offer in the operation of biological reactors. This does not mean that the exploitation of immobilised cells is new. Thus, the biological treatment of wastewaters has for some considerable time been aided by the presence of immobilised cells attached as films to solid surfaces in trickle filters and high rate filters (see Chapter 1), and the traditional process for industrial vinegar production involves *Acetobacter* cells immobilised on birch twigs. These processes, however, are examples of cases where immobilisation occurs naturally. It is now possible to immobilise any species of micro-organism, or indeed tissue cells, and it is this ability which is responsible for the sudden escalation in reported applications of immobilised cells in recent years [9.1]. Even in the case of wastewater treatment recent advances have enabled considerable improvements to be made to the conventional immobilised cell processes by increasing the specific surface area of supports in the system [9.2].

This chapter describes some of the techniques which can be used to achieve cell immobilisation and discusses the characteristics of immobilised cells. Due to the range of forms that immobilised cells can take, a wide variety of reactor configurations has evolved for use with different systems, and these will be considered together with some general performance characteristics. A detailed review of the literature concerning cell immobilisation will not be attempted here. There are a number of excellent reviews available, the most extensive and useful being that by Karel *et al.* [9.3]. For further detail the reader is also directed to two texts specifically concerned with immobilised cells, those of Cooper and Atkinson [9.2] which deals with biological fluidised beds for wastewater treatment, and of Webb *et al.* [9.4] which deals with engineering aspects of immobilised cell systems.

9.1.1 Why immobilised cells?

In principle cell immobilisation allows biological particles of any size, shape and density to be produced for a wide variety of both prokaryotes and eukaryotes. One of the major features of most immobilisation processes is the very high concentration of cells that can be achieved and this, combined with the ability to handle immobilised cells distinguishably from the fluid phase, offers a number of possibilities for process engineering improvements, namely:

(a) Continuous reactor operation at any desired liquid throughput without risk of cell washout. Immobilised cells can be retained in the reactor while the liquid phase is continuously passed through, enabling growth rate to be controlled independently of throughput. It is therefore feasible to operate continuously even with non-growing cells, an impossibility with freely dispersed cells.
(b) Increased overall productivity. This is a direct consequence of retaining a high concentration of cells in the reactor.
(c) Easy cell/liquid separation. Coarse screening or rapid gravity settling

enables liquid to be removed from a reactor vessel without removal of cells. This leads to the possibility of (d).

(d) Repeated batch operation using the same cells. Processed liquor can be drained at the end of a batch and the vessel recharged with fresh medium.

(e) Enhanced gas–liquid mass transfer. Viscosity problems often associated with high concentrations of dispersed cells are removed by immobilisation, enabling better gas–liquid mass transfer to be achieved. Similarly heat transfer to or from the bulk liquid can be improved.

(f) Plug flow operation. It is possible to maintain immobilised cells as a stationary phase in, for example, a packed bed and to pass process fluid through the reactor in a plug flow mode.

In addition to the above there are a number of other features of immobilisation which may lead to further possibilities. An immobilised cell system can, for example, withstand large fluctuations in liquid loading with no appreciable change in cell concentration. This offers the added possibility of controlling contamination in pure culture systems by 'washing out' the intruding species, enabling essentially non-aseptic operation. It is also possible that more than one species can be immobilised (independently if necessary) and used together in the same reactor so that a controlled mixed culture can be sustained. This offers the further possibility of the spatial location of different species in different parts of a reactor, the species performing different duties. Finally, since immobilised cells can readily be separated from the fluid phase, they may provide a convenient form of storage for large quantities of cells which can be brought into action almost immediately as required.

It should be pointed out at this stage that, although cell immobilisation can offer considerable advantage over freely suspended cell systems, there are limitations to the above claims. The existence of cells in high localised concentrations, for example, can result in considerably lower specific rates of reaction due to diffusional limitations, hence limiting the extent to which the overall rate of reaction can be increased. It can also lead to changes in metabolism and physiology resulting in poor productivity, or in the case of natural mixed cultures (as in wastewater treatment) to changes in the composition of the microbial population with possible undesirable effects. Immobilised cells are generally more expensive to prepare than freely suspended cells, since some form of support usually has to be supplied and reactor configurations are often more complex. It is therefore necessary that the various features of immobilisation referred to above be considered on merit for any given application.

9.2 TECHNIQUES FOR CELL IMMOBILISATION

A wide variety of immobilisation techniques has been developed, many of them taken directly from immobilised enzyme technology. To a certain extent the choice of technique is governed by the desired physiological state of the cells and the purpose to which they are to be put. Fig. 9.1 shows the range of physiological states of immobilised cells. It will be clear that some techniques will not be suitable for the whole range, while other techniques are equally applicable to the immobilisation of cells in any physiological state. The numerous techniques for achieving immobilisation can be divided according to the physical process involved, namely attachment, entrapment, containment, and aggregation. An important distinction should, however, be made between those techniques which allow the cells to become immobilised as a natural consequence of growth by simply providing a suitable surface/support, and those for which the cell population has to be pregrown and subsequently 'actively' treated in order to effect the immobilisation. Generally, 'active' techniques are more widely applicable and can be used for cells in any physiological state. 'Natural' techniques, on the other hand, involve no special input from the operator and are therefore generally easier and cheaper. Some of the more widely used techniques will now be described under the four major categories listed above, which are represented diagramatically in Fig. 9.2.

9.2.1 Attachment

All forms of immobilisation in which cells are in some way bound to the surface of a solid support come within this category. The attachment may rely on the forces of natural adhesion or be induced by chemical means.

Natural adhesion of cells to surfaces is a widespread phenomenon and has been the subject of many studies, although the mechanisms involved are still not fully understood [9.5]. It provides one of the simplest techniques for cell immobilisation and is the method used in both of the oldest industrial immobilised cell systems, vinegar production [9.6] and wastewater treatment [9.7]. Systems developed more recently prefer the use of particulate solid supports, often of material such as sand which, when used in a fluidised bed, for example, provide a greatly increased surface area for attachment per unit volume of reactor than in either of the traditional processes. The support particles, which are normally less than 1 mm in diameter, are simply placed in the reactor which is then inoculated (or seeded) in the normal way. Cells naturally adhere to the solid surfaces and establish an active film as they grow. The film thickness may be as little as a monolayer of cells, as often is the case when animal tissue cells are thus immobilised [9.8], or may be as much as several millimetres as shown in Fig. 9.3 for wastewater treatment organisms. Cells which do not naturally adhere to surfaces can sometimes be encouraged to attach by chemical means such as cross-linking by glutaraldehyde or silanisation to silica supports, or by chelation to metal oxides [9.3]. In such cases strength of attachment is similar to that in natural adhesion.

Attached cells are in direct contact with the surrounding environment and hence subject to any forces of shear or attrition which may result from the relative motion of particles and fluid. It is therefore likely that some cells will become detached and enter the bulk fluid phase, so this technique is unsuitable in situations where a cell-free liquor is required. It is also difficult

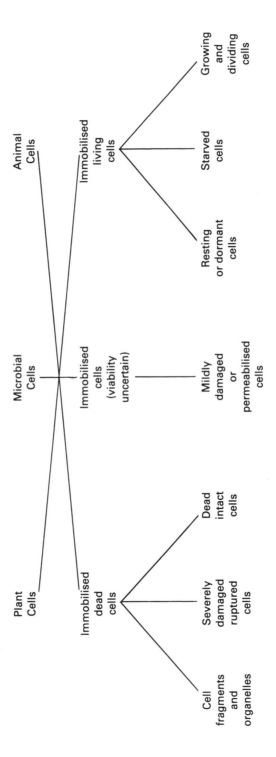

Fig. 9.1 — Physiological states of immobilised cells [9.71].

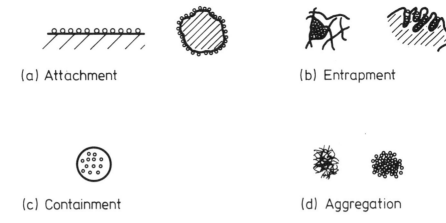

(a) Attachment   (b) Entrapment

(c) Containment   (d) Aggregation

Fig. 9.2 — Immobilisation processes.

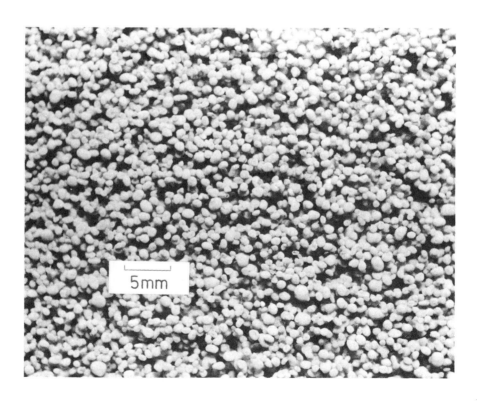

Fig. 9.3 — Wastewater treatment organisms immobilised by attachment to sand
particles in a biological fluidised bed.

to control or even determine the depth of the biofilm and this can be a future drawback with such systems.

The art of cell immobilisation by attachment is to provide the right surface in a suitable form for commercial use and colonised by the desired organism or population of organisms in as high a density as is possible [9.9]. The strategy needed for the selection of a support material for cell immobilisation has been reviewed very adequately by Kolot [9.10] and together with the review by Gerson and Zajic [9.11] provides information of the type needed to make the selection for a specific type of cell.

9.2.2   Entrapment

Cells can be entrapped within a variety of porous structures which are either preformed or formed *in situ* around the cells. Entrapment within preformed structures usually occurs as a natural consequence of cell growth and so, like natural attachment, the effectiveness of the immobilisation varies with cell type and support type. Porous structures which are formed *in situ,* on the other hand, can be used to immobilise almost any type of cell, though the conditions under which the support particle is formed may be harmful to the cells in some cases.

Techniques involving natural entrapment of cells within preformed porous structures are very similar to those used for natural attachment. The cells are allowed to diffuse into the pores of the structure and as they grow it becomes increasingly difficult for them to leave the pores and they become effectively entrapped. This can occur on a microscopic level with microporous particles such as brick, coke, ceramics, sintered glass or kieselguhr, where the sizes of the pores are similar in magnitude to those of the cells, or on a macroscopic level with particles having large pores (in excess of 0.1 mm). An example of such large pore particles are the Biomass Support Particles (BSPs) developed by Atkinson *et al.* [9.12]. These particles are large open structures fabricated from either knitted stainless steel wire crushed into spheres (Fig. 9.4a) or reticulated polyurethane foams cut into cuboid shapes (Fig. 9.4b). Immobilisation of such particles relies to a certain extent on the ability of the cells either to flocculate or to adhere to the strands of support material within the structure and should be considered as a 'cage-entrapment' process rather than pore-entrapment. The use of such BSPs for a range of applications has been summarised by Black and Webb [9.13]. Fig. 9.5 shows a porous BSP filled with a mixed microbial culture taken from an operating CAPTOR wastewater treatment plant [9.14] (see also Chapter 1). Naturally entrapped cells are protected from the shear field outside the particles but are not confined to the particle by any barrier. It is not therefore likely that the process fluid in such systems would be cell-free, but an advantage of this form of immobilisation is that cell growth can be controlled such that any cells growing beyond the boundaries of the particle are abraded by the flow field surrounding the particle or by particle–particle contact.

The most popular form of cell immobilisation currently in use, at least in the research laboratory, involves entrapment of cells within porous struc-

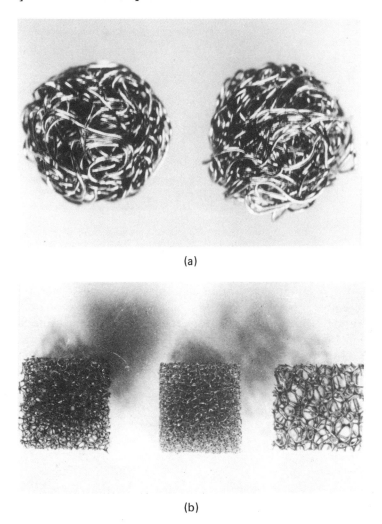

(a)

(b)

Fig. 9.4 — Porous biomass support particles (BSPs): (a) stainless steel spheres
(6 mm); (b) polyurethane foam cubes (6 mm).

tures which are formed *in situ* around the cells. The cells, in the form of a
slurry or paste, are generally mixed with a compound which is then gelled to
form a porous matrix under conditions sufficiently mild so as not to affect the
viability of the cells. The earliest use of such gel-entrapment involved the
polymerisation of acrylamide using a cross-linking monomer [9.15]. Unfortunately the treatment can be a little harsh due to the toxicity of the
monomer. Other synthetic polymers have also been used to effect this form
of immobilisation, but the majority of techniques involving *in situ* entrapment nowadays make use of polysaccharide gels [9.9]. Of these, which
include kappa-carrageenan, agar and alginates, calcium alginate gel is the
most popular.

Fig. 9.5 — Wastewater treatment organisms immobilised in porous biomass support particles as used in the CAPTOR process.

To entrap cells within calcium alginate could hardly be a simpler or gentler process [9.16; 9.17]. Cells are stirred into sodium alginate solution and the mixture extruded into a solution of a calcium salt. Surface gelation is instant but it is wise to leave gels for a least 20 min to allow complete gelation of the alginate to occur. Fig. 9.6 shows some calcium alginate beads.

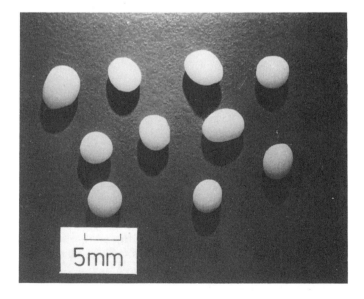

Fig. 9.6 — Calcium alginate gel beads containing yeast cells.

Protecting materials, such as osmotica or substrates, may be included in the alginate and calcium salt solutions. No heat treatment whatsoever is required and immobilised cells retain very high activities [9.16; 9.18]. The shortcomings of calcium alginate as an immobilisation medium are that gels can be destroyed when contacted with streams containing calcium chelators such as phosphate, and that it is relatively difficult to produce beads of calcium alginate with diameters of less than 5 mm.

Gel entrapment provides a controlled means of achieving what is quite a common occurrence in nature for certain organisms, e.g. slime-forming bacteria. The physical properties of gels are not dissimilar to such slimes, but whereas only a few species will form slimes, almost any organism can be immobilised by gel-entrapment. The gel is extruded either as droplets (to form beads of around 5 mm diameter) or in other desired shapes (e.g. 0.5 mm diameter 'mini-cylinders' [9.19]) or is set in sheets and then cut to the desired shape and size. Gel particles thus formed can be used in a wide variety of reactor configurations ranging from packed beds to stirred tanks. Cell growth within the particles can occur, though if the cell concentration exceeds approximately 30% v/v the gel will lose its integrity [9.20]. Gas evolution within the gels can also be a cause of particle disruption [9.19].

9.2.3 Containment

This category of immobilisation involves the containment of cells behind a barrier, either preformed or formed *in situ*. The barrier may be as simple as an interface between two immiscible liquids [9.21], in which case the cell suspension is emulsified with an organic solvent and resuspended as droplets in an aqueous phase. Pre-formed barriers include the semi-permeable membranes used for microfiltration and ultrafiltration [9.22]. Nutrients are able to diffuse to the cells retained behind the membrane.

The major applications of contained cells arise from the ability with such systems to maintain completely cell-free process liquors, and are mainly in the area of mammalian tissue cell culture [9.23].

9.2.4 Aggregation

By flocculating to form large aggregates, cells may become immobilised in the sense that it then becomes possible to retain them in continuously operated bioreactors, for example in the form of packed or fluidised beds. Natural flocculation of yeast cells occurs towards the end of fermentation and such immobilised cells have been exploited in beer production using tower fermenters [9.24]. Fungal mycelia also form aggregates in the shape of spherical pellets [9.25] and flocculation is a key feature of the activated sludge process for wastewater treatment [9.26]. Artificial flocculants may also be used to enhance the aggregation, though the mechanisms involved in flocculation are as yet still poorly understood [9.27].

9.3 REACTOR CONFIGURATIONS FOR IMMOBILISED CELLS

The first rational development of an immobilised cell reactor was probably that of Pasteur, who proposed an acetifier where the *Acetobacter* cells were immobilised on the surface of wood chips. This type of biological reactor, the trickling filter, is still used today for vinegar production and for wastewater treatment and is shown schematically in Fig. 9.7a (see also Chapter 1).

The majority of all current bioreactors are batch stirred tanks. However, the concept of cell immobilisation is intrinisically linked to continuous operation. Also the use of immobilised cell particles in a stirred tank often leads to particle break-up. In this context there is a need to develop novel reactor configurations suitable for use with immobilised cells. In contrast with the large amount of literature published in recent years on techniques for whole cell immobilisation, there is surprisingly little detailed analysis of immobilised cell reactors.

A multiplicity of factors influences the choice of reactor type for a particular process. These include immobilisation method, particle characteristics, (e.g. shape, size, density, robustness), nature of substrate, inhibitory effects and hydrodynamic and economic considerations. Immobilised cell reactors may be operated either batchwise or continuously, though in general, there are limited advantages for batch operation [9.28]. Continuous systems may be operated in a plug flow mode or may be completely mixed. Completely mixed reactors are usually advantageous if high substrate concentrations inside the fermenter are to be avoided due to substrate inhibition, though they are not particularly suitable for product inhibited reactions, as all cells are exposed to inhibitory levels of product. Plug flow reactors are difficult to supply with sufficient oxygen and are difficult to control.

9.3.1   Stirred tank reactors (STR)

The major problem encountered with the use of immobilised cell particles in STRs is related to the harsh treatment to which the particles are exposed. A high rate of shear may have severely damaging effects, especially in the case of gel particles. Modifications to classical STRs, e.g. enveloping the agitator in a porous mesh, can be made to allow mixing without destruction of the immobilised aggregates. The basket reactor shown in Fig. 9.7b, of which only laboratory applications are known, was developed in an attempt to protect catalyst particles from the disruptive action of the agitator. The catalyst is retained in mesh baskets that form the blades of the impeller. This gives good mixing and offers protection from attrition. Such adaptations allow the use of existing reactors but are not as satisfactory as the rational design of a purpose-built reactor.

9.3.2   Fixed bed reactors

Packed bed reactors are very common and, at least at laboratory scale, convenient to use. They usually provide the tool for the first test of the applicability of cells immobilised by novel techniques. They are, however, difficult to scale up and to quantify. Plug flow packed bed reactors operated on a once-through basis may offer high rates of reaction due to high substrate concentration but have relatively poor mass and heat transfer coefficients due to low liquid velocities. Packed bed fermenters with recycle show improved mass and heat transfer characteristics, plus improved controllability.

The size of the particulate carrier affects both pressure drop and internal diffusion resistance, see Fig. 9.7c. In well mixed packed bed reactors a compromise is sought for each process between pumping costs and mass transfer limitations. Qualitative factors like ease of handling may play a role in choosing the 'best' particle size. The size distribution should be as uniform as possible since pressure drop depends upon bed voidage.

Particle compression caused by the static weight of the bed and the pressure due to flow is usually a severe drawback in packed beds of gel particles. Compression leads to a considerable decrease of the bed voidage and consequent increase in the pressure drop across the bed. The compaction of the bed can also reduce drastically the activity of the immobilised cells due to the consequent decrease in the specific surface area of the particles presented to the fluid.

Particulate substrates may exclude the use of a packed bed due to plugging and channelling problems. Packed bed reactors can also present considerable drawbacks in three-phase operation. Gas–liquid contact is restricted, as is the release of gas from the voids of the bed. The release of gas is often observed to be slow, leading to gas accumulation in the form of stagnant slugs. This can cause gas flooding which in turn produces poor liquid distribution and hence poor performance [9.29].

In Japan, the Research Association for Petroleum Alternative Development (RAPAD) has developed two continuous pilot plant immobilised whole cell processes for the production of power alcohol from molasses [9.30]. One of these uses yeast cells entrapped in a photo-crosslinkable (polyethylene glycol) resin formed in the shape of sheets. These (0.8 to 1.0 mm thick) are arranged vertically in a parallel flow type reactor shown schematically in Fig. 9.7d. Such a novel fixed bed reactor, in spite of its reduced surface area when compared to particulate beds, can give high productivities. Its improved performance can be attributed to its open structure which allows good gas release and prevents blockage.

The rotating disc fermenter is an attached film fermenter developed for the cultivation of mycelial fungi [9.31]. The mycelia grow on the surfaces of a series of vertical polypropylene discs which rotate half-submerged in the culture medium, see Fig. 9.7e. The system can be operated aseptically and has been tested using a wide range of filamentous fungi.

By encouraging the natural attachment of the fungi, disc fermenters offer potential for the exploitation of filamentous organisms which are otherwise associated with high non-Newtonian viscosities in suspended cultures (with detrimental effects on the gas–liquid mass transfer rates). For instance, good performance in the production of citric acid by *Aspergillus niger* has been reported [9.32].

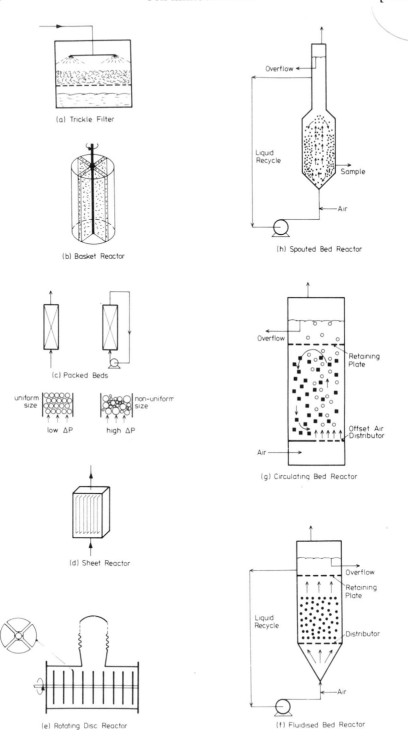

Fig. 9.7 — Immobilised cell reactors.

9.3.3   Fluidised bed reactors (FBR)

Fluidised bed reactors, in which particles become suspended as a result of the upflow of the fluid phase (usually a mixture of gas and liquid), have been the focus of much attention recently. Biological fluidised bed treatment of water and wastewater is a particular application of interest in which solid particles, e.g. sand, or porous particles (BSPs), can be used [9.2]. The use of FBRs has also been explored for aseptic systems [9.30; 9.33; 9.34] and Fig. 9.7f shows a fluidised bed fermenter.

The information available on biological fluidised bed behaviour is limited, while modelling is difficult. The problem is aggravated by the presence of a third phase. Despite these difficulties FBRs combine some of the advantages of STRs and packed beds and have few of their drawbacks. Their attractive features include good mixing and mass transfer properties. In three-phase operation gas–liquid contact and gas removal are facilitated as compared to packed beds. These are important characteristics for work with living cells. Thus higher volumetric oxygen transfer coefficients can be attained and gas flooding avoided. Cell density per unit reactor volume is potentially less in a FBR than in a packed bed due to packing considerations. However, the overall performance may be higher in the FBR due to operational conditions.

An interesting aspect of the fluid mechanics of three-phase fluidised systems is that gas hold-up shows a marked variation with particle size, particle density and fluid flow rates. The work on this facet of three-phase fluidisation was pioneered by Ostergaard in Denmark. For instance, gas hold-up and bubble size in beds of 1, 3 and 6 mm glass ballotini were measured and compared with those in the corresponding solids-free system (using a porous plate aerator). It was found that gas–liquid transfer is favoured in beds of 6 mm particles due to bubble break-up and greater gas hold-up [9.35; 9.36]. In this context there are reasons to justify consideration of particle size as a parameter in fluidised bed design, as well as concerning oneself with the biological limitations on particle size.

Particle density will also be an important parameter affecting pumping costs and mass transfer coefficients. The theoretical work (by means of dimensional analysis) of Riba [9.37] on mass transfer from a fixed sphere to a liquid in a fluidised bed suggested that the mass transfer coefficient (in the Sherwood number) depends upon the difference in density between particle and medium, expressed in terms of the density number — defined as $(\rho_s - \rho)/\rho$, where ρ_s and ρ are the densities of the particle and the liquid respectively. This was confirmed by subsequent experimental studies [9.38] which indicated an exponent of 0.37 for the dependence of the Sherwood number on the density number. It is therefore reasonable to suggest that the proper selection of the support matrix material may have beneficial effects on the rate of solid to liquid phase mass transfer in a fluidised bed. The density difference between a gel particle and the medium is usually very small. Immobilisation in gels is nevertheless one of the most popular techniques for whole cell immobilisation. Before attempting to use gel particles in a FBR it is important to be aware that, whilst pumping costs will be low, the low density difference between the solid and liquid will not result in high rates of mass transfer. Further, stable operation is difficult to obtain, due to the small difference between the fluidising velocity and the terminal settling velocity of the particles.

A specialised form of fluidised bed particularly suitable for use with mycelial fungi is the spouted bed fermenter shown in Fig. 9.7g. The increased shear occurring at the base of the bed of dense particles provides for attrition of the tough mycelial tissue, enabling steady control of biomass to be achieved [9.39].

9.3.4 Gas mixed reactors

The use of gas to circulate the contents of a fermenter through an external tube or internally using a draft tube is a convenient means (no rotating parts are involved) of achieving good mixing and aeration. Such 'airlift' fermenters are of simple construction and operation and are low power consumers. Consequently, they are very attractive for large scale operation. The hydrodynamic behaviour and mass transfer characteristics of gas mixed reactors have been studied by Blenke [9.40] and Schugerl [9.41]. In this context it is understandable that this type of bioreactor has been adopted by industry in a variety of processes using both free cells and cell aggregates, e.g. for cell mass production [9.42].

The production, at laboratory scale, of cyclosporin A (an immunosuppressive agent) by the filamentous fungus *Tolypocladium inflatum* immobilised in carrageenan beads (4–5 mm) using an airlift reactor with external loop was reported by Foster *et al.* [9.43]. The immobilisation of the fungal organism was aimed at producing a less viscous liquid medium than that found in the submerged fermentation, facilitating the maintenance of adequate dissolved oxygen levels.

Black *et al.* [9.34] have devised a 'circulating bed' fermenter (CBF) shown in Fig. 9.7h, which facilitates the mixing of biomass carriers of essentially neutral buoyancy, e.g. reticulated foam Biomass Support Particles. Particle motion is induced by introducing air and/or recycled gas below the distributor. It was found that good liquid and particle mixing is most effectively achieved by introducing the gas over only a segment of the distributor. The CBF was successfully operated continuously for extended periods for the production of alcohol by yeast cells.

9.3.5 Anaerobic reactors

Modern anaerobic reactors that are used for the treatment of wastewater tend to be operated as fixed biomass processes (see Chapter 2). Two such digester types require comment. They are the upflow sludge blanket reactor (USB) and the fluidised/expanded bed process. One of the essential aspects of USB reactors is the aggregation of the sludge into compact granules [9.44; 9.45] (Fig. 9.8). They are resistant to hydraulic shear forces and have a high settling velocity (0.012 m s^{-1}) [9.46]. However, the criteria necessary for their formation are ill-defined, although it does appear that calcium and phosphate ions may be involved [9.44; 9.47]. Anaerobic fluidised/expanded

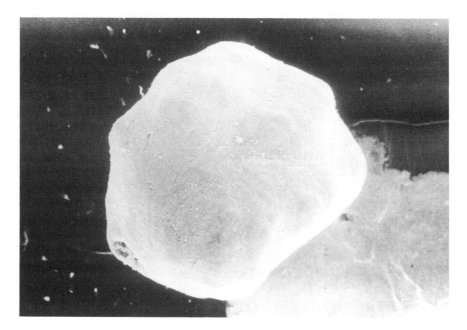

Fig. 9.8 — Electron micrograph of a sludge granule from a USB reactor
(bar = 300 μm).

beds operate in much the same way as their aerobic counterpart with a
biofilm developing on a solid support medium (e.g. sand). However, there
are some indications that the component microbes exist in two layers; an
inner zone of filamentous species, covered by an external layer of rods and
cocci [9.48] (Fig. 9.9). It must be stressed that the current state of knowledge
about the natural immobilisation of anaerobes, be it by flocculation or as a
film, is not good and is certainly much less than that concerning aerobic
species.

9.4   PERFORMANCE OF IMMOBILISED CELL REACTORS

With the exception of plant and animal tissue cell culture, the use of
immobilised cells would not appear to offer any operational advantages for
single batch culture and may, in fact, be disadvantageous, due for example
to immobilisation costs and lower specific rates of reaction. Significant
process engineering advantages are, however, evident for immobilised cells
in repeated batch, or 'draw and fill', operations, e.g. as used in vinegar
production. In such cases reactor performance can be considered to be
similar to conventional batch operation but with large inocula. The major
differences in performance between immobilised and freely suspended cell
systems are in continuous operation, hence the following sections are
confined to such systems.

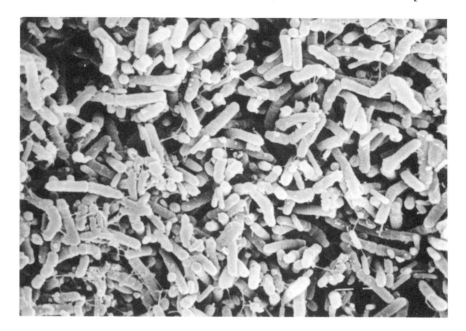

Fig. 9.9 — Electron micrograph of the surface of a USB reactor
(bar=1 μm).

9.4.1   Reaction properties

The performance of a fermentation system is dependent on the volumetric
rate of reaction (R_v) which can be defined as the product of the net specific
rate of reaction (R) and the amount of biomass in the vessel (the biomass
hold-up). For a continuous stirred tank fermenter (CSTF) where the cells
are freely suspended' this is given by Equation 9.1:

$$R_v = R_s\, x \tag{9.1}$$

The biomass hold-up (x) can be readily estimated for this system from a
small sample of the effluent. This results from the fact that microbial cells
have a similar density to that of the fermenter broth and are of microscopic
size, so that, in a well mixed vessel, any element of the fermenter broth will
contain an equal concentration of cells. For a CSTF the biomass hold-up
may also be predicted from consideration of the growth kinetics, e.g. for
Monod kinetics Equation 9.2 applies:

$$x = Y_c \left(S_{in} - \frac{DK_m}{\mu_{max} - D} \right) \tag{9.2}$$

The biomass hold-up in this case is a function of the dilution rate (D), the
maximum specific growth rate (μ_{max}), and the inlet concentration of the

limiting substrate (S_{in}), and falls to zero as D approaches μ_{max}. This latter condition, referred to as washout, imposes a severe limitation on the continuous operation of free cell systems. In immobilised cell systems the dependence of biomass hold-up on the parameters of Equation 9.2 is largely removed, thus providing the possibility of several major advantages over free cell systems, as described earlier.

Biomass hold-up in immobilised cell systems is not as readily estimated as in the CSTF, but may be defined as the product of the number of support particles per unit volume (n_p) and the average biomass hold-up per particle (m_p), plus any freely suspended cells that are present, i.e. $m_p n_p + x$.

A considerable diversity exists in the size and shape of particles used in immobilised cell reactors, and in the mode in which these reactors are operated. The validity of using an average value for particle biomass hold-up to predict the volumetric rate of reaction will therefore depend on the system being described but, in general R_v will be given by Equation 9.3 for particulate systems. In cases where the immobilised biomass is in the form of fixed films Equation 9.4 will apply:

$$R_v = R_p \, m_p \, n_p + R_s x \tag{9.3}$$

$$R_v = R_f \, n_p \, A_f \, L \, \rho_f + R_s x \tag{9.4}$$

In assessing the performance of immobilised cell reactors a problem is encountered concerning which volume to base calculations on, since productivity is measured as product concentration in the liquid phase times liquid flowrate divided by the relevant volume. Various volume bases have been suggested by different workers, as follows.

The total volume of the bioreactor, V_T [9.49]. This volume is useful at an industrial scale for comparing the productivity of one configuration with another but less so in the research laboratory where inefficient utilisation of reactor volume is likely, e.g. when the bed of particles occupies only a part of the working volume of the reactor.

The reaction zone volume, V_R [9.34]. The reaction zone is that part of the reactor occupied by the bed of particles and therefore responsible for the bulk of the productivity. Productivities based on V_R represent the potential for reactors if the whole volume V_T were occupied by particles, and are therefore more suitable for scale-up than productivities based on V_T.

The void volume, V_v [9.50]. This volume represents the bulk fluid phase volume and is equivalent to V_1, the liquid volume, if the gas hold-up is negligible. When dilution rate (the reciprocal of mean liquid residence time) is quoted this should always be based on V_v (or V_l if gas hold-up is large).

The volume occupied by immobilised cells plus supports, V_i [9.51]. Although less meaningful as a reactor term and totally meaningless as a basis for calculating dilution rate, this volume is the most important from the point of view of the reaction. Productivity based on V_i represents the amount of product produced per unit of immobilised biomass and as such is analogous to the specific productivity of cells. If this term is known it then becomes possible by analogy with Equation 9.1 to predict overall reactor productivities by multiplying by the fractional hold-up of particles in the reactor, f_p. Since f_p is an essentially physical, or hydrodynamic, parameter it seems sensible that it should be separated from the biological activity of the cells. The use of V_i does, however, involve the assumption that all of the productivity is attributable to immobilised cells, i.e. there are no freely suspended cells present in the fluid phase.

In situations where cell growth occurs during operation it is generally unreasonable to assume that the process liquor will be free of cells at dilution rates below about 10μ (where μ is the specific growth rate of the organism under the operating conditions). Black [9.52] has discussed the relative contributions of freely suspended and immobilised cells in such systems in more detail.

In situations where little or no growth occurs, e.g. the production of secondary metabolites, it is more likely that the relative amount of freely suspended cells will be negligible. In this case Equations 9.3 and 9.4 commute to the first terms only.

Specific rates of reaction for immobilised cells are generally lower than for freely suspended cells because of the need for substrates to diffuse into, and products out of, the immobilised cell aggregate. Prediction can be made of the diffusional effects on the specific rates of reaction by defining an effectiveness factor and this is dealt with by Mavituna [9.53].

9.4.2   Fractional particle hold-up (f_p)

It is generally desirable to minimise fermenter volume for any given duty. A major factor in achieving this for an immobilised cell system is in the number of support particles that can be accommodated per unit volume. By maximising the fractional particle hold-up ($f_p = V_i/V_T$) the proportion of the reactor volume not occupied by cells (the reactor voidage) is kept to a minimum.

The maximum attainable value of f_p for any system is given by a packed bed arrangement. For spherical particles a value of approximately 0.6 is usual, while for cubes and sheets values approaching unity are possible. The packed bed arrangement would therefore appear attractive, but unfortunately in practice, packed beds rarely prove satisfactory in terms of reactor performance, and arrangements with fewer particles must be used. Poor liquid distribution, resulting in channelling of both liquid and gaseous phases, is often the major reason for this. Packed beds may also suffer from gas flooding at only moderate levels of gas hold-up and the compressibility of support materials can limit the height of such systems. A further problem, that of bed blockage, can result if growing cells are used since effective control of biomass accumulation in packed beds is difficult. In other fixed bed reactors, such as sheet reactors and rotating disc reactors, f_p is low but is chosen to give the desired performance characteristics, i.e. it is fixed for a given duty.

Practical reactor systems employing immobilised cells are often operated as fluidised beds. In the case of small solid supports this mode of operation ensures that the surface area available for film growth is maximised. Fluidisation also leads to interparticle and particle–wall collisions which, in the case of immobilised growing cells, can effectively control the amount of biomass associated with each particle and hence prevent accumulation, which would otherwise result in eventual blockage of the reactor.

The fractional particle hold-up in such systems depends on the fluidisation characteristics of the immobilised cell particles and the operating superficial fluid velocity. In general, when a liquid flows upwards through a bed of particles, the pressure drop through the bed increases with increasing flowrate until it is equal to the buoyant weight of the bed. At this point the bed becomes fluidised and the fluid velocity (U) is referred to as the minimum fluidising velocity (U_{mf}). Beyond this point the pressure drop remains constant but the bed expands according to the relationship proposed by Richardson and Zaki [9.54]:

$$\frac{U}{U_i} = \varepsilon^n \tag{9.5}$$

where ε, the bed voidage, equals $(1 - f_p)$.

The two principal types of particle used in liquid fluidised bed fermenters are small solid particles such as sand, and stainless steel Biomass Support Particles (BSPs). Although a considerable amount of information describing the fluidisation characteristics of particles exists in the literature, there are special problems associated with the fluidisation of both solid support particles and BSPs in a fermenter environment.

The accumulation of a film of cells on a solid support particle leads to an increase in size and a decrease in overall density:

$$\rho_{pw} = \frac{\rho_s + \left[\left(\dfrac{1+L}{r_s}\right) - 1\right]\rho_{bw}}{\left(1 + \dfrac{L}{r_s}\right)} \tag{9.6}$$

As the film accumulates the change in size and density will lead to a change in minimum fluidising velocity. The bed voidage in an operating reactor will consequently vary throughout the bed, making it difficult to estimate overall values for f_p [9.55].

Stainless steel BSPs are fabricated from knitted fine-gauge wire and have a very open structure. They consequently differ from the types of particle used in classical fluidisation studies in that they are relatively large, rough, and porous. The effect of surface roughness is to increase the amount of hydraulic drag for a given liquid velocity, compared to that on a smooth sphere. The effect of porosity, on the other hand, leads to a reduced drag, due to a proportion of the liquid passing through the particle. In a fermenter employing stainless steel BSPs, particles start empty and gradually become filled with biomass. Clearly, the fluidisation characteristics will differ for empty and filled particles by virtue of the effects of porosity. The bed voidage and hence f_p can, however, be predicted for such a system [9.56] and in practice a value of 0.42 is sufficient to achieve satisfactory operation with 6 mm stainless steel BSPs [9.34].

Particles such as reticulated polyurethane foam BSPs and gel beads, because of their low density, have a near neutral buoyancy in the fermenter medium. Thus, such particles can be readily kept moving by the liquid motion induced by introducing gas into the reactor vessel. Studies of the hydrodynamics of such systems have shown that aeration over a part of the cross-section of the reactor, as opposed to the whole cross-section of the reactor, allows greater particle hold-ups to be used [9.57]. Operating values for f_p of around 0.5 for 6 mm foam cubes and 0.6 for gel beads are posssible.

Particle hold-up is, however, affected by many parameters including reactor geometry (especially aspect ratio), gas flowrate, gas distributor design, gas bubble size, and particle size, shape and density. These require extensive further study before such systems can be optimised.

9.4.3 Control of biomass hold-up

For systems in which cell growth occurs, the actual amount of biomass associated with an individual particle will depend, ultimately, on the organism being immobilised and the conditions within the fermenter. Reactor biomass hold-up is dependent both on biological parameters such as growth rate, and on physical parameters such as hydrodynamic shear. Under certain conditions, diffusional limitations within the immobilised biomass film or floc can lead to sloughing or to 'hollow centres'.

In attached film processes there will be a limit to the thickness to which a film of biomass can accumulate. This may be controlled either by the concentration of limiting substrate [9.58] or by the extent of attrition, resulting from interparticle or particle–wall contact [9.59]. The rate of attrition will depend on the balance between the shear forces imposed on the particle and the forces of adhesion binding the cells to the particle surface. These adhesive forces are organism dependent and vary widely for different species but may be measured using the LH-Fowler cell [9.60].

Although with solid support particles the use of preformed porous particles involves, to some extent, the ability of the organism to colonise the particle, biomass hold-up is readily controlled in both fluidised beds and gas-stirred reactors containing such particles. Whilst cells are retained within the pores of the particles any excess biomass occurring due to cell growth on the outside of the particles is effectively removed by the forces of attrition arising from interparticle and particle–wall contact. With organisms such as filamentous fungi the force required to remove excess biomass is considerable and in this case the spouted bed arrangement can be used in order to provide the necessary attrition. For conditions under which particles are not physically 'full' of biomass, particle biomass hold-up can be a function of the substrate concentration within the reactor and be controlled by the rate of diffusion into and out of the particle [9.61]. In foam BSPs, particle biomass hold-up is also dependent on the pore size of the particle [9.34], but this dependence is very organism-specific and general rules concerning the choice of particle pore size cannot be made.

With *in situ* immobilisation, e.g. gel entrapment, biomass hold-up is selected prior to reactor operation. This initial biomass hold-up will, however, only remain constant if no further cell growth occurs. In cases where cells continue to grow during reactor operation the biomass may become redistributed throughout the gel [9.51]. The overall biomass hold-up may also change as a result of the accumulation of gas leading to particle swelling. Although it may be controlled biologically by the concentration of limiting substrate in the reactor, physical control of biomass hold-up in such systems is not possible.

There are considerable difficulties associated with the measurement of biomass hold-up in most types of immobilised cell reactor. These difficulties arise from the problems of obtaining samples of particles from the fermenter, ensuring that samples are representative, and separating the biomass from the support material.

In non-aseptic systems such as those used for wastewater treatment, taking samples of particles may be relatively easy but this is not the case with aseptically operated reactors. However, sampling techniques have been developed for reactors containing BSPs [9.34] and for the rotating disc fermenter [9.31]. Both of these techniques involve taking the particles through a sterile lock arrangement. A similar technique may be suitable for sampling from reactors containing solid support particles in fluidised beds. No satisfactory technique for sampling particles from a packed bed reactor has yet been described.

Having obtained a representative sample of particles from the reactor, the biomass must somehow be separated from the support material in order to determine the actual biomass hold-up. The technique used for stainless steel BSPs involves drying the biomass with its associated support particle, and after weighing, removing the biomass by soaking in a sodium hypochlorite solution. The cleaned support particle is then reweighed and this weight subtracted from the total dry weight. Such a technique may also be suitable for determining biomass hold-up on solid support particles if the biomass cannot be successfully removed while it is wet. With foam BSPs the biomass can be removed from the particle simply by squeezing and rinsing. The dry weight can then be determined in the normal way by filtering, washing and drying the cells.

Biomass hold-up in gel particles can be measured before the immobilisation procedure. However, if growth occurs, this provides only approximate estimates during reactor operation. Once immobilised, it is very difficult to determine biomass hold-up, but estimates can be made if the gel is first solubilised [9.26] or indirectly by cell protein extraction [9.63].

9.4.4 Oxygen supply

One of the most serious limitations to the intensification of aerobic biological processes involves meeting the oxyen demand of the biomass. The problem is particularly acute in immobilised cell systems where oxygen has to diffuse through the solid phase. The ratio of immobilised cell activity to the activity of free cells is defined as the 'effectiveness factor', λ, where $0 < \lambda < 1$ [9.64].

da Fonseca [9.65] estimated effectiveness factors for oxygen in 6 mm stainless steel BSPs containing *Acetobacter* at various levels of particle biomass hold-up. The anticipated severity of the oxygen diffusion through the 'solid' phase was confirmed: at the maximum hold-up, i.e. with the particle 'full', the effectiveness factor was estimated as 0.025 when aerating with air and 0.06 when aerating with pure oxygen.

Briffaud and Engasser [9.66] studied oxygen diffusion in *S. lipolytica* adhering to the wood shavings of a trickling fermenter. From the calculated concentration gradient they estimated that the oxygen concentration approaches zero at less than 0.1 mm from the film interface. It is thus important to maximise the dissolved oxygen concentration at the solid–medium interface, the upper limit being the saturation value derived from the selected oxygen partial pressure. The volumetric oxygen transfer coefficient ($k_L a$) is dependent upon the geometric (type of distributor), hydrodynamic (bulk gas and liquid velocities), and physico-chemical (coalescence) conditions within the reactor.

Ostergaard and Suchozebrski [9.67] determined the effect of gas and liquid velocity and particle size on $k_L a$ in three-phase fluidised systems. The values were compared with those obtained in the absence of a solid phase. The $k_L a$ values for beds of 1 mm particles were approximately one-fifth of those for bubble columns at the same gas rates, whilst the $k_L a$ values for beds of 6 mm particles were approximately twice those for bubble columns. Lee and Buckley [9.68] reinforced the view that particles of 'large' diameter such as 4 mm and 6 mm are beneficial to aeration characteristics. Ostergaard and Suchozebrski [9.67] further verified that $k_L a$ was proportional to the superficial gas velocity and independent of the liquid velocity. The presence of gas bubbles can, however, have negative effects on the immobilised biomass. It induces, for instance, the stripping of biofilm from solid particles, e.g. in fluidised beds used for water treatment.

Dean and Webb [9.57] studied oxygen mass transfer in circulating bed systems and found a generally lower oxygen transfer rate in the presence of particles for a range of sizes, shapes and densities.

Processes for the production of acetic acid by *Acetobacter* are examples of systems with extremely high oxygen requirements. Ghommidh *et al.* [9.69] developed an immobilised *Acetobacter* fixed bed reactor characterised by an extremely good aeration capacity. The $k_L a$ value during operation with air (1 vvm) was as high as 4200 h^{-1}. The reactor column (1 litre liquid volume) contained cylinders (5 cm $\times$ 11 cm) of a porous ceramic material ('cordierite') onto which the cells were adsorbed. The high production rates obtained resulted from the efficiency of the aeration. Air was dispersed in the liquid medium by means of a pulsating pump located at the base of the column. The applicability of this aeration technique in fermentation has been discussed by Serieys *et al.* [9.70].

9.4.5 Cell physiology

The development and application of immobilised cell technology is posing many new, interesting, but difficult problems concerning the understanding and control of cell physiology. Optimisation of biocatalyst properties, particularly operational stability and catalytic activity, can only be achieved if appropriate attention is paid to the physiological 'status' of cells prior to, during, and after immobilisation. One of the most difficult aspects concerns the complex and poorly understood microenvironmental conditions, particularly physico-chemical gradients, to which cells are exposed within the support materials. Problems of oxygen supply and carbon dioxide removal have, for obvious reasons, received most attention but many subtler effects also operate. Numerous unpredicted changes in growth and metabolism, some beneficial and some detrimental to the process, have been observed with immobilised cells. These include increased operational stability of immobilised cells compared to free cells and have been discussed by Anderson [9.71]. It is clear that the physiology of immobilised cells is as yet poorly understood, though it is likely that this will become one of the most important aspects in the further development of immobilised cell technology.

REFERENCES

[9.1]   Linko, P. and Linko, Y. Y. (1984) Industrial applications of immobilised cells. *CRC Crit. Rev. Biotechnol.*, **1**, 289.

[9.2]   Cooper, P. F. and Atkinson, B. (eds) (1981) *Biological Fluidised Bed Treatment of Water and Wastewater,* Ellis Horwood, Chichester, UK.

[9.3]   Karel, S. F., Libicki, S. B. and Robertson, R. (1985) The immobilisation of whole cells: engineering principles. *Chem. Eng. Sci.*, **10**, 1321.

[9.4]   Webb, C., Black, G. M. and Atkinson, B. (eds) (1986) *Process Engineering Aspects of Immobilised Cell Systems,* Institution of Chemical Engineers Publications, Rugby, UK.

[9.5]   Berkeley, R. C. W., Lynch, J. M., Melling, J., Rutter, P. R. and Vincent, B. (eds) (1980) *Microbial Adhesion to Surfaces,* Ellis Horwood, Chichester, UK.

[9.6]   Greenshields, R. N. (1980) Acetic acid: vinegar. In *Economic*

Microbiology, Vol. 2, Primary Products of Metabolism, Rose, A. H. (ed.), Academic Press, New York, p. 121.

[9.7] Forster, C. F. (1985) *Biotechnology and Wastewater Treatment,* Cambridge University Press, Cambridge, UK.

[9.8] Rosevear, A. and Lambe, C. A. (1986) The potential of immobilised plant and animal cells. In *Process Engineering Aspects of Immobilised Cell Systems,* Webb, C., Black, G. M. and Atkinson, B. (eds), Institution of Chemical Engineers Publications, Rugby, UK, p. 225.

[9.9] Bucke, C. (1986) Methods of immobilising cells. In *Process Engineering Aspects of Immobilised Cell Systems,* Webb, C., Black, G. M. and Atkinson, B. (eds), Institution of Chemical Engineers Publications, Rugby, UK, p. 20.

[9.10] Kolot, F. B. (1981) Microbial carriers. Strategy for selection. *Process Bochem.,* **21**(5), 2; **21**(6), 30, 46.

[9.11] Gerson, D. F. and Zajic, J. E. (1979) The biophysics of cellular adhesion. *Am. Chem. Soc. Symp. Ser.,* **106**, 13.

[9.12] Atkinson, B., Black, G. M., Lewis, P. J. S. and Pinches, A. (1979) Biological particles of given size, shape and density for use in biological reactors. *Biotechnol. Bioeng.,* **21**, 193.

[9.13] Black, G. M. and Webb, C. (1986) An immobilisation technology based on biomass support particles. In *Process Engineering Aspects of Immobilised Cell Systems,* Webb, C., Black, G. M. and Atkinson, B. (eds), Institution of Chemical Engineers Publications, Rugby, UK, p. 277.

[9.14] Walker, I. and Austin, E. P. (1981) The use of plastic, porous biomass supports in a pseudo-fluidised bed for effluent treatment. In *Fluidised Bed Treatment of Water and Wastewater,* Cooper, P. F. and Atkinson, B. (eds), Ellis Horwood, Chichester, UK, Chapter 16.

[9.15] Mattiasson, B. (1983) Immobilised viable cells. In *Immobilised Cells and Organelles,* Vol. 2, Mattiasson, B. (ed.), CRC Press, Cleveland, Ohio, p. 23.

[9.16] Kierstan, M. and Bucke, C. (1977) The immobilisation of microbial cells, subcellular organelles and enzymes in calcium alginate gels. *Biotechnol. Bioeng.,* **19**, 387.

[9.17] Cheetham, P. S. J., Blunt, K. W. and Bucke, C. (1979) Physical studies on cell immobilisation using calcium alginate gels. *Biotechnol. Bioeng.,* **21**, 2155.

[9.18] Bucke, C. and Cheetham, P. S. J. (1981) *Production of Isomaltulose,* UK Patent Application No. 2,063,268.

[9.19] Emery, A. N. and Mitchell, D. A. (1986) Operational considerations in the use of immobilised cells. In *Process Engineering Aspects of Immobilised Cell Systems,* Webb, C., Black, G. M. and Atkinson, B. (eds), Institution of Chemical Engineers Publications, Rugby, UK, p. 87.

[9.20] Anon (1982) *Protanal alginates for cell immobilisation,* Information Sheet EF NO. 1006/1, Protan, Norway.

[9.21] Mohan, R. R. and Li, N. N. (1975) Nitrate and nitrite reduction by liquid membrane-encapsulated whole cells. *Biotechnol. Bioeng.*, **17**, 1137.

[9.22] Mehaia, M. A. and Cheryan, M. (1984) Hollow fibre bioreactor for ethanol production: application to the conversion of lactose by *Kluyveromyces fragilis*. *Enzyme Microb. Technol.*, **6**, 117.

[9.23] Ku, K., Kuo, M. J., Delente, J., Wildi, B. S. and Feder, J. (1981) Development of a hollow fibre system for large scale culture of mammalian cells. *Biotechnol. Bioeng.*, **23**, 79.

[9.24] Greenshields, R. N. and Smith, E. L. (1971) Tower fermentation systems and their applications. *Chem. Eng.*, **249**, 182.

[9.25] Metz, B. and Kossen, N. W. F. (1977) The growth of moulds in the form of pellets — a literature review. *Biotechnol. Bioeng.*, **19**, 781.

[9.26] Forster, C. F., Knight, N. J. B. and Wase, D. A. J. (1985) Flocculating agents of microbial origin. In *Advances in Biotechnological Processes*, Vol. 4, Alan R. Liss, New York, pp. 211–240.

[9.27] Atkinson, B. and Daoud, I. S. (1976) Microbial flocs and flocculation in fermentation process engineering. *Adv. Biochem. Eng.* **4**, 42.

[9.28] Black, G. M. (1983) *Immobilised Biomass Systems*, European Brewery Convention, Monograph IX, Nutfield, p. 218.

[9.29] Ghose, T. K. and Bandyopadhyay, K. K. (1980) Rapid ethanol fermentation in immobilised yeast cell reactor. *Biotechnol. Bioeng.*, **22**, 1489.

[9.30] Oda, G., Samejima, H. and Yamada, T. (1983) Continuous alcohol fermentation technologies using immobilised yeast cells. In *Proceedings of Biotech 83*, Online Publications, Northwood, UK, p. 587.

[9.31] Blain, J. A., Anderson, J. G., Todd, J. R. and Divers, M. (1979) Cultivation of filamentous fungi in the disc fermenter. *Biotechnol. Lett.*, **1**, 267.

[9.32] Anderson, J. G., Blain, J. A., Divers, M. and Todd, J. R. (1980) Use of the disc fermenter to examine production of citric acid by *Aspergillus niger*. *Biotechnol. Lett.*, **2**, 99.

[9.33] Lewis, P. J. S. (1979) *The Development of Immobilised Fungal Particles and Their Use in Fluidised Bed Fermenters*, PhD Thesis, University of Manchester, Manchester, UK.

[9.34] Black, G. M., Webb, C., Matthews, T. M. and Atkinson, B. (1984) Practical reactor systems for yeast cell immobilisation using biomass support particles. *Biotechnol. Bioeng.*, **26**, 134.

[9.35] Michelson, M. L. and Ostergaard, K. (1970) Hold-up and fluid mixing in gas–liquid fluidised beds. *Chem. Eng. J.*, **1**, 37.

[9.36] Ostergaard, K. (1978) Hold-up, mass transfer and mixing in three phase fluidisation. *A.I.Ch.E. Symp. Ser. No. 176*, **74**, 82.

[9.37] Riba, J. P. (1978) Thèse de Doctorat d'Etat, Institut National Polytechnique de Toulouse, Toulouse, France.

[9.38] Riba, J. P., Routie, R. and Couderc, J. P. (1978) In *Fluidisation*, Cambridge University Press, Cambridge, UK, p. 157.

[9.39] Webb, C., Fukuda, H. and Atkinson, B. (1986) The production of cellulase in a spouted bed fermenter using cells immobilised in biomass support particles. *Biotechnol. Bioeng.,* **28,** 41.

[9.40] Blenke, H. (1979) Loop reactors. *Adv. Biochem. Eng.,* **13,** 121.

[9.41] Schugerl, K. (1982) Characterisation and performance of single and multistage tower reactors with outer loop for cell mass production. *Adv. Biochem. Eng.,* **22,** 93.

[9.42] Scott, R. (1983) The design and evaluation of experiments to prove scale-up data. In *Proceedings of Biotech 83,* Online Publications, Northwood, UK, p. 235.

[9.43] Foster, B. C., Coutts, R. T., Pasutto, F. M. and Dossetor, J. B. (1983) Production of cyclosporin A by carrageenan — immobilised *Tolypocladium inflatum* in airlift reactor with external loop. *Biotechnol. Lett.* **5,** 693.

[9.44] Lettinga, C., van Velsen, A. F. M., Hobma, S., de Zeeuw, W. and Klapwijk, A. (1980) Use of the upflow sludge blanket (USB) reactor concept for biological wastewater treatment, especially for anaerobic treatment. *Biotechnol. Bioeng,* **22,** 699–734.

[9.45] Pipyn, P. and Verstraete, W. (1979) A pilot scale anaerobic upflow reactor treating distillery wastes. *Biotechnol. Lett.,* **1,** 495–500.

[9.46] Pette, K. C. and Versprille, A. I. (1982) Application of the USAB--concept for wastewater treatment. In *Anaerobic Digestion 1981,* Hughes, D. E. *et al.* (eds), Elsevier Biomedical Press, Amsterdam, pp. 121–136.

[9.47] Alibhai, K. R. K. and Forster, C. F. (1986) An examination of the granulation process in UASB reactors. *Environ. Technol. Lett.* **7,** 193–200.

[9.48] Oakley, D. L., Wase, D. A. J. and Forster, C. F. (1985) Bacterial attachment in relation to the operation of an anaerobic expanded bed reactor. *Advances in Fermentation,* **2,** 20–33.

[9.49] Karanth, N. G. (1982) Calculation of ethanol productivity in immobilised cell bioreactors. *Biotechnol. Lett.,* **4,** 2.

[9.50] Margaritis, A., Bajpai, P. K. and Wallace, J. B. (1981) High ethanol productivities using small Ca-alginate beads of immobilised cells of *Zymomonas mobilis. Biotechnol. Lett.,* **3,** 613.

[9.51] Wada, M., Kato, J. and Chibata, I. (1979) A new immobilisation of microbial cells. Immobilised growing cells using carrageenan gel and their properties. *Eur. J. Appl. Microbiol. Biotechnol.,* **8,** 241.

[9.52] Black, G. M. (1986) Characteristics and performance of immobilised cell reactors. In *Process Engineering Aspects of Immobilised Cell Systems,* Webb, C., Black, G. M. and Atkinson, B. (eds), Institution of Chemical Engineers Publications, Rugby, UK, p. 75.

[9.53] Mavituna, F. (1986) Activity of immobilised cell particles. In *Process Engineering Aspects of Immobilised Cell Systems,* Webb, C., Black, G. M. and Atkinson, B. (eds), Institution of Chemical Engineers Publications, Rugby, UK, p. 134.

[9.54] Richardson, J. F. and Zaki, W. N. (1954) Sedimentation and fluidisation: Part 1. *Trans. Instn Chem. Engrs*, **32**, 35.

[9.55] Webb, C. (1986) Biomass hold-up in immobilised cell reactors. In *Process Engineering Aspects of Immobilised Cell Systems*, Webb, C., Black, G. M. and Atkinson, B. (eds), Institution of Chemical Engineers Publications, Rugby, UK, p. 117.

[9.56] Webb, C., Black, B. M. and Atkinson, B. (1983) Liquid fluidisation of highly porous particles. *Chem. Eng. Res. Des.*, **61**, 125.

[9.57] Dean, J. F. and Webb, C. (1986) Oxygen mass transfer and particle circulation in an immobilised cell bioreactor. In *Bioreactor dynamics*, BHRA, Cambridge, UK, p. 1.

[9.58] Atkinson, B. and Davies, I. J. (1972) The completely mixed microbial fermenter — a method of overcoming washout in continuous fermentation. *Trans. Instn Chem. Engrs*, **50**, 208.

[9.59] Atkinson, B. and Knights, A. J. (1975) Microbial film fermenters — their present and future applications. *Biotechnol. Bioeng.*, **17**, 1245.

[9.60] Fowler, H. W. (1986) The evaluation of the forces involved in cell/surface attachment. In *Process Engineering Aspects of Immobilised Cell Systems*, Webb, C., Black, G. M. and Atkinson, B. (eds), Institution of Chemical Engineers Publications, Rugby, UK, p. 253.

[9.61] Atkinson, B., Cunningham, J. D. and Pinches, A. (1984) The biomass hold-ups and overall rates of substrate (glucose) uptake of support particles containing a mixed microbial culture. *Chem. Eng. Res. Des.*, **62**, 155.

[9.62] Shinmyo, A., Kimura, H. and Okada, H. (1982) Physiology of α-amylase production by immobilised *Bacillus amyloliquefaciens*. *Eur. J. Appl. Microbiol. Biotechnol.*, **14**, 7.

[9.63] Margaritis, A. and Wallace, J. B. (1982) The use of immobilised cells of *Zymomonas mobilis* in a novel fluidised bioreactor to produce ethanol. *Biotechnol. Bioeng. Symp.*, No. 12, 147.

[9.64] Atkinson, B., Davies, I. J. and How, S. Y. (1974) The overall rate of substrate uptake (reaction) by microbial films. *Trans. Instn Chem. Engrs*, **52**, 248, 260.

[9.65] da Fonseca, M. M. R. (1983) *Assessment of the Reaction Properties of Biomass Support Particles Using* Acetobacter, PhD Thesis, University of Manchester, Manchester, UK.

[9.66] Briffaud, J. and Engasser, M. (1979) Citric acid production from glucose, 1: Growth and excretion kinetics in a stirred fermenter. *Biotechnol.*, **21**, 2083.

[9.67] Ostergaard, K. and Suchozebrski, W. (1979) *Proc. 4th Eur. Symp. Chem. React. Eng.*, Pergamon Press, Oxford, p. 21.

[9.68] Lee, J. C. and Buckley, P. S. (1981) Fluid mechanics and aeration characteristics of fluidised beds. In *Biological Fluidised Bed Treatment of Water and Wastewater*, Cooper, P. F. and Atkinson, B. (eds), Ellis Horwood, Chichester, UK, p. 62.

[9.69] Ghommidh, C., Navarro, J. M. and Durrand, G. (1982) A study of acetic acid production by immobilised *Acetobacter* cells: oxygen transfer. *Biotechnol. Bioeng.*, **24,** 605.

[9.70] Serieys, M., Goma, G. and Durand, G. (1978) Design and oxygen transfer potential of a pulsed continuous tubular fermenter. *Biotechnol. Bioeng.*, **20,** 1393.

[9.71] Anderson, J. G. (1986) Immobilised cell physiology. In *Process Engineering Aspects of Immobilised Cell Systems,* Webb, C., Black, G. M. and Atkinson, B. (eds), Institution of Chemical Engineers Publications, Rugby, UK, p. 153.

10

Aeration of wastewater: basic physical factors†

A. W. Nienow
Department of Chemical Engineering, University of Birmingham,
UK

NOMENCLATURE

(In SI units — they may be different in the text and in the literature)

Symbol	Definition	Units
a	interfacial area of gas per unit volume of water	m^{-1}
A	interfacial area available for mass transfer	m^2
B	mass BOD removed	$kg\ d^{-1}$
c_i	concentration of oxygen in the liquid phase at the interface	$kg\ m^{-3}$
C_L	concentration of oxygen in the water away from the interface	$kg\ m^{-3}$
C_g^*	saturation concentration of oxygen in water for oxygen partial pressure p_g	$kg\ m^{-3}$
ΔC	water phase concentration driving force	$kg\ m^{-3}$
D	impeller diameter	m
D_L	diffusivity of oxygen in water	$m^2 s^{-1}$
d_B	mean bubble size	m
E	mass oxygen transferred per unit of energy	$kg\ kwh^{-1}$
F	energy required to remove unit mass of BOD	$kwh\ kg^{-1}$
Fr	Froude number, N^2D/g	dimension-less

† This chapter is based on a paper of the same title first published in the Proceedings of the Symposium on The Profitable Aeration of Wastewater (London, 1980), published by BHRA, Cranfield, UK. It is reproduced here by kind permission of BHRA, Cranfield. Section 10.7 is an editorial addition.

g	acceleration due to gravity	m s^{-2}
H	Henry's law constant	$\text{atm m}^3\text{ kg}^{-1}$
H_g	height of aerated liquid (see Fig. 10.4)	m
H_L	height of unaerated liquid (see Fig. 10.4)	m
J	oxygenation rate	kg s^{-1}
k_g	gas film mass transfer coefficient	$\text{kg s}^{-1}\text{ m}^{-2}$ atm^{-1}
k_L	liquid film mass transfer coefficient	m s^{-1}
M	mass of mixed liquor solids	kg
N	impeller speed	rev s^{-1}
OD	oxygen deficit as a fraction of maximum oxygen deficit	dimensionless
P	total pressure of the gas phase	atm
P_g	partial pressure of oxygen in the bulk of the gas phase	atm
P_i	partial pressure of oxygen in the gas phase at the interface	atm
r_{20}	endogenous respiration rate at 20°C	$\text{kg kg}^{-1}\text{s}^{-1}$
R	oxygen requirement for carbonaceous oxidation	kg d^{-1}
s	rate of surface renewal	s^{-1}
t	temperature	°C
t_e	time of exposure of an eddy before renewal	s
y	volume (or mole) fraction of oxygen in gas phase	dimensionless
δ_L	liquid film thickness	m
ε_H	hold-up $(H_g - H_L)/H_L$	dimensionless
ε_T	specific energy dissipation rate	$\text{m}^2\text{ s}^{-3}$
θ	temperature coefficient $= 1.07$	dimensionless
μ_a	(apparent) dynamic viscosity	$\text{kg m}^{-1}\text{s}^{-1}$

Subscripts
IN   in gas entering the aerator
OUT   in gas leaving the aerator
lm   log mean

10.1   INTRODUCTION

The unit operations involved in recovering usable water from wastewater are many but, no matter which combination is required for a particular application, aeration, or oxygenation to be more precise, is almost always one of them. Whether the level of contamination is specified by BOD or COD, the oxygenation rate must satisfy these demands.

The basic principles which underlie oxygenation are exactly the same as those which determine the rate of transfer of any sparingly soluble gas from the gas stream to the unsaturated liquid. The rate at which this transfer takes place is dependent on three principal parameters. These are: the area of contact between the gas and the liquid; the driving force available, i.e. the difference in concentration of gas in the two phases; and the hydrodynamics. In the case of oxygenation of wastewater, it is useful to consider a fourth factor, viz. the chemical composition of the impurities. Of course, once the oxygen is in the liquid phase, it will either react or be utilised by microorganisms. This chapter is specifically concerned with the transfer of oxygen from the gas phase (generally air) to the liquid.

10.2   THE BASIC MASS TRANSFER RELATIONSHIP

The first basic assumption in all physical mass transfer processes involving a soluble gas and a liquid is that equilibrium exists at the interface between the two phases. This assumption implies that, at the interface, the concentration of the gas in the liquid, C_i, is equal to its solubility at its partial pressure in the gas phase, p_i. Since, for sparingly soluble gases such as oxygen, there is a direct proportionality between the two, then

$$p_i = HC_i \qquad (10.1)$$

where H is the Henry's law constant. It is then assumed that as the gas is absorbed so its concentration falls progressively, firstly from the bulk concentration in the gas phase, p_g, to that at the interface, p_i; and then again from that on the liquid side of the interface, C_i, to that in the bulk liquid, C_L. Fig. 10.1 shows this phenomenological description diagrammatically and Fig. 10.2 indicates concentration relationships between the two phases.

The rate of mass transfer, J, is then assumed to be proportional to the concentration differences existing within each phase, the surface area between the phases, A, and a coefficient (the gas or liqid film mass transfer coefficient, k_g and k_L respectively) which relates the three. Thus

$$J = k_g A \ (p_g - p_i) \qquad (10.2)$$
$$= k_L A (C_i - C_L) \qquad (10.3)$$

Equations 10.2 and 10.3 are also the definitions of k_g and k_L. Combining Equations 10.1, 10.2 and 10.3 enables the unknown interfacial concentration, C_i, to be eliminated to give

$$J = A \left(\frac{p_g}{H} - C_L \right) \left(\frac{1}{k_L} + \frac{1}{Hk_g} \right)^{-1} \qquad (10.4)$$

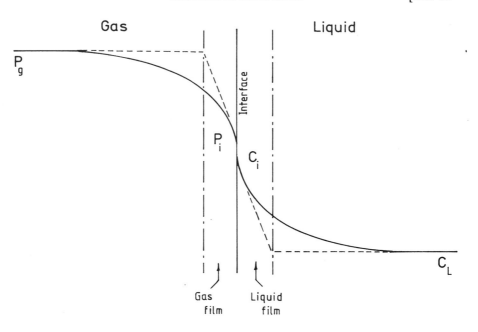

Fig. 10.1 — Oxygen concentration profiles.

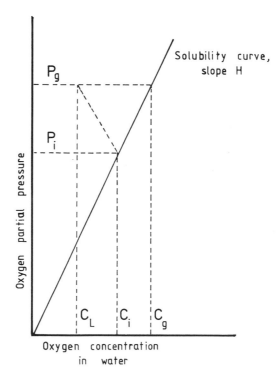

Fig. 10.2 — Solubility curve and concentraton relationship.

Since, for oxygenation, the transferring gas is sparingly soluble, so that H is large,

$$Hk_g \ll k_L \qquad (10.5)$$

Equation 10.4 can be simplified to

$$J = k_L A \ (C_g^* - C_L) \qquad (10.6)$$

since (from Fig. 10.2)

$$\frac{p_g}{H} = C_g^* \qquad (10.7)$$

This analysis neglects any possible resistance to mass transfer at the interface itself, and this point and the way k_L, A, C_g^* (or p_g and H) and C_L can be predicted, measured and controlled will now be discussed. In addition, it should be remembered that Equation 10.6 represents a time-averaged equation at a point in the aerated mixture and that, even at steady-state, all of the above variables will in general be a function of position. This effect of position will also be discussed, as well as a very brief consideration of economic factors.

10.3   THE MASS TRANSFER COEFFICIENT

10.3.1   Theoretical models

Fig. 10.1 shows an arbitrary relationship between concentration of oxygen in the two phases and distance from the interface. The precise spatial (and possibly time-dependent) relationship will depend on the hydrodynamics close to the interface. The simplest model is the Two-Film Theory of Whitman [10.1]. He considered the regions of changing concentration to be two hypothetical, stagnant layers (or films) across which mass was transferred by molecular diffusion and the dotted profiles in Fig. 10.1 represent this simple model. The effect that hydrodynamics have on the rate of transfer is accounted for by changes in the thickness of the films. Since oxygen is a sparingly soluble gas and, as was shown by Equation 10.6, k_g is unimportant, only the liquid film thickness, δ_L, need be considered:

$$J = k_L A \ (C_g^* - C_L) = \frac{D_L}{\delta_L} \cdot A(C_g^* - C_L) \qquad (10.8)$$

where D_L is the diffusivity of oxygen through the water and

$$\delta_L = f \ (\text{hydrodynamics}) \qquad (10.9)$$

In Equation 10.9, hydrodynamics refers to both the relative velocity between the two phases and the turbulence structure of the continuous liquid phase. Increases in either relative velocity or turbulence level enhance k_L and reduce the hypothetical δ_L but, of course, this reduction cannot be measured.

If turbulent eddies are the controlling hydrodynamic feature, then the Penetration Theory of Higbie is probably more realistic [10.2]. He proposed that fresh eddies move from the bulk at concentration C_L across the region of concentration change right up to the interface. There they remain for a definite length of time, t_e, and, during this time, unsteady state diffusion occurs from the fluid at the interfacial concentration, C_g^*. If it is assumed that t_e is sufficiently small so that within the eddy the concentration at its outer edge always remains at C_L, it can be shown that

$$k_L = \sqrt{\frac{4D_L}{\pi t_e}} \tag{10.10}$$

Again t_e cannot be measured, but enhanced turbulence should tend to a more and more rapid replacement of eddies and therefore to a reduction in t_e and an enhancement of k_L.

Since these early models, more and more sophisticated ones have been proposed. For instance, Danckwerts [10.3] suggested that to imagine that all eddies remained at the interface for the same length of time was unreasonable. He proposed that eddies remained there for a random distribution of ages. With this assumption,

$$k_L = \sqrt{D_L s} \tag{10.11}$$

where s is the rate of production of fresh surface per unit total area of interface. Progressively, more sophisticated models can be introduced but all suffer from the same problem in that they contain one or more parameters which cannot be measured!

Perhaps somewhat suprisingly, boundary layer models have rarely been used to analyse gas–liquid mass transfer. If the relative velocity is the governing hydrodynamic feature (and in bubble swarms moving through a relatively stagnant fluid this might be so), then boundary layer theory may be a more realistic model. This approach does not incorporate arbitrary parameters and has been applied successfully to turbulent particulate solid–liquid mass transfer in agitated systems with some success [10.4]. Laminar boundary layer theory would suggest that

$$k_L \propto D_L^{2/3} \tag{10.12}$$

If Equations 10.8–10.12 are compared, the main difference between each of the models is the exponent which relates k_L to diffusivity and through this difference the best model might be found. However, the difficulty of obtaining sufficiently accurate experimental data (for reasons which will become apparent later) makes such a differentiation a practical impossibility for the conditions found in wastewater treatment equipment.

10.3.2   Some practical considerations

Fortunately, which is the correct model is probably not a very important question. In general, more energetic fluid motion normally gives rise to higher k_L values. This is probably due to the dissipation of this energy as turbulence and more intense motion close to the interface. However, it should be noted that for solid–liquid mass transfer (where A is fixed by the particle size) a tenfold increase in power, i.e. energy-dissipation rate, ε_T, generally only gives a 50 to 60% increase in k_L [10.5]. In gas–liquid systems, increases of energy dissipation rate have a much greater effect on A and therefore the overall enhancement in oxygenation rate with ε_T greater than in solid–liquid systems. However, because of the interaction between k_L and A, the two have not often been measured separately and few k_L data are available. It should be obvious that increases in ε_T will also increase mass transfer of oxygen to microorganisms, but only marginally. In addition, it may lead to floc break-up if it is too high, thus leading to difficulties in sludge separation.

It is also possible that impurities collect at the interface, giving an additional resistance to mass transfer. Thus, oil contamination at the ppm level can reduce the mass transfer rate by as much as one-third [10.6]. On the other hand, ionic salts appear to enhance the mass transfer rate and often by an amount significantly greater than that due to the increase in surface area they provide [10.7].

The range of impurities that can be expected in sewage is very variable as are their effects. In practice, therefore, it is usual to consider an overall factor α, where:

$$\alpha = \frac{(k_L a)_{sewage}}{(k_L a)_{clean\,water}} \tag{10.13}$$

However, α itself can vary with a range of factors [10.8] (Table 10.1) These include:

— the degree of treatment
— the type of wastewater
— the nature of the solids in the aeration tank

Ideally, the precise value for α and the magnitude of any variations that occur during treatment ought to be determined for each and every case. If this is not possible, then a value of 0.7–0.9 may be used.

Table 10.1 — Values for the α factor [10.8]

Process	α
Surface aeration	0.63–0.94
Oxidation ditch	0.89–0.93
Fine bubble aeration	0.30–0.80
Diffused air	0.67–0.93

10.3.3 The effect of viscosity

Increasing viscosity reduces the mass transfer coefficient. Dimensional considerations of mass transfer generally link the kinematic viscosity with the diffusivity through the Schmidt number. The kinematic viscosity also appears in the Reynolds number which indicates the level of turbulence. However, none of the hydrodynamic/mass transfer models is sufficiently well developed to enable the overall effect of dynamic viscosity to be predicted accurately. Very often when fluids are significantly more viscous than water, they are non-Newtonian and shear thinning. Therefore an apparent viscosity must be estimated, related to the shear rate in the fluid in the region of interest.

If the fluid is Newtonian, the Stokes–Einstein relationship ($\mu \propto 1/D$) applies quite well. Thus the rate of mass transfer goes down due both to the decreased levels of turbulence (increasing δ_L, t_e or the boundary layer thickness) and to the reduction in diffusivity. If the fluid is shear thinning, especially if due to the presence of soluble polymers (e.g. Xanthan gum), diffusivity is almost independent of apparent viscosity.

Again, the complexity of the problem is such that in general the effect of viscosity has been considered only in relation to $k_L a$ rather than to k_L alone.

10.4   THE DRIVING FORCE FOR MASS TRANSFER, $\Delta C = C_g^* - C_L$

10.4.1   Introduction

Clearly to maximise the rate of mass transfer, it is necessary to have a large concentration driving force. This can be done by increasing C_g^*, though it and C_L will generally vary from point to point throughout the aerator. C_L itself may be approaching zero in places but clearly the water discharged should have a satisfactory level for subsequent use. Typical values of C_L on discharge fall in the range 3 to 6 mg l^{-1}, though design for a minimum throughout of about 2.0 mg l^{-1} is recommended [10.9]. However, provided C_L is greater than some critical value (typically 0.5 mg l^{-1}), biological activity is zero-order in oxygen concentration, i.e. higher values of C_L do not enhance it. Thus high values of C_L should be avoided [10.9].

In the main, this section will concentrate on the factors affecting C_g^* and its measurement, the measurement of C_L and the variation of ΔC throughout the equipment for different geometries and contacting patterns.

10.4.2   Oxygen solubility

C_g^* in Equation 10.6 is the saturation concentration related to the oxygen partial pressure in the gas phase, p_g, through Equation 10.7, Henry's law. In addition, the oxygen partial pressure is related to the total pressure, P, through Dalton's law of partial pressures, i.e.

$$p_g = Py \qquad (10.14)$$

where y is the mole (or volume) fraction of oxygen in the gas phase.

C_g^* (or alternatively H) is a function of the composition of the water and of the operating temperature, i.e.

$$C_g^* = \frac{468}{31.6 + t} \qquad (10.15)$$

for pure water where C_g^* is in ppm (or mg l^{-1}), t is the water temperature (°C) and the gas is air at 1 atm. This gives a solubility of 9.08 ppm (or 0.28 g mol m^{-3}) at 20°C. (The series of units used to define C_g^* illustrates a rather tricky arithmetic difficulty. Since p_g can also be expressed in many ways (atm, mm Hg, Pa), the units of $H = p_g/C_g^*$ are legion). For 35% w/w salt solution at 20°C, C_g^* falls to 7.4 ppm and, in wastewater, C_g^* will again be less than in pure water.

C_g^* must be determined by analytical methods if it is required accurately for a complex contaminated water [10.9]. It is important to note that C_g^* cannot be measured by oxygen electrodes because these instruments actually relate to p_g, i.e. the oxygen partial pressure in equilibrium with C_g^*. Therefore, regardless of the true value of C_g^* (or of H), two waters saturated with oxygen at the same partial pressure will always give the same reading on an oxygen electrode [10.10].

Because of the variations in C_g^* caused by impurities, it is usual, in practice, to adopt a factor β to incorporate the various effects. Thus:

$$\beta = \frac{(C_g^*)_{\text{sewage}}}{(C_g^*)_{\text{clean water}}} \qquad (10.16)$$

This factor has not been examined to the same degree as the α factor and a value of 0.9 is normally used.

Clearly from Equation 10.15 C_g^* is enhanced if operations are carried out under pressure either by imposing a back pressure on the aerator or by operating with large hydrostatic heads. The most extreme example of this is the ICI deep shaft aeration system where static heads up to 100 m are employed (Chapter 1). Alternatively, oxygen-enriched air (or pure oxygen) can be used, as in the Unox process (Chapter 1). This approach reduces the amount of off-gas to be handled, which may be an advantage, though oxygen recycling may be desirable, and excessively high dissolved oxygen levels may arise and cause problems for the microorganisms. However, increasing C_g^* through increases in either P or y generally requires additional costs either in compression or in oxygen production, and these must be offset against the enhanced aeration rate.

10.4.3 Measurement of C_L

This is normally carried out using an oxygen electrode. Providing that it has been calibrated to 0% for zero oxygen concentration and 100% for fully saturated, a reading of percentage of C_g^* is readily obtained. However, the absolute value of C_L cannot be found unless C_g^* is also known.

Many types of oxygen electrode are available [10.10] but they usually have two opposing characteristics. Either they tend to give readings which are sensitive to the velocity of the fluid past the probe and have fast response times; or, alternatively, they are slow instruments and insensitive to velocity. Though compromises and special micro-probes are possible ways between these two extremes, the type chosen must depend on the aeration system and the technique for determining J (or $k_L A$).

10.4.4 Bulk mixing pattern

The ICI deep-shaft system and the submerged air-sparged, agitated aeration system (Fig. 10.3) provide good examples both of the way the flow pattern alters the driving force throughout the equipment and of the two major flow patterns encountered. Between points (1) and (2) in the deep shaft (Fig. 10.4) oxygen is being transferred from the gas- to the liquid-phase and there it is being utilised by the microorganism. However, between (2) and (3), as the pressure falls, so C_g^* drops and, even though oxygen is being utilised, some will almost certainly desorb and there will be an extensive region of oxygen-supersaturated liquid. Thus there is precisely defined variation of oxygen concentration in both phases as they move in a manner approximating to plug flow around the loop [10.11].

In an agitated submerged aerator, the liquid can (except on the very large scale) be considered well mixed, i.e. C_L = constant. However, the gas-phase may be well mixed so that

$$p_g = \text{constant} = (p_g)_{\text{OUT}} \tag{10.17}$$

where $(p_g)_{\text{OUT}}$ is the partial pressure of oxygen in the exit gas and

$$C_g^* = (p_g)_{\text{OUT}}/H \tag{10.18}$$

This situation is most probable with fairly intense agitation and on the small scale.

On the other hand, for ease of application it is often assumed that no

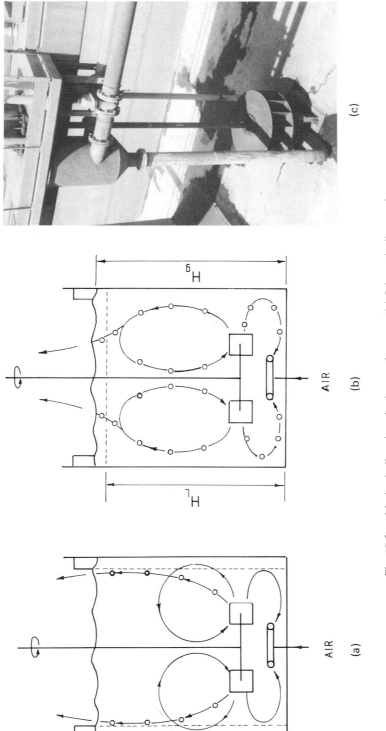

Fig. 10.3 — Mechanically-agitated submerged aerator: (a) Schematic diagram for plug-flow gas and well mixed liquid; (b) Schematic diagram for both phases well mixed; (c) As installed in an activated sludge aeration tank (by courtesy of Thames Water).

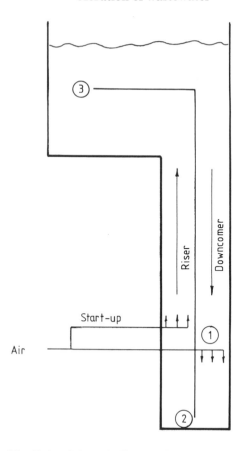

Fig. 10.4 — Schematic diagram of the Deep Shaft Process.

oxygen is utilised. This is the so-called no depletion model [10.12]. In this case,

$$C_g^* = (p_g)_{IN}/H$$

Again, it is most reasonable with low $k_L a$ values and on the small scale. Most of the data leading to $k_L a$ values in the literature (especially those collected in the review by van't Riet [10.13]) make this assumption.

For large scale plants, the gas-phase is best considered as being in plug-flow [10.14], so that a log-mean value of driving force is obtained, i.e.

$$\Delta C = \Delta C_{lm} = \frac{\Delta C_{IN} - \Delta C_{OUT}}{\ln(\Delta C_{IN}/\Delta C_{OUT})} \tag{10.19}$$

where

$$\Delta C_{IN} = (p_g)_{IN}/H - C_L \tag{10.20}$$

$$\Delta C_{OUT} = (p_g)_{OUT}/H - C_L \tag{10.21}$$

In addition, the effect of static head on p_g must be taken into account.

For more complex flows, more complex models are required. For surface aerators (Fig. 1.5) the well mixed model is often assumed. Yet in large basins C_L may vary dramatically with depth, and unless good liquid mixing is achieved, large proportions of the liquid may be well below acceptable oxygenation levels, even down to zero. No proper design can take place without adequate and quantifiable turnover of all the liquid in a basin.

10.4.5   The effect of viscosity

For most high-viscosity fluids, the assumption of a well-mixed liquid phase breaks down even on the small scale. This effect is particularly pronounced if the fluids are highly shear thinning when well-mixed regions develop in high shear zones, e.g. close to agitators, with almost stagnant fluid elsewhere [10.15].

High viscosity also makes the measurement of C_L difficult. It slows down the response of the oxygen electrode and the tendency for the reading of oxygen electrodes to be sensitive to liquid velocity is enhanced. This, it is often difficult to tell if the liquid phase is well-mixed [10.16].

10.5   INTERFACIAL SURFACE AREA

10.5.1   Production

The energy which is imparted to aerators must cause adequate fluid mixing and will have an effect on k_L. However, most of all, it will give rise to the all-important air–water interfacial area across which mass transfer can proceed, though this area may be only local to the point of energy input.

The submerged aerator, shown diagrammatically by Fig. 10.3 is, of course, a special application of the traditional agitated gas–liquid chemical reactor. The disc forces the sparged gas out through the gas-filled vortices at the back of the blades and the intense angular velocity in these vortices gives rise to gas break-up and dispersion as bubbles [10.17]. It is essential that adequate dispersion of the air occurs and, though this is very moderate in energy requirements on a small scale, the specific energy need increases with scale-up [10.18; 10.19].

The interfacial area produced depends quite critically on the average bubble size and this is determined to a considerable extent by the amount of bubble–bubble coalescences in the less intense energy-dissipating regions of the tank away from the impeller. In relatively pure water, coalescence occurs rather easily but traces of surface active agents, ionic salts [10.7; 10.20] and organic liquids [10.7; 10.21] all tend to migrate to the interfaces and stabilise the bubbles. Thus, most wastewaters will tend to be non-coalescing.

There are other important points. Firstly, even in non-coalescing systems, good gas-mixing will occur in the impeller cavities due to recirculation of the dispersed air [10.22]. Indeed, non-coalescing systems may have better gas-phase mixing through this mechanism than coalescing because the smaller bubbles inherent to the former recirculate more readily than the large bubbles of the latter. Secondly, an insignificant amount of surface aeration occurs to enhance that from the submerged air supply [10.22; 10.23]. Further details of this type of reactor are given in a recent textbook [10.24].

For this type of aerator, power (and capital) must be expended before air can be introduced through the sparger. However, if the impeller is of the self-inducing type, [10.7], no additional equipment is required (Fig. 10.5)

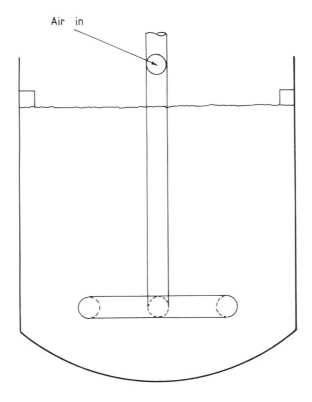

Fig. 10.5 — Schematic diagram of a self-inducing impellor.

for gas introduction, though it should be emphasised that the liquid circulation is often poorer with this type of agitator.

An alternative way of eliminating air compression is to use surface aerators, of which there are a very wide variety of types, though they may conveniently be subdivided into two categories: (a) those in which the impeller rotates about a vertical axis and which are broadly equivalent to the submerged aerators; (b) those in which the impeller rotates about a horizontal axis and in which water is initially dispersed as droplets in air, as well as air being dispersed in the water (see Chapter 1).

There are many different designs of vertical-shaft surface aerator (see, for example, Fig. 1.5a). A number of these have recently been compared by Zlokarnik [10.25], using his own data and that of other workers. His most interesting conclusion is that on an energy efficiency basis, i.e. kg O_2 transferred per kWh, scale-up should be done at constant Froude number Fr (Fr $= N^2D$ g^{-1}). This implies that efficiency decreases with the square root of the impeller size. A similar loss of efficiency on scale-up has also been suggested by the present author for submerged aerators [10.18], though many other workers have suggested that constant specific power is an adequate scale-up rule [10.13]. The impellers rotating about a horizontal axis typically have brushes which thresh the surface (Fig. 1.5b), throwing the water droplets into the air and producing a linear water flow which is ideal for use in the oxidation ditches for which they are designed [10.26].

There are also many types of static sub-surface aerator, all of which are designed either to produce fine bubbles or to extend the contact time between liquid and bubbles or to reduce bubble coalescence. The simplest and best established of these is the fine bubble diffuser (Fig. 10.6). The density of these diffusers can be arranged so as to provide an aeration intensity appropriate to the type of treatment required (carbonaceous oxidation, nitrification or de-nitrification). However, the design can suffer from clogging and it is also essential that the blowers providing the air should have a good 'turn-down' facility so that the aeration intensity can be reduced during periods of low load. The potential problems of providing a continuously variable supply of air have been discussed by Clough [10.27]. An alternative type of sub-surface aerator is that typified by the 'Helixor' system (Fig. 10.7). Thus, the upflow of fine bubbles into the Helixor-tube induces an upward turbulent flow of liquid which, in turn, promotes good mixing. The internal helical structure prolongs the bubble/liquid contact time and ensures good mass transfer.

A recent development has been the use of plunging water jets (Fig. 10.8) which have been studied in great detail by Smith and his co-workers [10.28; 10.29]. With this approach, both the impeller and compressor are eliminated since the plunging water jet entrains air as it enters the reservoir, which is then dispersed as it descends and coalesces around the jet as it reascends to the surface. At the same time, the jet causes good bulk flow. It has been shown to be applicable to large-scale operations [10.30]. Other types of jet-aeration are also available [10.31].

10.5.2 Measurement

The measurement of A is itself quite difficult. It depends on the bubble size and the hold-up, ε_H, and both of these will in general vary from point to point throughout the aerator [e.g. 10.18].

The bubbles will be present as a distribution of sizes, smaller in the regions of highest energy dissipation rate and larger elsewhere to an extent which depends mostly on whether it is a coalescing or non-coalescing

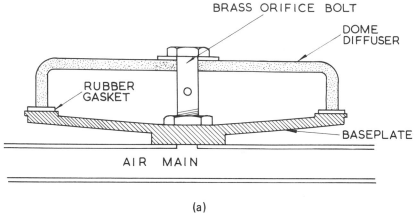

(a)

(b)

Fig. 10.6 — Fine-bubble diffusers: (a) Schematic diagram; (b) As installed in the aeration tank of an activated sludge system.

system. Area has been determined by light-transmission techniques [10.23], and size by suction probes [10.18], photographically and more recently by a highly sophisticated four-point conductivity probe [10.33]. In general, a mean size, d_B, is determined and similar techniques for evaluating ε_H lead to the specific area, a, per unit volume of liquid, since

$$a = \frac{A}{V} = \frac{6\varepsilon_H}{d_B} \qquad (10.22)$$

(a)

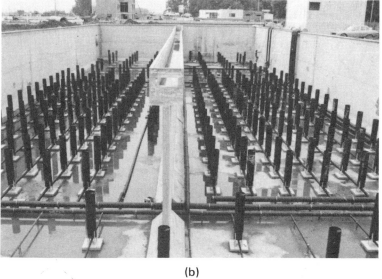

(b)

Fig. 10.7 — Sub-surface static aerators (by courtesy of Polcon Environmental Control Systems Ltd): (a) Schematic diagram; (b) As installed in an activated sludge aeration tank.

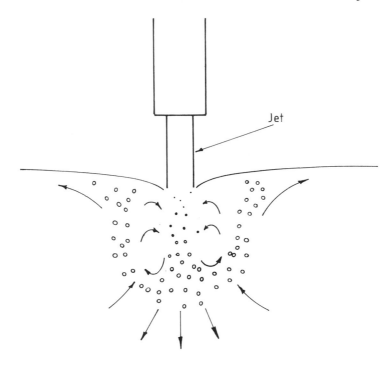

Fig. 10.8 — Schematic diagram of a plunging water-jet aeration (from [10.28]).

The above techniques have in the main been developed for the chemical reactor shown in Fig. 10.3 and used with clean water. Even so, integration of point values of ε_H have in general not given good agreement with the overall hold-up defined by

$$\varepsilon_H = \frac{H_g - H_L}{H_L} \tag{10.23}$$

The measurement and allowance for changes in A with position in large-scale equipment with wastewater is still a problem.

10.5.3 The effect of viscosity

There is a complex interaction between viscosity, bubble size and hold-up. Increasing viscosity and increased non-Newtonian behaviour tends to cause a marked change in bubble size and bubble size distribution. A growing proportion of the air is associated with very large bubbles due to the easier coalescence that occurs. In addition, large numbers of very fine bubbles are also produced [10.34; 10.35]. The large bubbles tend to have a rapid rise velocity and short residence time. The small ones on the other hand may remain in the fluid indefinitely. Depending on the balance of these two effects the hold-up may increase or decrease [10.16; 10.34].

10.6 MEASUREMENT OF OXYGENATION RATE

10.6.1 Introduction

The main method of measuring oxgyenation rate is, in fact, to eliminate the necessity to do so. This is possible if the water can be deoxygenated and the unsteady state oxygenation followed so that $k_L A$ (or $k_L a$) is determined directly. The most common ways of deoxygenation are sodium sulphite (and a standardised procedure is available) or nitrogen sparging [10.13]. A recent development has been the use of the catalysed-hydrazine reaction which has the advantage over sulphite that the reaction products are water and nitrogen which therefore have no effect on the system [10.25].

Apart from the possible effects of electrolytes on the bubble size, the main problems are that the probe response should be allowed for (though its effect may well be negligible) [10.10; 10.13] and, more seriously, the assumption that the gas phase and liquid phase are well mixed, i.e. of constant composition throughout. On the large scale, this can lead to serious errors [10.14]. If the liquid phase is well mixed, assumptions about the state of gas phase mixing can be eliminated by measuring the dynamic response of both the exit gas and the liquid [10.12]. A comparison of $k_L a$'s based on the no-depletion model (maximum driving force, minimum $k_L a$), complete mixing model (minimum driving force, maximum $k_L a$), plug flow model and the two-probe technique gives $k_L a$'s from the same raw data differing by as much as a factor of 3 [10.36]. The assumption that the liquid phase is well mixed has even been made for loop-type configurations [10.11]. Clearly, this assumption is often unreasonable, as it often is also in large scale stirred configurations. The errors arising from such assumptions in both loop and stirred type reactors have been examined by André et al. [10.37]. Steady-state methods can be employed and are certainly preferable for many situations [10.13; 10.29]. However, they do require knowledge of the true solubility if an accurate result is to be obtained and additional instrumentation is required if the mass transferred is determined by the change in concentration of the gas phase [10.16]. A review of the various ways of measuring the oxygenation rate in activated sludge aeration tanks has been provided by Boon and Chambers [10.38].

10.6.2 The effect of viscosity

When the viscosity is increased, $k_L a$ measurements become more difficult. Firstly, there is the difficulty of ensuring a well-mixed liquid phase and of measuring the quality of mixing. This effects both the dynamic and steady-state techniques. On the other hand, the dynamic method is particularly prone to errors due to the presence of small nitrogen bubbles being present following deaeration [10.39]. These then act as an oxygen sink which cause incorrectly low $k_L a$ values to be determined. The slowing down of the probe response also causes difficulties, though this can be allowed for [10.40].

The steady-state technique is preferred though the small nitrogen bubble problem may arise with deaeration/aeration vessels in a loop [10.29]. The use of yeast as an oxygen sink offers distinct advantages [10.16] but it requires much more complex instrumentation and equipment.

For submerged aerators, a number of workers have found, to a first approxiation, that

$$k_L a \propto \mu_a^{\frac{1}{2}}$$

(10.24)

for shear-thinning fluids [10.16].

10.7   OPERATIONAL ASPECTS

Since aeration can, in some cases, consume some 80 per cent of the total energy budget for a sewage treatment works, it is reasonable to suggest that the efficiency of energy usage is one of the most significant operational aspects. The first feature that must be considered is the efficiency, measured in terms of kg oxygen transferred kWh^{-1}, quoted by the supplier of the aeration equipment. This is nearly always quoted in relation to clean water (containing 5 mg anionic surfactant l^{-1} measured as Manoxol OT) and an unsteady state test (see Section 10.6.1). However, for surface aerators, whose efficiency varies with the depth of immersion, there are very wide fluctuations in the data quoted by manufacturers (see Fig. 1.6) [10.8]. It is essential, therefore, that, having selected a particular aeration system, the efficiency is checked during the commissioning stage and that appropriate 'penalty clauses' be written into the contract documents.

The second feature that must be dealt with is the control of aeration during operation. Control is usually effected by coupling oxygen electrodes to the aeration system (Section 10.4.3) so as to maintain the dissolved oxygen concentration in the mixed liquors within a predetermined range. Given this degree of control, the operational energy requirements ($F =$ kWh kg^{-1} BOD removed) should be kept low. Considered in theoretical terms [10.41],

$$F = \frac{R}{E \, \alpha \, (OD) . B}$$

(10.25)

$$R = B + 0.024 \, Mr_{20} \, \theta^{(T-20)}$$

(10.26)

These two equations can be combined to produce a single expression to define F, an expression which is heavily reliant on the values of E and α. Thus, all other factors being equal, to maintain a constant F-value, if α

decreases then E must be increased. This is not a feature incorporated into aeration control systems. In Fig. 10.9 curves based on this expression are superimposed on data from several full-scale plants, assuming a series of values for α and E. This shows not only the range of values which must be assumed for E and α if all the data are to be covered but also how low the aerator efficiency (E) must be at some works. An extension of these results would be to suggest that the product of E and α might be a more significant parameter to specify for design and operational purposes than E alone. Whichever is used, the data in Fig. 10.9 show that, at many plants, there is scope for improvement. The economic potential for this can be seen when it is realised that some $1.5 \times 10^6\,\mathrm{m}^3$ of domestic sewage are treated each day by some type of surface aeration activated sludge system. Assuming that there is an average BOD removal of 150 mg l^{-1} and that energy costs are 3.5p kWh^{-1}, the potential saving would be of the order of £0.72 × 10^6 each year if the F-value could be improved by 0.5 at half the works.

A similar situation exists with diffused air plants. In general, this type of aeration system has a higher clean water efficiency than that achieved by a surface aerator. However, a review of in-plant performances [10.42] has shown that efficiency values ranged from 1.08 to 2.13 kg kWh^{-1}. Indeed, Clough [10.27] has estimated that £0.5 × 10^6 could be saved annually if the transfer efficiency (E) at all plants could be maintained at 2.0 kg kWh^{-1}. The reasons for the poor performance of fine bubble diffusers include poor dissolved oxygen control, deviations from the design loading rates and air supply systems whose flexibility was less than adequate. Taking these factors into consideration, the basic criteria for achieving optimal efficiency have been defined [10.43].

There is, therefore, considerable scope for bio-engineers to develop systems for aeration or the control of aeration which are more energy efficient than those currently in use. Any development of this type will need to take full consideration of the basic concepts discussed earlier in this chapter.

10.8 CONCLUSIONS

This chapter has shown how the general mass transfer equation for gas–liquid systems can be simplified for the special case of aeration. It has then considered the various terms within the equation in turn, showing how they are varied, measured and optimised in real equipment. Although, for this purpose, the mass transfer coefficient, k_L, and the interfacial area, A, have been discussed separately, in practice, because both are extremely difficult to measure, especially in real aeration systems, they are lumped together as $k_L a$.

Many correlations for $k_L a$, exist in the literature for equipment broadly similar to the submerged aerator of Fig. 10.3, relating it to specific power input and aeration rate. However, because of the very considerable differences in contacting pattern in the various aerators and the profound effect of

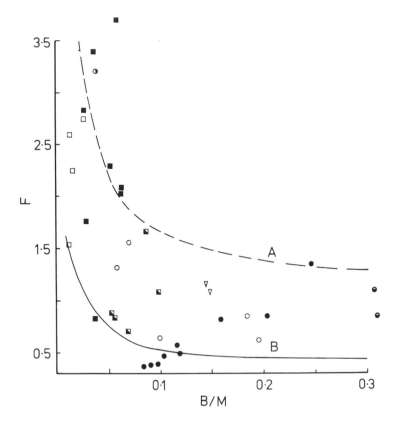

Fig. 10.9 — The interrelationship between energy aeration efficiency (F) and the specific BOD removal (B/M) for various plants, together with the theoretical curves, as follows:

Curve	$E\alpha$	α	E
A	1.12	0.3	3.73
		0.5	2.24
		0.7	1.60
B	3.36	0.7	4.8
		0.9	3.73
		1.1	3.05

trace impurities, it is very difficult to apply these data to real waste water in real equipment. This problem is enhanced by the lack of any well-established scale-up criteria.

At first sight $k_L a$ appears to be easy to measure. Using unsteady state techniques and assuming the no-depletion model, it is indeed very easy to get a number. However, it is doubtful whether in more than a very few cases this number is equal to the true $k_L a$ as implied by its strict definition. However, because of the complexity of improved methods of $k_L a$ measurement and because $k_L a$ is so extremely system-specific that it must be measured for every waste treatment process, in the opinion of the author it seems that on balance this simple method is the most practical one to use.

REFERENCES

[10.1] Whitman, W. C. (1923) The two-film theory of absorption. *Chem. Met. Eng.*, **29**, 147.

[10.2] Higbie, R. (1935) The rate of absorption of a pure gas into a still liquid during short periods of exposure. *Trans. A. I. Chem. E.*, **31**, 365.

[10.3] Danckwerts, P. V. (1951) Significance of liquid film coefficients in gas absorption. *Ind. Eng. Chem.*, **43**, 1460.

[10.4] Nienow, A. W. (1975) Agitated vessel particle–liquid mass transfer: a comparison between theories and data. *Chem. Eng. J.*, **9**, 153.

[10.5] Nienow, A. W. (1985) The mixer as a reactor: liquid–solid systems. In *Mixing in the Process Industries,* Hornby, N., Edwards, M. F. and Nienow, A. W. (eds), Butterworths, London, pp. 356–372.

[10.6] Warmoeskerken, M. M. C. G. and Smith, J. M. (1978) Surface contamination effects in stirred tank reactors. *Proc. Int. Mixing Symp.,* Mons, Belgium; EFCE, C13.1–16.

[10.7] Zlokarnik, M. (1978) Sorption characteristics for gas–liquid contacting in mixed vessels. *Adv. Biochem. Eng.*, **8**, 134.

[10.8] Forster, C. F. (1985) *Biotechnology and Wastewater Treatment,* Cambridge University Press, Cambridge, pp. 103–138.

[10.9] Hammer, M. J. (1975) *Water and Waste-water Technology.* John Wiley & Sons, New York.

[10.10] Lee, Y. H. and Tsao, G. T. (1979) Dissolved oxygen electrodes. *Adv. Biochem. Eng.*, **13**, 35.

[10.11] Blenke, H. (1979) Loop reactors. *Adv. Biochem. Eng.*, **13**, 121.

[10.12] Chapman, C. M., Gibilaro, L. G. and Nienow, A. W. (1982) A dynamic response technique for the estimation of gas–liquid mass-transfer coefficients in a stirred vessel. *Chem. Eng. Sci.*, **37**, 891.

[10.13] van't Riet, K. (1979) Review of measuring methods and results in non-viscous gas–liquid mass transfer in stirred vessels. *Ind. Eng. Chem. (Proc. Des. Dev.),* **18**, 357.

[10.14] Lakin, M., Salzman, R., Oldshue, J., and Gray, H. (1978) Data analysis of subsurface aeration systems. *Proc. Int. Mixing Symp.,* Mons, Belgium; EFCE, C2.1–40.

[10.15] Soloman, J., Elson, T. P., Nienow, A. W. and Pace, G. W. (1981) Cavern sizes in agitated fluids with a yield stress. *Chem. Eng. Comm.,* **11**, 143.

[10.16] Hickman, A. D. and Nienow, A. W. (1986) Mass transfer and hold-up in an agitated simulated fermentation broth as a function of viscosity. *Proc. Int. Conf. on Bioreactor Fluid Mechanics,* Cambridge, BHRA, Cranfield, UK., 301.

[10.17] Nienow, A. W. and Wisdom, D. J. (1974) Flow over disc turbine blades. *Chem. Eng. Sci.,* **29,** 1994.

[10.18] Nienow, A. W., Wisdom, D. J. and Middleton, J. C. (1978) The effect of scale and geometry on flooding, recirculation and power in gassed, stirred vessels. *Proc. 2nd European Conf. on Mixing,* Cambridge, BHRA, pp. F1.1–16.

[10.19] Nienow, A. W., Warmoeskerken, M. M. C. G., Smith, J. M. and Konno, M. (1985) On the flooding/loading transition and the complete dispersal condition in aerated vessels agitated by a Rushton turbine. *Proc. 5th European Conf. on Mixing,* Germany, BHRA, pp. 143–154.

[10.20] Lee, J. C. and Meyrick, D. (1970) Gas–liquid areas in salt solutions in an agitated tank. *Trans. I. Chem. E.,* **48,** T37.

[10.21] Nienow, A. W. and Machon, V. (1979) The effect of formaldehyde on hold-up in aerated, stirred tanks. *Biotech. Bioeng.,* **21,** 1477.

[10.22] Nienow, A. W., Chapman, C. M. and Middleton, J. C. (1979) Gas recirculation rate through impeller cavities and surface aeration in sparged, agitated vessels. *Chem. Eng. J.,* **17,** 111.

[10.23] Nienow, A. W., Chapman, C. M. and Middleton, J. C. (1983) Surface aeration in a small agitated and sparged vessel. *Biotech. Bioeng,* **22,** 981.

[10.24] Harnby, N., Edwards, M. F. and Nienow, A. W. (1985) *Mixing in the Process Industries.* Butterworths, London.

[10.25] Zlokarnik, M. (1979) Scale-up of surface aerators for waste water treatment. *Adv. Biochem. Eng.,* **11,** 157.

[10.26] Forster, C. F. (1981) Continously operated ditches. In *Oxidation Ditches in Wastewater Treatment,* Barnes, D., Forster, C. F. and Johnstone, D. W. M. (eds), Pitman, London, pp. 75–131.

[10.27] Clough, G. F. G. (1982) Implications and further applications. In *Sewage Treatment: Optimisation of Fine Bubble Aeration in Activated Sludge Plant,* Project Profile No 79, Department of Energy.

[10.28] van de Sande, E. (1974) *Air Entrainment by Plunging Water Jets.* PhD Thesis, University of Delft, The Netherlands.

[10.29] van de Donk, J. A. C., Lans, R. G. J. M. and Smith, J. M. (1979) The effect of contaminants on the oxygen transfer rate achieved with a plunging jet contactor. *3rd European Conf. on Mixing,* York, BHRA, Cranfield, UK, pp. 289–297.

[10.30] Dijkstra, F., Jennekens, H. F. and Nooren, P. A. (1978). The development and application of water jet aeration for wastewater treatment. *IAWPR Conference on Aeration,* Amsterdam.

[10.31] Pells, M. A. (1981) Construction of oxidation ditches. In *Oxidation Ditches in Wastewater Treatment,* Barnes, D., Forster, C. F. and Johnstone, D. W. M. (eds), Pitman, London, pp. 188–231.

[10.32] Calderbank, P. H. (1958) Physical rate processes in industrial fermentation. *Trans. I. Chem. E.,* **36,** 443.

[10.33] Figueiredo, M. and Calderbank, P. H. (1978) The effects of agitator configuration on mass transfer in large aerated mixing vessel. *Proc. Int. Mixing Symp.*, Mons, Belgium; EFCE, C3.1–19.

[10.34] Machon, V., Vlcek, J., Nienow, A. W. and Soloman, J. (1980) Some effect of pseudoplasticity on hold-up in aerated, agitated vessels. *Chem. Eng. J.*, **14**, 67.

[10.35] Nienow, A. W. and Machon, V. (1979) The effect of formaldehyde on hold-up in aerated, stirred tanks. *Biotech. Bioeng.*, **21**, 1477.

[10.36] Chapman, C. M., Nienow, A. W., Cooke, M. and Middleton, J. C. (1983) Particle–gas–liquid mixing in stirred vessels: Part 4 — Mass transfer and final conclusions. *Chem. Eng. Res. Des.*, **61**, 182.

[10.37] André, G., Robinson, C. W. and Moo-Young, M. (1983) New criteria for application of the well-mixed model for gas–liquid mass transfer studies. *Chem. Eng. Sci.*, **38**, 1845.

[10.38] Boon, A. G. and Chambers, B. (1983) Full scale evaluation of aerators. In *Reducing Aeration Costs,* Institute of Water Pollution Control, Maidstone, Kent, pp. 1–33.

[10.39] Heijnen, J. J., van't Riet, K. and Wolthius, A. J. (1980) The influence of very small bubbles on the dynamic $k_L a$ measurement in viscous gas–liquid systems. *Biotech. Bioeng.*, **22**, 1945.

[10.40] Soloman, J. (1980) *Mixing, Aeration and Rheology of Highly Viscous Fluids*. PhD Thesis, University of London.

[10.41] Johnstone, D. W. M. (1984) Oxygen requirements, energy consumption and sludge production in extended aeration systems. *Wat. Pollut. Control*, **83**, 100.

[10.42] Houk, D. H. and Boon, A. G. (1981) *Survey and Evaluation of Fine-bubble Dome-diffuser Aeration Equipment*. US Environmental Protection Agency, Report No. EPA–600/2–81–222.

[10.43] Boon, A. G., Chambers, B. and Collinson, B. (1982) Energy saving in the activated sludge process. In *Effective Use of Energy in the Water Industry*, Institute of Water Pollution Control, Maidstone, Kent, pp. 1–30.

11

Process engineering principles

M. S. Everett
Department of Chemical Engineering, University of Birmingham, UK

NOMENCLATURE

Symbol	Definition	Units
A	area	m^2
C	specific heat (heat transfer)	$J\,kg^{-1}\,K^{-1}$
	concentration (mass transfer)	$mol\,m^{-3}$
d	diameter	m
D	molecular diffusivity	$m^2\,s^{-1}$
F	shear force	N
g	acceleration due to gravity	ms^{-21}
H	specific enthalpy	$J\,kg^{-1}$
h	heat transfer film coefficient	$Wm^{-2}\,K^{-1}$
k	thermal conductivity	$Wm^{-1}\,K^{-1}$
m	mass	kg
$\dot{m}$	mass flow rate	$kg\,s^{-1}$
N	rate of diffusion per unit area	$mol\quad s^{-1}\,m^{-2}$
Q	rate of heat transfer	W
q	quantity of heat	J
R	thermal resistance (conduction)	KW^{-1}
	fouling factor (convection)	$m^2K^{-1}W^{-1}$
Re	Reynolds Number $= du\rho/\mu$ (dimensionless)	
t	temperature	K
u	velocity	ms^{-1}
U	overall heat transfer coefficient	$Wm^{-2}K^{-1}$
W	work done	J

x	wall thickness	m
y	distance (as defined in the text)	m
z	height above datum	m
μ	absolute viscosity	$kg\ m^{-1}\ s^{-1}$
		or $Ns\ m^{-2}$
ρ	density	$kg\ m^{-3}$
τ	shear stress	Nm^{-2} or
		Pa

Subscripts

A	*component A*
B	*component B*
c	*cold fluid or clean*
D	*design or dirty*
h	*hot fluid*
i	*inside*
m	*logarithmic mean*
o	*outside*
T	*total*
w	*wall*

1, 2, 3, etc. are used for different points in the system.

11.1   MATERIAL AND ENERGY BALANCES

11.1.1   Introduction

Whether one is designing a new plant or analysing the performance of an existing one, it is essential as a first step to carry out a *material balance* for the process. This involves a careful accounting of all materials flowing into and out of the plant and being formed, used up or accumulated within it. An *energy balance* can be carried out in a similar way but is concerned with the energy transferred when heating or cooling materials, the energy required to drive pumps and stirrers and the energy involved in chemical reactions. Both types of balance can be applied over any convenient part of a process (e.g. over a single cell in a culture medium, over an item of equipment or over a series of items) or over the process as a whole. The choice depends entirely on the data which either are already available or can be obtained and on the objects of the exercise.

An understanding of the material and energy flows in a process is essential (a) before a satisfactory design of the equipment can be carried out, and (b) for the efficient and economic operation of the equipment after it has been installed.

Material and energy balances involve the practical application of the Law of Conservation of Mass and the Law of Conservation of Energy, respectively, but it should be noted in passing that, strictly, these are not two separate laws but one. Mass and energy are inter-convertible and the sum of the two is constant. However, except when nuclear reactions are involved and/or when matter is moving at a velocity near to that of light, the conversion is undetectable. Thus for most engineering purposes and certainly in the field of biotechnology, mass and energy can be taken to be completely independent.

11.1.2   Material balances
Material balances are normally made in order to:

(1) check the consistency of measurements of flow rates and concentrations;
(2) calculate unmetered streams or unknown concentrations;
(3) determine the feasibility of a projected process;
(4) provide data for an assessment of the efficiency and profitability of a process.

Consider a simple processing system (which may, as already noted above, be a complete process or any arbitrary part of it):

Applying the Law of Conservation of Mass one can write the following material balance equation:

$$\begin{matrix} \text{Input} \\ \text{to system} \end{matrix} = \begin{matrix} \text{Output} \\ \text{from system} \end{matrix} + \begin{matrix} \text{Accumulation} \\ \text{within system} \end{matrix} \qquad (11.1)$$

The accumulation may be positive or negative.

Most continuous processes operate under steady-state conditions, so there is no accumulation ('what goes in must come out') and Equation 11.1 reduces to

$$\text{Input} = \text{Output} \qquad (11.2)$$

Equation 11.1 or 11.2, as appropriate, may be applied to all the material involved in the system (when the relationship is often referred to as an 'overall' or 'total' material balance) or to any component or group of components that passes through the system unchanged. The aim should be to set down as many independent material balance relationships as there are unknown flow rates or concentrations. It should then be a relatively simple matter to solve for the unknown quantities.

The most convenient units to be used for the material balances will, of course, depend on the nature of the problem being considered and must be consistent throughout a given set of equations. Flow rates are usually best expressed in mass units per unit time (e.g. kg s^{-1}, lb h^{-1}, tonne day^{-1}) or, occasionally, in molar units per unit time (e.g. kmol h^{-1}, tonne mol day^{-1}) but one must be careful when using the latter if chemical reactions are involved. Whereas mass and atom balances are always valid (in the absence of nuclear reactions), since neither can be destroyed, mole and radical balances are only valid when the entity concerned passes through the system unchanged.

Detailed discussions of the procedures for tackling material balance problems are given elsewhere [11.1–11.4], where information will also be found for dealing with processes which involve recycle, by-pass, make-up, or purge streams or unsteady-state conditions (e.g. at the start-up of a continuous and ultimately steady-state process). Computers obviously can play a significant role in solving material balance equations and their use is discussed in other texts [11.3; 11.5].

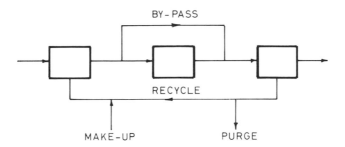

11.1.3   Energy balances

These are carried out for reasons which are very similar to those already outlined for material balances. A reliable accounting procedure for energy is the first step on the road towards the efficient use of the latter, the importance of which hardly needs to be emphasised in these days of high energy costs.

11.1.3.1   Forms of energy

The most important forms of energy that need to be accounted for in processing operations are:

(1) *Kinetic energy* $= \frac{1}{2}mu^2$ where u is the velocity of the material of mass m. The kinetic energy of a stream is usually small except when relatively high velocities are encountered, as in the jet from a nozzle (e.g. steam jet ejector or injector).
(2) *Potential energy* $= mgz$, where z is the height above an arbitrary datum. Changes in potential energy are generally small except, for example, when a liquid has to be pumped to an elevated tank.
(3) *Enthalpy* $= mH$, where $H =$ specific enthalpy (sometimes incorrectly called 'heat content') of the substance. H is a function of pressure and temperature and values can be obtained from standard reference books of data (e.g. from Steam Tables for the steam/water system). Absolute enthalpies are not obtainable and numerical values for a given substance are based on an arbitrarily defined datum, or standard state, for that substance. (The method is analogous to that of specifying heights above

sea level.) As all enthalpies are relative to an arbitrary datum, only enthalpy differences have any physical significance.
(4) *Heat added to the system* = q. By convention, heat added to a system is taken to be positive.
(5) *Work done by the system* = W. By convention, the work done by the system on its surroundings is taken to be positive.

There are many other forms of energy (surface, electrostatic, magnetic) but their effects can usually be neglected [11.1; 11.2; 11.4].

11.1.3.2 *Conservation of energy*

The Principle of Conservation of Energy (also called the First Law of Thermodynamics) states that energy can be neither created nor destroyed but only converted from one form to another. Thus, the conservation equations, 11.1 and 11.2, can also be applied to the conservation of energy:

For any process: Input = Output + Accumulation (11.1′)

For a steady-state process: Input = Output   (11.2′)

It is important to recognise that one particular form of energy (e.g. heat) is not necessarily conserved—in fact it usually will not be. Thus, partial energy balances (e.g. a heat balance) must only be used with great care and when one is certain that other forms of energy are either negligible or appear on both sides of the equation and so cancel out.

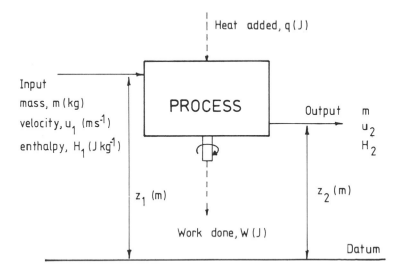

Fig. 11.1 — Energy balance for a simple process

In the steady-state process, shown diagrammatically in Fig. 11.1, mass m of material enters the process at a height z_1 above an arbitrary datum. The material enetering has a velocity u_1 and enthalpy H_1. The corresponding values for the output are z_2, u_2 and H_2 respectively. While the material passes through the equipment a quantity of heat q is transferred to it and the material does an amount of external work W. (If work is done *on* the material by, say, a pump or a mixer, the amount of work involved will, by the usual sign convention, be negative.)

Since this is by definition a steady-state process, Equation 11.2 applies, and so

$$\begin{array}{ccccccc} \text{Energy of input} & + & \text{Heat} & = & \text{Energy of output} & + & \text{Work} \\ \text{process stream} & & \text{added} & & \text{process stream} & & \text{done} \end{array}$$

$$(11.3)$$

Now,

Energy of a process stream = Kinetic energy + Potential energy +
+ Enthalpy

$$= \frac{mu^2}{2} + mgz + mH$$

$$= m\left(\frac{u^2}{2} + gz + H\right) \tag{11.4}$$

and so, from Equation 11.3:

$$m\left[\frac{u_2^2 - u_1^2}{2} + g(z_2 - z_1) + H_2 - H_1\right] = q - W \tag{11.5}$$

This equation can easily be adapted if necessary to allow for the presence of several input and output streams.

In many processes the kinetic energy and potential energy terms can be neglected and Equation 11.5 becomes

$$m(H_2 - H_1) = q - W \tag{11.6}$$

If no shaft work (W) is involved, the equation becomes a simple 'heat balance':

$$m(H_2 - H_1) = q \tag{11.7}$$

The above example is intended as an elementary introduction to the subject of energy balances and no account has been taken of accumulation or depletion of energy within the system, or of the energy changes involved in chemical reactions. A far more rigorous treatment of the subject, which also contains a large number of useful worked examples, is available elsewhere [11.1–11.5].

11.1.4 Conclusion

The information obtained from the carrying out of material and energy balances can usually be integrated with cost data to give a very revealing picture of the overall operation of a process. A critical examination of the information will then often indicate where modifications and improvements to the plant or its method of operation can be made, leading hopefully to increased efficiency and profitability.

11.2   FLUID FLOW

11.2.1   Introduction

Many operations in bioprocessing involve the transport of momentum, heat or mass from one phase to another. These transfer processes can be carried out singly, as in a heat exchanger, or in combinations of two or even all three. Transfer processes taking place simultaneously need not occur in the same direction, and in fact usually do not do so. In the fluidised bed drying of vegetables, hot air flows upwards through the bed of vegetables and momentum is transferred from the air to the solid particles to keep them in a fluidised state. Heat is transferred to the solid where the moisture is vaporised and passes, by a process of mass transfer, into the air stream. The entity being transferred will always tend to flow from regions of high concentration to regions of low concentration, the driving force for the process being the difference in concentration between the two regions.

The rate at which each of these three transfer processes occurs can be expressed in the form of a general equation:

$$\text{rate of transfer} = \frac{\text{driving force}}{\text{resistance}} \tag{11.8a}$$

This is analogous to Ohm's law, which relates to the rate of transfer of charge, i.e. electric current:

$$\text{current} = \frac{\text{potential difference}}{\text{resistance}} \tag{11.8b}$$

The most common transfer processes involve two phases and one, if not both of these will be a fluid. The way a fluid behaves when it flows has a profound effect on the rate of the transfer process (or processes) occurring within it.

11.2.2   Types of flow

When a fluid flows through a pipe, over a surface or around an object, the flow pattern depends on the velocity of the fluid, its physical properties and the geometry of the surface. Considering the simple case of flow through a circular pipe, two principal types of flow are possible—streamline and turbulent.

In streamline (or laminar) flow, which occurs at relatively low velocities, every element of the fluid moves in a direction parallel with the axis of the pipe. There is no bulk movement at right-angles to the direction of flow but there is a small amount of radial diffusion, which is a molecular process. The velocity of the fluid is at a maximum on the pipe axis and decreases rapidly as the wall is approached; the molecular layer actually in contact with the wall is stationary, the velocity profile across the pipe being parabolic (Fig. 11.2).

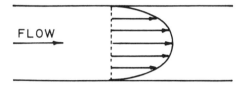

Fig. 11.2 — Velocity profile for laminar flow.

Above a certain critical velocity (which varies according to the nature of the fluid and the conditions of the experiment) the fluid begins to move erratically in cross-currents and eddies and the flow is described as turbulent. Under these conditions, due to the cross-mixing of the fluid, the velocity profile is flatter than for laminar flow (Fig. 11.3).

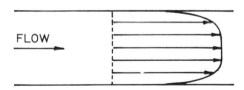

Fig. 11.3 — Velocity profile for turbulent flow.

Although the core of the fluid is in turbulent flow, there is always a thin layer immediately adjacent to the wall where the flow remains laminar and where the velocity gradient is very steep. Despite its small dimensions, this layer—known as the laminar sub-layer—exerts a controlling influence on many processes, such as heat transfer from the wall to the bulk of the fluid. The higher the velocity of the fluid the greater the degree of turbulence; although this results in a decrease in the thickness of the laminar sub-layer, the latter never disappears completely, no matter how high the velocity.

11.2.3   The Reynolds number

The conditions under which laminar and turbulent flow occur in a circular pipe were determined by Osborne Reynolds in 1883, who found that the transition from one type of flow to the other depends not only on the fluid velocity (u) but also on its viscosity (μ) and density (ρ) and on the diameter (d) of the pipe. He combined these quantities into a dimensionless group $du\rho/\mu$ (now known as the Reynolds Number, Re) and showed that if its value is less than 2100 the flow is always laminar. At values above about 4000 the flow is *usually* turbulent. Within the approximate range of Reynolds Numbers 2100–4000, known as the transition region, the flow pattern is unstable and conditions at any particular point oscillate in a random manner between laminar and turbulent. This transition from laminar to turbulent flow will usually occur over a different range of Reynolds Numbers if the bounding surface of the fluid is non-circular.

The physical significance of the Reynolds Number is that it represents the ratio of the inertial forces to the viscous forces in the fluid ([11.6] p. 48 *et seq.*). If the viscous forces predominate, the Reynolds Number is low and the flow is laminar. At higher Reynolds Numbers the inertial forces predominate and the flow becomes turbulent.

11.2.4   Advantages and disadvantages of turbulent flow

The chief characteristic of turbulent flow is the presence of eddies. These vary greatly in size, the largest approaching the pipe diameter and the smallest being only about 1 mm across. Within the eddies, the flow is laminar and, as even the smallest contain about 10^{16} molecules, turbulence can certainly not be considered a molecular phenomenon. Eddies that are less than about 1 mm across are rapidly destroyed by viscous shear and the mechanical energy is finally converted into heat. Thus, more power is required to pump a fluid in turbulent than in laminar flow. In spite of this, turbulent flow is almost invariably preferred for one or more of the following reasons:

(1) smaller pipes and processing equipment are required;
(2) heat transfer rates (for both heating and cooling) are considerably higher;
(3) mixing (which is important in both heat and mass transfer) is more effective.

Thus, the higher the Reynolds Number the smaller the plant required for a given throughput. However, since power consumption in turbulent flow is very sensitive to any increase in Re (the power required being approximately proportional to the square of the velocity), care needs to be exercised when choosing the operating conditions. Ideally an attempt should be made to optimise the conditions so that the total operating cost is at a minimum.

It can be seen by inspection of the Reynolds Number formula ($du\rho/\mu$) that with high viscosity liquids it would be necessary to achieve a corresponding high velocity in order to promote turbulent flow. In these circumstances, the power consumption and pressure developed could well be prohibitively high and viscous materials are, therefore, generally pumped and processed under laminar flow conditions.

11.2.5 More complex situations
The above discussion has been concerned almost exclusively with the behaviour of a single-phase fluid flowing through a circular pipe. This is clearly of direct relevance to the flow of process streams through pipes and heat exchangers. However, in most other types of equipment, particularly when two phases are being directly contacted, the situation is far more complex. Nevertheless, the basic concepts of laminar and turbulent flow (and, in the case of the latter, the laminar sub-layer) are still valid. For detailed information on these topics see Perry and Green [11.7] and Treybal [11.8].

11.2.6 Types of fluid
When a fluid moves in laminar flow over a stationary solid surface the latter presents a resistance to flow and shear stresses are set up in the fluid. As we have already seen, the molecular layer in contact with the surface is stationary and a velocity profile exists in the fluid (Figs 11.2, 11.4). The slope

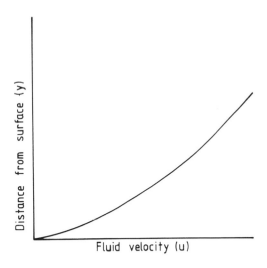

Fig. 11.4 — Relationship between fluid velocity and the distance from a surface.

of this velocity profile is dy/du and its reciprocal, du/dy, is the velocity gradient. This velocity gradient can be shown ([11.9] p. 49) to represent the time rate of shear and is often referred to by the latter name.

The shear stress (τ) at any point in the fluid is defined as the shear force per unit area. It is clear that the shear stress must be related to the velocity gradient (du/dy) set up—if a greater shear stress is applied to the fluid, the velocity at any particular point will be increased and so therefore will the velocity gradient.

For some fluids, the relationship between τ and du/dy (at constant temperature and pressure) is linear and passes through the origin (see Fig. 11.5). All gases, most liquids and solutions of low molecular weight are of

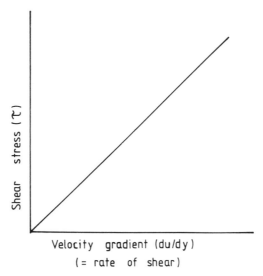

Fig. 11.5 — Relationship between shear stress and velocity gradient for a Newtonian fluid.

this type and are known as Newtonian fluids (since they obey the Newton law of viscosity, Equation 11.9 below).

If a different type of relationship exists between τ and du/dy (i.e. if it is non-linear and/or does not pass through the origin) the fluid is described as non-Newtonian. Examples include most high molecular weight liquids and solutions, and also gels, suspensions and slurries. Many foodstuffs exhibit non-Newtonian behaviour [11.10; 11.11] as do sewage sludges (see Chapter 5). For Newtonian fluids, where the shear stress (τ) is directly proportional to the velocity gradient (du/dy):

$$\tau = \mu \frac{du}{dy} \tag{11.9}$$

This relationship (the Newton law of viscosity) defines the *absolute* viscosity, μ, of the fluid.

Since the shear stress (τ) is shear force per unit area, we may write

$$\tau = \frac{F}{A} = \mu \frac{du}{dy} \tag{11.10}$$

or

$$\frac{F}{A} = \frac{\mu}{\rho} \frac{d(u\rho)}{dy} \tag{11.11}$$

The term μ/ρ is the *kinematic* viscosity of the fluid. Now the shear force (F) is a measure of the rate of transfer of momentum perpendicular to the surface, and $u\rho$ is the momentum of the fluid per unit volume (or volumetric momentum concentration). Thus, Equation 11.11 is analogous to the Fourier equation (11.12) for heat transfer by conduction (see next section) and to Fick's law of diffusion (11.30) which relates to mass transfer (see Section 11.5.2). All three equations are in the form of the general rate equation, 11.8.

11.3 HEAT TRANSFER

11.3.1 Introduction

Heat may be transferred by conduction, convection (natural or forced) and radiation, the driving force in each case being the temperature difference between the source and the receiver. Conduction, which involves the transfer of kinetic energy from one molecule or atom to another without bulk mixing, can occur in any material. In convection, the heat is transferred by mixing and the process can therefore only take place in a fluid. The rate of heat transfer is usually very much more rapid than in conduction. In natural convection, the mixing is induced by density differences arising from temperature gradients, whereas in forced convection the mixing is produced mechanically. Radiation, being of an electromagnetic nature and requiring no medium for its transfer, is of a different nature from conduction and convection. Also, there are no processes analogous to radiation in the transfer of momentum or mass.

11.3.2 Conduction

The rate of heat transfer by conduction in one dimension through a rectangular slab of material under steady-state conditions is given by the Fourier equation:

$$Q = kA\frac{\Delta t}{x} \tag{11.12}$$

where

Q	=heat transferred per unit time (J s^{-1} or W)
k	=thermal conductivity of the material (W m^{-1} K^{-1})
A	=cross-sectional area of the slab of material (perpendicular to the direction of heat flow) (m^2)
Δt	=temperature difference between the faces of the slab (K)
x	=thickness of the slab (m)

Equation 11.12 may be written as:

$$Q = \frac{\Delta t}{R} \tag{11.13}$$

where $R = x/kA$ = the *thermal resistance* of the slab.

Thus, Equations 9.12 and 9.13 are similar in form to Equation 9.8.

In many industrial situations conduction takes place through several layers in series, e.g. the flow of heat from an insulated storage tank will be through the metal wall and through the layer of insulation (see Fig. 11.6).

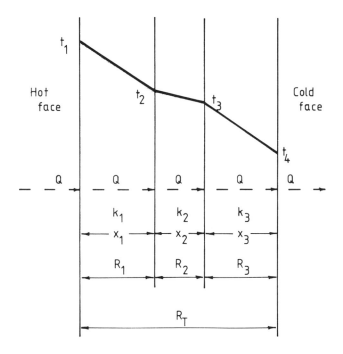

Fig. 11.6 — Conduction through several layers in series.

Equation 11.13 can here be used in the form

$$Q = \frac{\Delta t_T}{R_T} \tag{11.14}$$

where Δt_T = total temperature difference between the hot and cold faces
$= t_1 - t_4$

R_T = total resistance of the layers

$$= R_1 + R_2 + R_3$$

$$= \frac{x_1}{k_1 A} + \frac{x_2}{k_2 A} + \frac{x_3}{k_3 A} = \Sigma \left(\frac{x}{kA} \right) \tag{11.15}$$

i.e. the total resistance is equal to the sum of the individual resistances. This applies to any number of resistances, not just to the three shown in Fig. 11.6, and so a general expression can be written:

$$R_T = \Sigma R \tag{11.16}$$

Equations 11.13, 11.14 and 11.16 also apply to other shapes, e.g. cylinders and spheres, but the expression for the resistance then needs to be modified. For example, for a cylinder:

$$R = \frac{x}{kA_m} \tag{11.17}$$

where A_m = logarithmic mean of the outside and inside surface areas (A_o and A_i, respectively)

$$= \frac{A_o - A_i}{\ln (A_o / A_i)}$$

11.3.3 Convection and heat transfer coefficients

Very similar principles apply to natural convection and forced convection and regardless of whether the flow is laminar or turbulent. Since most heat transfer equipment is operated with forced convection and turbulent flow, an example of this type is used here by way of illustration. The equations employed (11.18–11.29) are equally valid for natural convection and for laminar flow.

Consider the simple tube-in-tube (or double pipe) heat exchanger (shown in Fig. 11.7a) through which two fluids are passed in turbulent flow and under steady-state conditions. Fig. 11.7b shows the temperature profile through a small section of the heat transfer surface (i.e. the wall of the inner pipe). In the turbulent cores of the two fluids the temperatures are essentially uniform across the section of the exchanger due to the rapid movement of the cross-currents and eddies. In the laminar sub-layers, however, there is no bulk movement in the direction of heat transfer (i.e. perpendicular to the pipe surface) and heat is therefore transferred solely by conduction. Although the thickness of a sub-layer is typically very small, most fluids have very low thermal conductivities and so the sub-layers form appreciable resistances to the transfer of heat. Between the sub-layers lies the pipe-wall which constitutes a third (albeit usually minor) heat transfer resistance. Thus we have three layers through which heat is being transferred by

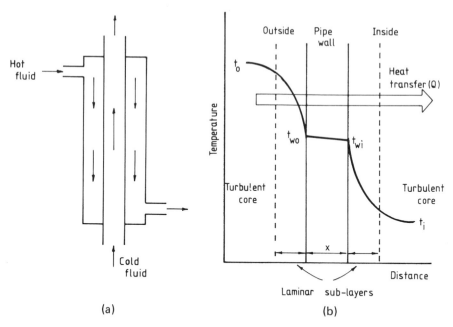

Fig. 11.7 — Heat exchanger: (a) Schematic diagram; (b) Temperature profiles.

conduction and the similarities between Figs 11.6 and 11.7b are self-evident. It is tempting, therefore, to try to apply the conduction equations (11.13–11.17) to the forced convection situation in Fig. 11.7. Certainly for the pipe wall itself, which has fixed boundaries (and which, in general, is cylindrical in shape), Equations 11.13 and 11.17 can be applied:

$$Q = k_w \, A_m \frac{\Delta t_w}{x} \qquad (11.18)$$

where $\Delta t_w = t_{wo} - t_{wi}$.

However, it is not valid to write similar equations for the fluid films on each side of the pipe wall; the laminar sub-layers do not have definite boundaries and so it is impracticable to ascribe precise thicknesses to them. This problem is overcome by the use of heat transfer film coefficients. Thus, for the fluid film on the outside of the pipe wall we can write

$$Q = h_o \, A_o \, \Delta t_o \qquad (11.19)$$

where A_o = outside surface of the pipe
$\Delta t_o = t_o = t_{wo}$
h_o = film coefficient of heat transfer

This film coefficient is defined by Equation 11.19 and is analogous to the ratio k_w/x in Equation 11.18. From Equation 11.19 it can be seen that the units of h_o in the SI system are W/m^2K.

Similarly for heat transfer through the inside film:

$$Q = h_i A_i \, \Delta t_i \tag{11.20}$$

where A_i = inside surface area of the pipe
  $\Delta t_i = t_{wi} = t_i$
  h_o = heat transfer coefficient for the inside film

Equations 11.18–11.20 cannot be used for estimating the area required for heat transfer, as they all involve the pipe wall temperatures (t_{wo} and t_{wi}) which are not usually known. What is needed is an equation (analogous to Equation 11.14 for conduction) that describes the overall heat transfer process in terms of the overall temperature difference, $t_o - t_i$. Ideally, this equation would be similar in form to Equations 11.19 and 11.20, for example:

$$Q = U_o A_o \, \Delta t \tag{11.21}$$

where $\Delta t = t_o - t_i$ and U_o = an overall heat transfer coefficient based on the outside area A_o.

It can be readily shown ([11.9] pp. 311–312) that U_o is related to the film coefficients by the expression:

$$\frac{1}{U_o} = \frac{d_o}{d_i h_i} + \frac{x d_o}{k_w d_m} + \frac{1}{h_o} \tag{11.22}$$

where d_m = logarithmic mean of the inside and outside diameters of the pipe wall (d_i and d_o respectively)

$$= \frac{d_o - d_i}{\ln (d_o/d_i)}$$

Equations 11.19–11.21 are all of the same form as the rate equation (11.8).

In Equation 11.19, for example, the total resistance is represented by $1/U_o A_o$, and $1/U_o$, in Equation 11.22, is seen to be the total (or overall) resistance per unit area of heat transfer surface. In a similar way, the terms on the right-hand side of Equation 11.22 represent the resistances per unit area of the inside film, the pipe wall and the outside film, respectively. So, as in the case of Equation 11.15 for conduction:

$$\text{Total resistance} = \text{sum of individual resistances} \tag{11.23}$$

11.3.4 Fouling of heat transfer equipment

In the above discussion, leading to Equations 11.21 and 11.22, it was tacitly assumed that the heat transfer surfaces were clean. However, when equipment has been in service for some time these surfaces usually become 'dirty' due to the deposition of scale, corrosion products, solid particles, biological growth or thermal decomposition products, etc. These layers of 'dirt', which usually have low thermal conductivities, present additional resistances to the transfer of heat and the performance of the unit deteriorates. This problem can, and usually must, be alleviated by periodic cleaning of the equipment but this is not the complete answer. Unless some fouling is allowed for at the design stage, the intervals between shut-downs for cleaning may be exceedingly short. It is important, by the careful selection and design of the equipment, to reduce fouling to a minimum and, whenever appropriate, to make suitable provision for subsequent cleaning (by chemical or mechanical methods). But, in addition, it is essential to anticipate the deposition of dirt by introducing into Equation 11.22 additional resistances called dirt, scale or fouling factors; i.e. if R_i = fouling factor for the inside surface, and R_o = fouling factor for the outside surface, then the 'design' or 'dirty' overall heat transfer coefficient is given by:

$$\frac{i}{U_{oD}} = \frac{d_o}{d_i h_i} + \frac{x d_o}{k_w d_m} + \frac{1}{h_o} + R_i + R_o \qquad (11.24)$$

From Equations 11.22 and 11.24

$$\frac{1}{U_{oD}} = \frac{1}{U_{oC}} + R_i + R_o \qquad (11.25)$$

where U_{oC} = the overall coefficient for the clean exchanger.

Thus, if performance tests are carried out on the clean exchanger (giving U_{oC}) and again when the unit has been in use for some time (giving U_{oD}) the total of the fouling factors $(R_i + R_o)$ can be estimated. The individual fouling factors can be determined by cleaning one of the surfaces (i.e. making either R_i or R_o equal to zero), putting the exchanger back on stream and again measuring the overall coefficient (U'_{oD} say). Then the remaining fouling factor is given by:

$$R = \frac{1}{U'_{oD}} - \frac{1}{U_{oC}} \qquad (11.26)$$

11.3.5 Use of fouling factors in design
In using Equation 11.24 for design purposes, experimental values of the fouling factors should be used whenever practicable and these values should ideally have been determined under conditions as similar as possible to those expected in the equipment being designed (see Section 11.3.6). Unless actual data on fouling are available, the use of fouling factors must be considered to be arbitrary [11.7]. In the absence of experimental values, approximate fouling data for use in design can be found [11.12; 11.13], but it is unfortunate in the present context that most of these data relate to petroleum-based materials.

The tabulated fouling factors are intended to protect the exchanger from delivering less than the required process heat load for a period of about 1–$1\frac{1}{2}$ years [11.13]. In the chemical and most non-food industries requiring very long uninterrupted production runs, the usual practice is to aim, at the design stage, to select suitable fouling factors for the various units so that they all become dirty at about the same time, regardless of the type of service. It is then possible to clean (by chemical or mechanical means) all these items of equipment during a single shut-down. This procedure is of course impracticable for units that foul very rapidly and spare or stand-by equipment must usually be installed.

It may well be feasible to follow the above practice for service streams in bioprocessing but, for the biological materials themselves, considerations of hygiene may have to take precedence over the thermal resistance aspects of fouling. Those considerations will therefore dictate the length of the intervals between shut-downs for cleaning and the design fouling factors should be selected accordingly.

There are, of course, bioprocesses in which hygiene is not of any importance (e.g. sludge processing; see Chapter 5). However, data for the fouling factors that can be applied when sewage sludge is being either heated or cooled are limited. Brade *et al.* [11.14] quote figures of 0.033 and 0.27 cal $cm^{-2}\,s^{-1}\,°C^{-1}$ for the sludge and water sides respectively of a concentric tube exchanger.

In all circumstances, if experience shows that the fouling factor allowed at the design stage was inadequate (i.e. too frequent cleaning is needed), then a larger value of R should be kept in mind for future design work.

11.3.6 Fouling factor optimisation

The estimation of fouling factors during the design of a unit involves both physical and economic considerations, many of which vary from user to user, even for apparently identical services. The main factors [11.12] which influence the choice of the appropriate fouling factor(s) are:

(a) Physical considerations, i.e.
— nature of fluid and material deposited
— temperature of fluid
— temperature of tube walls
— tube wall material and finish
— fluid velocity
— operating time between cleanings

(b) Economic considerations, including
— initial cost of exchanger
— variation of cost with size
— frequency of cleanings required
— cost of cleaning (including loss of production)
— fluid pumping charges

The optimum design fouling factor will be that which gives the lowest total annual cost for the heat exchanger. This is ideally based on past experience and current or projected costs.

It can clearly be seen from the above that the accurate estimation of fouling factors in the absence of practical data is virtually impossible due to the large number of factors which need to be considered. In addition, the effects of these various factors are not known quantitatively except in a few special cases [11.12; 11.13]. Even when experimental values are available, care must be exercised when applying these in design work unless the operating conditions are to be identical to those under which the fouling factors were obtained. When experimental data are not available, published figures may be used to give an approximate value for the design overall coefficient.

11.3.7   Mean temperature difference in heat exchangers
In the heat transfer rate equation $Q = U_o A_o \, \Delta t$, Δt is the difference between the bulk temperatures (t_o and t_i) of the two fluids (Fig. 11.7b). The magnitude of this temperature difference will usually change as the fluids pass through the equipment, as shown in Figs 11.8 and 11.9 for the simple cases of parallel and countercurrent flow.

Since Δt varies along the length of the exchanger, we need to be able to calculate a mean temperature difference, Δt_m, to use in the heat transfer rate equation which now becomes:

$$Q = U_o A_o \, \Delta t_m \qquad\qquad (11.27)$$

It can be shown ([11.6] pp. 169–171) that, for both parallel and counter-current flow, Δt_m is the logarithmic mean of the terminal temperature differences $\Delta t_1 - \Delta t_2$, i.e.

$$\Delta t_m = \frac{\Delta t_1 - \Delta t_2}{\ln(\Delta t_1/\Delta t_2)} \qquad\qquad (11.28)$$

This is usually referred to as the log mean temperature difference or LMTD.

When the flow is neither pure parallel nor pure countercurrent (as is the case, for example, in most shell and tube exchangers), a correction factor F is introduced into Equation 11.27. Graphical methods of obtaining values for this factor are available elsewhere [11.6; 11.7; 11.9; 11.12; 11.13].

11.3.8   Examples—heat transfer by forced convection
The ways in which the above series of equations can be used in practice can be illustrated by two simple examples:

(1) an outline design for a heat exchanger;
(2) the assessment of the performance of an existing exchanger.

In both cases, the calculations centre around the heat transfer rate equation (Equation 11.27) and a heat balance (see also Figs 11.8b, 11.9b and 11.10):

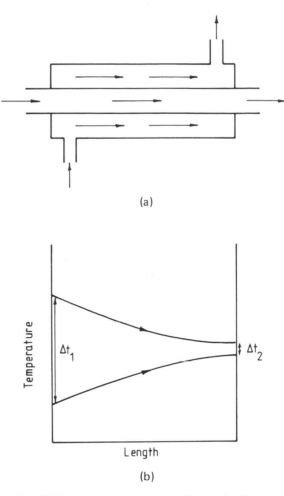

Fig. 11.8 — Parallel flow heat exchanger: (a) Schematic diagram; (b) Overall
temperature profile.

$$Q = \dot{m}_h C_h (t_{h1} - t_{h2}) = \dot{m}_c C_c (t_{c1} - t_{c2}) \qquad (11.29)$$

where $\dot{m}_h$, $\dot{m}_c$ = mass flow rates of the hot and cold fluids, respectively;
C_h, C_c = specific heats of the two fluids; and the temperatures (t) are as
defined in Fig. 11.10.

11.3.8.1 *Example 1—Outline design for a heat exchanger* (see Section
11.4)
(1) Determine the heat duty (Q) from the heat balance (Equation 11.29).
(2) Calculate LMTD (Δt_m) from Equation 11.28.
(3) Estimate overall heat transfer coefficient (U_{oD}) from Equation 11.24.
(4) Estimate the area (A_o) needed for heat transfer from the rate equation
(Equation 11.27).

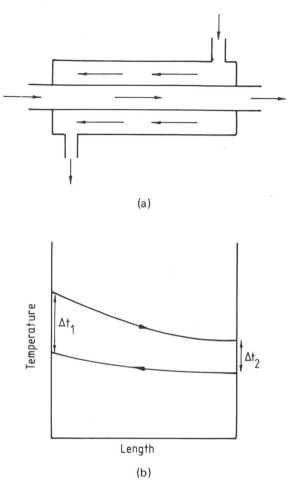

(a)

(b)

Fig. 11.9 — Counter current flow heat exchanger: (a) Schematic diagram; (b) Overall temperature profile.

11.3.8.2 Example 2—Performance of an existing exchanger

(1) Measure the fluid flow rates ($\dot{m}_h$ and $\dot{m}_c$) and all inlet and outlet temperatures (four in total). Then determine the heat duty (Q) from the heat balance (Equation 11.29). (If only five of the six quantities can be measured, the sixth can be calculated from the heat balance, but this neglects any heat losses to or gains from the surroundings.)

(2) Calculate LMTD (Δt_m) from Equation 11.28.

(3) Obtain a value for the heat transfer area (A_o) of the exchanger.

(4) Calculate the overall heat transfer coefficient (U_{oD}) from the rate equation (Equation 11.27).

(5) If required, fouling factor data can be obtained by carrying out further performance tests, as described in Sections 11.3.4 to 11.3.6 and then applying Equations 11.25 and 11.26.

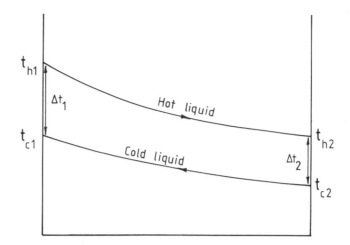

Fig. 11.10 — Temperature profile in a heat exchanger.

11.4   HEAT EXCHANGER SELECTION AND DESIGN

11.4.1   Introduction

In concept heat exchange is a simple process: in an exchanger heat is transferred from the warmer to the cooler stream by conduction and convection and sometimes, chiefly in the case of gases, also by radiation. In order for the heat transfer to proceed the two streams must be moved away from each other before equilibrium can be established so that a temperature difference between them is always maintained. This apparent simplicity is, however, deceptive. Due to, *inter alia*, the diversity of process requirements and the wide range of heat transfer equipment available, selection and design of the equipment is not a simple matter. It involves the interaction of many branches of technology and is most unlikely in practice to be carried out by a single individual.

11.4.2   Outline of design procedure

The complete design of a heat exchanger can be broken down into five major phases:

(1) *Process requirements*. It is necessary to specify or estimate flowrates, temperatures and temperature programmes, pressures and permissible pressure drops, condition of fluids (boiling, condensing, etc.), product specification, space available, etc.
(2) *Type selection*. The type of exchanger to be used will depend upon all the above factors plus material(s) of construction, fouling tendencies, mechanical features (for installation, inspection, hygiene, cleaning, modification and repair) and costs (both capital and operating).
(3) *thermal design*. This involves consideration not only of heat transfer but also of pressure drop; usually an attempt should be made to optimise the design on an economic basis.

(4) *Preliminary mechanical design.* Here one is concerned with operating temperatures and pressures, the corrosion characteristics of the fluids, the relative thermal expansions and the accompanying thermal stresses, the relationship of the exchanger to other process equipment, etc.

(5) *Design for manufacture.* This requires the translation of the physical characteristics and dimensions into a unit which can be built at a reasonable cost. Selection of materials, seals, enclosures and the optimum mechanical arrangement has to be made and the manufacturing procedures must be specified. Standard units or components are used wherever possible in order to minimise costs.

Phases 1, 4 and 5 are beyond the scope of this present chapter and readers are referred to the text by Schlunder [11–15]. Phase 2 (Type selection) is dealt with in the next section, and phase 3 (Thermal design) is discussed briefly in Section 11.4.4.

11.4.3 Type selection
11.4.3.1 Introduction
Heat exchangers can be classified according to the function that they perform, e.g. they may be termed coolers, heaters, evaporators, boilers or condensers, etc. However, a more useful classification is according to whether the heat is transferred by direct or indirect contact and, in the latter case, to subdivide further by the type of heat transfer surface, viz. whether it is made from straight tubes, coils, flat or curved plates, etc.

11.4.3.2 Direct-contact heat exchangers
In this type of exchanger the hot and cold streams, one or both of which will be a fluid, are brought into intimate contact with each other, so it is imperative that the two streams shall be compatible. The heat transfer area between the two streams is provided by the surfaces of particles, bubbles, droplets or liquid films. In most direct-contact operations there will be simultaneous transfer of mass between the phases, which often adds to the attraction of the process. High rates of heat and mass transfer are achieved and the equipment used is of simple design and relatively cheap. Direct-contact heat transfer is particularly useful for fluids which are highly fouling and for liquids containing suspended solids.

Most applications involve the contact of a gas or vapour stream with either a liquid or a solid. Examples of gas–liquid processes include gas quenching and desuperheating, humidification, water cooling and spray drying. In these cases it is, almost invariably, the liquid that is dispersed and the equipment usually consists of a chamber or column fitted with sprays. Often baffles or packed beds are incorporated to improve interphase contact and reduce back mixing. One example of a gas-dispersed process is submerged combustion where combustion gases are bubbled through the liquid to be heated and/or evaporated. Direct-contact heat transfer between a gas and a solid occurs in the fluidised bed quick-freezing of fruit and vegetables.

Since most of these processes involve simultaneous heat and mass transfer, the design techniques are more complex than for indirect-contact heat transfer. Design methods for most types of direct-contact heat exchanger are given by Perry and Green [11.7] and a number of references are also listed by Sinnott [11.16].

11.4.3.3 Indirect-contact heat exchangers

In these exchangers the two fluids are separated by a dividing wall, usually of metal (but sometimes of graphite, glass or plastic) and either tubular in shape or fabricated from sheet material (see Fig. 11.11).

The most common indirect-contact exchangers are:

— Shell and tube exchangers
— Tube banks (air-cooled exchangers)
— Double-pipe exchangers (including scraped-surface exchangers)
— Plate exchangers
— Spiral exchangers
— Vessels with coils and/or jackets

and these are discussed in the sections below. Because of space limitations it has not been possible to include information on equipment designed specifically for evaporation or condensation, fired heaters, heat exchangers for solids, graphite block exchangers, etc. For details of these and other types of heat transfer equipment see Perry and Green [11.7].

Design methods for most of these exchangers are well established and data are readily available [11.7; 11.15; 11.17]. However, the various types of both plate and scraped-surface exchangers are of proprietary design and, although some outline design techniques have been published, the final detailed specification is almost invariably left to the specialist manufacturers; some pilot-scale trials may be necessary.

The major factors to be considered in the selection of a heat exchanger for a particular application are:

(a) maximum operating pressure(s);
(b) temperature ranges of the fluids;
(c) material(s) of construction required;
(d) sizes available.

These and some other characteristics of several types of heat exchangers are tabulated in Table 11.1 [11.18; 11.19], which should enable a preliminary selection to be made. Further information about the special features of these exchangers (and of process vessels fitted with coils and/or jackets) is given below.

11.4.3.4 Shell and tube heat exchangers

A shell and tube (or 'tubular') exchanger consists of a bundle of tubes enclosed within a cylindrical shell. One fluid flows inside the tubes and the other flows outside the tube bundle (on the 'shell' side). The ends of the tubes are fitted into tube-plates which separate the two fluids. Baffles are fitted on the shell side both to support the tubes and to direct the flow of fluid

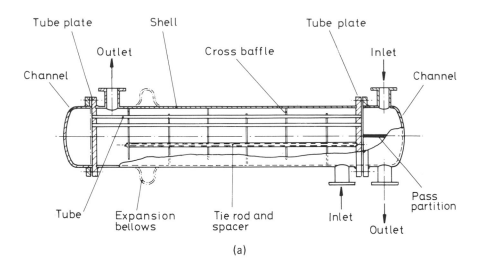

Tube plate Shell Tube plate

Outlet   Cross baffle Inlet

Channel   Channel

Tube Expansion Tie rod and Inlet   Pass
    bellows   spacer   partition

Outlet

(a)

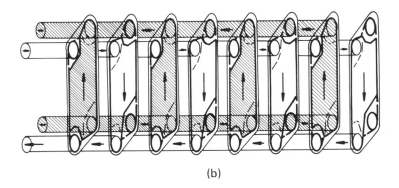

(b)

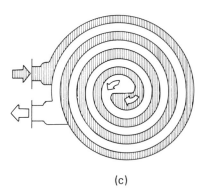

(c)

Fig. 11.11 — (a) Tubular heat exchanger; (b) Plate heat exchanger; (c) Spiral heat exchanger.

Table 11.1 — Chief characteristics of compact and tubular exchangers

	Plate	Spiral spiral-flow	Spiral cross-flow	Shell and tube	Double pipe	Air-cooled cooled
Heat transfer area per unit (m²)	0.1–1 200	up to 300	up to 300	10–1 000 per shell	up to 200[a]	5–200
Maximum liquid flow rate per unit (m³ h⁻¹)	2 500	400	8 000	Practically no limitation	Relatively low	Practically no limitation
Maximum gas flow rate per unit (m³ h⁻¹, 0.1 MPa, 0°C)	30 000	4 000	100 000			
Temperature range (°C)	−40 to 200	−40 to 400	−40 to 400	−200 to about 600[b]	−100 to about 600[b]	High on process side
Pressure range (depending on temperature) (MPa)	to 2.5	to 2.0	to 2.0	to 30.7[c]	to 30.7 (shell) to 140 (tubes)	High on process side

[a]For areas above about 20 m², shell and tube exchangers are usually cheaper.
[b]Higher with special materials.
[c]For higher pressures, design codes not applicable.

across the bundle, thus increasing the fluid velocity and the rate of heat transfer.

This is a particularly versatile method of construction and various additional features may be incorporated into the design if necessary, for example:

(a) to increase the number of passes made by each fluid as it travels through the exchanger;
(b) to allow for differential expansion between the shell and the tubes;
(c) to permit removal/replacement of the tube bundle;
(d) to facilitate mechanical cleaning of the outside of the tubes (cleaning inside the tubes being relatively easy).

Other important features of the shell and tube exchanger are:

(a) the heat transfer area/volume ratio is high;
(b) it can be constructed from a wide range of materials;
(c) it has an excellent shape for operating under pressure or vacuum;
(d) the design procedure is well established;
(e) fabrication uses standard techniques.

It is hardly surprising that the shell and tube exchanger is by far the most commonly used type of exchanger in the chemical and allied industries. This popularity should not, however, permit the undoubted merits of alternative types of equipment to be overlooked.

11.4.3.5 Double-pipe heat exchangers

Most double-pipe exchangers are fabricated from two concentric pipes, although multitube types (with seven or more tubes in a bundle) are also available. They are simple in construction and low in cost (at least in sizes up to about 20 m^2) and standard sections are offered by a number of manufacturers. The inner pipe is usually 20–100 mm in diameter and its outer surface is almost invariably fitted with longitudinal fins; these are of particular benefit when the fluid flowing in the annular has a relatively low film coefficient of heat transfer. The outer pipe diameter is normally within the range 50–150 mm although the shells of multitube units can be up to 300 mm. Because of the comparatively small diameters of the pipes only low flow rates can be accommodated, but the design is well adapted to high temperature and high pressure applications. Tube lengths are generally 3–7 m and heat transfer areas up to about 20 m^2; larger sizes are not usually competitive in price with shell and tube exchangers.

True countercurrent flow is readily achieved (or, indeed, true parallel flow if desired): a useful feature when very close temperature approaches are required and/or the fluid temperatures cover wide ranges.

11.4.3.6 Scraped-surface heat exchangers

These are generally of double-pipe construction with the process fluid flowing through the inner pipe and the cooling or heating medium in the jacket. Coaxial with the inner pipe is a rotating shaft carrying blades (usually spring loaded) which scrape the inside surface of the pipe thereby producing a high heat transfer coefficient. This type of exchanger is particularly useful where the process fluid is highly viscous or heat sensitive or where the heat transfer process is accompanied by crystallisation, solvent extraction or severe fouling.

11.4.3.7 Air-cooled heat exchangers

In an air-cooled exchanger, ambient air is caused to flow over a bank of externally finned tubes (through which the fluid to be cooled or condensed is passed) by fans mounted below or above the tube bank—forced and induced draught, respectively.

Air-cooled exchangers have long been used for process cooling and condensation in areas where water supplies are inadequate and/or expensive but they can also be competitive with water-cooled units when water is abundant. In Europe, where seasonal variations in ambient temperature are relatively small compared with some other regions of the world, most (and on some plants all) process cooling is carried out in air-cooled exchangers. It has been suggested by Frank [11.20] that, in moderate climates, air-cooling will usually be the better choice when the minimum process temperature exceeds 65°C and water-cooling when this temperature is below 50°C. Between these temperatures the choice is not clear-cut and a detailed economic assessment is needed.

The performance of an air-cooled exchanger can be adversely affected by nearby sources of heat and also by recirculation of heated air from its own outlet or those of other air-cooled exchangers. Recirculation will be influenced by wind direction and, for example, the presence of neighbouring buildings and other items of equipment. Thus the siting of an air-cooled exchanger is more critical than that of other types.

Air-cooled exchangers are usually purchased as packaged units and manufacturers should normally be consulted regarding the selection, siting and specification of suitable units. Approximate sizing can be carried out using the overall heat transfer coefficients in Table 11.2.

11.4.3.8 Plate heat exchangers

A plate heat exchanger (sometimes termed a plate and frame exchanger) consists of a stack of thin metal plates, separated by gaskets round the edges, and clamped together in a frame, the design principle being similar to that of a plate and frame filter press. The gaskets are so designed that the two fluids are made to flow through adjacent gaps between the plates and interleakage is virtually impossible. The plates are corrugated to impart rigidity, to improve the heat transfer characteristics and to ensure good flow distribution. Pressure drop is low and heat transfer coefficients are usually higher than in tubular exchangers.

Plates are available in a wide range of metals and a variety of gasket materials are used. The nature of the latter limits the operating temperature to a maximum of about 250°C. The pressure limit is about 20 bar.

One particular virtue of the plate exchanger is its compactness: a large

Table 11.2 — Typical overall heat transfer coefficients. (Reproduced with permission from Sinnott [11.16]).

Shell and tube exchangers		
Hot fluid	Cold fluid	U (Wm^{-2} °C^{-1})
Heat exchangers		
Water	Water	800–1500
Organic solvents	Organic solvents	100–300
Light oils	Light oils	100–400
Heavy oils	Heavy oils	50–300
Gases	Gases	10–50
Coolers		
Organic solvents	Water	250–750
Light oils	Water	350–900
Heavy oils	Water	60–300
Gases	Water	20–300
Organic solvents	Brine	150–500
Water	Brine	600–1200
Gases	Brine	15–250
Heaters		
Steam	Water	1500–4000
Steam	Organic solvents	500–1000
Steam	Light oils	300–900
Steam	Heavy oils	60–450
Steam	Gases	30–300
Dowtherm	Heavy oils	50–300
Dowtherm	Gases	20–200
Flue gases	Steam	30–100
Flue	Hydrocarbon vapours	30–100
Condensers		
Aqueous vapours	Water	1000–1500
Organic vapours	Water	700–1000
Organics (some non-condensibles)	Water	500–700
Vacuum condensers	Water	200–500
Vaporisers		
Steam	Aqueous solutions	1000–1500
Steam	Light organics	900–1200
Steam	Heavy organics	600–900

Air-cooled exchangers

Process fluid	
Water	300–450
Light organics	50–150
Heavy organics	300–700
Gases, 5–10 bar	50–100
Gases, 10–30 bar	100–300
Condensing hydrocarbons	300–600

Immersed coils

Coil	Pool	
Natural circulation		
Steam	Dilute aqueous solutions	500–1000
Steam	Light oils	200–300
Steam	Heavy oils	70–150
Aqueous solutions	Water	200–500
Light oils	Water	100–150
Agitated		
Steam	Dilute aqueous solutions	800–1500
Steam	Light oils	300–500
Steam	Heavy oils	200–400
Aqueous solutions	Water	400–700
Light oils	Water	200–300

Jacketed vessels

Jacket	Vessel	
Steam	Dil. aqueous soln.	500–700
Stcam	Light organics	250–500
Water	Dil. aqueous soln.	200–500
Water	Light organics	200–300

heat transfer area can be packed into a small volume. In addition, it can be readily opened for cleaning and inspection and the heat transfer area can be adjusted by adding or subtracting plates. If required, an exchanger can be designed for multiple duty, i.e. several different fluids can flow in different parts of the exchanger.

In plate heat exchangers the transition from laminar to turbulent flow occurs at very low Reynolds numbers (usually between 100 and 400 depending on plate design) and this makes them particularly suitable for use with very high viscosity liquids (up to 30 N s m^{-2}).

Even if none of these special features are of paramount importance, the use of a plate exchanger may well be justifiable on economic grounds compared with, say, a shell and tube exchanger. For example, if stainless steel tube-side construction needs to be specified, the plate exchanger will be competitive with a tubular unit. If all-stainless steel construction is essential, a plate exchanger will be cheaper than a tubular design.

Plate heat exchangers are of proprietary designs and the details of their specification will normally be established in consultation with the manufacturers.

11.4.3.9 Spiral heat exchangers

A spiral heat exchanger is made from two sheets of metal (typically about 1 m wide and up to 30 m or more in length) rolled, like a swiss roll, into a compact cylindrical shape. This provides two relatively long continuous spiral passages (each a narrow rectangle in cross-section) and gives a very close approach to true countercurrent or parallel flow.

The design of the spiral heat exchanger eliminates the problems caused by differential expansion, by-passing and flow reversals (with their associated pressure drop). Solids can be kept in suspension and turbulent flow is developed at a lower Reynolds Number than in straight tubes. Access to each spiral passage for inspection and cleaning is obtained by removing the respective end cover. Details of temperature and pressure limitations and materials of construction are given in Table 11.1.

11.4.3.10 Process vessels

Process vessels or tanks are simple and versatile and are particularly useful when a number of different processes are to be carried out in the same piece of equipment and/or when good access for cleaning is an important requirement. They can be used for batch, semi-batch or continuous processes and are usually equipped with mechanical agitation (internal stirrer or external pump) and fitted with internal and/or external heat-transfer surfaces (e.g. coils and jackets, respectively).

(a) Internal heat transfer surfaces

Coils are usually fabricated from metal but glass or PTFE coils are also available. Helical coils are recommended when a large heat transfer area is needed for rapid heating or cooling.

Finned tubing can be employed for fluids having poor heat transfer characteristics but cleaning may then become a problem. Spiral or serpentine coils give good bottom coverage which is particularly important when the material being processed solidifies on cooling.

Plate- or panel-coils are made from a pair of metal sheets with one or both of them embossed to form passages for the heating or cooling medium. Plate-coils may be flat or curved and are available in a range of standard sizes. Process vessels have been fabricated using plate-coils for the sides or bottom.

(b) *External heat transfer surfaces*

Jackets or external coils are often used for vessels that need frequent cleaning or those (for example, with glass linings) that are difficult to equip with internal heat transfer surfaces. One obvious disadvantage is that the area available for heat transfer is limited.

Even if external coils make good contact with the outside of the vessel, heat transfer rates are usually very low unless heat transfer cements are used. These putty-like materials of high thermal conductivity are applied so as to fill the spaces between the coil and the surfaces of the vessel.

A jacket gives a better overall heat transfer coefficient than external coils but usually lower than in a tubular or plate-type exchanger.

11.4.4 Thermal design

The key relationships in the thermal design procedure are the heat transfer rate equation (11.27):

$$Q = U_{oD} A_o \, \Delta t_m$$

and Equation 11.24 for the overall heat transfer coefficient:

$$\frac{1}{U_{oD}} = \frac{1}{h_o} + \frac{x d_o}{k_w d_m} + \frac{d_o}{d_i h_i} + R_i + R_o$$

Most of the factors on the right-hand side of Equation 11.24 depend not only on the physical characteristics of the fluids, the process requirements, etc., but also on the geometry of the exchanger. For most types of exchanger, therefore, one cannot arrive directly at the final design. First, an approximate design is obtained by a short-cut method (using an approximate value for the overall coefficient, U_{oD}). Then the performance of this exchanger is assessed and, if necessary, its design is modified by an iterative process until it is adjudged to be satisfactory. Comprehensive design techniques for particular types of heat exchangers (with the exception of proprietary designs) will be found in the references cited in the appropriate sections above.

No attempt is made here to present a detailed design procedure, but the method suggested will enable the approximate size of an exchanger to be estimated:

(a) Select an approximate value of U_{oD} from Table 11.2.
(b) Calculate Δt_m using Equation 11.28:

$$\Delta t_{\rm m} = \frac{\Delta t_1 - \Delta t_2}{\ln (\Delta t_1 / \Delta t_2)}$$

(c) From the process requirements evaluate Q using Equation 11.29;

$$Q = \dot{m}_{\rm h} C_{\rm h}(t_{\rm h1} - t_{\rm h2}) = \dot{m}_{\rm c} C_{\rm c}(t_{\rm c1} - t_{\rm c2})$$

(d) Estimate the heat transfer area $A_{\rm o}$ using Equation 11.27:

$$Q = U_{\rm oD} A_{\rm o} \, \Delta t_{\rm m}$$

While the heat transfer area obtained is only a first step towards the complete design of the heat exchanger, a knowledge of its approximate size may help in the selection process and/or enable a rough capital cost estimate to be made [11.19]. Note, however, that exchangers should not be selected solely on the basis of lowest capital cost. Before the design is finalised an attempt should be made to optimise the design on an economic basis (except for relatively small exchangers). The optimum design is the one that gives the lowest total annual cost (including the costs of operation, maintenance and depreciation).

11.5   MASS TRANSFER

11.5.1   Introduction

We now give brief consideration to some of the processes that are concerned with changing the compositions of materials, usually with the object of achieving at least a partial separation of the components. Some methods, such as filtration or centrifugation, are purely mechanical and will not be discussed here, but many others, such as drying, crystallisation, leaching, distillation, etc., involve changes in the composition of solutions—solid, liquid or gaseous. These changes of composition are encouraged to occur by establishing concentration gradients, under the action of which components will diffuse towards regions of lower concentration, i.e. these processes involve *mass transfer* (see also Chapter 10). The rates at which mass transfer processes take place can be expressed in the form of the general rate equation (Equation 11.8).

In most heat transfer processes the two phases are separated by a solid wall, although direct-contact heat transfer (as in heating with 'live' steam and in quick-freezing) is not uncommon. However, the most widely used mass transfer processes almost invariably involve direct and intimate contact between two immiscible phases; several examples were cited in the previous paragraph. In all mass transfer operations diffusion occurs in at least one of them and often in both. For example, in drying, liquid water diffuses through the solid towards the interface where it vaporises and then diffuses as vapour into the air stream.

11.5.2 Diffusion

Diffusion may result from molecular action alone or by a combination of molecular and turbulent action. In solids, diffusion is also influenced to a considerable extent by the internal structure of the material.

Molecular diffusion takes place as a result of the random movement of individual molecules through a substance by virtue of their thermal energy. It is the only mechanism by which mass transfer can occur in a homogeneous solid or in a fluid at rest. In gases (see Chapter 10), rates of true molecular diffusion are very low but in liquids they are even lower, by a factor of the order of 10^4; in solids, molecular diffusion is hardly detectable. However, much higher rates of mass transfer can readily be achieved in a fluid by rapid mixing (brought about, for example, by mechanical means or by convection currents), a process termed 'eddy' or 'turbulent' diffusion. In turbulent motion the rapid movement of the eddies is a highly effective means of transfer.

It is clear that molecular diffusion and eddy diffusion are analogous to conduction and convection, respectively, in heat transfer.

Whenever laminar flow exists, whether throughout the entire bulk of the fluid or, in the case of turbulent flow, inside the eddies and in the laminar sub-layer, molecular diffusion is the only means by which mass transfer can occur in a direction perpendicular to that of the flow of fluid. Thus, even when the bulk of a phase is in turbulent flow the laminar sub-layer adjacent to the interface forms an appreciable resistance to mass transfer.

In a mixture of two components **A** and **B** the rate of molecular diffusion of **A** is given by Fick's law:

$$N_A = -D_{AB}\frac{dC_A}{dy} \tag{11.30}$$

where N_A = molar rate of diffusion of **A** per unit area (mole unit time^{-1} unit area^{-1})

C_A = molar concentration of **A** (mole unit volume^{-1})

y = distance in direction of diffusion

D_{AB} = diffusivity or diffusion coefficient for the mixture **A** + **B** (area unit time^{-1})

The analogy has already been drawn between this equation and the corresponding ones for (a) the rate of transfer of momentum (Newton's equation, 11.11), and (b) the rate of transfer of heat by conduction (Fourier's equation, 11.12).

Diffusion is considered to be critical in controlling the transfer of nutrients (including oxygen) to microbes in many fermentations where the biomass has been immobilised either as a floc (activated sludge), or as a film (trickling filters) (see Chapter 1) or within a gel (see Chapter 9). Nutrient limitation by diffusion can also occur in some anaerobic reactors (see Chapter 2).

11.5.3   Mass transfer in solids

The mechanism of mass transfer in most solids is different from that in fluids due to the fact that most solids have a structure and are therefore not homogeneous. The structure is often complex and this is particularly the case with biological materials.

The effect of structure on mass transfer can be illustrated by considering again the process of drying. The rate of movement of water within the solid is of vital importance to the overall drying rate and varies markedly with the structure of the solid. With solids having relatively large open void spaces (characteristic of granular or crystalline solids, usually inorganic), the movement is likely to be controlled by surface tension and gravity forces within the solid. However, most foodstuffs and other organic solids are either amorphous, cellular, fibrous or gel-like. These materials hold moisture as an integral part of the solid structure or trapped within fibres or fine internal pores. Moisture movement is, therefore, slow and occurs by the diffusion of the liquid through the solid structure to the solid/gas interface. The diffusion through the solid is the rate-determining step in the overall mass transfer process carrying the moisture into the bulk of the gas phase.

11.5.4   Conclusion

We have seen that there are many similarities between heat and mass transfer. These extend into the field of transfer rates since *overall mass transfer coefficients* are often employed and these are derived from mass transfer *film coefficients* by the summation of *resistances*. Furthermore, the mean driving force in a mass transfer process is often expressed as the logarithmic mean of the terminal driving force (cf. LMTD in convection).

However, these similarities and others mentioned earlier must not be pressed too far. They do not extend to transfer through solids (discussed above) and there are other important differences, for example:

(a) The interfacial area can rarely be determined accurately for a mass transfer process involving the intimate intermixing of two phases.
(b) Diffusion is the physical flow of matter, which occurs at a definite velocity.
(c) A diffusing component leaves space behind it and room must be found for it at its new location.

These effects have no analogy in the transfer of heat. It should therefore come as no surprise to learn that mass transfer problems tend to be rather complex and to exhibit far greater variety than those occurring in heat transfer. Nevertheless, an understanding of the basic concepts of heat transfer is very useful—some would say essential—if one is to establish at least a qualitative appreciation of mass transfer.

'The relationship between mass and heat transfer is somewhat like the relationship between the English and American languages; if you know one you can get by in the other, but confusion and embarrassment are a consequence of not recognizing the difference between the two' [11.21].

REFERENCES

[11.1] Himmelblau, D. M. (1967) *Basic Principles and Calculations in Chemical Engineering,* 2nd edition, Prentice–Hall.

[11.2] Hougen, O. A., Watson, K. M. and Ragatz, R. A. (1943) *Chemical Process Principles, Part I, Material and Energy Balances,* 2nd edition, John Wiley.

[11.3] Shaheen, E. I. (1975) *Basic Practice of Chemical Engineering,* Houghton Mifflin.

[11.4] Thompson, E. V. and Ceckler, W. H. (1977) *Introduction to Chemical Engineering,* McGraw-Hill.

[11.5] Henley, E. J. and Rosen, E. M. (1969) *Material and Energy Balance Computations,* John Wiley.

[11.6] Coulson, J. M. and Richardson, J. F. (1977) *Chemical Engineering,* Vol. 1, 3rd edition, Pergamon.

[11.7] Perry, R. H. and Green, D. (eds) (1984) *Perry's Chemical Engineers' Handbook,* 6th edition, McGraw-Hill.

[11.8] Treybal, R. E. (1968) *Mass Transfer Operations,* 2nd edition, McGraw-Hill.

[11.9] McCabe, W. L. and Smith, J. C. (1967) *Unit Operations of Chemical Engineering,* 2nd edition, McGraw-Hill.

[11.10] Skelland, A. H. P. (1967) *Non-Newtonian Flow and Heat Transfer,* John Wiley.

[11.11] Science Research Council (1975) *Non-Newtonian Flow—A Review of Problems and Research,* SRC, London.

[11.12] Tubular Exchanger Manufacturers Association (1978) *Standards of TEMA,* 6th edition.

[11.13] Kern, D. Q. (1950) *Process Heat Transfer,* McGraw-Hill.

[11.14] Brade, C. E., Noone, G. P., Powell, E., Rundle, H. and Whyley, J. (1982) The application of developments in anaerobic digestion within Severn–Trent Water Authority. *Wat. Pollut. Control,* **81**, 200–219.

[11.15] Schlunder, E. U. (ed.) (1983) *Heat Exchanger Design Handbook,* Hemisphere.

[11.16] Sinnott, R. K. (1983) *Chemical Engineering. Vol. 6—Design,* Pergamon.

[11.17] Ludwig, E. E. (ed.) (1965) *Applied Process Design for Chemical and Petrochemical Plants,* Vol. 3, Gulf.

[11.18] Jensen, S. (1968) *Heat Exchanger Selection,* Chem. Process Engng., Heat Transfer Survey, 141.

[11.19] Linnhoff, B. *et al.* (1982) *A User Guide on Process Integration for the Efficient Use of Energy,* Inst. Chem. Engrs.

[11.20] Frank, O. (1978) Practical aspects of heat transfer. In *Chem. Eng. Prog. Tech. Manual,* A.I.Ch.E.

[11.21] Toor, H. L. and Condiff, D. W. (1970) *Chem. Eng. Education,* Fall 1970, p. 188.

12

Biopossibilities: the next few years

Christopher F. Forster,
Department of Civil Engineering, University of Birmingham, UK
and
D. A. John Wase
Biochemical Engineering Section, Department of Chemical Engineering, University of Birmingham, UK

12.1 INTRODUCTION

As can be seen from the preceding chapters, biotechnology currently has a significant role in protecting and rehabilitating the environment. Clearly, this will continue, in spite of future changes in popular or political policy, improvements in technology or merely expediency. However, because of this constantly changing situation, the authors must, of necessity, indulge in a degree of controlled speculation to provide some indication about how and in which direction biotechnology should develop to provide solutions for environmental problems over the next decade.

12.2 LIQUID WASTE TREATMENT

The biological treatment of wastewaters is a well proven technology (see Chapters 1 and 2). However, in their current form, the processes can only degrade (with any degree of control) carbonaceous compounds, which in structural terms are relatively simple, and ammoniacal compounds. Inorganics, toxic chemicals and structurally complex or highly substituted organics (which may also be toxic) are bound to the biomass or degraded to a degree but the removal that can be achieved is much less controllable. For example, no guarantee can be given for the removal of heavy metal ions by the activated sludge process (see Table 12.1). Although the concentrations of these 'uncontrollable pollutants' in municipal sewage can be and are limited by Trade Effluent Control measures [see 12.2], they still pose an

Table 12.1 — Metal removal efficiencies in activated sludge plants [12.1]

Metal	Removal efficiency (%)
Aluminium	70–98
Cadmium	30–92
Chromium	63–99
Copper	69–98
Iron	87–98
Lead	42–100
Manganese	25–31
Mercury	68–100
Nickel	25–74
Zinc	44–100

environmental threat by their passage through a treatment plant into the receiving watercourse. Alternatively, if they become incorporated into the sludge, they can become a problem when the sludge is disposed of to land. What is needed, therefore, is for the biomass (either in the main reactor or as a specialised treatment/pretreatment) to be given some controllable capability of degrading or de-toxifying more of these complex chemicals. This would entail either strain selection (see Chapter 6) or genetic manipulation (Chapter 7). This use of a specialised biomass could arguably be said to have started with the work at the British Coke Research Association on the treatment of phenols and thiocyanates [12.3; 12.4] and there are many other examples of acclimatised biomass being used to treat specific industrial wastes. However, these have tended to be natural developments rather than ones which were imposed by technological innovation. Nevertheless, this type of work can be considered as laying the foundations for the future. Indeed, continuing this analogy, one could say that the building has started. ICI, for example, are developing a treatment for cyanide based on fungi (for example *Stemphylium loti; Gloeocercospora sorghi* [12.5]). These species have the ability to transform the cyanide to formamide using the enzyme cyanide hydratase:

$$H_2 + CN \longrightarrow HCO\,NH_2 \tag{12.1}$$

Treatment can be effected with processes based on conventional treatment (i.e. activated sludge; trickling filters), artificially immobilised biomass (see Chapter 9) or even immobilised enzymes. Indeed, several companies market or are developing microbe mixtures for specialised applications such as the treatment of high carbohydrate wastes or petrochemical wastewaters. Cultures are also available for promoting the development of a flocculent rather than a filamentous flora in activated sludges [12.6]. However, there is some way to go before an operator can expect to have full control (over the complete spectrum of pollutants) of a biotechnologically or genetically engineered biomass. Indeed, this ideal may never be realised. Variations in the amounts and types of pollutant being applied to a process may well mediate against a 'synthetic' biomass since genetically engineered species might not survive within the highly competitive ecosystems which tend to exist in wastewater treatment processes. However, the concept must be tried. A subjective view of wastewater treatment would, almost certainly, highlight nitrification as a prime area for the application of genetic engineering. Is it possible either to reduce the mean generation time of nitrifiers or to transfer the essentials for nitrification to a faster growing bacterium and thereby reduce the minimum sludge age (compatible with full nitrification), to perhaps 2 days?

Another, quite different, area where biotechnological advances could enhance the treatment of wastewaters is that of heavy metal removal. Adsorption by polysaccharides is an established technique for removing metal ions from solution [12.7]. Polysaccharides have also been shown to be involved in the binding of metals by activated sludge [12.8; 12.9]. However, the current state of knowledge is not sufficiently adequate either to know what type of extracellular polymer needs to be produced by the sludge or what environmental/nutritional conditions are needed to maximise polymer production. It is, therefore, not possible at the moment either to optimise or to control metal removal by conventional biological wastewater treatment processes. One possible problem with this approach to metal removal is that the presence of large concentrations of polymer in the sludge may be incompatible with other of the required characteristics (e.g. settlement; filtration) [12.10]. In other words, a proper and complete understanding of the role of sludge polymers is of considerable significance in the development of wastewater treatment biotechnology.

The addition of phosphates to rivers and lakes is a major cause of eutrophication in these waters. Phosphates can be removed by chemical precipitation using lime [12.11] but this entails an extra process step and incurs an additional increment in running costs. Phosphates can also be removed biologically using the 'luxury uptake' principle [12.2]. However, this process has not been examined sufficiently for it to be reliable or amenable to full biotechnological control. If investigations were to show that an adequate reliability/control could not be achieved, then the biotechnologist might well examine alternative surface active agents, since most of the phosphates in wastewaters come from detergent 'builders'. A number of microbial species (e.g. *Nocardia erythropolis*) produce biosurfactants [12.13; 12.14] but the exploitation of these compounds, in commercial terms, is still in its infancy.

Nitrate is another anionic species which is of environmental significance in waters. The recommended concentration for nitrate-nitrogen (NO_3–N) in potable waters is 10 mg $^{-1}$ [12.15]. However, an increasing number of lowland rivers, which are used as supply sources, contain concentrations close to or in excess of this value. A significant proportion of this nitrogen stems from the discharge of nitrified sewage effluent to the river. It is certainly possible to remove nitrogen, almost completely, during the wastewater treatment process (using nitrification–denitrification) but, since there are other inputs of nitrate to a watercourse, in many cases, nitrate removal is deferred until the point of abstraction. Biological denitrification requires anoxic conditions and a carbon-source, such as methanol:

$$NO_3 + CH_3 OH \longrightarrow N_2 + CO_2 + H_2 + OH^- \qquad (12.2)$$

and the most recent technology is based on a fluidised bed reactor [12.16]. Results from this process have shown that up to 14 mg NO_3–N l^{-1} could be removed at temperatures as low as 2°C, the flow-rate being 2.8 Ml d^{-1}. Although these data are impressive, there is a temptation to wonder if an immobilised enzyme system (e.g. nitrate reductase) would be more cost-effective.

12.3 SOLID WASTES

It has been said that many solid wastes are generated as a result of an over-zealous protection of aquatic systems and that their generation merely transfers the problem of pollution from the water to the land. This is obviously a gross over-statement. The aquatic environment must be protected. So must other environments. In this context, therefore, one must question whether it is correct to spread metal-polluted sludges on agricultural land even if national or international guidelines are being followed (see Chapter 5). What happens at the end of the 30-year 'application period'? Might not a more logical and environmentally acceptable alternative be to use a pre-treatment based on de-toxification and metal recovery? The essential elements of such a process are already in existence. It would entail removing metal ions from the sludge with an acid treatment [12.17] and then re-absorbing the metals on specific biopolymers [12.7]. Given a greater understanding of the metal/polymer binding reactions, the polymers could be formulated so that the absorption phase would produce a material analogous to a low-grade ore which could then be processed as such to recover the metallic elements. A process such as this would, obviously, not alleviate the problem of waste solids contaminated with recalcitrant or toxic organic compounds. If a biotechnological process were to be used to stabilise or detoxify these solids, specifically adapted (or genetically engineered) microbes, or microbial consortia, would be required.

However, not all solid wastes are generated from the treatment of liquid wastes, nor are they all toxic. Domestic refuse is a prime example. As a general rule, this is disposed of as landfill with little, if any, control being exercised over its ultimate degradation. The recent development of recovering landfill gas (see Chapter 5) means that 'the tip' can no longer be allowed to operate in an uncontrolled manner but must be considered as yet another bio-reactor. The control and ultimate optimisation of this particular type of reactor may mean that an entire area of waste management policy will have to be re-evaluated. For example, if substrate control is necessary will there have to be a segregation of wastes with certain components of domestic and commercial refuse being proscribed? Such a philosophy poses, in turn, another question. Would this lead to the development of waste disposal policies based on reclamation rather than 'throw-away', destructive technologies? There is certainly sufficient knowledge (see Chapter 5) to control the biochemistry of landfill so that biogas production is optimised. What perhaps is lacking is the motivation to consider them as processes and to accept that this could mean a change in waste management policies.

Solid wastes, be they sewage sludge, domestic refuse or from agriculture, can of course be converted into compost using well-established technology (Chapter 4). However, there are other ways of processing solid wastes which are not so well established. Worm 'farming' (vermiculture) is one such example [12.18]. It is possible, therefore, to wonder if there are other scavenging/degrading/decomposing species which could be used in a controllable way for this purpose.

Biomass cultivation is a topic closely related to solid waste processing. The production of specific types of biomass, by photosynthesis, can also be coupled to the removal of plant nutrients (nitrogen and phosphorus) from water — clearly the concern of the environmental biotechnologist. This is true not only at the point of production but also at the processing stage since enzymic hydrolysis, anaerobic digestion, and fermentation are all used to transform the biomass into commercial products [12.19].

12.4   LAND

'The land is always there.' 'Land is the safest security there is.' This has, perhaps, been the view up to now, but times are changing. On the one hand, urbanisation relentlessly consumes good agricultural land throughout the western world, whilst, on the other hand, agricultural technology improves yields to the point where the EEC is consistently generating vast agricultural surpluses. Under these conditions, British land values are falling, and there is a tendency to regard our heritage rather lightly. However, it is likely that this view is misguided. Over the years, vast areas have been polluted with landfill (see Chapter 5), dumping or accidental spillage, with building residues or rubble. Currently more and more pesticides are being used; the concentration of inorganic ions applied grows whilst in many areas the amount of applied organic matter falls. Whilst the net effect of these changes is not known, not fully understood, and difficult to predict, it is clear that a modest fall in yields could, in the future, return us to the days of shortages. It is therefore germane to this problem to consider, even to speculate on, developments in control and alleviation of such pollution.

Some roles of microbes and microbially produced polymers have already been mentioned in this chapter in connection with the binding of metals in sludges (see Sections 12.2, 12.3). However, as our state of knowledge is insufficient to allow even general predictions (see Section 12.2), the extrapolation of these effects to soils is clearly some time away. There is little doubt that soil polymers together with clay minerals are responsible for binding considerable amounts of cation, but factors affecting the transition from the 'unavailable' cationic state are very imperfectly understood. Perhaps in the future one could extend this knowledge so that the addition of specific polymers when ploughing contaminated soil would ensure a plough layer essentially free of heavy metals for the succeeding season: further polymers added on seeding would promote the necessary slow release of trace elements or even macro-nutrients. Indeed, these effects could be further extended, for whilst organic matter is currently often removed from the ecosystem, political and economic pressures are increasingly forcing the return of such materials as chopped straw to the soil (see Chapter 4). The additon of specific inoculants to degrade this material has already been mentioned: perhaps a little genetic manipulation would permit the required polymers to be produced *in situ*, or at worst during a composting process, whilst a little more engineering could even eventually add nitrogen fixation, preventing the familiar nitrogen-starvation during degradation of the straw, and fertilising the following crop whilst the heavy metals are safely 'locked away'.

Oil can also be a persistent and serious soil pollutant. The natural microbial flora in the soil will, eventually, degrade this form of contamination. A recent development in the reclamation of oil-polluted soil involves mixing pine bark with the affected soil [12.20]. This project, known as 'the microbial regeneration of contaminated soil', depends on the microbes which exist at the bark/air interface and are acclimatised to growth on the complex hydrocarbons constituting the bark resins. It also depends on the ability of the bark to adsorb the polluting oil. In effect, therefore, the oil is concentrated in the presence of microbes acclimatised to degrading molecules of the same type as the oil. In its developmental form, the process utilises a natural absorbant and a natural microbial flora. It is pertinent, therefore, to ask whether the efficiency of the process could be enhanced by using a synthetic absorbant supporting a consortia of genetically engineered bacteria.

The use of co-metabolism/manipulated plasmids in connection with recalcitrant chloro-substituted pesticides is described in Chapters 6 and 7. These techniques are necessary because of land contamination with either pesticide or chemical residue: a distinction can be drawn because the former, whilst possibly cumulative, is applied in relatively low repeated dosages, whilst the concentration of the latter is relatively high. Recycling of organic matter (e.g. fungicide-treated straw) is hindered in the first case; the problem is likely to be alleviated by biological pesticides which are not usually strongly residual. For any serious attempt at reclamation of highly contaminated land (and this is going to be necessary to free potentially valuable sites for redevelopment) there is little doubt that a range of techniques including specialised genetically manipulated degraders, polymer applications, deep tillage and aeration will all prove beneficial.

12.5 AIR

Air pollution in the form of odour nuisance can arise from many processes. The molecules responsible for odours are, very often, organic compounds and as such should be amenable to microbial degradation. One problem is that these compounds are perceptible and, therefore, have the potential for constituting a nuisance, at very low concentrations (Table 12.2) [12.21]. The

Table 12.2 — Absolute threshold concentrations (ATC) for odour-producing compounds [12.21].

Compound	ATC (ppb)
Ethyl mercaptan	0.19
Methyl mercaptan	1.10
Skatole	1.20
Butyric acid	1.00
Valeric acid	0.60
Diallyl sulphide	0.14
Thiophenol	0.06

other is that 'non-point sources' of aerial contamination are not capable of being subjected to control. This, of course, is true whether one is considering the pollution of land, water or air.

However, for point sources, odour nuisances can be controlled by biological treatments. A typical reactor, as currently designed, would be either 'wet' or 'dry'. 'Wet' reactors or bio-scrubbers operate as packed beds with a counter-current flow of liquid (very often sewage) and gas (the contaminated air). The loading rate of the liquid is such that, although a biofilm is produced, its growth is severely limited. The odorous compounds in the gas are transferred to the liquid phase, as they would be in a normal scrubber, and are then oxidised by the flora within the biofilm. The overall benefits of the process are:

— scrubbing efficiency is high because the bio-oxidation reduces the concentration of the odiferous molecules in the liquid phase nearly to zero and thereby enhances mass transfer from the gaseous phase;
— liquid volumes needed for scrubbing are greatly reduced;
— there is no ultimate effluent disposal problem.

The 'dry' reactors are beds packed with biologically active, sorptive material (e.g. compost, peat). The contaminated gases are blown upwards through the bed.

Biological odour treatment is still in its infancy and, therefore, most designs are based, conservatively, on blanket 'rule of thumb' criteria [12.22]. In many cases, where a variable miscellany of odiferous compounds is involved, this is not a serious disadvantage since the process must be designed for the 'worst case' situation. If, on the other hand, the composition of the odours is both predictable and less variable, there is scope for more rational design procedures. In other words, determining which component was rate-limiting, quantifying its kinetic constants and then designing the process on the basis of their values. The potential for process development in this area is, therefore, very great. Not only must the process configurations be optimised (for example, in terms of mass transfer of the contaminating compounds from the gaseous to the liquid phase and pressure drop across the reactor) but also the biological consortia most appropriate for 'broad-spectrum' use need to be determined (or developed genetically).

A form of air pollution which is of considerable concern at the present is that produced by acid gases resulting from the combustion of fossil fuels. To be more precise, it is the effects that Acid Rain has on lakes and soils which is of concern. It seems unlikely that biotechnology will be able to offer any solution to removing the acidic components from the source gases. However, it does not seem unreasonable to suggest that there is considerable scope for developing biological formulations which, because of their tolerance to acidic environments, could initiate the rehabilitation of contaminated water and soil (see also Section 12.4).

12.6 CONCLUSIONS

This discussion has presented a number of areas which the environmental biotechnologist could rightfully and sensibly examine in the immediate or medium-term future. However, no mention has been made of control technologies or philosophies which can be applied to processes. Many of the processes which are currently in use are designed and operated on the basis of long-standing, *ad hoc* principles (see Chapters 1 and 2). This practice results in an over-stolid plant which, in general, performs well but does not have the capacity for being 'fine-tuned' in response to short-time-period variations in feedstock quality or product requirements. This type of control is necessary if the energy inputs (and, therefore, the process costs) are to be minimised. The two requirements for producing this type of plant are:

— a model which adequately describes all the essential features of the process;
— sensors which can provide on-line monitoring of the key determinants in the design/control model.

The activated sludge system is probably the best researched of the established processes used by environmental biotechnologists. The problems of developing models to describe this process have been discussed by Hamer (Chapter 8). Many of these problems will also apply to other processes. It may be that these difficulties are insurmountable but, until this has been resolved, modelling must remain as a major challenge in this field.

The sensors available for use in waste treatment processes have been reviewed by Briggs [12.23]. This review showed that, although instrumentation, control and automation (ICA) technologies are being used by water industries within the UK, their use is very limited when compared with many other major industries. The review also emphasises that any continuation of this rate of change to ICA depends on the production of low-cost sensors which are not only robust and reliable but also easily maintained by using modular replacements. This means that the instrumentation industry must also be considered as an integral part of environmental biotechnology, since the analytical problems of the water industry reflect those which exist right across the field, from measurements on landfill leachate to the estimation of organic acids in composting.

Environmental biotechnology is, therefore, really no different from any other area of biotechnology. It embraces many disciplines, the range varying with the demands of the problem. What is essential is that no discipline should ignore environmental problems nor should any discipline be ignored. The role of the biotechnologist (environmental or otherwise) is to ensure that this dictum is observed.

REFERENCES

[12.1] Brown, M. and Lester, J. N. (1979) Metal removal in activated sludge: The role of bacterial extracellular polymers. *Wat. Res.*, **13**, 817–837.

[12.2] Forster, C. F. (1985) *Biotechnology and Wastewater Treatment*, Cambridge University Press, pp. 312–348.

[12.3] Catchpole, J. R. and Cooper, P. L. (1972) The biological treatment of carbonization effluents — III. New advances in the biochemical oxidation of liquid wastes. *Wat. Res.*, **6**, 1459.

[12.4] Woodard, A. J., Stafford, D. A. and Callely, A. G. (1974) Biochemical studies on accelerated treatment of thiocyanide by activated sludge using growth factors such as pyruvate. *J. Appl. Bact.*, **37**, 277–287.

[12.5] Nazley, N. and Knowles, C. J. (1981) Cyanide degradation by immobilised fungi. *Biotech. Lett.*, **3**, 363.

[12.6] Saunders, F. (1985) An effective control of filamentous microorganism growth in wastewater treatment plants. *Wat. Waste Tr. J.*, **28**(1), 22–24.

[12.7] Wheatland, A. B., Gledhill, C. and O'Gorman, J. V. (1975) Developments in the treatment of metal-bearing effluents. *Chem. & Ind.*, 632–639.

[12.8] Forster, C. E. (1985) Factors involved in the settlement of activated sludge II. The binding of heavy polyvalent metals. *Wat. Res.,* **19,** 1265–1271.

[12.9]   Rudd, T., Sterritt, R. M. and Lester, J. N. (1983) Stability constants and complexation capacities of complexes formed between heavy metals and extracellular polymers from activated sludge. *J. Chem. Tech. Biotech.,* **33A,** 374–380.

[12.10] Steiner, A. E., McLaren, D. A. and Forster, C. F. (1976) The nature of activated sludge flocs. *Wat. Res.,* **10m,** 25–30.

[12.11] Gray, A. V. (1981) Phosphorous reduction studies. *Wat. Pollut. Control,* **80,** 333–340.

[12.12] Barnard, J. L. (1976) A review of biological phosphorus removal in the activated-sludge process. *Water Sa,* **2,** 136.

[12.13] Cooper, D. G. and Zajic, J. E. (1980) Surface-active compounds from microorganisms. *Adv. Appl. Microbiol.,* **26,** 229–253.

[12.14] Margaritis, A., Kennedy, K., Zajic, J. E. and Gerson, D. F. (1979) Biosurfactant production by *Nocardia erythropolis. Dev. Ind. Microbiol.,* **20,** 624–630.

[12.15] World Health Organisation (1984) *Guidelines for Drinking Water Quality,* Volume 1. WHO, Geneva.

[12.16] Croll, B. T., Greene, L. A., Hall, T., Whitford, C. J. and Zabel, T. F. (1985) Biological fluidised bed denitrification for potable water. In *Advances in Water Engineering,* Tebbutt, T. H. Y. (ed.), Elsevier Applied Science Publishers, London, pp. 180–187.

[12.17] Kiff, R. J., Cheung, Y. H. and Brown, G. (1983) Heavy metal removal from sewage sludge — Factors governing detoxification process efficiency. In *Heavy Metals in the Environment,* CEP Consultants, Edinburgh, pp. 401–404.

[12.18] Hartenstein, R. (1981) Potential use of earthworms as a solution to sludge management. *Wat. Pollut. Control,* **80,** 638–643.

[12.19] Moo-Young, M., Hasnain, S. and Lamptey, J. (eds) (1986) *Biotechnology and Renewable Energy,* Elsevier Applied Science Publishers, London.

[12.20] Anon. (1986) Microbes in harness. *Shell World,* October/ November, 18–19.

[12.21] Henry, J. G. and Gehr, R. (1980) Odour control: an operators' guide. *J. Wat. Pollut. Control Fed.,* **52,** 2523–2537.

[12.22] Toogood, S. J. (1986) *Biotechnological Methods in Odour Control.* Water Research Centre.

[12.23] Briggs, R. (1985) Instrumentation for waste treatment processes. In *Comprehensive Biotechnology,* Vol. 4, Robinson, C. W. and Howell, J. A. (eds), Pergamon Press, Oxford, pp. 1089–1106.

Index